LEO BAECK INSTITUTE
YEAR BOOK

1971

Norman Bentwich at a function of the Leo Baeck Institute in London, 1966
In the background, Richard Fuchs

PUBLICATIONS OF THE
LEO BAECK INSTITUTE

YEAR BOOK XVI

1971

EAST AND WEST LIBRARY
PUBLISHED FOR THE INSTITUTE
LONDON · JERUSALEM · NEW YORK

EDITOR: ROBERT WELTSCH

OFFICES OF THE
LEO BAECK INSTITUTE

JERUSALEM (ISRAEL): 33, Bustanai Street
LONDON: 4, Devonshire Street, W. 1
NEW YORK: 129 East 73rd Street

THE LEO BAECK INSTITUTE
was founded in 1955 by the
COUNCIL OF JEWS FROM GERMANY

for the purpose of collecting material on and
sponsoring research into the history of the
Jewish community in Germany and in other
German-speaking countries from the Emanci-
pation to its decline and new dispersion. The
Institute is named in honour of the man who
was the last representative figure of German
Jewry in Germany during the Nazi period.

The Council of Jews from Germany was established
after the war by the principal organisations of Jews
from Germany in Israel, U.S.A. and U.K. for the
protection of their rights and interests.

THIS PUBLICATION WAS SUPPORTED
BY A GRANT FROM THE
MEMORIAL FOUNDATION FOR JEWISH CULTURE

© Leo Baeck Institute 1971
Published in the East and West Library
by the Horovitz Publishing Co. Ltd.
5 Cromwell Place, London SW7
ISBN 0 85222 265 3
Printed in Holland
by N.V. Drukkerij Levisson, Rijswijk (Z.H.)

Contents

Illustrations

Introduction

BY ROBERT WELTSCH

After fifteen volumes of this Year Book we may perhaps be allowed to state, without being considered presumptuous, that the Year Book of the Leo Baeck Institute has emerged as a standard publication in the orbit to which it is devoted, namely the study of the history of German-Jewish relations in all aspects of human existence and activity, during the period from the beginning of the Enlightenment, through the final emancipation of Jews and beyond, up to the extinction of this relationship in 1933. For those of the older generation who still remember the unfathomable shock it was for German Jews when the entire foundation of their political, economic and cultural existence suddenly collapsed under their feet, and the amount of human suffering ensuing to the community and to innumerable individuals, it is somewhat curious to have to realise that almost forty years later this disturbing chapter of their life experience has receded to the shadows of un-reality, becoming the subject of historical research and of theses for academic degrees. Nevertheless, it is a cause of satisfaction to feel that the problem for the elucidation of which the Leo Baeck Institute was established in 1954 has indeed become the subject of serious research in a much wider setting. This concern is not confined to a group of so-called survivors, themselves deeply hurt and confused by the breakdown of the values in which they had believed.

That the German-Jewish case was of much greater than merely local significance has often been stressed and explained in these pages. It has its unique and peculiar character, but at the same time it is the classic example of an intellectually sophis-ticated minority group suddenly integrated into another dominant cultural struc-ture, with all the positive and negative reactions resulting from such an encounter. Moreover, it is the conspicuous case of the absorption of a sub-culture into the general post-Renaissance European civilisation which was mainly a system of spiritual and intellectual concepts before it became what we today call a technolo-gical way of life. Many features of a similar process can be observed elsewhere, especially in the post-colonial world today, where the clash of the adopted Western attitude with the old inheritance of local traditions and beliefs is one of the most intriguing aspects of the future.

German-Jewish history has a claim to be heeded because some of the results of this remarkable relationship had an enormous practical impact on the whole process of human thought as well as on concrete developments in some fields. For this and other reasons — some of them self-evident — the study of this period has recently been expanded to a surprising extent. After the pioneer work done by the Leo Baeck Institute in this sphere, a growing interest in this complex issue is noti-ceable at universities in the United States, in Germany, and in Israel, and perhaps

to a lesser degree also in other European countries. This fact is a great encouragement though it is perhaps to be regretted that sometimes the same material is the
subject of research in several places, without proper communication or co-ordina-
tion. True, it is difficult to say how such overlapping could be avoided. As far as
Germany is concerned, a praiseworthy beginning has been made by the Germania
Judaica of Cologne which regularly publishes *Arbeitsinformationen über Studien-
projekte auf dem Gebiet der Geschichte des deutschen Judentums und des Antisemitismus* listing
all research project of Jewish interest, and all work already in hand, so that anybody interested in these matters can find out whether a proposed research has
already been undertaken by others. Yet we have nothing comparable on a universal
scale.

It would be desirable that what is being done in this field all over the world
should be recorded somewhere. This is one of the reasons for the experiment made
in the current volume of the Year Book to put on record discussions not sponsored
or directed by the Leo Baeck Institute but devoted to the subject which the Leo
Baeck Institute regards as its concern. We are referring to a Symposium arranged
by the American Historical Association on the occasion of its annual meeting in
Washington, D.C. in 1969. This event had no direct link with the Leo Baeck Institute although it is easily seen that the publications of the Leo Baeck Institute
during the last fifteen years provided some of the source-material on which the
speakers could rely.

The position of the Jews, especially of the Jewish intellectuals in the last phase of
German-Jewish coexistence is, admittedly, a controversial one, and many of the
things said in this respect are open to further examination and discussion. The
judgment will often depend on the general views, political or otherwise, of the
speaker or author. In any case, discussion of the merits can be rewarding. Actually,
criticism was voiced at this very Convention. This is natural and serves clarification.
One of the principal obvious points of controversy is the impact made by the activity of left-wing intellectuals, e.g. the circle of contributors to periodicals like
Weltbühne and *Tagebuch*. In the debate held at Washington Wolfgang Sauer
objected to some of Donald Niewyk's views, but to our regret we are unable to
include in this report a further written reply sent to us by Niewyk as this would go
beyond factual reporting of the discussion as actually held. It is clear that Niewyk
belongs to those who believe that the radical publicistic outbursts of these Leftists —
though well-intentioned and for the most part substantially correct — actually impaired the stability of the Weimar Republic "by helping to terrify more conservative Germans of a left-wing threat". Such regrettable consequences, alas, are
perhaps inevitable in situations like these. In this connection Niewyk also mentions
George Mosse's recent book *Germans and Jews*[1] which contains a chapter on left-
wing intellectuals in the Weimar Republic, based on a lecture given at the annual
meeting of the American Historical Association in 1964. Thereby it may be seen

---

[1]George Mosse, *Germans and Jews. The Right, the Left, and the Search for a "Third Force" in Pre-
Nazi Germany*, New York 1970, London 1971.

that the 1969 session of the A.H.A. was not the first occasion on which the German-Jewish problem — or one of its important aspects — was raised in its councils.[2]

George Mosse who is, of course, a long-standing collaborator of the Leo Baeck Institute, has devoted much zeal to the study of contemporary sources and one of the results of this endeavour was his lecture given at the Symposium of the Leo Baeck Institute in Jerusalem in June 1970. This lecture in an enlarged form is included in the present Year Book. His conclusions will surprise many who are accustomed to regard left-wing parties which opposed the old conservative and nationalist trends as natural allies of the Jews in their fight for legal equality. But already Edmund Silberner in a Hebrew work (1956) which appeared later in a German translation *Sozialisten zur Judenfrage* (Berlin 1962) has pointed out how ambivalent — to put it mildly — has been the attitude of some leading Socialists to the Jewish question.

One episode mentioned in George Mosse's lecture which gave rise to a few comments at the Jerusalem Conference assumes a sad connotation today because of the man concerned. It was a reference to an article in the *Weltbühne* under the headline 'Hitler in Jerusalem', which expressed astonished disapproval of a nationalist students' demonstration against the inaugural lecture of Norman Bentwich in 1932 after his appointment as Professor of Political Relations at the University. The subject announced was Jerusalem, City of Peace; a noble idea, one would think, but apparently repulsive to those who believe in militancy alone. The noise and uproar and the throwing of stink bombs by students and other listeners forced the President of the University, Dr. Magnes, to call the police, but Bentwich was actually prevented from giving his course. When this happened, Arthur Ruppin, one of the protagonists of the idea of Jewish-Arab *rapprochement* and at the same time a promoter of Jewish colonisation (this, as he hoped, without infringement of Arab rights and possessions), wrote in his diary: "It seems that the whole world is mentally sick, much so we Jews. People who have spent their youth in the war and in its aftermath must be handled like the insane".[3] This was written, incidentally, in 1932, and the reference is to World War One, an almost forgotten event today. It might apply tenfold to the time which then was still in the obscurity of the future, the time of Hitler and Auschwitz and atom bombs and mutual nationalist and tribal massacres.

---

[2]The subject of the attitude of German left-wing intellectuals, most of them Jews, has recently been discussed on a number of occasions and dealt with in various publications, especially in the American Jewish monthly *Commentary*, where sometimes the position of Jewish intellectuals in America today is compared with that in Weimar Germany. See also Walter Z. Laqueur, 'The Tucholsky Complaint', *Encounter*, vol. *XXXIII*, No. 4, October 1969, pp. 76-80, now reprinted in his *Out of the Ruins of Europe*, New York 1971, pp. 445-454.

[3]Quoted also in Amos Elon's excellent book *The Israelis, Founders and Sons*, London 1971, p. 179. This book is by far the best analysis of Israel's reality and its European background that has appeared hitherto, although perhaps the "German" side of the story is not sufficiently appreciated. At the time of going to press the forthcoming publication of Ruppin's Diary in an English translation is announced by Weidenfeld & Nicolson, London.

The unsavoury incident in Jerusalem, which evoked the *Weltbühne's* criticism and affected the image of Jewish Palestine in the eyes of German intellectuals, must have been one of the most disheartening experiences in the long life of the man who died this year in London at the age of 88 and is deeply mourned by a vast circle of friends among whom also many Jewish emigrants from Germany would wish to be counted.

It is not for us to attempt a full appreciation of what this Grand Old Man of British Jewry has stood for, in his long career as civil servant, as promoter of humane ideas and philanthropic activities, and by his practical application of the maxim of loving one's neighbour, his indefatigable work for the Hebrew University and his concern for Arab-Jewish reconciliation. But the whole of former German Jewry will never forget his unrelenting effort for the alleviation of the lot of Hitler's victims, his frequent fearless interventions on the spot, his skilful and successful care for the refugees reaching British shores, and especially his difficult organisational work for the absorption of thousands of scientists, academics and other intellectuals who were stranded in a foreign country, often without sufficient knowledge of its language. It is difficult today to give a true picture of the desolation and despair of those times. Bentwich himself has left us a comprehensive matter-of-fact report on this great undertaking in his book *They Found Refuge*.[4] He was one of those who, without being patronising or callous, wholeheartedly identified themselves with Hitler's victims, and he became one of the most unflinching champions of their cause, also as regards restitution and indemnification from Germany. He was Chairman of the United Restitution Office from its very beginning.[5] Despite his great age he was always available where needed, and is it difficult to imagine Jewish life in England without him.

Coming back to the start of our discussion of German-Jewish history, we noticed that one of the lectures at Washington was devoted especially to Austria, and it is obvious that particularly in the field of literature no exact frontier can be drawn between Germany and Austria and consequently not between Jewish authors from one or other of these countries either. It is, however, different with regard to political thought and circumstances. This was particularly the case until 1918, i.e. during the period when literature produced by Jews in Austria flourished. Nevertheless, Austrian Jewry is of special importance and also characteristic as a group of German-speaking Jews who played a major part in Jewish tradition as well as in general culture. They were the bearers of a certain sort of German-Jewish erudition, both in the purely Jewish sense and also in respect of participation in general culture.[6] German-speaking Jews in old Austria after 1782 (the year of Emperor Joseph II's Edict of Toleration) were different from German Jews because they lived

---

[4] *They Found Refuge*. An account of British Jewry's work for victims of Nazi oppression with an introduction by Viscount Samuel, London 1956.
[5] See the moving obituary by Eva Reichmann in *AJR Information*, May 1971.
[6] Cf. also Introduction to *LBI Year Book III* (1958), p. X.

among other nationalities which formed the old Austrian Empire, and from there could bring many influences to bear on general Jewish life and make a special contribution to the colourful Austro-Jewish culture, and naturally there was also much antagonism. In Austria, the national problem was ever-present. By contrast, a clash between nationalities (except in the case of minorities in border districts) was not of primary importance in the monolithic German world and therefore did not affect German Jewry proper.

The fact that in the Austro-Hungarian Empire — comprising such different provinces as Polish-(or in its Eastern part Ruthenian-) speaking Galicia, Czech-speaking Bohemia and Moravia, Italian-speaking Trieste and so on — the Jews lived mainly within a sphere of German-language culture and preserved this allegiance during more than a century of assimilation almost until 1914, is one of the outstanding phenomena in European-Jewish history. The Jews filled a gap in the social organism as traders and merchants and later in the professions, but culturally they were an enclave, German as well as Jewish, with their own schools and educational systems in villages and small towns before the migration to the big cities gathered momentum. It was a unique situation, and it was apt to engender conflicts especially after the other nationalities, many of them consisting predominantly of peasants, underwent social changes and developed their own middle class and also their own national cultural consciousness. Despite the common pattern there were differences between the single provinces because the encompassing nationalities were different; some of them had a strong historical physiognomy, like the Poles or the Italians, and accordingly they gradually also attracted some of the educated Jews, as did the Czechs at a later stage, from the end of the nineteenth century onward; others were more "backward" and on a lower social level, like the Ruthenians or Slovaks. This chapter is of the highest significance for the study of German-speaking Jewry of modern times because many people who came from these surroundings attained positions in German cultural life and never doubted their own German character.[7] The problem cannot be enlarged upon in the present context. The point to be made here is the complexity of the nationality problem in Austria and its impact on the position of the Jews, after a large section of the Jewish population of the Empire, especially of its Eastern provinces, had developed, at the end of the nineteenth century, its own Jewish national consciousness, primarily spurred by the Zionist idea. The granting of general suffrage in 1908 made it possible to nominate Jewish-national candidates in

---

[7]The facts have frequently been referred to in individual biographies or family chronicles, but the historical and psychological particularities and their impact have not, as far as I know, been objectively and exhaustively studied. Anyhow, it is known that Sigmund Freud's family had originally come, via Moravia, from Galicia, Gustav Mahler and Karl Kraus were born in the Jewish community of a small Czech town. Robert Neumann, a noted German writer, has described his provenance from ancestors in Slovakia. Karl Emil Franzos came from Eastern Galicia as did Joseph Roth, both undoubtedly prominent German writers. And in the recently published history of the S. Fischer Verlag by Peter de Mendelssohn we find a detailed record of the youth of the famous German publisher Samuel Fischer and his migration from his parental home in the Slovakian Carpathians to Vienna and later Berlin. These are only a few examples chosen *ad libitum*.

Galicia and Bucovina in districts with a dense, mostly Yiddish-speaking Jewish population, and a number were elected to the central Parliament in Vienna, where they formed the "Jewish Club". In the last stage of the Empire's existence the Jewish national movement had vigorously pushed its demand for official recognition of a Jewish nationality, in order to spare the Jews the humiliation of having to declare themselves as of Polish, Ukrainian, Ruthenian etc. nationality according to the place where they lived, and where the majority of the population was antisemitic and did not accept the Jews as co-nationals, although at election time their votes were wanted.

The majority of the Jews of Western Austria including Vienna and such regions as make up Czechoslovakia today were always opposed to the recognition of a Jewish nationality. They preferred to be counted with the dominant races, Germans in Vienna and Hungarians in the Hungarian regions to which also parts of present-day Czechoslovakia or Rumania belonged. In Galicia the upper-class Jews identified themselves with the dominant Poles. There as in Hungary they were supporting the dominant nations even though speaking German at home.

But in Vienna, which had always been the centre of the Empire, there lived many people of Eastern origin, and in addition the growing Zionist movement was in favour of Jewish nationality for ideological reasons. In Czechoslovakia the popularity of the Jewish national idea grew during the war when the signs of a dissolution of the Empire and of the creation of new nationalist states became evident. Many of the Jews who had hitherto voted German thought it now more opportune to declare themselves Jewish in order not to provoke the anger of the Czechs. This is the reason why in 1918 the problem of voting Jewish became topical both in Czechoslovakia and — to a certain degree — in the newly created Republic of German Austria (first called *Deutsch-Österreich*), where many Jews originating in the former Eastern provinces were resident, especially in the second district (Leopoldstadt). In 1918, under the impact of the British Balfour Declaration and what was considered the victory of the Zionist idea over its Jewish opponents, the temptation was very strong to try to get a Jewish-nationalist candidate into the new parliament, and also Jewish-national representatives into municipal councils, mainly in Vienna. But the bulk of the Viennese Jews, both liberal and socialist, remained hostile to a separate Jewish party which they regarded as a return to the ghetto and a disadvantage to their own political interests because of loss of votes.

Why socialists following Karl Kautsky opposed Jewish nationality is explained in George Mosse's essay in this volume. The Jewish-nationalist propaganda was carried on with fervent enthusiasm, and thanks to an electoral agreement with another splinter party, one Jewish-national candidate, Robert Stricker, was elected to the first Austrian *Nationalversammlung* in 1919. He sat there as the only and lonely representative of a national minority in the new state. But rump Austria, different from the old Empire, was not a "nationality state", not composed of various nationalities, and the Jewish-nationalist movement had no prospects as a

political party. Stricker was not re-elected.[8] (He later perished in Auschwitz.)
This is the background to the statistical survey which Walter B. Simon, a
Canadian professor, is publishing in the present volume.

Migration was for the Jewish people always an intrinsic part of its history, more
so than for any other people in the world. In the course of centuries it contributed
to the transformation of whole Jewish communities and individuals who both
profited by and suffered from the close contact with different cultures. This process
determined the Jewish people's multi-faceted existential character throughout the
ages. What is usually called *Ashkenazi* (German) Jewry because its character was
formed during its residence in German lands from the Middle Ages onwards, had its
encounter later with many peoples of Europe outside the German-speaking orbit,
primarily in Slav, and to a lesser extent, in Western countries. As far as contemporary Jewry is concerned, migration has perhaps even a more pronounced
effect because in the modern world where the principles of emancipation and —
to a certain degree — equality, prevail assimilation takes place more rapidly. A
phenomenon *sui generis* is American Jewry today, the majority of whom consists of
the offspring of Eastern European *Ashkenazi* (Yiddish-speaking) imigrants, and
while in the nineteenth century German Jews had laid the foundation of American
Jewish institutions this element of the immigrants' conglomeration was substantially enlarged over the last forty years by Jews from Central Europe fleeing from
Nazi persecution. The problems of acculturation with which these new Americans
are confronted, especially in the second and third generation, are discussed in the
article by Herbert Strauss in this volume. This analysis is concerned with the future
of Jewish life in one — albeit most important — country, but considering migration
as an overall phenomenon, it is a fact that during the nineteenth century German
Jewry was changed considerably by movements of population both inside Germany
from the villages to the cities and to regions overseas. All this is an inexhaustible
subject of sociological studies beyond the mere statistical aspect. Jacob Toury, who
is engaged in research on these facts, brings to our notice an interesting chapter
relating to a number of Bavarian communities which provide an instructive pattern
of these happenings and their demographical results. As one sidelight of such
changes it may be observed that the origin of families is often indicated by their

---

[8]In a Hebrew lecture given at the Jerusalem Symposium of June 1970 I tried to give the present
generation an idea of the tremendous impact of the First World War on the political thinking
of the German-speaking Jews. The problem of East European Jews in all its aspects and in its
full complexity revealed itself for the first time during the German occupation of Poland and
other Russian provinces. The destiny of these Jews also became, or was thought to have become (as long as Germany was deemed victorious), a direct responsibility of German Jews. In
consequence, all the leading German organisations, including the so-called assimilationists,
supported the Zionist demand for granting minority rights and protection of their cultural
interests to the Jews in the new East European states. That some theorists confused this demand
with the philosophy of personal national autonomy according to the doctrine of Karl Renner
and Otto Bauer was perhaps unavoidable because of the newness of the concept. On Otto
Bauer's attitude to the Jewish problem see *LBI Year Book IV* (1959), pp. XVII ff.

name. When one of Toury's examples is the town of Kissingen and its Jewish community, we become aware that the name Kissinger, borne by a man of considerable political responsibility in our day, is derived from this little town whose Jewish community has practically ceased to exist in its original home.

We are glad that Professor Liebeschütz, himself originating from Hamburg, devotes an essay to Aby Warburg on the occasion of Professor Ernst Gombrich's great biography. Liebeschütz knew Warburg personally and as contributor to the two series of the Institute's Hamburg publications he observed the working of the *Warburg Bibliothek* from close quarters. He is one of the few people alive who are familiar with the surroundings in which Warburg worked and built up his famous library from which later the Warburg Institute in London emerged.

A figure like Warburg is of the greatest relevance to the subject of the studies with which the Leo Baeck Institute is concerned. Scion of a famous family clan which had always been conscious of its Jewish identity and of the obligations ensuing from this, he devoted himself totally to the investigation of the sources of culture, especially the hidden deeper forces of the soul asserting themselves in the creation of works of art, and their dependence on ancient traditions buried in the depths of the human mind. Warburg was especially aware of the impact of the revival of pagan symbols and ideas at the time of the Renaissance as revealed in art, and their blending with Christian mythology, but it is remarkable that despite his consciousness of his own Jewish origin he never fully directed his attention to the part played by Judaism and Jewish ideas in Western thought, or their crystallisation in the mystery world of the Kabbala, which had many strong links with the world of astrologers and alchemists in which Warburg was so keenly interested. Perhaps one has to take into account that at that time Kabbala was not yet taken seriously, in any case was not yet as accessible to Western scholarship as it has now become owing to the work of Gershom Scholem. Be that as it may, Warburg was conscious of the fact that he himself was a mixture, a product of the combination of various powerful elements whether of his own choosing or not, and he expressed this in the formula printed as a motto on the title-page of a lecture which Gertrud Bing gave at the Hamburg *Kunsthalle* on the 31st October 1958:

> Ebreo di sangue
> Amburghese di cuore
> d'anima Fiorentino

It is a moving confession, indicative also of the complicated psychological dilemma of erudite German Jews at the climax of assimilation, when their most sophisticated and learned individuals passionately tried to absorb in all its profuse dimensions the European culture to which they owed so much.

While this Year Book was going to press, the first copy was received at the Leo Baeck Institute in London of the new English translation of Franz Rosenzweig's *The Star of Redemption.*[9] This is, by any standard, a major event for all those in the

English-speaking world who are taking an active interest in Jewish theology and religious thought. Coming only one year after the Hebrew edition which was published by the Leo Baeck Institute in Jerusalem in co-operation with Mossad Bialik, it is most gratifying that this great book will now be accessible to Jewish and non-Jewish students of Judaism in those countries where the most important sections of World Jewry live. There is something typically "German" in Rosenzweig's writing, not only in the linguistic sense, but also in the way of expressing his thoughts, often with associations taken from German literature and philosophy. Of this difficulty the translators were aware; the English translator William W. Hallo, who deserves congratulations on completing this most difficult enterprise after seven years of work, gives in his Preface an account of his endeavours to overcome the obvious difficulties. On Rosenzweig's particular relationship to language, in this case the German language, Nahum N. Glatzer, himself a veteran Rosenzweig scholar and editor of great merit, contributes appropriate explanations in his concise and instructive Foreword to the English edition.

The Star of Redemption is regarded as the crowning spiritual achievement of German-Jewish coexistence in that final though short-lived period which Leo Baeck sometimes described as a "Jewish renaissance" in Germany. Actually, many students of Jewish theology, especially in the United States, have acquired a working knowledge of German or are themselves descendants of German-speaking families, so that even without translation Rosenzweig was not a complete stranger to them, as can be deduced from frequent quotations from and references to Rosenzweig's works in English-language periodicals and scholarly treatises. Now, however, the book will reach a much wider readership.

Another proof of the impact of Rosenzweig on contemporary Jewish studies can be found in the essay by Dr. Moshe Schwarcz in this volume. His original lecture at the Leo Baeck Institute Symposium in Jerusalem relied on the Hebrew translation of *The Star of Redemption*; the English version of the lecture could not yet make full use of the new English translation, which appeared only after the essay had been completed.

OBITUARY

Julie Braun-Vogelstein, who died early this year, was a member of the Board of the Leo Baeck Institute in New York, and took a very active and alert part in its work despite her age (88) and frequent ailments. She was an extraordinary woman of the highest cultural and intellectual qualities and of many-sided interests (her main professional occupation having been history of art). Scion of a notable German-Jewish family, the Vogelstein clan, she has described with great care and devotion the environment of her youth and the Jewish and non-Jewish influences exerted on her life and studies, in her autobiography *Was niemals stirbt* which was

---

⁹*The Star of Redemption*. By Franz Rosenzweig. Translated from the Second Edition of 1930 by William W. Hallo. The Littman Library of Jewish Civilization. Routledge & Kegan Paul, London 1971. (Holt, Rinehart & Winston, New York.)

published by the Leo Baeck Institute in 1966. Apart from the fascinating story of her growing-up and the experiences of a gifted and adventurous woman, this book also portrays in a most instructive way Jewish life in pre-Hitler Germany at the peak of assimilation. Julie Braun was highly esteemed in the councils of the Leo Baeck Institute for her unerring intelligence and her warm-hearted approach, and the unremitting support she gave to the cause of the Institute.[10]

Another personality of high standing who died in March of this year is Professor Hans Kohn who collaborated with the New York branch of the Institute for many years, gave it his invaluable advice and placed at its disposal his vast experience of academic life both in the United States and in Europe. Kohn was a prominent historian whose principal concern was the study of nationalism, its philosophical sources and its effect on world politics, but he was also astonishingly versed in the literature of all Western nations. Particularly brilliant in his analysis of the close connection existing between literature and poetry on the one hand, and philosophical and political thinking on the other hand, he was the man to show how the "mind" of a nation expresses itself, and how this ultimately determines its place in world history. Hans Kohn's contributions to the publications of the Leo Baeck Institute are mainly literary in character. His *Heinrich Heine: The Man and the Myth* was printed as text of the Leo Baeck Memorial Lecture 2 in New York in 1959, while his book on the Jewish aspect of Vienna at the turn of the century, mainly devoted to three characteristic figures — *Karl Kraus, Arthur Schnitzler, Otto Weininger* — was published in German in the Schriftenreihe wissenschaftlicher Abhandlungen des Leo Baeck Institutes (Tübingen 1962). An extract of this book in an English version was printed in Year Book VI (1961).[11]

Finally, we have to announce also the death of a man who, perhaps mainly for geographical reasons, was not formally linked with the councils of the Leo Baeck Institute, but represented one remnant of the old pre-1938 establishment of organised German Jewry. Alfred Hirschberg died at the age of 70 in São Paulo, Brazil, in September, just when this Year Book was going to press. He was for many years a leading functionary of Germany's largest Jewish organisation, the *Centralverein*. At the last stage, when life in Jewish organisations had become most uncomfortable, Hirschberg was appointed syndicus of the C.V. and editor-in-chief of its organ, the weekly *C.V.-Zeitung*. After his emigration Hirschberg's house in São Paulo became a centre of Jewish activity in many fields, and he was concious of the difficult duty to transmit to the new, Portuguese-educated, generation of immigrants' descendants an inkling of the achievements and values of German Jewry. Hirschberg contributed a character sketch of the C.V. leader Ludwig Hollaender in Year Book VII (1962), but owing to his illness he was unable to fulfil the plans of collaborating in an objective critical history of the *Centralverein* projected by the London branch of the Leo Baeck Institute, for which Hirschberg had collected much documentary material.

---

[10]See also *LBI News*, spring 1971.
[11]See also Robert Weltsch, 'The Philosopher of Nationalism', in *AJR Information*, May 1971.

JULIE BRAUN-VOGELSTEIN

(1883 - 1971)

HANS KOHN

(1891 - 1971)

By courtesy of
Mrs. Patricia H. Henson, Texas

Religious Trends

Religious Currents and General Culture*

BY MOSHE SCHWARCZ

It is not my purpose in this paper to give a description of religious Jewry in Germany in all its multi-coloured diversity. I do not consider myself competent to do this because I have no personal experience of its way of life within the communal and congregational framework. All my knowledge concerning the nature and the manners of one of the most important and illustrious centres of Diaspora Jewry over the centuries is derived from literary sources.

The features of traditional Jewry in Germany have been depicted by Professor Baruch Kurzweil with artistic skill and acumen in an essay on S. R. Hirsch and Isaac Breuer. He has expertly dwelt upon the phenomenon of German orthodoxy "in its serious, as well as its strange and even ludicrous aspects".[1] As for the intellectual features of the liberal Judaism of the nineteenth century, this has been thoroughly and forcefully delineated by Max Wiener in his classic work *Jüdische Religion im Zeitalter der Emanzipation.*[2]

My treatment of the subject will be confined to the intellectual, or as it were the philosophical, layer of the burgeoning personality of German Jewry. It has frequently been pointed out that the Jewry of Germany had, of its own volition, to search for its roots or its Jewish identity. The alternative was social assimilation and spiritual absorption in the general society and culture. It was a characteristic feature of German Jewry that the striving after an interpretation of Jewish identity was pursued among all its religious currents and trends, ranging from the Reform Movement to extreme Orthodoxy. Cultural integration became one of the conspicuous distinguishing marks of religious Jewry in Germany. S. R. Hirsch expressed this position when he said that German Jewry became "a Jewry that knew itself". But what was the nature of its self-awareness, and what were its limitations? Where did the religious Jewry of Germany stand in relation to general culture? And what was the theological significance of the confrontation of Judaism with general culture?

In connection with this subject, a great deal of importance attaches to the polemic which Leo Strauss conducted against Julius Guttmann in his review of the latter's book *Die Philosophie des Judentums.* And although the main topic of the controversy was "the struggle between the old and the new in Jewish philosophy"[3] it contained

*This contribution is based on a lecture given in June 1970 by the author in Hebrew at the Conference on the Research into the History of Central European Jewry from the Emancipation to its Destruction organised by the Jerusalem Leo Baeck Institute.

[1]Baruch Kurzweil, *Be-ma'avak 'al 'Erekhei Ha-Yahadut*, Schocken, pp. 267-290; and also 'Lezikhro shel Yitzhak Breuer Zal', *Ha-'Aretz*, 1.11.46.

[2]Berlin 1933.

[3]Leo Strauss, *Philosophie und Gesetz*, Berlin 1935. — On Julius Guttmann and his book see Fritz Bamberger, 'Julius Guttmann — Philosopher of Judaism', in *LBI Year Book V* (1960), pp. 3-34.

3

a kind of summary, one-sided yet penetrating, of the achievements and the short-comings of the religious thought of German Jewry.

Julius Guttmann — it would seem from his book *Die Philosophie des Judentums* — regards the meeting of Judaism and general culture in recent years as a positive and fruitful alliance, which enabled the two different cultures to become substantially integrated because of the kinship of their ideals and the similarity of values existing between Judaism and general culture, i.e., a culture of enlightened learning. In his view it is possible to speak without the slightest reservation of a Judaeo-German *symbiosis*, whether because of the original character of the ideas of Judaism which is founded upon two enduring principles, viz. *the ideals of humanity* and *the aspiration towards clarity of religious thought*, or because of the character of the Enlightenment, deistic and Kantian, in which also two bases became dominant: fundamental humanistic values on the one hand, and clear, critical religious thought on the other. "The firmness with which Judaism consistently clung, throughout all the convolutions of the colourful religious development of the previous century, to the ideals of humanity and to the aspiration towards lucidity of religious thought — on this firmness was imprinted not only the stamp of the spirit of Judaism but also the fact that Judaism had entered modern culture by virtue of the ideas of the Enlighten-ment and especially by virtue of the ideas of Kant".[4]

On the one hand, Judaism was able to become "a special factor in world history",[5] since by good fortune it combined with the Enlightenment at a time when it was governed by the desire to facilitate this aspiration,[6] and on the other hand Jewish religious thought was able, as a result of its familiarity with general thought and with modern religious consciousness, to adopt the strict and confident method essential for a critico-philosophical approach. In Guttmann's view, it is to the credit of modern religious thought, both general and Jewish, that it rejected the identification — so widespread among the thinkers of the Middle Ages — of scientific, speculative truth with the truth of religious perception. There-fore modern thinkers of Judaism have a better understanding of the nature of religious experience and of various aspects of religious tradition, as a result of the combination with modern, general, philosophical culture.

Leo Strauss, on the other hand, rejects the notion that modern philosophy provides a better means of understanding the quality and content of religious tradition than did the philosophy of the Middle Ages.[7] He argues that Jewish philosophical consciousness, which had crystallized in Germany under the influence of a general philosophy of religion, was not only incapable of creating modes of comprehension that were in accord with religious thought, but also utterly contra-dicted the "spirit of Judaism". It drew its sustenance from the basic values of secular, enlightened humanism, which perforce brought about the destruction of the foundations of Jewish tradition.[8]

[4] J. Guttmann, *Dat U-madda*, Magnes Press, Jerusalem 5715 (1945), p. 222.
[5] *Ibid.*, p. 218.
[6] *Die Philosopie des Judentums*, Munich 1933, p. 263.
[7] Strauss, *op. cit.*, p. 35.
[8] *Ibid.*, p. 11.

The basic concepts of religion — creation, revelation, redemption — lost their original significance through their "internalisation" *(Verinnerlichung)* and as a result of the negation of their objective, "external" significance. In place of supranatural revelation as the exclusive sanction of the religious way of life there appears the concept of "faith" *(Glaube)* which is not Jewish in origin, and which is the modern metempsychosis of the mystical fear of heaven and of pietistic, religious feeling. In the Middle Ages, Strauss goes on, divine precept was the sanction even of philosophical activity, whereas in recent years the sanction even of religious behaviour is subjective feeling or experience.

It seems to me that both these standpoints, i.e. that of Guttmann and that of Strauss (which are poles apart in their evaluation of the meeting between Judaism and general culture) lack completeness and are possibly wide of the mark. Guttmann is inclined to paint an idealized picture by limiting general culture to the basic values of Enlightenment and defining Judaism in terms of messianic idealism and social humanism. His view is not far from that of Hermann Cohen, which was programmatically formulated in his anti-Treitschke pamphlet. "A theoretical pre-condition", Cohen writes there, "to a deepening and genuine understanding between Germanism and Judaism is that the value of Jewish monotheism for a general idealistic conception of life should more and more gain free and profound recognition and appreciation."[9] Cohen continues: "And as for our own spiritual life, we have already experienced an intimate religious partnership in the accord that exists *between Jewish messianism and German humanism*".[10]

Guttmann does not go as far as Cohen in emphasising the kinship between Jewish messianism and German humanism. But he does emphasise the kinship between Judaism on the one hand and general and Kantian enlightenment on the other, seeing therein the secret of the greatness of modern Judaism. Leo Strauss, however, is inclined to paint a negative picture of the subservience of modern Judaism to subjectivity, in which "faith", religious experience, and devoutness substitute for the transcendental and supra-natural approach of original Judaism. Guttmann thus approximates the two cultures to such an extent that the considerable tension between them goes altogether unnoticed, a tension that has in my opinion produced and fostered the best and most original elements in modern Jewish thought; while Strauss separates authentic and modern Judaism to such an extent that modern Judaism is deprived of all connection with anything Jewish.

In order to clarify the special modes of cultural integration which led to the various attempts at self-definition on the part of the religious Jewry of Germany one must, as in the case of the characteristic marks of general culture, give prominence to three principles, as a result of the opposition or partial adaptation to which the religious awareness of German Jewry was built up and nurtured.

[9]Hermann Cohen, 'Deutschtum und Judentum', in *Jüdische Schriften*, vol. II, Berlin 1924, p.312.
[10]*Ibid.*, p. 316.

1. In the first place, one must emphasise that the general culture into which the Jews of Germany were catapulted, and by the light of which they were educated, was basically a Christian culture. In this respect there certainly existed a difference in principle between the intellectual position that obtained in the Middle Ages and the position that arose in the New Era. In the former case, the thinkers of our people were confronted, on the one hand, by a Christian or Muslim civilisation, and on the other hand by a Greco-philosophical consciousness. Hellenism and Christianity, Hellenism and Islam, did not originally find their organic fusion. But from the period of the Reformation and from the commencement of the New Philosophy, there occurred a unique fusion of Christianity and general philosophical consciousness. One may describe the emergence of a consciousness of general philosophical culture, through a growing recognition of Christian principles, as the basic characteristic of Western civilisation as a whole. The first stage in its conquest of Western philosophical consciousness was bound up with the Reformation and the philosophy of subjectivity, as also with the reflection which was reared by the former. The Reformation brought the good tidings of salvation for individual freedom, of the liberation of the human conscience from the shackles of the metaphysical guilt of original sin, and in particular of the invigoration of the inner life, without making this consciousness of freedom a basis for religious and speculative radicalism, without bringing in its train revolutions in Church, State, or Society. In the strengthening of this awareness of inner freedom, the Reformation movement joined with German mysticism (Meister Eckhart, Jakob Böhme), and it was this spiritualization *(Vergeistigung)* that paved the way for the spiritual life of Germany: "The spiritual life of the Germans received through the Reformation a distinctive theological quality."[11]

Philosophical activity in Germany was impressed with the stamp of self-reflection, "which cannot be described apart from Christian self-consciousness".[12] It is, therefore, not surprising that German idealism in its entirety was regarded by one of its brilliant representatives, F. W. J. Schelling, as a direct descendant of Christianity. "Idealism belongs entirely to the New Era; yet one cannot deny the fact that it was Christianity that opened the gates which had been closed to it."[13]

Hermann Cohen, too, much later emphasised the part played by Christianity in the fashioning of the spiritual image of Western culture when he stated: "The significance of Christianity for the history of civilisation consisted in this, that under the dogmatic veil of the humanisation of God it brought about the humanisation of religion, and thereby laid the foundation of the modern 'idea of ethical autonomy', as developed particularly in the German Reformation and in Kantian philosophy."[14]

---

[11]W. Lütgert, *Die Religion des deutschen Idealismus und ihr Ende*, Reprographischer Nachdruck der Ausgabe Gütersloh 1930, Hildesheim 1967, vol. I, p. 1.

[12]K. Löwith, *Gott, Mensch und Welt in der Metaphysik von Descartes bis zu Nietzsche*, Göttingen 1967, p. 28.

[13]*F. W. J. Schellings Sämmtliche Werke*, Stuttgart und Augsburg 1859, Part 1, vol. 5, p. 649.

[14]Cited according to Franz Rosenzweig, *Zweistromland. Kleinere Schriften zur Religion und Philosophie*, Berlin 1926, pp. 201-202.

But with Kant, and especially through the development of certain elements of Kantian philosophy in German idealism and in romanticism, a further deepening occurred in the partnership between Christianity and Western philosophical consciousness. In this development of philosophical thought, two opposing aspects are of importance from the point of view of the rise and crystallisation of Jewish philosophic consciousness.

2.   Cohen did indeed mention in the same context the German Reformation and the teaching of Kant — since in his own view there is an identity of ideas between Jewish messianism and German humanism — but one must not overlook the basic contradiction that exists between the notion of freedom that arose in the Reformation and the Kantian notion of autonomy. In spite of the fact that reflection or internalisation in Kant's teaching attained a depth and an acuteness unparalleled in earlier philosophical systems — and thereby Kant is revealed as the heir to the modern, "evangelical gospel" — one must stress, as a specially ideal trait, its identification by Kant with the "notion of ethics and the notion of absolute subjection to the categorical imperative".[15]

Through this inner connection between the principle of freedom, the notion of ethics, and the law as a source of moral duty, it became possible for Jewry in spite of the inner, subjective source of freedom to obtain a spiritual foothold in the intellectual sphere of Germany. One of the most surprising phenomena in connection with Jewish thought in Germany is the conceptual subservience of all thinkers, no matter to which current in Judaism they belonged, to the philosophy of Kant. Not in every centre of Judaism in the Diaspora would the words of the leader of the *Agudat Israel* in Germany have been accepted as self-evident, viz. that "if we want to know how pure humanity finds its necessary culmination in Judaism, all we have to do is to study Kant".[16]

3.   A further stage in the consolidation of the association of Christianity with Western philosophical consciousness is connected precisely with the period in which German Jewry began to take an active part in the general intellectual life; therefore we must emphasise the tension which arose from the different directions in which Jewish thought and general culture were developing. At the end of the eighteenth century the consciousness of the identity between Greek culture and Christianity deepened to such an extent that these two areas of culture became the exclusive supports of the coping-stone of Western culture. The commencement in this process of historiosophical reconstruction may be seen in the aesthetic classicism of Winckelmann, and its culmination in German idealism and in romanticism which strove for the crystallisation of a Christian-Hellenistic conception of the world.[17]

---

[15]Guttmann, *op. cit.*, p. 277.
[16]Isaac Breuer, *Der Neue Kusari, Ein Weg zum Judentum*, Frankfurt a.M. 1934, p. 359.
[17]For a comprehensive discussion of this subject see Georg Stefansky, *Das Hellenisch-Deutsche Weltbild*, Bonn 1925.

The outstanding representatives of the view that European culture is a Christian-Hellenic symbiosis were Schiller, the brothers Schlegel, Schelling, and Hegel. Anyone who examines carefully the great systematic philosophical and aesthetic theories of the period will realise that characteristic of them all was an identification with the concept of "aesthetic idea", the chief significance of which was the demand for a union of opposites — necessity and freedom, nature and history — which had been regarded as identical by both the Christian and the Greek historical schools of thought. As an example, we need only cite Schelling's "construction" of the "new mythology" as a long-awaited blending of pagan Greek mythology — which is basically a general, "natural" conception of reality — with the historical, Christian mythology based on a universalistic-ideal conception of reality. "The subject-matter of mythology is nature, i.e. the general perception *(Anschauung)* of the universe as nature, while the subject-matter of Christianity is the general perception of the universe as history, a world of Providence."[18]

The new mythology in actual fact, Schelling continues, is not at all identical either with Greek mythology or with Christian mythology, but should be a union of both. The time will come, Schelling prophesies, when the "this after this" of the modern (Christian) world will become the "this beside this" of the Greek world, a faithful reflection of the identity of history and nature.[19]

This culture — to judge from its most mature philosophical manifestations — consequently expelled Judaism from its midst, by belittling its spiritual stature and defining it as a merely legalistic religion, completely opposed to meditation, to a life of inwardness, to subjectivity. Kant looked upon Mendelssohn's book *Jerusalem* and upon the whole attempt at a spiritual and philosophical renewal of Judaism as nothing more than "shrewd tactics", the main purpose of which was to defend Judaism against Christianity. A historiosophical conception which traced general culture from the association of Hellenism and Christianity had no difficulty in squeezing out of it the spiritual reality of Judaism.

How did Judaism make its way in a society which opened its gates to it on the legal and political plane but took pains to exclude it from its mental, ideological sphere?

In answering this question, it should first of all be emphasised — against Guttmann — that it was not the culture of Enlightenment, which was well disposed towards Judaism, that served as the basis for the most positive and vital works of religious thought of German Jewry, but precisely the general culture in its Hellenic and Christian combination and in its — from the Jewish point of view — problematic composition. In the second place it must be stressed — against Strauss — that to arrive at a positive assessment of the encounter between German Jewry and general culture is possible only if attention is paid to the original attempts at grappling with the theoretical problems which were forced upon Jewry as a result of its encounter

---

[18]Schelling, *op. cit.*, p. 427.
[19]*Ibid.*, p. 448.

with general culture, not by dint of self-effacement but rather by dint of the desire and the need to wrestle with it.

A first response to the challenge of this demand for a cultural struggle and its resulting theological conclusions is to be found in liberal theology.

THE INTEGRATION OF JUDAISM INTO GENERAL CULTURE WITHIN THE FRAMEWORK OF LIBERAL THEOLOGY

However surprising it may appear to us, it is precisely liberal theology (the central theme of which is commonly regarded as being the integration of Judaism into general culture) that confronted general culture, not by self-effacement but by a critical examination of the nature of general culture and of its — from the Jewish point of view — problematic composition. This theological trend — the outstanding representatives of which were Salomon Formstecher, Samuel Hirsch and to a certain extent also Ludwig Steinheim — was meant to come to grips with the spiritual and historiosophical assumptions of the prevailing general philosophical ideas, and sought to crystallise a theoretical position which would harmonise with the *Weltanschauung* of Judaism.

In this theological endeavour three aspects could be discerned which mark its contribution to its own as well as to later generations.

Firstly, the uncompromising, critical attitude to Christianity. One might have expected that during the period of the emancipation when desire for assimilation spread among the people and demands for the introduction of religious reforms were raised, Reform Jews would incline either to deprecating their own or to aping the dominant religion. But this was not the case. Nothing as strong as the criticism that was heard in liberal theology against Christianity was to be found in the neo-orthodoxy of S. R. Hirsch or, for altogether different reasons, among thinkers of religio-national sensibility, like Franz Rosenzweig and Martin Buber. Let us cite only Abraham Geiger's stern words of criticism. In his view Christianity not only did not constitute a positive factor in human advancement or in man's aspirations for a better world; it also showed itself to be the greatest enemy of culture and human progress. "During the sovereignty of the Christian Church, no new discipline was called into being, no new literature was created, not even a popular literature of vitality and freshness. There was just a vast desolation of learning and tedious burrowing in incomprehensible thoughts."[20] And these words do not refer only to Catholicism. "It was not only that the Catholic Church wages war openly against all spiritual advancement ... but also the attitude of the Evangelical Church to all scientific and artistic progress in the life of the state and the citizen becomes increasingly worse."[21] As against German idealistic historiosophy, Geiger

[20]Abraham Geiger, *Das Judentum und seine Geschichte*, Part II, Breslau 1865, p. 176.
[21]*Ibid.*, Part III, p. 162.

argued that Western culture was based not on Hellenism and Christianity, but on Hellenism and Judaism: "From the point of view of religion, modern culture derived from Jewish monotheism; from the point of view of science and art, from the Greeks. It ignored the peculiar Christian elements or thrust them aside."[22] Geiger's bold words were directed against a historiosophical opinion which sustained the best products of the thought and creations of German Enlightenment, i.e. against the assumption of an integration of Hellenism and Christianity whether as a given reality or as an aesthetic, philosophical ideal. Therefore we must state that the cultural integration to which Jewry aspired within Western culture was not possible without refuting and demolishing the philosophical assumptions and ideas prevailing in Western culture. This was achieved within Jewish liberal theology with acumen and without restraint, unparalleled in other theological trends in Judaism.

Secondly, but more significant from the Jewish theological point of view, there is the criticism which pervades the works of the liberal theologians Samuel Hirsch, Salomon Formstecher and Ludwig Steinheim. As has been stated, Geiger still conceived the structure of Western culture as a blending of Judaism and Hellenism. He substituted Judaism for Christianity, but retained the historiosophical conception of romanticism and Western aesthetic culture (of Schiller and others), namely that Western culture as a whole was indeed constructed of a synthesis of heterogeneous elements; and that out of a historical re-orientation based on a proper view of the spiritual importance of Judaism, salvation would burgeon not only for the Jew but also for Western man generally. As opposed to this, the systematic liberal theologians saw in the main realms of Western culture, in the ancient world of myths, in Greek philosophy and in the Christian world, a manifestation of a joint entity that was in principle the very antithesis of Judaism. In doing so, they did not intend merely to argue against Christianity, after the manner of Geiger; their purpose was to refute the basic standpoint of idealistic historiosophy as a whole. Steinheim in his book *Revelation according to the Torah-concept of the Synagogue* establishes an intellectual separation of an extremely severe form, between Judaism on the one hand and Greek and Christian thought on the other, although elements of this view are also found, with varying emphasis, in the works of Hirsch and Formstecher. According to them Judaism and Western philosophy did not spring from the same spiritual source. The culture of Greece and of Christianity was based upon the idea of immanence. There God is defined as the principle that manifests itself in the world through self-realisation, and not as a personal God revealing himself to the world: "Revelation as self-manifestation indicates the embodiment *(Verlieblichung)* of spiritual being, the representational concretisation *(Versinnlichung)* of the supernatural being; revelation as a Torah-concept means the disclosure of the nature and attributes of the Spiritual Being, i.e. of the Supreme One, of God."[23] From the

---

[22]*Ibid.*, Part II, p. 189.
[23]Ludwig Steinheim, *Die Offenbarung nach dem Lehrbegriff der Synagoge*, vol. IV, Frankfurt a.M. Leipzig Altona 1835-1865, p. 133.

point of view of the Torah-concept of religion there is no distinction in principle between the elements of knowledge in various pagan myths and the primary principles of rational philosophical doctrines. "Paganism in its twofold image of religion and philosophy expressed itself in the negation of freedom."[24] These doctrines are based on the concept of necessity, the *Ananke* of myth; on the Christian idea of the Incarnation; on the philosophical concepts of causation and emanation. In all these, any possibility of action without theoretical motivation is negated at once. Concepts which are basic in Judaism — creation, revelation, prophecy, ethical action — are excluded.

This brings us to the third aspect, the most important and problematic in liberal theology. As a result of the release from the prolonged metaphysical guardianship, a categorical change of values became essential. That is to say that as a result of the widening credibility gap between Judaism and general philosophical culture, thinkers of the new era were required to form more adequate concepts and more authentic ways of interpreting Judaism. To meet this need, Steinheim went much further than his liberal contemporaries when he declared that Judaism not only demanded a release perforce from mythological, philosophical and Christian attitudes (to use the term of R. Bultmann, it demanded a strict "demythologization"); it also established the criteria for deliverance from every mythological and Christian *Weltanschauung*. With Steinheim's strict insistence on the idea of *creatio ex nihilo* as the intellectual and methodical dividing line between Judaism and paganism, the door was opened to the conceptual renewal of Jewish theology.

Nevertheless, one must also see the problematical side of this line of development in liberal theology, inasmuch as this demand for the renascence of theological speculation was, according to these theologians, equivalent to a social and cultural Utopia. Since Judaism was "an active religion of freedom" (in the words of Hirsch) or "an ethical monotheism" and not "aesthetic" (in the words of Formstecher) or "a religion of the Torah" (in the words of Steinheim) it proclaimed the message of freedom which Christianity had dimly felt, without attaining a full awareness of its implications.

Judaism then fulfils, according to these thinkers, a sublime cultural mission, by the light of which mankind will march towards self-redemption. Thus the aim of this theology is disclosed as equating Judaism with general culture, and it was precisely this that alarmed those thinkers whose theological aim was not centrifugal, i.e. severance from national particularism towards universal human existence, but centripetal, i.e. coalescence and strengthening of Jewish national existence.

THE INTEGRATION OF GENERAL CULTURE INTO JUDAISM: THE WORK OF S. R. HIRSCH

The problem of the relationship between Judaism and general culture occupied a central position also in the speculative and educational activity of S. R. Hirsch. In

---

[24]*Ibid.*, p. 86.

programmatic fashion, Hirsch emphasises that it is not the function of Jewish theology to measure Judaism with the yardstick of general culture but rather to measure general culture with the yardstick of Judaism. In this emphasis on a change of direction in cultural integration there is possibly an indirect suggestion in favour of a categorical re-valuation of values, that is needed in order to preserve the authenticity of Jewish theological speculation. The feeling that Hirsch was in fact bent on the renewal of religious thought on the basis of Judaism grows when one considers the sharp words of criticism directed by him against Maimonides.

Hirsch is known for his opposition to Maimonides. The speculative method of Maimonides is severely condemned, since it sought — in Hirsch's view — to subject Judaism to principles and values which did not originate in Judaism.

> "The spiritual direction peculiar to him was Arab-Greek, and so, too, was his conception of life. He penetrated Judaism from the outside and carried with him views which he had maintained anyhow . . . His highest aim, too, was self-perfection through recognition of the truth; the practical side was subordinated."[25]

Western (Arab-Greek) philosophy could not (in Hirsch's opinion) serve as a basis for a Jewish *Weltanschauung* because in its view the highest value of life consists in intellectual perfection and contemplation, that is, theoretical activity *par excellence* and not in the practical ethical life which is a basic principle of Judaism.

For this reason Hirsch considered Mendelssohn's attitude preferable to that of Maimonides. While on the one hand Steinheim, the liberal contemporary of Hirsch, condemned Mendelssohn for having eliminated from Judaism every epistemological and metaphysical element and based it on law alone; and while on the other hand, Hermann Cohen praised Mendelssohn for "imbuing Judaism with the spirit of Germanism" and making an important contribution "to the revival of the Jewish religion in general",[26] Hirsch has a positive approach to Mendelssohn because he "demonstrated to his brethren and to the world that it is possible to be a strictly religious Jew and yet be distinguished and highly respected as a German Plato".[27]

Mendelssohn's opposition to the theologisation and dogmatisation of Judaism and his interpretation of Judaism as revealed law and not as revealed religion was heartily approved of by Hirsch. The *Torah* was not given to the Jewish people to serve as a basis for transcendental dogma or to make of "faith" an inner cult or an inner intention. Consequently Hirsch considered the method of liberal theology to be a continuation of Maimonides' system of compromise, while defining his own method (that of *Torah* and *Derekh Eretz*) as a continuation in the development of Mendelssohn's system.[28]

One could of course take this analogy further and argue that Hirsch even deepened the approach of Mendelssohn, and in this change are disclosed both the

---

[25]Samson Raphael Hirsch, *Neunzehn Briefe über Judentum*, Frankfurt a.M. 1920, p. 80.
[26]Cohen, *op. cit.*, p. 260.
[27]Hirsch, *op. cit.*, p. 84.
[28]*Ibid.*, p. 15.

virtues and the defects of his teaching. Paraphrasing the remarks in which he characterised Mendelssohn, one could say that S. R. Hirsch sought to demonstrate to his contemporaries that insofar as a Jew is devoted to his religion he could pride himself on being, if not a Plato, then at any rate a German Kant or Schiller.

Two, apparently contradictory, trends struggle in the spiritual world of Hirsch. The positive one was a vision of Judaism as a substantial entity rooted in itself, a spiritual, autarkic, self-contained entity. The concept of Judaism as a totality that is self-sufficient assuredly singles out Hirsch's view of Judaism as different from that of his liberal contemporaries. But accompanying this view was a second trend which cannot be understood apart from the cultural encounter of German Jewry with German culture, i.e. the trend to identify revealed law with general, human culture; Yisroel with Man; *Torah* with *Derekh Eretz*.

How strongly Hirsch felt about this identification can be exemplified by his description of the various dimensions of experience and the part played by Judaism within them.

Judaism rests entirely upon Law, upon the precepts of the *Torah*. But the Law is not, as it is for Mendelssohn, a particular force which obligates a definite people in whose presence the Law was revealed at a definite moment in history, but the Law is a principle of all being, concerning all the structures of existence. There are three main orders: nature, humanity and Yisroel.

The law of nature is the law of general obedience, the law of blind necessity, in which there is no room for knowledge or will. "Everything from the smallest to the greatest is a force emanating from God, in order to be effective according to the laws of God by means that are pre-determined, and in a place that is designated, and within a compass that is fixed — to take only in order to give . . ."[29]

Human law is the law of freedom and pure will. Like Kant and idealism, Hirsch interprets the law of freedom not as a free, arbitrary will, but that man "shall subordinate himself voluntarily to the law which all other creatures must serve of necessity . . ."[30]

The third, and supreme, dimension of existence is the law of the *Torah*. Just as the law of freedom does not reject the law of nature but interprets and complements it by adding the dimension of self-consciousness, so, too, does the law of the *Torah* add a new dimension to the realm of the law, by emphasising the obligatory bond between the will of God and His laws, which sustain the whole world.

Judaism is thus the bearer of a sublime mission to all mankind, through which, by virtue of the people's attachment to the *Torah*, there is revealed the indispensable link between law and the pure Divine will, which Kant laid down as basic to autonomous morality.

From this it is evident that Hirsch's criticism of the proponents of "compromise" in Jewish (liberal) theology did not at all aim at the dissolution of the spiritual partnership between general culture and Judaism, nor did it result in the reshaping

[29]*Ibid.*, p. 16.
[30]*Ibid.*

of the modes of thinking in Judaism. On the contrary, it was meant as an argument in favour of an inner organic partnership with mankind which a Jew could acquire through his unreserved loyalty to the law of the *Torah*. One must agree with the words of Max Wiener, that "Hirsch in no way lagged behind the most radical liberalism", and that he was in fact a "modern" and an "intellectual, no less than any of his opponents".[31] We may go further and argue that Hirsch was not even aware, in the way the liberal theologians were aware, of the problems and complexities which called in question every attempt at a total harmonisation of Judaism with general culture. That ideal and idyllic picture of the ethico-humanistic culture portrayed in the work of Hirsch is shown to be naive and anachronistic by the liberal thinkers who were more alive than he was to the crystallising process of modern culture and were more sensitive to the negative, philosophical fluctuations in the intellectual life of Germany. They drew from them the necessary theological conclusions.

This criticism is not intended to deprecate the educational work of Hirsch or his considerable contribution to the creation of a cultural framework which kept alive the flame of Judaism upon German soil. It is only an indication of doubt as to his theological achievement and the vitality of thought of the man who founded the New Orthodoxy of Germany. The symbolical-romantic hermeneutics of Hirsch, which he developed so systematically, were a faltering beginning to the meeting of cultures by way of simulation and after the manner of a cringing sycophant.[32] And the anchoring of Judaism in law, as explained by Hirsch, left it in the orbit of German culture, since the emphasis upon the categorical imperative as the source of moral behaviour is a substantial part of the heritage of Kantian philosophy, even though the sanction of the precept is the will of God and not the autonomous human will.

THE JEWISH INTEGRATION OF GENERAL CULTURE: THE WORK OF FRANZ ROSENZWEIG

It is in Franz Rosenzweig's speculative work that we notice a revision in the understanding of the relationship between Judaism and general culture, which in its intellectual demands and Jewish authenticity was superior to all the previous attempts made by Jewish thinkers in Germany.

All the assumptions about a possible encounter between religious Jewry and general culture appeared to Rosenzweig to be questionable and basically invalid. And even though the thought had never entered his mind that the partnership between Judaism and Germanism in civil, social, and cultural life might be brought

---

[31]Max Wiener, *Jüdische Religion in Zeitalter der Emanzipation*, Berlin 1933, p. 72.

[32]Criticism, by no means wide of the mark, in connection with Hirsch's style can be found in the afore-mentioned article of B. Kurzweil: "Already forty years ago the style of S. R. Hirsch aroused in me profound unpleasantness and disappointment. This style is replete with unbearable pathos, which is reminiscent of the pathos in the poorer works of Schiller; to be more exact: Schiller as he was understood by the petty-bourgeois classes." *Be-ma'avak 'al Erekhei Ha-Yahadut*, p. 275.

to an end, inferences which deviated from the personal conclusions of Rosenzweig himself followed from the criticism which he levelled against previous forms of this partnership, both the liberal and the orthodox.

One can distinguish in Rosenzweig's teaching at least two elements of thought which necessitate the abandonment of any possible symbiosis between Judaism and general culture.

The first element is bound up with the historiosophical outlook, which entirely rejected the historical mode of observation found in the theology — both liberal and orthodox — of the nineteenth century, as well as the Enlightenment and Hegel, which constituted the basis of the ideas in this theology. Rosenzweig severely criticises the historistic approach when he emphasises the negative character of historical temporality and of secular historical reality. The general, historical sphere was subject to the authority of irrational, arbitrary forces, and there was no foundation for deifying historical reality as a spiritual, divine entity, as taught by the Hegelian school. It is a fact that the world is tearing itself apart with wars, and history is the drama of a cruel battle-field drenched with blood and violence. The negative, destructive elements unceasingly overcome the positive, constructive elements.

Liberal theology, which pinned its faith on historical progress by which the ideals of social justice and prophetic morality would become a reality, created the false hope that a harmonious relationship would exist between a messianic Utopia and an ideal social order, which was in the course of being gradually realised. But when this faith in historical progress was lost, the cement that bound Germanism and Judaism together began to crumble.[33]

At the same time that Hermann Cohen, Rosenzweig's teacher, was still referring to "Jewish messianism" and "German humanism" as identical cultural conceptions, Rosenzweig was already speaking of the "paganism of the human idol-worshipper" and the "Christianity of Christian man" in one and the same breath. In his opinion, Western humanism as a whole was basically pagan, because it was based on the idea of the closeness of the mythical world, on the autarkic nature of humanism and on the immanence of Western culture, in which there was no room for revelation, for the rule of God upon earth. Ideas of historical progress and the ideals of humanity, which constituted the world of liberal theology and of the neo-orthodoxy of S. R. Hirsch, were anathema to Rosenzweig and many of his contemporaries.

His main reason for opposing "Jewish messianism" in the style of German humanism is disclosed by Rosenzweig in one of his letters to his cousin Hans Ehrenberg. It was an accepted thing in the nineteenth century to "see God in

[33]This post-liberal attitude, which was fed by the cultural pessimism of Schopenhauer, Nietzsche, and Spengler, was shared by Isaac Breuer, who in his outlook is much closer to Rosenzweig than to his grandfather, S. R. Hirsch. He writes in *Der Neue Kusari:* "One cannot grasp the historical nature of Judaism without an insight into the nature of general history and of the tragic fate of the nations of history, over which the meta-history of the Jewish nation rears itself as a necessarily recognised divine corrective." *Ibid.*, p. 324.

history", because history had acquired an independent, autochthonous image. It became the sphere of God's revelation. But — asks Rosenzweig — why do we still need God, if history is itself divine? Only Hegelians, liberal theologians and adherents of *Wissenschaft des Judentums*, who followed in their footsteps, were able to put all their stake in history and divest religion and the real relationship that exists between the individual and his God,[34] of their essential impact.

The second element in Rosenzweig's teaching which lead to a rejection of cultural integration was his meta-historical conception of Judaism. It is possible to speak about the integration of different cultures, but only on condition that they share a boundary. Judaism, however, is not contiguous to any other culture since "the secret of the people's eternity lies in a most profound rootedness within its own substance".[35] Judaism acquires a reality for itself as a result of a constant turning inwards towards its substance. The law, in which S. R. Hirsch saw the source of the Jewish people's eternity and the secret of its existence, could be given a spiritual-intellectual interpretation, and in fact the national continuity is thus explained by Hirsch. As opposed to this, the national element in Rosenzweig's opinion does not permit of a conceptual explanation, since it is the mighty reality of Jewish existence, which as a result of concealing its innermost being from spiritual exposure has fashioned a shield for its self-protection.[36]

Does not this withdrawal on the part of the people from any reflective attitude towards itself provide a sufficient reason, from Rosenzweig's standpoint, for condemning, in any shape or form, attempts made by Jewish thinkers in Germany to bring about cultural integration?

It is symptomatic of the extent to which German Jewry became attached to German culture that even Rosenzweig, who held fast to a conception of existential nationhood free of all compromise, which involved the abandonment of any partnership in fate or culture between Judaism and Germanism, not only refrained from taking a stand that derived its justification from the efforts of German Jewry to achieve cultural integration but, on the contrary, it was precisely he who arrived at a much more radical standpoint than any of his predecessors in the way he defined the nature of cultural integration. The ideal of "a Judaism that knows itself" in all the severity of its significance became part of the world of Rosenzweig.

In a manner that is particularly explicit, Rosenzweig formulates his point of view when discussing the Jewish Teutonism of Hermann Cohen: "It is only right that, also for a Jew, his Judaism should be all-embracing, all-permeating, all-combining no less than is Christianity for the Christian man or paganism for the human idol-worshipper".[37]

And in another context he goes on to say: "The main thing is *not* to show 'relationship' between the Jewish and non-Jewish spheres; this attempt was made

---

[34]F. Rosenzweig, *Briefe*, No. 46.
[35]*Der Stern der Erlösung*, III, Heidelberg 1954, p. 57.
[36]Rosenzweig, *Zweistromland*, p. 70.
[37]*Ibid.*

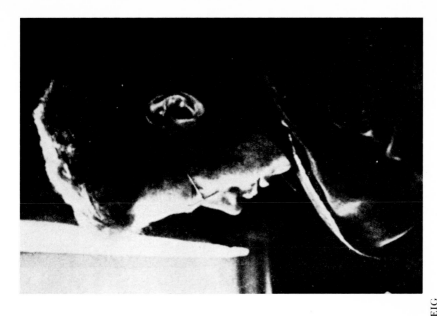

As a young man

FRANZ ROSENZWEIG

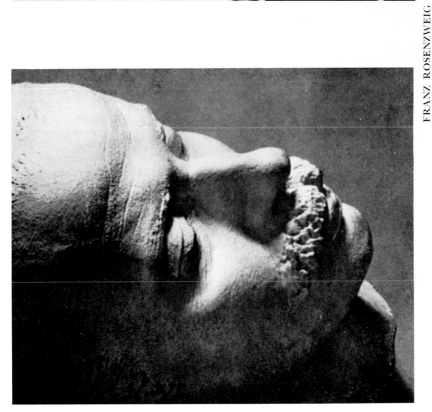

Death-mask

long ago. Not to vindicate Judaism, but to find the way to the heart of our life, and to make sure that this heart is a Jewish heart, for we are Jews."[38]

In place of an attitude of self-vindication with a sidelong glance at general culture for the purpose of building a bridge, no matter how rickety, between Judaism and general culture Rosenzweig demands a global relationship which will no longer tolerate a separation between a person's Jewishness and his humanity. Without a Jewish integration into general culture, the Jewish substance falls victim to the environment, as can be seen in liberal theology, or it remains empty of all meaning, as can be observed in the nationalist, atheistic ideology (against which Rosenzweig protested very strongly in his article 'Atheistic Theology').

This view, in which one can discern the nucleus of the systematic conception found in *Stern der Erlösung* (Star of Redemption) is in fact based upon the meta-historical conception of Judaism. For the uniqueness of Jewish reality consists in the primary identity, embodied within it, of existence and speculation, of national entity and its significance. "He [the Jew] does not believe in something, he is himself belief; he is a believer within an immediacy that no Christian dogmatist could ever attain."[39] In other words, Judaism is a national substance, lacking indeed an explicit consciousness of itself, but nevertheless steeped in the significance of a Divine world order in thought and in deed. In the language of Rosenzweig: "The Jewish people gathers within itself the elements of God, World, and Man who constitute one whole".[40] The uniqueness of the people lies in universal particularism, in its enfolding the totality of being within its separate, particular substance.

As has already been pointed out, Rosenzweig's conception with regard to the interpretation of a Jewish national identity sustained his thought and led him to construct "a system of philosophy resting upon a special, Jewish base". In his severe approach as systematically set out in the *Stern der Erlösung* German Jewry, at the termination of the problematical coexistence of Judaism and Germanism, assumed a new attitude in their relationship with general culture, an attitude which completely rejected the two previous standpoints: that of orthodoxy and that of liberal theology. Rosenzweig's uncompromising demand for a re-integration, from the Jewish point of view, of the culture of humanity, through the creation of concepts that would be in harmony with the spiritual image of Judaism, and which contains the elements to lighten the path of the Western world (paganism, Islam, Christianity, etc.) in a special way — this is the most glorious achievement of the religious Jews of Germany.

[38] *Ibid.*
[39] *Der Stern der Erlösung*, III, p. 105.
[40] *Ibid.*, III, p. 57.

Jewish Religious Reform and Wissenschaft des Judentums

The Positions of Zunz, Geiger and Frankel*

BY MICHAEL A. MEYER

Only four truly important intellectual movements appear in the Jewish history of the nineteenth century. Two emerged in its last decades, and despite individual support in the West, owed their successes to East European Jewry: Zionism and Jewish socialism. The other two were both initially centred in Germany and grew out of the German-Jewish experience of the last century. They are the movement for Jewish religious reform and the scholarly enterprise termed *Wissenschaft des Judentums (WdJ)*. The first pair gave birth to the ideology upon which the modern State of Israel was founded; the second pair has to a large extent shaped the conception of Judaism held by Jews of the Diaspora.

Although Jewish religious reform and *WdJ* have been intensively studied since the beginning of this century, they have usually been treated discretely, as separate movements with separate goals easily identified.[1] While such a division has the advantage of convenience, it removes the possibility of probing a complex of basic problems, both ideological and methodological, which can be properly understood only when these two movements are considered together. Only from an integrated study can we hope to learn how particular conceptions of Judaism helped to shape varying definitions of *Wissenschaft*; how *Wissenschaft* could be used — or as some claimed, misused — for the purpose of religious change; and how religious tenets could place definite restraints on scholarly inquiry. The necessity for dealing with the two movements together becomes the more apparent when we realize that religious reformers and Jewish scholars in the early period were almost always the same men, faced with the task of developing for themselves concepts of religion and scholarship which would harmonize their own twofold activity.

*The author wishes to express his appreciation to the following individuals for their assistance in preparing this study: Dr. Jakob J. Petuchowski, Dr. Israel Lehmann, Mr. Martin Tattmar, and Mr. Barry Kogan.
[1] The best general treatment is still Max Wiener, *Jüdische Religion im Zeitalter der Emanzipation*, Berlin 1933. Here too, however, *Reform* and *Wissenschaft des Judentums* are discussed in separate chapters. See also Nahum N. Glatzer, 'The Beginnings of Modern Jewish Studies', *Studies in Nineteenth-Century Jewish Intellectual History*, ed. Alexander Altmann, Cambridge, Mass. 1964, pp. 27-45.- Both *Reform* and *Wissenschaft des Judentums* have also been frequently discussed in this *Year Book*, cf. A. Altmann in *Year Book* I and VI (on Zunz), H. Liebeschütz in *Year Book I, II, V*, F. Bamberger in *Year Book V* (on Julius Guttmann), E. Rosenthal in *Year Book VIII* (on Elbogen) a.o.

I

The embryonic movements for religious reform and *Wissenschaft des Judentums* were both secondary products of the process of acculturation which had originated within Central European Jewry during the previous century. Only in the wake of the *Aufklärung*, once it had become possible to identify with a new and freer society, did many Jews feel the urge to adjust their faith — first out of political and aesthetic considerations, and later from deeper religious and intellectual motivations — to the model presented by the world around them. And only after the *Aufklärung* did they gradually become aware of the canons of modern scholarship and begin to conceive of a type of Jewish learning different from the traditional study of Jewish texts.

Enlightenment was followed, first in France and then more restrictedly and less permanently in Germany, by the granting of political equality. In part it was precisely the limited and uncertain nature of this "emancipation" in Germany which produced a great deal of the initial stimulus for both religious reform and *WdJ*. But for the only partly fulfilled hope of political equality, the frequent claim — made especially by the earliest reformers — that religious reform would finally remove all arguments against complete political acceptance, would have lost its force against orthodoxy. Had political equality been nearly complete, as in France since the Revolution, or undreamed of, as in Russia, the reform movement would not have been able to establish itself so easily. *WdJ* would probably also have been severely hampered in its development had not the universities been open to talented Jewish students, exposing them to modern scholarship but at the same time remaining unwilling to grant them academic chairs in any discipline whatever. Young Jews with aspirations to scholarship were thus forced either to convert, to enter business, or to use their humanistic studies in the cause of Judaism while serving as rabbis of Jewish communities or as teachers in Jewish schools.

Of the history of Jewish religious reform it may be said briefly that its seed-time and its flowering both occurred in Germany within the first half of the nineteenth century.[2] Beginning with the practical changes in the religious service during the first two decades of the century, it became in the thirties an intellectual movement that was developing a distinctive concept of Judaism. By the forties there was a sufficient number of progressively oriented rabbis to organise three rabbinical conferences which discussed issues as general as the nature of the Sabbath and as specific as circumcision. They were held between 1844 and 1846 in Braunschweig, Frankfurt am Main, and Breslau. Although towards mid-century the bulk of German Jewry remained rural demographically and orthodox in belief and practice, in the larger cities the feeling for religious change — reconciliation of *Leben* and *Lehre* — ran very deep. The non-orthodox section of Jewry had already split into

---

[2]On the Reform movement, see David Philipson, *The Reform Movement in Judaism*, New York 1931; Caesar Seligmann, *Geschichte der jüdischen Reformbewegung von Mendelssohn bis zur Gegenwart*, Frankfurt a.M. 1922; and Simon Bernfeld, *Toldot ha-reformatsyon ha-datit be-Yisrael*, Cracow 1900.

three parts: a radical faction which successfully formed its own *Gemeinde* in Berlin, soon under the leadership of Samuel Holdheim; a liberal or reform section whose mentor was Abraham Geiger; and a conservative *Richtung* which looked to Zacharias Frankel. In fact the forties represent a high point of enthusiasm and activity in the promotion of Jewish religious liberalism; the years after 1848, by contrast, brought somnolence and apathy.

Not quite the same is true of *Wissenschaft des Judentums*. Although its presuppositions and aims were formulated before mid-century, and although both important individual works and academic journals had been published, Jewish scholarly creativity — dependent on individuals rather than on the masses — continued unabated even in the less favourable political climate following 1848.[3] It began as an idea within a circle of highly intelligent and promising Jewish students at the University of Berlin who in 1819 formed a *Verein für Cultur und Wissenschaft der Juden*. As a number of its members, especially the president, Eduard Gans, had come under the influence of Hegelian philosophy, their programme for *WdJ* leaned heavily on Hegelian concepts.[4] But the amalgam of Hegelian philosophy of history and Jewish studies remained unstable. Most members of the *Verein* were less interested in Jewish scholarship than in philosophy and literature. After five years of existence and the publication of one volume of its *Zeitschrift für die Wissenschaft des Judentums* the *Verein* disbanded in 1824.[5] Not until the thirties and forties did Jewish scholarship receive renewed and lasting impetus as other men, mostly serving in rabbinical positions, now began to combine practical activity with scholarly endeavours. This time, however, the movement took hold and within two decades succeeded in producing a significant number of important scholarly works and in creating a distinctly modern type of Jewish study.

Of the Jewish scholars who laid the foundations of *WdJ* three individuals especially stand out. The first, Leopold Zunz, who had been the editor of the *Zeitschrift*, the journal of the *Verein*, was perhaps the least philosophically inclined of the group, and the sole founding member to devote his entire life to Jewish scholarship. The other two were both practising rabbis: Abraham Geiger and Zacharias Frankel. Each of these three was a significant personality in his own right; each held a view of religious reform and *jüdische Wissenschaft* clearly differentiable from the other two; and each has left a legacy measured not only by the continued influence of his works, but also by the continuing utilization of his basic approach to Jewish religion and scholarship on the part of one sector or another of the contemporary Jewish community. More than any other single individuals they illustrate by their writings, both

[3]For a survey, see Ismar Elbogen, 'Ein Jahrhundert Wissenschaft des Judentums', *Festschrift zum 50 jährigen Bestehen der Hochschule für die Wissenschaft des Judentums*, Berlin 1922, pp. 103-144.
[4]See the text of this programme, first published in an English translation: Immanuel Wolf, 'On the Concept of a Science of Judaism (1822)', *LBI Year Book II* (1957), pp. 194-204.
[5]On the *Verein*, see Siegfried Ucko, 'Geistesgeschichtliche Grundlagen der Wissenschaft des Judentums', *Zeitschrift für die Geschichte der Juden in Deutschland*, V (1935), pp. 1-34; Hanns G. Reissner, 'Rebellious Dilemma: The Case Histories of Eduard Gans and some of his Partisans', *LBI Year Book II* (1957), pp. 179-193; and this author's *The Origins of the Modern Jew: Jewish Identity and European Culture in Germany, 1749-1824*, Detroit 1967, pp. 162-182.

public and private, the various dimensions inherent in our subject. I shall here devote my main attention to a presentation of each man's basic position. Then a discussion of the specific issue of the religious limits of *Wissenschaft* will follow, and finally a look at the personal relationships between these central figures.

II

Of the three, Leopold Zunz was the most devoid of ideological bias. He did not serve as the rabbi of a large community, he was not the publicly acknowledged leader of a particular direction in Judaism. As a *Privatgelehrter* in Berlin he devoted himself with the least external motivation to the cause of *Wissenschaft* for its own sake. His scholarship most closely approximated the ideal of studying the past merely because it is the past and seeks to be rescued from oblivion. And yet even for Zunz Jewish scholarship existed within the context of the contemporary life of the Jewish people, and his own unique devotion to the discipline must be related to his experiences as a Jew growing to maturity in early nineteenth-century Germany.

From Detmold, where he was born in 1794, Zunz migrated shortly after his father's death to Wolfenbüttel where he received at first a thorough, traditional Jewish education and then, due to the influence of the new director of the Samson Free School, S. M. Ehrenberg, an introduction to secular studies and to the currents of the Jewish enlightenment. In 1815 he went to Berlin in order to study at the newly-founded Berlin University, and from then on spent almost the entire remainder of his life — he lived to the age of ninety-one — in the Prussian capital.

Zunz's university years in Berlin were filled with two forms of activity, which the young Zunz, however, surprisingly kept separate: participation in the life of the Jewish reform circle revolving around the figures of Israel Jacobson and David Friedländer, and a first effort at incorporating the new influences of the university into a programme for the scientific study of Judaism.

For a little over a year, from 1821 to 1822, Zunz served as one of the preachers at the modernized services conducted in Berlin which boasted greater decorum, use of an organ, slight changes in the prayer-book, and most notably, a sermon in German. As evidenced by his earliest writings and letters, Zunz was at the beginning a fervent advocate of the reform of Jewish life and highly cognisant of the need to replace the old-style rabbinical leadership with one more appropriate to the changed political and cultural climate. As he wrote to his teacher Ehrenberg, he felt strongly that the rule of the Talmud must be broken.[6] Even in middle age, at a time when he was turning towards greater traditionalism in practice, he wrote to the Jewish community in London that he favoured the abolition of the Kol Nidre prayer and most of the medieval poetry as well as conducting the confirmation ceremony and prayers in the language of the country.[7] Although it is true that in the

---

[6]Nahum N. Glatzer (ed.), *Leopold and Adelheid Zunz. An Account in Letters, 1815-1885*, London 1958, p. 13.

[7]'Zunz' Tätigkeit für die Reform', *Liberales Judentum*, IX (1917), pp. 113-120.

course of his life Zunz became more enamoured of tradition as the subject of his research began to appeal to his emotions as well as to his intellect, he never allowed attachment to his subject to influence his critical faculties. Both dogmatism and religious romanticism remained totally foreign to his mode of thinking.

Zunz's basic conception of *jüdische Wissenschaft* as essentially "philology" can be clearly traced to the influence of his mentor at the University of Berlin, the great classical philologist Friedrich August Wolf, and to Wolf's younger colleague August Boeckh. With Boeckh Zunz agreed that truth must be the aim of all historical studies, not uncritical veneration of the past, and not making the past seem more modern and enlightened than it really was. He agreed also that the past should not be studied merely in order to provide inspiration for the young. Through the years he remained true to this ideal by vehemently rejecting the servile apologetics and popular didactics which have characterized so much of Jewish historiography before his time and ever since. From Boeckh, too, Zunz probably derived the notion that philology was much more than linguistics, rather "a rediscovery and exposition of the totality of human knowledge", unlike history, however, not principally concerned with political events.[8] Such a discipline must have seemed to Zunz ideally suited to studying the past of a people which he believed deserved its place in history only on account of its literary productivity.

Yet, even more deeply, and indeed personally as well, it was Friedrich August Wolf who exerted a lasting influence on the young Zunz, and may indeed have served as a lifelong model. Wolf was not a popular instructor at the University; he even eschewed the position of Professor Ordinarius because he preferred to have maximum time available for his own research. His classes were poorly attended, often cancelled for lack of enrolment.[9] Yet, by Zunz's own testimony, he was extraordinarily attracted to the sober, historical, critical method of this noted scholar of Homeric poetry. And it is remarkable how the isolation of Zunz's scholarly life and his own disdain for scholarly popularity paralleled those of his teacher. Zunz did serve as head of a Jewish teachers' seminary in Berlin for about ten years and gave occasional lectures. But after the failure of his efforts in the Berlin reform circle and the break-up of the *Verein* in 1824, he lived mostly for his scholarship. When a burst of political initiative in pursuit of liberty and democracy came to nought with the demise of the Revolution of 1848,[10] Zunz once more and finally found refuge in his study of the Jewish past in all its intricacy and detail. Not a Jewish ideologist and not a popularizer, he remained aloof and was largely ignored by the bulk of the Jewish community. "No public exists for what I am doing", he complained in 1843.[11] Insofar as the Jewish public was interested in Jewish scholarship at all, it sought only to derive from the past some benefit for the present or the future.

---

[8]August Boeckh, *Die Staatshaushaltung der Athener*, 2nd ed., Berlin 1851, I, p. 2; idem, *Enzyklopädie und Methodologie der philosophischen Wissenschaften*, ed. Ernst Bratuscheck, Leipzig 1877, pp. 5-25.
[9]Wilhelm Körte, *Leben und Studien Friedr. Aug. Wolfs, des Philologen*, Essen 1833, II, pp. 11-72.
[10]See the Hebrew article by Nahum N. Glatzer, 'Zunz and Jost and their Relation to the Revolution of 1848', *Papers of the Fourth World Congress of Jewish Studies*, Jerusalem 1968, II, pp. 199-202.
[11]Nahum N. Glatzer (ed.), *Leopold Zunz. Jude—Deutscher—Europäer*, Tübingen 1964, p. 224.

To be sure, giving relevance to Jewish scholarship was also not foreign to Zunz's own orientation. From his very first work, *Etwas über die rabbinische Litteratur*, published in 1818, Zunz had introduced at some point in nearly all of his writings, especially in the earlier period, one or more explicit motives beyond the intrinsic interest of the subject-matter. The most common justification which we find in the Jewish scholarship of the early nineteenth century, and also in Zunz's work, is that promoting a proper understanding of the Jewish past will make governments less prejudiced against Jews and hence more likely to accord them full political and religious rights. Zunz presents this motive most explicitly in introducing his *Die gottesdienstlichen Vorträge der Juden*, the first of his major works, published in 1832, and he refers to it in other writings as well.

> "Mit der bürgerlichen Hintansetzung der Juden steht die Vernachlässigung jüdischer Wissenschaft im Zusammenhange. Durch grössere geistige Cultur und gründlichere Kenntnis ihrer eigenen Angelegenheiten, würden nicht allein die Juden eine höhere Stufe der Anerkennung, also des Rechts, errungen haben: auch so manche Missgriffe der Gesetzgebung, so manches Vorurtheil gegen jüdisches Alterthum, so manche Verurtheilung neuer Bestrebungen ist eine unmittelbare Folge des verlassenen Zustandes, in welchem seit etwa 70 Jahren, namentlich in Deutschland, sich jüdische Literatur und Wissenschaft des Judenthums befinden."[12]

In addition to political considerations there was also his desire for religious reform. It appears most prominently in Zunz's early writings, to disappear gradually in the thirties and be almost totally absent from Zunz's later work. He enunciated it most clearly in 1818: "Thus, in order to recognize and to distinguish what is old and useful from what is obsolete and harmful, to recognize what is new as well as desirable we must proceed carefully to study the [Jewish] people and its history, in its political as in its moral aspects."[13] As Zunz reached middle age, this motivation, so basic both for Geiger and for Frankel, receded to the point of virtual disappearance. But it was not displaced by a desire to accept the past *in toto* as a norm for the present, even if the past as a whole and not just those elements most acceptable to modern life needed scholarly attention. Although Zunz wrote a short piece on the *Tefillin*, published in 1843, in which he defended the practice of putting on the phylacteries, he did not go so far as to advocate their use by the contemporary Jew. "I know only too well that I cannot restore the practice of putting on *Tefillin*," he wrote to Ehrenberg, "yet is this what I really want? It is the scoffers I want to silence; it is always better to tie on *Tefillin* than to tie up heretics."[14] Zunz's increasing attachment to Jewish tradition, insofar as it was not influenced by external considerations, is best explained not as a return to any sort of orthodoxy but as the product of a decades-long preoccupation with the substance of the Jewish

---

[12]*Die gottesdienstlichen Vorträge der Juden*, Berlin 1832, p. vii.
[13]*Etwas über die rabbinische Litteratur*, Berlin 1818, p. 5. Four years later Zunz is still convinced that if it be possible to discover the inner life and striving of Jews under all conditions in the past, "then we will find again in every chapter of Jewish history the great laws of history and of nature, of that which is permanent and that which is transient, and be able to distinguish the human from the divine." *Zeitschrift für die Wissenschaft des Judenthums*, I (1822-23), p. 118.
[14]Glatzer, *Leopold Zunz*, p. 226.

past which necessarily made him not only its investigator but to a large extent also its champion. He could not look dispassionately upon efforts to belittle and mock that past to which he was so intensely and continuously devoted. He did indeed see his scholarly activity as a defence, but not as a defence of a static orthodoxy. In 1844 he wrote to Ehrenberg:

> "Now I am to become the support of Judaism; first I re-established the dignity of the phylacteries; now I am to fight for the *Milah* [circumcision], and in my mind's eye I can see the Shabbat coming next. I began with the re-establishment of *Wissenschaft*, then had to defend the *Derashah* [sermon], then the names of Jews, after that the freedom of development of worship, and now even the *Torah* itself."[15]

Yet this scheme of defending the Jewish past against its detractors also faded to be replaced in later years by loving absorption in the most recondite and forgotten creations of mediaeval liturgical poetry — which Zunz was not, however, suggesting should be introduced into the synagogue services.

There is only one thread which runs through Zunz's work from first to last. It is his firm belief that the study of the Jewish past must be raised to the level of a *Wissenschaft* and that *WdJ* might thus gain its rightful place within the constellation of academic disciplines. "How has it come about that our discipline [*Wissenschaft*] alone is languishing?" Zunz had already complained in 1818.[16] And in one writing after another he outlined what such a *Wissenschaft des Judentums* would include, and what needed to be done. That Zunz's primary interest all along was neither political nor religious, but oriented to the greater world of scholarship he had first encountered at the University of Berlin, becomes evident when one moves beyond the introductions and endings of his works to their substance. His *Gottesdienstliche Vorträge* is ostensibly a defence of the antiquity of the Jewish sermon; it is intended to provide grounds for persuading the Prussian government to allow sermons in German to be given in synagogues. But the content of the work is above all bibliographical. Under the guise of *Gottesdienstliche Vorträge* the reader is presented with a learned survey of the midrashic literature of the centuries, which renders the book still today a valuable bibliographical tool. Zunz was copiously illustrating just how rich a field of investigation Jewish literature offers. Perhaps the best example of Zunz's basic motive, i.e. to convince the scholarly world of the legitimacy of the specific area of Jewish research, is his *Zur Geschichte und Literatur*, published in 1845. It is noteworthy that the word "Jewish" does not even appear in the title of the book. No doubt quite intentionally, Zunz was thereby indicating that the various individual erudite studies which make up his work are intended as contributions to the broad field of literature and history in general, not to some parochial appendage of Jewish theology. "If the sum total of spiritual activity is an ocean then one of the rivers flowing into this ocean is indeed Jewish literature. . ."[17] It is recognition of scholarly equality that Zunz is most fervently seeking.

[15] *Ibid.*, p. 228.
[16] *Etwas über die rabbinische Litteratur*, p. 5.
[17] *Zur Geschichte und Literatur*, Berlin 1845, p. 2.

"Already the society of oriental philologists has introduced Jewish literature into its range of subjects. Its introduction into the academies and universities cannot be long in coming. For my part I would like to have at least contributed towards the reader establishing, even if only between the lines, a connection between the various fields of study, towards a participation of *everyone* in education and progress, and towards the existence of a humaneness that liberates from set forms."[18]

Because Zunz had the academic community, both Jewish and Christian scholars, principally in mind, he conceived of *Wissenschaft des Judentums* in broader and more secular terms than either Geiger or Frankel. Already in his first published work, which contained the designation *rabbinische Literatur* in the title, Zunz had expressed his preference for some other, broader term such as *neuhebräische* or *jüdische Literatur*. By 1845 he had rejected the title "Rabbinic literature" entirely, considering it a term imposed by Christian theologians. For him Jewish literature was not limited to works of a religious content. Like the literature of other peoples, the literature of the Jews must be understood to include writings on every conceivable subject: geography, natural science, secular poetry, as well as religion. "Our science should first of all emancipate itself from the theologians," he wrote. [19] But as a scholar who was neither a practising rabbi nor a theologian, Zunz was almost alone among the Jewish writers of his day. Geiger and Frankel were both theologians. Therefore their conceptions of *Wissenschaft des Judentums* would necessarily differ markedly from his.

III

The intellectual life of Abraham Geiger may be best understood as a continuing fluctuation between the aims and goals of the scholar and the desire to exert the immediate influence upon the present which is possible only for the active rabbi. Devotion to scholarship and concern with community leadership and direction created a tension which Geiger could never completely resolve.

Geiger, who was born into an observant Jewish family, in Frankfurt in 1810, was, like Zunz, something of a child prodigy, gaining competence in the traditional Jewish disciplines at an extremely early age. When he entered university he was uncertain whether to concentrate his interest in Semitics (Orientalia) or in theology. At first, in Heidelberg, most of his courses were in the field of language studies, and even after his transfer to Bonn he continued with Semitics. But during his student years in Bonn he developed an interest in philosophy and history which made him dissatisfied with philology. He recalled that his favourite subject had been Orientalia, but added, "once my mind had developed in the direction of philosophy I could no longer enjoy it [the study of Orientalia] as before, and so I sat alone in my room, at times in quite low spirits."[20]

In turning to philosophy, however, Geiger did not fall under the influence of any particular philosophical system, least of all the reigning Hegelian one. He appre-

---

[18]*Ibid.*, p. iv., cf. Glatzer, *Leopold Zunz*, p. 54.
[19]*Zur Geschichte und Literatur*, p. 20.
[20]Ludwig Geiger (ed.), *Abraham Geiger's Nachgelassene Schriften*, V, Berlin 1875-1878, p. 18.

ciated the lectures of an unknown young teacher in Bonn by the name of Bobrich precisely because he did not simply expound a system. From contact with Bobrich, Geiger hoped "to best achieve what I want most: an introduction to the philosophical mode of thought without having to swear allegiance to a system."[21] This goal of thinking philosophically without espousing a particular system remained basic for Geiger all his life. Unlike the Jewish philosophers of the early nineteenth century, who produced Jewish versions of Kant, Hegel, or Schelling, Geiger's thought remained free of such adaptations. The crucial intellectual influence upon him during his student days seems to have been Herder.[22] When he was only fourteen or fifteen he had already read this eighteenth-century philosophical historian who became, as he said, his favourite writer and ideal. At Bonn he re-read him and was, it appears, very definitely and permanently affected. His rediscovery of Herder coincided with his movement away from philology and towards a distinctly Herderian kind of historical study. After much critical reflection, recorded in his diary during the last weeks of 1830, Geiger finally noted that he had regained his appreciation of Herder, and concluded: "I must go along with him, but with more research of my own, so as to make clear and intelligible to myself that which he surmised, obscurely though vividly felt in his soul."[23] Upon consideration, it is not surprising that Herder should possess a special appeal. This pre-romantic thinker was not interested in history in the sense of political developments, to which he devoted very little attention, but in order to discover the evolution of the human spirit. In his work *Auch eine Philosophie der Geschichte zur Bildung der Menschheit*, which we know Geiger read at this time, Herder was able with broad, almost impressionist strokes of the pen to present a lively image of past ages without the burden of detail. While maintaining a critical view of the present, he could point out the continual striving forward as age followed age upon the "Schauplatz der Gottheit," as Herder called history. In marked contrast to Zunz, Geiger was to aim at just such an approach to Jewish history; his goal was to be able to characterize an era of the Jewish past as a particular manifestation of the Jewish spirit and to advance from bibliography to intellectual history. By April 1831 he could write definitively to his student friend, Samson Raphael Hirsch, later to become leader of Neo-Orthodoxy and Geiger's arch-opponent:

> "Nicht wahr, liebster Hirsch, Sie müssen mich bei unserem ersten Zusammentreffen, da ich noch in die Fesseln philologischer Kleinlichkeitsjagd geschlagen war, recht oft für sich ausgelacht haben. Freilich hat sich nun das Interesse hieran gar nicht verloren, aber Alles ist doch einem höheren Zwecke untergeordnet und die kleinste Bemerkung in der Sprache gewinnt neues Leben durch Zurückgehen auf ihren Ursprung aus dem menschlichen Geiste und wie hierin sich gerade die eigene Ansicht der Dinge und des Lebens bei jedem Volke abspiegelt."[24]

Under different circumstances Geiger might have become a professional historian.

---

[21]*Ibid.*, p. 28.
[22]This early and decisive impact of Herder's approach to historical scholarship upon Geiger has never been properly emphasized.
[23]Geiger, *op. cit.*, p. 34.
[24]*Ibid.*, p. 49.

But for a Jew in early nineteenth-century Germany an academic position was clearly out of the question. Moreover, Geiger longed not only to write, but also to make history and, ideally, somehow to combine the two. He could see himself neither as the pure scholar in the style of Zunz nor could he identify fully with the functions of a rabbi. Despite his later insistence upon the prerogative, making decisions of ritual law like a rabbi of the old type held little attraction for him. Nor was he entirely satisfied with the new rôle of preacher exemplified by such men as Eduard Kley and Gotthold Salomon at the Hamburg Temple. Practical rabbinics of any kind, though he is supposed to have performed them well, held little attraction for him. Between the pure scholar, the antiquarian, and the practically oriented rabbi, the young Geiger discerned an intermediate rôle which he chose as his own: that of the theologian. By theology, however, Geiger did not mean the formulation of a theological system; he rather meant scholarly study of religious history with the intention of grasping the expressions of the religious spirit in each age and its development in the course of time — a study undertaken not wholly from scholarly motives, but with the intent of providing perspective and direction to religious development into the future. With this conception in mind, Geiger in 1835, at the age of only twenty-five, began to publish a periodical entitled *Wissenschaftliche Zeitschrift für jüdische Theologie* which was to run for a total of six volumes. In introducing the first issue, he plainly put forward the notion that only Jewish theologians, fully familiar with the entire historically formed structure of the Jewish religion and at the same time in accordance with the "level appropriate to the age" (a Herderian expression), could advance the cause of Israel through their scholarly and practical activity.

The task of such scholarly Jewish theology, as Geiger understood it, was twofold. As a first step, the history of Judaism must be understood in its own terms, each period in its own context possessing relative validity as the revelation of the religious consciousness of the community of faith at a particular point in Jewish history. But that is not enough. Geiger was too conscious of the contemporary situation to allow such a non-evaluative historicism to exhaust the purposes of Jewish theology; the Jewish theologian is not to be solely a sympathetic investigator of the spiritual eras of the Jewish past. He should also commit himself to an evaluation of the previous manifestations of Jewish religion in terms of their organic connection or lack of connection with the present and their viability for the future. In the fourth volume Geiger wrote that the student of the Jewish past has to attempt an answer to the question:

> ". . . wieviel der Gegenwart von ihrem Besitze nicht bloss äusserlich überkommen ist, sondern auch innerlich angehört—ihm kann es nicht genügen, die Zeiten und die Zeit zu verstehen, er wird auch mit sehnsüchtigem Blicke in der Zukunft lesen und den Weg ebnen wollen, damit diese in der geziemenden Weise sich bewegen könne."[25]

Geiger wanted to dispel the notion that contemporary Judaism was an integral unity whose components all shared in its sanctity. Historical study, in his view,

[25] *Wissenschaftliche Zeitschrift für jüdische Theologie*, IV (1839), p. 322.

would show that not all parts of the tradition were equally ancient or historically of equal significance; some elements were grafted onto it — *parasitenmässig ange-schmiegt* — as a result of external influences. Exposing the origins and historic rôle of each individual element would offer liberation from the static view which regarded every custom, ceremony, and belief as indispensable to Judaism.

The ultimate task of the theologian was, then, to bring the results of his research to bear upon the Jewish life of the present and to utilize his newly-won historical perspective to propel the present into the future. Because he was more knowledgeable about the Jewish past in all the vicissitudes of its development, the Jewish theological scholar was in the best position to provide direction, to participate actively in shaping Jewish history; he would resist being simply driven along by the mass. The salvation of Israel, according to Geiger, lay neither in cutting off the past nor in passively allowing history to take its course, but:

> ". . . in the endeavour to develop historically that which has evolved historically, even now since we have become agents of history, restraining here, encouraging there, here following the wheels of time, there grasping and accelerating them with a strong arm."[26]

In his conviction that the theologians must take upon themselves the responsibility for religious change, Geiger differed both from Zunz, who mistrusted any "hierarchy" of rabbis or theologians, and from Frankel who, as we shall see, felt strongly that the will of the community as a whole, not of the theologians, should rule.

Geiger's *Zeitschrift* was formally issued under the aegis of a *Verein jüdischer Gelehrter*, sixteen Jewish scholars whose names, including Zunz, the historian Jost, and the Galician scholar and rabbi S. L. Rapoport, were listed on the inside cover. Thirteen of them held doctorates; nearly all contributed at least one article or review to the *Zeitschrift*. They constituted a grouping of individuals formally educated both in Jewish and secular studies which could scarcely have been put together a generation earlier: the beginnings of the community of modern Jewish scholarship. But despite this *Verein*, which existed only on paper, the *Zeitschrift* was largely a personal organ for Geiger's own ideas. He wrote the leading articles and he determined its direction.

The historical studies which Geiger composed for his periodical were clearly chosen because their subjects were of more than mere antiquarian interest. Geiger could not conceive the study of each phase or current of the Jewish past as of equal value. Those aspects of Jewish experience closest to the present in terms of *Weltanschauung* were selected for elucidation. His first subject, 'Die wissenschaftliche Ausbildung des Judentums in den zwei ersten Jahrhunderten des zweiten Jahrtausends bis zum Auftreten des Maimonides', attracted Geiger because it seemed to him a period of "many-sided and joyous development."[27] The modern scholar finds the men of this period congenial; he admires their scholarship and their creativity. They serve as historical proof that Jewish creativity is not by nature narrow, but became so only when external persecution narrowed its horizons.

[26]*Ibid.*, I, (1835), pp.2-3.
[27]*Ibid.*, pp. 13 ff.

Still, Geiger maintains his historical perspective and will not make this or any other period of Jewish history normative for the present. The works of an Ibn Ezra, a Yehuda Halevi, or even a Maimonides, admirable in their own right, were created "in the spirit of their time", and for Geiger this meant in an intellectual environment which, for all its close relation with philosophy, was still devoid of *Wissenschaft* in the modern sense of historical criticism directed to its own origins.

For all Geiger's desire to find a precedent in the past, he was well aware that modern *Wissenschaft*, with its critical independence, remained very different from even the non-Talmudic Jewish learning which he found and admired in various stages of the Jewish past. It took over elements from the old but brought them into association with hitherto uncontemplated scholarly considerations, thus raising Jewish learning for the first time "to a scientific level".[28] Although Geiger himself wrote a number of scholarly articles in Hebrew, he had qualms about using the language of traditional Jewish scholarship precisely because he feared use of the old linguistic expressions might subtly disguise the novelty of the scholarship and obscure the contradictions between past and present which would be quite obvious in an article written in German.[29]

It is characteristic of Geiger's early historical studies that he consistently aimed at penetrating to the essential character of a period and to the progress of the Jewish spirit from age to age. Like Herder, he was basically uninterested in political history for — at least with regard to the Jews — he found their changing political circumstances uncontrolled by any rational principle of development and hence incapable of treatment in a scientific manner. Individual events or individual writings were for Geiger only building blocks for the understanding of a total developing *Gestalt*. They needed to be brought together into an integrated picture. Although Geiger frequently wrote the most erudite and detailed articles and reviews, and although for a time he included a column of specifically Jewish news items in his *Zeitschrift*, his mind was disdainful of detail for its own sake. He criticized Zunz for dwelling upon it too exclusively in his learned researches and he belittled Ludwig Philippson's *Allgemeine Zeitung des Judentums* for serving up to its readers nothing more than the surface froth of current events.

While for Zunz it was essential that the history of Jewish literature achieve equal status in the *Literaturgeschichte* of the nations, for Geiger it was Jewish theology that must be given its rightful place beside the theological investigations of Protestants and Catholics. A column in Geiger's *Zeitschrift* called *Nachrichten aus der Synagoge* by the fourth volume had its title shortened simply to *Nachrichten* and was used to report on, and subject to criticism, the latest articles of interest in Christian theological journals. Zunz's larger intellectual community was that of the literary historians; Geiger's that of the historians and critics of religion. When the important critical movement which produced David Friedrich Strauss's *Life of Jesus* (1835) succeeded in shaking Christianity to its foundations, Geiger felt his readers should be acquain-

---

[28]*Ibid.*, V, (1844), pp. 24-25.
[29]*Nachgelassene Schriften*, II, p. 286.

ted with the results in terms of the New Testament and what the application of similar principles of higher criticism to Jewish sources might imply. It was a movement, Geiger concluded, which having had such an impact upon Christianity must not be ignored by Jewish theologians, especially those who do not want to live isolated from their period, "a movement which will affect not merely the sources of Judaism, but, as things now stand, even Judaism itself."[30]

But Geiger's most basic concern was not the status of Jewish scholarly activity in the eyes of the world; it was not Jewish scholarship for its own sake at all. Geiger wanted to reshape the present and the future of Jewish life and needed a more than arbitrary basis on which to proceed. He almost always rejected the approach of the early reformers, and even of Samuel Holdheim in his own day, which was to argue dialectically with orthodoxy on its own legal grounds.[31] For Geiger the link of *halakha* which bound the religious community of Israel to its past and had unified the group in each age, was broken. A new link had to be found and a new criterion for assessing religious life. For Geiger that link was the spiritual heritage of Israel seen as a developing entity, past generations appearing not as vessels of divine law but, in Geiger's words, as "living bearers of the moral, religious and scientific spirit at its historical stage".[32] The Jew of the present would relate to the past by gaining an understanding of Jewish spiritual development. The committed Jew thus became a student of Jewish intellectual history where previously he had been a student of Jewish law.

Geiger began his *Zeitschrift* shortly after he received his first rabbinical position in the Rhineland town of Wiesbaden where he remained for six years until in 1838 he was invited to become rabbi in Breslau. The thirties were years which allowed Geiger much leisure for scholarly pursuits. But in the forties the Breslau rabbinate and the controversies attendant upon his appointment as well as the rabbinical conferences in the middle of the decade made him devote a much greater portion of his time to practical activities. By then Geiger did indeed feel that the time for action had come. The scientific basis had been laid in the thirties; the forties were used to apply the fruits of *Wissenschaft* to life.[33]

Caught in the storm of political events leading up to the Revolution of 1848, Geiger had to suspend publication of his *Zeitschrift* after the sixth volume in 1847. But he remained convinced that it had performed a necessary task which required further efforts. In a hitherto unpublished letter of 1854, he wrote:

"Uns thut eine periodische Schrift noth, die mit Kräften in das Geistesleben eingreift, wie um es ohne Unbescheidenheit zu sagen, zu ihrer Zeit meine Zeitschrift war. Ich warte schon lange auf das Jüngelchen, das an einem noch irgend unbekannten Orte sitzt und in sich hineinquält und in sich hinein murrt, bis es herausplatzt und sich die Aufmerksamkeit erzwingt. Dieses jugendliche Streben will ich freudig begrüssen und gern auch das in mir noch nicht erloschene Jugendsein anfachen um es auf das gemeinsame Alter

[30]*Wissenschaftliche Zeitschrift für jüdische Theologie*, III (1837), p. 302.
[31]*Ibid.*, VI (1847), p. 14.
[32]*Ibid.*, V (1844), p. 22.
[33]*Ibid.*, VI (1847), pp. 1-2, 91.

zu bringen. Mit romantischem Brilliantfeuer und mit verlöschenden bibliographischen
Kohlen schafft und unterhält man kein Organ der Zeit.''[34]

Eight years later, in 1866, Geiger himself again took up the editorship of a periodical which this time he entitled, appropriately enough, *Jüdische Zeitschrift für
Wissenschaft und Leben*. And during the second half of the century, until his death in
1874, he maintained this dual and related devotion to *Wissenschaft* and to life — first
in Breslau, then in Frankfurt, and finally in Berlin. [35] The latter he exercised in his
practical rabbinate, the former in his prolific writings, most notably his magnum
opus of 1857, *Urschrift und Übersetzungen der Bibel*, to which we shall return. Yet
there were those in the Jewish community, equally devoted to both *Wissenschaft* and
life, who felt that Geiger subverted the former for a highly questionable conception
of the latter. Their most notable spokesman in the first half of the nineteenth century was Zacharias Frankel.

IV

Unfortunately we know much less about the intellectual influences which shaped
Zacharias Frankel than about those exerted upon Zunz and Geiger. Very few letters
from his early years have been published, and Frankel himself produced no scholarly
work until 1840, when he was already thirty-nine years old. It may be that it was
the Jewish atmosphere of the city of his birth, Prague, that stimulated in the young
Frankel the very deep attachment to all things Jewish which was consistently to
determine his attitude to theoretical as well as practical issues. After a thorough,
traditional Jewish education in his home city, he went to study at the university in
Pesth where he also received his doctorate. Thereafter he served in rabbinical
positions in Teplitz in Bohemia, and in Dresden, before becoming the first president
of the Jewish Seminary in Breslau in 1854, a position he held for more than twenty
years until his death in 1875.

It was during the early 1840s, while he was rabbi in Dresden, that Frankel
swiftly rose to prominence in German Jewry. At that time he began to publish
scholarly works and sermons in rapid succession; he was offered but declined the
prestigious rabbinate of Berlin; and in 1844 he began to publish his own periodical,
the first of two he was to edit during his lifetime. His journal was called *Zeitschrift
für die religiösen Interessen des Judenthums* and it lasted for three volumes until, like
Geiger's *Zeitschrift*, it was destroyed by the convulsions of 1848. In its pages we find
spelled out for the first time Frankel's unique approach to *Wissenschaft* and religious
reform.

[34]Abraham Geiger, Breslau, 23rd October 1854, to Meir Wiener, Hanover. Abraham Geiger
file in the German section of the Archives of the Hebrew Union College Library, Cincinnati,
Ohio.
[35]Other aspects of Geiger's approach to scholarship are treated in Max Wiener, 'Abraham
Geiger's Conception of the "Science of Judaism"', *YIVO Annual*, XI (1956/57), pp. 142-162 and
in H. Liebeschütz, 'Wissenschaft des Judentums und Historismus bei Abraham Geiger',
Essays Presented to Leo Baeck, London 1954, pp. 75-93.

ABRAHAM GEIGER

(1810 - 1874)

ZACHARIAS FRANKEL

(1801 - 1875)

With respect to goals and even to the language employed, Frankel's programme is remarkably similar to Geiger's. The latter would have had to endorse heartily Frankel's statement of purpose: "This journal has primarily assumed the task of illuminating Judaism in its religious aspects from the standpoint of theology and promoting further development from its present stage."[36] No less must Geiger have agreed with Frankel's repeated call for the reconciliation of faith and life and with his plan to hold up as models certain outstanding periods of Jewish history in which Jewish life underwent significant evolution.

Yet for all of this genuine similarity, their differences were profound. Frankel's warm regard for Jewish tradition made it quite impossible for him to advocate a conception of *Wissenschaft* sufficiently free and independent to stand outside Jewish historical experience and render judgment upon it. *Wissenschaft* must be conducted "on a positive historical basis" Frankel argued, even before the Frankfurt rabbinical conference of 1845.[37] Unlike the orthodox, Frankel held that Judaism had indeed evolved in the course of time and it was the task of *Wissenschaft* to point out the advances which had already occurred. But it was not its function to set up external criteria for evaluating the process of development in the future. Scholarship was not the sole prerequisite for deciding the direction development should take. The religious reformer — and Frankel did not reject the term "reform" — must be more than a scholar: he must be intimately involved in the Jewish life of his day. He must be existentially engaged with the present, not just intellectually but emotionally. The Jewish present "must be lived through, felt through ['muss ein Durchgefühltes sein']," Frankel tells us. And Frankel himself did indeed possess just such an intimate knowledge of the contemporary Jewish community and its religious values — to a degree beyond Geiger.

Frankel correctly realized that what mattered to the average Jew was not theology but practice and that his attachment to customs and tradition was much less a matter of intellectual consideration than of simple emotion. He could therefore quote approvingly the Talmudic dictum that what the people accept and what is part of their way of life no authority may abolish. And he could argue that present practice constituted an "irrefutable norm for attempts at reform."[38] This meant that no Jewish theologian or conference of rabbis ever had the right to abolish a custom or ceremony held sacred by the people. It also meant that the traditionally inclined Jew would never have to justify his practices by any intellectual criterion. The observances of the community were self-justifying simply because they were the observances of the community. Over and above the impersonal criterion of *Wissenschaft* Frankel thus sets another entirely different measuring rod for change, which he calls the *Gesamtwille* of the community. The theologians in fact have little more to do than clarify this common will and bring it to full consciousness. Change may be desirable, but only because so many Jews are dissatisfied with the present form of Judaism, and any significant change in Judaism would have to be the product of a

---

[36]'Anzeige und Prospectus', *Zeitschrift für die religiösen Interessen des Judenthums*, 1843, p. 6.
[37]*Ibid.*, p. 5.
[38]*Ibid.*, I (1844), p. 19.

synod of laymen and rabbis, not of rabbis alone. No Jewish leader, one must assume, has the moral right to make the people intellectually dissatisfied with any element of Jewish tradition to which they are still emotionally attached. Such criticism would be not only unjustified, but a religious desecration. For Frankel the will of the people is nothing less than holy, nothing less than a form of revelation: "The general consciousness of a religious community contains a revelation which so long as it is viable constitutes the common possession of the faith and must be accorded no less a recognition than the direct, divine one."[39] Not surprisingly, therefore, the only changes in religious practice that Frankel was willing to consider were those already made by a large section — perhaps the majority — of his community in Dresden: abolishing the second day of certain holidays, allowing the eating of *Hülsenfrüchte* (pulse) on Passover, and the abolition of certain customs associated with mourning and circumcision.[40]

Unlike Geiger and Zunz, Frankel held that *Wissenschaft* must always remain subservient to religion and should never be allowed to become its master. The only valid *Wissenschaft* is that which respects the primacy of revelation and indeed takes revealed truth as its zenith. Frankel himself summed this up well in the second volume of his journal.

> "Eine positive Religion kann den Fortschritt nur bis zu einem gewissen Ziele kennen; sie sagt schon durch ihre Benennung, dass sie ein Gesetztes, Unauflösbares habe, das erhalten werden muss, sie ist Offenbarung und nicht Wissenschaft, und das Judenthum darf noch überdies mit gerechter Freude erwähnen, dass seine Basis auch zugleich der Wissenschaft höchster Punkt sei."[41]

Given Frankel's conception of Judaism and of *Wissenschaft* as he outlined them in his *Zeitschrift*, we can easily understand the direction taken by his scholarly work. Conceiving Judaism as a religion of actions, ceremonial and moral, Frankel did not lavish interest upon the development of ideas within Judaism, as did Geiger, nor upon the creativity of individuals as did Zunz, but upon the evolution of Jewish law. Often the immediate motivation for his writing was political, such as removal of the degrading "Jewish oath" or other Jewish disabilities in serving as witnesses in court. More basically, however, and increasingly in the course of time, Frankel's goal was to gain respect for the Jewish legal tradition among Gentiles and even more among Jews. By approaching Jewish law with the tools of *Wissenschaft*, Frankel hoped to bring it into contact with modern modes of thought. Ultimately, he aimed at writing a complete history of the *Halacha* which would present it as a dynamic and evolving entity.

---

[39] *Ibid.*, II (1845), p. 15.

[40] While referring to the will of the people made a certain amount of sense for a conservative religious leader in the first half of the century, increasing erosion of religious practice in the course of time made this position less and less tenable. On this subject see Ismar Elbogen, 'Der Streit um die "positiv-historische Reform"', *Festgabe für Claude G. Montefiore*, Berlin 1928, pp. 24-29. In Geiger's view, Frankel even in 1844 knew at first hand only the life of the traditional section of the community; see *Nachgelassene Schriften*, V p. 177.

[41] *Zeitschrift für die religiösen Interessen des Judentums*, II (1845), pp. 16-17.

Frankel did not achieve that goal, though he did much to arrange and analyze the legal literature on specific subjects. He comes closest to his aim in his magnum opus, *Darche Ha-Mishna*, published in 1859. In the most important second chapter Frankel provides a view of the historical development of the earliest stage of Rabbinic law by arranging the most significant opinions expressed in the Mishna in chronological order according to the *Tannaim* who set them forth. But like Zunz, Frankel is a compiler rather than a historian. Far more than Geiger or Zunz, Frankel takes his model from the Jewish scholar of the old type, whose status is attained by his knowledge of Jewish law. In fact at one point he equates *Wissenschaft* with "knowledge of the law."[42] Though he must have realized the difference, Frankel uses the terms *Wissen* and *Wissenschaft* in conjunction with each other in such a way as to obscure the great gap between the essentially uncritical stance of past Jewish intellectual activity and the critical canons of the present. He desires to maintain continuity with the past and does so by finding precedent for modern *Wissenschaft* in earlier periods of Jewish history, thus making it seem indigenous to Judaism and rendering it innocuous and not at all threatening to constituted Jewish life. Frankel justified modern scholarship not only as a basis for development, but also as a brake upon over-hasty change; it was to be a stabilizing influence, a counterweight to the destructive pressures of the *Zeitgeist*: "Without *Wissenschaft* no reform, no reformation; an attitude of tearing down only, of all-destructive negation does not bring improvement and salvation."[43] But even Frankel, the religious conservative among our trio of scholars, is irresistibly drawn to the term *Wissenschaft* and never publicly uses the old Yiddish expression *Lernen*. "The very vitality of Judaism lies in its scholarship," he wrote.[44] With Zunz and Geiger, he shared the belief that *Wissenschaft* and *Wissenschaftlichkeit*, the shibboleths of the academic community, must be applied to any intellectual enterprise claiming respect.[45] Where he differed from them was in its definition, its goals, and its limits.

V

The question of whether *Wissenschaft* has any fixed limits is the really crucial issue in any discussion of the relationship between the spheres of science and religion. Orthodoxies have always restricted free inquiry to a separate realm and prevented it from attacking the fundamentals of the faith. When modern historical criticism emerged, it claimed the ability to determine origin and composition of sacred texts, and thus posed the severest challenge to their established status. Not surprisingly, orthodox Jewry barred its application to either the written law of the Bible or

---

[42]*Ibid.*, I (1844), p. 22.

[43]*Vorstudien zu der Septuaginta*, Leipzig 1841, p. x.

[44]*Zeitschrift für die religiösen Interessen des Judenthums*, I (1844), p. 293.

[45]Even the orthodox, though definitely opposed to unfettered scholarship, appropriated these value terms for their own purposes, eventually declaring that true *Wissenschaft des Judentums* meant precise knowledge of Jewish ritual law. They termed any other scholarly enterprise related to Judaism "Wissenschaft *vom* Judentum," a surrogate for the genuine article. *Der Israelit*, XLIV (1903), p. 2096; XLV (1904), p. 2069.

the oral law of the Talmud. When Frankel in his *Darche Ha-Mishna* questioned the Sinaitic origin of certain laws contained in the Talmud, he called down upon himself the wrath of Samson Raphael Hirsch and his fellow orthodox.

But for Frankel, too, there was a definite limit to *Wissenschaft*, which he set at the text of the Pentateuch. And when he wrote on the Septuagint translation of the Bible, his unwillingness to doubt the precise exactitude of the Masoretic text severely limited his freedom of conceptualization.[46] For him the Pentateuch (Five Books of Moses) remained *sanctum sanctorum*, not to be touched by secular inquiry. In his work he was careful to avoid the higher biblical criticism and he excluded it also from the journals which he edited.

Geiger's attitude was different. Unlike Frankel, he set no limits to the range of *Wissenschaft*. For him the written law as well as the oral, the text of the Bible as well as the text of the Talmud, needed philological and historical criticism to determine their place in the development of religious ideas. Concluding the last volume of his *Zeitschrift* in 1847, Geiger wrote that the time for Jews to engage in biblical studies had not yet arrived, but it would come — and surely sooner than many expected. Seven years later, in 1854, Geiger himself began to devote serious attention to the late biblical period and to the traditions of the Bible in the first centuries after its canonization. As the last part of the title of his *Urschrift und Übersetzungen der Bibel*, published in 1857, tells us, his goal was to relate his philological findings to the "inner evolution of Judaism" in these early centuries. He did not doubt that this development had wrought changes in the very text of the Hebrew Bible.

In its day, Geiger's *Urschrift* received a mixed reception.[47] A French journal reviewed it very favourably, as did the Hungarian rabbi Leopold Löw. Zunz wrote more circumspectly: "Geiger's book *Der Urtext* has scientific value but, despite the author's assurance to the contrary, a tendency derived from contemporary influences."[48] Writing for a non-Jewish scholarly journal, Zunz himself later published the most radical kind of Pentateuch criticism in which he denied the Mosaic authorship of the Torah and ascribed various sections to different periods of time.[49] The fault he found in Geiger was not his radicalism in assailing the sanctity of the text, but his not very carefully veiled desire to find a powerful precedent for religious change in a formative period of Jewish history.

---

[46]Markus Brann, a teacher at the Breslau Seminary, admitted: "Bei Frankel fällt allerdings *eine* Aufgabe der Septuaginta-Forschung weg, die griechische Version zur Controlle des M.T. benutzen zu wollen, ihm steht die Authenticität gleichsam die Uncontrollierbarkeit des letzteren fest, die hebräischen Codd., aus denen der griechische Vert. übersetzt, sind ihm nichts als entstellt durch Unkunde der Leser, Abschreiber u.s.w. . . ; dass sie einer anderen unabhängigen Hdschr. Familie mit gleichem Anspruch auf Berücksichtigung angehörten, das anzunehmen perhorrescirt natürlich Frankel nach seiner ganzen theolog. Richtung." See *Zacharias Frankel: Gedenkblätter zu seinem hundertsten Geburtstage*, Breslau 1901, p. 65.

[47]Ludwig Geiger (ed.), *Abraham Geiger: Leben und Lebenswerk*, Berlin 1910, pp. 324-325.

[48]Glatzer, *Leopold and Adelheid Zunz*, p. 286.

[49]*Gesammelte Schriften von Dr. Zunz*, Berlin 1875-1876, I, pp. 217-270. Geiger, who appreciated the substance and spirit of Zunz's biblical work, published Zunz's conclusions in his *Jüdische Zeitschrift für Wissenschaft und Leben*, XI (1875). In this periodical Geiger himself had earlier published some of his own short studies in Pentateuchal criticism.

More traditionally inclined Jewish scholars regarded the *Urschrift* as trespassing the permissible bounds of Jewish scholarship. The Italian Jewish scholar S. D. Luzzatto condemned it for what he regarded as its "rationalism." Frankel, as far as we know, made no public statement whatsoever. The periodical which he founded in 1851 in Dresden and edited until 1868, the justly famous *Monatsschrift für Geschichte und Wissenschaft des Judentums*, contains no review and no mention of the work. One assumes that Frankel — whose work on the septuagint Geiger criticizes in his introduction — had decided it best to pass over the book in silence, hoping it might be forgotten. Now, however, thanks to a previously unknown letter, we may determine just how strong Frankel's feelings were and to what extent religious and personal considerations entered into his editiorial decisions. In 1864 Meir Wiener, head of a Jewish school in Hanover, and a regular contributor to the *Monatsschrift*, submitted a review of the recently published new edition of the anonymous old work on the Masora, *Ochlah W'ochlah*. The editor, S. Frensdorff, had chosen not to mention Geiger's *Urschrift* in his explanatory notes, and for this omission Wiener criticized him in the review which he sent to Frankel. Here is Frankel's reply:

> "Hinsichtlich der Recension des *Ochlah W'ochlah* wird sie die baldigste Aufnahme finden, nur gebe ich Ihnen anheim folgendes gef. [älligst] zu erwägen. Dr. Frensdorff hat unstreitig recht gehabt, Geigers Buch nicht zu erwähnen. Das *Ochlah W'ochlah* ist ein Werk für Jahrhunderte; und sollte er G.'s Schandbuch ins Schlepptau nehmen, um ihm Unsterblichkeit zu verschaffen? Ich lobe sehr Ihren Eifer für die Monats und -schaft, und Ihre Meinung *kabel emet mimi she'omro* [receive truth from whoever speaks it] aber G. ist es nicht um emet [truth] zu thun und er hat keinen *emet*: sein Buch ist voller Frivolität und böser Absichtlichkeit. Sie werden mir daher hoffentlich gestatten diesen Passus in welchem Sie Frensdorff zum Vorwurfe machen, dass er G. nicht berücksichtigt, auszulassen und werde die Recension daher im f. [olgenden] Hefte bringen. Ich würde sehr bedauern, wenn Sie auf diesen Passus bestehen und so dann die M'schrift die Recension nicht bringen könnte."[50]

The review did indeed appear with no references to Geiger's *Urschrift*; Wiener apparently succumbed to Frankel's censorship.[51]

The irony of this matter is that Geiger of course considered his work motivated by just that search for truth in which Frankel declared him lacking. Here, too, there is an unpublished letter worthy of quotation. It was written by Geiger to Wiener in 1857 and contains a defence of Geiger's religiosity in general and of his *Urschrift* in particular.

> "Dass ich dem alten Buchstaben- und Inspirationsglauben nicht huldige, dass mich überhaupt ein romantischer Nimbus nicht blendet, daraus habe ich nie ein Hehl gemacht; diesen Glauben habe ich immer als einen blossen Phantasierausch, von dem man bloss katzenjämmerlich erwacht, der weder Geist noch Herz erfüllt und ohne alle weitere Poesie ist, gekennzeichnet. Hingegen habe ich den gesünderen geistigen Glauben, der in der grossen Geschichtserscheinung des Judenthums mit seiner vollen Entwicklung, von seiner ersten Entstehung an bis zur Gegenwart die volle Evolution der höchsten Wahrheit sieht und nicht von der Wegnahme irgend eines Buchstaben erschüttert wird. Mein Glaube umfasst liebevoll die Jahrtausende, vertraut seiner Kraft für alle Zukunft;

[50]Zacharias Frankel, Breslau, 20th September 1864, to Meir Wiener, Hanover, Zacharias Frankel file in the German Section of the Archives of the Hebrew Union College Library, Cincinnati, Ohio.

[51]*Monatsschrift für Geschichte und Wissenschaft des Judenthums*, XIV (1865), pp. 31 ff.

jener Glaube, den Sie durch mein Buch verdunkelt fürchten, klammert sich ängstlich an eine Zeit, die er nicht kennt, an Buchstaben die er nicht verbürgen kann, ruft schwächlich von aussen Verständigungsmittel auf, sieht schwarzen Blickes in die Zukunft, kurz ein solcher Glaube ist ohne Glauben. Dem einen Streich zu versetzen, soll mich um das Prädicat eines *tsaddik gamur* [fully righteous man] wenn ich je die Prätention hätte es in Anspruch zu nehmen, bringen? Da sei Gott für!

Uebrigens habe ich, wie ich es im Vorworte bemerkt, mein Buch ohne alle Tendenz als die der Wissenschaft u. d. Wahrheit geschrieben; und was von diesen aus mir entgegengehalten werden wird, werde ich mit der grössten Aufmerksamkeit und Unbefangenheit prüfen. Was mir von ketzerrichterlicher Seite ins Gewissen geschoben wird, werde ich je nachdem entweder ignorieren oder gebührend abfertigen. Dass Sie nicht in solcher Weise verfahren werden, glaube ich überzeugt sein zu dürfen."[52]

VI

The controversy over the *Urschrift* was only one of many disputes that split the small community of Jewish scholars in Germany during the whole of the nineteenth century. No two of our three protagonists enjoyed fully cordial relations for the entire span of their adult lives. Perhaps the closest ties were those between Geiger and Zunz. From the very beginning of his own scholarly career, Geiger expressed the highest regard for Zunz's immense learning and always considered himself Zunz's student. When Geiger came to live in Berlin for a little over a year from 1838 to 1839, a personal relationship was established between the two men, which would later be strained but was never entirely broken off. Zunz had bemoaned the fact that there was hardly anyone in Berlin with whom to discuss Jewish literature and he therefore welcomed Geiger of whom he had written: "Geiger's spirit, knowledge, and scientific integrity form a beautiful whole, I know few like him."[53] It appears that as a result of their very close contact during this time Zunz successfully persuaded Geiger to become less involved in projects and to concentrate more on basic research. Toward the end of his stay, Geiger wrote:

"Habe ich mich schon früher ernstlich und mit Liebe mit der Geschichte des Judenthums beschäftigt, so habe ich mich nun, durch den Umgang mit Zunz angeregt und denselben benützend, noch specieller darauf geworfen. Ohne die Tagesbegebenheiten zu ignorieren, mag ich doch mich nicht mehr hineinmischen . . ."[54]

Once in Breslau, however, Geiger's activism reasserted itself and found expression in the rabbinical conferences of the 1840s. The relationship between the two men soon became strained and was not fully restored until some years later. Geiger grew increasingly critical of Zunz's unwillingness to come to grips with the problems of contemporary Jewish life, while Zunz looked down upon the work of the rabbinical conferences with contempt, claiming that they had no mission. It seems that Geiger had disappointed the other man by choosing to re-enter the active battle for reforms, and in Zunz's view he thereby invalidated his scholarly credentials: "People

---

[52]Abraham Geiger, Breslau, 23rd September 1857, to Meir Wiener, Hanover, Abraham Geiger file, Hebrew Union College Archives.
[53]Glatzer, *Leopold Zunz*, p. 174.
[54]*Nachgelassene Schriften*, V, p. 148.

committed to the party line [*Parteileute*] lose their judgment."[55] But there are un-questionably deeper personal factors responsible for these strains. Geiger's admiration for Zunz was always mingled with envy of his far greater learning. Zunz, for his part, even as he chose the secluded life of the scholar, could not avoid feelings of resentment about not enjoying the status and the monetary rewards that came with a major rabbinate. His reaction was to view the current scene with a cultivated cynicism and to tell his friends — almost with pride — that he read no Jewish news-papers. When Geiger specifically invited Zunz to the third rabbinical conference in Breslau, Zunz declined, claiming he could not afford to go. He had no congregation to pay his expenses.[56]

Zunz's resentment of the prestige-laden rabbis also affected his relationship with Zacharias Frankel, an association which was never very close and which seems to have soured in the course of time. Initially, during the thirties and forties, the two men were apparently on cordial terms. Unlike Geiger they shared an appreciation of the close relation between moral and ceremonial elements in the Jewish tradition. Zunz's writings were reviewed in Frankel's first periodical and Frankel sent a gift copy of one of his writings to Zunz.[57] A strain first developed when Frankel became a candidate for the Berlin rabbinate in 1842 and expressed his intention of control-ling the teachers' seminary of which Zunz was in charge. It appears also that in the late 1840s, when Zunz became an active proponent of the cause of democracy in Germany, Frankel remained far more inclined to conservatism.[58] During the nearly twenty years that Frankel edited the *Monatsschrift*, Zunz contributed not a single article or review and, except once in the context of a general survey, his works were never discussed there. Zunz, for his part, was not even a subscriber.[59] Yet the rela-tionship between Zunz and Frankel never developed into bitter animosity. That happened only between Zunz and Frankel's protegé, the historian Heinrich Graetz. The latter in his foreword to the fifth volume of his history insulted Zunz by writing that he had derived little benefit from "Dr. Zunz's confusing rather than enlighten-ing jumble of notes and dry nomenclatures."[60]

Not surprisingly, the final set of relations, those between Geiger and Frankel, were ultimately the worst of all. In the earlier years there was at least a degree of mutual respect between these two men. Frankel reviewed Geiger's *Zeitschrift* favourably in his own first journal and wrote that he thought in the case of Geiger — though not in that of Holdheim — there was no reason to question his scholarly qualities and his

---

[55]Glatzer, *Leopold and Adelheid Zunz*, p. 132.

[56]Glatzer, *Leopold Zunz*, p. 240, n. 2. On this relationship cf. Ludwig Geiger, 'Leopold Zunz und Abraham Geiger', *Liberales Judentum*, VIII (1916), pp. 131-139.

[57]Zunz's copy of Frankel's *Der gerichtliche Beweis nach mosaisch-talmudischem Rechte*, Berlin 1846, at present in the Hebrew Union College Library, is marked in Zunz's hand: "Zunz *(don. aut)*."

[58]This would seem implied by Zunz in a letter written in 1849 to Bernhard Beer: "Ihr Wunsch, dass ich weniger dem[okratisch] seyn möchte ist mir erklärlich; nicht aber Ihre Voraussetzung, dass ich es seyn wollte: Hier scheint [Zacharias] Frankels Einfluss zu spre-chen, nicht wahr?" Glatzer, *Leopold Zunz*, p. 301.

[59]*Hebrew Union College Annual*, XXXVIII (1967), p. 250.

[60]*Geschichte der Juden*, V, Magdeburg 1860, p. vi.

love of truth.[61] Geiger visited Frankel in Dresden in October 1844 and the men seem to have got along fairly well together then, sufficiently so for Frankel to participate with Geiger in the rabbinical conference of the following year.[62] As we have seen, both men were trying to do much the same thing. They shared the belief that Jewish literature is essentially religious; they possessed a common concern for scholarly relevance and the search for positive models in the Jewish past; and each liked to regard himself as a man of the centre. But after Frankel walked out of the Frankfurt conference on the question of the significance of Hebrew, and especially after he received the presidency of the Breslau Rabbinical Seminary to which Geiger felt rightfully entitled, all cordiality disappeared. The two men henceforth ignored each other's work or condemned it; neither was able to appreciate the genuine accomplishments of the other.

Differing religious concepts, differing ideas about the rôle of *Wissenschaft des Judentums*, and personal rivalries thus all contributed to an atmosphere of regretable antipathy which soon after the emergence of the reform and scholarly movements split the small group of Jewish scholars and detracted from their achievements. "It is really a shame," Ludwig Philippson wrote in 1863, "how the dozen Jewish scholars devour each other and forcibly crush the scarcely reviving respect of the Jewish and Christian public."[63]

VII

By the middle years of the nineteenth century the movements for religious reform and *Wissenschaft des Judentums* had produced three distinct positions which were sufficiently contradictory to prevent harmony. For Zacharias Frankel revelation, as expressed at Sinai and in the will of the Jewish people, had to remain the controlling influence restraining religious change and limiting the scope of *Wissenschaft*. For Geiger any significant scholarly endeavour had to direct itself to the broadest questions of Jewish intellectual history and to serve the interests of the future as he envisaged it. And for Zunz *Wissenschaft des Judentums* ultimately became a discipline which needed to remain independent of all religious considerations, whether directed towards preserving or towards innovating; it had to be free of theology.[64] In the century which has elapsed since their time no single one of these

---

[61]*Zeitschrift für die religiösen Interessen des Judenthums*, I (1844), pp. 270-273, 327.

[62]*Nachgelassene Schriften*, V, p. 177. A letter in the Geiger file of the Archives of the Leo Baeck Institute in New York, dated 30th April 1837, reveals that Geiger also invited Frankel to attend the informal conference of rabbis which he convoked in Wiesbaden in August, 1837. Frankel, however, declined.

[63]Ludwig Philippson, Bonn, 1st May 1863, to Meir Wiener, Hanover, Ludwig Philippson file, Hebrew Union College Archives.

[64]In the final decades of the nineteenth century *Wissenschaft des Judentums* in Germany followed the pattern of Zunz more than any other. It dwelt upon detail; it became more "microscopic" in its focus; it was concerned less with the present. No doubt this was due in part to the influence of positivism upon the historical sciences in this same period and the growing disrepute of grand generalizations. But it also meant that *WdJ* failed to become the guide for

points of view has been able totally to displace the other two. With variations, all three are still held today as they were then, with the same conviction and the same fervour.

religious life envisaged by the reformers. At the end of the century one youthful liberal rabbi complained: "*Wissenschaft des Judenthums*, the spoilt darling of the fathers of the Jewish renaissance, has not turned out to be the Messiah one saw in it. That is because the whole highly praised *Wissenschaft* is merely philology, archaeology. A sad testimony. As if Judaism were only ancient and not new!" (Caesar Seligmann in *Die Deborah*, 5th July 1894, p. 4). Cf. the remarks of Ludwig Philippson in *Allgemeine Zeitung des Judenthums*, XLIII (1879), pp. 706-707.

Emigration and Immigration

Jewish Manual Labour and Emigration

Records from some Bavarian Districts (1830—1857) *

BY JACOB TOURY

The scantiness of primary source-material on early Jewish emigrants from Germany has often been commented upon[1] and is also mirrored in recent bibliography on German Jews in the U.S.A.[2] It therefore seems appropriate to dwell at some length upon several hitherto forgotten Bavarian statistics for the period between 1830 and 1857, which contain rather detailed figures on emigration from the Bavarian Palatinate and from the district rabbinate of Kissingen in the county of Lower Franconia[3]. These records also provide significant data on Jewish "productivization", i.e. the taking up of manual occupations, and on the emergence of Jewish artisans and peasants.

The statistics for the Palatinate were drawn up by Government officials and are suspect of anti-Jewish bias insofar as they tend to minimize the Jewish effort of productivization. On the other hand they reported only those instances of emigration that had been officially registered, thus concealing the fact of a "hidden" draining away of Jewish (and non-Jewish) inhabitants from the province.

The Kissingen records were assembled by the district rabbis Dr. Adler and Dr. Lippmann for the purpose of launching petitions for the amelioration of the Jewish plight in Bavaria. They contain reports by the communities of the district, which are in part rather outspoken, but in part more reticent than might have been expected. Thus, these internal reports, too, do not always mirror the real state of affairs and have to be interpreted with care.

*This study is a small part of a historical and sociological survey on 'Jewish Entrance into German Citizenry', undertaken under the auspices of the Diaspora Research Institute of the Tel Aviv University, with generous financial aid from the Memorial Foundation for Jewish Culture, New York.

[1]Cf. Adolf Kober, 'Jewish Emigration from Württemberg', *Publications of the American Jewish Historical Society*, XLI, 1952, No. 3, pp. 225-273, who himself had at his disposal only the sources for one district. Rudolf Glanz in his essay 'The "Bayer" and the "Pollack" in America', *Jewish Social Studies*, XVII, 1955, No. 1, pp. 27-42, uses only biographical material and cuttings from the Jewish press. Also in his later essay 'The German Jewish Mass Emigration 1820-1880', *American Jewish Archives*, XXII, 1970, No. 1, pp. 49-66, he uses secondary material.

[2]H. G. Reissner, 'The German-American Jews (1800-1850)', in *LBI Year Book X* (1965), pp. 112-116; Rudolf Glanz, 'The German Jew in America', *Bibliographia Judaica No. 1*, Cincinnati 1969.

[3]The records for the Palatinate: Staatsarchiv Speyer, Reg. Pfalz K.d.I./Extr. 1897, No. 187, fol. 79. The records of the Kissingen district, formerly kept in Würzburg, have been transferred to the Jerusalem Central Archives for the History of the Jewish People (CAHJP) and bear the following signatures: Statistics on emigration 1830-1854: D/WR 15; other statistics for 1843-1844 and 1847-1848: D/WR 16; population figures for 1850: D/WR 495, especially the letter dated 20.3.1850. Where figures in the above documents are incomplete, estimates based on the average percentage have been interpolated, but the records on emigration are complete. Obvious errors in the original statistics have been corrected. Further quotation of the above signatures will be dispensed with, if documents are not quoted verbatim.

Before scrutinising the details of the Palatinate and Kissingen records the place of these districts in the overall statistical picture for the whole of Bavaria has to be established. The geographical and occupational distribution of the Jewish population of the Kingdom in 1847/48 can be seen in Table I.

TABLE I

Main types of Jewish occupations in Bavaria (1847/48)[4]

Governmental Districts	Jewish Inhabitants			Jewish Families engaged in:				
	Fami-lies	Persons	Average persons per family	Agri-cul-ture	Crafts	Joint average %	Com-merce	(Including Peddling)
Upper Bavaria	152	663	4.4	6	48	35.5	49	—
Swabia	1,474	6,764	4.6	193	346	36.4	634	(122)
Upper Palatinate	151	774	5.1	2	35	24.5	94	(21)
Middle Franconia	2,562	11,451	4.6	189	523	27.8	1,290	(233)
Upper Franconia	1,313	6,017	4.7	135	417	42.4	474	(233)
Lower Franconia	3,535	16,255	4.7	453	1,004	41.2	1,456	(348)
Palatinate	3,182	15,574	4.9	80	636	22.8	2,126	("a large part")
Total	12,369	57,498	4.7	1,058	3,009	32.9	6,123	(c. 1,950)

The table reveals that the Palatinate to the west of the river Rhine was inhabited by rather large Jewish families (4.9 souls), but came last in the percentage of "productivization", with only 22.8% of the householders occupied in agriculture and crafts. Unlike the Palatinate, Lower Franconia with the rabbinical district of Kissingen was inhabited by average-sized families (4.7 souls), while its rate of productivization (41.2) was almost the highest for Bavaria and took second place only to that of Upper Franconia. However, this rate was still rising and in 1851 reached a peak of 45.1% (30.8% craftsmen and 14.3% agriculturists)[5]. Moreover, in Lower Franconia only 348 householders lived by peddling (9.8% of the bread-winners), thus leaving 622 heads of families (17.6%) for all other occupations including employees of the community (4.1%), the professions, *rentiers* and those living on charity[6] (together 13.5%).

In the Palatinate pedlars were not separately listed, but the statistical tables expressly state that they comprised "a large part" of the 2,126 householders engaged in commerce. No other occupations are mentioned, except for 340 householders

[4]Official statistical tables of the Bavarian Ministry of the Interior printed in Stefan Schwarz, *Die Juden in Bayern im Wandel der Zeiten*, München & Wien 1963, p. 350. No Jews were found in the whole of Lower Bavaria, and reference has been omitted by the present author. The total of 10,190 occupied as against 12,369 householders leaves a margin of 2,179 bread-winners, of whom about 450 were engaged in rabbinical and other religious occupations. The remaining 1,730 householders belonged either to the so-called "capitalistic" and "free" professions or had some occupation other than the tabulated ones. But a very large number of them must have been old or destitute. Further sources cf. note 5.
[5]Government statistics for the Bavarian districts (excluding the Palatinate on the left bank of the Rhine): Bayerisches Haupt-Staatsarchiv, München, MH 9634.
[6]Schwarz, *op. cit.*, p. 349.

making their living from "commerce and agriculture". This problematical figure will be considered later. Here it may suffice to state that the numbers of destitute heads of families and of employees of the community must have been rather small[7].

Now the district of Kissingen with its 2,400 Jews, living in 24 communities near the banks of the river Saale, averaged only about four persons per Jewish family, while the percentage of householders occupied in "productive" callings varied from place to place between 28% and 60%. Among the 360 heads of families in fifteen communities, from which more or less exact data of population and occupation are preserved, no less than 154, or 42.8%, were either craftsmen or farmers in 1847. Although the Kissingen percentages correspond closely enough to those for the whole of Lower Franconia, it is inadvisable to compare the figures of a mere district with those for the whole of the Palatinate. Therefore, a similar small unit of the latter province, i.e. the *Land* Commissariat of Germersheim[8], has been selected for the purpose of comparison with the Kissingen district.

TABLE II

Comparison between the Jewish inhabitants of two Bavarian districts (1847)

District	Germersheim (Palatinate)		Kissingen (Lower Franconia)	
Communities	14			15
Persons	1,192		c.	1,500
Families, number (and average members)	246	(4.9)	c.	360 (4.2)
Productive occupations, number (and % of householders)	53	(21.1%)		154 (42.8%)

These data confirm the previous impression that the Kissingen district as well as the whole of Lower Franconia had a distinctly higher percentage of productive occupations and a definitely lower family average than the Germersheim district and the Palatinate as a whole.

Could this be the result of a statistical distortion? We have already mentioned that 340 householders in the Palatinate (almost 11%) were described as engaged in "commerce and agriculture", which probably means that they were part-time farmers, augmenting their income from agriculture by some commerce. And indeed, for one of the Palatinate districts a note has been added to the statistical table, stating that "although twenty-five families own land, they nevertheless leave its cultivation to tenant-farmers, while they themselves pursue their craft or commerce which constitutes their main source of livelihood"[9]. In other words, at least a part

[7]*Ibid.* The number of householders belonging to the last-mentioned callings might correspond roughly to the number of unmarried artisans, traders and agriculturists, who apparently were included in the respective columns. Anyhow, the problem of those living on charity must seem to have more or less vanished from the Palatinate, while a generation earlier about ten per cent were still deemed utterly destitute; Staatsarchiv Speyer, Reg. Pfalz K.d.I., No. 8249, Statistical Abstract for the Speyer district, 17th June 1815.
[8]Figures for the district of Germersheim: Staatsarchiv Speyer, Reg. Pfalz K.d.I./Extr. 1897, No. 187, fol. 65.
[9]Note attached to the figures for the district of Rülzheim, *ibid*, fol. 65.

of these 340 heads of families may be regarded as craftsmen or landowners, i.e. as "productively" occupied.

But even so, although the rate of "productive" occupations in the Palatinate can thus be raised, it nevertheless remains far below that for Lower Franconia. Moreover, in the Germersheim district, serving as a medium for comparison with the Kissingen district, not a single provider is listed under this problematical heading, leaving the discrepancy unresolved.

The real explanation for the inconsistencies in the social development of the districts under consideration ought not therefore to be sought in statistical intricacies, but in their different legal status under the Bavarian Jew laws.

Both these provinces had been annexed to Bavaria as an outcome of the Napoleonic wars — Lower Franconia in 1814, the Palatinate in 1816. But whereas in the former district the Bavarian Jew laws of 1813 were introduced by decree of 5th December 1816, the Jews of the Palatinate continued, even under Bavarian rule, to enjoy almost full rights which had been bestowed upon them during the French occupation (1793-1814). Although their equality was curbed since 1808 by Napoleon's *décret infâme*, they were not unduly bothered by it, even when it was prolonged under the Bavarian rule[10]. For, in compensation for this iniquity, they were spared the other "educational" measures of the Bavarian legislation, which were far more oppressive than those of the Napoleonic decree of 1808. Thus, they entirely escaped the cruel provisions embodied in the *Matrikel* ordinances enforced in all the other provinces of the Kingdom (see below). The Palatinate Jews had to contend, however, with the growing problem of wresting a livelihood from the congested ground of rural trade, by cattle and corn-dealing or by peddling; their response to the governmental policy of "productivization" — which in fact had already been pursued to a lesser extent by the French authorities — was obviously weaker than that of the Jews in other parts of the kingdom, because it was not enforced by a Bavarian law.

Contrary to the relative freedom of the Palatinate Jews from the coercive Bavarian legislation, the Jews of Lower Franconia and the Kissingen district were compelled to bear its full viciousness. They had to be enrolled in the local *Matrikel*, for holders of a *Matrikel* number alone were recognized as legal inhabitants of the community. Only when a number became vacant at a certain place could another Jew claim a right to setting up lawful residence and establishing a family — provided that he was not earning his livelihood by *Schacherhandel* (bartering, trafficking or peddling), and provided that he could meet all the other requirements, such as a separate dwelling-place and a trade that was not "overcrowded". There were, however, certain hypothetical exceptions from the *Matrikel* laws, in accordance with their professed aim of "educating" Jewish pedlars and cattle-dealers to "productivity": Settlement in excess of the fixed number was theoretically declared open to Jewish peasants, master craftsmen and members of the so-called free professions.

[10]They also were excluded from the suffrage to the assemblies of the Bavarian County Estates.

First page of the Westheim roll of emigrants (1854)

Second page of the Westheim roll of emigrants (1854)

But even they were forbidden to settle in places where Jews had not previously been living. Moreover, even in places where Jewish communities existed they, too, had to obtain permission from the local magistrate and — in case of artisans — also from the respective craft-guild, before governmental consent to their establishing residence in excess of the *Matrikel* numbers would be forthcoming. Thus, the declared "educational" intention of the law was obviated by the hidden, but nevertheless prevalent, determination of local and state authorities to control and even deplete the Jewish population of Bavaria.

But at first, Bavarian Jews did not decrease. They responded with surprising alacrity to government pressure. Their offspring were prevailed upon to learn a craft or to take up farming. The success of this trend after about one generation is amply borne out by the figures for 1847/48, summarized above in Table I.

The Kissingen district made no exception. Although no overall percentages can be worked out from the extant records, full figures for five out of the twenty-four communities establish the trend without a doubt. The data for the year 1847 are shown in Table III.

TABLE III

Occupations of Jewish householders in five places of the Kissingen district (1847)

Place	Occupations in %			Employees of the community and teachers	Day labourers %	Population		
	Commerce	Handicrafts	Agriculture			Others & without occupation %	Bread-winners	Persons
Westheim	30.0	20.0	20.0	6.0	20.0	4.0	46	183
Hessdorf	52.0	19.0	9.0	—	—	20.0	45	153
Massbach	35.5	45.0	13.0	6.5	—	—	31	147
Steinach	23.5	26.0	16.0	10.5	5.5	18.5	38	137
Völkersleier	66.0	21.0	9.0	4.0	—	—	24	105

These figures do not include apprentices, journeymen and agricultural trainees. Their numbers, together with those of master craftmen and peasants, were recorded for the year 1843/44 in four of the places mentioned above, and are given in Table IV (figures for 1847 in brackets).

TABLE IV

"Productive" occupations of Jewish inhabitants in four places of the Kissingen district (1843/44)

Place	Master craftsmen	Journey-men	Appren-tices	Farmers	Trainees
Hessdorf	8 (8)	9	4	3	3
Massbach	14 (14)	10	3	5	1
Steinach	7 (9)	11	2	7	—
Völkersleier	5 (5)	1	2	3	4
Total	34 (36)	31	11	18	8

A comparison of the respective number of apprentices with that of journeymen and master craftsmen, and of the agricultural trainees with the already established farmers points to an interesting fact: the rush to manual occupations, in response to the "educational" *Matrikel* laws, was in the first generation rather striking; but by 1844 it had already slowed down to a significant extent: in three out of the four places mentioned the number of apprentices and agricultural trainees had fallen below the level of journeymen and master craftsmen or farmers. This trend can be verified by additional figures from thirteen other communities in the Kissingen district: compared with 55 master craftsmen and 101 journeymen, only 17 new apprentices were to be found in 1844, and not more than 8 trainees followed the example of the 30 farmers already settled in the district.

It seems likely that the reason for the slackening in "productive" zeal is not only bound up with the acute crisis in all the crafts during the thirties, owing to growing imports and to mechanization of production; at least to the same extent it was inherent in the specific difficulties that beset Jewish youngsters when attempting to establish themselves in a trade or in agriculture: they did not easily find a Gentile master craftsman or farmer willing to take them on, even if they would have consented to forego kosher food and observing the Sabbath which in Bavaria they generally declined to do. Moreover, even if Jewish trainees and journeymen successfully finished their training and started looking for a place to settle as master craftsmen or farmers, the real obstacles still lay before them: it has already been mentioned that the establishment of a new master at a given place was dependent upon the consent of magistrates and craft-guilds and that the right of settlement was generally refused to a Jew. This refusal was often backed up by the claim that the place was already overcrowded by Jews in similar occupations. There was some truth in this allegation, since Jews tended to concentrate in certain manual occupations which consequently had become almost a Jewish domain.

The reason for this one-sided choice of certain crafts is easy to detect. The Jewish entry into manual occupations was by no means a normal process: the first generation of Jewish craftsmen was not physically prepared for heavy work. They preferred occupations suited to their strength and possibly even looked for those that offered room for some commercial enterprise, like butchering, tailoring and shoemaking. The difficulty of finding a place also influenced the choice of vocation:

many boys became apprenticed to weavers, whose proverbially meagre livelihood made them agreeable to take on Jewish apprentices for a relatively reasonable payment. Later on, the "Jewish" trades perpetuated themselves by the establishment of Jewish masters, who in turn accepted Jewish apprentices for training.

Anyhow, tailoring, weaving, butchering and shoemaking were the preferred Jewish crafts. In the 17 townships of the Kissingen district, from which vocational statistics are available, they together accounted in 1844 for 190 out of 249 craftsmen, or for over 75 per cent of the total. The exact figures are: 61 butchers, 61 weavers (including a few cloth and hose-makers), 42 shoemakers and 26 tailors[11].

The overcrowding of these branches and the difficulties of settling outside one's birth-place and in excess of the fixed quota of *Matrikel*, left many craftsmen without a place to live in, and often even without adequate means of subsistence. Thus some of them reverted to trafficking and peddling, which brought them into conflict with the law of the land.

The plight of Bavarian Jews — whether predominantly tradesmen or pedlars, as in the Palatinate, or artisans and farmers, as in the Kissingen district — drove many to emigration. The whole extent of the exodus from Bavaria is evident in the development of the Jewish population during fifty years[12], as shown in Table V.

TABLE V

The Jewish population of Bavaria, 1822-1871

Year		Jews	% of general population
1822		53,402	
1840		59,376	1.40
1843/44	c.	61,000	
1847/48		57,498	
1851	c.	54,200	
1871		50,648	1.04

In other words, while the Jewish population in almost every one of the German States was steadily increasing up to its peak in the seventies, Bavarian Jews had already reached their peak in the forties and began to diminish in absolute numbers, and still more so in their percentage of the general population.

As a matter of fact emigration of Bavarian Jews seems to have started as early as 1830. But from the Palatinate and the Germersheim district exact figures are available only for the five years between 1842 and 1846. During this period 463 Jews left the Palatinate. From the records it is not evident whether bread-winners only were listed, or whether this number included all the members of the emigrating

---

[11]The rest is made up by 11 soapmakers, 8 carpenters, 8 bakers and pastry-cooks, 6 tanners, 6 ropemakers, 5 makers of gold and silver lace, 4 saddlers, 3 bookbinders, 3 furriers, 2 turners, 2 glaziers and 1 miller.

[12]Figures from *Sabbath-Blatt*, 1844, p. 142 (1843/44); Schwarz, *op. cit.*, p. 349 (1847/48); Bayerisches Haupt-Staatsarchiv, München, MH 9634 (1851 — Palatinate interpolated); 'Bavaria', in *Jüdisches Lexikon*, vol. I; 'Statistics' (1822, 1840, 1871), *ibid.*, vol. V.

families. But even if we take the latter view which is probably the correct one, as we shall see with regard to the Kissingen district — emigrants during the short period of five years accounted for a loss of almost 3% of the Jewish population. The numbers of emigrants, according to districts, are shown in Table VI.

TABLE VI

Jewish emigration from the Palatinate, 1842-1846

District	Families	Persons	Emigration	Emigration as % of persons
1. Bergzabern	286	1,371	101	7.4%
2. Kusel	130	599	—	—
3. Frankenthal	472	2,361	70	3.0%
4. Germersheim	246	1,192	34	2.9%
5. Homburg	120	627	6	0.9%
6. Kaiserslautern	254	1,267	76	6.0%
7. Kirchheim	347	1,787	10	0.6%
8. Landau	457	2,241	74	3.3%
9. Neustadt	328	1,532	5	0.3%
10. Pirmasens	216	1,101	55	5.0%
11. Speyer	241	1,040	29	2.8%
12. Zweibrücken	85	456	3	0.7%
Total	3,182	15,574	463	3.0%

It is interesting that no uniform picture emerges. The rate of emigration varies from district to district, from nil to 7.4%, without any apparent reason, if one neglects to take into account the geographic position of the three counties most affected by emigration: Bergzabern, Kaiserslautern and Pirmasens almost straddle the French border, and emigration from there to Alsace, either for family or other reasons, was easy. None of the other counties had nearly as high a rate of emigration as the three border districts, and Germersheim — chosen here to be compared with Kissingen — happens in any case to conform exactly to the central value in the above table, thus remaining quite suitable to its purpose.

During the five years in question, 34 Jews from seven villages left the Germersheim district to go abroad, while in seven other villages all of them stayed on. The Jewish inhabitants of that county were probably neither too hard hit by economic difficulties, nor did they shelter entirely destitute persons. And, indeed, we have already surmised from the absence of unspecified occupations from their records that the Jews of Germersheim were rather well-to-do. Anyhow, extremely poor people could seldom emigrate owing to lack of funds. Emigrants to countries overseas had to provide money for the passage, and even emigrants to adjoining states, if they did not slip through the border, had to have some resources in order to start a business, for beggars were everywhere chased away. The only people who could easily move without money were apprentices going abroad for training, and journeymen who traditionally spent part of the years before taking their master examinations in journeying from place to place. Although we have no indication as to the occupation of the emigrants from the Palatinate, it seems safe to assume that not all of them were tradespeople and that at least some of them were journeymen. For they could openly leave the country without a special authorization from the authorities and without a valid passport. They were also free to enter another country on the strength of a journey-book (*Wanderbuch*) of their craft alone[13]. Thus, at least some of them even retained the possibility of returning to their home towns, and in any case evaded the statisticians for many years after their disappearance. The number of such conditional emigrants from the Palatinate might therefore have been even larger than indicated in the records.

All these surmises may amply be proved by the figures preserved in the records of the Kissingen district.

First of all, in 1844, at the time of the first census taken by the rabbinate, no fewer than 69 journeymen and apprentices — out of a total of 151 in thirteen of the villages — were reported absent. Some of them might have been apprenticed in a larger township and others could have journeyed according to custom — or so at least state the records. But nevertheless it appears that the figure of 69 lies rather high and suggests that certainly some or other of them might have already left for good.

Indeed, Table VII summarizing some data on the emigration from the Kissingen district, establishes the fact that out of 234 emigrants, whose time of departure is known, no less than 104(44.4%) had already left before 1848. The table also establishes that the total number of emigrants for the time between 1830 and December 1854 was at least 588. This means that during a quarter of a century the district had been deprived of about 20% of its Jewish inhabitants, which is rather more than the percentage found for the Palatinate and the Germersheim district $(5 \times 3\% = 15\%)$.

It is interesting to note that out of 336 emigrants whose destination was ascertainable only eleven went to European countries, mainly France, whilst all the others went to the United States.

The percentage of emigrants settling in a German State outside Bavaria seems to have been small. But at least some of the absent journeymen, whose intention of emigration was not openly stated in the records, must have settled there. For although our tables contain only one single instance of emigration to Hessen Nassau, while Frankfurt, Hamburg or Prussia are not mentioned at all, ultimately a sizeable number of Bavarian craftsmen could be found there[14]. It may be, however, that some of the men intending to leave for America got stranded on their way in some German town.

Up to now we have assumed that the emigrants from the Kissingen district belonged generally to the class of manual workers. As the above table contains an analysis according to occupations, this surmise is easily checked. Out of 178 male emigrants from fourteen places, whose occupations are ascertainable, 116 were in-

---

[13]Cf. Bayerisches Staatsarchiv Nürnberg, Best. K.d.I., Abg. 1932, Tit. I, No. 10, and also further below on Kissingen.

[14]On this subject the present author hopes to report in a separate paper. Meanwhile, cf. CAHJP, D/AHW 260 c, fasc. 1, where the extraction of some 54 Hamburg tailors is given.

Jacob Toury

TABLE VII

Emigrants from the Kissingen District 1830-1854 according to time and direction of emigration and occupation

No. Place	Number of Emigrants			to America	Occupation of male emigrants				Females	
	1830-1854	before 1848	after 1848		Commerce	Crafts	Agriculture	other males	with occupation	without occupation & children
1. Neuhaus	51	?	?	All	1	20	—	4	—	26
2. Neustadt	5	1	4	All	—	3	—	1	—	1
3. Unsleben	48	38	10	?	1	14	1	2	—	30
4. Lebenhahn	22	?	?	All						
5. Eichenhausen	17	?	?							
6. Hammelburg	29	?	?	All	4	7	—	5	—	13
7. Westheim	83	13	70	All	4	28	1	7	15	28
8. Rieneck	21	14	7	18	2	9	—	4	—	6
9. Weikersgrüben	32	?	?	2*	2	?	?	?	?	21
10. Burgsinn	9	7	2	2	—	2	—	3	—	4
11. Untererthal	27	?	?	All	3	1	1	—	6	16
12. Dittlofsroda	15	?	?	14	1	6	—	1	—	7
13. Kissingen	17	?	?	All						
14. Völkersleier	28	11	17	All	10	2	1	—	—	15
15. Adelsberg	5	2	3	?	—	4	—	1	—	—
16. Thundorf	1	?	?	?	—	1	—	—	—	—
17. Steinach	36	?	?	?	—	12	3	6	4	11
18. Massbach	23	?	?	All						
19. Poppenlauer	27	?	?	?						
20. Rödelmaier	37	?	?							
21. Oberthulba	6	5	1	All						
22. Hessdorf	29	13	16							
23. Höllrich	20	?	?							
24. Gemünden	0	0	0							
Total	588	104	130		28	109	7	34	25	178

*Destination of the other emigrants not stated.

deed peasants and craftsmen (very many of them apprentices and journeymen), to which one has to add two other manual workers (porters). Thus, the percentage of manual occupations among men amounted to 66.8%. But this is not all. Of the 25 working women in our list 23 were servant-girls, one a soapmaker and one a midwife[15], boosting the total of "productive" workers among the emigrants to an exceptionally high level.

But some other occupations were also represented: 28 (15.7%) of the male emigrants had entered commerce, most of them being self-employed, but at least four had served as assistants (*Commis*). 14 had trained as rabbis or teachers (7.9%), 4 belonged to the professions (2.2%; among them two physicians!), 3 were rag-and-bone men (1.7%), and 10 did not specify their occupations (5.6%). In short, only

[15] A specification of women's occupations exists only for three places. It can therefore safely be assumed that the number of servant-girls was in reality far higher.

relatively small numbers of older tradespeople and pedlars left Bavaria. The bulk of the emigrants consisted of professional people and predominantly of the most active and work-accustomed younger manual workers[16]. The "educational" policy of the Bavarian Kingdom had miserably backfired, presenting the U.S.A. with a generally fit and active influx of newcomers.

What was the exact composition of the people leaving the Kissingen district, and what were the means at their disposal for founding a new home overseas? Table VIII summarizes the available data on these questions.

TABLE VIII

Emigrants from the Kissingen district according to family status and exported capital[17]

Place	Jewish families 1850 (changes since 1847 in brackets)	male	female	married (widowed added in brackets)	single & child- ren	Total	Amount of exported capital (if stated)
Neuhaus	27	28	23	2 (+1)	48	51	9,500 fl.
Neustadt	11	4	1	—	5	5	?
Unsleben	} 40	24 (?)	24 (?)	22 (+2)	24	48	16,100 fl.
Lebenhahn		11 (?)	11 (?)	2 (+2)	18	22	3,500 fl.
Eichenhausen	7	?	?	?	?	17	?
Hammelburg	27	14	15	4	25	29	22,900 fl.
Westheim	46 (–10)	39 (?)	44 (?)	2 (+3)	78	83	?
Rieneck	?	14	7	—	21	21	7,250 fl.
Weikersgrüben	6	15 (?)	17 (?)	4 (+1)	27	32	8,200 fl.
Burgsinn	?	5	4	—	9	9	3,900 fl.
Untererthal	(vide Hammelburg)	16	11	8	19	27	12,950 fl.
Dittlofsroda	12	9	6	2 (+1)	12	15	4,900 fl.
Kissingen	50	11 (?)	6 (?)	0 (2?)	15	17	6,000 fl.
Völkersleier	24 (–4)	14 (?)	14 (?)	4 (+1)	23	28	8,800 fl.
Adelsberg	?	5	—	—	5 (?)	5	?
Thundorf	17	1	—	—	1	1	?
Steinach	38 (–6)	23	13	4	32	36	10,800 fl.
Massbach	31 (+6)	?	?	?	?	23	?
Poppenlauer	18	16	11	2	25	27	?
Rödelmaier	32	23 (?)	14 (?)	4	33	37	5,000 fl.
Oberthulba	?	2	4	—	6	6	2,000 fl.
Hessdorf	44	?	?	—	29	29	?
Höllrich	?	11 (?)	9 (?)	2	18	20	120-150 fl.
Gemünden	no emigrants						
Total (less than 600)		285	234	62 (+13)	473	588	121,950 fl.

[16]This is not to say that all immigrants to the U.S. continued to work as craftsmen and peasants. It is known that rather large numbers of them returned, under the different conditions of America, to peddling and commerce, especially in the so-called frontier regions.

[17]Contrary to Table VII, which has been compiled from scattered figures, this table is based on an original document, drawn up by the district rabbi Dr. Lippmann on the 4th December 1854, according to the reports sent to him by the communities (CAHJP/D-WR 15, fol. 1 a). But his table is neither complete, nor are his calculations above reproach. As the various local reports have been preserved, I took the liberty of amending and correcting the original.

The property that emigrants took with them was pitifully small. The total amount taken by 398 persons did not exceed 122,000 florins. That would mean an average of 8,130 fl. per village, and of 306 fl. per head. It is interesting to note from an entry for the community of Kissingen that a single fare to America was then estimated at 300 fl.[18] In other words — emigrants owned on average just their passage-money, and not a whit more.

But averages are unreliable. For instance, from Höllrich twenty people emigrated and from Lebenhahn 22, yet only one Höllrich family had 120-150 fl. to its name, while on the other hand two Lebenhahn families accounted for the whole of 3,500 fl. exported from there. But this may be of little consequence, for people might have been reluctant to declare their property, and the heads of the community, filling out forms for the district rabbinate, might have had their reasons for not assessing emigrants whose families were left behind. Thus, eight community-heads entirely ignored the question of the emigrants' property, and four named only a lump sum for all of them.

It may therefore be indicated to take a closer look at the specifications for the twelve communities, from which fuller data are extant: 157 property entries, representing 290 emigrants, totalled 107,300 florins. This sum averages about 370 fl. per caput, or 683 fl. per family entry. This again is close enough to the general average, but in reality things were rather different. Table IX will prove it.

TABLE IX

Division of capital, relating to 157 entries

under 300 fl. (i.e. below the average passage money)	48 entries
from 300 to 500 fl.	63 ,,
from 600 to 900 (i.e. passage money for two to three)	17 ,,
from 1,000 fl. upwards	29 ,,
Total	157 entries

In other words: 30% of the emigrants lacked sufficient funds to finance immediately their passage to America. Part of them might — as already indicated — have taken up temporary residence in one of the larger German towns. Forty per cent had passage money for one, and another thirty per cent for two or more people.

It is perhaps of some interest to take a glance at the 29 "rich" emigrants, who incidentally accounted for more than half (55.5%) of the whole capital specified in our 157 entries.

They came from ten out of the twelve places (Rieneck and Oberthulba seemingly being poor communities), but the biggest number and the largest percentage of well-to-do emigrants originated from Hammelburg (4 out of 29) and Unsleben (6 out of 48). These seem to have been the only places which were abandoned by better-off families. From most of the other villages only poor people emigrated.

---

[18]While in Table VIII a total of 6,000 fl. is entered for Kissingen by Dr. Lippmann, he himself had in the local report accounted for 5,400 fl. and "two fares", thus setting the single fare at 300 fl.

As to the professions of the 29 better-off emigrants and the distribution of property among them, this is shown in Table X.

TABLE X

Occupations and property relating to 29 better-off families

3	families of farmers (1,000; 1,500; 4,000 fl.)	6,500
2	families of horse and cattle-dealers (2,000; 6,000)	8,000
2	families of merchants (1,600; 4,000)	5,600
1	single merchant (1,000)	1,000
2	single salesmen (1,000; 1,000)	2,000
1	family of a rag-and-bone man (1,000)	1,000
1	single candidate for the rabbinate (1,000)	1,000
1	family of a teacher (1,000)	1,000
2	families of butchers (1,200; 1,500)	2,700
1	single butcher (1,000)	1,000
3	families of craftsmen (1,500; 1,800; 8,000)	11,300
5	single craftsmen (1,000; 1,000; 1,500; 4,000; 4,000)	11,500
5	families without specification (1,000; 1,000; 1,200; 1,500; 2,000)	6,700
29		**59,300 fl.**

Stripped to the essentials this means: Fifteen families owned almost three quarters of the money declared by the better-off people (42,000 fl.), or 40% of all the capital specified in 157 entries. Another fourteen single persons owned the fourth quarter of the property declared by the well-to-do, or an additional 15.5% of the money belonging to all the specified emigrants. Contrasted with this "upper crust", the rest did in fact look extremely indigent. But even those 29 better-off people were by no means really wealthy, for many of them were travelling with three or more dependants, and their voyage accordingly became more expensive.

Contrary to expectation, traders do not take first rank among the well-to-do, even if one adds the butchers to their number (as government statistics generally did). Some craftsmen seem to have done better than the pedlars and shopkeepers The top rank includes a saddler, a weaver (each 4,000 fl.) and a ropemaker (8,000 fl.). The saddler might have traded horses as a sideline (one horse-dealer was assessed at 6,000 fl.!); but how a weaver and a ropemaker gained their wealth and why they then decided to emigrate, is open to speculation.

Now we turn to the demographic picture of the emigration from the Kissingen district. The exact number of Jewish families living there in eighteen different places is known for the year 1850. Although by then a goodly part of the emigrants had already left, it is fairly safe to assume that the number of households (431) in that year corresponds more or less to the *Matrikel* granted by the authorities and that the vacated numbers must have been filled quickly by applicants eagerly waiting for a chance to settle (the number of these in Lower Franconia, as far as the authorities could make out, was 284 in 1848[19]). But in three villages — Westheim, Steinach, Völkersleier — the number of households had nevertheless decreased

[19]Living at a place "in excess of the *Matrikel*", Schwarz, op. cit., p. 349.

significantly since 1847, while only in one place — Massbach — had it risen since
then and 1850. Those discrepancies might mean that the lists were drawn up on
different principles, viz.: at one time and place they included unmarried people,
while at the other they excluded them. Later on, this supposition will be proved
correct without, however, effacing the overwhelming fact that already by 1850 the
shrinking of the Jewish population in Lower Franconia had made itself clearly felt.

The mean rate of emigration from eighteen communities accounted for during
the years 1830-1854, was 1.17 souls per family, when 505 emigrants left dwelling-
places inhabited by 431 families. Ten villages furnished rather more than the
average number and six rather less. Outstanding at the one end of the scale were
Gemünden with no emigrants at all, and Thundorf with a low rate of 0.06 per
family. At the other end of the scale, Eichenhausen, Hammelburg and Untererthal
had double the average rate of emigrants, while the village of Weikersgrüben
excelled with an emigration rate of 5.33 souls per family unit (i.e. more than the
size of an average household!). This would suggest that the Jewish community
there was in the throes of disintegration. And indeed, in 1854 there remained only
six householders at that place, consisting of one family of 4 persons, 2 widows with
12 dependants and 3 unmarried persons with another 3 dependants[20].

Two villages — Rödelmaier and Völkersleier — approximated the mean value
of 1.17 emigrants per family, and we shall hear more about one of them later on.

It is not surprising that the number of men among the emigrants was larger than
that of the women (285:234, in twenty places from which complete reports are
extant). They had learned a trade and they were naturally more eager than the
women to try their luck in a new country. But it is surprising that women constituted as many as 45% of all the emigrants. This means that unmarried women staying
behind had only a small chance of finding a husband with a free *Matrikel* number and
consequently preferred to follow the men to an unknown but free world, instead of
facing a barren future in Bavaria. Perhaps this is also the cause of the abnormally
low rate of married people among the emigrants. Whoever had succeeded in wresting a *Matrikel* number from the reluctant authorities was more agreeable to linger-
ing on, trying to make a living at his birth-place. Some "matriculated" heads of
families nevertheless sent their children overseas. and the records show various instances of 2 or 3 youngsters, more often female than male, travelling alone to the
New World[21]. Anyhow, only 31 married couples and 13 widowed people, probably
older and possibly persuaded to emigrate by relatives abroad, compare with 473
single persons (in twenty-one places), or in other words: for every married emigrant
there were more than six unmarried ones.

The word "unmarried" has been chosen on purpose, for it seems that several of
the emigrants, especially the servant-girls, can neither be called spinsters, nor
single. Some were probably engaged to one of the male emigrants or went overseas
to join their betrothed, who had made good there. Some unmarried mothers with

[20]CAHJP/D-WR 15, fol. 8b. Remark made by the head of the community.
[21]Boys had to serve in the Bavarian army, and their early departure was apt to arouse the
    suspicion of draft-dodging; see below.

their infants, and some other "undesirable elements", too, are expressly mentioned in the lists of emigrants: one case concerns a whole family from Sulzbach that was sped on its way with financial help from the community and from individual donors[22]. In another instance the unmarried Regina Raab of Westheim with her three children was "deported by the community"[23]. The same explanation was given for the emigration of the widow of a former Westheim cantor and her six children. It was probably cheaper for the community to pay their fare to America than to keep them on charity for years to come.

Now, neither that widow nor the above-mentioned Regina Raab, although listed as emigrated from Westheim in 1854, can be traced in the 1848 list of Jewish inhabitants for that township. Such omissions occasionally happen also in other communities with regard to some marginal people, both female and male, and might be explained either as an oversight or as a deliberate attempt at keeping the number of Jews as near as possible to the quota of *Matrikel*. Yet in Westheim this assumption is not only provable beyond any doubt, but the discrepancies exceed the normal margins of error: out of 69 Jews reported as having emigrated between 1848 and 1854, no less than 30 cannot be traced at all in the lists of inhabitants for the year 1848, and five more may only be identified with a stretch of the imagination with regard to their names and occupations. In short, it must be assumed that about one half of the ultimate emigrants were either transients or living "underground" in that township, before embarking upon their voyage to America. As to the transients, a goldsmith and his family of four are expressly recorded in the 1854 list as "not resident" (*hier nicht am Platze*), as if this were a reason for their leaving. Yet, considering that more than 30 persons are not accounted for in the list of 1847/48, one cannot escape the conclusion that — side by side with Westheim's "official" Jewish households, which had reportedly decreased from 46 families with 183 souls in 1847 to 36 in 1850 — there lived in the community scores of single persons or even of whole families, unregistered and without legal right of residence, but somehow provisionally sheltered by the community. Some of them emigrated, while others probably tried to gain a legal foothold in the community by competing for *Matrikel* numbers vacated by emigration.

Their chances were however rather slim, for the number of *Matrikel* falling vacant must needs have been small. Probably it was even smaller than the number of the emigrating married couples, as may be surmised from the reasons for emigration adduced in the records. The Westheim record, including the largest number of emigrants (83), gives the most detailed account,[24] shown in Table XI.

As expected, the reason most often adduced was "no acceptance". It explains the departure of many master craftsmen and journeymen, but also of some merchants and pedlars. It was sometimes phrased as "no subsistence", meaning either lack of a

---

[22]CAHJP/D-GA Sulzbach, 54 (unpag.). As this place, located in the Upper Palatinate to the east of the river Rhine, is outside our enquiry, the case will not be reported here in detail.
[23]*Ibid.*, D-WR 15, fol. 15 b: 'Von der Judengemeinde dahin geschafft'.
[24]*Ibid.*, fol. 17 a-c.

TABLE XI

Reasons for emigration from Westheim (Kissingen district)

No acceptance or no means of existence	34	(see below)
Not indigenous (*nicht am Platze*)	5	(see above)
Deported by the community	11	(see above)
Family reasons	13	(4 of them engaged, 5 going to relatives in the U.S.)
Men — reason for emigration not stated	11	(including a rabbi, a teacher and a soldier — see below)
Women — reason for emigration not stated	9	
Total	83	

Matrikel number or lack of a livelihood, or both. In this form it almost certainly pertains also to the emigrants for whom no special reasons are adduced. In other words, most of the people leaving for overseas did not vacate a *Matrikel* number, but were forced to emigrate precisely because they themselves had failed to obtain one.

In a quite unusual form this predicament is expressed on the last page of the Westheim record by a pun of the compiler: Among the emigrants were two physicians, after whose names appears the following reason for emigration: *Paradieserlangung* (gaining paradise). The intention is clear: *Praxiserlangung* (gaining a practice), as they probably had not obtained the right to settle and to practise above the limits of the *Matrikel* quota. Whether the slip of the pen was intentional or not, it reveals much bitterness on the part of the writer and reduces to one word the reason behind all other reasons for emigration: From the hell of iniquity to the paradise of equality!

Although the Westheim list contains the fullest particulars as to the reasons for emigration, some lists from certain other places also occasionally explain the motives of the emigrants: four women between 30 and 36 years from Oberthulba left in order to marry, while two men from the same place could not gain acceptance by guild and magistrate. In Adelsberg three men complained of the same, while in Rieneck their number was as large as eight. Of one teacher from Adelsberg it was stated that "his profession was no longer in much demand" and the dwindling of the livelihood of rabbis and teachers with the declining number of Jewish inhabitants is borne out by a remark from Rödelmaier[25], and by entries from Westheim. In the latter place one candidate for the rabbinate and one teacher appeared among the emigrants, but they were listed without specifying their reason. So was a Westheim soldier, of whom it is only stated that he "had finished his tour of duty".

The emphasis on this point makes one wonder whether this applied to all the youngsters on the lists. The above-mentioned letter from Rödelmaier makes it clear. It speaks disapprovingly of the often occuring "illegal emigration of youngsters who

[25]*Ibid.*, fol. 29 a, in an accompanying letter to the 1854 statistics: ". . . wie die Verhältnisse der Herrn Rabbiner, Lehrer und sonstigen Gemeinde-Bediensteten, deren Existenz sich grösstentheils auf Privatverdiensten gründen, gefährdet seien . . ." (how precarious were the circumstances of the rabbis, teachers and other employees of the community whose living depend mostly on private honoraria).

are dodging conscription"[26]. In a letter from Neuhaus it was even explained that "only a few of the 51 emigrants had received the consent of the King's Government, while most undertook their voyage across the ocean only on the strength of their journey or labour-books, and among them some who went to the new homeland in order to evade conscription. Thus, it has been seen fit to omit the names of the 51 families"[27].

Now it is becoming clearer why some of the communities gave only scant information on their emigrants. Could there not have been more draft dodgers and more "underground" people than the numbers we have reconstructed from the Westheim record? Might not their mention have seemed inadvisable to the heads of the community even if they reported only to the rabbi of the district and not to the government? Better to be careful than to compromise the community and those members of the emigrated families that had stayed on. But if this reasoning is correct, might not then the overall figure of emigrants have been even larger than the 588 accounted for in our records? The same inference has already been drawn above, with regard to the emigration from the Palatinate.

In any case, Jewish emigration fron Bavaria did not stop in 1854. On the contrary, it seems to have continued unabated until *Matrikel* laws were abolished in 1861. This is also established by government figures on emigration for the year 1857[28], reproduced in Table XII.

TABLE XII

Emigration from Bavaria in 1857

Province	General emigration	Jewish emigration overseas	Europe	(b) and (c)	% of general emigration
	(a)	(b)	(c)	(b) and (c)	
Lower Bavaria	319	—	—	—	0.0%
Upper Bavaria	296	2	3	5	1.7%
Palatinate	3,450	144	12	156	4.5%
Upper Palatinate	585	6	0	6	1.0%
Upper Franconia	1,432	36	3	39	2.7%
Middle Franconia	741	25	9	34	4.6%
Lower Franconia	2,077	109	16	125	6.0%
Swabia	546	17	8	25	4.5%
Total	9,446	339	51	390	4.1%

While for the twenty-five years between 1830 and 1854 the annual mean of Jewish emigration from the Kissingen district, with about 17% of the Jews of Lower Franconia, was 23.5 persons, the official government statistics for 1857 reveal the annual number for the whole of Lower Franconia as being 125. Now, 17% of

[26]*Ibid.*, fol. 29 b.
[27]*Ibid.*, fol. 27 a, b.
[28]Hauptstaatsarchiv München, Abt. I, Allgemeines Staatsarchiv, M. Inn., 43339-43341.

this for the Kissingen district would again indicate an "official" emigration of 21.5 persons from the already depleted district. Although this figure, as all the other Jewish emigration figures, is already far in excess of the Jewish part in the Bavarian or Franconian general population, the unofficial, i.e. real rate of emigration may have been still higher, but cannot be ascertained with any degree of accuracy.

The annual mean for the Palatinate, which in the years 1842-1846 was 92.6 persons, showed a marked increase for the year 1857: no less than 156 Jews left the province during this one year. Jewish emigration from the Palatinate in that year constituted 4.8% of the combined Jewish and non-Jewish wave of emigration (3,450); but in Lower Franconia it amounted to 6% of the 2,077 emigrants, vastly exceeding the Jewish percentage of population.

Thus, the rate for 1857 also establishes the impression gained during the whole of our analysis: in Lower Franconia, and especially the Kissingen district, Jewish discontent was particularly widespread, and hence the proportion of emigrants, especially to the United States, was strikingly large there.

The Immigration and Acculturation of the German Jew in the United States of America*

BY HERBERT A. STRAUSS

INTRODUCTION

The migration of the refugees from Hitler's Germany between 1933 and 1945, at first glance, appears to constitute one chapter in the great movement of population that characterises modern industrial civilisations. Jews have been part of the great Western *Binnenwanderung* from countryside to city over the past two hundred years. They moved from East to West, as has been the general trend of migration (with some exceptions, for example, the emigration of Irish factory workers to England). Jews also moved across the Atlantic Ocean with the great European population trek that led forty million of the sixty million emigrants from Europe to the United States of America between 1830 and 1939. Today the labour force of Western European states is composed of up to 30% of foreigners mostly subsumed under the term of "migratory worker". The Second World War that uprooted about sixty million people from their homes has made Europe, too, not only America, in some respects a continent of migrants.[1]

But different from earlier waves of emigration, the forced expulsion of the Jew from Germany was part of the great catastrophe that Germany had brought upon itself, upon the rest of Europe, and upon the Jewish people through the Nazi regime. Most sophisticated attempts at explanation end with the admission that the accumulated malfunctions of German history, a breakdown of German civilisation, not anything Jews might have done, forced them into exile.[2]

*The author previously dealt with this subject in an essay entitled 'Die kulturelle Anpassung der deutschen Juden in den Vereinigten Staaten von Amerika', in *Emuna Horizonte*, vol. V, No. 1, January 1970, pp. 19-36.
[1]Of the vast literature on migration and US immigration history the following may be relevant: M. L. Hansen, *The Immigrant in American History*, Cambridge, Mass. 1940; E. E. Hirschler, *Jews from Germany in the United States*, New York 1955; Louise Holborn, 'The World Refugee Problem', in *International Encyclopedia of Social Science*, vol. XIII, 1968, pp. 361-373; H.S. Linfield, *Statistics of Jews and Jewish Organizations: historical review of ten censuses 1830-1937*, New York 1939; M. J. Proudfoot, *European Refugees 1939-1952*, Evanston, Ill. 1956; J. B. Schechtman, *European Population Transfers 1939-1945*, New York 1946; M. Wischnitzer, *To Dwell in Safety*, Philadelphia 1949.
[2]Interpretations of antisemitism are offered by Eva G. Reichmann, 'Diskussionen über die Judenfrage 1930-1932', and Robert Weltsch, 'Schlussbetrachtung', both in *Entscheidungsjahr 1932. Zur Judenfrage in der Endphase der Weimarer Republik*, Ein Sammelband herausgegeben von Werner E. Mosse unter Mitwirkung von Arnold Paucker, Tübingen 1965, 1966 (Schriftenreihe wissenschaftlicher Abhandlungen des Leo Baeck Instituts 13), pp. 503-562. For relevant summaries of the problems of Nazi "origins" and the links of Nazism with German, Austrian, or

I. AMERICAN IMMIGRATION POLICY
AS A FACTOR IN EMIGRATION FROM HITLER'S GERMANY

The United States, to which 250,000 to 300,000 refugees of all kinds fled from Nazi-dominated Europe between 1933 and 1944 has traditionally been the goal of migrants fleeing persecution. Germany, in fact, has been a consistent source of emigrants escaping from religious, political, or economic oppression: "... not a single decade of American history when Germany has not provided part of the American immigration."[3] Christian immigrants who fled from persecution at home have, in their turn, established patterns of intolerance and oppression not only towards the Negro slave but also towards those who deviated from the branch of Christianity confessed by locally prevailing majorities: Puritan persecutions of alleged heretics, Protestant intolerance towards Catholics. Even in the twentieth century, American immigration legislation has tended to discriminate against the Oriental, the Catholic, the East and South European for a mixture of "racial", religious, economic, and social reasons.

The image of America as a "haven for the huddled masses" of decadent Europe must thus be tempered by the realities of American immigration legislation as it developed in response to economic pressures and the status and prejudice patterns influencing public opinion, lobbies, and lawmakers over the years. As early as 1885, a provision against contract labour was enacted into law to protect the unwary immigrant from the worst exploitation. The Immigration Act of 1882 empowered immigration authorities to deny admission to a person who was "likely to become a public charge" (LPC provision). Under the impact of the social Darwinism and racism that permeated the forty-eight volumes issued by a US Immigration Commission in 1911 as the latest "scientific" findings on North-West European racial superiority, and of isolationism, anti-Catholicism, antisemitism and general xenophobia, immigration legislation became restrictive and in effect, discriminatory. The national quota system embodied in the Quota Act of 1921 and in the Immigration Acts of 1924 and 1929 was backed also by American labour (American Federation of Labor) and by the lower and lower middle-class segments of the urban population who thus added their voice to the narrow nationalism that

European antisemitism see K. D. Bracher, *Die deutsche Diktatur*, Köln/Berlin 1969, pp. 1-60; E. L. Ehrlich, 'Judenfeindschaft in Deutschland', in *Judenfeindschaft, Darstellungen und Analysen*, ed. K. Thieme, Frankfurt/Hamburg 1963, pp. 209-257; H. Greive, *Theologie und Ideologie. Katholizismus und Judentum in Deutschland und Österreich 1918-1935*, Heidelberg 1969; E. Nolte, *Three Faces of Fascism*, New York 1966; P. G. J. Pulzer, *The Rise of Political Anti-Semitism in Germany and Austria*, New York 1964; Eva G. Reichmann, *Hostages of Civilization*, London 1950; E. Sterling, *Er ist wie du. Aus der Frühgeschichte des Antisemitismus in Deutschland (1815-1850)*, München 1956; H. A. Strauss, ed., *Conference on Anti-Semitism*, New York 1969; idem, 'Die preußische Bürokratie und die anti-jüdischen Unruhen im Jahre 1834', in *Gegenwart im Rückblick. Festgabe für die Jüdische Gemeinde Berlin 25 Jahre nach dem Neubeginn*, ed. H. A. Strauss and K. R. Grossmann, Heidelberg 1970, pp. 27-55.
[3] See F. L. Reinhold, 'Exiles and Refugees in America', in *The Annals of the American Academy of Political and Social Science*, May 1939, No. 203, pp. 63-73.

appears to have affected immigration legislation in all countries during the 1930s.[4]

As a result, the total annual quota of immigrants was not to exceed 153,774 persons a year under the 1929 Immigration Act. Not included in this figure were non-quota immigrants (including clergymen), students, entrants on visitors' visas, and immigrants born in the Western hemisphere. With the onset of the depression, the administration of the Act was tightened up. President Herbert Hoover, on the 8th September 1930, responded to widespread pressure and ordered the State Department's Visa Division to advise local consuls that the LPC clause was to be rigidly enforced forthwith. Hoover's rule, in force until 1937 — although somewhat relaxed for prospective immigrants from Germany in 1935 — was thus Immigration and Naturalization Service and State Department (Visa Division) practice when Hitler struck in Germany on the 30th January 1933, at a time when the Roosevelt Administration was turning inward to deal with unemployment, the business slump, and the general misery and hardship of the "Great Depression".[5]

During the first years of the Nazi regime, Jewish and political refugees fleeing Germany did not enter the United States in any appreciable numbers (see Table I).

TABLE I

Jewish immigration from Germany to the United States of America, January 1933 to June 1938

January 1933 to December 1933	535	
January 1934 to December 1934	2,310	
January 1935 to June 1935	658	
July 1935 to June 1936	6,750	(estimated)
July 1936 to June 1937	6,750	
July 1937 to June 1938	10,000	
Total (approx.)	27,000	

From Werner Rosenstock, 'Exodus 1933-1939. A Survey of Jewish Emigration from Germany' in *LBI Year Book I* (1956), p. 376.

[4]Critical and well-balanced scholarly analyses will be found in H. L. Feingold, *The Politics of Rescue. The Roosevelt Administration 1938-1945*, New Brunswick, N.J. 1970, and D. S. Wyman, *Paper Walls. America and the Refugee Crisis 1938-1941*, Amherst, Mass. 1968. An angry and somewhat selective account is offered by A. D. Morse, *While Six Million Died. A Chronicle of American Apathy*, New York 1967. Of human interest for the author's personal experiences is Kurt R. Grossmann, *Emigration. Geschichte der Hitler-Flüchtlinge 1933-1945*, Frankfurt 1969. A war-time review based on public material and influenced by the ongoing public struggle to liberalize immigration procedures is offered by A. Tartakower and K. R. Grossmann, *The Jewish Refugee*, New York 1944. Maurice R. Davie, *Refugees in America*, New York/London 1947, avoids the issue of US immigration policies almost entirely. Davie's study is based on solid questionnaire and interview research but suffers from its orientation towards the "Americanization" problem then current in American (war-time) evaluation of the refugee's "contribution" to America as a factor in his worthiness of being admitted.

[5]See Feingold, *op. cit.*, pp. 16, 126-127; Wyman, *op. cit.*, pp. 3-13.

Thus the annual quota for immigrants who were natives of Germany (25,957) remained largely unfilled. How far American restrictions affected this result is difficult to determine (actually a large number of emigrant aliens left the United States during those years of up to twelve million American unemployed, and early refugees from Germany appear to have been politically and culturally attracted by continental Europe[6]; see Tables II and III).

The restrictive immigration policy, to be sure, was supported by practically all segments of the American people: antisemitic and xenophobic attitudes appeared consistently in all opinion polls of the period. Condemnation of such universally despised acts as the *Kristallnacht* of the 9th-11th November 1938 did not lead to a basic change in public opinion on matters of immigration.[7] Bills introduced in Congress to liberalize the system of national immigration quotas were countered by numerous other bills calling for the end of all immigration and for the deportation of aliens during the "Roosevelt recession" of 1937-1938.[8] President Franklin D. Roosevelt — whose attitudes towards immigration have been scrutinized by recent research — succeeded in extending "12,000-15,000" visas to refugee visitors already in the USA in 1938, but an attempt to open the gates to 10,000 non-quota refugee children (the Wagner-Rogers Bill) made by liberal forces in 1938-1939 was rejected by two-thirds of the American people (as evidenced by opinion polls), and would not have passed the House Immigration Subcommittee had it been brought to a vote there.[9] Roosevelt, aware of the hysteria a debate on immigration might have unleashed among his vociferous conservative opponents, also failed to support the bill, while Labor and State Departments, in charge of immigration procedures, maintained "neutrality". The number of children admitted under unaccompanied childrens' immigration programmes to European countries has been estimated at 9,000 (United Kingdom, November 1938-September 1939), 2,000 (Holland), 1,500 (Belgium), 600 (France), 250 (Sweden), as compared with 240 for the United States of America (all November 1938-May 1939).[10] A movement to admit British children following the fall of France, in contrast, was widely supported by public opinion and the Washington bureaucracy. It led to the admission of about 4,000

[6]See Morse, *op. cit.*, pp. 141-143, for some cases culled from the files of the American Consulate in Rotterdam, Holland. The evaluation of the refugees' motives in not selecting (or coming to) the USA in larger numbers offered in the text was first stated by W. Rosenstock, 'Exodus 1933-1939 — A Survey of Jewish Emigration from Germany', in *LBI Year Book I* (1956), p. 380; cf. Morse, *op. cit.*, pp. 130-149; Wyman, *op. cit.*, pp. 33-34, 155-162. J. Carlo Menotti's short opera *The Consul* is one of the few artistic attempts known to the author to deal with the consulate-emigrant situation.

[7]For public opinion polls on Jews in America see G. J. Selznick and S. Steinberg, *The Tenacity of Prejudice*, New York 1969, and Ch. H. Stembler a.o., *Jews in the Mind of America*, New York 1966. See also Feingold, *op. cit.*, pp. 42-44, and Wyman, *op. cit.*, pp. 14-23, 67-75.

[8]For a list of the anti-immigration bills of that year see Wyman, *op. cit.*, p. 69.

[9]For the story of the Wagner-Rogers bill see Wyman, *op. cit.*, pp. 75-98, and Feingold, *op. cit.*, pp. 148-154. The estimate of the voting trend in the House Committee on Immigration and Naturalization on the Wagner-Rogers bill was based upon a private poll "known to the State Department" as reported by Wyman, *op. cit.*, p. 91.

[10]For statistics on the admission of unaccompanied children from Germany and Austria to Western countries (1938-1939) see the figures quoted by Wyman, *op. cit.*, pp. 97-98.

TABLE II

Total number of immigrants from all countries arriving in the United States of America, 1933-1944

	From all Countries	From Europe	Number of Refugees Gross Estimate	Number of Refugees Refined Estimate
1933	23,068	14,400	11,869	1,919
1934	29,470	19,559	16,323	4,241
1935	34,956	25,346	21,915	5,436
1936	36,329	26,295	22,875	6,538
1937	50,244	35,812	31,537	12,012
1938	67,895	50,574	44,848	44,848
1939	82,998	68,198	61,882	61,882
1940	70,756	56,254	50,581	50,581
1941	51,776	36,989	30,808	30,808
1942	28,781	14,881	12,620	12,620
1943	23,725	8,953	6,629	6,629
1944	28,551	8,694	6,348	6,348
Total	528,549	365,955	318,235	243,862

From Maurice R. Davie, *Refugees in America*, Harper & Brothers, New York/ London 1947, p. 24 (reproduced with the permission of the publishers).

TABLE III

Admissions and departures of immigrants to the United States of America, 1931-1944

Year	Immigrant Aliens Admitted	Emigrant Aliens Departed	Net Entries
1931	97,139	61,882	35,257
1932	35,576	103,295	— 67,719
1933	23,068	80,081	— 57,013
1934	29,470	39,771	— 10,301
1935	34,956	38,834	— 3,878
1936	36,329	35,817	512
1937	50,244	26,736	23,508
1938	67,895	25,210	42,685
1939	82,998	26,651	56,347
1940	70,756	21,461	49,295
1941	51,776	17,115	34,661
1942	28,781	7,363	21,418
1943	23,725	5,107	18,618
1944	28,551	5,669	22,882
Total	661,264	494,992	166,272

From Maurice R. Davie, *Refugees in America* (from *Annual Reports of the Immigration and Naturalization Service*, for the appropriate years), Harper & Brothers, New York/ London 1947, p. 21 (reproduced with the permission of the publishers).

British children in the few months before the programme came to an end in the late summer of 1940, following the sinking of the *City of Benares* by German submarines with the loss of 79 children.[11]

In spite of this persistent opposition to changing the national quota system of immigration, the Roosevelt Administration liberalized the LPC clause in 1937, and instructed local consuls — the final arbiters of the admission of prospective immigrants under the prevailing system — to permit full use of the combined legal quota for German and Austrian-born immigrant refugees. Immigration statistics for the fiscal years 1939 and 1940 thus reflect not only the increasingly desperate situation of Jews in Germany and Austria but also American economic recovery and changed immigration policies.

The outbreak of the war, with its increased transportation difficulties, once again changed the policies of the Visa Division of the State Department (presided over by Breckinridge Long,[12] the former ambassador to Italy): the stricter rules governing proof of support (affidavits) and the difficulties of obtaining a paid steamship ticket brought rejection to many applicants in German and Austrian consulates, with applicants in transit countries (United Kingdom, Shanghai, Portugal) taking their places in the quota queue. The figures for the fiscal years 1939 and 1940 reflect this policy which unwittingly, of course, condemned most applicants rejected in Germany and Austria to death (see Table IV).[13]

TABLE IV

Percentage of the German-Austrian quota fulfilled, and number of German and Austrian immigrants admitted to the United States, 1933-1944

	Total quota	1933	1934	1935	1936	1937	1938
Per cent:	100	5.3	13.7	20.2	24.3	42.1	65.3
Numbers:	27,370	1,450	3,740	5,530	6,650	11,520	17,870
		1939	1940	1941	1942	1943	1944
Per cent:		100	95.3	47.7	17.4	4.7	4.8
Numbers:		27,370	26,080	13,050	4,760	1,290	1,351

Calculations of absolute numbers prepared by the author, based upon percentages adapted by M. Davie, *op. cit.*, p. 29, from G. Krichefsky, 'Quota Immigration, 1925-1944', *Immigration and Naturalization Service Monthly Review*, II, 12, June 1945, pp. 156-195.

[11]See Wyman, *op. cit.*, pp. 116-128.
[12]The best source for the shabbiness of some State Department officials is *The War Diary of Breckinridge Long. Selections from the Years 1939-1944.*, ed. Fred L. Israel, Lincoln, Nebraska 1966. Long's attitudes are analysed in Feingold, *op. cit.*, and Wyman, *op. cit.* (see indices s.v. Long). Not available to the author: Saul S. Friedman, *Official U.S. Policy towards Jewish Refugees 1938-1945*, Ph.D. thesis (typewritten), Ohio State University 1969, 418 pp. (Reference by courtesy of Prof. H. Friedlaender, New York.)
[13]Wyman, *op. cit.*, pp. 173-183.

With the fiscal year 1940, however, a new motive entered into the implementation of American immigration policy: American officials believed — or pretended that they believed — that Nazi and Communist agents were being infiltrated as a "fifth column" into the United States by the Soviet and Nazi governments to subvert the U.S. government in case of war, as the military resistance of France was believed to have been subverted by Nazi and Communist agents in May-June, 1940. To deal with this threat, or imagined threat, the Immigration and Naturalization Service was transferred from the jurisdiction of the Labor to that of the Justice Department, and the issuing of visas was ordered to be delayed or stopped (Visa Division cable of 29th June 1940). American diplomatic personnel (Bullitt, Steinhardt) warned publicly or in dispatches against the danger of Communist or Nazi infiltration, while a wave of hysteria swept newspapers, magazines and public opinion in the latter half of 1940. The Smith Act (famous for its use during the anti-Communist drive of the late 1940s and early 1950s) was passed by the Senate in June 1940 (the House version had dated from 1939); it legislated, as its third title, for the registration and finger-printing of all aliens in the United States of fourteen years and older. Refugees from Germany and Austria suffered restrictions, but were at least spared the internment considered necessary by the French and British governments (and meted out by the US government, in a decidedly brutal manner, to its Japanese and Nisei populations in California following Pearl Harbour). Immigration procedures were reorganised to allow additional screening and review procedures. Immigration figures for 1941 register the result of this policy: only 3,000 visas were issued between July and December 1941. Then the war produced a new situation, as only immigrants who could be expected to be "beneficial" to the interests of the United States were allowed to enter.[14]

Judgment on these policies and attitudes, and on the decision-making authorities involved, will have to be attempted against the background not only of the general closing of doors to immigration, Western policies towards Nazi migration blackmail, the treatment of refugees from Germany in other countries, and the American self-image as a haven for the oppressed: a judgment also involves questions concerning Jewish policies towards resettlement and immigration, and ultimately, the fact, pointed out by Henry L. Feingold,[15] that the American tradition of restrictionism set the pattern for American policy makers. When the ultimate emergency of the holocaust called for bold and imaginative measures, the American people and government proved incapable of responding adequately.

These then were the circumstances under which between 129,000 and 132,000 German refugees of all kinds reached the United States between 1933 and 1944. Of the total number of refugees from European countries, (see p. 67) about 160,000

[14]*Ibid.*, pp. 169-205. On Ambassador William C. Bullitt, see Feingold, *op. cit.*, p. 129, and Wyman, *op. cit.*, p. 189. On Ambassador Laurence Steinhardt, see Feingold, *op. cit.*, pp. 285-289. Heinz Pol answered Bullitt's Philadelphia speech of the 18th August 1940, in *The Nation*, vol. CLI, 31st August 1940.

[15]On Zionism as a possible factor in aborting resettlement schemes in countries other than Palestine, see Feingold, *op. cit.* pp. 123-125, 166, 295-305.

identified themselves as "Hebrews", the ethnic/racial/religious tag prescribed for Jews by the Immigration Act of 1924. About 57.9%, or 97,374 persons thus identifying themselves, were born in Germany. Non-quota immigrants, immigrants on legalized visitors' visas, and persons educated in Germany but born elsewhere and falling under other than the German national quota must be added to this figure to yield the approximate number of Jews coming from Germany to the United States during the Hitler years.[16] Following World War II, under special legislation admitting "displaced persons", about 105,000 Jews entered among the 300,000 war-time refugees; the rest were ethnic Germans, Ukrainians, Poles, nationals of the former Baltic States etc., many of whom had moved from East to West with the Nazi army and SS-troops when the Soviet Union advanced into Germany. The number of German Jews among "displaced persons" in the USA, and the number of immigrants from transit areas (Shanghai, South and Central America, Europe) has not been clearly established at this time of writing.[17]

II. THE AMERICAN EXPERIENCE: PATTERNS OF ACCULTURATION

The United States of America has been a major social laboratory for contacts between ethnic and racial groups, and for contacts between the "old" and the "new" immigrants that make up the non-native (non-Indian) population of the United States. The different sociological models developed to describe these processes of culture contact have, in some sense, corresponded to different phases of American history. They were also made to serve the social, economic, or political interests of various groups that used models of this acculturation process to construct ideological superstructures for their segmental interests. As a result, the analytic *Ansatz* has remained fluid not only with respect to the specific Jewish situation, but also as applied to ethnic groups generally.[18]

---

[16]At this time of writing, no precise or unambiguous data are available on non-quota refugees, extended visitors' visa entrants, and persons raised in Germany but admitted to the United States under the quota of their country of birth. Some of the statistical difficulties are described by Davie, *op. cit.*, pp. 24-27.

[17]At this time of writing, no comprehensive analysis of the immigration of Jewish "displaced persons" to the USA is available. Written works deal primarily with the D.P. as a psychiatric or social "problem", not with his acculturation. See, for example, D. Crystal, *The Displaced Person and the Social Agency*, Rochester, N.Y. 1958; Philadelphia Study Committee on Refugee Integration, *Refugees in Philadelphia*, Philadelphia 1962 (inter-denominational, stressing "success" in integration); W. G. Niederland, 'Psychiatric disorders among persecution victims', in *Journal of Nervous and Mental Diseases*, vol. 139/5, 1964, pp. 458-474; J. Goldstein, I. F. Lukoff and H. A. Strauss, 'A Case History of a Concentration Camp Survivor', in *OSE-Review*, vol. 8/1, 1951, pp. 11-28; H. Paul and H. J. Herberg, *Psychische Spätschäden nach Politischer Verfolgung*, Basel-New York 1963; W. R. von Baeyer, H. Haeffner and R. P. Kisker, *Psychiatrie der Verfolgten*, Berlin 1964.

[18]Theoretical models of acculturation are developed by S. N. Eigenstadt, *The Absorption of Immigrants*, Glencoe, Ill. 1955; N. Glazer and D. P. Moynahan, *Beyond the Melting Pot*, Cambridge, Mass. 1963; N. Glazer, 'A New Look at the Melting Pot', in *The Public Interest*, vol. 16, 1969, pp. 180-187; M. Gordon, *Assimilation in American Life*, New York 1964; O. Handlin, *The Uprooted*, New York 1951; *Conference on Acculturation*, ed. H. A. Strauss, New York 1965; W. L. Warner and L. Srole, *The Social System of American Ethnic Groups*, New Haven, Conn. 1945; A. Weinberg, *Migration and Belonging*, The Hague 1961.

Perhaps the oldest view of American immigration history, a view that prevailed during the first period of US immigration from the colonial period to the onset of mass immigration in the 1880s, is held by historians who identify the culture of a country primarily by its political, legal or linguistic system. America, in this view, is an Anglo-Saxon country that was settled in its formative period primarily by Protestant English, Dutch, Scotch, Irish, German, Scandinavian, or French settlers, all of whom adopted English political institutions. Other immigrant groups or cultures would have to adjust to the prevailing culture but would be permitted, due to the separation of church and state, to pursue their religions as "private affairs". This view of culture contact appeared to describe, with some realism, the actual social processes of early America, at least in areas that were not too isolated from Anglo-Saxon settlements. It has been used by nineteenth-century Protestants to discriminate, for example, against the Irish-Catholic immigration of the 1840s and 1850s, and has inspired the anti-Catholic "Know-Nothing" movements of that period to demand restrictive immigration laws and bar the foreign-born from political office. This "Anglo-Conformity" also served racial trends of thought that were directed against Negroes, Catholics, foreigners (Ku-Klux-Klan), or Orientals (Oriental exclusion laws), or it was linked with anti-German trends (World War I), antisemitism (inter-war period), or anti-Japanese trends (World War II). It has generally expressed the most hard-faced demand for the "assimilation" of all immigrant groups, and has produced a historiography in which the political-legal-linguistic pattern of America, more or less complete by 1830, more or less located along the Eastern sea-board and in the colonial South, has tended to dominate the story. European historians, little versed in social analysis, have tended to accept "Anglo-Conformity" as the expression of "true America" in line with their own monolithic images of the modern *Nationalstaat*. Many non-Protestants, non-Anglo-Saxons, non-Whites have found the ideal of an open Anglo-American social structure, ready to accept those willing to assimilate, nothing short of a myth when it came to the realities of primary group contacts in periods of mass migration or in urban mass societies, even in the second generation.[19]

Thus, a second view of American immigration patterns offered itself, the famous "melting-pot" model described as early as 1782 by J. Hector St. John (Crèvecoeur) (1735-1813), formulated later by Ralph Waldo Emerson (1845), and popularised by Israel Zangwill's drama *The Melting Pot* (1908).[20] It claimed, in response to both the old rural "frontier" and the new urban "frontier" that America was a product of an amalgamation between the different ethnic strains and cultures, that here, on the new continent, ethnic groups that had been separated by national rivalries,

[19]Trends in American opinion directed against immigrants and aliens are discussed by J. Higham, *Strangers in the Land. Patterns of American Nativism 1860-1925*, New Brunswick, N.J. 1955; R. A. Billington, *The Protestant Crusade 1800-1860*, New York 1938; Gordon, *op. cit.*, pp. 91-103. The story of the evacuation of Japanese and Nisei citizens will be found in A. Bosworth, *America's Concentration Camps*, New York 1967; A. Gridner, *The Great Betrayal*, New York 1969; J. ten Broek, E. N. Barnhart, and F. W. Matson, *Prejudice, War, and the Constitution*, Berkeley, Cal. 1954.

[20]On the "melting pot" see Gordon, *op. cit.*, pp. 114-131.

religious or racial hatreds in their countries of origin, met, "acculturated" with one another, intermarried and produced "that new man, the American" (Crèvecoeur, 1782). There can be no question that this model describes another part and period of American social history:

> "a substantial proportion of the descendants of the non-English immigrants of colonial times and the first three-quarters of the nineteenth century (with the exception of the Irish-Catholics and the German Jews) have by now been absorbed into the general, white, sociologically Protestant sector of American life".[21]

This leaves out all the non-Whites, and a considerable sector of the "new immigration" whose very number and sectional cohesion have so far prevented them from disappearing into the "melting pot" as prescribed by this theory. Not only have the three major religions managed to stay quite separate: traces of ethnic separateness and consciousness abound even in "White" America. The model is to be judged in effect either as a version of Anglo-Conformity designed to make it easier for the ethnic immigrant to accept Anglo-Saxon Protestant status and power patterns, or as a description of the process of the amalgamation of some external features of the various ethnic strains (e.g. American cooking), or as an ideological tool for the descendants of new-comers to pry open older Anglo-American power patterns by appeals to the "melting-pot" ideology.

If these two models assume, ultimately, the disappearance of "ethnicity" in America, the idea of "cultural pluralism" lays bare another segment of America's social realities to analytic understanding, and may yet become the most important tool for the harmonisation of racial tensions, or religious and ethnic differences. This model accepts the obvious facts upon which the other two models base their claims. The political-legal-linguistic pattern of the country is, of course, American-English, and considerable inter-mixtures of cultures and peoples have taken place, and are taking place, under the umbrella of this political pattern. Yet, large segments of old "immigrants" — especially the American Negro population of at least twenty million men, women and children — as well as the "new immigration" continue to lead lives that are not adequately described by either "melting-pot" or "Anglo-Conformity" models: Protestants, Catholics, and Jews maintain not only their religions but will probably continue to marry within their groups in the majority of cases in the future; ethnic groups, even in the second or third generation, tend to settle in identifiable neighbourhoods, even when they move to the new suburbs of the more or less affluent; group contacts after work tend to be restricted for most groups to members of the same ethnic or religious groups ("the five-o'clock shadow", intellectuals and artists forming a major exception); clubs and similar leisure associations cater to distinctly separatist interests and exclude "lower prestige" groups, however defined. In addition, recent attempts by Black activists to prise open residential areas, to win priority in the allocation of government funds, or break down monopolistic economic practices — e.g. among trade unions — have led to an awakening of a "new ethnicity" among lower-middle-class Irish,

[21] *Ibid.*, p. 126.

Italian, Ukrainian, Polish etc., American Catholics, even of the second generation, that cannot be explained by either of the two previous models of culture contact in America: in 1966, thirty-four million Americans were foreign-born or first-generation descendants of foreign-born parents.[22]

In origin, the idea of cultural pluralism derives from the internationalist, idealistic, tolerant liberalism of men like John Dewey, Horace M. Kallen, and the educators and social workers who needed to account for the facts of acculturation during mass immigration. Cultural pluralism avoided the "ethnic self-hatred" i.e. self-rejection forced upon many "new immigrants" by the Americanization process, and gained new impetus in the humane revulsion of American social analysts against the perverse consequences of Nazi racism and super-nationalism. As a tool or rationalisation, it seems to serve those interests best who search for a coexistence of ethnic groups, nationalities, races and religions in the face of strong or weak prejudice, or those political publicists who wish to extend the right of the individual to a separate existence to *groups* (like the Jews) in the modern world. America, in contrast with the Soviet Union as much as with Switzerland, would thus become a *Nationalstaat* of a special character. It would grant its small Jewish minority — and its larger other minorities — the right to continued ethnic, cultural, and group existence, although all minorities would speak one common language, and would provide "universal" areas of co-operation in the "general society" (universal "social rôles") without disturbing intimate primary group contacts or "social rôles" in the ethnic group context. Cultural pluralists, like adherents of the other two social models, are able to cite an impressive body of data for their view of America. In sum, one is led to conclude that a more differentiated breakdown of social behaviour reveals the operational and analytic usefulness of each of the models for a segment of the culture-contact situation in America. Pluralism is, of course, ethically superior, psychologically healthier, and less repressive than the other two models. On its proper harmonisation with American nationalism may yet depend the resolution of America's racial dilemmas.[23]

III. THE JEWISH COMMUNITY IN AMERICA, 1933 AND AFTER

When the first refugees from Nazism arrived in small numbers in the United States in the mid-thirties, its Jewish population fell into three groups and traditions. The oldest groups had been part of the colonial settlement of the continent, of Sephardi or Ashkenazi provenance, small in number and long-range impact. Prior to the

[22]On the "new ethnicity" see A. M. Greeley, *Why can't they be like us?*, New York 1969; M. H. Engel, in *International Migration Review*, III/1, 1968, pp. 50-53; N. J. Russo, *ibid.*, III/2, 1969, pp. 3-17, and J. Vecoli, *ibid.*, III/3, 1969, pp. 58-61; Reports on the *National Consultation on Ethnic America* (e.g. in *The Wall Street Journal*, 24th April 1969; *The New York Times*, 19th November 1969); P. Schrag, 'The Forgotten American', in *Harper's Magazine*, August 1969 (reprint, n. pp.); A. Greeley, *Ethnicity as an influence on behavior*, ed. National Consultation on Ethnic America, New York n.d. (mimeo.), and similar mimeographed material published by the same organisation, a group supported by the American Jewish Committee.

[23]On social rôles see S. N. Eisenstadt, D. Weintraub and N. Toren, *Analysis of Processes of Role Change*, Jerusalem 1967.

1880s, a few hundred thousand Jews from Germany (or as Lloyd Gartner has shown, from countries bordering Germany to the East but identifying themselves as German Jews and with German culture) had joined the first settlers. This group proved to be not only enormously successful economically: it also created the main pattern of Jewish organised life in the United States. The largest and most influential group of Jewish immigrants began to arrive from Eastern Europe in the early 1880s.[24] Their arrival coincided with the beginning of a social antisemitism in the United States that was probably not uninfluenced by its contemporaneous German counterparts. "German Jews" generously, if often condescendingly, like other upper-middle class charity efforts, responded to the social and "Americanization" challenge provided by the new immigrants. In the large cities where the new immigrants congregated, a diversified cultural life in the Yiddish language erupted in the religious and secular areas; the new immigrants constituted a genuine Jewish proletariat and entered the labour market, like similar immigrants before them, largely unprotected against the harshness of unbridled laissez-faire capitalism. They settled in dense "Jewish" neighbourhoods — like New York's Lower East Side, or Brooklyn's Williamsburg, Flatbush, or Bushwick sections — formed labour unions, protective and social associations, *shtübls, heders, shuls, hevres* in the rich associational pattern of the East European ghetto.

"The rise in socio-economic status of this group and of Eastern European Jews and their descendants is . . . the greatest Horatio Alger story in American history." At the end of this process — today, in 1970 — their occupational distribution resembles that of the (highest-status) Protestant denominations in the country as a whole. In New York and other cities of similarly concentrated Jewish settlement, about one third of all Jews gainfully employed in 1930 worked in manufacturing (textiles and related areas) as blue-collar workers, but another third was employed in trades, and 11.3% in the professions. In 1900, according to one estimate, about 60% of all gainfully employed Jews worked in industry; nation-wide, the percentage had fallen to about 13%–14% by 1930.[25]

This economic and social mobility was accompanied by a process of acculturation. Success on the socio-economic ladder implied a climb out of the Yiddish environment via education. Orthodoxy became identified with "grandfather" and "the old country"; the very nostalgia, the aura of quaintness with which the American-educated second or third generation Eastern Jew surrounds this aspect of his past today, testifies to the psychological break he has made with it. The great

[24]On Jewish immigration to the USA see Note 1, and M. Richin, *The promised city: New York's Jews 1870-1914*, Cambridge, Mass. 1962 (with good bibliography); B. Sherman, *The Jew within American Society*, Detroit 1961; A. Tartakower and K. R. Grossmann, *op. cit.*; M. Wischnitzer, *op. cit.* The social etc. composition of German-Jewish immigrants to nineteenth-century America is discussed by E. E. Hirschler, *op. cit.*; H. G. Reissner, The 'German-American Jews (1800-1850)' in *LBI Year Book X* (1965), pp. 57-116 (including a good bibliography, pp. 112-116); L. P. Gartner, 'The Jewish Community in America, Transplanted and Transformed', in *Conference on Acculturation*, ed. H. A. Strauss, New York 1965, pp. 7-17.

[25]See Gordon, *op. cit.*, pp. 173-195; B. Sherman, 'Demographic and Social Aspects', in *The American Jew. A Reappraisal*, ed. O. Janowsky, Philadelphia 1965, pp. 27-51; N. Reich, 'Economic Status', *ibid.*, pp. 53-74; B. Sherman, *op. cit.*, pp. 97-116, 173-189.

Yiddish-based culture in literature, journalism, the theatre, religious learning, politics that had characterized the first generation declined inexorably, but the emotional tie, the intense communal loyalty, remained and intensified in America as a tool of survival in a harsh new economic environment. Social contacts with non-Jews — as far as one can generalise on the basis of the available data — remained mostly confined to business and professional associations, even in the second generation, with the important exception of the intellectual and artistic group and some professions. In quite a few areas, discrimination and prejudice against the "pushy Jew" existed; antisemitic movements, radio preachers, and organisations sprang up, formed in reaction against Jewish social or economic upward mobility in the 1920s, and as the xenophobic aspect of post-World-War-One isolationism. American history knows other examples of social and economic conflicts taking on the coloration and overtones of religious, ethnic, or racial prejudice against such upwardly mobile groups.[26]

This, then, was the Jewish community in the 1930s and 1940s which the German Jew entered. It was a community in the true sense of primary group cohesion, similar culture consciousness, similar reactions to a like perception of the social self. A new type, the "American Jew" was emerging, as marriages between the socially compatible layers of the different immigrant strains took place (or across classes among college youth). The descendant of the Eastern immigrant created a secular religion of social responsibility that led him into the arena of trade-union politics, liberal causes, the Left. In his Jewish culture, the new "American Jew" was still showing a dependence upon the older European centres of Jewish education and learning in the 1930s. But different from the "German citizen of the Jewish faith" (the average member of the *Centralverein deutscher Staatsbürger jüdischen Glaubens*) American Jewry remained intensely conscious of its group character, its ethnicity: it was universally and became, as it were, naturally, pro-Zionist, as its differentiated structure of charitable organisations led by professionals of Yiddish-speaking origin, prepared itself to face one of the two greatest challenges of its history, the care for the refugee on a world-wide basis, and the financial, political and propagandistic concern with the dream that was to become Israel. The images or recollections – some true some false – of Jewish professionals, of what had happened to their migrant parents and grandparents in Germany and at the hand of "German Jews" in the United States, were not always free of distortions and resentment: the "German Jew" of the nineteenth century had become a symbol of "upper-class" charity, of coldness and tight organisational drives, of "assimilation" and, in Freudian terms, of "identification with the aggressor", the Gentile world into which American Jews were just about to move themselves — but not just yet. America was offering a picture of "cultural pluralism", and even in the mid-forties it seemed as if Americans were being "melted down" culturally, economically, politically, while maintaining separate religious identities

[26]See N. Glazer and D. P. Moynahan, *op. cit.*, pp. 137-180; B. Sherman, *op. cit.*, pp. 137-156.

and the rich cluster of associations that temples and synagogues, churches and cathedrals were developing around the core of ritual observances: "Catholic, Protestant and Jew"[27], religious pluralism. The isolating influences of concern with Israel's survival and of the new sub-urban return to the Temple; the dismally low and static level of religious or Jewish knowledge and education; the disintegrating influence of increasing intermarriage, secularism, and loss of cultural dynamics in an increasingly mobile society; these forces of the 1940s and 1950s were as yet dimly visible. The 1960s, finally, would pose a new challenge in the revolution of rising Negro expectations and the fundamental doubts the new Negro consciousness and pride would raise for the model by which America was to perceive its future, as backlash, including Jewish backlash, threatened to destroy liberal hopes for the political and social community of the New World, and Jews felt a new and sudden decline in their national position. The effect of the new group situation on Jewish survival in America, the difficulties created by conservatives who may or may not be flirting with antisemitism while fighting "the Eastern liberal establishment", the potential dilemma for Jewish politics that may be posed by Israel, and the propaganda of the "Old" and "New" Left and its Jewish adherents — these will be the challenge and problems of tomorrow.

IV. SOME CHARACTERISTICS OF GERMAN JEWRY, 1933

The 564,519 Jews recorded by the German census of 1925 were a heterogeneous population, varying in geographic distribution, occupation and class, customs and intellectual characteristics.[28] There had been the megalopolitan uniqueness of Berlin where, alone of all German cities, a sizable Jewish proletariat had come into being with the (often forced) immigration of Jews from Eastern Europe during and after World War I.[29] There had been the urban Jew, and the Jew of the small rural community who lived in a subculture and *"Milieufrömmigkeit"* (Baeck) of his own. In cities like Frankfurt, Würzburg, or Hamburg, a German-Jewish orthodoxy had developed an intense intellectual and religious commitment and theological culture.[30] Elsewhere, religious reform was attracting its upper-class clientele. German Jewry had developed its outstanding figures within its own culture. Jews had taken part in German politics and German culture since the eighteenth century, and their presence in Germany — apart from some flaws — had borne glorious fruit in spite of, and perhaps, also on account of, the outcropping of antisemitism.

Compared to the Christian environment in which they lived in Germany, the German-Jewish group had distinct demographic characteristics.[31] More than the

---

[27]W. Herberg, *Protestant-Catholic-Jew*, New York 1955.
[28]See W. J. Cahnman, 'The Three Regions of German-Jewish History', in *Jubilee Volume dedicated to Curt C. Silberman*, ed. H. A. Strauss and H. G. Reissner, New York 1969, pp. 1-14.
[29]On Berlin Jewry see H. A. Strauss, 'The Plural Worlds of German Jewry. A Postscript', in *Gegenwart im Rückblick*, pp. 317-329.
[30]For a short history of German Orthodoxy see M. L. Munk, 'Austrittsbewegung und Berliner Adass Jisroel-Gemeinde', *ibid.*, pp. 130-149.
[31]Most concise source for the statistics of Jews in Germany is Esra Bennathan, 'Die demographische und wirtschaftliche Struktur der Juden', in *Entscheidungsjahr 1932*, pp. 87-134.

Christian population, Jews had engaged in *Handel und Verkehr* (trade and commerce, 61.3%, as compared to 19.4% of the general population in 1933) and in professions and public or private service jobs (12.5% as compared to 8.4%); fewer Jews had been occupied in industry or the crafts (23.1% as compared to 40.4%), in agriculture or forestry (1.7% as compared to 28.9%). Socially, also, Jews differed: almost half of the Jewish population was self-employed (46% as compared to 16.4%), one third were white-collar employees (as compared to 17%) and only 8.7% classified themselves as workers (as compared to 46.4% of the general population in Germany; all figures from the 1933 census). Politically, this essentially middle-class group of German Jews tended to liberalism, in a middle-of-the-road way, its traditions and beliefs tied in with the middle-class parties of the centre.[32]

Ever since 1912, the demographic demise of German Jewry had been predicted as a function of low fertility and high intermarriage rates.[33] The German Jew, it had been remarked correctly by Werner J. Cahnmann[34], was not an "assimilated Jew". He was German, and he was Jewish in the difficult-to-define sense of an organisational and religious co-culture (a term more suggestive than the usual "subculture" of the social anthropologist). His Jewishness ranged from rejection and repression, via a balanced fusion to orthodox intensity, with a majority occupying probably the broad middle spectrum between self-hatred and Zionism. Still, it was a primarily religious identification. Community of destiny differs from ethnic identification. It was different from the ethnic separateness of the United States.

V. THE JEW FROM GERMANY IN AMERICA — EXTERNAL ASPECTS OF RESETTLEMENT

The most easily observable and external aspect of immigrant adjustment, the integration with the economy of the country, is seen by immigrant and outside observer alike as an unqualified success. Statistics on the occupational structure of immigrants (which include groups from other European countries as well) suggest that it corresponded roughly to the structure of the German Jewish group. The "refugees" represented an unusually large percentage of professionals, amounting to about 16% (adjusted total) of those indicating a profession, or between 7.3% and 7.4% of the total number of immigrants (including dependants) admitted during those years.

The economic settlement of the refugee would have been impossible without the generous help he received from American-Jewish welfare organisations: most of this story is still to be written. The former immigrant from Germany now in the

---

[32]For the rôle of German Jews in German politics see passim, and Arnold Paucker, *Der jüdische Abwehrkampf gegen Antisemitismus und Nationalsozialismus in den letzten Jahren der Weimarer Republik* (Hamburger Beiträge zur Zeitgeschichte Band IV), second edition, Hamburg 1969.
[33]F. Theilhaber, *Der Untergang der deutschen Juden*, 2nd ed., Berlin 1921 (first edition not available to the author).
[34]W. J. Cahnman, 'Comments on the American-Jewish Scene', in *Conference on Acculturation*, ed. H. A. Strauss, New York 1965, pp. 17-27.

TABLE V

Percentage Distribution by Occupation of Immigrant Aliens admitted to the United States, for Five-Year Periods, Fiscal Years ended 30th June, 1911 to 1944

	By selected European races [sic] 1933-1944	By Europe as last permanent residence 1933-1944
Total	100.0	100.0
Professional	7.7	7.4
Commercial	11.6	11.0
Skilled	12.5	11.3
Farmers	1.4	1.3
Servants	4.3	5.3
Labourers	3.6	3.4
Miscellaneous	2.6	2.7
No occupation (women & children)	56.3	57.6

SOURCE: Davie, *op. cit.*, p. 40, as adapted from Immigration and Naturalization Service data (reproduced with the permission of the publishers).

Estimated Number of Refugee Immigrants admitted to the United States, Fiscal Years ended June 30, 1933-1944, who had followed certain Professional or Commercial Occupations

Occupation	Estimate based on arrivals by selected European races [sic] or peoples
Professional pursuits	
Actor	767
Architect	402
Chemist	507
Clergyman	2,489
Editor	457
Engineer (technical)	2,818
Lawyer	1,989
Musician	1,501
Nurse	707
Physician	5,516
Professor and teacher	3,569
Scientist and literary person	1,900
Sculptor, artist	702
Other professional	2,211
	25,535
Commercial pursuits	
Accountant	253
Agent	6,045
Banker	805
Manufacturer	2,115
Merchant/Dealer	30,000

SOURCE: *ibid.*, p. 41 (reproduced with the permission of the publishers).

United States owes a lasting debt of gratitude to these agencies although, in many cases, the well-known over-organisation and bureaucratism of American social workers took their toll of human patience and cultural friction when dealing with a clientele that saw a social worker for the first time in their lives in New York City.[35]

German Jews arrived in the United States at a time when the country was slowly working its way out of the depression of the thirties: the typical course of economic resettlement often meant a first menial or household job for the wife — the migration was primarily a family migration; about 56% of the immigrants are presumed to have been dependent members of families. The experiences of German-Jewish middle-class couples working as butler-cook teams in upper-class American-Jewish households and being treated "like members of the family" ranged from the painful to the hilarious and absurd, as rôle expectations and status fantasies clashed with each other. The English spoken on working-class levels, by other dishwashers, lathe operators, or stock-clerks of Puerto Rican, Negro, Eastern-Jewish, Italian, etc. descent presented some difficulties to people whose English, if they had learned the language before immigration, had been based on the conventions and the grammar of another class and circumstance. The immigrant worker, sent out of Germany (from 1937 on) with his furniture in a crate and $4.00 (Reichsmark 10.—) in cash, experienced his position of menial worker as a loss of status. He had trouble penetrating the linguistic mysteries of the American luncheonette, and found himself impotent in the face of the unaccustomed ways of the new culture on the most elementary food-shelter-clothing level. It was an emotionally debilitating struggle with a strange way of life that these often middle-aged men and women faced in the first months or years following the shock of uprooting and arrival.

Thus, the refugee from Germany was expected to start from the traditional "bottom". However, soon after the bulk of immigrants arrived, the American economy began to climb out of the depression under the impact of rearmament and renewed world demand for American food and industrial goods. The unique characteristics of the German-Austrian refugee would not keep him for long at the bottom reserved for immigrant labour: the American *Wirtschaftswunder* of 1940-1960 gave thousands of refugees their first solid jobs in factories and offices, once the prejudice against them as "enemy aliens" had lessened. More than one thousand immigrants contributed their expertise to various levels of government service. The younger men served in the Armed Forces. Women contributed to the war effort. Still, in 1940, the average weekly income of refugees in New York was for:

professionals	$19.00
managers	23.00
unskilled labour	16.00
(often women were so classified)	
"service"	15.00
(primarily domestic)	

[35]Autobiographical statements by immigrant refugees will be found in *The Annals of the American Academy of Political and Social Science*, passim; M. Davie, *op. cit.*; D. P. Kent, *The Refugee Intellectual*, New York 1953, passim.

Only one person in 300 earned as much as $110.00 per week; the average for the group was a meagre $19.00. (Figures must be considered as lower-limit estimates, since the fight to liberalize US immigration laws was still waged when they were published; also the reader of 1971 must be aware of the difference in purchasing power.)

By 1946, the situation had changed considerably: professionals had risen to a weekly average income of $79.60 for men, and $42.30 for women (lower limit estimates)[36]. In addition, the deeply-rooted drive for economic independence among Jewish white-collar employees reasserted itself, as a number of independent firms were now being established by refugees: this group comprised craftsmen (butchers, bakers, carpenters, opticians, furriers, tailors, corsetmakers, etc.), retail store-owners of all kinds, wholesale and export trades, service stores (radio, television, air-conditioning repair services) etc. Also founded were small or middle-sized manufacturing firms that introduced new products in the United States, and a few rather large industrial, banking and brokerage houses (most or all of which had already been established in Germany or other European countries, and had been able to transfer capital, expertise and/or goodwill from Europe to the United States). Less fortunate were the about 500 refugee families settled by *Umschichtungs**-minded agencies in agriculture, primarily chicken farming. Most of these settlers were unable to prosper in the face of rising costs, agricultural concentration, and decreasing farm yields.[37]

Responsible for this upsurge of independent business ventures, however, was not only the enterprising spirit of the refugee who managed to realise his dream of independence: capital was contributed for some by Jewish aid societies, banks, or relatives; for many others, it came from their savings. Deviating from more adventurous American business methods, refugees practised their "solid German" virtues of thrift and frugality until the money needed for the great step was available.[38] Since the early 1950s, those refugees who were still young enough to profit by them, were aided also by the funds that became available from West Germany's restitution and indemnification legislation.[39] Those, in turn, especially of the younger age group, who preferred to pursue white-collar careers in the larger retail or wholesale corporations profited from the increase in the gross national product.

---

[36]Data on refugee income are offered by S. M. Robinson, *Refugees at Work*, New York 1942; J. and E. Hirsch, 'Berufliche Eingliederung und wirtschaftliche Leistung der deutsch-jüdischen Einwanderung in die Vereinigten Staaten (1935-1960)', in *American Federation of Jews from Central Europe, Twenty Years*, New York 1961, p. 59. Lists of new business establishments founded by refugees are offered by Davie, *op. cit.*, pp. 247-248.

*occupational re-training seen, in part, as a "normalization" of Jewish social and economic life.

[37]Comments on Jewish chicken farmers and on German Jews settling as farmers are based on information supplied by social workers of Selfhelp, Inc., and from the author's impressions gathered during service on a scholarship committee of the Nehemia Robinson Scholarship Fund of Selfhelp, Inc., New York.

[38]The "German virtues of thrift" shown by refugees have been observed by J. and E. Hirsch, *op. cit.*

[39]No precise data on the rôle of German restitution payments in the economic adjustment of refugees are available at this time of writing. Comments are based on the author's impressions .

Aided by the trade unions' collective bargaining, and an expanding need for white-collar jobs in service industries, increased productivity produced rising salaries and wages for the middle levels and the unionised segments of the skilled labour force.

A special chapter in this saga of economic integration was written by the intellectual and professional refugee from Hitler's Germany. It has no parallel in the history of any other group of immigrants in the United States. If available statistics are reliable, the percentage of those professing the Jewish religion among this group was relatively small, especially for refugees from Germany. (Christian [then so-called] "non-Aryans" made up two thirds or more of the group.)[40] The German-Austrian group included 7,622 individuals listed as professionals: 2,352 physicians, 1,090 educators, including university teachers, 811 lawyers, 682 journalists, 645 engineers, and additional numbers of musicians, artists, clerics, actors, architects, scientists, writers and others. [See Table V, p. 78.] For some members of this group, especially the lawyers, writers, and journalists, the new language and culture often posed serious problems, as when mature attorneys-at-law returned to school and undertook the enormous task of getting acquainted with another system of law. Many others had to find substitute ways of professional employment, and succeeded in doing so frequently after much hardship. Others found serious obstacles in government or professional practices that were designed to restrict professional careers to White Protestant or "assimilated" groups. The American medical profession, especially county and state licensing boards, and the (politically) conservative to reactionary American Medical Association (AMA) and its local branches, were frequently felt as hostile by immigrant physicians: they restricted licensing in many states, made membership in medical societies (and thus access to hospitals and beds for patients) dependent upon American citizenship (AMA House of Delegates, 1942 recommendation) while naturalization procedures were suspended for "enemy aliens" during war time, and the German Jew was an "enemy alien". Competent observers agree that the main motives were: the intense parochialism with which American physicians viewed their medical training; the desire to limit economic competition *(Futterneid);* the differences between the German general practitioner and the American preference for specialization; the desire to maintain high medical standards, and a strong tradition of xenophobia and antisemitism. (It will be remembered that Jewish students, until twenty-five years ago, had faced serious difficulties in being admitted to most American medical schools.) The immigrant physician, on the other hand, was equally convinced that he had enjoyed quite superior training, and resented the difficulties he faced in learning a new terminology and taking examinations alongside young resilient American medical students. It is easy to visualise the clash of conflicting expectations and images in these situations.[41]

[40]On the religious affiliations of refugee intellectuals and professionals, see Kent, *op. cit.,* p. 18.
[41]In addition to informal interviews conducted by the author in New York and Pittsburgh, data on refugee physicians and their view of US attitudes towards them are based on Davie, *op. cit.,* pp. 257-286; Kent, *op. cit.,* pp. 125-131.

Former German university professors, too, under the different conditions of higher education in the United States, faced not only open or hidden discriminatory practices against Jews in the academic professions. The older group among them also had to change their attitude towards students, course content, teaching methods, and team work to an extent that often amounted to a mental revolution, before they blended into the human and professional environments of those colleges and universities that were willing to accept them. Many academics made excellent adjustments as teachers, scholars and administrators, assisted by organisations like the *American Committee for Intellectual Refugees* initiated by Alvin Johnson, Karl Tillich and others.[42]

Exempt from such difficulties were those experts among refugee intellectuals — natural scientists, social scientists, musicians, *Germanisten*, architects, *Geisteswissenschaftler*, etc. — who arrived with internationally established reputations. This is not the place to detail the contributions made by European representatives of *gestalt* psychology, quantitative sociology, political science, psycho-analysis, physics, chemistry, biology, architecture, economics, history, mathematics, art and history of art, music and musicology, and other fields, to American intellectual life; the record is not fully evaluated at this time of writing.[43] However, most professional and intellectual refugees from Germany and Austria overcame the initial obstacles within themselves and in the professional world into which they were moving. Eventually, most physicians were practising or teaching after passing their licensing examinations and becoming citizens, and university teachers found niches commensurate with their talents and energy, as society at large, shocked by the holocaust, recognised the unique talents of this group: "Hitler's present to the American people". Today, relations between many intellectual refugees and their colleagues in Germany have become closer, and some former refugees now well established in the USA are among the most active "bridge-builders" between America and Germany. Sociology, political science, history, the humanities have been greatly advanced by this cross-fertilization, and exchanges of personnel between American and German universities and learned institutes have contributed to better international understanding. Relations with Israeli institutions also appear to have developed to some extent.

Thus, the immigrant from Central Europe who arrived in the USA before the end of World War II had, on the whole, moved towards the economic and social level that he had occupied in his country of origin. Few data are available about the economic success or failure of post-war "displaced persons", or about the German-born immigrants and professionals among them. Their Yiddish-speaking majority,

[42]For refugee academics see *The Annals of the American Academy of Political and Social Science*; Davie, *op. cit.*, pp. 300-323; Kent, *op. cit.*, pp. 110-124.

[43]For attitudes towards established "experts" see e.g. L. Fermi, *Illustrious Immigrants*, Chicago 1968; D. Fleming and B. Baylin, eds., *The Intellectual Migration: Europe and America, 1930-1960, Perspectives in American History*, vol. 2, Cambridge, Mass. 1968. A closer study of the Graduate Faculty of the New School for Social Research, New York City, would also reveal some of the in-group tendencies and limitations of academic and political refugees from Weimar Germany controlling the humanities and social sciences departments there and determining what was to be defined as "Weimar Germany", "social science", etc.

it appears, formed another labour class, like earlier Eastern European Jewish immigrants. The impression persists that many former D.P.s have remained in blue-collar work, or advanced the usual small step to lower-middle-class independence as luncheonette owners, cleaning-store operators, small service craftsmen, etc. Adjustment probably varied depending on energy, skill, and psychological make-up. The long-range psychological effects of the holocaust and the concentration camp, according to qualified observers, persist even among men and women who are not clinically classified as psychotic or neurotic.[44] Much poverty, or at least, relative poverty, exists among some white-collar segments of all ages, and among aged immigrants from Germany and, especially, Austria whose attitude towards restitution and reparation are too well known to be detailed here. Their plight is mitigated by German pensions or American social security payments, and by the social services built up by German Jews. In most cases, it appears, support from younger members of the family helps to prevent the worst, but the lack of financial reserves (typical for comparable classes in the general population) renders their situation more precarious.

VI. THE SOCIAL INTEGRATION OF THE IMMIGRANT

The economic integration reviewed above serves as an index of individual adjustment to the immigrant situation. However, the immigrant adjusted also through a collective effort that combined the traditions of his country of origin with the organisational pattern of America. Led by rabbis, community leaders, social workers, lawyers, etc., immigrants established a network of organisations from coast to coast, wherever they settled in sufficient numbers in the *landsmannschaftlich* fashion known from the history of American immigration.[45]

One large group of organisations consists of "self-help" and social welfare organisations. They provide a broad range of individual aid and advice, including employment services, financial aid, or cheap credit, and began providing professional services on matters of restitution and indemnification as soon as post-war German restitution legislation had become operative. In New York and elsewhere, concern for the aged — who comprise an ever-growing part of the group — led public-spirited community leaders to establish old age homes and apartment buildings, and to enter into arrangements with existing old age and nursing homes for places

---

[44]See Note 17 and H. March, ed., *Verfolgung und Angst in ihren leib-seelischen Auswirkungen. Dokumente*, Stuttgart 1960.

[45]For the history of the organisational efforts of the Hitler refugee immigration see American Federation of Jews from Central Europe, Inc., *Annual Meeting 1956, Reports and Addresses*, New York 1956; *idem, Ten Years American Federation of Jews from Central Europe, Inc., 1941-1951*, ed. Kurt R. Grossmann, New York 1952; *idem, Twenty Years American Federation of Jews from Central Europe, Inc., 1940-1960*, ed. H. G. Reissner, New York 1961; *idem, The Twenty-Second Year. American Federation of Jews from Central Europe, Inc., 1961-1962*, ed. H. G. Reissner, New York 1962; *Conference on Acculturation*, ed. H. A. Strauss, New York 1965; *idem*, 'Zur Problematik der deutsch-jüdischen Einwanderung in den USA', in *Council Correspondenz*, Jerusalem 1966 (mimeo.); *Aufbau*, passim, offers primary material on the continuous organisational activities of US refugee organisations.

and beds for elderly immigrants — part of a general effort by society to care for the ever larger percentage of elderly people in modern industrial states. They were financed initially by contributions from all segments of the immigrant group and by contributions from those among its affluent who honoured the tradition of Jewish welfare "giving". (There is some evidence that American Jews of Eastern-European descent adhere to this tradition in larger numbers and with greater generosity than Jews from Central Europe where welfare used to devolve primarily upon government agencies and tax levies.)[46]

Jews from Germany never founded a German-Jewish school for their children concentrating, instead, on the resettlement of the parents and on care for the aged. This policy was in line with that of earlier immigrant groups: the American public school system, like the Israeli army, is a prime tool of acculturation, and foreign-language or foreign-culture school systems (École Française, Rudolf Steiner School, etc.) are reserved for the socially or culturally ambitious elites of the big cities. The failure to found a "German-Jewish school" reflects a more basic dilemma, to be discussed below.

German Jews founded a number of religious congregations led by German-

[46]Major old age homes are located in Newark, New Jersey (Newark House, an inter-denominational foundation), San Francisco (Residence Club), Cleveland (Montefiore Home; Schnurman Foundation), all of which were supported by funds supplied by the Council of Jews from Germany from Jewish Restitution Successor Organization funds, and distributed in the USA by the American Federation of Jews from Central Europe, Inc., through United Help, Inc., an organisation originally founded as the welfare arm of the American Federation. The latter, for a variety of reasons and motives, asserted its independence from the parent organisation. (This view is based on statements made by the late Dr. Hermann Muller, Executive Director of the American Federation from 1941 to 1963, to the author during the 1960s.) United Help also erected two major apartment houses for aged refugees (Kissena Apartments One, Kissena Apartments Two) with the help of JRSO restitution funds and sizeable mortgages obtained from the State of New York. These apartment houses represent new departures in purpose-built and dignified housing for the aged. A nursing home sponsored by the New York Foundation for Nursing Homes, Inc. was opened in August 1971. It was financed by private funds contributed by refugees, a New York State mortgage, and support from the Jewish Philanthropic Fund, Inc., the fund-raising and welfare arm of the American Federation. It, too, aims at providing dignified (rather than merely adequate) care for refugees. All homes are, by law, committed to a non-discriminatory admissions policy; fund-raising groups are, a.o., Blue Card; Help and Reconstruction; The Jewish Philanthropic Fund of 1933; The Combined Campaign (all located in New York); most refugee organisations conduct their own fund-raising drives, benefit concerts, etc. — Among social and fraternal organisations are The American-Jewish K.C. (*Kartell-Convent*) Fraternity; The Jewish Veterans Association; Maccabi Athletic Club (sports); New World Club, Inc. (founded in the 1920s, owner of *Aufbau-Reconstruction*); Prospect Unity Club; Theodor Herzl Society; Association of Jews from Württemberg; Achduth (Washington, D.C.); The Central Club of Philadelphia (Philadelphia); Chevra Ahavas Chesed (Baltimore); Club of 1946 (Denver, Colorado); The Friendship Club (Pittsburgh, Pennsylvania); Immigrants Mutual Aid Society (IMAS) (Boston, Mass.); The Jewish Club of Seattle (Seattle, Washington); The Jewish Club of 1933 (Los Angeles, California); The Jewish Council of 1933 (San Francisco, California); The New Home Club (Milwaukee, Wisconsin); The New World Club of Minneapolis, Minnesota; The Jewish Unity Club of Newark, New Jersey; Self-aid, St. Louis, Missouri; Selfhelp, Chicago, Illinois. (This list is presumed to be incomplete; it is based on membership lists of the American Federation of Jews from Central Europe, the co-ordinating agency of refugee organisations in the USA.) — It is estimated that German communal restitution funds made available to American refugee organisations for charitable purposes total about 4 million dollars (16 million DM). (Information supplied by the late Dr. Hermann Muller.)

speaking and German-preaching rabbis along denominational lines that continued the German division into *Einheitsgemeinde*, orthodoxy, and (mild) *Reform (Liberalismus)*. Since German Jews, at least in cities like New York, settled in distinct neighbourhoods, e.g. Washington Heights (Manhattan) or Kew Gardens (Queens) most congregations (with a few important exceptions) reflected, to some extent, the geographic and social character of their neighbourhoods (e.g. Southern-German, rural, urban, lower-middle class, etc.). Sociability and much mutual aid originated with these religious congregations. Sunday schools served the young, and a variety of cultural and artistic activities developed for all age groups. Today, care for the elderly and "Golden Age Clubs" form an important part of their work, while a second generation of (often) American-trained rabbis is beginning to take the mantle from the shoulders of the founder generations.[47]

In the more narrowly-defined field of cultural institutions, only the orthodox Jewish community from Germany developed a wider range of organisations including a school system, *yeshivot*, and adult education groups. One weekly newspaper in the German language, *Aufbau*, grew into a major cultural force among immigrants providing a wide range of information on politics, literature, music, theatre, films and miscellaneous *Generalanzeiger*-style intelligence that attracted a broad social spectrum of readers. The New York Leo Baeck Institute, the American branch of the international archive and research foundation, is devoted to preserving the history and culture of German Jewry through a (primarily German-language) programme of scholarly publications. It has also assembled an excellent library on German-Jewish history and culture.

Politically, German Jews began to feel the need for a central representation when refugees from Germany were included in the legal category of "enemy aliens" and subjected to a series of rather ridiculous restrictions (see above, part I, for background information). The American Federation of Jews from Central Europe,

---

[47]The following congregations founded by refugees from Germany are affiliated to the American Federation of Jews from Central Europe:
  American Congregation of Jews from Austria
  American Jewish Congregation
  Congregation Adath Jeshurun of Westbronx, Inc.
  Congregation Adath Machsike Hadath
  Congregation Ahavath Torah of Washington Heights, Inc.
  Congregation Beth Hillel of Washington Heights, Inc.
  Congregation Chevra Gemiluth Chesed
  Congregation Emes Wozedek
  Congregation Habonim, Inc.
  Congregation Machane Chodosh, Inc.
  Congregation Ohav Sholaum
  Congregation Ramath Orah
  Congregation Shaare Hatikvah
  Congregation Shaare Tefillah
  Congregation Shaare Zedek of Astoria
  Congregation Tikwoh Chadoshoh
  Congregation Gates of Hope, Inc. Cleveland Heights, Ohio
  Congregation Gemiluth Chassodim, Detroit, Michigan.
(Smaller, non-affiliated congregations, or congregations functioning merely during the high Jewish holidays, are not included in this list.)

founded in 1941 as the coordinating agency of German Jews in the USA, has represented the German-Jewish viewpoint in response to successive and changing tasks, ranging from aliens legislation to immigration, naturalization, the founding of the State of Israel, restitution, indemnification, German policies affecting Jewish matters and, during the last few years, developments in the American-Jewish community, migration history, and Jewish communal affairs generally.[48]

This network of service and cultural organisations reflected, to some extent, the organisational experience the immigrant had brought along from Germany in religious, charitable, and politico-cultural life. It provided him with immediately needed services, and created a semblance of an immigrant sub-culture in which the German, the American, and the Jewish intermingled, and individuals and families found support in shared anxieties, shared problems of adjustment, shared needs for information and spiritual comfort. The *landsmannschaftlich* organisations fitted, however, also into the pattern that other immigrant groups had followed in the USA before the Hitler period. Organisations like the Association of Jews from Württemberg and the Jewish Veterans Association (Jewish veterans of the German Army of World War I, the former *Reichsbund jüdischer Frontsoldaten*) indicate the extent to which local communality or group loyalty survived under changed cultural circumstances.

Like all *Landsmannschaften*, these organisations gave the immigrant the all-important assurance that he did not have to face his fate alone; his mental balance, his integration as a personality and, correspondingly, his ability to take his place, or find a place for his children, in the "wider" community, depended, to some extent, on his participation in these groups. For the immigrant, this was "pluralism", although he may not have known the word, an important step in his Americanization as an ethnic group. Here, among peers, the often galling loss of status was minimised: a lawyer doing menial work was still a lawyer to those who had known him "at home", the cultural shock decreased, the uprooted immigrant succeeded in maintaining continuity with his past self-image, while smaller intellectual avant-garde and professional groups found opportunities to employ their energies in a way that American culture, as yet distant, denied the immigrant during the first phases of his arrival and resettlement.[49]

---

[48]See *Newsletter* (irregular; mimeo.); *Conference on Acculturation, Conference on Anti-Semitism*, and *Conference on American-Jewish Dilemmas* (held on the 28th February 1971) for the range of the Federation's cultural activities. A project on migration history, to be carried out by an independent Research Foundation for Jewish Immigration, Inc., an affiliate of the Federation, is being organised at this time of writing in co-operation with similar ventures in the United Kingdom and France. The range of interests connected with the American Federation is also indicated by the *Jubilee Volume dedicated to Curt C. Silberman* and *Gegenwart im Rückblick*; the latter *Festschrift* was not a project sponsored by the Federation but carried out with its help, the Executive Vice-President of the Federation serving as editor (with K. G. Grossmann) and a sizeable number of contributors being connected with the work of the Federation.

[49]The importance of primary group contacts for a psychologically balanced acculturation has been stressed by Crystal, *op. cit.*, Davie, *op. cit.*, Eisenstadt, *op. cit.*, Gordon, *op. cit.*, Greeley, *op. cit.*, Handlin, *op. cit.*, Sherman, *op. cit.*, Warner-Stole, *op. cit.*, H. A. Strauss ed., *op. cit.* (1965, 1966).

Today (late 1970) efforts to study the structure and write the history of this organisational network are about to begin; reliable, adequately documented, information through which the development of these organisations could be traced is as yet scarce. To this participant-observer, a few tentative observations suggest themselves, subject to correction as better information becomes available.

In organisational structure, it appears, religious congregations founded by German Jews had taken over the forms used by American-Jewish congregations, such as boards of directors, brotherhoods and sisterhoods, afternoon religious schools staffed by cantors and (frequently marginal) part-time teachers etc. Personal observation in a few such congregations would suggest that the all-powerful lay boards that have alienated many younger American rabbis are not the rule among immigrant congregations: the rabbi, on the whole, appears to have retained the position of leadership. Some congregations have succeeded in creating a high level of cultural activities (lectures, discussions, art), depending on the social and intellectual composition of the membership. Other congregations have seen the level of their cultural activities decline as the need for senior citizens' programmes arose, and the friction that fuelled the earlier intellectual excitement created by immigration and acculturation was not supplemented by energetic participation in current Jewish or American public or intellectual affairs. (Only one such congregation appears on the ascent in its cultural activities today [1970].) In most congregations, the disappearance of the older founding generation will lead to a decline. On the other hand, the speed of "Americanization" rather than the process itself are the subject of intense debates, as younger couples stay loyal to their "father's temple", and "outsiders" begin to arrive. Where social changes in a formerly German-Jewish neighbourhood — e.g. in sections in New York and Philadelphia — have led to the intermingling of White and Black or Puerto Rican with immigrant groups, the social problems faced by many members of these minority groups — drug addiction, unemployment, juvenile *anomie* and its attendant social ills, primarily increased criminality — are having a serious impact on their sense of security. Young couples move to the suburbs, leaving behind the old people, who fear to venture into the streets after dark or without companions. At least in one area (Washington Heights, New York) a social programme is being introduced by the local Young Men's Hebrew Association, an immigrant congregation, and a refugee social welfare agency, to deal with the various aspects of this situation, but in other areas the disappearance of the young and the flight of Whites to the suburbs will spell the end of local synagogues or temples and with it of refugee congregations. No German-Jewish congregation seems to have been founded by refugees in the suburbs. They are being absorbed by local American-Jewish organisations if they remain Jewish at all.

The social welfare organisations founded by Jewish immigrants from Germany see themselves as being set apart from the "typical" American-Jewish social agency by the style of concern with the individual, a more personal relationship between social worker and client (both of the same ethnic and historic experiences), and have started some new programmes. German restitution money provided by the Council of Jews from Germany, from Jewish Restitution Successor Organization and Jewish Trust Corporation funds via the American Federation of Jews from Central Europe) allowed the most important of these organisations to move beyond their initial employment-exchange rôle — primarily for employees and "homemakers" i.e. domestic service — to programmes dealing with the aged, with student aid and others as outlined above. Organisationally these welfare organisations, headed by boards and managed by American and European educated professionals, had tended to become independent of their founding organisation (e.g. the American Federation of Jews from Central Europe): this trend, to some extent, ran counter to organisational developments in the American-Jewish welfare field where the Council of Jewish Federations and Welfare Funds wields a certain influence over its constituents across the country. For German-Jewish social agencies, the decrease in German restitution payments calls for reappraisal of future rôles: as funds become available from US government and other public sources for programmes serving the "general community" (i.e. Black and Puerto Rican constituents), shifts in emphasis are being felt. These issues are earnestly discussed at responsible board meetings to assure that services for the "refugee community" will not suffer, and the allocated funds will be used "correctly". Difficult also are problems of staffing as older German-speaking social workers retire from the scene. These developments parallel those observable in established American-Jewish social institutions (like hospitals or neighbourhood centres) many of which were founded by earlier German-Jewish immigrants: they have long ceased to serve a primarily or exclusively Jewish clientele. How the problem of transition is solved will decide organisational survival — an expansion of functions to serve other needy groups, or the ultimate demise of an agency originally conceived to serve refugee needs. At the board level, younger (second generation) members have been available in adequate numbers so far to co-operate with the founding group in directing the future of these welfare groups.

Cultural organisations share the structural characteristic with social welfare organisations in that they follow the American pattern of control by boards. As a result they are not subjected to the formal democratic checks and controls available to religious congregations, i.e. the dues-paying members of these organisations, if any, have no voice in selecting their boards, and the available funds, including German restitution payments, are administered without public accounting (but with great private propriety, as behoves "German Jews". This corresponds to the general pattern of American-Jewish organisational and political life, expressed historically, for example, in the tensions between "uptown" New York "aristocratic" Jewish organisations and the "downtown" (immigrant) lower class "democratic" groups arriving from Eastern Europe before World War I. They resemble the classical *landsmannschaftlich* structure as far as they define their objectives primarily as intellectual and emotional concern with the particular German-Jewish past, and appeal to a public of like interest, thus restricting the rôle they might play for other groups through changes in the focus for their historic concerns.

As to the largest of these cultural institutions, the German-Jewish group's publication programme may ensure that in the future, too, it will, as a research and publication foundation, occupy a respectable if marginal place in American intellectual life. There is, however, certainly a danger that interest in the Leo Baeck Institute may decline as the immigrants who support it fade away, unless it succeeds in reaching out to the broader American-Jewish community. This it is well qualified to achieve thanks to its impressive intellectual heritage (ranging from giants like Buber, Baeck, Rosenzweig, Hermann Cohen, Taeubler, Kafka, to the *littérateurs* of the 1920s, Jewish social criticism etc.), and to benefit the wider Jewish community further by the paradigmatic lessons to be learned from the German-Jewish experience. Thus it should play a far more important rôle than merely that of serving the interest of scholars and students concerned with German-Jewish history — a group whose number will remain limited by the sociology of American academic life and appointments.

The German-language weekly *Aufbau* founded by immigrants also depends for its survival on a German-reading clientele. It will be difficult to turn the paper into an English-language weekly of cultural American or American-Jewish interest, since its contents reflect a specific historic experience and nostalgia that would need to be transformed — not merely translated — to be understandable to another age and another generation. Although concerned with American politics and Israeli foreign affairs, the main thrust of the paper, under its present editorial leadership, concerns German politics. This political direction, in general, has led the paper away from facing the problem of its ultimate *American* rôle, i.e. its possible transformation into an American political weekly or an American-Jewish community paper offering the cultural fare that is urgently needed for Jewish middle America. For the moment, the paper is widely read in more than fifty countries: its future is earnestly debated and pondered by its friends and directors.

Thus, the institutions created by the Jewish immigrant from Germany to assist him materially, satisfy his spiritual needs, express his concern with the poor and the aged, or represent his political and social will have entered the maelstrom of acculturation. They face the difficult problem of translating their experiences into the sensitivities and attitudes, the language and culture of their Americanized second and third generations, while near-revolutionary changes grip the big cities where most immigrants settled. Even if their organisational life spans should be limited, these institutions form an important chapter in the history of American immigration and of Jewish resilience in the face of uprooting and resettlement. Could German-Jewish immigrants have developed a strong second generation if they had truly transmitted their cultural heritage and ventured into unknown educational territory instead of — or in addition to — concentrating on the poor, the aged, the sick, the traditional social welfare tasks, i.e. if the immigrants had not despaired of transmitting more than the personal values of their past, if they had been Jewish-German rather than German-Jewish? It would have been the first time in American immigration history that a group had succeeded in maintaining its language and culture unchanged: future planning has to start with these historic realities, not Utopias.

VII. MELTING POT, PLURALISM, OR ENDURING ETHNICITY?

The true drama of the immigrant's life was not reflected in his *external* success or failure: the story of his economic and social response was repeated, with variations, many times over in the history of all refugees all over the world in the twentieth century. What made his story memorable was the complex *internal* process, his *seelische Einordnung* that went on beneath the socio-economic adjustment, yet conditioned it all the same.[50] Veterans of this experience share memories that set them apart as a special fraternity among the victims of twentieth-century history.

Many influences, personal and psychological, determined the course of this *Einordnung*. During the late thirties and the war years, the Jewish immigrant faced the psychological dilemma of having been — in fact, of being — German; the unfolding story of Nazi policies in Occupied Europe, and the news of the holocaust, produced a lasting wound of sorrow that made it difficult for the sensitive person who felt himself to be a Jew to maintain his identity as a *German* Jew. Here, the synagogues and temples established by German Jews provided two important comforts: the German-Jewish heritage of Moses Mendelssohn, Hermann Cohen, Martin Buber, Franz Rosenzweig, and Leo Baeck, of *Wissenschaft des Judentums*, or Samson Raphael Hirsch, Isaak Breuer, Esriel Hildesheimer, Esra Munk, or the German literary and artistic heritage provided a "home away from home" which was often embraced with an intensity that revealed the underlying insecurity. (For some immigrants, such outstanding figures of German culture as Thomas Mann and a host of lesser men gave assurance that there still existed a German culture of humanism and liberality.) For many others, however, the solution lay in stressing their *Jewish* identification,[51] a rediscovery of Jewish existence as an ethnic group, a concern with (the then) Palestine where almost every immigrant had friends or relatives. The leadership of the immigrant community turned to favouring

[50]The following comments are based primarily on the author's personal observations; see also M. George, 'Geistige Einordnung in die Neue Welt', in *Ten Years American Federation*, pp. 78-85.
[51]There is evidence that the recovery of "Jewish identity" among German Jews was not produced by Nazism but, rather, followed World War I when sensitive young members of Jewish youth groups searched for new roots in a crisis society. Men like Fritz Schwarzschild, Paul Eppstein, Hugo Hahn, Max Wiener, Paul Lazarus, and many others met in this endeavour with older men like Franz Rosenzweig, Martin Buber, Leo Baeck, Eugen Taeubler, and in the Lehrhaus movement, or neo-orthodox groups. Similar observations may be made about the attitudes gaining ground among the "young Turks" of the *Centralverein deutscher Staatsbürger jüdischen Glaubens* in the 1920s. See Herbert Strauss, 'The Jugendverband. A Social and Intellectual History', in *LBI Year Book VI* (1961), pp. 206-235; and *idem*, 'The Jewish Press in Germany, 1918-1938 (1943)', to be published in Tel Aviv in 1971/1972 (*Handbook of the Jewish Press of the Holocaust*, tentative title). For a sensitive presentation of the effect of World War One on Jewish attitudes see Eva G. Reichmann, 'Der Bewußtseinswandel der deutschen Juden', in *Deutsches Judentum in Krieg und Revolution 1916–1923*. Ein Sammelband herausgegeben von Werner E. Mosse unter Mitwirkung von Arnold Paucker, Tübingen 1971. (Schriftenreihe wissenschaftlicher Abhandlungen des Leo Baeck Instituts 25), pp. 511–612. This analysis is based on the published and periodical literature of the period. Fully conscious of the methodological problems involved in basing broad judgments about "consciousness" or the "spirit of a period" on sources of this kind, Eva Reichmann presents a succinct portrait of Jewish reactions to the events of the war, and of the immediate post-war period, establishing beyond doubt that the Jewish renaissance among German Jews began with World War One and its antisemitic shocks, not with the Nazi period.

Zionist policies like the broader American-Jewish group: Zionism and Palestine belonged to the great philanthropic and political preoccupations of American Jews, and German Jews soon took part in it.

Whatever the *Jewish* solution of the immigrant's dilemma, the *general* cultural trend was a uniform urge for speedy "Americanization" which, in some ways, resembled a *Flucht nach vorne* (aggressive defence). One major factor in this energetic acculturation was, of course, the immigrant's drive towards economic success and recovered status, his high educational level that allowed him to overcome the language barrier with unparelleled speed, his occupational history, in sum, his middle-class character and the social psychology inherent in his class and the Jewish group in general. In some ways, the Jewish immigrant from Germany followed the precedent of Christian-German immigration waves before him: they, too, tended to lose their cultural identity through Americanization while maintaining social and religious ties within their group, even after "Americanization" became an accomplished fact. The Hitler refugee, in addition, was driven to speedy acculturation by the attitude taken by his environment towards his German origin: immersed in the sea of revulsion and impotent rage over the unfolding story of war crimes committed by Germans he was under strong pressure to place the largest possible distance between himself and a Germany that, at the time, appeared like an obedient, monolithic war machine supported by all segments and groups of the German population, and, in the anguish of the war period, appeared to blacken all that was once good and beloved in German culture and humanity. As sons or daughters served in the Armed Forces against Hitler, the average parent at home strove to yield to the pressures that demanded that he divest himself of the cultural insignia of his Germanism and become "an American". That he remained "German" nevertheless, in customs, mannerisms, accent, and basic values (the degree of acculturation depending on psychological and educational factors) also defined the extent to which he was able to move in American, especially American-Jewish society, where the sympathy and compassion his fate aroused were occasionally tempered by his new friends' — or his children's — silent awareness of how much he had remained "a German". As a result — except for such contrary groups as opportunists and idealists, the very old and the very young, left-wing intellectuals, a few German nationalists, academicians, or writers — the average Jewish immigrant from Germany, it appears, emerged from the war with a thoroughly broken relationship to his German past. Since 1945 the situation has changed in a number of ways. The Federal Republic of Germany has eased the burden of the Nazi heritage, at least in its material aspects. Some of its representatives proved sensitive towards the mentality of the Nazi victim and, on professional and social levels, new links have been forged. For some émigrés the material rewards offered proved irresistible. The policy of goodwill and support for Israel that appears to have been followed in Bonn, and the well-noticed German concern with the Israeli-Arab War of 1967, have been as important as has been the generally changing image of a new democratic Germany that already has lasted longer than Weimar, and appears to have weathered, so far, its radical Right and its (anti-Zionist) New Left. Still, reactions to Germany range from the return of confidence to indifference, or an abiding rejection and alienation, often among the most sensitive. Much of this depends on the age of the immigrant and his psychological and ideological make-up.

In addition, the Jewish immigrant from Germany has long reached the age where new cultural influences tend to be integrated into existing patterns of thought and feeling, where new intellectual or cultural adventures are no longer undertaken. Acculturation, it appears, proceeds in an as yet unrecognised rhythm, passing through a stormy confrontation followed by intense insecurity and doubt about the environment until a level of economic and social satisfaction is reached that is linked, in some way, to the previous cultural creativity or receptivity of an individual and other psychological or social factors. A new sub-culture, American-German-Jewish, had developed on this plateau. As far as it is based upon German folkways, language, or literature it will disappear as the immigrant fades from the scene, and turn into history or memory for the second and third generations.

Still another factor in the Americanization of the immigrant was his initial image of America and of its ethnic patterns, especially in New York where the bulk of immigrants had settled. There is little doubt, from the available evidence, that the immigrant knew very little about the social, economic, or cultural life of the country he was moving to, often in great distress, in line with the general ignorance of Europeans, at that time, about American life. His German experience had prepared him to tend towards the "Anglo-conformity" or the melting-pot models of society, the more so as most immigrants to the USA appear to have been following the ideology of the *Centralverein deutscher Staatsbürger jüdischen Glaubens* before emigration. (With notable exceptions, including some German-Jewish immigrants from Israel, this, at least, appears to have been the mentality of the group of German-Jewish communal leaders that arrived here.) In the process of acculturation, however, neither model proved to be quite adequate to explain what actually happened. Personal experiences, as well as communal interest, led to the discovery of the "cultural pluralism" model, the idea that America was, in Louis Adamic's words, a "nation of nations". In the big urban centres where most immigrants found themselves, the immigrant's socio-cultural history paralleled that of the American Jew in important respects. He, too, was upwardly mobile in the second generation. He, too, had created a web of social links and religious and defence organisations. He, too, had an intense interest in education for his children, and like the best American Jews he, too, was groping for a modern Judaism that would allow him to live as a Jew and as an American without a break. Like the American Jew, the German Jew, whatever internal differences there may have been, was experiencing a threat to his Jewish existence. Antisemitism neither was nor is alien to the American scene. He soon shared, on his own, an intense concern with Palestine/Israel and the as yet unresolved threat to its existence. In many American-Jewish institutions the thoughtful immigrant recognised, after a while, the organising hand of the "German Jew" of the nineteenth century — *B'nai B'rith*, theological and scholarly Jewish institutions, the American Jewish Committee, Reform Jewry, conservatism, even orthodoxy (as distinct from Eastern Chassidism or Talmud-oriented religiosity).

Socially, too, the immigrant Jew from Germany met either his own peers or, with the exception of professional and intellectual groups, other Jews, American Jews, even if he or his children joined the Reform Democratic clubs in New York in the 1950s.

Politically, to be sure, the "average" Jew from Germany, with important exceptions, showed none of the penchant for radical criticism or political action that is typical at least for some of the children and grandchildren of Jewish immigrants from the East. Few German Jews play a rôle in trade union politics, few have been able to make the weight of their group felt in city halls or state Capitols, to say nothing of national politics. Few descendants of German Jews have chosen politics as a career, again excepting very few New York-based figures. German Jews never learned to feel at home in the rough-and-tumble that characterises not only politics but other aspects of public life in America as well. The solid virtues of the *Bürger*, the ideals of hard work and professionalism, appear to have been enduring features of the twentieth-century Jew from Germany as they have been typical for his nineteenth-century precursor.

Thus the Jew from Germany has joined the American-Jewish community. Its fate will be his. German-Jewish immigrants form a temporary ethnic group within an ethnic group. As the affluent leave the decaying urban centres for the once-exclusive and once-green suburbs, they meet other Jews — German or non-German — who had moved there before them, and join the religious or communal centres that influence sociability — primarily with other members of the same ethnic group. With American Jews, German-Jewish immigrants face the social upheaval presented by urban problems, student impatience, Black racialism, New Left anti-Zionism, and persistent antisemitism. Israel and the common concern for Jews everywhere are also our concerns, even where we still support separate welfare or political organisations to represent us. The future of America, and of the Jew in America, will also determine our future.

The German Jew and his descendants, as far as he and they remain committed to Judaism (data are missing on this important subject) face, in addition, a challenge that could assign to them an important rôle in the future of American-Jewish life. Most observers agree that American Jewry's organisational and philanthropic excellence is not paralleled by its cultural achievements. The American-Jewish middle class, like much of the rest of its peers in other religions, has not used its affluence and its ethical and political culture to create an aesthetically or intellectually satisfactory style of life, away from mass media, sports, small talk, or status-seeking consumerism.[52] Its restless children, the new youth movement of the late

---

[52]Observations on Jewish middle-class life in the USA will be found in Glazer-Moynahan, *op. cit.*, Herberg, *op. cit.*, Janowsky, *op. cit.*, M. Sklare, *Jewish identity on the suburban frontier. A study of group survival in the open society*, New York 1967. For continuing observations on Negro-Jewish relations see the relevant issues of *Commentary*, the American Jewish Committee's *Der Morgen*. Opinion data will be found in the sources quoted in note 19. For a discussion of the contemporary American-Jewish situation from the perspective of the younger Jewish professionals see *Conference on American-Jewish Dilemmas, 1971*, ed. Herbert A. Strauss, American Federation of Jews from Central Europe, New York 1971.

1960s, like to point to what is unauthentic, hypocritical, or routinized about the great suburban wasteland of American affluence. For the German-Jewish immigrant, his descendants and his organisations, this might present a last, final, opportunity to recreate the personal inwardness, the intellectual and emotional culture that was his, in a new language and a new environment. This group has begun to be questioned by alert Jewish intellectuals about the lessons its experience may offer to Jewish self-understanding in America. The group will leave an enduring legacy, in addition to the contributions made by individual immigrants and their children, if it succeeds, in however modest a way, in helping to create a style of life that will continue what can be preserved for the future. However, the former German Jew is convinced today that he is the last of the line, the survivor of an extinct culture. The course of his acculturation in America, his failure to believe enough in himself or his Jewish heritage and in his ability to transmit his cultural values, threaten to turn this conviction into a self-fulfilling prophecy.

Jews in Austrian and German Politics

The Jewish Vote in Austria

BY WALTER B. SIMON

Before Austria became part of the Third Reich, about ten per cent of Vienna's population was Jewish. Seven years later, after the Third Reich collapsed, the Jewish population of Vienna amounted to only a fraction of one per cent.[1] Viennese Jewry had virtually disappeared. The subject-matter of this historical chapter may one day fit into the larger picture of a comprehensive history of the Jews of Central Europe, a history yet to be written. Also, the present essay may perhaps contribute to the study of Jewish assimilation in particular and of cultural pluralism in general.

The constitution of the 21st February 1867 guaranteed the Austrian Jews equal rights as citizens. The Jews emancipated from the ghetto found themselves well prepared for entry into the economy of the Danube Monarchy. This fitness resulted from the past relationship of the ghetto with the economy of the community at large.[2] For centuries the Jews had combined the traditional rôles of the stranger and the trader,[3] and in this capacity they had become carriers of trade throughout most of the world of Christendom. The business sense and commercial acumen thus acquired were at a premium in the expanding economy of nineteenth-century capitalism.

The values and traditions of the ghetto fitted the Jews for entry into cultural and intellectual life. Within the confines of the ghetto learning was always valued for its own sake, while money was valued mainly because of the importance given to it by the world outside. Illiteracy was virtually unknown in the ghetto at a time when in the world beyond the ghetto the ability to read remained a mark of rare distinction.[4]

When the doors of the ghetto opened the emancipated Jews devoured with voracious appetite whatever learning and knowledge became accessible. Soon Jews in Central Europe became prominent in academic life, in literature, in science, and in the professions. This prominence continued throughout the nineteenth and the first part of the twentieth century. In the Danube Monarchy the Jews contributed to art, science, and literature, were numerous in the professions, and dominated the press. In the years 1888-1889 more than half of the lawyers and physicians in Vienna

[1]The last official census, held in the First Republic of Austria on the 22nd March 1934, showed 191,481 Jews; the first official census in the Second Republic of Austria, held on the 1st June 1951, put the number of Jews at 11,224. Over ninety-five per cent of all Austrian Jews lived in Vienna.
[2]Werner Sombart, *Die Juden und das Wirtschaftsleben*, Leipzig 1911.
[3]Georg Simmel, "*The Stranger*". *The Sociology of Georg Simmel*, translated and edited by Kurt H. Wolff, Glencoe, Ill. 1950, pp. 402 ff.
[4]Thus we find in a twelfth-century poem a German knight introduced as follows: "Ein Ritter so gelehret was dass er selbet in den Buchen las ..." ("a knight who was so learned that he could even read books"). See Hartmann Von der Aue, *Der Arme Heinrich*, ed. John G. Robertson, London 1895, p. 25.

were Jewish, as were 48 per cent of the medical students, 22 per cent of the law students, and 15 per cent of the philosophy students enrolled at the University of Vienna.[5]

The writer Jakob Wassermann recorded the following observations on his move from Munich to Vienna in 1898:

> "One circumstance puzzled me before I had been long in Vienna. In Germany I had associated with Jews scarcely at all; only now and then did one appear in my circle, and no special stress was laid by either himself or others on the fact that he was Jewish. Here, however, it developed that all with whom I came into intellectual or friendly contact were Jews. I soon realized that all public life was dominated by Jews. The banks, the press, the theatre, literature, social organizations, all lay in the hands of Jews. The explanation was easy to find. The aristocracy would have nothing to do with such things; with the exception of a few non-conformists who had been ejected from the fold, a few who saw things in a different light, they not only maintained a respectful distance from intellectual and artistic life but feared and condemned it. The small number of untitled patrician families imitated the aristocracy; the original upper middle class had disappeared, leaving a gap now occupied by government functionaries, army officers and professors; then came the closed circle of the lower middle class. The court, the lower middle class and the Jews gave the city its stamp. And that the Jews, as the most mobile group, kept all the others in continuous motion is, on the whole, not surprising. Yet I was amazed at the hosts of Jewish physicians, attorneys, clubmen, snobs, dandies, proletarians, actors, newspapermen and poets."[6]

The Jews continued to play a major rôle in the intellectual and cultural life of Vienna until 1938, the year Austria became part of the Third Reich. In Austria Jews had been excluded from the civil service, but up to 1938 they had predominated in law and medicine, the press and the arts, as well as in commerce and finance. A continuous process of assimilation alienated large numbers of Jews from their Jewishness. At the same time a large Jewish proletariat continued to be replenished by migrants from the Eastern provinces of the Danube Monarchy.[7] This process of integration and assimilation calls for some brief comments before we proceed with our discussion of the Jew in Austrian politics.

INTEGRATION AND ASSIMILATION[8]

> "A Society is similar to a house divided into rooms and corridors. The more a society resembles ours in its form of civilization, the thinner are its internal partitions and the wider and more open are its doors of communication."[9]

[5]Karl Eder, *Der Liberalismus in Altösterreich*, Vienna 1955, p. 222.
[6]Jakob Wassermann, *My Life as German and Jew*, translated by S. N. Brainin, New York 1933, pp. 186-187.
[7]Peter G. J. Pulzer, *The Rise of Political Anti-Semitism in Germany and Austria*, New York 1964, pp. 3-27.
[8]The theoretical formulations that underlie this section were presented by the author at the annual meeting of the American Sociological Association in Los Angeles in August 1963. See also: Walter B. Simon, 'Assimilation, Integration and Identity in Pluralist Society', *Mens en Maatschappij*, Amsterdam, vol. 38, No. 1, pp. 9-12. An expanded version of this article with references to the Jewish situation in Germany and Austria was republished in *The Wisconsin Sociologist*, vol. 3, No. 3, Sept. 1964, pp. 7-14.
[9]Arnold van Gennep, *The Rites of Passage*, translated by Monika B. Vizendom and Gabrielle L. Caffee, Chicago 1960, p. 26.

The dimension of integration is distinct from assimilation. Assimilation refers to the replacement or modification of cultural characteristics as a consequence of contact with hereto-fore alien cultures. Integration refers to the extent to which a minority actually forms a part of the body politic of its society. Thus German "non-Aryan" Christians were fully assimilated but, in the Third Reich, certainly not integrated into German society. Usually, the dimensions of integration and assimilation will vary jointly, but they may vary independently. The instances where their variations are disparate are of special interest.

The preservation of a distinct cultural heritage requires a measure of apartness, and such apartness is desired to the extent to which the group in question desires to preserve its cultural distinctness. In its original meaning the term "minority group rights" actually referred to the right of cultural distinctness, be it linguistic or religious or both, while in possession of rights of citizenship.

Persecution of and discrimination against cultural minorities usually aim at the establishment of cultural homogeneity. To this end a cultural minority may either be kept at arm's length or expelled altogether, or on the other hand, pressured and enticed to assimilate. We are here concerned first with the pressures against cultural pluralism and for homogeneity that operate in addition to — and even in the absence of — persecution. From there we shall proceed to a discussion of the situation that confronts an integrated cultural minority when it encounters pressures towards exclusion while the process of assimilation is progressing.

Emancipation from the community of the ghetto to citizenship in the newly emerging society of the nineteenth century opened dazzling prospects of infinite achievement and fulfilment among those brought up in the messianic faith of the Hebrew prophets. They entered the Age of Reason and Enlightenment with special fervour and zeal.

With the emancipation from the ghetto a puzzling and often painful problem emerged: *how to strike a balance between membership in the Jewish community and citizenship in the new society.* Such problems of balance arise universally from the stresses and strains between the maintenance of divergent cultural identities in pluralist societies. Such problems arise even in societies where the preservation of cultural pluralism is valued for its own sake and is not merely accepted as a matter of expediency.

All members of cultural minorities who combine membership in the community of their group with citizenship in their pluralist society find themselves confronted by this dilemma. *The more integrated a cultural minority into the society of which it forms a part, the more precarious will be the minority's cultural identity; conversely, the more pronounced the identity of a cultural minority the greater its apartness from society at large.*

As a cultural minority becomes integrated into a pluralist society its identity is bound to become attenuated. This attenuation takes place gradually and may be said to begin with an attenuation of the degree of the rejection accorded to the defector or apostate. The more the minority group becomes integrated the more the defector remains a fellow citizen. A shift of aspirations away from the fold of the group to society at large devalues membership in the group in favour of citizenship in society. This in turn will fragment the leadership of the group and attenuate the degree of rejection of the defector or apostate still further. A selection of leaders upon the basis of their achievements outside the group and an identification with successful defectors then become symptoms of the disintegration of the group itself.

The more apart a cultural group, the more clearly its identity will find expression in the rejection of its defectors; the more a cultural group is integrated into a society at large that encompasses diverse cultural groups, the more the rejection of defectors must be tempered by considerations that are due to fellow citizens. Such a modification of the group's rejection of its defectors attenuates group ties for all members of the group and thereby weakens the group's cohesion and its distinct identity.

The ghetto Jew had been living in the world of the Gentiles, but without being part of this world. His dealings with Gentiles were dealings with aliens, and he perceived his place for better and for worse within the fold of the Jewish community. The relationship with those who had turned their backs upon the community was clear and unequivocal: the converts were dead to the Jewish community and were literally mourned as dead by their next of kin. As soon as the Jews became citizens the defectors from Judaism remained fellow citizens.

In order to maintain its identity a cultural group must transmit its cultural heritage. The more apart it is, the more effectively can the group concentrate its efforts upon transmitting its culture. The more thoroughly a group is integrated into a pluralist society, the more preparation for citizenship in society at large will compete with and take precedence over the teaching and transmission of its cultural heritage. The more such preparation for citizenship in society at large takes precedence over initiation into the culture of the group, the more the cultural identity of its members will become nominal rather than essential.

The entire intellectual and spiritual efforts of the ghetto Jews had been bent upon the transmission of the heritage of Judaism to the coming generation who, in turn, ignored all knowledge and thought which did not form part of the sacred tradition. The aspirations and expectations of the ghetto Jews for themselves, for their children, and for their children's children were firmly fixed within the fold of Israel-in-exile.

Many emancipated Jews continued to cherish the faith of their fathers and took pride in their heritage. They wanted to bequeath this heritage to their children — but they also wanted their children to take their place in the society of which they now formed a part.

Secular knowledge has always been — and is even more so today — essential for admission to and competent participation in an industrial urban society. The more the Jews became integrated into society at large, the more did secular education compete with or even replace the transmission of traditional Judaism. The Jewish tradition of learning was readily transferred from a study of the sacred scriptures to the study of secular knowledge of the age of science.

The more apart a group from society, the more will the aspirations and expectations of its members be confined to the fold of the group. Conversely, the more integrated a group into the pluralist society of which it forms a part, the stronger will be the aspirations of its members to achieve success in that society.

Aspirations to succeed in society at large rather than within the group itself already constitute some degree of alienation from the group. Such alienation is actually compounded when the aspirations for success in society at large are motivated not only by the rewards offered by society but also by the rewards offered by the group for success in society. The prospect of dual reward for success outside the group will orient the expectations and aspirations of group members away from the group to the society of which it forms part. Such orientation of aspirations away from the group will take place in direct proportion to the group's integration into society and will further weaken the distinct identity of the group and its members.

After emancipation from the ghetto, expectations and aspirations shifted more and more from within the Jewish community to society at large. The second generation of Jews emancipated from the ghetto and those who followed them were deemed to work and strive in society at large while retaining their allegiance to the Jewish community. On one side was the slowly fading memory of forebears who had chosen the martyrdom of exile and stake as witnesses of their faith, on the other beckoned achievement and position in society. Such achievement was doubly welcomed, first for its own sake and then because of its favourable reflection upon the Jewish community as a whole. The high status accorded within the Jewish community to those who had won a prominent place in society at large also helped to orient aspirations from within the Jewish community to society at large.

The value placed by the group upon achievement outside the community in society at large undermines and fragments the leadership of the group. The more apart a group, the more its leadership positions will be the focus of the respect of the group and the object of the aspirations of its elite. The more a group becomes integrated into a pluralist society, the more will the shift of aspirations from the group downgrade and fragment its own leadership.

The greater the respect given by the group to its members for success outside the group, the less attractive the leadership positions within the group will become. At first, leadership positions will be filled by those whose aspirations have been limited to within the group; eventually, leadership positions will attract those who have obtained status within the group by their success outside.

The leaders whose aspirations have been focused upon the group to begin with most likely embody the values and traditions of the group but are apt to be marginal to society at large; those who achieve positions of leadership within the group on the basis of their success in society at large are likely to be marginal to the group in their values and orientations. The more integrated a group into a pluralist society, the more prevalent will be the influence of the latter among its leaders. The resulting fragmentation and downgrading in the group's leadership positions is bound to attenuate the identity and cohesion of the group still further.

Secular leadership of the Jewish community of Vienna was accorded primarily upon the basis of achievement in society at large. The degree of alienation of these men from Judaism may be surmised by the extent to which many of their immediate descendants changed their religion. Among such converts, just to cite one conspicuous instance, we find the poet, Hugo von Hofmannsthal, son of one of the illustrious presidents of Vienna's Jewish community in the nineteenth century.[10] Jewish leaders whose ties with Judaism were so attenuated that they failed to transmit identification with Judaism to their immediate offspring were not likely to strengthen the vitality of Judaism within the community that they led.[11]

The shift of aspirations from within the group to society not only fragments the leadership of the group, but also modifies further the rejection of those who have defected. On the whole, success in society will be more easily achieved by those who conform than by those who do not. Consequently, defection or near-defection from the group will in many cases facilitate success in society. In the resulting conflict between respect for the achievement of success in society at large and rejection of the defector, rejection of the defector is apt to be modified by pride in the defector's success when such success is sufficiently conspicuous.

The respect for success achieved outside the group thus undermines the cohesion of the group in two ways: marginal members are recruited into leadership on the basis of achievements in society at large; and the rejection of defectors from the group, initially modified by considerations due to fellow citizens, is tempered further by pride in and even identification with the defectors' achievements in society at large outside the group.

A society composed of different cultural groups is always characterised by a certain amount of conflict and of accommodation. The mode of accommodation and conflict will depend upon the nature and the degree of cultural differences — whether they be in language, religion, or both — but strains towards greater homogeneity and conformity will always be in evidence. Such strains may appear in the form of acculturation and accommodation, or in the form of exclusive pressures designed to keep the nonconformists at arm's length or even to expel them altogether. Exclusionary pressures may or may not encourage assimilation and eventual complete acculturation.

Where one cultural group is dominant in a pluralist society, its opposition to cultural diversity and the straining towards conformity it imposes may express itself in the form of pressures for the assimilation or against the integration of those of a different culture. These two types of pressures are combined to the extent that rights of citizenship are contingent upon assimilation while non-assimilation leads to exclusion from citizenship or even expulsion. These two types of pressures may, however, operate at cross-purposes when they originate without consistency from different sectors of the dominant cultural group with varying intensity.

[10]On Hofmannsthal see the chapter 'Geschichte einer Assimilation' in Hermann Broch, *Hofmannsthal und seine Zeit*, München 1964, pp. 90-105. *Ibid.*, on the phenomenon of "the strange inner antisemitism of the assimilated Jew", p. 105.

[11]The psychologist Kurt Lewin deals with this problem of leadership under the heading 'Leaders from the Periphery'. In his condemnation of such leaders Lewin overlooks the sociological imperatives of the relationship between the leaders and those they lead. The leaders were not turning their backs upon their cultural heritage in order to further personal ambitions; their ambivalence towards their cultural heritage reflected the ambivalent attitudes of those they led. See Kurt Lewin, *Resolving Social Conflicts*, New York 1948, pp. 193-195.

The more apart a cultural minority is from the dominant cultural group, the greater its inner cohesion and solidarity. Thus, its members will sustain and be sustained by their group in their resistence to outside pressures. The more a cultural minority is integrated into its society, the more the group as a whole and its individual members will be exposed unsustained to pressures of all kinds. These pressures include those for their complete assimilation, as well as those opposed to their integration and for their exclusion and expulsion. The group whose cohesion and solidarity is anchored in its cultural identity is able to confront both types of pressure and cope with them through its institutions and traditions.

The more a cultural minority forms part of its society, the weaker its inner cohesion and the more vulnerable the group and its members become to pressures. As group cohesion weakens, its members will be compelled to come to terms with society at large on their own, and they will have to cope with all the pressures exerted upon them as individuals.

For the Jew in the ghetto the assimilationist pressures were all of a piece: either to discard his own religion for the religion of the dominant group and become completely assimilated and integrated into the dominant society, at the price of complete separation from his group — or to stay in the ghetto, unassimilated and apart from the alien society within which his group has formed an isolated enclave. The emancipated Jew not only has to cope with the pressures of the dominant culture with little support from the Jewish community, but the pressures he is under are fragmented in a way that precludes an effective confrontation: on the one hand promises of full citizenship exert pressure towards complete assimilation; but threats to the citizenship of the church-going descendants of completely assimilated Jews counteract these assimilationist pressures.

From their emancipation to full citizenship in February 1867 until the incorporation of Austria into the Third Reich in March 1938 Austrian Jews were confronted by an infinite array of combinations of contradictory assimilationist and exclusory pressures. Jewish participation in Austrian politics must be viewed against this background of diverse combinations of contradictory pressures.

THE LIBERAL ERA

Jews entered Austrian politics under the banner of liberalism and its disappearance left the assimilated Jewish middle class of Vienna politically homeless.

Jews first appeared in public life in Austria during the Revolution of 1848. The revolutionaries fought for the establishment of constitutional government, including freedom of speech, of the press, and of assembly. With this went the demand for equal rights for all subjects of the Crown, irrespective of religious denomination. Jews played a prominent part in the revolutionary movement, and Jewish students manned the barricades side by side with their non-Jewish fellows in order to fight the forces of the autocratic regime.[12]

[12]Wilhelm Stein, 'Austria', in *The Universal Jewish Encyclopedia*, vol. I, ed. Isaac Landman, New York 1939, p. 628.

From 1867 until the turn of the century the powerful liberal movement continued to rally the Jewish bourgeoisie and the anti-clerical German bourgeoisie of Imperial Austria of which most members of the Jewish bourgeoisie formed a part. Jews played a prominent rôle in the *Deutsch-liberale Partei*, the political party of Austria's German-speaking anti-clerical bourgeoisie, which upheld the ideals and traditions of the Revolution of 1848.

In the seventies the future looked promising. Throughout the Middle Ages the antagonism towards the Jews had been directed against them as religious dissenters in a society professing one religious faith. The constitutional sanction of religious pluralism removed the disabilities previously imposed upon the Jews, and they were confident that anti-Jewish sentiments would vanish altogether. They trusted in the ultimate triumph of the Age of Reason over unreasoning faith, and their own faith in progress was to prove remarkably hardy.

In the eighties and nineties matters began to take a turn for the worse for the Austrian Jews. Antagonism to Jews on religious grounds persisted. It was supplemented by antisemitism directed at Jews as a "race" and thus threatened the assimilated and even those who had turned their backs upon Judaism.

Jewish prominence in the economic structure of capitalism led to a fusion of anti-capitalism and antisemitism. An early proponent of this fusion had been Karl Marx with his statement that ". . . public credit rests upon the confidence that the state will allow itself to be exploited by the Jews of Finance."[13] Men aspiring to popular leadership in Germany and Austria time and again found antisemitism a useful platform from which to reach and stir the dissatisfied masses. At the turn of the century the above-quoted pithy statement of Karl Marx became popular with anti-Jewish propagandists and agitators in Vienna, and a generation later the sentiments of these phrases were to become part of the ideology of Hitler's National Socialist movement. Before this, the effectiveness of anti-capitalist anti-semitism had been enhanced considerably by Jewish disciples of Marx who went to great lengths to emulate their master's Jewish self-hatred in order to dissociate them-selves from Judaism as much as possible.

The first half of the nineteenth century had been the golden age of German culture. All over the world men of learning studied German for the privilege of reading Goethe and Kant in the original. Soon German universities attracted students from all over the world — among them, incidentally, the leading educators and scholars of the United States. It was therefore not surprising that after their emancipation from the ghetto the Jews were eager to step from the narrow confines of the ghetto or from outlying provinces of the Austrian Empire into the magic circle of German culture; they partook of its offerings and contributed to its scope and glory.

The Jews who embraced German culture had to learn, however, that those who

---

[13]Karl Marx, *The Class Struggle in France (1848-1850)*, New York 1938, p. 46. — Objections that the above quotation is cited out of context are without merit because Karl Marx had himself inserted this statement without qualification of any kind. His Jewish self-hatred poses a problem for his apologists.

arrogantly proclaimed their monopoly of being German did so from positions of uncompromising chauvinism that in no way reflected the humanism that had endowed German culture with its greatness. In the decades that followed the middle of the nineteenth century Jews had been welcomed into German clubs and fraternities throughout the Austrian Empire. But by the turn of the century membership in many of these associations had been restricted to "Aryans", that is to ethnic Germans whose four grandparents had undergone baptism in their early childhood.[14]

The Jews who had suffered persecution during the Middle Ages had borne their lot as witnesses to their faith. The Germanized Jews were expelled from the *völkisch* German clubs, societies, and fraternities, and ostracised. The German Jew could seek solace in Kant, Goethe, Herder, and Lessing and so reassure himself that he had a more valid claim to the heritage of German culture than his raucous detractors. To the precursors of Hitler in Austria, Goethe's stoic principle *Nichts Menschliches ist mir fremd* was itself degenerate alien nonsense. Already at the turn of the century the anti-clerical German-speaking intelligentsia of Austria turned their backs on the humanist tradition and became pioneers of rabid racialism.[15]

The *Deutsch-liberale Partei* espoused a position of moderate German nationalism. The leading Jewish intellectuals supported the spread of the German language into every corner of the polyglot Empire, but without chauvinism.

This liberal position is well expressed by Adolf Fischhof, one of the celebrated heroes of the Revolution of 1848 and later the Grand Old Man of Austrian liberalism. In his statement Fischhof comments on the efforts of some German elements in Imperial Austria to establish their dominance over the other ethnic groups or *Nationalitäten* by means of rigidly centralised government:

> "Inasmuch as it is the purpose of modern constitutional representation to preserve for the people the right of self-determination there can hardly exist a more flagrant violation of the principle of constitutional government than the transfer of the centralistic principle of a *Nationalstaat* [a monolithic state with a homogeneous ethnic population] to the *Nationalitätenstaat* [a multi-national state with several *Nationalitäten* or ethnic groups, such as Imperial Austria]. Centralism in Austria is an anachronism, a sin against the spirit of our time. The German does not have any need of this sin. He stands above his non-German countrymen without placing himself upon the pedestal of special privilege. His moral superiority offers him more lasting guarantees than artificially contrived parliamentary power. He should not be a guardian but a model to the nations. By his efforts to germanize the German does not fulfil his cultural mission, but only wakens the hatred of the other *Nationalitäten* and promotes the [Panslavic] objections of Russia."[16]

[14]This definition of "Aryan" is based upon the stipulations of the Nuremberg Racial Laws enacted in the autumn of 1935 in Germany and later extended to all territories over which the Third Reich had jurisdiction.

[15]For a detailed account of the break between the German-nationalist chauvinists and the Liberals see the chapter 'Schönerer and the Liberal Split' in Pulzer, *op. cit.*, pp. 148-160.

[16]Cited with approval by Friedrich Funder in his autobiography; Funder was one of the cofounders of Lueger's antisemitic pro-clerical *Christlich-Soziale Partei*. See Friedrich Funder, *Vom Gestern ins Heute. Aus dem Kaiserreich in die Republik*, Vienna 1952, p. 87. Friedrich Funder recognises in Fischhof's statement the sentiments that might have preserved the Danube Monarchy.

In the above Fischhof spoke primarily for those German-speaking liberal Austrians who identified themselves with the heritage of German humanism and the culture it represented.[17] Pan-Germanic chauvinists, however, considered a conciliatory attitude in matters of culture and language as treason. Many of them had a vested interest in limiting as far as possible the use of languages other than German in the administration, in the judiciary, and in the school system. Mixed with this was nationalistic pride as well as aversion to intellectual effort.

It is highly significant that racial antisemitism, as well as other "ideological" attributes that were to characterise Hitlerism, originated within Austria's pan-Germanic movement. Their stronghold was in the German-language areas that were in 1918 to become part of the Czechoslovak Republic, and which later became known as Sudetenland. There the racialists *(Völkische)* polled significant majorities in free elections, and there we find a *Nationalsozialistische Arbeiterpartei* already before the First World War.

The pan-German Austrians designated themselves as *freiheitlich* in order to set themselves apart from what they referred to contemptuously as *Juden-liberal*.[18]

Nevertheless many German-speaking Jews sided with the German chauvinists and tried to gain their approval and acceptance. Many others found themselves at a loss as to where to turn. In the words of Theodor Herzl:

> "The Jews, whose culture is German [in Bohemia] and whose formative years coincided with the time when liberal ideals predominated attached themselves with all their hearts to the German nation . . . too closely, it would seem. Then all of a sudden they found themselves shaken off. All of a sudden they were told that they were parasites . . . One jerk only, and they were no longer Germans but Jews."[19]

In the mixed-language areas of the Danube Monarchy, especially in Bohemia and Moravia, their equivocal position exposed the Jews to attacks from all sides.[20] Before the First World War the advance of racial *(völkisch)* theories had noticeable repercussions also in Vienna, as a large proportion of its intelligentsia was Jewish. At the same time as the Austrian Jews were confronted with the racial antisemitism of the anti-clerical pan-Germans who had broken with liberalism, they also found themselves vis-à-vis the vigorous pro-clerical antisemitism of Karl Lueger's newly-founded and extremely popular *Christlich-Soziale Partei*.

The emancipated Jewry of Imperial Austria, deriving their political philosophy from the Enlightenment, first came into conflict with the Catholic Church when many Jews actively and prominently participated in the struggle for constitutional

---

[17]For a discussion of the influence exerted by Fischhof on the Jewish intelligentsia see Werner J. Cahnman, 'Adolf Fischhof and his Jewish Followers', *LBI Year Book IV* (1959), pp. 111-139.

[18]The contemptuous rejection of liberalism, strangely enough, did not prevent some Nazis from associating themselves with liberal traditions of 1848; the biographical sketch of a prominent Nazi recorded with pride his descent from Robert Blum, the famous revolutionary who had been shot in Vienna in 1848 after the city's surrender to the Imperial troops. See Baldur von Schirach, *Die Pioniere des Dritten Reiches*, Essen 1933, p. 20.

[19]Theodor Herzl, 'Die Jagd in Böhmen', written in 1897, published in *Gesammelte Zionistische Werke*, 3rd edition, vol. I, Berlin 1934, p. 217.

[20]*Ibid.*, pp. 216-222.

government and against the autocratic absolutism with which the Church had been closely allied. During the heyday of the liberal era many Jews viewed Catholicism — like all religions — as the vanishing heritage of an unenlightened past. All that was vanishing, however, was the staid *Konservative Partei* of the landed aristocracy and high-ranking civil service. They were replaced by a new and vigorous party of great popular appeal: Lueger's anti-liberal, antisemitic and pro-clerical *Christlich-Soziale Partei*, which soon put an end to the Liberal Party's control of Vienna's city hall. The ill feeling between the Jews and the Catholic Church was fanned but not caused by Lueger's campaign.[21] The causes lay deeper.

The emancipated Jewish intelligentsia of Vienna absorbed, endorsed, propagated, and contributed to the doctrines of the positivist-rationalist philosophy so characteristic of the liberal era. In the words of a contemporary writer:

> "Through all these Jews ran a quality of rationalism that cast a gloom over any more intimate relationship. Among the base it found base expression, in worship of success and wealth, in self-seeking and lust for gain, in greed for power and in social opportunism. Among the nobler it manifested itself in impotence in the ideal and intuitive realms. Science was set up as an idol, intellect as the sovereign lord."[22]

Some Jewish writers, among them men of high rank and reputation and endowed with creative talent, engaged in attacks on articles of faith and on the dogma of the Catholic Church. Thus one of the most celebrated playwrights of pre-war Vienna in one of his plays confronted a Jewish doctor with a Catholic priest in a dispute over whether a dying Catholic patient was to be offered the final unction of the last sacrament. While the priest insisted on preparing the patient for the hereafter the doctor wanted to spare the patient the horror of his approaching certain death. This reference is pertinent here because the author weighted the argument in his and the doctor's favour to the extent of having the priest admit off the record to strong doubts about his own position.[23]

The conservatism of political clericalism sustained the image of the Church as a politically reactionary factor. Members of the lower clergy engaged openly and uncharitably in vicious antisemitic propaganda; some priests even spread the ritual murder charge, despite the official position of their Church.

It should be added here that the antisemitism of the *Christlich-Soziale Partei* remained largely on the level of rhetoric and softened over the years. As mayor of Vienna, Lueger dispelled many of the apprehensions previously occasioned by his colourful and inflammatory demagogy. Under his able and fair administration the prospering metropolis continued to attract Jews as well as non-Jews from the

[21]For a detailed treatment of Austrian pro-clerical antisemitism in general and Lueger's antisemitism in particular see Pulzer, *op. cit.* The material presented here should help to clear Lueger from the taint of Hitlerism. For all his demagogic antisemitic rhetoric Lueger has long been remembered with real fondness by friends and foes — Jews included — for his fair and competent administration of Vienna, his joviality, and his genuine sense of humour. These human (and very Viennese) qualities set Lueger poles apart from the insane criminal with whom he is often compared by superficial observers. — See also *LBI Year Book X* (1965), pp. XIV, 50 ff.

[22]Wassermann, *op. cit.*, p. 189. — See also *LBI Year Book III* (1958), p. XV.

[23]Arthur Schnitzler, *Professor Bernhardi*, Berlin 1912.

provinces of the Danube Monarchy.[24] Nevertheless traces of virulent antisemitism remained characteristic of Lueger's party for years to come. Also, his powerful style of oratory in which he linked Jews and capitalist gold remained a rich source of reference for demagogues of lesser calibre.

The defection of the German-nationalist chauvinists and the extension of suffrage to non-propertied wage earners eliminated political liberalism as a factor in Austrian politics. In the provinces of Imperial Austria which were to form the post-1918 Austrian Republic the Liberal Party lost its dominant place to the Socialists, the *Christlich-Sozialen*, and the party of the German-nationalists *(Großdeutsche)*.

The Socialists officially rejected antisemitism. The *Christlich-Sozialen* appealed primarily to the lower middle class and the peasants. This slowed down but did not prevent the ultimate disappearance of political liberalism; the upheavals of the revolution of 1918 also led to a temporary upsurge of a "Jewish-nationalist" party. When this party disappeared, too, the Jewish middle-class voters were confronted at the polls with a painful choice. They had to vote either for the Social Democratic Party that deliberately refrained from appealing to the middle classes or to abstain altogether, if they did not find an excuse for supporting the *Christlich-Sozialen*. For the Jews of Vienna the "Age of Reason and Progress" thus ended in a blind alley.

THE AUSTRIAN JEWS AND SOCIALISM

As political liberalism declined Austrian Jews were more and more attracted to socialism. But only intellectuals alienated from Judaism could accept socialism without reservations; liberalism permitted continued attachment to Judaism but socialism did not. What may have influenced Jewish intellectuals — consciously or unconsciously — was socialism's quasi-messianic promise of a classless society founded on universal brotherhood in perfect justice and peace. They also endorsed the Socialist Party's extensive educational programme that served to stimulate and to satisfy the thirst for knowledge of industrial workers whose formal education had been limited. This programme provided many Jewish intellectuals with opportunities for dedicated and idealistic service. Jewish intellectuals had been prominent among the founders of Austria's Socialist Party, and long continued to remain political leaders, especially as theorists of what became known as "Austro-Marxism".

Marxist ideology, however, was highly repugnant to many members of the Jewish middle class engaged in commerce, finance, and manufacture. They resented Jewish and non-Jewish Marxist agitators alike who labelled private enterprise as "parasitic". Anti-religious Marxism was also repugnant to those Jews who cherished the traditions of their religion. However, after the decline of political liberalism the Socialist Party remained the only major party opposed to antisemitism. But the Socialist Party argued that the Jewish question would be solved

[24]According to Hannah Arendt the era of Karl Lueger as mayor of Vienna has even been referred to as ". . . actually a kind of golden age for the Jews". See Hannah Arendt, *The Origins of Totalitarianism*, New York 1951, p. 44.

automatically through assimilation in the classless society of the future. This idea did not please those Jews who cherished their spiritual and cultural heritage. Nor did such a position provide a platform from which to fight antisemitism with vigour.

Jewish intellectual leaders displayed great courage when they stood up for their political convictions. By contrast, their quasi-apologetic response to antisemitic attack may only have spurred on and encouraged their opponents. Their ineffective efforts to ignore and even deny their Jewish background corroded their self-respect and reduced them to objects of contempt; an affirmation of their Jewishness would have strengthened their self-respect and blunted anti-Jewish attacks. Such an affirmation, however, seemed incompatible with socialist theory.

When heckled repeatedly by shouts of "Jew" during a speech before the Lower Austrian diet,[25] Dr. Victor Adler, founder of the Austrian Socialist Party, first tried to ignore the interruptions. Finally he replied: "Now tell me frankly: Aren't you getting bored with this 'Jew, Jew, Jew'? I most certainly am!" Adler's obvious discomfort only incited his hecklers who proceeded to taunt the speaker with his "Hebraic ancestry". In reply, Adler reminded the hecklers, one of whom was a member of the lower clergy, that stooping to racial antisemitism was hardly proper for devout Catholics whose Church had just recently enthroned one Theodor Kohn as archbishop.[26]

Victor Adler set the pattern of response to antisemitism for other Jewish Socialists when he limited his references to antisemitism in his campaign speeches to charges of inconsistency on the part of antisemites whom he accused of associating with rich Jews and of doing business with Jews. Thus Adler declared in a campaign speech that ". . . even though the antisemites have recently invited the richest Jews to the annual ball of the City of Vienna they maintain that the Socialist Party is led by Jews." This *non sequitur* is taken from a campaign speech held on the 28th February 1897.[27]

On the 2nd March 1897 Adler found himself before his constituents in a debate with his German-nationalist opponent Dr. Mayreder. This speaker had called on the working-class audience to ". . . elect one of their own kind rather than someone like Dr. Adler . . . who owes his position of power to the activities of his forebears . . ." Adler responded in front of his constituents as follows:

"Dr. M. takes the position that the socialist workers are fine fellows but that their leaders are evil men. Here the gentlemen speak however only of 'Jewish' leaders *(as an aside, there are among the antisemites more Jews than among us)*[28] but they never speak of the great mass of leading Aryan [sic] comrades . . ."[29]

Towards the end of his speech Adler finally replied to Mayreder's slur upon his

[25]Session held on the 16th July 1902.
[26]Victor Adler, *Aufsätze, Reden und Briefe*, Vienna 1929, p. 161.
[27]*Ibid.*, p. 106.
[28]Author's italics.
[29]Adler, *op. cit.*, p. 109. Readers may note here Adler's self-effacing emphasis upon the large number of "Aryan" leaders, and that he can accuse his antisemitic opponents of nothing beyond themselves mixing with Jews.

ancestry as follows: "My parents were Jews; but for that my parents were no worse than yours, Herr Doktor."[30]

The above appears to have been an example of the maximum of affirmative response ever achieved by Jewish Socialist leaders in Vienna when confronted by antisemites. Their response revealed that they themselves viewed their Jewish background with disdain and agreed with the antisemites that it constituted a stigma.[31]

Nearly all the non-Jewish leaders of the Austrian Socialist Party took a firm stand against antisemitism. But the Jewish self-hatred of many Jewish Socialists provided excellent cover for Socialists who indulged in and subscribed to anti-semitism. Furthermore, the position of the Jewish leaders, described above, was highly repugnant to Jews who were not at all apologetic about their Jewishness and their "Hebraic ancestry".

In the First Republic of Austria Jewish voters of all classes and shades of opinion voted increasingly for the Socialist Party. They had no real alternative.

A characteristic note may be added here. A few years ago an ageing veteran leader of the Austrian Socialist Party published his autobiography.[32] During his childhood and adolescence antisemitism became a major political and social force in his native Vienna, and when he had achieved a position of prominence his opponents rarely referred to him without pointing to his Jewishness. During his eleven years in exile following the Nazi occupation of Austria, the Jewish community of Vienna was reduced by expulsion and mass murder to a pitiful remnant of survivors and straggling returnees. Yet such words as *Jude* or *jüdisch* do not appear anywhere in the book. We learn from this veteran Socialist what his mother packed into his father's lunch box, but not a single word about their religious affiliation — in Austria a matter of public record, and at a time when religious knowledge was an obligatory subject of instruction at school. The author does express his disapproval of what the Nazis did, in a few passing references to their *Rassenwahn*, their obsession with racialism.

JEWISH NATIONALISM

Most of the assimilated Jews of Vienna continued to dismiss the upsurge of anti-semitism at the turn of the century as a belated manifestation of a vanishing dark age. They were disturbed when Lueger's *Christlich-Soziale Partei* ousted Vienna's liberal city administration, but they were reassured by its subsequent policies. The

---

[30]*Ibid.*, p. 109.
[31]For further details see the chapter 'The Social Democrats' in Pulzer, *op. cit.*, pp. 259-270. Pulzer refers to a significant incident at the International Socialist Congress at Brussels in 1891. The American Jewish delegation had proposed a resolution condemning antisemitism, but it was opposed by Singer (a German Socialist of Jewish birth) and by the Austrian, Victor Adler. The Congress finally condemned "anti-Semitic and philo-Semitic agitation as one of the manoeuvres by which the capitalist class and reactionary governments try to make the Socialist movement deviate [presumably, from its course] and to divide the workers ..." *Ibid.*, pp. 265-266. This incident is also referred to in Edmund Silberner, *Sozialisten zur Juden-*

emergence of racial antisemitism among the anti-clerical nationalist middle class and especially in the universities was a shock, but eventually the Jewish middle class had to live with the disabilities this imposed upon them. The optimistic faith of the assimilated Jews in progress and reason was nearly as impervious to the pressure of adverse experience as the messianic faith of their fathers had been to the threatening terrors of expulsion and the stake.

Only a small minority of the Jewish intelligentsia recognised in this upsurge of antisemitism a threat to their future. Out of the vision of one of the members of this far-seeing minority arose the movement of political Zionism. Its founding father, Theodor Herzl, had come to the conclusion that there was no future for Jews in Central Europe.

As is well known, Herzl's ideas, expressed in his pamphlet *Der Judenstaat* (1896) found very few supporters among the Viennese Jews, and many vociferous opponents. On the other hand he found an enthusiastic echo among the Jews of Eastern Europe, including the Eastern provinces of what was then Imperial Austria. They formed the bulk of Herzl's following in Vienna, but he also attracted supporters among the more sensitive members of the assimilated Jewish intelligentsia and especially among the students.

The Zionists also challenged the assimilationist control of the Jewish community council of Vienna, the *Jüdische Kultusgemeinde*. This was an official body legally authorised to levy taxes and entrusted with the administration and supervision of Jewish religious and cultural life in Vienna, and with the management of welfare institutions. After 1918, the Zionist opposition made considerable progress in their bid for the *Kultusgemeinde*. It was not until November 1932 (two months before Hitler became Chancellor of Germany), however, that the Zionists succeeded in mustering a majority among those Viennese Jews sufficiently interested in Jewish matters to cast their votes in elections to the Jewish community council.

From 1919 until 1930 the Zionist *Jüdisch-nationale Partei* in Vienna also put up lists of candidates in national and city elections to represent Jewish interests.

THE JEWS AT THE POLLS[33]

Before the First World War the Jewish bourgeoisie of Vienna had no difficulty in making their choice at the polls. They voted Liberal. At the beginning of the century the Liberal Party was, however, reduced from a major political force to a splinter group by two developments, the defection of the anti-clerical non-Jewish middle class to the antisemitic German-nationalists, and the introduction of universal male

frage, Berlin 1962, pp. 235-236. — On Victor Adler see also Julius Braunthal, *Victor und Friedrich Adler, Zwei Generationen Arbeiterbewegung*, Vienna 1965, and 'The Jewish Background of Victor and Friedrich Adler. Selected Biographical Notes', in *LBI Year Book X* (1965), pp. 266-276.

[32]Julius Deutsch, *Ein weiter Weg*, Vienna 1961.

[33]Another version of part of this section has been published in *Jewish Social Studies*, New York, vol. 23, No. 1, Jan. 1961, pp. 38-48.

suffrage. Before its introduction all representative bodies were divided into so-called *Kurien*, electoral colleges composed according to economic classes.

In Table I we tabulate the party representation in the Vienna City Council for 1894 and for 1896. For the elections held in March 1896 we also record the numbers of votes cast.[34] The data show how Liberal representation in the City Council of Vienna declined in two years from 80 out of 138 to 42, while the antisemitic parties (pro-clerical and German-nationalist) increased their representation from 56 to 96. We also note that the Liberal Party was strongest and held on to its strength most effectively in the 1st *Kurie* that consisted of members of the upper class. The Liberal Party was weakest to begin with and then suffered its heaviest losses in the 3rd *Kurie* representing the lower middle class; the development regarding the 2nd *Kurie* representing the upper middle class was somewhere between the trends in the other two *Kurien*.

While each of the three *Kurien* elected the same number of city councillors the voters of the 3rd *Kurie* were nearly ten times as numerous and those of the 2nd nearly five times as numerous as the voters of the 1st. This explains why the Liberal Party was doomed to become insignificant as soon as suffrage was extended to the working class.

TABLE I*

Elections to the City Council of Vienna in 1894 and 1896

Voting to City Council by *Kurie*, electoral bodies that represented different classes of taxpayers in accordance with amount of direct taxes paid. Every *Kurie* elected 46 councillors

	Number of councillors elected in 1896 (results of 1894 in parenthesis)		Votes cast in 1896***	
	Antisemitic parties	Liberals	Antisemitic parties	Liberals
1st *Kurie*	18 (6)	28 (40)	1,677	2,753
2nd *Kurie*	32 (15)	14 (29)**	11,796	9,332
3rd *Kurie*	46 (35)	— (11)	33,556	9,074
			47,029	21,159

*Ibid., p. 186.
**The source does not indicate the affiliation of the remaining two councillors.
***Voting data are given for the elections in March 1896.

The Liberal Party continued to remain a minor factor in the politics of Imperial Austria even after the introduction of universal suffrage. In the First Republic, however, it had no prospects whatever of carrying a candidate. This confronted the Jewish middle-class voters in the First Republic of Austria with a difficult choice.

[34]Pulzer, *op. cit.*, p. 186. The source gives the voting data only for the March 1896 elections.

They could vote for the Socialists and against their class interest; many Jews voted Socialist in 1923, and still more Jews did so in 1932. They could vote in line with their class interest for one of the two major anti-Socialist parties and ignore certain antisemitic tendencies; some of the upper and middle-class Jews actually voted for Dr. Schober's fusion of anti-clerical and anti-socialist (and predominantly German-nationalist) parties in 1930 and for the *Christlich-Soziale Partei* in April 1932. In the municipal elections up to April 1932 the Jewish voters in Vienna were also able to vote for a Jewish-nationalist (i.e. Zionist) ticket or for the dwindling Liberal Party; neither party had any prospects but otherwise their appeal to Jewish voters was untarnished. They could abstain from voting altogether.

THE LIBERAL AND THE ZIONIST VOTE

In the First Republic the Liberal Party dwindled from a minor party to a nonentity. At different elections political liberalism presented itself to the voters of Vienna under diverse names but without avail. Under the designation *Bürgerliche Arbeitspartei* the Liberal vote in Vienna dropped from 4.4 per cent in 1920 to 1.8 per cent in 1923; in 1927 a *Demokratische Liste* polled 1.3 per cent of the Viennese vote, and in 1930 a *Demokratische Mittelpartei* a mere 0.5 per cent; in the municipal elections held in Vienna in 1932 the Liberals did not even put up candidates of their own.[35] Intellectually, however, political liberalism did remain a factor, mainly through its press and publications, among which the daily paper *Neue Freie Presse* was the most outstanding. It played the rôle of *The Times* in Vienna from its foundation in 1867 until closed down by the Nazi regime in 1938.

The Liberal vote had been concentrated in Vienna's middle-class districts.[36] It declined fastest in the districts with comparatively few Jews and slowest in the districts where proportions of Jews had been highest.

The traditional stronghold of liberalism in Vienna was the First District with a Liberal vote of 27 per cent in 1920, 10 per cent in 1923, 5 per cent in 1927, and 3.6 per cent in 1930. These data do not bear upon our proposition that non-Jewish voters defected from liberalism faster than Jewish voters because the First District ranked highest in middle-class composition and second-highest in proportion of Jews (24 per cent). We may, however, infer the rate of Jewish defection and that

[35]The election results for the municipal districts of Vienna for 1920 and 1923 are taken from *Statistisches Jahrbuch der Stadt Wien*, 1929, published in Vienna by the Magistrat, Abt. f. Statistik in 1929, pp. 270-271. The results of the elections held on the 24th April 1927 appear in *Die Nationalratswahlen vom 24. April 1927*, published in Vienna in 1927 by the Bundesamt für Statistik, and the results of the elections held on the 9th November 1930 are from *Die Nationalratswahlen vom 9. November 1930*, published in Vienna by the Bundesamt für Statistik in 1931.

[36]The 21 districts of pre-war Vienna have been ranked according to economic class on the basis of the following criteria: proportion of women employed as domestic helps and proportion of professional men as indication of middle-class composition, and proportion of privately employed wage earners as indication of working-class composition. Rank orders of Vienna's districts by the first two criteria are nearly identical with one another as well as with the reversed rank order according to the third criterion. See Robert Dannenberg, *Die Entwicklungsmöglichkeiten der Sozialdemokratie in Österreich*, Vienna 1924, p. 50.

of non-Jewish defection from liberalism if we compare rates of defection in middle-class districts containing different proportions of Jews. The Second District of Vienna, ranking highest in proportion of Jews (34 per cent) and eighth in middle-class composition, in the proportion of Liberal votes, held tenth place in 1920 and in 1923, fifth in 1927, and third in 1930. The Ninth District, third in proportion of Jews (23 per cent) and fourth with respect to middle-class composition, ranked third in proportion of Liberal votes in 1920 and 1923, and second in 1927 and in 1930. Conversely we find that the Fourth District, eighth in proportion of Jews (9 per cent) and second as middle-class district, was in proportion of Liberal votes second in 1920 and 1923, seventh in 1927 and in 1930. It follows that the Liberal vote declined most rapidly in middle-class districts with a comparatively small proportion of Jews, and more slowly where the proportion of Jews was comparatively high.[37]

The efforts of the Zionists to rally Jewish voters in general elections in support of a "Jewish-nationalist" list of candidates were not very successful. It was only in 1919 that their representative (Robert Stricker) entered the Austrian parliament but he was not re-elected in 1920. In 1920 and again in 1923, the Second District sent one "Jewish-nationalist" counsellor to Vienna's City Hall but in 1927 he, too, lost his seat.

While about 10 per cent of Vienna's voters were Jewish, a *Jüdisch-nationale Partei* received 2 per cent of Vienna's vote in 1920, a *Jüdische Wahlgemeinschaft* received 2.4 per cent of the vote in 1923, a *Jüdische Partei* polled 0.9 per cent of the vote in 1927, and a *Jüdische Liste* polled 0.2 per cent of the Viennese vote in November 1930. When the last municipal elections of the First Republic of Austria were held in Vienna in April 1932, the Zionists, like the Liberals, did not put up candidates.

Vienna's Zionist stronghold was, of course, the Second District, 34 per cent Jewish. Here the Zionists polled 11 per cent of the vote in 1920 and again in 1923, 5 per cent in 1927, and 1.1 in 1930.

After 1920 the Zionist vote declined fastest in Vienna's Jewish working-class district, the Twentieth, and at first increased and then comparatively slowly decreased in the Jewish middle-class districts.

The Zionist gain in Vienna from 2.0 per cent of the vote in 1920 to 2.4 per cent of the vote in 1923 resulted from Zionist gains in Vienna's middle-class districts that were in part balanced by a Zionist loss in the Twentieth District, Vienna's working-class district with the highest proportion of Jews. The Twentieth was Vienna's only district which ranked higher with reference to proportion of Jews (15.3 per cent or 4th in rank among Vienna's 21 pre-war districts) than in middle-class composition since it ranked only fifteenth with reference to middle-class composition. With a drop in the Zionist vote from 4 per cent in 1920 to 2.6 per cent in 1923 the Twentieth dropped with reference to the proportion of Zionist votes to total votes from third place to seventh. Conversely, the share of the Zionist vote in the First, Sixth, Seventh, and Nineteenth, all middle-class districts, more than doubled.

[37]Cf. Tables II and III.

TABLE II

The Liberal and the Zionist vote in Vienna
(in percentages)

District	Liberal*				Zionist**			
	1920	1923	1927	1930	1920	1923	1927	1930
I	27.0	10.0	5.0	3.6	3.0	6.8	2.0	0.4
II	5.0	1.8	2.0	1.4	11.0	11.0	5.0	1.1
III	9.0	2.5	1.5	0.7	1.5	2.2	0.7	0.1
IV	14.0	4.6	1.5	0.8	0.9	1.6	0.6	0.2
V	3.0	1.6	0.9	0.1	0.5	0.8	0.2	0.05
VI	5.5	3.7	1.2	1.0	2.0	4.0	1.6	0.2
VII	6.0	3.6	2.2	1.2	1.7	4.1	1.7	0.2
VIII	5.0	3.9	2.3	1.0	2.4	3.4	1.3	0.3
IX	10.0	3.7	2.5	1.5	5.0	6.5	2.4	0.4
X	0.7	0.7	1.0	0.1	0.7	0.6	0.2	0.04
XI	0.3	0.4	0.4	0.05	0.04	0.1	0.03	—
XII	1.0	0.7	0.8	0.2	0.3	0.4	0.1	—
XIII	2.5	1.4	1.2	0.3	0.4	0.8	0.2	—
XIV	1.0	0.6	1.0	0.2	0.5	0.6	0.2	—
XV	1.5	1.0	1.2	0.2	0.5	1.0	0.2	0.01
XVI	0.8	0.5	0.9	0.1	0.5	0.5	0.1	0.03
XVII	1.5	0.7	0.5	0.2	0.7	0.7	0.1	0.08
XVIII	6.0	1.9	1.1	0.5	0.9	1.4	0.5	0.07
XIX	8.0	3.0	1.6	0.8	1.0	2.4	0.8	0.1
XX	0.9	0.5	0.2	0.2	4.0	2.6	1.5	0.2
XXI	1.0	0.4	0.4	0.1	0.1	0.2	0.2	—
VIENNA	4.4	1.8	1.3	0.5	2.0	2.4	0.9	0.2

*1920 and 1923: *Bürgerliche Arbeitspartei*
       1927: *Demokratische Liste*
       1930: *Demokratische Mittelpartei*
**1920: *Jüdisch-nationale Partei*
    1923: *Jüdische Wahlgemeinschaft*
    1927: *Jüdische Partei*
    1930: *Jüdische Liste*

SOURCES: For 1920 and 1923: *Statistisches Jahrbuch der Stadt Wien, 1929*, published by the City of Vienna, pp. 270-71.
For 1927 and 1930: *Die Nationalratswahlen vom 24. April 1927* and *Die Nationalratswahlen vom 9. November 1930*, published in Vienna by the Bundesamt für Statistik.

The contrast between the Zionist decline in the working-class Twentieth and the Zionist advance in the middle-class districts becomes even more obvious if we compare the developments in the Zionist share of the Jewish vote only.[38] From 1920 to 1923 the Zionist share of the Jewish vote in Vienna increased from 21 per cent to 26 per cent. In 1920, the working-class Twentieth had ranked second highest among the 17 districts in regard to the Zionist share of the Jewish vote. Between

[38]We calculate the Zionist share of the Jewish vote on the assumption that Jewish voting participation did not differ significantly from non-Jewish voting participation. Since voting participation in Vienna is traditionally around 90% such an assumption appears fairly safe and reasonable.

TABLE III

The Municipal Districts of Vienna

Column I: Percentage of Jews according to census of 1934.
Column II: Percentage of privately employed wage earners in industry, trade, commerce, and transportation.
Column IV: Percentage of self-employed professional men.

District	Col. I % of Jews	Col. II* % of male wage earners	Col. III % of domestic help (women)	Col. IV % of professional** men
I	24.1	16.5	18.2	11.8
II	34.0	25.0	4.6	3.4
III	9.2	30.6	5.2	3.6
IV	9.6	18.4	7.8	7.2
V	4.4	37.8	3.0	3.3
VI	15.1	23.2	6.1	5.7
VII	14.8	21.1	5.8	4.8
VIII	13.2	18.5	7.0	7.3
IX	23.3	19.6	6.1	6.3
X	2.3	54.8	1.8	1.2
XI	1.0	50.6	1.6	0.6
XII	2.3	44.5	2.0	2.0
XIII	3.9	33.9	3.6	2.9
XIV	4.3	47.0	1.5	1.4
XV	4.7	37.3	2.1	2.6
XVI	2.7	54.1	1.6	1.5
XVII	3.6	43.0	1.7	1.7
XVIII	6.2	24.6	4.3	4.0
XIX	9.0	29.9	5.5	4.0
XX	15.3	45.7	1.6	1.2
XXI	1.7	52.6	1.6	1.0
VIENNA	9.4	37.2	3.8	3.1

*Wage earners in private employment only.
**Self-employed only.

SOURCES: For Col. I: The official Austrian census of 1934;
for Col. II, III, IV: See Dannenberg, *op. cit.*, p. 50.

1920 and 1923 the Zionist share of the Jewish vote in the Twentieth declined from 27 to 17 per cent and the district became the second lowest in Zionist share of the total Jewish vote.

If we take Vienna's ten districts above the median in middle-class composition we find that all but the Second and the Ninth were in 1920 below the city average regarding the Zionist share of the Jewish vote. In 1923, we find that in seven of these ten districts the Zionist share of the Jewish vote was above its city-wide average.

As a result of the defection of non-Jewish voters from the Liberals and of the defection of working-class Jewish voters from the Zionists we find that in 1927 and in 1930 Vienna's top three districts by proportion of Liberal votes were the First, the Ninth, and the Second, and by Zionist votes the Second, the Ninth, and the First.

These were the only districts with more than 16 per cent Jews,[39] and they ranked eighth, first, and fourth by middle-class composition. Thus we find that votes for the declining Liberal and Zionist Party list declined slowest among the Jewish middle class.

THE JEWISH VOTE FOR THE SOCIALIST PARTY

From the very beginning, as we have seen, socialism had appealed to large numbers of Jewish intellectuals. As the one major party opposed to antisemitism, the Socialists in the First Republic of Austria now also attracted increasing majorities among Jewish voters of all classes at the polls.[40]

Table III shows the municipal districts of Vienna with their proportions of Jews and the proportions of occupational groups that reflect working-class, or middle-class composition respectively. In Table IV we tabulate the Marxist vote in the districts of Vienna for the elections of 1923, 1932, and 1949.

In Table IV we omitted data for the elections in 1920 because the Socialist increase from 47 per cent to 55 per cent in 1923 was fairly evenly distributed over all twenty-one districts, since it nowhere exceeded 10 per cent and nowhere fell below 6 per cent. Table IV shows how the Socialist vote in the non-Jewish working-class districts changed but little from 1923 till 1932, while considerable increases took place in middle-class districts where the proportion of Jews was high. The stability of the Socialist vote in the working-class districts from 1932 till 1949 again contrasts with the Socialist vote drop in the middle-class districts, accounted for by the elimination of the Jews.

We are listing the Communist vote for 1923 and for 1932 in spite of the party's insignificance in order to avoid a false impression and to account for the Socialist decline in the working-class districts.

---

[39]The Second District contained 34% Jews, the First 24%, the Ninth 23%. Cf. Tables II and III.
[40]A similar development can, of course, be traced in the Weimar Republic. On the shifting of the Jewish vote to Social Democracy and the increasing co-operation of Jewish organisations with the German Socialists, see Arnold Paucker, *Der jüdische Abwehrkampf gegen Antisemitismus und Nationalsozialismus in den letzten Jahren der Weimarer Republik* (Hamburger Beiträge zur Zeitgeschichte Band IV), second edition, Hamburg 1969, pp. 89, 90, 96-97, 273, and passim; and by the same author, 'Searchlight on the Decline of the Weimar Republic. The Diaries of Ernst Feder', in *LBI Year Book XIII* (1968), pp. 166, 169. On the Jews and the political parties both in Imperial Germany and in the Weimar Republic, see also Ernest Hamburger, 'One Hundred Years of Emancipation', in *LBI Year Book XIV* (1969), pp. 3-66 passim. Two important publications of the Leo Baeck Institute have dealt with the political allegiances of the German Jews before 1918: Jacob Toury, *Die politischen Orientierungen der Juden in Deutschland. Von Jena bis Weimar*, Tübingen 1966; Ernest Hamburger, *Juden im öffentlichen Leben Deutschlands – Regierungsmitglieder, Beamte und Parlamentarier in der monarchischen Zeit, 1848-1918*, Tübingen 1968 (Schriftenreihe wissenschaftlicher Abhandlungen des Leo Baeck Instituts 15 & 19). – On Jewish political allegiances in the Weimar Republic see also the most recent publication of the Leo Baeck Institute: Ernst Feder, *Heute sprach ich mit . . . Tagebücher eines Berliner Publizisten* 1926-1932, edited by Cécile Lowenthal-Hensel and Arnold Paucker, with a Biographical Index compiled by Ernst G. Lowenthal, Stuttgart 1971, in particular the introduction, pp. 19-23.

Table IV shows clearly that the Socialist advance from 1923 until 1932 was concentrated in the middle-class districts with a larger proportion of Jews. There was the Socialist advance of 18% in the 1st District, of 12% in the 2nd, and of 7% to 8% in the 6th, the 7th, the 8th, and in the 9th. Moderate Socialist advances around 3% appear in all the other middle-class districts, while the Socialist Party actually suffered minor losses in all the working-class districts except the 20th.

In 1949 a drop of 4% since 1932 just about put the Marxist vote of Vienna back to where it had been in 1923. Marxist losses in some of the districts are accounted for by shifts in population not involving Jews, such as the incorporation of non-working-class suburbs into the 13th, the 14th, and the 16th Districts. But on the whole, Socialist losses are heaviest in the formerly Jewish middle-class districts where the Socialist advance had been biggest in 1932.

In order to illustrate the impact of the Jewish middle-class vote upon the proportion of Socialist votes in the 21 districts (pre-war districts) of Vienna we shall

TABLE IV

The Marxist vote in the Districts of Vienna in 1923, 1932, and 1949

(Left of comma the Socialist percentage. Right of comma the Communist percentage)

	1923		1932			1949		
District	% Soc.	% Com.	% Soc.	% Com.	Difference 1932-1923	% Soc.	% Com.	Difference 1949-1932
I	26.0,	0.0	43.8,	—	+18	26,	4	—14
II	53.4,	0.8	65.2,	1.3	+12	47,	11	— 8
III	46.8,	0.8	51.1,	1.0	+ 3	44,	6	— 2
IV	29.4,	0.2	35.8,	0.4	+ 6	34,	5	+ 3
V	54.1,	0.9	57.5,	1.2	+ 4	48,	6	— 5
VI	40.3,	0.2	46.7,	0.5	+ 7	37,	5	— 5
VII	37.3,	0.3	44.8,	0.4	+ 8	35,	5	— 5
VIII	33.8,	0.4	41.1,	0.6	+ 7	36,	4	— 1
IX	45.2,	0.4	53.6,	0.6	+ 8	40,	5	— 8
X	70.3,	2.5	71.3,	3.6	+ 2	66,	12	+ 3
XI	66.2,	1.4	67.9,	1.3	+ 2	62,	9	+ 2
XII	60.9,	1.4	64.1,	2.0	+ 4	58,	8	0
XIII	54.6,	2.0	57.7,	2.0	+ 3	39,	6	—15
XIV	64.3,	1.6	64.1,	2.6	+ 1	54,	8	— 5
XV	55.1,	0.8	56.9,	1.5	+ 2	55,	7	+ 5
XVI	68.9,	3.0	66.5,	4.3	— 1	59,	9	— 2
XVII	58.4,	1.8	57.2,	2.7	0	50,	7	— 3
XVIII	41.9,	0.4	44.7,	0.9	+ 4	38,	5	— 3
XIX	49.1,	0.6	53.4,	1.1	+ 6	43,	5	— 7
XX	69.4,	1.8	71.4,	2.3	+ 3	65,	9	0
XXI	69.0,	1.7	68.9,	2.1	0	58,	12	— 1
VIENNA	54.9,	1.3	59.0,	1.9	+ 5	49,	8	— 4

SOURCES: For the data of 1923: Dannenberg, *op. cit.*, p. 19.
For 1932: Hans Riemer, *Auf dem Wege zur Mehrheit*, Vienna 1946, pp. 20-21.
For 1949: official election statistics published by Österreichisches Statistisches Zentralamt.

(in Table IV) rank the districts in three adjacent columns as follows: by percentage of industrial workers employed in private industry, by percentage of Socialist votes in 1923, and by percentage of Socialist votes in 1932.

If we compare the rank order of the districts of Vienna as tabulated in Table V with respect to working-class composition and with respect to the Socialist vote we notice, first of all, the nearly perfect correlation between the rank order by industrial workers and the rank order by Socialist vote in 1923. We have circled the four districts with more than 15% Jews and we notice that as early as 1923 the 20th, the 2nd, and the 9th ranked higher in their Socialist vote than in their percentage of workers. This becomes a great deal intensified in the elections of 1932 Not only do we find that the 20th, the 2nd, the 9th, and the 1st rank a great deal higher in their Socialist votes than in their working-class composition, but also that these shifts in rank are accompanied by shifts in the opposite direction in the comparatively non-Jewish middle-class 3rd, 4th, 8th, and 18th.

As further statistics on the Jewish vote we may quote the 1930 election figures for Unter-Eisenstadt, a suburb of Eisenstadt, the capital of Burgenland.[41] According to the census of 1934[42] there were 225 Jews among Unter-Eisenstadt's population

TABLE V

The 21 Districts of Vienna, ranked according to their proportion of industrial workers and according to their proportion of Socialist votes in 1923 and in 1932

By % of Workers	By % Socialist in 1923	By % Socialist in 1932
X	X	(XX)
XVI	(XX)	X
XXI	XXI	XXI
XI	XVI	XI
XIV	·XI	XVI
(XX)	XIV	(II)
XII	XII	XIV
XVII	XVII	XII
V	XV	XIII
XV	XIII	V
XIII	V	XVII
III	(II)	XV
XIX	XIX	XIX
(II)	(IX)	(IX)
XVIII	III	III
VI	XVIII	VI
VII	VI	VII
(IX)	VII	XVIII
VIII	VIII	(I)
IV	IV	VIII
(I)	(I)	IV

Districts in ( ) were more than 15% Jewish.

[41]*Die Ergebnisse der Volkszählung vom 22. März 1934*, p. 48.
[42]*Die Nationalratswahlen vom 9. November 1930, op. cit.*, pp. 148-149.

of 364. Of 217 registered voters 179 cast their ballots, 172 for the Socialist Party, 4 for the *Christlich-Sozialen,* and 3 for Schober's moderately German-nationalist fusion list of candidates.

OTHER ASPECTS OF THE JEWISH VOTE

In order to sift the evidence as to whether or not there was a Jewish vote for moderate German-nationalism in 1930, and for the pro-clerical *Christlich-Sozialen* in 1932, we shall now analyse in greater detail the election results of the 1st District in contrast with the results for Vienna as a whole. In doing this we keep in mind that the 1st District was 24.1% Jewish and mostly upper-class in its composition.

We can account for the Nazi vote of 201,411 in Vienna on the 24th April 1932 by looking at the election results in Vienna, on the 9th November 1930. On that day the Nazis polled 27,540 votes in Vienna, the fascist *Heimatblock* polled 26,377, Schober's moderately German-nationalist grouping received 124,375 votes, and the *Christlich-Soziale Partei* 282,879. The Nazi gain of 174,000 appears just about accounted for by the vote of the then eliminated fascist *Heimatblock,* by the vote of Schober's party (but for the 8,850 who voted in 1932 for the pan-German *Großdeutsche Volkspartei*), and by the 30,000 votes lost by the *Christlich-Sozialen.* In every district in Vienna the 1932 vote for the Nazis results from 100% of the 1930 vote of Schober's ticket, plus the vote for the Nazis and the *Heimatblock,* plus anywhere up to 25% of the 1930 vote for the *Christlich-Soziale Partei.*

In all the districts of Vienna but the 1st District, we find that the Nazi vote of 1932 exceeded the total combined 1930 vote of Schober plus Nazis plus *Heimatblock,* just as in Vienna as a whole. In the 1st District we find for 1930 a Schober vote of 4,267, a *Heimatblock* vote of 699, and a Nazi vote of 446. The Nazi vote of 1932 in the 1st District came to 3,579; this is about half of what the Nazi vote would have been, had the 1932 vote of the 1st District developed from the 1930 elections as it did in such middle-class districts as the 8th, the 4th, and the 18th. The 1st District had been traditionally unfavourable towards German nationalism in the First Republic with the exception of the elections in 1930. This suggests that Schober's moderate German-nationalist group did indeed succeed in attracting Jewish middle-class votes, as it was considered an effective barrier to further Nazi advance.

From 1930 until 1932 the vote of the *Christlich-Sozialen* in the whole of Vienna dropped from 23.72% to 20.16%. In none of the working-class districts (the 10th, 12th, 14th, 15th, 16th, 20th, and 21st) did the drop exceed 3%. In the working-class 11th there was even a gain of about 300 votes and 1.4%. In middle-class districts the losses of the *Christlich-Sozialen* were high, 6% in the 18th, and 5% in the 2nd, 3rd, 4th, and 8th.

In the whole of Vienna and especially in the city's middle-class districts the vote for the *Christlich-Sozialen* in 1932 had reached an all-time low. Meanwhile the proportion of votes for the *Christlich-Sozialen* had increased in the 1st District from

1930 until 1932 from 33.82% to 36.94%, while the vote itself had declined from 8,018 to 7,522. The discrepancy between developments in the 1st District and in other middle-class districts and the city as a whole strongly suggests that the *Christlich-Soziale Partei* had also attracted Jewish voters in the upper-class 1st District in 1930 as well as in 1932.

SUMMARY

The Jews entered Austrian politics as ardent champions of liberalism. They were among the revolutionaries of 1848, and they were among the founders and leaders of the Liberal Party that became dominant after the enactment of the Constitution of 1867.

The defection of the German-nationalist chauvinists and the extension of suffrage to non-propertied wage earners eliminated political liberalism as a decisive factor in Austrian politics. In the provinces of Imperial Austria which in 1918 were to form the Austrian Republic liberalism was replaced by socialism, clericalism, and German-nationalism. None of these appealed to middle-class Jews.

Our analysis of election data indicates that some of the Jews in the upper-class First District of Vienna voted in 1930 for a moderate German-nationalist list that was to lose just about all its non-Jewish votes to the Nazis within seventeen months; some of the Jews in that district seem to have supported the *Christlich-Sozialen* in 1932. Fluctuations in the Socialist vote in Vienna's middle-class districts leave no doubt that in 1932 the bulk of the Jewish middle-class voters voted Socialist. The Socialist Party was the only major party without overt antisemitic tendencies, but its Marxist ideology made it unattractive to Jews in finance and business (also, the Jewish self-hatred of Jewish Socialist leaders rendered the Socialist Party even less effective as a possible shield against antisemitism).

In the First Republic of Austria political preference correlated highly with economic class. The comparative lack of such correlation in the case of the Jewish vote may serve as an index of the extent to which the Jewish voters had become alienated from their society:[43] none of the three major parties solicited their support at the polls.

---

[43]For a discussion of the general implications of this relationship see Walter B. Simon, 'Integration and Apartness of Minority Groups as Reflected in Election Results', *The Sociological Quarterly*, vol. 3, No. 2, April 1962, pp. 123-134.

German Socialists and the Jewish Question in the Weimar Republic*

BY GEORGE L. MOSSE

It has been asserted that in the final phase of the Weimar Republic the Jewish question played a minor rôle in the propaganda and journalism of the Left.[1] This statement could be extended to cover the whole period of the Republic, for while Leftist thought on the Jewish question varied in the emphasis given to it, the theories on which it was based remained much the same from the end of the First World War to the Nazi seizure of power. But while, as we shall see, there is some truth in the contention that the Jewish question played a minor rôle in Leftist thought, it did so only as the peak of an iceberg which determined the attitudes of the Left towards the Jewish problem. That problem was an integral part of a general theory about man and society, and as such it was highly significant during the Republic, and is of topical interest even today. Not only does an analysis of the Jewish question in this context throw some light upon a much-neglected phase of socialist theory and action, but it also affected the position of German Jews embattled against Rightist antisemitism.

What sort of Left should concern us here? The Social Democratic Party, obviously, and the Communists as well. But in addition we must pay some attention to the left-wing intellectuals, most of whom were themselves Jewish. But before we analyse these various positions on the Jewish question we must be aware of socialist theory as it had been elaborated earlier, for all discussions on the Jewish question during the Republic originate in pre-war socialism, a necessary background to which they had to relate.

I

The foundations for modern German socialist thought on the Jewish question were laid by Karl Kautsky. This "pope" of the pre-war *Sozialdemokratische Partei Deutschlands* (SPD) set the tone for discussions about Jewish assimilation and Zionism even when, after 1914, he himself had fallen out of favour. The "German" must be emphasised here although, as we shall see, Kautsky's analyses of the Jewish

---

* This is a considerably expanded version of a paper delivered in June 1970 at the Conference on Research into the History of Central European Jewry from the Emancipation to its Destruction, organised by the Jerusalem Leo Baeck Institute.

[1] Hans-Helmuth Knütter, 'Die Linksparteien [zur Judenfrage]', in *Entscheidungsjahr 1932. Zur Judenfrage in der Endphase der Weimarer Republik*. Ein Sammelband herausgegeben von Werner E. Mosse unter Mitwirkung von Arnold Paucker, Tübingen 1965, 1966 (Schriftenreihe wissenschaftlicher Abhandlungen des Leo Baeck Instituts 13).

question were spread beyond German-speaking countries by such men as Lenin and Stalin. In France, however, as George Lichtheim has shown, the foundation for a hostile socialist view of the Jewish question was laid as early as the decades following the French Revolution. Edmund Silberner has demonstrated the existence of German socialist antisemitism up to the First World War, but its direction was different from that of many French Socialists. The Marxist tradition prevailed in Germany, but not in France, where the anti-Jewish attitudes of men like Fourier and Proudhon could have greater scope.[2] We should be careful, then, with the use of the word "antisemitism" for, in Germany at least, what might be regarded as hostility towards the Jews was always part of a larger socialist doctrine which, whatever its immediate effects, looked towards a future society where all mankind would live in peace and equality.

Karl Marx had been the first to deal with the Jewish question, but it was Kautsky who produced its modern socialist formulation. His first important contribution to the Jewish problem was an article, written in 1903, called 'The Massacre of Kishinev and the Jewish Question'. Here, as in his later writings, his ideas were based on Karl Marx's pamphlet on the Jewish question written half a century earlier. Kautsky accepted the thesis that Jews, through the evolution of their history, had become the representatives of the worst aspects of capitalism: the fetichism of goods, love of money and devotion to commerce. Judaism as a religion was merely the objectification of commercial transactions.[3] Kautsky's own contribution to this analysis did not change its fundamental direction but provided an updating of Marx's mid-nineteenth century tract. Jews are an urban people — Kautsky again and again emphasises this point — and as city dwellers show all the peculiarities of their milieu, not only in trade but intellectually as well. In his later book, *Rasse und Judentum* (Race and Judaism), 1914, he attributes the negative, critical and "dissolving" *(zersetzend)* spirit of Jews to this milieu.[4] Both Marx and Kautsky continued a tradition begun in the Enlightenment of the eighteenth century. The Jew who was faithful to his Jewishness was wholly corrupt, an evil force in society, who must be re-educated to shed his Judaism and enter the age of progress and enlightenment. Marx did not stress the re-education of the Jews, but believed that Judaism would end only with the fall of capitalism. Kautsky, for whom a revolution was far in the future, was closer to the Enlightenment when he wrote that the Jewish masses have to be enlightened in order to counteract their Judaism. For both Marx and Kautsky the Jews' supposed lack of humanity was of crucial concern. Jews were alienated from their own humanity by their intimate involvement with capitalism and with their religion. Eugene Kamenka has stressed the young Marx's preoccupation with human dignity, which was at its height at the

---

[2]George Lichtheim, 'Socialism and the Jews', *Dissent*, July-August 1968, pp. 314-342; Edmund Silberner, *Sozialisten zur Judenfrage*, Berlin 1962.

[3]Karl Kautsky, 'Das Massaker von Kischeneff und die Judenfrage', *Die Neue Zeit*, XXI, vol. 2 (1902/03), pp. 303-309. Although this article had the greatest impact, Kautsky had witten another article, 'Über das Judentum', in *Die Neue Zeit*, VIII (1890), pp. 23-30, in which he put forward the same theses in a less complete analysis.

[4]Karl Kautsky, *Rasse und Judentum*, 2nd edition, Stuttgart 1921, p. 70.

very time he was writing his tract on the Jewish question. Emphasis on human dignity, coupled with opposition to servility, was deeply entrenched in the socialist tradition: the Jew seen as an urban merchant, linked to the ghetto both physically and spiritually, typified a state of dependence which perpetuated the feudal Middle Ages within the dialectical progress of mankind.[5]

The "vanishing of Judaism" is a phrase of Kautsky's which was to be repeated by many Socialists. It means not only the vanishing of the Jewish religion, but also an end to the "Jewish peculiarities" of devotion to commerce and the "negative" spirit.[6]

Kautsky always looked at the Jews from the standpoint of Western culture to which the Socialists, despite their revolutionary vocabulary, were deeply committed. The enlightenment of the East European Jewish masses would serve to elevate them to the plateau of Western culture, a viewpoint which Kautsky shared with his liberal contemporaries. Jews everywhere must become "modern people", as he put it in *Rasse und Judentum*, and he fully accepted the stereotype of the ghetto as it had grown up in the nineteenth century.[7] Moreover, physical factors were taken into consideration, and Kautsky (though he attempted to minimise them) wrote with enthusiasm about the necessary infusion of fresh peasant blood to strengthen the physical constitution of Jewish city dwellers. Finally, Jews are always "strangers", and thus it seems only logical that they cease to be strangers by intermixing with the local population.[8]

Given these premises, the rejection of Zionism was a logical consequence. For Kautsky, the Zionist movement merely reinforced "Jewish peculiarities" and Jewish isolation. In his own mind that movement was connected with the ghetto and the commercialism of the "medieval" Jewish religion.[9] Kautsky never changed his mind on Zionism or, indeed, on the Jewish question in general. At the very time when his own star was being eclipsed in the socialist movement, his analysis of the Jewish question received new impetus. For the article on the Kishinev massacre was received with enthusiasm by Lenin. He not only reprinted it in *Iskra*, but based his own analysis of the Jewish question largely on Kautsky's earlier article. Stalin, in turn, took over the argument in his own work on nationalities which stated that

---

[5]*Ibid.*, pp. 108, 55; Karl Kautsky, 'Das Massaker von Kischeneff und die Judenfrage', *loc. cit.*, p. 306; Eugene Kamenka, *Marxism and Ethics*, London and New York 1969, p. 9. While much nonsense has been written about Marx's *Judenfrage*, David McLelland's *The Young Hegelians and Karl Marx*, London 1969, puts the tract in its proper chronological and ideological setting. As a matter of fact, Marx borrowed heavily from Moses Hess's article 'On the Essence of Money'. Hess and Marx both agreed in viewing money as the primary symbol of alienation, and on their solution to the Jewish problem. McLelland even holds that Marx copied Hess's ideas at this stage. *Ibid.*, p. 158. Marx's attitude on the Jewish question was not unusual at the time but, unlike Hess, he remained constant in his advocacy of the ideas he had put forward in 1844.
[6]Kautsky, 'Das Massaker von Kischeneff und die Judenfrage', p. 304.
[7]Kautsky, *Rasse und Judentum*, p. 107. For the ghetto stereotype see George L. Mosse, *Germans and Jews. The Right, the Left, and the Search for a "Third Force" in Pre-Nazi Germany*, New York 1970, pp. 44-46.
[8]Kautsky, 'Das Massaker von Kischeneff und die Judenfrage', pp. 305, 306.
[9]Kautsky, *Rasse und Judentum*, pp. 83 ff.

Jewish nationhood and nationality must be denied,[10] and had Lenin's full blessing. Surely, given his premises, Kautsky was correct in asserting that Jews must not merely move from one medieval ruin (capitalism) to another (Zionism). Their disappearance would not be a tragedy, like that of the Red Indians or the Tasmanians; instead it would lead to greater strength, well-being, and prosperity.[11]

From a socialist standpoint such ideas were fully justified. The end product of socialism was to be a new man, a new humanity, encompassing Jews as well as all mankind once capitalism had been abolished. "Where the Jew is regarded as free and equal he vanishes." Socialist theory was reinforced by Lamarckian theories of biological evolution. The materialist and environmental explanation of how life on this planet evolved helped to explain how Jews could shed their "Jewish" characteristics with the triumph of socialism.[12]

Jews were destined to a process of denationalization. Kautsky had already added to his other arguments in the 'Kischeneff Massaker' the fact that Jews had lost their own territory hundreds of years ago. Moreover, ever since 1887 Kautsky had clung to the idea that a common language is necessary in order to make a nation. The importance of language he traced to economic roots.[13] Obviously the Jews had no such recognised common language to offer, for they spoke not only Yiddish but also, for the most part, the languages of the host nations. Historical claims to Jewish nationality could not be accepted as valid by Socialists. Austrian Marxists like Otto Bauer agreed with Kautsky's arguments. More important still, Lenin and Stalin were ready to grant such autonomy to other suppressed nationalities, but not to the Jews, who were not granted separate political rights. They applied Kautsky's theories to the Jewish question — an analysis which did not apply to other peoples either in the Soviet Union or elsewhere.

These views on the Jewish question and Jewish nationality remained the prevailing opinion among Socialists until the end of the First World War. When, for example, in 1916 the Zionist labour movement, *Poale Zion*, was finally admitted to

---

[10]See Werner Blumenberg, *Karl Kautsky's Literarisches Werk*, The Hague 1960. For Kautsky's influence on Lenin and Stalin see Marc Jarblum, *Le Problème Juif dans la théorie et practique du Communisme*, Paris 1935, p. 18; the influence of Kautsky is obvious in their works, and he is cited with respect. Both, however, devote more space to Otto Bauer's analysis of the nationalities question, partly because he disagreed with them on certain points. Both were, above all, concerned to polemize against the *Bund*; W. I. *Lenin über die Nationale und die Koloniale Nationale Frage*, Berlin 1960, especially pp. 143, 147; Stalin, *Marxismus und Nationale Frage*, Vienna n.d., especially pp. 40, 51. In spite of these critiques of Bauer, this leader of Austrian Social Democracy as well as many others of that party shared Kautsky's basic views on the Jewish question, and carried them over into the post-war world through their discussions of the ever-present Austrian nationalities problem. However, we are here concerned with Germany and not with Austria. On Bauer, see Introduction by Robert Weltsch to *LBI Year Book IV* (1959), pp. XVIII-XIX.

[11]Kautsky, *Rasse und Judentum*, p. 108.

[12]*Ibid.*, p. 73. Hugo Iltis, Kautsky's friend and admirer, expressed his open agreement with the fundamentals of Lamarckianism. Hugo Iltis to Karl Kautsky, 9th April 1930, Kautsky Familien-Archiv, Portf. 3, Mappe 4; International Archive for Social History, Amsterdam.

[13]Hans-Ulrich Wehler, *Sozialdemokratie und Nationalstaat*, Würzburg 1962, p. 198.

the Second International, it entered as a national organisation of Palestinians and not as a representative of proletarian Zionist Jewry.[14]

Kautsky's major work on the subject, *Rasse und Judentum*, first published in 1914 and republished in 1921, added nothing new to his original analysis. It apparently did not sell well, and in spite of Kautsky's repeated urging was not republished again.[15] The reason for this failure may lie in Kautsky's own increasingly isolated position within socialism. The Social Democrats were having a change of heart about the Jewish question, as we shall see, and the Communists were publishing their own literature which derived from the early Kautsky but ignored the old Kautsky who had refused to join their party. Certainly the subject itself never lacked interest in Germany.

Disappointed, the ageing Socialist published a new article on Zionism after the Palestine massacres of 1929.[16] These events seemed to him to confirm his analyses of Zionism; not only was it a movement of the Jewish petty bourgeoisie, as he had held in *Rasse und Judentum*, but it had proved to be an unrealiseable Utopia. The Jews in the Holy Land were the victims of the Zionist movement, closely linked with the imperialist aims of British policy. Yet here Kautsky seems to be weakening. The blanket condemnation of Jewish nationalism is replaced by the statement that Zionism is attractive as a solution to the persecution of Jews, but that Palestine is not the land where this can be accomplished. It is too small and not fertile enough. Moreover, Islamic culture predominates and the Jews are Europeans. One wonders what has become of the mass of primitive Jews who must first be raised to the level of Western culture. Kautsky now admires the Zionist pioneers, but deplores their useless sacrifice. All this does not prevent him from repeating almost word for word his earlier analyses of the Jewish question.

With the passing of time Kautsky seemed to be weakening in his polemics and in his hopes. At the same time that he wrote his article after the Palestine massacres he received a circular letter from Ben Gurion and Eleazar Kaplan asking him to join in founding a united socialist party in Erez Israel. There is no record of his reply. It is certain that in 1937, by now an exile, he was on very friendly terms with Berl Locker of the General Federation of Jewish Labour in Palestine.[17] Kautsky must have felt deeply the Nazi onslaught upon the Jews. But for all the scattered evidence of a certain new ambivalence in his attitude, there was no fundamental

[14] Arjeh Tatakower, 'Zur Geschichte des Jüdischen Sozialismus V. Vom Ausbruch des Weltkriegs bis zur Nachwirkung der Russischen Revolution', *Der Jude*, VIII (1924), pp. 642, 643.
[15] At least in 1929 the publisher and a party newspaper in Leipzig still possessed a good many copies which they wanted to sell. This was the reason why the Dietz publishing house did not want to republish it at that time, as Kautsky was urging. Adolf Schultz to Karl Kautsky, 18th April 1929, International Archive of Social History, Amsterdam, K.D. IX, 62; Adolf Schultz to Karl Kautsky, 18th May 1929, International Archive for Social History, Amsterdam, K.D. IX, 64.
[16] Karl Kautsky, 'Die Aussichten des Zionismus', International Archive for Social History, Amsterdam, K.A. 154. The article was printed in *Vorwärts* on the 4th and 6th October, 1929.
[17] Hectographed invitation, 12th December 1929, International Archive for Social History, Amsterdam, K.D. IV, 128; Berl Locker to *Chaverim* Louise and Karl Kautsky, 18th September 1937, International Archive for Social History, Amsterdam, K.D. XVI, 30.

change in his outlook. Indeed the muted tone of the article of 1929 may have been due to quite a different factor. Kautsky realised sharply that the socialist consensus on the Jewish question and Zionism was dissolving. He wrote this article, at least in part, in order to put an end within socialism to divided attitudes about this "romantic and reactionary Utopia".[18] That this division affected his own Social Democrats must have been especially painful to him. That the Communists continued his line of thought on the Jewish question must have seemed equally distressing to one who hated the "Bolshevist terror".

II

Under the pressure of growing antisemitism and reaction many Social Democrats began to have a change of heart. Anton Fendrich, a party publicist after 1918, may have been at least partially correct when he wrote, in 1920, that Marx's work on the Jewish question had always been rejected by those Social Democrats who were capable of a greater spirituality. For Fendrich, Social Democrats rejected the bitter judgments heaped upon the Jews by Marx, the convert and missionary. But he also believed that Germans and Jews must be united through the emergence of a new species of man.[19] Indeed it must have seemed after the war that Marx's Jewish stereotypes would play into the hands of the racists. Antisemitism was on the rise and this was clearly connected with the thrust of the Right against the new Republic. At that moment, shortly after the end of the war, Social Democratic criticism of the traditional Marxist analysis of the Jewish problem started. The Communists never followed the Social Democrats along this road, and instead published a new edition of Marx's work on the Jewish question. Within Social Democracy a different trend was to emerge which not only liquidated Marx's own standpoint but also the older socialist attitudes towards Zionism.

For example, Paul Kampfmeyer, one of the chief Social Democratic writers against antisemitism, sought to demolish the idea that Jews were wedded to the spirit of usury and materialism. After all, he wrote, Marx himself, although he was a Jew, had nothing of this spirit. His system originated in the philosophy of German idealism: for him the negative Jewish spirit did not exist. Marxism was flexible and German. Typically enough Kampfmeyer was influenced by Ferdinand Lassalle as much as by Karl Marx. He condemned the "Bolshevist terror" and the soldiers' and workers' councils which had sprung up briefly during the German revolution of 1918. Red terror, he held, always ended in white terror. Though his patriotism made him condemn the Treaty of Versailles and see in the French a continuing "enemy", his defence of the Weimar Republic and of the Jews was straightforward and unambiguous.[20] Such a defence by the Social Democrats could be combined

[18]Kautsky, 'Die Aussichten des Zionismus', *loc. cit.*, p. 2.
[19]Anton Fendrich, *Der Judenhass und der Sozialismus*, Freiburg i. Br. 1920, II, p. 19.
[20]Paul Kampfmeyer, *Streifzüge durch die Theorie und Praxis der Arbeiterbewegung*, Stuttgart 1907, p. 3; Kampfmeyer, *Die Sozialdemokratie im Lichte der Kulturentwicklung*, Berlin 1920, p. 147;

with a stress upon the "German" nature of Social Democratic Marxism as well as with a rejection of "materialism". (It should be added that much of the material the Social Democrats used in combatting antisemitism stemmed from Jewish sources.) These arguments were often repeated by Social Democrats in the early post-war years, usually combined with an appeal to the solidarity of the oppressed, though it must be added that at times the physical stereotype was accepted only to be brushed aside in the name of a common humanity.[21]

Eduard Bernstein, the revisionist, played a leading part in changing the accepted picture of Jews and Zionists. During his youth the normal world had seemed to him non-Jewish, and the Jewish world abnormal. Just before the war he had also condemned Zionism as an ecstasy which would pass, though it had found its way into the heads of some Socialists who he felt should have known better.[22] Bernstein was, no doubt, encouraged in this stand by his general aversion to nationalism, though this was never without ambivalence. The First World War and its aftermath changed his views; and Kautsky was right in deploring the fact that the war had given Zionism a new beginning.[23] But, typically enough, in revising his stand on Zionism, Bernstein also liquidated Marx's and Kautsky's picture of the Jews as a whole. For though the earlier Socialists (and later the Communists) attempted to distinguish between Jews and the reactionary Zionist Utopia, their viewpoint towards Zionism and the Jews proved to be organically linked.

Bernstein's bridge to a re-evaluation of his position was the Austrian view of the nationalities question elaborated by Karl Renner and Otto Bauer. For Bernstein, nationality had always been a sociological fact which Socialists could not ignore. Now he held that the concept of national autonomy surpassed ideas of socialist centralism in their democratic potential. Jews should, if they so desired, be granted "Jewish nationality" within individual European countries, a situation which might eventually lead to the establishment of a Jewish state. This argument was in line with much of the ideas of the Zionist movement, as was his contention that all nationalism was only a step towards the organisation of humanity as a whole.[24]

Kampfmeyer, *Jüdischer Marxismus*, Berlin 1923, pp. 4, 5, 7. Similar arguments to those of Kampfmeyer were made from the Jewish side in a leaflet of the C.V. See Arnold Paucker, *Der jüdische Abwehrkampf gegen Antisemitismus und Nationalsozialismus in den letzten Jahren der Weimarer Republik* (Hamburger Beiträge zur Zeitgeschichte Band IV), second edition, Hamburg 1969, p. 208.

[21] *Was muss das schaffende Volk vom politischen, wirtschaftlichen, religiösen Juden- und Rassenhass des reaktionären Faschismus wissen?* Für Redner und Funktionäre, herausgegeben von der Sozialdemokratischen Partei Deutschlands, Ortsverein Hannover 1924. — It has been pointed out to me by Arnold Paucker that this Social Democratic pamphlet is to a very large extent based on defence material of the *Centralverein deutscher Staatsbürger jüdischen Glaubens*. According to his C.V. informants it was probably supplied in toto as was also most of the propaganda material on the Jewish Question (and much of that on Nazism) distributed by the SPD, *Reichsbanner*, etc. during the last years of the Republic.

[22] Eduard Bernstein, 'Der Schulstreit in Palästina', *Die Neue Zeit*, XXXII, vol. I (1914), p. 752; Bernstein, 'Wie ich als Jude in der Diaspora aufwuchs', *Der Jude*, II (1917/18), p. 191.

[23] Kautsky, 'Die Aussichten des Zionismus', *loc. cit.*, p. 2.

[24] Eduard Bernstein, in *Sozialistische Monatshefte*, June 1907; 'Die demokratische Staatsidee und die Jüdische Nationalbewegung', MS. in the International Archive for Social History, Amsterdam, A. 114.

Bernstein became an ardent champion of Zionism: "a free human community on free soil."[25] He aided the *Poale Zion* in its quest for entry into the Second International. Salman Rubashow (Zalman Shazar, now President of Israel) wrote that when Kautsky made accusations against this Jewish proletarian party, Bernstein came to its defence.[26] As late as 1930 the secretary of the Socialist Committee for a Labour Palestine asked for Bernstein's support in the executive of the Socialist International against attacks by Otto Bauer and Victor Adler.[27] Obviously Bernstein was an important contact for the *Poale Zion*. In gratitude Rubashow linked together what he considered to be "three great Jews": Lassalle, Marx, and Bernstein.[28] Bernstein's sympathy for Zionism also led him to adopt a positive attitude towards the masses of East European Jewry. Contrary to Marx or Kautsky, Bernstein considered these Jewish masses, still involved in their ghetto, on the whole just as "moral" as the Germans.[29] He carried his regard for the downtrodden masses to its logical conclusion. Certainly a defence of the ghetto Jews runs through some, but by no means all, Social Democratic literature. It enabled Socialists like Bernstein to engage in a straightforward defence against the forces of antisemitism, for most Social Democrats refused to concede the reality of a Jewish stereotype.

The close relationship between such men of the SPD's moderate right wing and Jewish efforts at self-defence should not be surprising. Arnold Paucker has documented this fact, and has shown how the Social Democratic press consistently used material given to it by the *Centralverein deutscher Staatsbürger jüdischen Glaubens* (C.V.), the Jewish defence group. This did not hold true for other German political parties. Typically enough, this relationship dated only from the end of the First World War, and became increasingly more intimate after the elections of 1930.[30] The change of heart on the Jewish question not only encompasses Zionism, but also collaboration with Jewish non-Zionist and anti-Zionist efforts at self-defence.

Bernstein's views were shared and forcefully expressed by men important in the Socialist International, like Paul Löbe, Camille Huysmans, and Émile Vandervelde. Löbe, the Social Democratic President of the *Reichstag*, admitted that the Social Democrats had been critical of Zionist experiments. But by 1929 he believed that Zionism was of the greatest significance for International Socialism. For unlike the Bolshevik regime in Russia, Zionist Socialists attempted to bring about a new society without the use of force. Others also took the opportunity of the 1929 Palestine riots in order to proclaim their support.

The French right-wing Socialist Renaudet republished Kautsky's 'Die Aussichten des Zionismus' in his journal *La Vie Socialiste* in 1929. Both Huysmans and Vander-

---

[25]Eduard Bernstein, review of Émile Vandervelde, *Schaffendes Palästina*, handwritten MS. in the International Archive for Social History, Amsterdam, A. 126.

[26]Salman Rubaschow, *Eduard Bernstein*, MS. in the International Archive for Social History, Amsterdam, B. 23, p. 8.

[27]Marc Jarblum to Eduard Bernstein, 20th April 1930, International Archive for Social History, Amsterdam, D. 305.

[28]Rubaschow, *op. cit.*, p. 7.

[29]Eduard Bernstein, 'Die Ostjuden in Deutschland', International Archive for Social History, Amsterdam, A. 790.

[30]Paucker, *op. cit.*, pp. 57, 95, 96.

velde answered Kautsky in that same issue. Huysmans, while stressing the fertility of Palestine, also broke a lance for Utopias in general. Vandervelde believed that Zionists did not practise traditional colonization, but that between fellaheen and Chaluzim there was a community of interests directed against all capitalists.[31] Vandervelde was sent to Palestine by a Zionist committee; in his book, *Le Pays d'Israël* (1929), subtitled *A Marxist in Palestine*, he not only repeats his faith in the building of a socialist state in that country, but also praises "one of the most wonderful idealistic efforts of our time". The failure of assimilation and the continued oppression of Jews was evidence of the need for a Jewish state. The vitality of the Zionist ideology was proof against the Bolsheviks (and Kautsky, it would be safe to add) who believed that economic considerations played a primary rôle in solving the Jewish question.[32] It should be added that it was Huysmans, the secretary of the Second International, who sponsored the admission of *Poale Zion* into that organisation during the First World War.[33]

Clearly an important cadre of Social Democratic leadership, then, was pro-Zionist after the war, taking a firm and unbending stance against all antisemitism. These men stood, for the most part, on the right wing of their respective parties, for their attitude implied a break not only with Marx's own view on the Jewish question but with orthodox socialism as it had developed since Marx's death. Their attitude on the Jewish question was part of a more general revisionism which tended towards gradualism, while those who moved further to the left put their faith in revolution and in the ideal of the new man. Revolutionary socialism desired to put an end to Jews and Judaism. We shall come back to such movements, but even for Social Democracy the path was never as straight as men like Bernstein would have it.

In 1933 Kurt Blumenfeld, a leading German Zionist, declared that hardly any Jewish Social Democrats were being appointed to public positions. To be sure, he made this statement with respect to every German political party, and at a time when Hitler had just become Chancellor in a coalition government. Blumenfeld concluded that now Jews would have to become conscious of their Jewishness and keep their distance from the German world.[34] For all his obvious partisanship, there is truth to his contention. Nevertheless, the Social Democrats never tried to beat the Nazis at their own game by adopting a nationalist stance, as the Communists did

[31]'Socialisme et Sionisme', *La Vie Socialiste*, VII, Série Nouvelle No. 168 (14th December 1929), pp. 7, 9. — For Löbe see *Die blutigen Ereignisse in Palästina (1929) und der Internationale Sozialismus*, Vienna n.d., p. 79.

[32]Émile Vandervelde, *Le Pays d'Israël. Un Marxiste en Palestine*, Paris 1929, pp. 9, 11.

[33]H. H. Van Kol, *La Démocratie Socialiste Internationale et le Sionisme*, Lausanne 1919, p. 5. He also documents the change in Socialist attitudes after the war. Jean Longuet supported the *Poale Zion, ibid.*, pp. 4, 11.

[34]Kurt Blumenfeld, 'Die Zionistische Haltung', *Jüdische Rundschau*, XXXVIII, No. 17 (28th February 1933), p. 81; the SPD's reluctance to nominate Jewish candidates is also referred to in the contribution by Werner Jochmann, 'Die Ausbreitung des Antisemitismus', in *Deutsches Judentum in Krieg und Revolution 1916-1923. Ein Sammelband herausgegeben von Werner E. Mosse unter Mitwirkung von Arnold Paucker*, Tübingen 1971 (Schriftenreihe wissenschaftlicher Abhandlungen des Leo Baeck Instituts 25), pp. 498/99; he also gives an excellent bibliography on the antisemitic currents in the KPD for the years 1920-1924, on p. 498, n. 331.

during the last years of the Republic. The pressures upon the Social Democrats were more subtle, and they resisted them as best they could. The obvious successes of the German Right in their use of antisemitic actions and slogans put the Social Democrats ever more on the defensive. It had already been said in some of their pamphlets that Marxism could not be a mere "Jewish" concept because Engels, after all, was a Christian.[35] For example, the SPD police president of Berlin, Albert Grzesinski, instituted legal actions against those who "insulted him" by spreading the rumour of his Jewish descent. As Grzesinski wrote to the editor of the *Vorwärts* (who was Jewish himself): by spreading the rumour that he was the product of an affair between his servant-girl mother and the Jew Cohen, the rumour-mongers were insulting his mother and presenting him as a *Judenstämmling*."[36] By 1932 it was no longer desirable to be considered a Jew, at least for anyone in a public position. Though the SPD fully supported Grzesinski's Jewish deputy, Bernhard Weiss, they too could not escape the influence of a growing antisemitic atmosphere.

Another factor may well have entered here, one which is difficult to document properly. The relationship between the SPD and its intellectuals was both stormy and full of strain; these intellectuals were for the most part Jews. Was this fact important in weakening the Social Democratic attitude on the Jewish question? As far back as 1894 August Bebel had felt that Jews "undoubtedly" lacked tact when dealing with the Christian world, that they were apt to be brilliant and pushing. He had put this forward in a speech arguing against antisemitism in which he offered arguments lifted in part from Marx and leaning on Kautsky.[37] When Kautsky himself spoke about the "negative spirit" as one of the Jewish "peculiarities" he may well have had the party's troublesome intellectual critics in mind.

The tension between party and intellectuals came to the fore at the SPD party congress of 1903. At that point the leadership suggested that intellectuals might undergo a special probationary period before being admitted to full party membership, in order to test their ability to become integrated with the working classes. This integration was supposed to be proven through their loyalty to party dogma and leadership.[38] Much later, at the party congress of 1931, young comrades who revolted against the leadership's lack of militancy were at once likened to those intellectuals who constantly criticised the party.[39] Hugo Marx, who tried to found an *Intellektuellenbund* (League of Intellectuals) within the SPD, saw his hopes dashed and the council dissolved by the beginning of the 1930s.[40] Fritz Naphtali reflected the official party position when in 1930 he called for an end to such leagues. He held

---

[35]I.e. *Was muss das schaffende Volk . . .*, p. 12.

[36]Albert Grzesinski to Friedrich Stampfer, 13th September 1932, International Archive for Social History, Amsterdam, G. 2319.

[37]This refers to Kautsky's article of 1890 (see note 3); August Bebel, *Sozialdemokratie und Antisemitismus*, Berlin 1894, p. 31.

[38]*Protokoll über die Verhandlung des Parteitags der Sozialdemokratischen Partei Deutschlands*, Berlin 1903, pp. 174, 225.

[39]*Sozialdemokratischer Parteitag in Leipzig, 1931, Protokoll*, Berlin 1931, p. 265.

[40]Hugo Marx, *Werdegang eines jüdischen Staatsanwaltes und Richters in Baden*, Villingen 1965, pp. 195 ff.

that the intellectual needed contact with the worker, and the worker needed a sense of the cultural dimensions of his struggle.[41]

Naphtali was more polite towards intellectuals then Bebel had been. However, in no case did anyone in the party officially link intellectuals and Jews. In fact, both Hugo Marx and Naphtali were Jewish, but it could perhaps be proved that Marx was more representative of the articulate Jewish party membership. Here Theodor Lessing, the maverick philosopher, was closer to the mark when he characterised the League of Intellectuals as crucial, for the party had to be provided with a conscience.[42]

The effect which these strained relationships had upon the general attitude towards the Jewish problem can only be surmised. Those who wrote about the failures of the intellectuals in the party do not mention this particular aspect of the problem. Among the workers themselves the matter may well have been different and more clear-cut. Hans Jaeger reports that when giving a course for workers on behalf of the Communist Party at the beginning of the 1930s he was asked, "what are intellectuals? Are they (the same) as Jews?"[43] The problem posed by Jews as socialist intellectuals may well have been one dimension of the pressures put upon the party's posture as a bulwark against Rightist antisemitism. Certainly the existence of the left-wing intellectuals who constantly criticised the party from without, and who were overwhelmingly Jewish, must have added to this tension. The young radicals within the party were, in 1931, likened to these intellectuals who gathered around the *Weltbühne*, a journal to which we shall return.[44]

Yet the problem posed by intellectuals was only one factor in the party's situation at the end of the Republic, and certainly not the most important. The antisemitic dynamic of the Right collided with a party which refused to move off centre. SPD support of the Brüning government was combined with an official optimism about the ineffectiveness demonstrated by the Nazi movement. The Nazis would not succeed, said Rudolf Breitscheid, a member of the party directorate, to the Congress of 1931, because they rested their appeal upon a slender theoretical foundation directed towards the lower human instincts of hatred and envy. The Social Democrats never descended to these depths, but while this gave them moral strength in retrospect, it also blinded them to the real Nazi menace. The Brüning government, in their eyes, was supposed to prevent a coalition between the bourgeoisie and the Nazis;[45] their revisionism made them believe in the strength of middle-class liberalism, and they ignored the fact that National Socialism was, in large measure, a bourgeois movement in the first place. The result of their political analyses was the need they felt to survive this crisis and wait for better times to come.

---

[41]*Konservative Tendenzen in der Sozialdemokratie? Eine Rundfrage*, Heidelberg 1930, p. 8. This a was publication of the *Intellektuellenbund*.
[42]*Ibid.*, p. 12.
[43]Hans Jaeger, *Antinaziarbeit bis 1933*, Wiener Library, London, Personal Reports, 3000 Series, No. 3006, p. 3.
[44]*Sozialdemokratischer Parteitag in Leipzig, 1931. Protokoll*, p. 265.
[45]*Ibid.*, pp. 107, 102.

Social Democrats had an abiding faith in the strength of their organisation, exemplified by Friedrich Stampfer in his funeral oration for Eduard Bernstein. Even in 1932 he held that the "disorganised mob" of Nazis would never be able to conquer the firm organisation of the traditional German workers' party.[46] We shall see later that the left-wing intellectuals also had an abiding belief in the strength of the working classes in face of the Nazi menace. However, for them this faith was founded on the strength of socialist belief as it existed in every worker, and not upon a glorification of party organisation. The very organisation of the Social Democrats may have dulled their revolutionary and militant fervour.

How typical that Rudolf Hilferding, the economic expert of the SPD, sounded a warning against stupid adventures which would only breed nervousness within the party — though he saw his party hemmed in between Communists and Nazis. Julius Deutsch, the founder of the *Republikanischer Schutzbund* (league for the protection of the Austrian Republic), attempted to persuade Kautsky to take violent action. But he, too, was resigned; the large majority of party members was opposed to revolutionary Marxist action and would do everything possible through democratic means.[47] This was written in Austria in October of 1933, and the Nazis had been in power in Germany all that year. Survival for the Social Democrats never meant entering into competition for the nationalist masses, as the Communists attempted to do. But it did mean the use of "discretion", both generally and as far as the Jews were concerned. Such discretion could have been made easier through the general antisemitic atmosphere of the times, the under-estimation of the Nazi menace, and by the party's own internal problem with its intellectuals as well.

When all is said and done, the attitude of the Social Democrats towards the Jewish question and towards the defence of the Jews was firmer than that of other Socialists. They had largely succeeded in liquidating the heritage of Marx's *Jewish Question*, and Kautsky's became an increasingly lonely voice within his party. The Communist Party continued the older traditon, and was here indeed the inheritor of orthodox Marxism.

III

This continuity with Marx and Kautsky was established almost immediately upon the founding of the *Kommunistische Partei Deutschlands* (KPD). The party could not very well republish the works of the "renegade" Kautsky on the Jewish question, and so they returned to Marx instead. Marx's *Jewish Question* appeared under party auspices in 1919. Its behind-the-scenes sponsor was Ernst Meyer of the central committee of the KPD and editor of the *Rote Fahne* — a man destined in a few years to become one of the most influential and durable German Communist

---

[46]Gustav Mayer, *Erinnerungen*. Vom Journalisten zum Historiker der deutschen Arbeiterbewegung, Zürich-Wien 1949, p. 362.
[47]Rudolf Hilferding to Karl Kautsky, 1st December 1932, International Archive for Social History, Amsterdam, K.D. XII, 650; Julius Deutsch to Karl Kautsky, 19th October 1933, International Archive for Social History, Amsterdam, K.D. VII, 410.

leaders. The publication rights of the pamphlet belonged to the literary estate of Franz Mehring, who had edited it as part of his edition of Marx's collected works *(Nachlass)*. Mehring had joined the Communists in the last year of his life (1918) and consequently left his literary estate to the party. Meyer had no trouble, therefore, in asserting the party's rights to the book, much to the chagrin of Kautsky, who wanted to republish it himself.[48] Kautsky, as we have seen, republished his *Rasse und Judentum* instead, two years later. The fact that Meyer was in such a hurry to bring out Marx's pamphlet once more is in itself interesting. Both Meyer and Kautsky, for all their enmity, had the same goal in mind. The traditional position on the Jewish question had to be reaffirmed at a time when, as we have seen, some socialists were beginning to depart from the orthodox line.

Stefan Grossmann, left-wing writer and himself a Jew, wrote the preface to this edition of Marx's *Jewish Question*. The technique of using sympathisers who were not party members for such tasks in order to give them a wider audience was to become standard procedure. The Rowohlt publishing house which published the pamphlet was not one of the party's many enterprises. Grossmann stressed that Marx was neither a friend nor an enemy of the Jews, but rather the herald of a new world. Moreover, those who wrote insultingly about the "Jew Marx" could now judge for themselves Marx's own critical attitude towards the Jewish question.[49] The Jew was never to be defended as a Jew — that approach to the Jewish question was now set for the future.

The traditional socialist arguments continued, together with the contention that for the workers it made no difference whether the means of his oppression were in Jewish or in Aryan hands. This could lead to a laudable emphasis upon equality which required all Socialists to fight antisemitism regardless of the existence of the Jewish capitalist stereotype. For example, the *Rote Fahne* wrote in 1932: "When the Nazis sing in the streets that Jewish blood will drip from the knife, they mean by this not only the blood of poor Jewish proletarians but also the blood of the working classes. That blood will flow in the mutual interest of German and Jewish capital."[50] Whenever Jewish firms are mentioned in the communist press, they are described as capitalist, and nothing is said about their Jewish stereotype as encountered in Marx's own writings. But communist attitudes were not so simple or straightforward. The traditional view of the Jewish question exemplified by Marx and Kautsky became enmeshed in the struggle against National Socialism. Moreover, the attempted solution of the Jewish question in the Soviet Union was bound to have a crucial effect upon the German party. These factors were to keep the traditional socialist attitudes alive and even to deepen their portent.

On a rather superficial level in the struggle against the Nazis, the *Rote Fahne* was

---

[48]W. Dietz to Karl Kautsky, 27th April 1920, International Archive for Social History, Amsterdam, K.D. VIII.

[49]*Zur Judenfrage von Karl Marx*, edited by Stefan Grossmann, Berlin 1919, p. 5. Grossmann, the founder of the *Tagebuch*, had become disillusioned with communism and the Soviet Union by 1921. *Das Tagebuch*, II, No. 46 (19th November 1921), p. 1399.

[50]*Die Rote Fahne*, XV, No. 92 (29th April 1932).

fond of featuring every occasion when Jews seemed to support National Socialism or when National Socialism flirted with the Jews. Thus, for example, it claimed that a wildly antisemitic Nazi had turned out to be of Jewish ancestry.[51] Such glosses served the purpose of making the Nazis look ridiculous rather than providing an anti-semitic thrust. But this dividing line was easily crossed in the effort to show that Jewish and Aryan capital were identical and that therefore the Jewish problem as stated was irrelevant. "Nazis support Jewish capital" appeared as a headline in the *Rote Fahne*,[52] while *Der Rote Aufbau* went even further: it asserted that there were many Jewish capitalists among the financiers of National Socialism, while numerous Nazi leaders carried names which pointed to Jewish descent or were shown to be the offspring of mixed marriages. When this could not be proved, then physical appearance makes the point, and Goebbels was cited as an example. Kurt Kersten, who wrote this piece, was quick to end by asserting that ideas of racial purity are nonsense.[53]

To be sure, "Hitler was the saviour of rich Jews",[54] but communist analyses went beyond such a claim in order to link Jews and National Socialists more intimately. They thus accepted the stereotype (at least for non-proletarian Jews) of physical appearance (though this seems rare) to the point of castigating the "Jew editors" of the *Völkischer Beobachter*.[55] It must be stressed, however, that such accusations were the exception rather than the rule. Yet emphasis upon the class struggle meant the linkage of Jews and Nazis, on the surface deadly enemies, but in reality joined in the common struggle of all capital against the new order. "Jewishness" was irrelevant in the face of this overriding consideration.

These ideas were deepened through the sporadic efforts of the party to compete with that nationalism which the Right exploited so well. This competitive course was adopted in 1923 when Karl Radek advocated an alliance between communism and German national aspirations. In a famous speech, Radek praised the good patriotic intentions of Albert Leo Schlageter, the Nazi martyr executed by the French in the Ruhr. He was lauded as a truly courageous soldier of the counter-revolution who should have joined the working classes in fighting French imperial-ism. Radek also dealt with the Jewish question in his advocacy of the new party line. The union of the workers with the nationalist petty-bourgeois masses would end the rule of both "circumcised and uncircumcised capital". Jewish capital would opt for fascism in this struggle, and "we will witness how Messrs. Warburg, Litwin and Bosel pin on the Swastika". Antisemitic propaganda was considered stupid by Radek because it did not distinguish between Jewish capitalists and Jewish workers.[56]

---

[51]*Ibid.*, XV, No. 175 (23rd August 1932). This was the first reference to Jews in the paper since the 14th July.

[52]*Ibid.*, XV, No. 182 (7th September 1932).

[53]*Der Rote Aufbau*, V, No. 1 (1st January 1932), p. 13.

[54]*Die Rote Fahne*, XV, No. 76 (9th April 1932).

[55]*Der Rote Aufbau*, IV, No. 3 (March 1931), p. 158.

[56]*Kommunismus und Nationale Bewegung, Schlageter, eine Auseinandersetzung*, Berlin 1923, pp. 5, 7; Karl Radek, 'Kommunismus und deutsche nationalistische Bewegung', *Die Rote Fahne*, VI, No. 188 (16th August 1923), p. 50.

Unfortunately there were very few Jewish workers in Germany. Nationalists could easily focus their notions of the Jew upon the Jewish capitalist classes and indeed for them the figure of the "Jewish banker" played a leading rôle.

The nationalist course of the party in 1923 was not as dangerous as the resumption of that course after 1930. By that time it was explosive stuff, for an increasingly dynamic antisemitism also concentrated on the Jew as the exploiter of the masses, though, in this case, he had a monopoly of exploitation. In a speech of 1930 the Communist leader Heinz Neumann called on the Nazi masses to join the Communists in a common struggle and not to continue the "fratricidal war"[57], but the new nationalist course was never quite as blatant. The conversion from National Socialism to communism of Lieutenant Richard Scheringer, who had been imprisoned for spreading Nazi propaganda in the army, was exploited to the fullest extent. Here was a patriotic officer whose phrases of "national and social liberation" were backed up by an unblemished nationalist past.

When Scheringer came to deal with the Jewish question in 1931 his nationalist past was easily adjusted. For the new communist convert, the Jewish question, the "Jewish spirit of commerce and usury", was part of the capitalist *hubris*. But Scheringer also struck a different note when, at the conclusion of his analyses of the connection between Jews and capitalism, he stated that "no Jew had a seat in the Central Committee of the Communist Party". However, there were nine "representatives of this race" in the nationalist and anti-Marxist Scherl Publishing House.[58] Where Scheringer adopted an almost apologetic tone in his claim that no Jew sat in the Central Committee, the Communist mass circulation newspaper *Welt am Abend* in that same year reacted against a Nazi accusation of Jewishness with unrestrained fury. Not a single Jew sat in its editorial office, the paper claimed, and among their collaborators not one had the "terribly Jewish" appearance of Goebbels.[59] Such remarks must be seen in the context of polemics against Nazi attacks, and on this level such a reply is not much different in technique from those put forward by some Jewish organisations. If Jews were pictured as bad, they countered with examples of Jews who were moral; if Jews were said to be "un-German", stories were published of Jews who had sacrificed their lives in war. Thus if communism is said to be "Jewish," it was asserted that there were no Jews in the Central Committee or working for the *Welt am Abend*. Even the Social Democrats, as we have seen, at times succumbed to this technique of reply: Marx did not have the "Jewish spirit", or it was the "Christian" Engels who systematized socialist doctrine. Such counter-arguments were inevitable once the Nazi contentions were accepted at face value and taken seriously. The arguments put forward against them therefore had to depart from antisemitic premises in putting forward examples which might defeat Nazi contentions. The Nazis were successful in forcing their adversaries to argue

[57]Ossip K. Flechtheim, *Die Kommunistische Partei Deutschlands in der Weimarer Republik*, Offenbach a.M. 1948, p. 89.
[58]*Erwachendes Volk, Briefe an Leutnant a.D. Scheringer*, Berlin 1931, pp. 13, 21.
[59]*Welt am Abend*, IX, No. 179 (4th August 1931); but it also reprinted a translation of Mike Gold's *Jews without Money* to show the fate of proletarian Jews under capitalism. *Ibid.*, IX, No. 229 (1st October 1931).

within a framework which they themselves had laid down, however absurd this may have seemed to those who opposed them. This factor was one of the chief purveyors of the antisemitic atmosphere of the time, whose importance has already been noted. Much of the defence against National Socialism seemed, however reluctant, to accept the fact that Jews were a special and problematic element within the German population.

The Communists went further in this direction than other organisations, not only in order to reply to Nazi polemics but also to capture the nationalist masses for themselves. They did emphasise Germany's exploitation through French and British imperialism, but the Jewish question was involved as well. No doubt traditional socialist theory made it easier to adopt such a posture as all matters specifically "Jewish" fell under a blanket condemnation.

Alfred Kantorowicz, then a young Communist literary critic, summed up the party's attitudes towards the Jewish question as discussed up to this point. Writing in 1932, he asserted that the Jewish problem would be solved when the specifically "Jewish", and therefore parasitic class of *Luftmenschen*, of unproductive capitalist middlemen, was made productive — when the Jew ceased to be merely a capitalist merchant. This feat had already been accomplished in the Soviet Union; there innkeepers, middlemen and usurers had become peasants and soldiers.[60]

Kantorowicz's proposed solution already existed, and the impact of the Soviet Union upon communist attitudes towards the Jews was of decisive importance. It meant the acceptance of Lenin's and Stalin's contention that the Jews, unlike other territorial minorities, were not a nation with claims to separate political rights. But it also meant a concern with the Jewish settlement at Birobidjan, then new and attracting world-wide interest and attention. From this point of view the traditional rejection of Zionism was kept and, in fact, deepened; there could be no change of heart on this question.

Willi Münzenberg put his enormous organisational talents at the disposal of propaganda on behalf of Birobidjan. The organisation he created for this purpose became the leading Communist forum for the discussion of the Jewish question. Moreover, its scope was soon broadened beyond a concern with Birobidjan or anti-Zionist polemics, to encompass agitation and propaganda on behalf of all the political aims of the party. OZET (Society for the Rural Placement of Jewish Toilers) was originally founded in 1924 in the Soviet Union in order to attract settlers for Birobidjan and the short-lived Jewish settlement in the Crimea.[61] The German branch of OZET, *Geserd* (a Yiddish term for OZET), was founded in 1928. Its sponsors were largely fellow-travellers rather than party members and included many Jews. This, as we have noticed earlier, was in accordance with the technique of broadening the appeal of such organisations by keeping party control in the background. No doubt the general enthusiasm for the Soviet Union played a

---

[60]Alfred Kantorowicz, 'Liquidation der Judenfrage', in: *Klärung. 12 Autoren und Politiker über die Judenfrage*, Berlin 1932, pp. 159-60, 168. Typically enough, Willi Bredel, a leading Communist writer, in a novel, *Die Prüfung*, 1935, pictured the Jew as an unpolitical petty bourgeois.

[61]Salomon Goldelman, *Löst der Kommunismus die Judenfrage?*, Prag 1937, p. 277.

large part in the support *Geserd* received. For example, Ernst Toller's words of greeting to the organisation praise the Soviet Union but never mention the settle-ment idea. But for others like Kurt Hiller the Soviet Union seemed to provide a meaningful alternative to Zionism at a time of heightened Jewish persecution.[62]

Geserd published some literature, but above all it sponsored public discussions and courses for workers. The topics generally concerned communism versus Zion-ism but later, in the years after 1930, were also addressed to the general struggle against fascism. The Soviet Union itself asked with some interest what the *Geserd* groups were doing within the general framework of anti-fascist activity.[63] Never-theless, the Jewish question was the foremost reason for *Geserd's* existence. Otto Heller was appointed secretary of the organisation, undertaking many lecture tours on its behalf. Heller had studied at the University of Prague, the son of a wealthy accountant. Once he had left the University he joined the Communist Party and became the editor of a local party newspaper. He left Bohemia for Berlin in 1925 and there he caught the eye of Willi Münzenberg. He wrote for the *Welt am Abend* until he was dismissed in the late twenties for some disagreement with the party. Yet Münzenberg continued to befriend him, making possible Heller's trips to the Soviet Union and consequently his glowing reports about conditions in the workers' and peasants' state. Münzenberg undoubtedly suggested his appoint-ment as secretary to *Geserd*, which must have been attractive for Heller who was himself Jewish. He was killed by the Nazis in Mauthausen in 1945.[64]

Heller's real "fame" came in 1931 with the publication of his *Der Untergang des Judentums*. The book has been called, with some justification, a "breviary" of *Geserd*,[65] but it also became an instant classic the day it was published — the only full-length German communist book on the Jewish question. Part of its contents should be familiar to us: Jews as Jews are always in tune with capitalism; their fetishism of goods is not an inborn trait, but derives from their milieu; not only is trade their way of life but they have also acquired other undesirable characteristics: they are a nervous people who gesticulate; the Jewish religion springs from the necessity of inventing rules for the pursuit of commerce; it is a "dead ceremonial religion".[66] The Social Democratic journal *Die Gesellschaft* was largely justified when it fulminated against such "Communist Marxism" which is plagiarised from begin-ning to end.[67] After all, Kautsky was associated with that journal. But Heller's plagiarism was confined to the first part of the book. His solution of the Jewish question had to go beyond the advocacy of assimilation in order to take into account the Jewish settlement in the Soviet Union.

[62]*Auf eigener Scholle*, Berlin 1928, pp. 28, 37. This was a propaganda publication of *Geserd*.
[63]Jaeger, *op. cit.*, p. 1. Stalin dissolved *Geserd* in 1938/39.
[64]Babette Gross, *Willi Münzenberg*, Stuttgart 1967, p. 175; Tilly Spiegel, *Österreicher in der belgischen und französischen Résistance*, Monographien zur Zeitgeschichte. Schriftenreihe des Dokumentationsarchivs des österreichischen Widerstandes, Vienna 1969, pp. 43-44, n. 41. [I am indebted to Professor Georges Haupt for this reference.]
[65]*Jüdische Rundschau*, XXXVI, No. 99/100 (23rd December 1931), p. 581.
[66]Otto Heller, *Der Untergang des Judentums*, Berlin 1931, pp. 115, 116, 141, 337. The book was translated into French in 1933.
[67]Review by Otto Mänchen-Helfen, *Die Gesellschaft*, II, vol. 7-12 (1932), p. 461.

Heller did this by confining his advocacy of assimilation to Western European Jews. The Eastern European Jewish masses have different needs, he said, though these cannot include the assertion of a non-existent Jewish nationality. This led him into some mental gymnastics. Birobidjan was not a Jewish state but a proletarian settlement where Jews could practise their culture and their language (Yiddish). Because it was in the Soviet Union, it was a living culture, not a dead religion, and served to assimilate the Jewish to the Russian proletariat. We might add that, in contradiction to such proletarian assimilationism, *Geserd* propaganda itself now and then stressed the importance of Jewish nationalism. For example, with reference to the Birobidjan settlement they quoted Lenin as saying that nations are all-important and nationalism is a necessity.[68] As for Heller himself, it soon became evident how tenuous his construct proved to be. The Jews in the West were to be assimilated, and yet the masses of Eastern European Jewry were to retain their own culture without sliding into nationalism, which for Jews was one more manifestation of capitalist repression. Heller called Zionism a movement of the petty bourgeoisie, a movement that sought to compensate for growing class differences. For him Zionism had no connection with antisemitism but instead was part of the universal capitalist conspiracy. While in Palestine Jews who are exploited go from the land to the cities, in Birobidjan, while the Jew still gesticulates, "his hands are heavy from manual work".

It is worth noting that a year later the same Communist Party publishing house which brought out Heller's book, republished *W. I. Lenin on the Jewish Question* (1932). Lenin's pre-war polemic against the *Bund* ("General Jewish workers' Union" in Russia and Poland) for its advocacy of Jewish nationality and opposition to assimilation still seemed relevant to the party's position on the Jewish question at that time. We have seen how, earlier, the party had republished Marx's own tract on that problem. In the preface to this short collection of Lenin's writings the publisher pointed to Heller's work as showing concretely how the Soviet Union had managed to solve the problem of the Jews.[69]

Heller repeated the theses of his book in lectures throughout the German-speaking countries, and in books and articles about his further travels in the Soviet Union. *Die Welt am Abend* published long excerpts from *Der Untergang des Judentums* for its mass readership, contending that here, for the first time in contemporary literature, the Jewish problem had been analysed from a Marxist standpoint[70] (thus choosing to ignore Kautsky's work). The Jewish reaction to the book was not as hostile as might be imagined. The *C. V.-Zeitung* gave it large coverage, and while it had no objection to Heller's anti-Zionism it did strongly object to the idea of a vanishing of Judaism in the West. Above all, it disagreed with Heller's materialism. This criticism was one of the main objections to the communist point of view raised by the anti-Zionist liberals. Alfred Wiener, the Syndicus of the C.V.,

[68]Heller, *op. cit.*, pp. 77, 212, 337, 153, 165; M. Alberton, *Birobidschan, die Judenrepublik*, Vienna 1932, p. 211.
[69]*W. I. Lenin über die Judenfrage*, Berlin 1932.
[70]*Welt am Abend*, IX, No. 285 (7th December 1931).

asserted that the C.V.'s attitude towards communism was largely influenced by the communist warfare against religion. The C.V. always refused to collaborate with the Communists, in spite of sporadic exchanges of anti-Nazi material. In 1932, for example, the C.V. declined to make a financial contribution towards the creation of an SPD-KPD united front against Hitler.[71] The German organisation to combat antisemitism, the *Verein zur Abwehr des Antisemitismus*, raised similar objections, but concluded that "the book is not as frightening as its title".[72] Jewish liberals, involved in the struggle against the Nazi menace, showed a certain ambivalance here as they had done in their relationship with the Soviet Union.

The Zionists reacted with greater vigour, as might be expected. They had good cause to do so, for communist attacks on Zionism did not stop with Heller's book or the activities of *Geserd*. In 1932 a party publishing house produced a novel in its popular "red series" glorifying the heroism of a young Arab in the 1929 uprising against the Jews and the British in Palestine. The young hero leads the revolt, even against the advice of the Grand Mufti (not known for his love of Zionism). The *Day of the Fellahin* by Hadad (himself a Jew) served to popularise communist theory and give it an added edge.[73] Where Kautsky had been disappointed to find his prophecies about Zionism fulfilled in 1929, this book praised the uprising and glorified its leader. Once more it must be stated that such attitudes towards Zionism were not irrelevant to attitudes towards Jews in general. Otto Heller expressed this well when he stated that the Jewish question regarded from the standpoint of the Jews was without interest to him.[74] The main Zionist response to Heller was a book by Eli Strauss devoted to a point by point refutation of his theses.[75] But for all such "self-defence" Felix Weltsch was undoubtedly closest to the mark when, in the *Jüdische Rundschau*, he stressed Heller's basic indifference to any "Jewish" concerns. Party dogma and the Soviet Union were for him all that counted.[76]

It became impossible to remain even a fellow-traveller and support the Zionist cause. The case of the Jewish journalist Arthur Holitscher is instructive in this regard. Shortly after the end of the First World War he sang the praises of Zionist Palestine; once again, the war had strengthened a Jew's feeling of his identity. By 1928 he could recall how he had known three great movements for man's liberation: Bolshevism, the Chinese liberation movement, and Palestinian Zionism.[77] However,

---

[71]*C.V.-Zeitung*, IX, No. 9 (26th February 1932), pp. 77/78; *ibid.*, XI, No. 43 (21st October 1932), p. 430; Paucker, *op. cit.*, pp. 116, 274.

[72]*Abwehr-Blätter*, XLII, No. 1/2 (February 1932), p. 103.

[73]L. Haddad, *Tag der Fellahen*, Rote Reihe, MOPR Verlag, Berlin 1932. MOPR is a Russian abbreviation for International Class War Prisoners Aid; this was a branch of a Moscow publishing house.

[74]*Jüdische Rundschau*, XXXVII, No. 9 (2nd February 1932), p. 41.

[75]Eli Strauss, *Geht das Judentum unter?*, Vienna 1933.

[76]*Jüdische Rundschau*, XXXVII, No. 9 (2nd February 1932), p. 41.

[77]Arthur Holitscher, *Mein Leben in dieser Zeit*, Potsdam 1925, p. 188. He also published a book which praised the Zionist experiment: *Reise durch das Jüdische Palästina*, Berlin 1922; on the effects of the war, see the work by Egmont Zechlin, *Die deutsche Politik und die Juden im Ersten Weltkrieg*, Göttingen 1969. – The intensification of Jewish consciousness as a consequence both of the war and of growing antisemitism has now been discussed extensively in the monograph by Eva G. Reichmann, 'Der Bewußtseinswandel der deutschen Juden', in *Deutsches Judentum in Krieg und Revolution 1916–1923, pp. 511–612*.

by that time he was a firm supporter of *Geserd*; Zionism had lost its heroic phase and was doomed to failure. Unlike Zionism, the Soviet Union had managed to maintain its socialist and proletarian impetus while in Palestine capitalism and the "barren" Jewish religion had triumphed.[78]

Holitscher constantly looked for heroics and for a mystical spirit which could sustain the approaching new world. He was not a party member, not even an orthodox Communist, but thought of himself as an intellectual in the service of the proletarian ideal. Unlike other left-wing intellectuals, to whom we shall return, he accepted work in party front organisations and consistently glorified the Soviet Union. For this kind of Jewish left-wing intellectual, commitment to communism meant ever closer adherence to the party line and, therefore, a necessary (though perhaps deeply felt) repudiation of a momentary enthusiasm for the resurgence of Jewish nationality.

Communist attitudes towards the Jewish question back up the recollection of Hans Jaeger, a party lecturer during the last years of the Republic, that Communists were not deeply troubled by antisemitism.[79] It must be clear from our analysis that such a lack of concern was built into their socialist theory. This is why Communists could side-step the issue of antisemitism in their flirtation with the nationalist masses. Jaeger, who was also a member of the KPD "anti-Nazi" commission, documents the manner in which the party tried in the last years of the Republic to de-escalate the struggle with the Nazis. Communists and Social Democrats equally underestimated the strength of the enemy.[80] For the *Rote Fahne*, in 1930, the resurgence of fascism did not mean a decline of the proletarian movement. It was, instead, the inevitable sign that a revolutionary situation was in the making.[81] This mistaken assessment of National Socialism must be joined to their attitude towards the Jews in order to understand the full dimension of the Communists' relationship to the Jewish question.

Those groups which broke with the established Socialist parties in order to advocate greater militancy against fascism paid little attention to the Jewish question. The "KPD-Opposition", led by Heinrich Brandler and August Thalheimer, was preoccupied with preventing the masses from drifting to the Right. The economic crisis of capitalism which seemed decisive, could only be overcome by immediate militant and revolutionary action. They did believe that a Jew like the president of the powerful Danat Bank (Jakob Goldschmidt) would join the advocates of a Third Reich in order to preserve finance capital. But they also regarded antisemitism as the lowest form of reaction, exemplified by Czarist Russia. The "KPD-Opposition" held that the Communist Party had abdicated the leadership of the proletarian masses through its flirtation with nationalism. They

---

[78]Arthur Holitscher, *Mein Leben in dieser Zeit*, p. 238; he made similar statements in the *Geserd* publication *Auf Eigener Scholle*.
[79]Jaeger, *op. cit.*, p. 2.
[80]*Ibid.*, p. 10.
[81]Quoted in Enzo Collotti, *Die Kommunistische Partei Deutschlands 1918-1933*, Milan 1961, p. 35.

republished Trotsky's attack upon "national communism" which, so he charged, had substituted Scheringer for Liebknecht.[82]

The "Red Fighters", who had been driven out of the SPD in 1931, to a large extent shared the ideology of the "KPD-Opposition" though the two were fighting each other. Here also, revolution was the call of the hour and no compromise with any part of the fascist movement was possible. They, too, accused the Communists of having accepted the nationalist ideology. Neither Communists nor Social Democrats were any longer the allies of the proletariat, but instead based their ideas upon the petty bourgeoisie.[83] As we have seen, the "Red Fighters" had some truth on their side. For such groups a truly revolutionary and proletarian thrust against the existing order, meeting force with force, made the Jewish problem irrelevant within the framework of the struggle.

Within the established Socialist parties the Jewish problem did play a part. For the Communists, in particular, it was an integral part of their outlook on man and society. Both Social Democrats and Communists had to face the Jewish problem, and the way in which they did this influenced the kind of support Jews could expect from them during their period of crisis.

IV

The Communist Party was hardly a reliable ally in meeting the Nazi attacks against the Jews. The Social Democratic Party took a firmer stand, but even here we notice some ambivalence during the last years of the Republic. What about the left-wing intellectuals, most of whom, as stated earlier, were themselves Jews? They were critical spirits who, although Socialists, could not be expected to accept unquestioningly the dogmatism of the past.[84] As illustrated earlier, intellectuals were troublesome to the orthodox Marxists, whilst at the same time they rejected the established Socialist parties. Such men, for example, deplored the bureaucratic and pragmatic nature of the Communist Party. Their organ, the *Weltbühne*, accused the *Rote Aufbau* of being obsessed with economic considerations, of fulminating against those with true revolutionary spirit.[85]

Yet the *Weltbühne* carried an ecstatic review of Heller's book, stressing that the collapse of bourgeois civilisation would also mean the vanishing of the Jew.[86] To be sure, Bruno Frei, author of the review, was one of the few contributors to the *Weltbühne* who consistently favoured the Communist Party. He was also the editor-in-chief of the Berlin communist daily *Berlin am Morgen* which, like the *Rote Aufbau*,

[82]*Gegen den Strom*, IV, No. 5 (28th February 1931), p. 49; *ibid.*, VI, No. 7 (July 1933), pp. 32-33; Otto-Ernst Schüddekopf, *Linke Leute von Rechts*, Stuttgart 1960, pp. 292, 293.

[83]*Der Rote Kämpfer*, I, No. 8 (10th July 1931), pp. 5, 6; *ibid.*, I, No. 4 (15th February 1931), p. 8; see also Olaf Ihlav, *Die Roten Kämpfer*, Meinsenheim am Glan 1969, pp. 40, 41.

[84]For a general discussion of such intellectuals, see George L. Mosse, *Germans and Jews*, ch. 7.

[85]*Die Weltbühne*, XXVII, No. 25 (23rd June 1931), p. 938; for a breakdown of the preponderance of Jews on the journal see Istvan Deak, *Weimar Germany's Left-Wing Intellectuals. A Political History of the Weltbühne and its Circle*, Berkeley and Los Angeles 1968, p. 24.

was controlled by Willi Münzenberg. The review of Heller's book is therefore not really typical of *Weltbühne* attitudes, even though at times the journal linked Jews to antisemitic parties which they were said to support out of mistaken self-interest. The *Weltbühne's* view of Eastern European Jewry was not much different from Kautsky's; for example, it accused Eastern European Jews of engaging in white-slave traffic.[87] On the whole, however, the approach of the left-wing intellectuals differed from that of the Communists. They thought of themselves as Socialists, as the true heirs of Karl Marx, and yet Marx's analysis of the Jewish question is mentioned only by Bruno Frei.

More typical was Manfred George's *Weltbühne* article on the Jewish revolutionary, a reflection of the left-wing intellectual's personal dilemma. George rejects the bourgeois Jew and the nationalist Jew. There remains only the Jew as revolutionary, but he is doomed to isolation. For the Jew believes in justice and therefore cannot be effective in a time of terror, which is an integral part of revolutionary action. The Jew will be a fertilizer of revolution, but nothing more.[88] This analysis affords deep insight into the make-up of these intellectuals. In 1930, when this article was written, they were indeed isolated and had themselves rejected participation in all political parties. Their view of themselves as Jews, however ambivalent, appeared in stark relief and, in the last resort, made it impossible for them to view the Jewish question in concert with the Communists.

It was a subject they would have liked to avoid altogether, but this was impossible in those years of turmoil. George may have spoken the truest words about their situation, but they themselves attempted to face it by dwelling upon the shallow nature of antisemitism and by brushing aside the rising power of antisemitic National Socialism. Carl von Ossietzky, the editor of the *Weltbühne*, characterised antisemitism as a shallow by-product of nationalism. It does not run deep, he said, but has the character of a popular ballad.[89] Walter Mehring, in 1931, agreed with this analysis when he wrote that antisemitism was merely the external symptom of the sickness of capitalism. The Nazis did not really believe in their own rhetoric, he said, and Goebbels would just as soon march with the Red Army if it suited his purpose. But his party was dependent on the money contributed by heavy industry and rich Jews as well.[90]

Antisemitism could not possibly represent a deeply-held conviction; all these men agreed on this point. The rationalism and idealism of the left-wing intellectuals blinded them to the depth and strength of anti-Jewish feeling. Their belief that man is essentially good and that a bad society has only perverted his nature also stood in the way of a realistic assessment of the situation. Ossietzky firmly believed that

---

[86]*Die Weltbühne*, XXVIII, No. 1 (5th January 1932), pp. 14-17.
[87]*Ibid.*, XXIX, No. 8 (21st February 1933), p. 298; on Bruno Frei: Deak, *op. cit.*, p. 239; *Jüdische Rundschau*, XXXV, No. 101 (23rd December 1930), pp. 683-684.
[88]*Die Weltbühne*, XXVI, No. 9 (25th February 1930), pp. 313-316.
[89]*Ibid.*, XXVIII, No. 29 (19th July 1932), p. 89.
[90]*Ibid.*, XXVII, No. 5 (3rd February 1931), pp. 168-171.

those writers who advocate antisemitism come close to advocating pogroms, for they can claim no case of intellectual substance.[91] Two years earlier, in 1930, the *Weltbühne* had assured its readers that no one takes antisemitism seriously; there was no need to get passports and pack one's luggage.[92] This reassurance was needed, for the Nazis had just scored their first spectacular electoral triumph in the *Reichstag* elections. It is typical that Ossietzky ends his discussion of antisemitism with the statement that antisemitism had never taken root in the working class.[93] It is this faith which enabled the left-wing intellectuals to brush aside the Nazi successes. After all, the workers were, in their eyes, the least corrupt elements in a corrupt society.

In 1931 it was still possible to believe that if Hitler attempted to come to power as Mussolini had done, a general strike would stop him.[94] Those holding this view reassured themselves with the thought of the general strike which had stopped the *Kapp-Putsch* thirteen years earlier. However, it was pandering to illusions to state in February of 1933 that while the Italian working classes were exhausted when Mussolini came to power, the German proletariat was ready and willing to fight.[95] Such an article in the *Weltbühne* demonstrates the extent to which the left-wing intellectuals had lost contact with reality. As we saw earlier, the Austrian Social Democrat, Julius Deutsch, was nearer the mark when he wrote about the German workers' rejection of revolutionary experiments. The only realistic note in the *Weltbühne* was sounded by Ernst Toller, who had some experience in making revolutions. Toller stated that Hitler once he came to power would not give it up. But Toller, in 1930, also thought that the working classes, through the trade unions, could still do someting to stop National Socialism.[96]

The intellectuals tried to overcome their feeling of isolation by putting their faith in the working classes. For they saw themselves not as Jews but as the vanguard of an internationalism based upon justice, reason, and the abolition of the capitalist system. In this they were at one with the Jews in the Communist Party, and with those who were among the militant opposition to established socialism as well. Arnold Zweig's review of Simon Dubnow's *History of the Jews* can give us further insight into these attitudes. He treats Dubnow's *History* as the story of a minority which was able to sustain itself against all adversaries, not through an archaic religious faith, but because of its belief in the power of reason. In Zweig's view the Jews were needed in order that nationalism might be defeated and the barriers between peoples torn down.[97] Carl von Ossietzky shared Zweig's feelings which were, in turn, close to the liberal concept of the supposed "mission of Jews". The solution to the Jewish question lay not in the creation of a separate Birobidjan but in a fusion with a vigorous and unbeaten proletariat. However, this idea of

[91]*Ibid.*, XXVIII, No. 29 (19th July 1932), pp. 96-97.
[92]*Ibid.*, XXVI, No. 39 (23rd September 1930), p. 480.
[93]*Ibid.*, XXVIII, No. 29 (19th July 1932), p. 88.
[94]*Ibid.*, XXVII, No. 4 (27th January 1931), p. 120.
[95]*Ibid.*, XXIX, No. 6 (7th February 1933), p. 199.
[96]*Ibid.*, XXVI, No. 4 (7th October 1930), pp. 537-539.
[97]*Ibid.*, XXVII, No. 1 (6th January 1931), pp. 25, 27.

fusion was ambivalent. The original prospectus of the *Weltbühne* called the intellectuals the "council of the wise". They must lead, for only they can have an overall view of society and culture. These intellectuals were not class-bound.[98]

This leadership ideal sprang from their impotence, but it introduced an element of ambivalence into their assimilationist ideal. They looked back to 1918/19 when Jewish intellectuals had made a revolution in Bavaria; Jews who wanted to be not Jews, but part of the progressive brotherhood of all humanity. Their idealism not only blinded them to the reality of National Socialism: it also made them impassioned enemies of Zionism. Their attitude towards Zionism had some similarities with that of the Communists, but it also had its own peculiar twist in tune with their outlook upon the world. The *Weltbühne* stressed that conditions in Palestine were no better than in the Germany of the early thirties. "Where once upon a time love was preached, hatred has remained strongest." In ancient times Jewish sects warred with one another in Palestine, while now Christians, Jews and Mohammedans lived in a warlike state. These were *Unholy Memories of the Holy Land*.[99]

For these men Palestine was no Utopia, no island where rationalism reigned; instead it was a mirror of all the world's ills. These left-wing intellectuals, unlike the Communists, did not make much of the capitalist exploitation of the Jews. Instead they pictured the Holy Land as unleashing all that is worst in human nature. As committed pacifists they asserted that the word "peace" is as hated in certain Zionist circles as it is in the rest of the world. A lecture in 1932 at the Hebrew University in which Norman Bentwich extolled Jerusalem as a potential centre for world peace was interrupted by stink-bombs, whistles, and foot-stamping. The Zionist *Jüdische Rundschau* reported the event with outright condemnation. The misguided revisionist youths, who were responsible for the disturbance, imitated the nationalism current at German universities or in Poland which took offence at the very word "peace".[100] The *Weltbühne* took up this report, sharpening its tone and making the analogy with Germany more outspoken: Nazi riots on the Kurfürstendamm in Berlin, it said, were reproduced on Mount Scopus. We do not know whether it is true that in the subsequent trial a revisionist lawyer praised Hitler for being the saviour of Germany (he was, after all, still nearly a year from seizing power), as the *Weltbühne* contended. Nor is it certain that he pledged support for the Nazi leader provided Hitler dropped his antisemitism. This alleged remark prompted the *Weltbühne*, however, to hazard that next to the call "Germany awake", humanity would finally hear cries of "Zion awake". The headline of the *Weltbühne* article was "Hitler in Jerusalem".[101]

This article is symptomatic of the intellectuals' attitude towards Zionism. The *Weltbühne* took this opportunity to go far beyond the strictures of the *Jüdische Rundschau:* it made an explicit analogy with National Socialism, an analogy not

---

[98]George L. Mosse, *Germans and Jews*, pp. 185-186.

[99]This was the title of a book by Horace B. Samuel which had just appeared in England and was reviewed in *Die Weltbühne*, XXVII, No. 7 (17th February 1931), p. 247.

[100]*Jüdische Rundschau*, XXXVII, No. 13 (16th February 1932), p. 62, and leading article in No. 16 (26th February 1932).

[101]*Die Weltbühne*, XXVIII, No. 22 (31st May 1932), pp. 835, 836.

lightly made in 1932. In its view Zionism (and not only the revisionists) had prevented the true universalist and socialist mission of the Jewish people, and of the left-wing intellectuals. Zionist Palestine was indeed an unholy land. But unlike Heller's attack, there was no talk in the *Weltbühne* of the vanishing of the Jewish people, nor was there any reference to Kautsky's or Marx's "Jewish peculiarities" under capitalism.

The absence of the Jewish stereotype did not mean a clear confrontation with National Socialist antisemitism. Unlike the Communists they did not toy with the Nazi movement; it was firmly rejected. However, the Jewish question was ultimately dissolved into the general longing for human brotherhood and a more rational world.

In some left-wing intellectuals this produced a painful tension between their "humanity" and their Jewishness. Lion Feuchtwanger, himself a member of the *Weltbühne* circle, provides a good example of this dilemma in his *Josephustrilogie*. The first volume of the novel, *Der jüdische Krieg*, published in 1932, is a song of praise for reason amidst the passion and violence of the age. Reason must triumph if a war in which all truth collapses is to be avoided. Josephus, the hero of the book, opposed both the fanaticism of the Jewish warriors and the barbarism of Rome. Small wonder that another journal close to left-wing intellectuals, the *Tagebuch*, praised the book upon its appearance as an attack upon chauvinism. But it also saw fit to make an analogy with the year 1932. Compared with the excessive nationalism of the Jews of the first century A.D., the Nazis seem like advocates of internationalism. It is surely significant that the review dwells at some length on Jewish chauvinism and ignores Feuchtwanger's description of an even greater Roman ruthlessness.[102] Jews were once more reminded that they must identify themselves with cosmopolitanism, rationalism, and love for all humanity. Nationalism, as we have seen, was opposed to these ideals in the minds of left-wing intellectuals — here no compromise was possible.

The second volume of the trilogy, *Die Söhne*, which appeared in 1935 after the Nazis had seized power, still exalted reason, but by now despaired of its effects. Reason can fossilize into a rigid and unbending system especially when it is used on behalf of a theocratic nationalism. Moreover, the conflict between Feuchtwanger the left-wing intellectual and Feuchtwanger the Jew comes out in stark relief. He cannot, as yet, resolve this dilemma and both parts of his loyalty exist side by side without joining hands. Feuchtwanger makes Josephus give this description of his famous book on the Jewish war: "It is a Jewish book, but the spirit which informs it is that of a citizen of the world."[103]

The final volume, *Der Tag wird kommen*, written during the Second World War, and published in 1945, goes one step further. Josephus now "sickens" because of his rationalism. He is said to have betrayed the Jewish state in favour of a cosmopolitan Utopia. "He wanted to proclaim the kingdom of reason, of the Messiah . . . He who

---

[102]*Das Tagebuch* (17th December 1932), pp. 1755-1757.
[103]Lion Feuchtwanger, *Die Söhne*, Amsterdam 1935, p. 81.

makes such a prophecy has to pay for it with too many sacrifices. However, it is sweet and honourable to pay allegiance solely to one's people, one's nation."[104] Feuchtwanger the left-wing intellectual had passed from using the Jews as symbols for humanity and rationalism to an attempted confrontation with Jewish nationalism. To be sure, this was confrontation rather than acceptance, and yet the change from the previous volumes is obvious. One might add that even in the first volume of the trilogy Josephus leaves his people only when the battle is lost. Before this he has fought heroically as a leader of the Jewish cause.[105] Feuchtwanger's Josephus is a very human creature, attracted to wordly power and might. However, the emphasis changes in the three volumes, and together they portray the torn soul of a Jewish left-wing intellectual in his journey from a disillusionment with universalism and rationalism to a confrontation with his Jewishness.

During that journey, typically enough, Feuchtwanger made a foray into communism and paid allegiance to the promise of the Soviet Union. This also ended in disillusionment. He was unwilling to give up altogether what he called "practical socialism as exemplified by the Communists", but was quick to add that his heart and feeling could not affirm it. He never contemplated settling in Communist East Germany. Moreover, in his book *Arms for America* (1947) he returned once more to a belief in the "slow, very slow, yet certain growth of human reason between the last ice age and that which is to come".[106] Feuchtwanger's evolution and hesitations are typical of the generation of intellectuals which had once gathered in the offices of the *Weltbühne*.

V

Confrontation with the Jewish problem was for left-wing intellectuals who travelled this road a consequence of the Nazi triumph and of their own exile. For the majority of such intellectuals, however, exile did not markedly change their political attitudes. The (non-Jewish) novelist Heinrich Mann, for example, whom they admired most, in 1933 criticised the dominance which the persecution of the Jews exercised over all anti-fascist mass meetings. Hatred of the Jew in National Socialism, he said, took second place to the hatred of human freedom. Humanity was an integral whole all of which was menaced by fascism. The Jews as Jews had no special claim to attention.[107]

In a critique of their own failure the Social Democrats attempted to find a new *élan* which would give them a more successful political posture. Some continued to call for a pragmatic approach to politics, but others believed that the masses had to be wedded to the leadership through a renewed emphasis upon the class struggle.

[104]Lion Feuchtwanger, *Der Tag wird kommen*, Stockholm 1945, pp. 61 ff.
[105]I.e. Gustav Krojanker, 'Vom Weltbürgertum', *Jüdische Rundschau*, XXXVIII, No. 18 (3rd March 1933), p. 87.
[106]George L. Mosse, 'The Heritage of Socialist Humanism', *Salmagundi*, No. 10-11 (Fall 1969-Winter 1970), pp. 132-135.
[107]*Ibid.*, p. 129.

The rationalism which seemed to have led to the party's pragmatic politics came under attack. Youth especially, so it was said, could not live by reason alone.[108] Many Social Democrats came to share with intellectuals like Feuchtwanger a despair in the efficacy of human reason. But the failures with which we have been concerned did not arise from a preponderance of reason, but came rather out of illusions fostered by a Marxist heritage, however much it had been diluted and changed by such men.

The Communists continued to take their stand on the same ground that they had occupied under the Republic. Their attitude on the Jewish question remained unchanged. The *Neue Weltbühne*, for example, now published in Prague under Communist auspices, asserted that an anti-fascism based upon the persecution of Jews was mistaken; for Jews themselves were split into social classes and for some the profit motive was more important than anti-fascist activity. Anti-fascism must be set in the framework of the international working classes both inside and outside Germany.[109] Soviet attitudes towards Zionism and the Jewish question did not change, and therefore those of the German Communist Party remained constant as well.

The failure of the German Left to present a united and consistent front on the Jewish question was a tragedy for German Jews during this crisis. The Left had let them down in the end, and there seemed little to cling to in the way of allies in the battle which had to be waged. The poignancy of this situation was fully understood by Eva Reichmann in 1932. The general process of radicalization had also gripped Jewish youth, and as they could not join the antisemitic radical Right, they joined the radical Left.[110] For such young Jews the failure of the Left must have been particularly harrowing. The centre parties to which many Jews confessed allegiance had shown signs of collapse even before National Socialism arrived on the brink of power. The Right was impregnated with antisemitism, though some Jews turned in that direction to find a bulwark against National Socialism. There is hardly any evidence that any Jewish capitalist in desperation turned to the Nazis themselves[111].

Only the Social Democratic Party seemed to present a barrier of Republicanism against the rising tide of the Right. Yet on the whole, a promising avenue of hope had been closed. The noble humanitarian confessions of faith and the Left's utter rejection of racism could not erase the fact that the Jew as a Jew had no place within their ideology. Some Social Democrats like Eduard Bernstein did believe that the affirmation of Jewish identity was a necessary step to world brotherhood. Such men shared the idealism of Gustav Landauer and Martin Buber, but not that of Marx or Kautsky. It was difficult, at best, to combat Nazi racism which attacked the Jew as a Jew, if one could only reply that the Jew as a Jew did not in fact exist. But the inherently noble ideals of the Left seemed sullied when the Jew remained a

[108]Erich Matthias, *Sozialdemokratie und Nation*, Stuttgart 1952, pp. 61 ff.
[109]*Die Neue Weltbühne*, 2. Halbjahr (1933), p. 1154.
[110]Eva Reichmann-Jungmann, 'Der Untergang des Judentums', *Der Morgen*, VIII (1932), p. 64.
[111]It is, of course, possible that some isolated Jewish capitalist contributed money to the Nazis. Ruth von Mayenburg, *Blaues Blut und Rote Fahnen*, Vienna 1969, p. 86, mentions one such case.

stereotype, though this was one of their not unexpected consequences. The theories of the Left served to betray the Jew at a moment of crisis while many Jewish intellectuals, after the Nazis had triumphed, were torn between their left-wing allegiance and their Jewishness. Political illusions were added to that world of illusions in which so much of the German Left lived. The lessons of failure are not easily learned. This may be one reason why the attitudes of German Socialists towards the Jewish question in the face of National Socialism have not yet found their historian[112].

---

[112]Since these lines were written Donald L. Niewyk has published his *Socialist, Anti-Semite, and Jew: German Social Democracy Confronts the Problem of Anti-Semitism, 1918-1933*, Baton Rouge 1971. Based largely on an examination of the most important segment of the party press, the book constitutes a valuable documentation on the opposition of Social Democracy to antisemitism. However, Niewyk rather tends to explain away the importance of those factors which may have induced an ambivalence in the party towards the Jewish question, especially in the final phase of the Republic. He mentions the use of the Jewish stereotype, the hesitation in appointing Jews to public office, and suspicion of Jewish intellectuals. But these factors deserve a much more thorough investigation. The unambiguous condemnation of antisemitism in the last years of the Republic (p. 165) was accompanied by the use of a certain discretion on the Jewish problem and, above all, by the fact that the Nazis defined the territory from which the struggle against antisemitism had to be waged. This did mean an acceptance of the difference between German and Jew, even if it was expressed ironically through the use of the Jewish stereotype to defeat the Nazis at their own game and to show up their inanity. Thus one *Reichstag*-deputy asked the Nazis whether they had been reared in a *Judenschule* because they made so much noise (p. 212) while on another occasion the SPD broadcast the fact of the Jewish descent of a candidate for speaker of the *Reichstag* in order to get their own man elected (Heinrich Brüning, *Memoiren 1918-1934*, Stuttgart 1969, pp 199-200). These and similar exploitations of the Jewish problem cannot be passed over by stressing the straightforward opposition to antisemitism by the official party press.

The complex and ambivalent interplay of the Left and the Jewish problem has received more adequate treatment in another book just published: Hans-Helmuth Knütter, *Die Juden und die deutsche Linke in der Weimarer Republik 1918-1933*, Bonner Schriften z. Politik und Zeitgeschichte, 4, Düsseldorf 1971. The title defines his emphasis: the book begins with a definition of the special characteristics of Jews which led them into idealistic and messianic forms of socialism. What he has to say here will be controversial, partly because the Jewish attitudes he discusses follow trends which are obvious among German youth as a whole. Yet he is correct in emphasising the *Weltbühne* as the specific organ of a "Jewish" socialism and many of his examples throughout the book are drawn from that source. Because of his analysis we must correct our statement that the Jewish stereotype was absent from that journal. Knütter proves that it was present despite the *Weltbühne's* fight against antisemitism. Slightly more than half as well as the weakest part of the book is devoted to the problem of antisemitism and the positions of the Jews within the German Left.

As he discusses the attitudes towards Jews of the KPD or SPD, the emphasis falls upon their adjustment to the times, rather than upon the importance of a specifically socialist heritage. The section on the KPD brings much that is new, but omits mention of *Geserd* and does not analyse the importance for Germany of the Soviet Jewish settlements. The SPD gets short shrift, though Knütter provides a necessary antidote to Niewyk by his discussion of the concessions which that party made to the German national spirit. Quite rightly, he also deals with the problem of the intellectuals as opposed to workers and party organisation.

Knütter's framework seems somewhat narrowly confined to specifically German sources and he might have found new problems and different emphases if he had used some of the English language literature and foreign archives, such as that in Amsterdam. To give one example: there he would have found the story of the publication by Ernst Meyer in 1919 of Marx's pamphlet on the Jewish question and that might have made his discussion of the attitude of the early KPD towards the Jewish question still more complex. His analysis of left-wing attitudes towards the Jews could have been extended, but then this is only a part of what he is trying to accomplish. Knütter's book will be useful in future studies and discussions of socialism and the Jews.

It is a tribute to the richness of the subject that despite differences in emphasis and documentation between Knütter and myself our general conclusions agree with one another. Indeed this essay and the two books are complementary. There are enough differences in the use of sources and in the sources used to warrant further research into a subject which is only beginning to find its historians.

A Symposium on Central European Jews

At its Convention in December 1969, the American Historical Association held a Symposium on The Cultural and Economic Rôle of the Jews in Central Europe with Professor R. John Rath of Rice University in the chair. The aim was to clarify, and comment on, the situation of the Jews in the Weimar Republic of Germany and in the last stage of the Habsburg Empire. This is, of course, a subject on which the studies of the Leo Baeck Institute are focused. The fact that a section of this great American Association of scholars submitted it to close scrutiny shows that the development of the Jewish problem during a comparatively liberal period in Central Europe, on the eve of disaster, is accepted as a matter of general historical significance. Its impact widely transcends the narrow limits of the special case or of purely Jewish relevancy. Not only have some of the outstanding figures produced by the cultural integration of Jews in Central Europe left their mark on the thought of the century, but the very problem of integrating a minority, with its own characteristic features, into a society from which they had been separated for centuries, with all the resulting consequences — both positive and negative — is a matter of great general psychological and sociological interest, not only to historians.

We are grateful to the participants of this American discussion for permission to print their papers in this Year Book. Nothing essential has been changed in the original texts nor has the editor interfered with the spontaneity of the speeches, so as to preserve the actual character of the event. We have also avoided criticism or comment on some of the more controversial points. The intention here is to let our readers know how the speakers of that Conference, all well-versed students of the material, look at these problems so close to ourselves. As to our own position, readers of the fifteen volumes of this Year Book and of other publications of the Leo Baeck Institute may be familiar with it. We consider that one single study could hardly do justice to a subject of such vastness and complexity, which requires detailed research. The two volumes which the Leo Baeck Institute has published deal with the situation at two particularly critical moments of the Weimar Republic, 1916-1923* and 1932**, and place the Weimar era in the context of German history as a whole. But we agree with Professor Sauer that one more concise and unitary survey of the subject would be desirable and particularly valuable to those readers for whom the whole Weimar epoch is gradually receding into a legendary and hazy past. Meanwhile, it will be noticed that publications of the Leo Baeck Institute are frequently quoted by the speakers. Some pertinent remarks in the general introduction to this volume refer to this fact.

We believe, however, that members of the Leo Baeck Institute and readers of the Year Book will be greatly interested to learn the views of some American historians and their approach to a problem which is of special concern to the work of the Institute.

*Deutsches Judentum in Krieg und Revolution 1916-1923. Ein Sammelband herausgegeben von Werner E. Mosse unter Mitwirkung von Arnold Paucker, Tübingen 1971 (Schriftenreihe wissenschaftlicher Abhandlungen des Leo Baeck Instituts 25).
**Entscheidungsjahr 1932. Zur Judenfrage in der Endphase der Weimarer Republik. Ein Sammelband herausgegeben von Werner E. Mosse unter Mitwirkung von Arnold Paucker, Tübingen 1965, 1966 (Schriftenreihe wissenschaftlicher Abhandlungen des Leo Baeck Instituts 13).

The Jews in the Habsburg Empire, 1879-1918

BY WILLIAM A. JENKS

In a recent essay on Richard Wagner's interpretation of the rôle of the Jews in the nineteenth century, the British theatre critic and television personality Bryan Magee offers a stimulating theory to explain the explosion of talent and great accomplishments that marked the first century of Jewish emancipation in Europe. First, he is sure that the "intellectual and artistic output of Jews in this century relative to their numbers is a phenomenon for which I can think of no parallel in history since Athens five centuries before Christ". Why? Not because they were "chosen" to be "masters," an idea he deems "superstitious, obviously false, and nasty", but because they were integrating with a Western cultural tradition that was disintegrating to meet them half-way. The Jew who had recently come from the ghetto or who knew of his parents' life there was likely to be more emotionally involved in and better prepared to articulate the deepest concerns of the age in which he lived. Rootlessness, alienation, and adjustment were not novelties for him, and so he became the archetypal modern man. At the cost of renouncing what Magee calls "that most tribal, observance-ridden and past-oriented of religions", the greatest of the Jews — Marx, Freud, and Einstein — "have produced theories about man and his environment which in depth, originality and scope are equal to almost any before them".[1]

I should like to suggest that the atomization of society and the individual's loneliness and vulnerability therein also help to explain the rise of the great Jewish capitalists. The man whose ancestors weathered the uncertainties of money-lending, door-to-door selling, and personal insecurity was likely to comport himself with coolness and toughness when panics, tariffs, or switches in governmental favours menaced his holdings. He had to be a "matador of the Bourse", to use one of the antisemitic phrases of the day that paid unconscious tribute to the grim laws of economic survival.

Indubitably the outstanding Jewish contributions to Austro-Hungarian culture and material prosperity came from those who were neutral about their faith, officially *konfessionslos*, or converts to Protestantism or Catholicism.[2] The question of

---

[1]Bryan Magee, *Aspects of Wagner*, New York 1969, pp. 39-50.

[2]For the Jews of Austria, the best bibliography is the one prepared by Ilse R. Wolff in Josef Fraenkel, (ed.), *The Jews of Austria*, London 1967, pp. 547-566. For Hungary, one must still rely on Klaus Schickert, *Die Judenfrage in Ungarn*, Berlin, Essen, Leipzig 1937, pp. 183-189, and on the suggestions made by P. Hanák, 'Skizzen über die ungarische Gesellschaft am Anfang des 20. Jahrhunderts', in *Acta Historica Academiae Scientiarum Hungaricae*, X, 1963, No. 1-2, pp. 42-45. In order to ascertain which persons were of Jewish descent the reader is referred to the following works: Julius von Farkas, *Der Freiheitskampf des ungarischen Geistes 1867-1914*, Berlin 1940; Hans Tietze, *Die Juden Wiens*, Leipzig and Vienna 1933; Saul Raphael Landau, *Der Polenklub und seine Hausjuden*, Vienna 1907; Max Grunwald, *Geschichte der Wiener Juden bis 1914*, Vienna 1925;

classification obviously is difficult and can be tendentious. Several examples should suffice. What of Vilmos Fraknói, born Frankel, who became a Catholic priest at twenty-two, eventually the titular bishop of Arbe (Rab), and respected by Leo XIII and the Hungarian public for his historical studies of Pázmány, Hunyadi, and the liberation from the Turks? Or of Tobias Ludwig Österreicher, who renounced Judaism at twenty-five, served with distinction in the navy, especially in the geodetic survey of the Adriatic coasts, and retired as *Conteradmiral* in 1882?[3] That either of them consciously felt close to his heritage is questionable, but a recent comment on Gustav Mahler is apposite. Henry-Louis de la Grange projects a "definitive biography" of the composer by 1970, and he already has recorded the participation of Mahler's father in Jewish communal life in Iglau and his son's regular attendance at the synagogue. He concludes that his subject "did not practise Catholicism to any greater extent than he had practised the religion of his fathers, but there is no doubt that his orthodox Jewish education exercised a considerable influence on his character".[4] Solid biographical studies of others who deserted the synagogue would probably lead to similar conclusions.

Prior to 1867 Jewish individuals and families in the Habsburg dominions made their more significant contributions in the economic sphere. The Rothschilds were the best known of the entrepreneurs, shoring up the state's finances when deficits regularly appeared, securing the funds needed for the great railway lines, and establishing the banks needed for the expansion of industry, commerce, and mining. After 1879 the influence of the great families diminished only in the field of rail transportation, where the state assumed control of all important lines save, temporarily, the *Nordbahn*. To meet the cost of occupying Bosnia-Hercegovina, the Rothschild consortium in Vienna disposed of six per cent state obligations on the world's money markets.[5] Wilhelm Guttmann, the "coal king", collaborated with the same family in exploiting the Moravian-Silesian coal-fields,[6] and the Jewish production of textiles in Brünn and of sugar in Bohemia was a commonplace of political and economic discussions. The great houses of the Todesco, Schey, Königswarter, and Springer clans along the Ringstraße emphasised the great importance of the Viennese Jews in leather goods, furniture, ready-to-wear clothing, beer, and food processing. Today the name Gerngross reminds visitors of the techniques developed decades ago to place a variety of goods under one roof of a department store.

In Hungary the railway lines and textile factories were the creations of Viennese

Aurelia Gerlach, *Der Einfluss der Juden in der österreichischen Sozialdemokratie*, Vienna and Leipzig 1939; Robert Körber, *Rassesieg in Wien*, Vienna 1939. As some of these were published under the Nazi regime they must be consulted with extreme caution, and all should be checked against S. Wininger, *Große Jüdische National-Biographie*, 7 vols., Czernowitz 1925-1936 which also, however, in a few instances, makes erroneous attributions.

[3] Unless otherwise noted, biographical material has been taken from Wininger's alphabetized entries.

[4] *Saturday Review*, 29th March 1969, pp. 47-48.

[5] Heinrich Benedikt, *Die wirtschaftliche Entwicklung in der Franz-Joseph-Zeit*, Vienna and Munich 1958, p. 110.

[6] Erich Zöllner, *Geschichte Österreichs*, Vienna 1961, p. 448.

finance, but it was not long before Jewish families of Budapest, whether of recent or distant provenance, moved from flour-milling into leather goods, distilleries, presses, banks, coal-mines, and railway carriage construction. The oligarchy which dominated the Bourse and the grain sales in the capital usually founded its fortunes in the production of flour, and such names as Weiss, Wolfner, Deutsch, Ullman, Brüll, and Herzog might become Magyarized when a second or third generation dabbled in chauvinism or mere *belles-lettres*.[7] Thanks to their early experience as tradesmen in grain, the prosperous millers tended to buy or lease farmland to an extent rivalled in Austria only by some sugar magnates. The truly spectacular career was that of Manfred Weiss. Born in 1857, he created an industrial complex on Csepel Island in the 1880s to turn out impressive quantities of the cartridges, rifles, and munitions that the Austro-Hungarian army would practise with and then use in 1914-1918. His many other interests included textiles, the shipping industry at Fiume, the presidency of the Pest Hungarian Commercial Bank, and membership in the House of Magnates. Fifty great families, the majority Jewish by origin, dominated Hungarian industry, banking, and, in reality, the marketing of agricultural commodities. Thanks to their ties with Vienna and Germany, they were a most necessary part of Hungarian society, a fact realized by the magnates rather than by the gentry and peasantry.[8]

Closely allied to the world of business was that of politics and the press. With the advent of Dualism and true emancipation, the Jews of both realms at first gravitated to liberal parties which stressed basic civil rights and minimal governmental interference in economic affairs. In the 1870s Julius Glaser and Josef Unger were Austrian cabinet members, and in the 1880s Emil Steinbach, symbolizing intellectual discontent with *laisser-faire*, prepared the social legislation of the Taaffe era. A decade later Rudolf Sieghart was accomplishing wonders for prime ministers in the Austrian parliament by cajoling and threatening obstructionist deputies into voting "the right way". It was widely noted in the re-negotiations of the economic *Ausgleich* in 1907 that he, born Singer, was the chief Austrian bargainer, while József Szterényi, the son of a rabbi, represented the Hungarian point of view.[9] Persons of Jewish background who served in both parliaments did not tend to embrace Jewish nationalism until the empire's last decade, and then really only in Austria. A Rudolf Auspitz, factory owner and doctrinaire liberal, might sit in the same chamber with an Alois Zucker of the Czech Club and a Rafael Luzatto of Trieste. Four or five nearly always helped to represent Galicia, and their demonstrated loyalty to the Polish Club was comparable to the tendency of the Jews of Vienna and Prague to opt for German culture, to the rapid Magyarization of the Jews of Budapest, and the Jewish affinity with Italian culture in Trieste. After 1900 a specifically Jewish National Party sent a few deputies to the *Reichsrat*, but their

[7] V. Sándor, 'Die Entfaltung der Großmühlenindustrie in Budapest nach dem Ausgleich i. 1867', in *Acta Historica Academiae Scientiarum Hungaricae*, X, 1964, pp. 264-265.
[8] Hanák, *loc. cit.*, p. 11. See also Nathaniel Katzburg, 'Hungarian Jewry in Modern Times', in Randolph L. Braham, ed., *Hungarian-Jewish Studies*, New York 1966, pp. 144-146.
[9] For Rudolf Sieghart's opinion of Szterényi, see his *Die letzten Jahrzehnte einer Großmacht*, Berlin 1932, p. 110.

inability to shake the cultural allegiances of their co-religionists was all too apparent in the elections of 1907 and 1911.

In Hungary outstanding Jewish physicians, businessmen, journalists, and jurists sat in parliament as part of the Liberal machine perfected by the Tiszas or, less often, with the Party of Independence. In either case their adherence to Hungary's social and national policy was undeniable, and a watch-maker turned Agrarian Socialist like Vilmos Mezöfi was very much an anomaly in the Lower House.

In both realms the emergence of Marxian Socialist parties complicated the general tendency of the Jews to blend with an historic nationality (the Czech excepted). Among the founding fathers in Austria were Victor Adler of prosperous middle-class origin, the ex-clerk Friedrich Austerlitz, who taught himself the intricacies of law and literature, and Ignacy Daszyński, the son of a minor Galician district official who organised over ninety of the first Polish trade unions. In Hungary some of the earliest Marxian activists were Jakob Schlesinger and Leo Frankel, and among the leaders who still were battling without much success against "the system" in Hungary after 1900 were Miksa Grossmann, stalwart of the Butchers' Union, Jakab Kardos (born Israel), the ex-tinsmith, and Zsigmond Kunfi, pedagogue and journalist.[10] In the German-Austrian, Polish-Austrian, and Magyar branches of Social Democracy then, persons of Jewish ancestry who almost always had become estranged from their faith were prominent. In the Czech branch this was not the case, since the Jews of Bohemia and Moravia tended to espouse German cultural patterns.[11]

Direct involvement in parliamentary affairs of the Jewish community and its often agnostic sons paled in comparison with their involvement in press affairs. Who has not read of the Hungarian Christian-Social paper, edited by a one-time Jew? If the story is unprovable, it at least lies in the sphere of probability. The *Neue Freie Presse* and the *Pester Lloyd* were two of Europe's best journals, though such powerful editors as Moritz Benedikt, Miksa Falk, and Leo Veigelsberg enraged readers who did not equate happiness with liberalism and the steady growth of the gross imperial product. It was no surprise, consequently, to find Austerlitz editing the *Arbeiter-Zeitung* and Kunfi active on *Népszava*. Possibly the best known of Viennese publishing tycoons was Moritz Szeps, the Crown Prince's friend, and certainly Vienna's best-known gadfly was Karl Kraus. Whether one wanted the discreet official line, cabaret-type satires on the foibles of the mighty, or dogged analyses of society's ills, the Viennese press obliged, and its owners and writers were overwhelmingly Jewish.[12] In Budapest there was need for more editorial discretion, but

[10]See G. D. H. Cole, *A History of Socialist Thought*, vol. III, Part II. — *The Second International 1889-1914*, London 1956, pp. 575-576, 584-585, and Tibor Süle, *Sozialdemokratie in Ungarn. Zur Rolle der Intelligenz in der Arbeiterbewegung 1899-1910*, Cologne and Graz 1967.

[11]For a general picture of the Jews in Bohemia and Moravia, see Ruth Kestenberg-Gladstein, 'The Jews between Czechs and Germans in the Historic Lands, 1848-1918', in *The Jews of Czechoslovakia*, Philadelphia and New York 1968, and Ernst Wodak, *Prag von Gestern und Vorgestern*, Tel Aviv 1948.

[12]See Richard Grunberger, 'Jews in Austrian Journalism', in *The Jews of Austria*, pp. 83-95, and J. W. Nagl, Jakob Zeidler, and Eduard Castle, *Deutsch-Österreichische Literaturgeschichte*, vol. III, Vienna 1930, pp. 867-904.

the picture was much the same.[13] In Prague the German-oriented *Bohemia* had a series of Jewish editors, but organs of Czech nationalism looked elsewhere. The chance to write *feuilletons* and to criticize music and literature furthered the careers of many of Jewish background. Eduard Hanslick and Julius Korngold are still worth reading, even if the former offered an over-supply of unfortunate verdicts. Geza Molnár did much the same for the *Pester Lloyd*, exemplifying with his *Theory of Hungarian Music* (1903) the Budapest Jewish community's tendency to further the march of Magyar pride. Theodor Herzl, Anton Deutsch, Alexander Bródy, Felix Salten, and dozens more — in political reporting, economic analysis, naturalistic short stories or discriminating pen pictures of the era, made a substantial contribution in educating and entertaining the literate public.

Politics and press had the law as their solid underpinning, and here, too, in commentaries and in exposition legal scholars of Jewish origin made their mark. Julius Glaser struck a great blow for civil rights when his ideas triumphed in a new code of civil procedure for Austria. Josef Unger was the great analyst of the civil law, and the two, through lectures and casebooks, educated several generations of students. A galaxy of jurisconsults wrote expertly on property, marriage, labour relations, patents, military law, and even canon law. As is quite well known, a sizeable percentage of law students were Jewish, and their contribution to strengthening the rule of law is likewise worth mentioning.[14] In Hungary Károly Csemegi and László Fayer redrew the criminal code, while Anton Almasi was the great codifier in the field of civil law. Emancipation was not simply the opportunity to move into all of society's activities. The unending struggle to secure the law and to expand its benefits likewise attracted hundreds.

Medicine as well was a lure for the altruistic, the ambitious, and the scientifically curious. Victor Adler was the "poor man's doctor" before turning wholly to radical politics, as was Wilhelm Ellenbogen. Arthur Schnitzler worked at laryngology for a while, but medicine was no half-way station for dozens of others who held posts at the universities and treated every kind of ailment in their clinics. Sigmund Freud's work made a tremendous impact on the generation that survived World War I, and Alfred Adler's breach with the master in 1911 merely exposed the richness of the field Freud had opened up. In more orthodox fields, Emil Zuckerkandl used wit and sarcasm to illuminate anatomy, Adam Politzer and Henrik Neuman eased the frustrations of the deaf, Moritz Kaposi laboured to heal the afflictions of the skin, and Julius Mauthner's research on cholesterine afforded our generation a never-ending topic for debate. In every field — embryology, internal medicine, radiology, neurology — there were masters to instruct the students in Vienna, Prague, and Budapest. Even a bustling textile town like Brünn could boast later that Siegmund Kornfeld had lectured regularly on anatomy at the *Technische Hochschule* before

---

[13]For example, such editors as József Vészi on the *Pesti Napló*, József Csukássy of the *Pesti Hirlap* (until he founded, with Eugen Rákosi, the *Budapesti Hirlap*) Menyhert Palagyi of *Uj Nemzedék*, and Emil Makai of *A Hét*. Outstanding publishers were Singer & Wolfner and Mór Révai.

[14]See Franz Kobler, 'The Contribution of Austrian Jews to Jurisprudence', in *The Jews of Austria*, pp. 25-40.

embarking upon psychiatry in Vienna. The great reputation for medical training which the capital enjoyed owed much to the brilliant teachers and clinicians of Jewish ancestry.[15]

From rostrum and printed page other scholars added to the empire's cultural wealth. If a Theodor Gomperz conveyed the serenity of the classical world while his brothers played leading rôles in Brünn's and Vienna's moneyed circles,[16] other specialists were likely to identify themselves with a dominant national culture. Heinrich Friedjung was the prize example of German Austrian patriotism, while Henrik Marczali, Ignác Acsádi, and Ármin Vámbéry dug deep into the Magyar past. If a Ludwig Gumplowicz at Graz attempted to discern the emergence of "the state" through *Rassenkampf*, his son Maximilian, trained in history at Lvov, laboured on early medieval Polish texts at the University of Vienna. The most striking example of scholarship turned to ethnocentric considerations was Zsigmond Simonyi's search for the origins of Magyar when he was a professor at the University of Budapest.

In literature the emancipated generation was quite active and impressive. *Liliom* seems picturesque, even bland, when compared with the polemical broadsides of our time, and *The Guardsman* calls for Thespian finesse of a high order if it is to work. But who, better than Ferenc Molnár, acquainted the rest of the West with the empire's creative impulses? Possibly Schnitzler in Vienna, who was concerned in his writings with the problems of conversion to Christianity and who debated in private with Herzl the future of the Jews.[17] Both pointed to the ugliness and stupidity that marred their period in time, but it was their fate to suffer audiences and critics who chose to look for sentiment and the purely bitter-sweet in their creations. A host of less famous figures in the two capitals involved themselves in every facet of literary life. Peter Altenberg was the rebel against hypocritical convention, Alexander Bródy preached naturalism, Karl Kraus was the eternal moralist, and Ignotus (Hugo Veigelsberg) led yet another "Young Hungary". In sociological discourses, essays on aesthetics, literary debates, and satirical squibs there was a thorough ventilation of man's faults when he governed, and his errors when he described his condition.[18] Standing in the wings, heirs to such adventurousness and imagination, were young men of the calibre of Franz Kafka, Stefan Zweig, Franz Werfel, and Egon Friedell.

In music Mahler helped bring to a close the great romantic tradition, and Arnold Schönberg inaugurated the freedoms that preceded our electronic and aleatory experimentation. Could any other statement better encapsulate the ability of the first truly free generation to master the accepted canons and yet strike out in a

---

[15]See Moshe Atlas, 'Großjüdische Ärzte Wiens im neunzehnten und zwanzigsten Jahrhundert', *ibid.*, pp. 41-65.

[16]On these brothers, see *Österreichisches Biographisches Lexikon 1815-1950*, 6. Lieferung, Graz and Cologne 1957, pp. 31-32.

[17]Harry Zohn, 'Three Austrian Jews in German Literature: Schnitzler, Zweig, Herzl', in *The Jews of Austria*, pp. 69-71.

[18]For this period in Hungary, see Zoltán Horváth, *Die Jahrhundertwende in Ungarn. Geschichte der zweiten Reformgeneration 1896-1914*, Budapest 1966.

masterfully original manner? The same cannot be said for Imre Kálmán's charming but superficial operettas and Hermann Rosenzweig's fiery gipsy music. But musicologists like Guido Adler and Egon Wellesz, a publisher like Emil Hertzka, conductors like Bruno Walter and Arthur Bodanzky, even singers like Selma Kurz and Leopold Demuth attested to the general involvement in the musical life of Vienna, Budapest, and Prague.

Jewish contributions to painting, sculpture, and architecture were surprisingly meagre. A Philippe de László made a great reputation as a portraitist in England, but no one in the empire rivalled Pissarro, Modigliani, or Soutine.[19] Viennese society might seethe over the designs offered by Otto Wagner, Olbrich, and Josef Hoffmann, but antisemitism could not be invoked.

An appreciation of Jewish contributions to Austro-Hungarian culture and life requires caveats, of course. In all the fields covered above, non-Jews also played their part. One near-exception was psychiatry, where Freud's unorthodoxies, rivalled only by Schönberg's in originality and shock-value among the creations emanating from the Jewish community, seemed to inhibit or repel the traditional Christian man of medicine. A second field in which non-Jews had but a supporting rôle was journalism, for the rise of Catholic-Conservative, Catholic-Social, and antisemitic papers did not seriously threaten the prestige and the profits of the older dailies.

But industrialism owed a great debt to an Alexander Schoeller and other Gentile industrialists and artisans from what eventually would be the German Empire. In political life the members of cabinets and parliaments were substantially of long-established Catholic and Protestant families. As for Jewish influence in Liberal and Marxian political circles, it is next to impossible to decide where the emancipated generation had its greater influence. Within Social Democracy the incidence of Jews as leaders was high, but who can say that this fact was more decisive than the influence of moneyed circles in Vienna, Budapest, Prague, and Brünn upon Liberal policies? Whatever the verdict, one must remember the masses of non-Jewish workers and intellectuals who voted the Socialist way and the marked non-Jewish control of Liberal electoral and parliamentary strategy. In law, medicine, literature, and music the Jewish contributions were great, but not monopolistic. Richard Strauss had the lead on Mahler in 1914, to give an obvious example.

Another serious challenge to a proper appreciation of the Jewish contribution lies in the still under-explored field of economic history. The Nazis were able to ascertain and put on record all the Rothschild holdings in Austria in the 1930s, but the full extent of the famous house's influence during Dualism is known only in general outline. No one is unaware of the need of a history of the Mauthner family, of the Deutsch-Hatvany family, of all the great Jewish families, but who is hopeful that many of the records have survived? Also, one must face the fact that the spread of capitalism and the building up of great fortunes has not always seemed to all

---

[19]A conclusion arrived at from reading Karl Schwarz, *Jewish Artists of the 19th and 20th Centuries*, New York 1949.

observers to be in the general interest. Eduard März has made serious charges about the selfishness of the great banks in his theory that they impeded the flow of capital to areas ready for take-off.[20] Here, of course, an entire hierarchy of economic power is on trial, with accused and accusers from the Jewish and non-Jewish communities.

The many controversialists who denounced the Germans, Magyars, and Poles for their condescension towards, and sometimes repression of, other nationalities, have not spared the Jews some of their reproaches. The attitude of the self-sufficient Jewish burgher of Vienna and Prague was nearly always pro-German, certainly in the cultural sense. In Galicia there was a tendency not to oppose Polish pre-dominance over Ruthenes and Jews alike until Landau and Benno Straucher raised the banner of Jewish nationalism. Without the brains, the wealth, the actual numbers of the Jews in Hungary, could Magyarization have been as effective as it was? Czechs, Ruthenes, South Slavs, and Rumanians resented the Jewish collab-oration with those most responsible for Jewish emancipation, and the participation of Jewish intellectuals in Social Democratic plans for appeasing national bitterness meant little to them. In short, should one call the Jews of the empire a centripetal force, and question of questions, was this a bad thing?

Finally, there is the problem of creative originality in Franz Joseph's Dual Monarchy. In medicine research was undoubtedly first-rate. In operetta and gipsy music there was an atmospheric note rarely duplicated elsewhere. But in other fields there was a tendency to follow, to copy. Naturalism, symbolism, expression-ism, art for art's sake — the phrases and the creations seemed more at home in Paris, London, and Berlin. Nevertheless, Freud and Schönberg profoundly in-fluenced man's thinking. Like practically all persons of the emancipated generation, their loyalty to traditional Judaism was tepid. Freed of the constraints that prejudice and inwardness had forged, they epitomized in their works a conscious-ness of a dissolving society and its ills. Hundreds from the Jewish community made their contribution to the empire's last years. These two simply represent the best that was offered, and their best was rivalled but not surpassed by anyone else in the Western world.

---

[20]Eduard März, 'Besonderheiten in der Entwicklung des österreichischen Bankwesens', in *Schmollers Jahrbuch für Gesetzgebung, Verwaltung und Volkswirtschaft*, 77, 1957, No. 2, pp. 62-70.

The Economic and Cultural Rôle of the Jews in the Weimar Republic

BY DONALD L. NIEWYK

The rôle of Jews in the economy and culture of Weimar Germany has been exaggerated by both Nazi and anti-Nazi writers, the former to disparage alleged Jewish decadence and domination, the latter to praise Jewish achievements and to identify antisemitism as being in part rooted in jealousy and envy.[1] And yet, there can be no question that Jews contributed to some aspects of German economic and intellectual progress between 1919 and 1933 in numbers disproportionate to their representation in the population. The roughly 600,000 Germans of Jewish faith constituted just under one per cent of the German population before 1933, while there was probably an equal number of Jews who had broken all ties with the Hebrew religion.[2] The census figures, on which most economic analysis must rely, provide information only about Jews who adhered to Judaism. In identifying Jews in Weimar culture, however, it is essential to include all who had Jewish ancestors and who were therefore regarded as Jews by antisemites. A great many Jewish intellectuals and businessmen had long since ceased to think of themselves as Jews, and it was in large part the persistence of Judaeophobia that prevented their full assimilation. Indeed, the tension between social discrimination and opportunities for advancement in German economic and cultural life was instrumental in forming the productive pattern of Jewish participation in German society before 1933.

The overwhelming majority of German Jews was engaged in bourgeois occupations between 1918 and 1933. Almost three quarters of them made their living from trade, commerce, banking, and the professions, especially medicine and law. At the same time only about one quarter of the non-Jewish population of Germany was similarly employed. While professed Jews made up at most 0.9 per cent of the German population in the Weimar period, they held slightly more than 3.5 per cent

---

[1]Typical of the Nazi point of view are two publications of the Institut zum Studium der Judenfrage: *Die Juden in Deutschland*, Munich 1939, and F. O. H. Schulz, *Jude und Arbeiter: Ein Abschnitt aus der Tragödie des deutschen Volkes*, Berlin 1944. Anti-Nazi sources erring in the same direction are: Arnold Zweig, *Bilanz der deutschen Judenheit 1933, Ein Versuch*, Amsterdam 1934. Mit einem Nachwort von Achim von Borries, Neudruck, Cologne 1961. Marvin Lowenthal, *The Jews of Germany*, New York 1936, pp. 333-335; and Sidney Osborne, *Germany and Her Jews*, London 1939.

[2]For detailed demographical and sociological information about the Jews of Weimar Germany, consult: Erich Rosenthal, 'Trends in the Jewish Population in Germany, 1910-39', in *Jewish Social Studies*, VI, 1944, pp. 233-274; Esra Bennathan, 'Die demographische und wirtschaftliche Struktur der Juden', in *Entscheidungsjahr 1932. Zur Judenfrage in der Endphase der Weimarer Republik*, Ein Sammelband herausgegeben von Werner E. Mosse unter Mitwirkung von Arnold Paucker, Tübingen 1965, 1966 (Schriftenreihe wissenschaftlicher Abhandlungen des Leo Baeck Instituts 13), pp. 87-131; and Arthur Ruppin, *The Jews in the Modern World*, London 1934, 182-85, 218-20, 329-31.

of all positions in these trades.[3] The reasons why so many Jews belonged to the middle class are well known. For centuries virtually all German Jews had been obliged to live in cities and work in such artisan, retail sales, and banking occupations as Christians found undesirable. Often the very survival of local Jewish communities depended on their ability to provide the princes with substantial taxes and compulsory loans, and Jews therefore became adept at accumulating capital against the day of arbitrary official harassment. Having been freed from all legal disabilities comparatively recently — less than fifty years before the establishment of the Weimar Republic — insufficient time had passed for them to have lost their characteristic economic predilections. And, indeed, there was no compelling reason why they should have wanted to do so. Certainly there were Jewish artisans and retailers whose incomes compared unfavourably with those of their non-Jewish competitors or even of some skilled industrial workers. But the comfortable niches that most Jews occupied in the machinery of German capitalism provided them with a degree of social prestige and wealth that few of them could have held in contempt. Moreover, they experienced little difficulty in finding a measure of security from Judaeophobia in the independence of self-employment or the semi-independence of managerial positions. The great majority of German Jews, therefore, appeared to be reasonably content in the bourgeois occupations history seemed to have prescribed for them, at least until 1929 brought economic depression and increasingly successful Nazi agitation.

More than sixty-one per cent of all gainfully employed Jews in Weimar Germany were engaged in some form of trade or commerce. Of these, slightly more than one half were self-employed and nearly three quarters were retailers. Strong Jewish proclivities for economic independence kept most of these firms small or medium in size. Jewish business houses were of particular importance in the textile and clothing trades. In 1930 Jews owned four thousand of Germany's wholesale textile firms, or 40 per cent of the total, while nearly 60 per cent of all wholesale and retail clothing businesses were in Jewish hands, again divided among many hundreds of concerns. Around a quarter of all wholesalers of agricultural products were Jewish, although they and all other agricultural middle-men were increasingly challenged by farmers' co-operatives in the 1920s. Jews were also important in the wholesale metal trades and the retail grocery business.[4]

While most Jewish firms were neither large nor individually conspicuous, Jews were highly visible as owners of great department stores and chain-stores. In 1932 department stores owned by Jews accounted for 79 per cent of all business done by such enterprises. Just before the turn of the century the Jewish brothers Hermann and Leonhard Tietz had introduced department stores to Germany in conscious imitation of the American model. Later the brothers separated. Leonhard operated a chain of department stores in southern Germany and the Rhineland, while

[3]Bennathan, *loc. cit.*, pp. 104-113. Unless otherwise noted, all figures concerning Jews in the German economy are taken from this excellent essay, which is based on official census statistics.
[4]A. Marcus, 'Jews as Entrepreneurs in Weimar Germany', in *Yivo Annual of Jewish Social Science*, VII, pp. 175-203.

Hermann Tietz established his concern in Berlin and, together with his nephew, Oscar Tietz, made it into the city's largest in 1926 when he purchased the KDW *(Kaufhaus des Westens)* from another Jew, Adolf Jandorf. The brothers Franz, Georg, and Wilhelm Wertheim operated three large department stores in Berlin, as well as branches in Breslau and Rostock. Outside the capital Salman and Simon Schocken ran a chain of thirty department stores,[5] while two important chains of shoe shops, the Salamander and Leiser companies, were also Jewish-owned.[6]

Jews were similarly prominent as bankers in Weimar Germany. Almost half of all private banks, the number and importance of which declined after 1920, were owned by such famous Jewish banking families as the Mendelssohns, Bleichröders, and Schlesingers. On the other hand, Jews directed fewer than one per cent of Germany's more numerous and increasingly important credit banks, although those with Jewish managers included some of the largest and most successful of these financial institutions. Arthur Salomonsohn directed the *Disconto-Gesellschaft* and engineered its fusion with the *Deutsche Bank* just before his death in 1930, thus creating the famous *DD Bank*. Salomonsohn employed his considerable skills to consolidate the German potash industry and to help revive and rebuild Germany's heavy industry and merchant navy after the First World War. The equally important *Dresdner Bank* was directed by Eugen Gutmann and, after his death in 1925, by Henry Nathan. Jakob Goldschmidt, director of the *Darmstädter und Nationalbank*, was largely responsible after 1923 for acquiring substantial loans of working capital for German industry from Holland, Sweden, and North America. The University of Heidelberg in 1927 awarded him an honorary doctorate for his "services to the reconstruction of the German economy".[7]

Jews were less prominent in the leadership of German industry, although they were well represented in a few fields. Two major areas of Jewish participation were the mining and chemical industries of Upper Silesia, a region where Jews had encountered few barriers to careers in industry as a result of the relative indifference of the great landowners to Silesia's industrial potential. By 1919 the Friedländer coal concern had branched out into the coke, petroleum, and coal-tar industries. The largest of the Silesian iron and steel concerns, founded more than thirty years earlier by Georg von Caro, was ably directed until 1930 by Leo Lustig. Indeed, in contrast to conditions in the Rhineland, more than half of Upper Silesian industry was owned or directed by Jews before 1933.[8] Elsewhere the proportion was much smaller. After the murder of Walther Rathenau in 1922 and the retirement in 1927 of Paul Mamroth, Jewish influence in the *Allgemeine Elektricitäts-Gesellschaft* virtually disappeared; in 1933 the firm required no official "aryanization". While a number

[5]Siegfried Moses, 'Salman Schocken — His Economic and Zionist Activities', in *LBI Year Book V* (1960), pp. 73-104.

[6]For brief biographies of these and many other Jewish businessmen, consult: Daniel Bernstein, 'Wirtschaft: Handel und Industrie', in Siegmund Kaznelson (ed.), *Juden im deutschen Kulturbereich*, rev. ed.; Berlin 1959, 760-797.

[7]Daniel Bernstein, 'Wirtschaft: Finanzwesen', in Kaznelson, *op. cit.*, pp. 720-759.

[8]F. R. Bienenfeld, *The Germans and the Jews*, New York n.d., pp. 16-17; Osborne, *op. cit.*, pp. 18-19; Zweig, *op. cit.*, pp. 166-167.

of skilful Jewish scientists worked for the *I. G. Farben* trust, the only Jewish member of its board of directors was the distinguished chemist Carl von Weinberg. Only in the publishing industry were Jews unquestionably leaders. The two largest publishing houses in Germany, the Ullstein and Mosse concerns, published large numbers of books, magazines, and newspapers, and Jewish journalists were notable across almost the entire spectrum of the liberal and left-wing press.[9]

Since most Jews had been excluded from the judiciary, the civil and diplomatic services, and many corporative posts before 1918, large numbers of them concentrated in law and medicine, both then and during the Weimar years. In 1933 they made up 11 per cent of Germany's doctors, more than 16 per cent of its lawyers and notaries public, and around 13 per cent of its patent lawyers.[10]

Not all Jews in Germany enjoyed more or less comfortable middle-class lives. Nearly 20 per cent of them were refugees from Eastern Europe — *Ostjuden* — of whom the great majority were industrial workers, minor artisans, or itinerant salesmen. Of all the Jews in post-war Germany, these suffered the hardest lot. Before 1914 nearly ninety thousand of them had taken refuge in Germany from Russian pogroms.[11] During and after the war they were joined by another seventy thousand, some of whom were enlisted by the wartime German military government in Poland as workers for war industries, whilst others sought refuge in Germany from the antisemitism of the Tsarist and White Russian armies or from Communism. Crowded in the industrial centres of Upper Silesia, Berlin, and the Rhineland, they were subject to chronic unemployment, sporadic official harassment, and the resentment of both Jewish and non-Jewish Germans. Their presence in Germany after the armistice proved a boon to racist propagandists, who alternately carped on the nation's inability to absorb the *Ostjuden* and sought to obscure the distinctions between the newcomers and German Jews.[12]

Although concentrated in relatively few occupations, increasing numbers of German Jews took advantage of Weimar society's permeability to forsake mercantile pursuits in favour of positions in government, the arts, and academic careers. However, the trend towards assimilation was slow, and after 1929 National Socialist agitators had no trouble exploiting the Jews' vulnerable position in the German economy as part of their campaign against capitalism. Petty bourgeois businessmen resented the competition of both small Jewish tradesmen and Jewish department stores, while some workers harboured similar feelings about *Ostjuden* who were willing to work for lower wages than German citizens. The fact that Jews of all classes were as hard hit by the depression as other Germans was frequently ignored. Close traditional Jewish ties with finance capitalism encouraged the Nazis

[9]Bernstein, 'Wirtschaft: Handel und Industrie', in Kaznelson, *op. cit.*, pp. 772-781; Siegmund Kaznelson, 'Verlag und Buchhandel', in Kaznelson, *op. cit.*, pp. 131-146.
[10]Bennathan, *loc. cit.*, pp. 111-112.
[11]Jacob Toury, 'Ostjüdische Handarbeiter in Deutschland vor 1914', *Bulletin des Leo Baeck Instituts*, 21 (1963), pp. 81-91.
[12]S. Adler-Rudel, *Ostjuden in Deutschland, 1880-1940. Zugleich eine Geschichte der Organisationen, die sie betreuten*, Tübingen 1959 (Schriftenreihe wissenschaftlicher Abhandlungen des Leo Baeck Instituts 2), pp. 60-119.

to make blanket demands for the destruction of "interest slavery" to "rapacious" Jewish capital. Resentment against Jewish capitalists was intensified by the concentrations of Jewish employees in Jewish-owned establishments, in-growth that in some firms reached levels of 40 per cent of all employees.[13] There was, of course, no truth in Nazi charges that Jews dominated the German economy. Of the nine wealthiest men in Weimar Germany only one, Baron Maximilian von Goldschmidt–Rothschild, was Jewish, while Hugo Stinnes, the richest man in Germany and ruler of an enormous industrial empire in the early 1920s, was no friend of the Jews.[14] By the same token it would be a mistake to over-estimate the importance of Jewish contributions to the Weimar economy. Certainly many Jewish business and professional men constituted a vigorous and progressive element in the Republic, but the "economic miracle" in largely *judenrein* post-war Germany after 1948 suggests that Jews were useful rather than essential in the functioning of that economy.[15]

Jews were much more important and creative in almost every branch of cultural life in Weimar Germany. This phenomenon is usually traced to the Hebrew religion's long-standing affirmation of the life of the mind and to Jewish longings to overcome discrimination and attain security and social esteem through intellectual achievement. It is the latter influence that most interests us here, for their position as "outsiders" encouraged Jews to question popular ideas and to take risks in defying authority. In this sense most Jewish intellectuals harboured ambivalent attitudes towards the culture of the Weimar Republic. Undeniably many of them were enthusiastic about its emphasis on rationality and its faith in human progress, the strength and vigour of German cultural institutions, and the degree of emancipation that permitted Jews to use these institutions without giving up their identity as Jews. At the same time most remained acutely aware that they enjoyed less than full social equality, and this consciousness of rejection was a major stimulus to creativity. As outsiders they were in a position to view popular assumptions without reverence, and as a minority deprived of full social equality they were unlikely to accept the status quo with equanimity.[16]

This qualified alienation expressed itself in three ways: From some Jewish intellectuals it elicited overt criticism of majority values. In others it prompted radical departures from established cultural and artistic norms. For still others it stimulated efforts to excel in accepted forms and modes of thought.

Weimar theatre accurately mirrored the diverse ways in which alienation impelled some German Jews towards innovation and criticism. It would be no exaggeration

---

[13]Bennathan, *loc. cit.*, pp. 109-110, 119-120.
[14]*Was muss das schaffende Volk vom politischen, wirtschaftlichen, religiösen Juden- und Rassenhass des reaktionären Faschismus wissen?* Für Redner und Funktionäre herausgegeben von der Sozialdemokratischen Partei Deutschlands, Ortsverein Hannover, Hanover 1924, p. 9.
[15]Henry C. Wallich, *Mainsprings of the German Revival*, New Haven 1955, pp. 270-271.
[16]Oscar Handlin, 'Jews in the Culture of Middle Europe', in Max Kreutzberger (ed.), *Studies of the Leo Baeck Institute*, New York 1967, pp. 159-175; Istvan Deak, *Weimar Germany's Left-Wing Intellectuals. A Political History of the Weltbühne and its Circle*, Berkeley and Los Angeles 1968, pp. 24-29; Howard M. Sachar, *The Course of Modern Jewish History*, New York 1963, pp. 394-405.

to describe the Weimar stage as decisively influenced by Jewish directors, actors, and playwrights. Max Reinhardt, already Berlin's most influential director, further developed an expressionist technique that integrated music, dance, pantomime, and other related arts into the obsessive naturalism that had dominated the pre-war stage. He also found time to convey his skills to a new generation of disciples, among whom were two Jews who became prominent as directors of expressionist and neo-objectivist theatre in the capital: Leopold Jessner at the State Theatre, and Victor Barnowsky at the House of Comedy.[17] The German screen, too, was profoundly influenced by Jewish writers, actors, and directors, including Carl Mayer, co-author of *The Cabinet of Dr. Caligari*, and Fritz Lang, who directed *Caligari* and several other notable expressionist and neo-objectivist films.[18]

Of the five or six leading expressionist playwrights of the Weimar years, three — Ernst Toller, Carl Sternheim, and Franz Werfel — were Jews who stood in the vanguard of the movement, while Toller subsequently went on to become one of the pioneers of the "new objectivity" *(Neue Sachlichkeit)* of the mid-1920s.[19] Toller was clearly the one most alienated from the norms of German society. Transformed into a Leftist and a pacifist by World War I, he became one of the leaders of the Bavarian Soviet Republic in 1919, for which he was sentenced to five years' imprisonment. His plays attempted to rouse the masses from apathy by passionately denouncing capitalism and militarism. Toller's first play, *Die Wandlung* (Transfiguration) was partially autobiographical in that it told of the conversion of an ardent young patriot into an idealistic revolutionary socialist by the grotesque horrors of war. Expressionist devices like dancing skeletons and speaking choruses, however effective in *Die Wandlung*, turned into *clichés* in Toller's subsequent dramas, as did his self-righteous harping on the war and the revolution. Deepening pessimism over his inability to influence the course of events was mirrored in his 1927 neo-objectivist play *Hoppla, wir leben!* (Hoppla, such is life!), in which a revolutionary Leftist commits suicide in despair over mankind, following his failure to assassinate a former Socialist comrade who had been rewarded with a high government post for betraying the revolution. A similar end awaited Toller himself in a New York hotel room in 1939. Another Jewish critic of German society, Carl Sternheim, was, unlike Toller, virtually unknown outside his homeland. His 1926 play *Die Schule von Uznach* carried his pungent satires on bourgeois morality into the Weimar period with cynical mockery of the ethical nihilism and sexual licence that post-war German youth took for emancipation. Less overtly alienated was yet a third popular Jewish playwright, Franz Werfel, an Austrian who found his most receptive audience in Germany. Together with the non-Jews Oskar Kokoschka and Ernst

[17]H. F. Garten, *Modern German Drama*, revised ed., London 1964, pp. 84-85, 168-169; Fritz Engel, 'Theater', in Kaznelson, *op. cit.*, pp. 201-205; E. G. Lowenthal, 'Die Juden im öffentlichen Leben', in *Entscheidungsjahr 1932*, pp. 65-67; a useful review of research on Jews in all phases of German expressionism is Hans Tramer, 'Der Expressionismus. Bemerkungen zum Anteil der Juden an einer Kunstepoche', in *Bulletin des Leo Baeck Instituts*, 5 (1958), pp. 33-46.

[18]Siegfried Kracauer, *From Caligari to Hitler: A Psychological History of the German Film*, Princeton, New Jersey 1947, pp. 61-66, 96-106, 149-151, 218-223, 248-250.

[19]Of the others, Paul Kornfeld and Ferdinand Bruckner were Jews, Carl Zuckmayer a "half-Jew", whilst Fritz von Unruh, Georg Kaiser and Bertolt Brecht were not Jewish.

Barlach he had helped to pioneer the expressionist drama immediately prior to World War I. While Toller fulminated against capitalism, and Sternheim lampooned the middle class, Werfel concerned himself with the more personal problem of human wavering between the divine and the demonic. A master of the psychological dissection of characters, Werfel was at his best in the 1920 play *Der Spiegelmensch* (The Mirror Man), in which the central figure was made aware of his lower instincts by an implacable mirror-image that induced him to commit suicide in atonement for his sins. Similar themes marked Werfel's historical dramas about the Austrian Archduke Maximilian (short-lived Emperor of Mexico) and the Apostle Paul. Underlying Werfel's preoccupation with ethics was a profound religious mysticism that stemmed from his Jewish background.[20]

In literature, the Jewish novelist Jakob Wassermann was one of the Republic's five leading impressionist novelists,[21] while Arnold Zweig and Alfred Döblin helped to introduce expressionism to German fiction. Zweig's novels denounced German militarism as forcefully as the plays of Toller. Zweig had experienced the brutality of the Prussian bureaucracy at first hand as a member of the press section of the German high command on the eastern front in World War I. The most notable of his pacifist novels, *Der Streit um den Sergeanten Grischa* (The Case of Sergeant Grischa), appeared in 1927. It told of a Russian prisoner of war who escaped from his German captors and assumed the name of a comrade who had deserted, only to be executed as a spy when recaptured by the Germans. Although made aware of the Russian's true identity and thus of his innocence by a compassionate divisional officer, headquarters heartlessly refused to reverse the sentence. Zweig's personal response to the persistance of Prussian bureaucracy in Weimar Germany was to associate himself closely with the Zionist movement.[22]

In contrast to Zweig, Weimar Germany's most popular Jewish novelist, Jakob Wassermann, was neither angry nor particularly creative. Although a skilfull craftsman who attained international popularity, his style was derived essentially from Balzac and Dostoyevsky, employing themes that described the attainment of humility and selflessness through suffering. Little of his sentimental fiction has enjoyed lasting appeal, and Wassermann is best remembered as the author of an eloquent autobiographical sketch, *Mein Leben als Deutscher und Jude*, published in 1921. Sometimes mistaken for a pure and simple denunciation of German anti-semitism, the essay is also an expression of faith that the suffering caused by virulent

[20]Garten, *op. cit.*, pp. 96-101, 111-115, 138-147; Richard Samuel and R. Hinton Thomas, *Expressionism in German Life, Literature, and the Theatre*, Cambridge 1939, pp. 45-47, 58-61; Richard Beckley, 'Ernst Toller', and W. H. Fox, 'Franz Werfel', in Alex Natan (ed.), *German Men of Letters*, III, London 1968, pp. 85-128; Solomon Liptzin, *Germany's Stepchildren*, Philadelphia 1948, pp. 195-208; Paul Stoecklein, 'Franz Werfel', in Hermann Friedmann and Otto Mann (eds.), *Deutsche Literatur im zwanzigsten Jahrhundert*, Heidelberg 1954, pp. 264-287; Ernst Toller, *I Was A German*, translated by Edward Crankshaw, London 1934.

[21]The four major non-Jewish impressionists were Heinrich and Thomas Mann, Hermann Hesse, and Hermann Stehr. A useful bibliography of Jewish authors is C. A. Stonehill (ed.), *The Jewish Contribution to Civilization*, Cheltenham 1940.

[22]Jethro Bithell, *Modern German Literature*, London 1939, pp. 422-423; Liptzin, *Germany's Stepchildren*, 281-284.

post-war Judaeophobia would purify and reconcile German and Jew. Wassermann must have been encouraged about the prospects of reconciliation by the enormous popularity of his 1928 novel *Der Fall Maurizius;* this prompted him to deliver public lectures on the main character, Etzel Andergast, before adoring crowds that included the cream of the German intelligentsia. [23]

Wassermann's penchant for subjecting his fictional characters to lengthy psychological scrutiny was imitated and given a psycho-analytical twist by several Jewish *Literaten.* The best of them, Alfred Döblin, was a Berlin neurologist — a practitioner of the science widely associated in the public mind with Jews. Döblin produced both historical novels and sophisticated science-fiction stories, but his most popular and enduring novel, *Berlin Alexanderplatz*, was a naturalistic attempt to capture the mental processes of a down and out Berlin worker who had become a common criminal out of stupidity and bitterness. Not only is it a remarkable record of the thoughts of a proletarian tough, but it compassionately delineates dehumanised urban conditions from the viewpoint of the political Left. The historical novels of Lion Feuchtwanger and Alfred Neumann similarly attempted to penetrate the minds of their subjects, but with considerably less skill and perception. Psychoanalytical devices also marked the almost universally popular biographies by Emil Ludwig of such diverse historical characters as Bismarck, Jesus, and Cleopatra. [24]

Jews found considerable opportunities to comment on Weimar society as journalists in the moderate and left-wing press. They edited and contributed to Weimar Germany's best newspapers, including the *Frankfurter Zeitung* and the *Berliner Tageblatt*, as well as a host of lesser publications. Most of their journalism was notable for its terse clarity of style as well as its moderate and democratic attitudes; it trenchantly criticized the Republic's short-comings without implying that there was no hope of improvement within the Weimar framework. [25] The same cannot be said for a small group of independent Jewish journalists who made up nearly two thirds of the *Weltbühne* circle, of whom Siegfried Jacobsohn, Kurt Hiller, and Kurt Tucholsky were most prominent. Their grim, frequently satirical attacks on the enemies of radical socialism and on the leaders of the Republic, some of them written from comfortable retreats in neighbouring countries, helped to disillusion elements of the intellectual Left with political democracy. It may be that they and their non-Jewish colleagues were not influential enough to have reversed the trend towards a catastrophe, but — recent attempts to rehabilitate them notwithstanding [26] — there can be no question that these irresponsible ideologues did their best

[23] Bithell, *op. cit.*, pp. 332-338; Liptzin, *op. cit.*, pp. 178-184; Jakob Wassermann, *Mein Weg als Deutscher und Jude*, Berlin 1921.

[24] Bithell, *op. cit.*, pp. 416-417, 434, 436; Victor Lange, *Modern German Literature, 1870-1940*, Ithaca 1945, pp. 86-87; Robert Minder, 'Alfred Döblin', in Friedmann and Mann, *op. cit.*, pp. 249-268; W. E. Yuill, 'Lion Feuchtwanger', in Natan, *op. cit.*, III, pp. 179-208.

[25] Lowenthal, *loc. cit.*, pp. 59-64.

[26] Deak, *op. cit.*, Harold L. Poor, *Kurt Tucholsky and the Ordeal of Germany, 1914-1935*, New York 1968.

to discredit free institutions in Germany at a time when they needed every possible support. [27]

The most original musical mind of the twentieth century was that of Arnold Schönberg, a Viennese Jew who chose to make Berlin his home in 1925. There he received the recognition that Vienna had begrudged him. He was called to succeed Ferruccio Busoni as professor of composition at the Berlin Academy, and there was considerable scope for the performance of his compositions in the German capital. Not that the average Berlin audience found Schönberg's atonality particularly assimilable or that he was without professional critics, but Berlin produced little of the widespread petty carping that had plagued the composer in Vienna. In Germany Schönberg not only completed eight new compositions, but he exerted a strong influence on virtually all Weimar composers, including three young Jews — Kurt Weill, Hans Eisler, and Paul Dessau — all of whom have earned more recognition on account of their setting to music the political verses and songs of Bertolt Brecht than for their abstract compositions. An enthusiastic champion of the new atonality was the Jewish music director of Berlin's Kroll Opera, Otto Klemperer. [28] However, the other major Jewish conductor of the day, Bruno Walter, had difficulty in understanding the post-romantic idiom and never included such works in his concerts with the Berlin Philharmonic and Leipzig Gewandhaus orchestras. [29] Of the three great Jewish instrumentalists of the Weimar years, Fritz Kreisler, Arthur Schnabel, and Emanuel Feuermann, only the last-named displayed genuine interest in performing atonal compositions. [30]

One of Weimar Germany's most original architects, Erich Mendelsohn, was Jewish. He and Walter Gropius led the frontal attack for modern architecture against the heavy formalism that popular taste had inherited from the Second Reich. Both insisted that buildings, in addition to being functional, must be *organic* — that they must be active participants rather than passive intruders in their settings. But while the architects of the *Bauhaus* fashioned geometric structures, Mendelsohn designed sculptured buildings with boldly curving forms. Arguing that nature abhors the pedantic geometry of man he proved that steel and concrete can appear plastic with his first and most radical creation, the famous Einstein tower near Potsdam, which resembles an enormous submarine conning tower with windows and doors, crowned by an observatory. His subsequent designs for a variety of department stores and office buildings pushed structural framework far behind the glass façades, making the upper stories seem to float. In some respects his architecture presaged our own disillusionment with the antiseptically functional,

[27]Gordon A. Craig, 'Engagement and Neutrality in Weimar Germany', in Walter Laqueur and George L. Mosse (eds.), *Literature and Politics in the Twentieth Century*, New York 1967, p. 55; Kurt Sontheimer, *Antidemokratisches Denken in der Weimarer Republik*, Munich 1962, p. 395.

[28]Hans Heinz Stuckenschmidt, *Arnold Schoenberg*, translated by Edith T. Roberts and Humphrey Searle, New York 1959, pp. 92-109; Oswald Jonas, 'Schaffende Musiker', in Kaznelson, *op. cit.*, pp. 158-160.

[29]Bruno Walter, *Theme and Variations*, translated by James A. Galston, New York 1946, pp. 169-170, 233-299.

[30]David Ewen, *Men and Women Who Make Music*, New York 1949, pp. 129-135; Rudolf Kastner, 'Nachschaffende Musiker', in Kaznelson, *op. cit.*, pp. 171-172, 174.

and it has been an important inspiration to the school of contemporary architecture that prefers to call itself "modern baroque".[31]

German Jews furnished no equivalent of the innovative genius of Schönberg and Mendelsohn to the painting of the Weimar years. Max Liebermann, the Grand Old Man of German impressionism and president of the German Academy of Arts, remained the most popular artist in Germany — probably because he never developed beyond the austere techniques he had mastered well before World War One.[32] Among younger Jewish painters only Ludwig Meidner and Jankel Adler departed radically from pre-war impressionism, and neither of them approached the boldly abstractionist experiments of Kandinsky and Klee or the bitter social comments of Dix and Grosz, all of whom were non-Jews.[33]

The addition of notable Jewish scholars to the faculties of German universities enormously enriched Weimar academic life. Ernst Cassirer, the originator of the philosophy of symbolic forms, verified the compatibility of Einstein's theory of relativity with his own neo-Kantianism.[34] In the field of history, Gustav Mayer perceptively analysed the German labour movements from a bourgeois point of view while Arthur Rosenberg dissected the Second Reich from the standpoint of a left-wing Social Democrat.[35] The sociologist Karl Mannheim fought with some success to preserve his discipline from embracing unreservedly deterministic explanations of human consciousness while he investigated irrational influences on mass behaviour.[36] Hermann Kantorowicz argued persuasively in favour of basing German law on sociological concepts rather than dogmatic legal constructions alone.[37] Jewish contributions to scientific advancements were hardly less distinguished. No fewer than five of the nine Nobel prizes won by German citizens during the Weimar years were won by Jewish scientists, three for medicine and three for physics.[38]

---

[31]Wolf von Eckardt, *Eric Mendelsohn*, New York 1960, pp. 9-23; Peter Gay, *Weimar Culture: The Outsider as Insider*, New York and Evanston 1968, pp. 97-101; Barbara Miller Lane, *Architecture and Politics in Germany, 1918-1945*, Cambridge, Mass. 1968, pp. 32-33, 52-56, 60, 61.

[32]Karl Scheffler, *Max Liebermann*, Wiesbaden 1953; Heinrich Strauss, 'Judentum und deutsche Kunst. Zum Problem Max Liebermann', in Robert Weltsch (ed.), *Deutsches Judentum, Aufstieg und Krise*, Veröffentlichung des Leo Baeck Instituts, Stuttgart 1963, pp. 289-304.

[33]Max Osborn, 'Bildende Künste', in Kaznelson, *op. cit.*, pp. 88-94; Franz Roh, *German Art in the Twentieth Century*, Greenwich, Connecticut n.d., pp. 14-180; Peter Selz, *German Expressionist Painting*, Berkeley and Los Angeles 1957, pp. 32-38, 274-311; Bernard S. Meyers, *The German Expressionists: A Generation in Revolt*, New York n.d., pp. 71-294.

[34]Felix Kaufmann, 'Cassirer's Theory of Scientific Knowledge', in Paul Arthur Schilpp (ed.), *The Philosophy of Ernst Cassirer*, Evanston 1949, pp. 183-214; Harold Landry, 'Philosophie', in Kaznelson, *op. cit.*, p. 261.

[35]Gustav Mayer, *Erinnerungen. Vom Journalisten zum Historiker der deutschen Arbeiterbewegung*, Zürich-Wien 1949.

[36]Ernst Noam, 'Volkswirtschaft und Soziologie', in Kaznelson, *op. cit.*, pp. 703-704.

[37]Max Pinn, 'Rechtswissenschaft', in Kaznelson, *op. cit.*, pp. 600-601.

[38]The five were: for physics, Albert Einstein, 1921 (for formulating the law of photo-electric effect); James Franck and Gustav Hertz, 1925 (for discovering the laws governing the impact of electrons upon atoms); for medicine, Otto Meyerhof, 1922 (for research in the metabolism of energy in human muscles); and Otto Warburg, 1931 (for discovering the nature of respiratory ferment).

Without these and other Jewish participants, the cultural life of Weimar Germany would have lost much of its richness and diversity. Their achievements in virtually every area reached a minimum level of first-rate technical competence, while in music, science, and architecture some of their contributions earned them lasting international recognition. Success in almost every case can be attributed to their openness to new ideas and their willingness to attempt bold experiments. Ironically, precisely the same achievements and characteristics helped Hitler convince more than a few Germans that Jews alone were responsible for much of what bewildered and antagonised many ordinary people: Marxian socialism, pacifism, internationalism, expressionism, psycho-analysis, atonal music, and organic architecture. In truth, Jews were no more solely responsible for modern culture in Germany than they were for the abuses of capitalism. The left-wing plays of Bertolt Brecht by far excelled those of Toller, and occasioned more controversy than those of any Weimar dramatist. None of the psychological novels by Jewish authors could stand comparison in popularity and quality with the best works of Thomas Mann. Nor were Hindemith or Gropius less controversial and creative than Schönberg and Mendelsohn. What made Hitler's myth plausible was the disproportionately large number of Jews among the critics and innovators of Weimar culture, supplemented by occasional National Socialist attempts to fasten the Semitic label on non-Jewish intellectuals. As a result, the Nazi-led revolt against cultural modernism and economic capitalism inevitably destroyed the basis of life for German Jewry, with results that were almost as disastrous for German culture as they were for Germany's Jews.

Comments on the Papers of William A. Jenks and Donald L. Niewyk

BY ANDREW G. WHITESIDE

The subject of Jewry is a delicate one. Writers about Jews, whether they themselves are Jewish or not, have tended to be uncritically philo-Semitic or venomously antisemitic. In a recent review in *The New York Times* of Ernest van den Haag's *Jewish Mystique* — an attempt like the papers of Professor Jenks and Professor Niewyk to illuminate the history of the Jews in a Christian culture — Anatole Broyard observes that for Jews, ambivalence about the world in which they live has been almost a way of life and they have usually preferred that the truths about themselves be wrapped in jests, custom-tailored by their own comics. These two learned and informed papers are a valuable contribution to knowledge of what we may call the Jewish mystique. Both papers have dealt with those schismatics who left the conservative political and social traditions of the old Jewish communities and of the rabbinic elite and who became, as Salo Baron put it, "followers of Marx or Spinoza, or altogether materialistic".

It is generally recognized that these emancipated Jews-without-Judaism did not achieve perfect integration into German national culture. The rising force of racism after 1880, which declared that Jews could never become Germans, made the path to assimilation increasingly difficult. The Jewish response to antisemitism was complex and diverse. Some assimilationists became, as Oscar Jaszi observed, — thinking perhaps, among others, of Moritz Benedikt of the *Neue Freie Presse* — "a loud and bigoted bodyguard of the German and Magyar national leadership". Others sought to become the "conscience of the German people", *das andere Deutschland,* and to correct the excrescences of the German national spirit by criticism through the media of literature and the arts. Still others turned away from assimilation towards Zionism. These are only the main responses.

The assimilationists were troubled not only by antisemitism. Most of them found intellectual and psychological difficulties in combining their Jewish heritage with at least some of the main currents of German national culture. One tragic and typical victim of the fascination which Teutonic nationalism exercised over a number of Jews was the brilliant young Viennese philosopher Otto Weininger. His attraction to a mixture of Aryan racism and romanticized Christianity such as was found in Richard Wagner and Houston Stewart Chamberlain caused him to become possessed of a violent hatred of his Jewishness and to renounce Judaism in favour of Protestantism, — only to find that the Aryan *Weltanschauung* to which he was so attracted denied the possibility of Jewish assimilation. His despair ultimately led to his suicide at the age of twenty-three. That act reflected in magnified form all the tensions that afflicted the assimilationist Jewish intelligentsia of Central Europe.

174

Theodor Lessing, a German philosopher of Jewish extraction, in his work *Der jüdische Selbsthaß*, cited Weininger's death as evidence that emancipated Central European Jews suffered from intense selfhatred. The Nazis pointed to Weininger's suicide as the only logical step which could be taken by a Jew anxious to solve the Jewish question.

Masochistic antisemitism seems to have been a characteristic feature of many German and Austrian Jewish intellectuals of the era before the advent of Hitler. Examples can be found in the works of Heine, Marx, Lassalle, Walther Rathenau, Maximilian Harden, Theodor Lessing and Karl Kraus. Kraus, who had abandoned Judaism at an early age, became famous for the mercilessness of his attacks on the failings of other Jews.

This was more than a violent reaction against his father, or against the corrupt Viennese press of his day, and the philistinism of the purse-proud Viennese liberal bourgeoisie, many of whom, as Professor Jenks notes, were Jewish. He attacked his own people as the Old Testament prophets castigated the unworthiness of the Israelites for betraying the trust that God had placed in them. The bitterness of his alienation was a symptom of the importance that inheritance played in the formation of his personality. Like many German-speaking Jewish intellectuals, Kraus was both a victim and a critic of the situation in which the Central European Jewish intelligentsia found itself at the opening of the twentieth century. It was a class that had become alienated from a Judaism which it regarded as parochial, and was attracted by what it perceived as the moral seriousness of the German cultural tradition — a tradition in which it found deep affinity to that of Judaism. Yet many of these Jews were aware that the society in which they lived was one in which they could never be accepted. Lassalle once quipped that he hated two things, Jews and *Littérateurs*, and that he had the misfortune to be both. Kraus criticized Heine, a classic case of German-Jewish symbiosis, on aesthetic grounds as a vulgar and superficial cosmopolitan, but his great dislike of Heine stemmed from his conviction that Heine was facetious and lacked the moral seriousness of both the German and Jewish traditions. For Kraus, Heine was "a Moses who struck the rock of the German language and brought forth nothing but Eau de Cologne". In his poem 'A Prayer to the Sun of Gibeon' Kraus called down the vengeance of Jehovah on the Jewish people for its worship of false gods.

For racism of every kind, be it noted, Kraus had of course infinite contempt, but the esteem in which antisemites held him, from Lanz von Liebenfels and H. S. Chamberlain to, it was rumoured, the *Reich* Ministry of Popular Enlightenment, is a reflection of the fact that he was, as Theodor Lessing observed, a significant example of the alienation and self-hatred of the assimilated Central European Jew.

Zionism was one possible response to the Jewish situation. The movement derived much of its inspiration from the very civilization — German and Russian — that it repudiated. Before moving to his rediscovery of the treasures of Chassidism, even Martin Buber — a Viennese contemporary of Karl Kraus — had experienced the temptations of assimilation and in his revolt against modern materialism and his search for moral certitude in the values of a reinvigorated Judaism, Buber was greatly indebted to nineteenth-century German Romanticism and to the thought of Friedrich Nietzsche. When attempts are made to trace too simple a line from German thought to Nazism, we should also ponder the contribution of German thought to the formation of modern Israel.

The return of the Jewish intellectual to his roots can also be seen in circles far removed from Zionism. In 1900 Sigmund Freud[1] affirmed that he regarded himself as Jewish by joining the Vienna lodge of the B'nai B'rith society. Thirty years later he told one of his visitors that "my language is German. I considered myself a German intellectual until I noticed the growth of antisemitism in Austria. Since that time I prefer to call myself a Jew." Franz Kafka ultimately reaffirmed his Jewish allegiance and rejected the habit of the Bohemian Jewish middle class to identify with the Germans against the Czechs. Richard Beer-Hofmann slowly came to abandon his belief in assimilation and in the end proclaimed his faith in his destiny as a Jewish artist. Arnold Schönberg — Jewish by origin, brought up a Catholic, and a convert to Protestantism at the age of eighteen — embarked on a long spiritual Odyssey which began with the unfinished oratorio *Jacob's Ladder* of 1913, and ended with his formal return to his ancestral faith, after the advent of Hitler and his own exile.

Some Jewish intellectuals chose to ignore the signs of tension between themselves and their environment or were crudely ignorant of its existence. Walter Laqueur recently recalled, in the magazine *Encounter*[2], in a perceptive analysis of the position of German-Jewish intellectual circles, that the young Jewish writer Moritz Goldstein believed in 1912 that the country's Jewish journalists, theatre directors, actors, musicians, and writers, were split personalities, divorced from the people amidst whom they were living, and therefore that they refused to face the questions raised by their virtual management of German culture. This refusal, he maintained, was a dangerous fallacy for "the others [that is, the rest of Germany] do not feel that we are Germans" and much of the cultural achievement of the Jewish intelligentsia with its liberal and "good-European" values was rejected by the German people. In literature and the arts, he said, "any major initiative must be rooted in a popular and national framework", and this "rootedness" the Jews lacked, "despite all their intellectual and emotional efforts". Goldstein's article produced a storm of denunciation, as may be imagined, the essence of which was that Jews would become fully integrated in the future as the last vestiges of antisemitism and exclusion disappeared.[3]

Whether or not Moritz Goldstein was correct in his analysis, Laqueur points out that when the Weimar Republic did away with at least the last formal restrictions, Jewish intellectuals remained not only radicals in politics but alienated and de-

[1]For a detailed study of Freud as a Jew see Ernst Simon, 'Sigmund Freud, the Jew' in *LBI Year Book II* (1957), pp. 270-305. — Ed.

[2]Walter Z. Laqueur, 'The Tucholsky Complaint', *Encounter*, vol. XXXIII, No. 4, October 1969, pp. 76-80. — Ed.

[3]See also Moritz Goldstein, 'German Jewry's Dilemma. The story of a Provocative Essay', in *LBI Year Book II* (1957), pp. 236-254. — Ed.

structive critics. He cites Kurt Tucholsky and the circle that wrote for *Die Weltbühne* as classic examples. By making no effort to differentiate between patriotism and maniacal chauvinism, they disqualified themselves even in the eyes of their friends on the Left, Socialists and Communists alike. They lacked sensitivity for the patriotic feelings of their fellow citizens and were incapable of understanding anybody who reacted differently from the way they did.

This "Tucholsky Syndrome" as he calls it, Laqueur fears has been spreading as a prominent feature of the New Left in Europe and America, where many of its leaders are Jewish. Works like *MacBird!*[4] and the columns of *New Left Notes* reflect a rejection of the American way of life and the aspirations of the American people that are remarkably similar to that found in Tucholsky's *Deutschland, Deutschland über alles*. The New Left in America, like the *Weltbühne* circle of authors in Germany, opposes not just its country's policy at home and abroad, but insists that its judges are hangmen; its jails are worse than Auschwitz, its police worse than the Gestapo, its massacres worse than Babi Yar. It derides all patriotism, every national symbol, and all the country's venerable traditions and traditional values. It is of no consequence for the general public's view of these radicals that the vast majority of American Jews has no sympathy with the New Left. It is, as Laqueur observes, Mark Rudd, not the Chassidic rabbis of Brooklyn, who determines the public image. This is not the place to attempt an analysis of the rôle of the Jewish intelligentsia in the cultural life of the United States or in its radical movements, but concerned observers point out that the destructive criticism of everything German in pre-1933 Central Europe and of everything American in this country today, by alienated young intellectuals, represents a continuing and peculiar characteristic of the emancipated Jewish intelligentsia, and is a serious perversion, not a continuation, of the great age-old Jewish tradition of championing progress and social justice. Historical analysis of the rôle of Jews in Germany and Austria offers today unusually attractive opportunities for achieving that elusive quality of relevance that our students demand of us.

---

[4]The satirical play "MacBird!" by Barbara Garson (a Jewish student) was published in the United States in 1966, and in England in 1967 in "Penguin Modern Playwrights". It is an unpalatable parody of Macbeth applied to the murder of President Kennedy. — Ed.

Comments on the Paper of Donald L. Niewyk

BY WOLFGANG SAUER

The following remarks will deal with Mr. Jenks's paper only as far as structural and conceptual problems are concerned. In all substantive matters I will concentrate on Mr. Niewyk's paper as I cannot claim expertise on the Habsburg monarchy. In addition the state of research as evidenced by the two papers seems to suggest that the study of the Jews in the Weimar Republic is still more in need of work and help.

Our subject concerns what is certainly one of the most agonizing problems of modern German history, and historians are apparently moving only slowly into it. To be sure, we have a number of valuable monographs contributing to the subject, among others those of the Leo Baeck Institute.* But we do not as yet have an all-embracing comprehensive study of the subject itself. The more do we owe our thanks to the programme committee for having drawn our attention to this lacuna of modern German history.

As formulated for today's session, the subject presents us with the difficulty of finding a common denominator for economy and culture, and I doubt that we can find such a denominator. Mr. Niewyk has not addressed himself to the question while Mr. Jenks tried to build a bridge between the two fields by including politics and the press, thus expanding his subject to a point where it borders on the social rôle, generally, of the Jews in their host societies. But this must remain a compromise. The reason for singling out economy and culture was probably that these were the fields with the highest concentration of Jewish activities. But by isolating these fields we tend to lose sight of the important question as to just why Jews were concentrating in them. Mr. Niewyk has attempted some explanation which, however, for the reasons mentioned remains somewhat impressionistic. In addition his explanation is essentially historical, and this still leaves us with the question as to why the historical pattern did not change in the Weimar Republic. Or did it? Was there a change or the beginning of it? We do not know, but we would like to know.

Another, more general and more difficult problem is how we are to define the term "Jew" for our purpose. Both authors are aware of the problem, and Mr. Jenks has touched on what is the particular difficulty — that religion as the clearest and simplest dividing line is inoperative here because in social terms the converted or

---

*The two large symposia, *Entscheidungsjahr 1932. Zur Judenfrage in der Endphase der Weimarer Republik*. Ein Sammelband herausgegeben von Werner E. Mosse unter Mitwirkung von Arnold Paucker, Tübingen 1965, 1966 (Schriftenreihe wissenschaftlicher Abhandlungen des Leo Baeck Instituts 13) and *Deutsches Judentum in Krieg und Revolution 1916-1923*. Ein Sammelband herausgegeben von Werner E. Mosse unter Mitwirkung von Arnold Paucker, Tübingen 1971 (Schriftenreihe wissenschaftlicher Abhandlungen des Leo Baeck Instituts 25) — the latter published more than a year after the speech printed here had been delivered — deal only with limited periods.

assimilated Jew is not necessarily the "lesser" Jew (or none at all), nor does he necessarily face the lesser problems. This fact must be borne in mind if Mr. Niewyk's statistics are to be read correctly, as they are based on the official German census which identified, of course, only the professed Jews. Unfortunately, what seems to be the only alternative — defining an "objective" concept of Jewishness, a Weberian ideal type of "the" Jew — is probably no more promising, and both authors have avoided it. But that leaves the job essentially undone.

My own preference, if I may make a suggestion, would be to take consciousness as a criterion — the consciousness of an individual of either being a Jew in religious terms or stemming from a Jewish background. The criterion works because such consciousness can indeed be lost — see the bizarre case of Theodor Duesterberg, top leader of the *Stahlhelm*, one of Weimar Germany's most anti-republican paramilitary organisations, who had to be reminded by the Nazis that his grandfather was a Jew. Compare with this the case of Kurt Tucholsky who tried all his life to forget his Jewish extraction but re-identified with Jewry in the face of Nazi persecution. Obviously, Tucholsky falls within our context while Duesterberg does not. Admittedly this does not solve all problems either, but it has the great, and for the historian crucial, virtue of preserving the autonomy of the individual rather than subjecting it to artificially, and perhaps anachronistically, construed concepts.

No less troublesome may be the job of explaining what we mean by "rôle". What do we want to know? The degree of prominence or accomplishment? Overall participation in terms of quantity? Political attitudes and influence? Contribution of specific cultural and social values? Mr. Jenks thinks mainly in terms of prominence and accomplishment and applies the theory that the break-up of the traditional structures of the host societies allowed for an explosion of Jewish talent, even in the economic field. This is an interesting suggestion and deserves to be pursued further. In the history of the Weimar Republic the theory of the Jewish talent explosion leads to a perplexing and perhaps fruitful paradox. It is widely held today that Weimar was weak on democracy and that especially Weimar intellectual history was little but an antecedent to Nazism. If that is so, and if the Jews made, as they undoubtedly did, a great contribution to Weimar cultural life, do we have to conclude that they, too, contributed to the rise of Hitler? Or was there, during the "golden twenties", the possibility if not the reality of "another Weimar"? The first conclusion strikes us as absurd, but if it is, are we justified in drawing the second one?

Turning to Mr. Niewyk's paper specifically, I should like to deal briefly with some of its problematical aspects. First, there are some conceptual confusions and lacunae, with regard to German twentieth-century intellectual history. The author's use of concepts such as naturalism, impressionism, and neo-objectivism is perplexing to the intellectual historian, and so is his classification of Franz Werfel as a playwright without mentioning that Werfel's main achievements were in poetry and in the novel. Literary historians might also rank Alfred Döblin and even Lion Feuchtwanger above Jakob Wassermann. In addition, there are omissions that, with all due regard to time and space problems, should not have occurred. It may be debatable whether or not we can include Austrians in a survey of German intellectual history, but if one mentions Werfel and Max Reinhardt, one should not ignore Karl Kraus, the greatest German satirist and stylist in our time, and Franz Kafka, the leading representative of the German expressionist novel. Neither should a reference be missing to poetry in general, and in particular, to Else Lasker-Schüler, the greatest German poetess in the first half of the twentieth century. A survey of science and scholarship should include the names of Albert Einstein, the great physicist; Edmund Husserl, philosopher of phenomenology; and Hugo Preuß, the father of the Weimar constitution.

Another problem concerns Mr. Niewyk's own conceptual framework: his main thesis seems to be — at least in terms of an underlying theme — that the Jews, because of their peculiar social situation, showed a tendency towards ambivalent attitudes. He then goes on, however, to distinguish *three* varieties of Jewish attitudes: (1) overt criticism of majority values; (2) radical departure from established norms; and (3) efforts to excel in accepted forms and modes of thought. I do not see a substantial difference between the first and second of these categories, and in terms of ambivalence it would in any case be clearer to distinguish only two basic attitudes — attempts to change a hostile environment either by reform or revolution, or by changing the "insufficient" individual by adjustment (or over-adjustment). Needless to say such framework would need considerable refinement, perhaps along the lines exemplified by Mr. Jenks and Mr. Whiteside in their dealings with the same problem.

Mr. Niewyk is probably right in his thesis of Jewish ambivalence, although this was at least matched by that of Gentile Germany. Upon closer investigation we might also find that Jewish behaviour was often pretty normal. Jews could be found in all political camps and parties; they showed great accomplishments but also mediocrity; and there were even famous criminals, like the Barmats and the Sklareks.

It is perhaps owing to the nature of Mr. Niewyk's categories that he does not really apply them. He deals at length with people who might pass as representatives of his first two categories but he does not show us examples of the third one. And yet there were such examples. There were a surprisingly large number of Jews in or at the margin of the Stefan George circle: Friedrich Gundolf, noted literary historian; Ernst Kantorowicz, biographer of the medieval historian Frederick II; and the poets and essayists Rudolf Borchardt and Karl Wolfskehl. Another example of Jewish conservatism is Paul Nikolaus Cossmann, publisher of the *Süddeutsche Monatshefte* and leading propagandist of the stab-in-the-back legend. But there were also *Vernunftrepublikaner* such as Walther Rathenau. More than anything else such examples serve to expose the paranoia of German antisemitism.

On the other hand there is no doubt that the majority of Jews gravitated to the left of the political and cultural spectrum. But this is a universal phenomenon; whether there was anything specifically German in it, must remain a matter of speculation until further study. What needs to be emphasised, however, in any discussion of the rôle of the Jews in Weimar Germany, is the important part their gravitating to the left played in the strengthening of the democratic and humanist tendencies in German twentieth-century history. This brings us back to the question of the "other" Weimar raised earlier. I think there was such a democratic, humane, and civilized Weimar. That it came to life, at least for a brief historical moment, was to a considerable degree owing to the help of the German Jews. I would extend this evaluation, in disagreement with Mr. Niewyk, also to the *Weltbühne* circle. It is now time for us to stop fighting the battles of the cold war, nor should we let ourselves be deterred by the preference, among *Weltbühne* writers, for the continental, especially the French, political culture over the Anglo-American one. Whoever reads the writings of Siegfried Jacobsohn, Kurt Tucholsky, Kurt Hiller, etc. cannot fail to recognize their deep commitment to democracy and humanism. They have to bear their share of responsibility for the errors of the time, but this problem can be evaluated correctly only in the context of the agonizing dilemmas arising in a society in deep crisis.

Memoirs and Documents

Jewish Petitions to the
German National Assembly

in Frankfurt 1848/49

BY R. MOLDENHAUER

"It was the liberation struggle of 1813 and the blood of the Jewish youths who had joyfully laid down their lives for Germany's liberation by which the Jews' covenant with their new fatherland was solemnly and irrevocably sealed before the Judgment seat of world history; and the soil which has been soaked in this blood and which has been watered with the tears of sorrow of the older Jews, even those of the strictest persuasion, who dedicated their sons to a hero's death for the fatherland — this soil can nevermore disown its newly-won children with impunity. Since those days the German Jew has been a German, whether or not he be recognised as such by the law of his state."

Die Gegenwart, vol. X (1855), p. 563.

Before discussing individually the petitions addressed to the Frankfurt Parliament by Jews or Jewish communities and presented in this publication, we shall have to deal briefly with the situation of the Jews in the individual Federal States of nineteenth-century pre-imperial Germany. We are here touching on problems of acute concern to very wide circles, problems thrown into relief by the poignancy of so many of the petitions addressed to the National Assembly — and of others as well for that matter — which are particularly revealing when studied in toto.[1]

The lines prefixed as a motto to this investigation were written by an unknown author in 1855.[2] Reading them today, a quarter of a century after the terrifying events in Germany which changed the world, we are inclined to react with almost incredulous amazement at the optimism which at that time appeared to be possible when judging the situation, and with bitterness over the baleful course of Germany's recent history which acted as a force engendering chaos. Indeed, any observer who

---

[1]So far the following treatises have appeared: W. Klötzer, 'Die nassauischen Petitionen an die Frankfurter Nationalversammlung 1848/49', in *Nassauische Annalen,* vol. 70 (1959), pp. 145 f.; R. Moldenhauer, 'Die Petitionen aus Oberhessen an die deutsche Nationalversammlung 1848/49', in *Mitteilungen des Oberhessischen Geschichtsvereins,* vol. 51, p. 120; *idem,* 'Die Petitionen aus Kreis und Stadt Wetzlar an die deutsche Nationalversammlung 1848/49', in *Mitteilungen des Wetzlarer Geschichtsvereins,* No. 23 (1967), p. 134 f.; *idem,* 'Die Petitionen aus der Freien Stadt Frankfurt an die deutsche Nationalversammlung 1848/49', in *Archiv für Frankfurts Geschichte und Kunst,* No. 51 (1968), p. 201; *idem,* 'Die Petitionen aus den preußischen Saarkreisen an die deutsche Nationalversammlung in Frankfurt 1848/49', in *Zeitschrift für die Geschichte der Saargegend,* XVII/XVIII (1969/70); *idem,* 'Die Petitionen aus der Stadt Berlin an die Nationalversammlung 1848/49' (to be published shortly in Berlin).

[2]'Die Gegenwart, Eine enzyklopädische Darstellung der neuesten Zeitgeschichte für alle Stände', vol. 10, Brockhaus, 1855, article 'Das Judentum'. See also *ibid.* vol. 1, 1848, 'Die bürgerlichen Verhältnisse der Juden in Deutschland. Die Ursachen der neuesten Judenverfolgungen', pp. 353 ff.

studies the history of the Jews in Germany will have to admit that the course of events might well have been very different.

For a whole century the Jews in Germany fought for their civic emancipation.[3] This striving for equal rights received a powerful impetus from Napoleon's measures. Emancipation was first introduced in the territories of the old *Reich* occupied by France. In 1808 emancipation was enacted in Hessen. The rights of the Jews were extended in 1833 in Kurhessen (completely), and with substantial limitations in 1838 in Saxony, and in 1842 in Hanover. In Frankfurt — at the time the largest Jewish community in Germany — the rights of the Jews were augmented in 1811. Even earlier the Jews had been granted State citizenship in Baden, where however they still required permission from the sovereign and the commune concerned if they wanted to settle in a locality where no Jews had lived before, and even when admitted their status was not that of citizens in their communes, but only that of protected persons.

In 1828 the emancipation of the Jews was introduced in Württemberg. Old Württemberg considered itself a rigorously Protestant State. Under the regional statutes of 1521, Jews had been strictly debarred from residence, but attempts were made subsequently to establish more favourable conditions. Yet even after the emancipation Jewish rights were still subject to restrictions which the *Ständeversammlungen* (Estates Conventions) of 1833, 1836 and 1845 did not see fit to remove despite urgent entreaties.

In Bavaria legislation affecting the Jews was comparatively liberal, but there was a ban on the immigration of Jews from other regions and there were restrictions on eligibility for public office and on marriage. They were able to acquire citizenship by presenting their original certificate of admission, accepting a fixed family name and taking the oath of allegiance. The only public offices from which they were excluded were those of *Landrat* (District Officer) and Diet Deputy. They were liable to military service but not eligible for commissions. All trades, with the exception of brewing, the selling of spirits, and catering, were open to them.

In Austria Joseph II had in 1782 promulgated the *Toleranzedikt* which, however, did not grant the Jews citizenship of either the State or the communes but continued to treat them as protected persons. The Jews were excluded from the civil service, but they were liable to military service and even eligible for elevation to the ranks of the nobility. Acquisition of land was generally not permitted.

In Bohemia the number of officially admitted Jews was restricted to 8,600 and a Jewish community in the proper sense existed only in Prague. A revision of the laws affecting the Jews was started in 1833 but had not brought any conclusive results by 1848.

In Prussia emancipation was introduced in 1812 when all the Jews holding *Generalprivilegien*, patents of naturalisation, certificates of protection, or concessions were declared native residents and State citizens. But they continued to remain

[3]See two recent studies published in this Year Book: Ernest Hamburger, 'One Hundred Years of Emancipation', and Reinhard Rürup, 'Jewish Emancipation and Bourgeois Society', in *LBI Year Book XIV* (1969), pp. 3-66, and pp. 67-91 respectively.

excluded from State offices and the rights of the estates. Later they were again debarred from academic and other teaching posts and the validity of Hardenberg's Law of 1812 was confined to the territories which had been Prussian at the time. The various *Provinziallandstände* (Provincial Estate Assemblies) made repeated attempts to curtail the Jews' newly-won rights. This was the case especially at the *Vereinigter Landtag* (Unified State Diet) of 1847.

Although Article 16 of the Act of the German Confederation laid down that the conditions of the Jews should be governed by uniform regulations throughout Germany, many of the individual States deliberately delayed its implementation. A number of States — including Hanover, Frankfurt, and Hamburg — actually imposed new restrictions on civic rights.

The basic rights proclaimed by the first German Parliament included the proposition that the full enjoyment of civic and political rights should not be conditioned or restricted by an individual's religious faith. In actual fact, although the Jews were no longer stripped of all rights, their status fell far short of legal equality. In many States it was at least difficult for a Jew to be admitted to a career in the civil service or the professions and virtually impossible to become an officer. One of a later generation, pondering on the lost chances of that period, the undreamt-of opportunities that were missed, is struck by the profound tragedy of that failure. Achievements quite out of the ordinary could have been accomplished in the fields of culture and art, in commerce and politics. Can it not be said that the two "peoples" complement one another? Has not nature in so many respects given the one what it denied the other? It was the failure to recognise this which lay at the root of the tragedy of the relations between "Jews" and "Germans" in the nineteenth century.

Before looking in detail at the various petitions to be discussed here, it will be necessary to make some general observations on the rôle of petitions in nineteenth-century Germany.

The March Revolutions of 1848, coming as they did after decades of restoration and immobility as well as resignation, gave rise to political stirrings of unprecedented vitality in all German towns. The feeling of "people's sovereignty", almost unknown before, was alive everywhere, and there was a mushroom growth o political clubs and associations. Even in the smallest localities — which only too soon were to sink back into their age-old political slumbers — efforts were made to take part in the formation of a political will. Unfortunately the search for the documents of those associations has so far been in vain.[4]

One manifestation of that movement, however, has been preserved: the numerous petitions addressed to the German National Assembly in Frankfurt which had been solemnly opened on 18th May 1848. On this Assembly were focused the hopes of all the liberal elements which looked to it for the attainment of the objectives they had long been yearning for: political unification, the establishment of a unified State and a central government; the Assembly was plied with political advice and demands both of public and private import; the Assembly was expected to perform

---

[4]Presumably they were either confiscated by the police or destroyed by the associations themselves during the subsequent period of harsh reaction.

the miracle of creating a new strong *Reich* of the Germans. Even today a close study of these petitions reveals an impressive picture of that institution which was later scathingly described as the "Parliament of professors".[5]

The right to submit petitions was by no means unchallenged in Germany in the middle of the nineteenth century, least of all when the petitioners were not private individuals. In many places the old notions of the position of a subject in an absolutist State were dying hard; according to these the *particulier* was allowed to hand a petition to his prince at a specified spot[6], or to pass it to him in some other way. Collective petitioning on the part of political groups and associations, if tolerated at all, would have been regarded as a seditious or even revolutionary action and severely punished. In the Constitution of the German Confederation no provision was made for activities of that kind; indeed, the Confederation had repeatedly attempted to impose restraint on governments of individual States, especially in Southern Germany where a more liberal trend was in evidence. All this was characteristic of the political climate of Germany before the Revolution of 1848, a Germany cast in the mould of Metternich's ideas. Fifty years had gone by since the French Revolution, the United States had achieved freedom in America, a fresher breeze had long been blowing into Germany, the Rhineland as well as other major German territories had been under French rule and liberal ideas had gained ground. Yet in most of the Federal States the old, strict police regimes continued in power.

It is all the more astonishing that the newly-aroused political interest should have manifested itself at once throughout Germany in the form of such petitions as well. The register of petitions of the National Assembly office, which has been preserved, lists over 8,000 entries (the total number is much larger still) not all of which, unfortunately, have been preserved. The intellectual level and the length of these documents naturally vary a great deal, but there can be no doubt as to the inestimable historical and sociological value of this material which as yet has hardly been studied as a coherent whole.

Before dealing with the substance of the individual Jewish petitions we must discuss the part played by petitions in general in helping to shape the attitude of

---

[5]This is not the place for a bibliography of the revolutionary movement of the years 1848/49. Next to the official records of the National Assembly and the Provisional Central Authority, which are preserved only in part, the most important source is the publication of the shorthand reports of the proceedings of the National Assembly, edited by F. Wigard: *Stenographische Berichte über die Verhandlungen der deutschen constituierénden Nationalversammlung zu Frankfurt am Main*, Frankfurt 1848/49 (quoted hereafter as St B). The authoritative work is still V. Valentin, *Geschichte der deutschen Revolution*, 2 vols., Berlin 1930/31. See also J. Droz, *Les Révolutions allemandes de 1848*, Paris 1957; F. Eyck, *The Frankfurt Parliament 1848-1849*, New York 1968.

[6]E.g. the "petition lime-tree" by the Castle of Potsdam, preserved until 1945. See F. Schnabel, *Deutsche Geschichte im 19. Jahrhundert*, 4 vols., Freiburg 1955, p. 570. Up to the Revolution of 1848 the enlightened civil service, thinking exclusively in fiscal terms, notwithstanding the efforts of Frederick William IV, retained its unchallenged power in nearly all German States. As late as 1848 Karl Vogt wrote a pamphlet, preserved in the Giessen University Library (M 26169/1), in which he demanded the "uncurtailed right of petitioning" for everyone.

Parliament. It appears that they exerted great influence.[7] The petitions, having been registered, were not immediately filed away, as is likely to have been the practice of many parliaments after that period. No attempt was made in Frankfurt to cope with the spate of incoming petitions with the aid of a "parliamentary steam engine"[8], but they were taken for what they actually were: manifestations of the popular will.

To begin with, an incoming petition was registered by the bureau (secretariat),[9] then conveyed to the plenum for further consideration and the production of a report by one of the many specialised committees. To settle the order of proceedings a special committee for the priority of instructions and petitions was set up.[10] This committee heard reports from its members and then arranged for petitions to be referred to the appropriate committees. Later the bureau was able on its own initiative to forward petitions directly to the committees. Other petitions again were sent by the petitioners directly to the committees, and these are not recorded in the register of petitions but can be found among the records of the individual committees in so far as these have been preserved. The committees themselves heard reports on the petitions referred to them; more broadly-conceived reports were submitted to the plenum. Only then were the petitions either filed with the parliamentary records or passed on to the government departments of the Provisional Central Authority.

In my earlier regional investigations of the petitions addressed to the National Assembly I arranged them for the purpose of discussion according to subject. Since there are only a very few "Jewish petitions", this procedure does not appear to be useful here. Out of fifteen petitions traced in these investigations, five have not been preserved, two were direct applications to the *Reich* Ministry of Justice, filed together with the resulting decisions, and four are examples of antisemitic sentiment. The petitions of that last group were chance finds, but are of great interest in this connection.

The present paper — as has been made clear before — is concerned exclusively with the petitions that were addressed to the German National Assembly of 1848/49 and are now kept at the Frankfurt-on-Main branch office of the *Bundesarchiv*. It goes without saying that petitions were also addressed to the individual Confederate German States. As early as 1815 Jewish wishes and grievances had been ventilated at the Vienna Congress in the form of petitions, and many more petitions pleading

---

[7]A glance at the register of the St B, p. 55, reveals how often and in what detail the plenum dealt with the treatment of petitions. See also the official minutes of the Assembly committees in K. D. Hassler, *Verhandlungen der deutschen verfassungsgebenden Reichsversammlung zu Frankfurt a. M.*, vol. II., *Ausschuss- und Kommissionsberichte Nr. 1-180 der amtlichen Protokolle*, Frankfurt 1848/49.

[8]Cf. the well-known cartoon of the "parliamentary steam engine", reproduced in P. Wentzke and W. Klötzer, *Ideale und Irrtümer des ersten deutschen Parlaments (1848-49)*, Heidelberg 1959, p. 96.

[9]The bureau or secretariat was in charge of the administration of the National Assembly. It was composed of the Deputies Biedermann, Fetzer, Jucho, Möring, Riehl, Ruhwandl, Schüler, and Simon von Trier.

[10]Set up under National Assembly resolution of 24th May 1848. See StB 1, pp. 67, 74.

for equal rights were sent by Jewish official bodies (communities) and by private individuals to Governments and Parliaments. This is the general background against which the documents quoted here must be seen.

The first extant petition, bearing no registration number, was addressed not to the *Paulskirche* (the National Assembly) but to the President of the Committee of Fifty.[11] It came from the Board of the Israelite Community, which offered its prayer room in the Predigerstraße opposite the Dominican Church for extraordinary meetings.[12] The room is described as heatable and provided with a gallery capable of accommodating an audience of 500. The letter is signed by the President of the Community, Dr. Mannhayn[13], and by Isaac Rothschild[14]. The document carries the endorsement "At the meeting of 17th April the chairman (of the Community) Abegg reported that the offered hall did not appear to answer the purpose." Jewry had particular reasons to look to the first German Parliament for a solution of its problems. That is presumably what prompted the Frankfurt Jews to make this offer as a token of their goodwill.

Some time before 28th July 1848 — the date can only be inferred from the registration — the theology student Israel Schwarz[15] submitted a *Sendschreiben an das teutsche Parlament in Frankfurt am Main für die Aussprechung der Judenemanzipation und ein offenes Wort an den christlichen Klerus* (Message to the German Parliament in Frankfurt-on-Main for the promulgation of the emancipation of the Jews and an open word to the Christian clergy), Heidelberg 1848.[16] In it Schwarz declares: "I believe that just as the force of custom is enormous in all things, so it comes that in the matter of the emancipation of the Jews execution is so difficult only because the people are accustomed to see the Jew not free, not emancipated, but always oppressed and submissive. How distressing the thought, how lamentable the reading we should get from a light-gauge measuring the degree of human enlightenment if it were true that the force of custom and the fact of things being as they are carry the greatest weight even where the most sublime treasures of life, where honour, right and freedom are at stake! And yet, however distressing, however lamentable, it is true and incontrovertible. For indeed, all the objections to a suggested emancipation put forward now or in the past on account of our teachings and our mode of life are such as to blow away and scatter like chaff as soon as they are examined a

---

[11]The Committee of Fifty was appointed by the *Vorparlament* and was in office from 7th April 1848 until 18th May of the same year when the National Assembly was constituted. The Committee was to assist the *Bundestag* in guarding the national interest, and to advise the Committee of Seventeen (delegates of the individual States) in constitutional matters.

[12]Located in the Compostelhof building.

[13]Dr. jur. Samuel Michael Mannheimer (29.9.1800-22.10.1878) changed his family name in 1823 to Mannhayn. In 1825 he applied for admission to practise law. In 1842 he married Auguste, daughter of the trader Abraham Hayum Halle. (Senatssuppl. Frankfurt, vol. 132, No. 42.)

[14]Israel Rothschild (24.6.1802-18.4.1852), trader. (Senatssuppl. Frankfurt, vol. 286, No. 25.) In 1834 he married Julia Henrietta Halle; the document was countersigned by the lawyer Dr. Michael Mannhayn.

[15]Born about 1828 in Hürben near Augsburg, the son of a rabbi, he enrolled at Heidelberg university in 1846.

[16]No. 1313. Published in full in the Appendix.

little more closely." "If we now cast a glance upon the life of the Jews we shall find that in general it stands on a relatively higher level of moral accomplishment than that of any other creed, because it is precisely their severe ritual and their faith which nurture the qualities of frugality and humanity in them. But as for the infirmities that can be seen in some of them, it is the State itself which brought them about by imposing its bondage and oppression, by hindering any liberal development." The "open word to the Christian clergy" ends on a note that sounds somewhat solemn to our ears: "You are not unaware of the difficult position occupied by the Church in our modern era, — and it is only through the truth that she can save herself, if she should set out on devious paths she would be lost forever. In your own interest I beg and entreat you to strive for her preservation. Show before the world how unjustly the Church is judged when she is believed to be obstructing progress, stifling the free intellect, blocking the paths of truth. Oh priests, bear witness to this through your teachings and the righteous cause will triumph and you, too, will show yourself in the hue and complexion that befits your exalted rank. Our whole generation will pay tribute to your merit, the people of Israel will tender their thank-offering, and all posterity will bless your memory."

This "open word" elicited from Christian quarters an open answer culminating in the following appeal: "Therefore, you priests of the Christian religion, desist from accusing and abusing your brothers in the ministry if one or another of them run ahead of the rest in his correct appreciation of our time and its great tasks: do not incite congregations against their pastors when the latter are tirelessly engaged in elevating their flock to a higher level of religious and even of political understanding. Never utter words of hate against Christians of a different denomination and work with all your energies for a Germany that, though she cannot for a long time yet be united in creed, shall yet be united in love. And from this love do not exclude the Israelites whose hands are raised to us in entreaty; lead them into the paternal home and they will shed the faults naturally engendered by the exclusion, discrimination and mistreatment to which they have been exposed. Upon you, preachers of the gospel, will rest the shame if during the imminent emancipation of the Jews the Christian people will refuse to accept it, if the brutality and fiendish malice of those blind to the truth should be vented on the defenceless minority in vile excesses such as we ourselves witnessed in our Bavaria recently. Set your hands to the task, you messengers of peace, and the peace of Jesus Christ, which the world cannot give, will be with you. And herewith I proffer my brotherly hand to the Jewish theologian in Hürben."

On 17th July 1848 the Evangelical Pastor J. G. Lehmann, of Nussdorf near Landau in the Palatinate, sent a memorandum of thirty foolscap pages to Parliament, entitled "Emancipation of the Israelites within the German peoples' commonwealth and their instatement in all civic and political rights".[17] This memorandum is the fruit of prodigious industry and application, using all the sources available to the author at the time. As a unique document it is published in part in the

---

[17]No. 1170. Excerpts are published in the Appendix.

Appendix. The Pastor's covering letter accompanying the memorandum runs as follows:

"German men of the *Reich* Diet: To contribute dutifully my modest mite to the fashioning of the weal of our common fatherland, and in order, if possible, to help facilitate and advance the debates on what constitutes one of the most momentous and vital issues of the German peoples' commonwealth, I send you here enclosed a memorandum on the emancipation of the Israelites and the granting to them of legal equality with the members of all other religious communities, hoping that you will see fit to make it the subject of your inquiry and deliberations. The good of the German Confederation of States that must be solidly established; the advancement of human well-being in general; and the encouragement of the practice of true Christian brotherly love — these are the basic ideas which have guided and inspired me in drafting this memorandum. May it be received by you in the same spirit of patriotic zeal which prompted me to write it and present it to you, and may it meet with your sympathy and indulgence! This is the fervent desire of your obedient servant."

In July 1848 the Israelite teachers in Württemberg pleaded in a petition for their Jewish denominational schools to be turned into common elementary schools.[18] This petition has unfortunately not been preserved, neither has that of their Christian colleague J. Weil, of Kochendorf in Württemberg,[19] entitled "Motion for the vesting of the existing public Israelite schools under State supervision with the rights of the Christian elementary schools".

However, a similar request by the Jewish teachers of Baden has come down to us.[20] The petition bears the title: "Plea of the undersigned Israelite teachers of Baden against freedom of instruction and for the investment of elementary schools with the character of State institutions and the establishment of communal schools; in the interest of the intellectual and material well-being of the people, and notably out of consideration for the minority of religious communities living in mixed communes."

Here the case for the non-denominational school is put with arguments which seem surprisingly modern: "That communal schools present no danger to the Christian religion has not only been pointed out by statesmen who are good Christians, but it has actually been proved by one Christian State in Germany, the Grand Duchy of Hessen, where such schools have functioned for some time without detriment to the faith. In the same way we have noted their religious innocuousness as regards our own faith. For since the Israelites were required by law to learn the secular subjects of instruction the Israelite children in most localities have been attending Christian schools, and there has so far been no indication that the Jewish children became Christians. Why then should it not be admissible for a Jewish teacher to instruct Christian children, a Catholic teacher Evangelical children, an Evangelical teacher Catholic children in secular subjects? Are not the secondary

---

[18]No. 1395.
[19]No. 1944.
[20]No. 2734. Published in full in the Appendix.

industrial schools and the *Gymnasien* (classical grammar schools) mixed already? And are not members of the clergy themselves sending their children to such schools without fearing any danger to their religion?" Unification rather than separation would be achieved by not allowing every religious party to misuse the school for party ends.

In conclusion the petitioners anticipated ideas which have since made a not inconsiderable contribution to the establishment of our modern *Mittelpunktschule* (central school — a lower secondary school serving several rural communes). There is so much that could have been done better and more favourably if only such progressive ideas had been taken up earlier.[21]

Among the petitions that have not been preserved there is one from a Rabbi Moses of Schwerte, dated August 1848, pleading for an amnesty for his daughter.[22]

In September 1848 the Central Committee of German Butchers made representations to the Frankfurt Parliament with the request to liberalise imports of livestock from abroad in view of the poor quality of domestic animals[23]. It is remarkable that the signatories to these petitions include many Jewish butchers who — surprisingly in view of kosher slaughtering — were ordinary members of the guilds, just like the non-Jews. Signatures of Jews to these petitions have been ascertained, among other localities, in Anderhain (Rheingau), Thewald and Essen.

The "German Jews of the Mosaic faith" in Schwäbisch-Hall sent an address of thanks to the German *Reich* Assembly in September 1848 occasioned by the defeat of the motion tabled by Mohl[24]. The petition, which has not been preserved, was forwarded with a covering letter by the Stuttgart Deputy Zimmermann who, as we shall see, was very active in support of Jewish interests.

Another document that has not been preserved is a report submitted by the Association for the Advancement of Artisans among the Israelites, informing the Assembly of its existence and describing its activities.[25]

[21]It goes without saying that such progressive suggestions especially as regards education were not made from Jewish quarters only. See Moldenhauer, 'Die Petitionen aus Oberhessen . . .', *loc. cit.*, p. 94. The petition of a Grünberg schoolmaster published there includes among its noteworthy suggestions the idea of an alternative access to higher education for young people who had left school early, on the lines now instituted in Western Germany as the *zweiter Bildungsweg*. A study of the petitions generally reveals an astonishing wealth of ideas and shows how many ideas accepted as intellectual achievements of our age were in fact widely current 120 years ago.

[22]No. 2138.

[23]No. 2781. Signatures of Jewish fellow citizens are very frequent. See Moldenhauer, 'Die Petitionen aus Oberhessen . . .', *loc. cit.*, p. 106. The signatories to Petition No. 8900 concerning the implementation of the *Reich* Constitution of 4th May 1849 included several Jews (one of whom added the rider: "without law no life"). At the time the village of Bönstadt had only about 450 inhabitants and 35 Jews. Relations with the non-Jews were excellent up to 1933 and beyond.

[24]No. 3139. This refers to Mohl's motion of 24th May 1848, which called for the inclusion of "civic equality, in particular abolition of the nobility, its titles and privileges" among the German people's basic rights. See Hassler, vol. V., pp. 18 ff.

[25]No. 4893.

In February 1849 Dr. Ephraim Moses Pinner[26] presented three copies of his pamphlet *Offenes Sendschreiben an die Nationen Europas und an die Stände Norwegens und die politische Stellung der Juden* (Open letter to the nations of Europe and the Norwegian estates and the political position of the Jews)[27]. The pamphlet, which is by no means unknown, is not filed with the records, which is explained by the following note: "No longer dealt with by the Priority and Petitions Committee"; the three copies were therefore handed on 29th August to the librarian, Dr. Plath, for the *Reichsbibliothek*.

Another petition that has not been preserved was submitted by the widow of Salomon Katz, née Goldschmidt, of Helsen (Waldeck), who complains about the Government banning her remarriage.[28] A personal petition to the *Reich* Ministry of Justice was made by the orientalist Dr. L. H. Löwenstein[29] of Steinbach in the Kingdom of Württemberg, at the time staying at Rödelheim, in order to complain about his expulsion from Frankfurt by the police. His "most humble remonstrance and request concerning his political expulsion ordered without any judicial proceedings" was conveyed to the Ministry with a covering letter from the Deputy Zimmermann, whom we have met already. The decision was drafted personally by the Minister of Justice, Robert Mohl.[30] In his rejoinder Löwenstein said: "The highly esteemed rescript of the 1st/4th inst. [the ministerial decision was dated 1st November 1848, presumably received on the 4th] has been a source to me of fresh reassurance inasmuch as in it I find my claim to the protection of the *Reich* on the strength of the Basic Law fully recognised and founded on a *Reich* Law and its authentic interpretation, so that it only remains for the Ministry to take cognizance of an utterly notorious and unquestioned matter of fact to enable me to look forward in quiet confidence to the early granting of my most humble request and

[26]Ephraim Moses Pinner was born in 1803 at Pinne (Province of Posen) and died in 1880 in Berlin. After extensive travels in Eastern Europe he settled in Berlin. In several writings and appeals of a political and religious nature he championed the betterment of the political position of the Jews and at the same time opposed any modification of the liturgy. His main works are a translation of the Talmud tract *Brachot*, published in Berlin in 1842, a prospectus on Hebrew manuscripts in Odessa, published together with S. Pinsker, and a volume of collected tombstone inscriptions, published in 1861. See *Jüdisches Lexikon*, vol. IV, pp. 948 f., Lewin, 'Aus der Vergangenheit der jüdischen Gemeinde zu Pinne', Pinne 1903; Meisl, *Haskalah*, Berlin 1919.

[27]No. 6243.

[28]No. 7536.

[29]Lipmann Hirsch Löwenstein, a Hebrew scholar, worked for a publisher at Rödelheim, and wrote a number of learned works; died in Frankfurt about 1850. Rödelheim, up to 1806 a possession of the Counts zu Solms, then part of Hessen, from 1866 in Prussia, since 1910 belonging to Frankfurt, always had a sizeable Jewish community. In E. Hartmann, P. Schubert, *Alt Rödelheim, Ein Heimatbuch*, Frankfurt 1921, there is no mention of Löwenstein. One Esselen and one Pelz were expelled from Frankfurt together with Löwenstein. This was the subject of a protest by E. Montignay of Frankfurt in Petition No. 69. Many artisans from outside the region who had attended the Journeymen's Congress endorsed the petition. See Moldenhauer, 'Die Petitionen aus der freien Stadt Frankfurt ...', p. 27. Löwenstein's complaint was printed. (Biogr. ff. Coll. 553[13] 1848.)

[30]Rough draft in Mohl posthumous papers, Tübingen University Library, fair copy filed with the records.

to the termination of my undeserved sufferings as a result of the application of the pronouncements of the selfsame highly esteemed rescript."

This incident, although regrettably not exceptional,[31] appears important enough to be fully documented in the appendix.

On 9th February 1849 the widow Rebekka Bamberger, Berlin, Königstraße 54, addressed a "most humble application" to the same Ministry, "concerning the realisation of Westphalian Reich bonds Litt. A classes and series of the Westphalian forced loan, dating from the years 1808, 1810 and 12, which were certified in 1814 on instructions of the Royal Prussian Government by the Court Steward, Counsellor von Madai, and of which the three interest coupons which fell due on 31st December 1813, 30th June 1814 and 31st December 1814 respectively were marked with the Royal Prussian red stamp F.W. and were fully accepted in lieu of payment by all treasury offices of the former Kingdom of Westphalia in settlement of personal taxes".[32] She was informed by the Ministry of Justice on 14th February 1849 to the effect "that the negotiations having regard to this subject which were initiated with the Governments of Prussia, Hanover, Kurhessen and Brunswick have not yet reached completion". In her rejoinder of 29th March 1849, Rebekka appealed to the Ministry to "expedite the negotiations initiated in this matter and make the result public at the earliest opportunity".

The document is hardly likely to have been written by Mrs. Bamberger personally, but it is drafted so skilfully, expertly and effectively, that it is not devoid of topical interest in present-day Germany, where twice within one generation the citizen has been cheated of possessions and his life's savings by financial manipulations. The rejoinder is therefore published unabridged in the appendix.

This exhausts the list of known Jewish petitions. It remains to discuss the accidentally discovered antisemitic petitions. It is noteworthy that these petitions do not come from intellectual circles. This is scarcely fortuitous, and it is likely that this result will not be changed by a further systematic search. There was no absence of resentment against the Jews even in intellectual circles, yet emancipation was still looked upon as the most expedient way of normalising relations with the Jews. The artisan and the small man, on the other hand, were still in the habit of seeing the Jew as the usurer and the haggling trader; moreover the blame for the economic difficulties of the past few years had been laid on the Jews, as usual. The intensity of the hatred engendered in this way is a matter of common knowledge. The diatribe of an anonymous petitioner of Karlstadt[33] is an illustration of the mood resulting from an incitement campaign in certain circles. The document is all the more significant as very few petitions were received from the less educated sections of the people. The rather incoherent text reads:

---

[31]It was not only Jews who were affected by such expulsions, for at that time the right of domicile was certainly not acquired within Germany simply by registering in a commune. The Economic Committee conducted prolonged discussions on a liberal new law.

[32]DB 55 (*Reich* Ministry of Justice).

[33]Unnumbered, undated, filed on 9th May 1848.

"As consequently there can no longer be a *Reich* unless the Jews are driven out of Germany, because it is only the downfall of the people what they are after, they ruin the trade, they issue false mortgage bonds against each other, only to cheat the Christian out of all he has. They go bankrupt, in short all they are after is the downfall of the Christians, if they are not moved to another country we will be compelled to drive them out by force, but we do hope the people's association in Frankfurt will stem this evil, because otherwise the *Reich* will not be united or stay united, because the Jew is the friend of no Christian."

In August 1848 the leaders of the guilds at Eschwege petitioned against "Jewish usury"[34], after dealing in their voluminous application at length with the situation of the artisan trades. They opposed freedom of trade and favoured the preservation of the ancient guilds. Their twenty-one demands are concerned above all with the improvement of the social and economic situation of the artisans and envisage restrictions on the operation of factories. Demand No. 12 refers to the Jews. It says: "Relegation of the Jews within the confines of the natural civil trades, so that they shall not learn trades by way of pretence, in order to be able to exploit their position by trading."

In an earlier passage the petition complains about the way in which "the sons of Israel have contrived to get control of nearly all goods". "What then, the National Assembly will ask, are the flaws and the baneful consequences of that freedom of trade that has been so strongly under attack? We venture to point them out in detail. To begin with, it has given rise to overpopulation. Before, while closed guilds existed, the young man desirous of independence had to prove his qualification for mastership by producing a masterpiece. Now the youth who has scarcely completed his apprenticeship is offered the opportunity of building up an independent livelihood, and few care to ask whether thereby the livelihood of other breadwinners, already wretched, is not further impaired; innumerable families come into being; sales, and consequently incomes, are drying up; people resort to selling at give-away prices, to deception and various artificial devices. Morality and contentment get lost and lead to the parlous situation in which we find ourselves already. But the conditions are no different as regards concessions and market licences. A glance at the markets shows how the sons of Israel have contrived to get control of nearly all goods: beginning with the haberdasher's booth where ribbons are sold by the ell, and with the sale of odds and ends at 6 kreutzers a piece, up to the great world-famous clothiers shops where a coat is offered for $1^1/_2$ thaler, we see nothing but charlatanry and deception. And who are those knights of industry as a rule? They are the sharp-witted sons of Israel and people who do not earn their bread by the sweat of their brow, but who intend, at the expense of the honest artisan, at the expense of truth, to make their own lives pleasant and to amass riches over and over again. And it is not only at the fairs but in the hawker's bundle, too, that our products are degraded. Who at the trade fairs is more adept and keen-eyed and, making a mockery of human charity, dares to part the faint-

[34]No. 2600.

hearted and intimidated artisan forcibly from his products, often for barely half of their true value? Alas, it is again those whom we should have wished to see granted the same rights as we enjoy, if only our German nature, the inner man, did not raise a warning voice, saying: take care, remember that grapes can never be reaped from thistles; remember your past experience."

In addition the masters, journeymen and guild members of Eschwege saw themselves prompted in a special petition of 30th September 1849 to protest against "unfair trade practices of the Jews".[35] The document, signed by about 300 petitioners, demands that Parliament "in laying down the basic rights of the German people should not proclaim unconditional freedom of trade but the principle of a trade statute 'for our time'." Strictly speaking, the petition is not downright antisemitic, as it expresses the belief that once their demand was fulfilled the mood towards the Israelites would improve. "If we may venture on this occasion to adumbrate another idea and recommend that it be given thorough consideration, it is this: that it is most desirable that a stop should be put through the trade statute or, if that takes too long in materialising, through an earlier legal measure, to the malpractices especially of the Israelites in the field of trade, who indulge in such practices to the greatest detriment of other, mostly Christian, tradesmen by intermeddling in every type of business, so that one of them often runs several or even many businesses, acting not seldom as a wholesaler, retailer, manufacturer, general merchant, etc. rolled in one. Such a measure, serving the interests of the Christian population at whose expense the Israelites seek to enrich themselves and to whose disadvantage they exploit any business that promises any gain, would have a most salutary effect and would contribute to eliminating most of the causes of the hostile mood against the Israelites of which there have been such widespread manifestations."

A few days earlier the Council of the Commune of Walldürn had made a plea to be "freed from the pressure of the Jews".[36] The Council explicitly opposed the emancipation of the Jews, since "their religious creed marks them as aliens rather than 'Germans'."

It clearly emerges from these petitions that one of the main elements of antisemitism has its roots in the situation created by the general industrial development, which of course was by no means launched by Jews, but as a result of which certain vocational groups felt their livelihood threatened. So they set their faces against the — objectively inevitable — new economic tendencies and vented their resentment on the Jews who represented, for all to see, a new element of the economic structure carried to the top by the liberal wave.

---

[35]No. 3331.
[36]No. 3651. Published in full in the Appendix.

APPENDIX

I

Petition Nr. 1313

Sendschreiben an das teutsche Parlament in Frankfurt, am Main für die Aussprechung der Judenemanzipation und ein offnes Wort an den christlichen Klerus von Israel Schwarz stud. theol. Heidelberg. Druck der G. Reichard'schen Buchdruckerei 1848.

Hochzuverehrende allgeschätzte teutsche Volksvertreter!

Kaum seid Ihr, edle Männer, angelangt an dem Platze Eurer Bestimmung, kaum vermogtet[!] Ihr nur die Pläne Eurer Verhandlungen zu ordnen, kaum durchblicktet Ihr das Chaos der Wünsche, Begehren und Forderungen, die von allen Ländern, wo die deutsche Zunge sich bewegt, Euch hoffnungsvoll zugesendet worden, und, siehe da! Euer Auge blickt erstaunt ein Sendschreiben an Euch für die Aussprechung der Judenemanzipation. Ha! der Jude, der aufdringliche, arrogante Jude — steht auch an der Almosenpforte, fleht auch um die so oft verwehrte Gnadengabe, um ein Gehör für seine Herzenswsorte. O! verzeiht es diesem Unglücklichen, daß er keine Gelegenheit, die sich ihm günstig zu gestalten scheint, anwendungslos vorübergehen läßt, weil sich eine solche so überaus selten ihm darbietet. Und wahrlich! der schon so viele Jahrhunderte unter Euch Wohnende glaubt gewiß jetzt den Ort gefunden zu haben, um für seine Freiheit Euch angehen zu dürfen, um sie jetzt fordern zu müssen, da Ihr es doch Euch zur Hauptaufgabe machtet, diese dem teuschen Vaterlande und vielleicht einer ganzen fremden Nation darzureichen.

Männer des teutschen Volkes! zu Euch blickt jetzt, vertrauend auf den hohen Zweck, den Ihr Euch zu lösen setztet, vertrauend auf Euer Rechtsgefühl, das Auge des gesammten teutschen Judentumes. Gestützt auf sein uraltes, Zeit und Nationen überlebendes Glaubensbekenntnis, entquollen aus dem Borne der ewigen Wahrheit, des lautersten Lichtes, der heiligsten Gottheit; gestützt auf seinen es noch nie verlassenen[!] himmlischen Schutzherrn, gestützt auf diese Stützen, die nicht wanken und nicht beben, blickt es zu den Menschen, zu den nicht nur von den mächtigen Zeitverhältnissen, sondern von einer hoch über dieselben erhabenen Vorsehung bestimmten Erlösern von Millionen — zu Euch, Parlamentsmitglieder, blickt das Judentum, um aus Euren Händen seine Erlösung zu empfangen. Sprecht sie aus, die Gleichstellung der Juden, sprecht es aus, daß endlich gewichen sei in bürgerlicher und politischer Hinsicht die Verschiedenheit der Konfessionen, sprecht es aus, daß ohne Unterschied der Religion und des Glaubens Jedermann die allgemeine Freiheit erblühe. Haben wir doch jüngstens wieder zu ihrer teilweisen Erringung auch unsere Kräfte, unser Gut und Blut aufgeopfert, haben wir doch in allen Hauptstädten hinter und auf den Barrikaden für unsere christlichen Mitbürger gekämpft; haben wir so edlen Samen mit Euch in einen Erdenschoß gelegt, durfte dieser im Tode das Grab mit Euch teilen, so gebet ihm auch Anteil beim Leben an den heiligen Gütern der Freiheit und des Menschenrechtes, so lasset den überbliebenen doch frisch ersprossen, und ertötet ihn nicht in seinem Keime.

Wurde so oft der bittende und mahnende Ruf um Emanzipation der Juden, der die unumstößlichsten Beweise für die Gerechtigkeit seiner Forderung niemals vermißte, da, wo er von wirklichem großen Gewichte sein konnte, bei den ständischen Verhandlungen erstickt durch den Aufweis einer simplen, obskuren Gesetzgebung hinter welchen Wällen des toten Buchstabens sich immer die herausgeforderte Feigheit verkriechet; wurde sie erstickt durch die Einwürfe böswilliger Fanatiker, so wird zweifelsohne dieser schon tausendmal ertönte Ruf da geachtet werden, wo eine ganz neue Gesetzgebung verfaßt werden soll, wo nicht der Buchstabe, sondern das lebendige Wort und der freie Geist ihre Stelle behaupten werden, und wo die Hellsehendsten, fern von jedem Zelotismus, im ächtesten Sinne der Humanität die Menschenrechte interpretieren. Und dieser Ruf, der läßt sich nun einmal nicht unterdrücken und nicht beschwichtigen, und seit die Presse ihren Einfluß übt, und seit das Wort nicht mehr durch die Sklaverei gehemmt und die allgemeine Stimme auch gehört ward, und seit die Sonne der Aufklärung ihre wärmende Strahlen sendet und der Geist der Menschenwürde Menschen zu beseelen anfing, seitdem schon hört man an den Toren der Gerechtigkeit, an den Sitzen der Wahrheit und an den Fenstern des hereinblickenden Lichtes diesen Ruf für der Unterdrückten Befreiung. Und wenn diese Stimme in Deutschland noch immer keine Aufnahme findet, dann wandert sie hinauf zu ihrem Meister, der sie vorangesendet, und kehrt dann zum letzten Male zurück mit begleitenden Tönen, die keine Bitte mehr orgeln und kein Armutslied mehr singen, aber alle verstopfte Ohren zu öffnen, und in des Herzens tiefste Tiefen durch die Macht des göttlichen Rechtes und durch die Kraft der himmlischen Wahrheit einzudringen weiß. —
Ich glaube, daß, wie bei allen Dingen der Gewohnheit Macht so ungeheuer ist, ebenso sei auch bei der Emanzipation der Juden nur darum die Ausführung so schwer, weil man nun einmal gewöhnt, daß der Jude nicht frei, nicht emanzipiert, sondern immer gedrückt und untertänig ist. So betrübend freilich es sein muß, und so traurig der Lichtmesser für die Aufklärung des Menschen seine Grade angeben kann, wenn auch bei den höchsten Gütern des Lebens, bei Ehre, Recht und Freiheit die Gewohnheit und das Einmalsoseiende an der Spitze der ganzen Bewegung steht, so wahr und so unumstößlich ist es nun dennoch. Denn wahrlich! die Einwürfe gegen eine mögliche Emanzipation, die man wegen unserer Lehre und unseres Lebens machte, waren und sind alle der Art, daß sie wie Spreu zerstieben, wenn man sie auch nur ein wenig genauer betrachtet.

Wer unsere Lehre, unsern Glauben, unsere ganze jüdische Religion kennt — und der Ignorant darf sich kein Urteil anmaßen — der wird ein erhabenes, heiliges, ehrwürdiges Gebäude vor sich finden, das nur durch das in Strömen vergossene Blut seiner Märtyrer — wodurch es freilich sich mehr und mehr befestigte — nie aber über die Leichen anderer, wie es bei dem christlichen der Fall war, emporstieg: ein Gebäude, das schon seit dem Exile keine Spanne Erde mehr besitzet, einen Glauben der nur durch ewige Enthaltsamkeit und Entbehrungen sich erhält, und nur unter einer Vorsehung seine Existenz fristet. Natürlich hat unsere Religion, wie jede andere, auch ihre mannigfachen Zeremonien und symbolischen Gebräuche, die man aber im unzertrennbaren Ganzen, in der lebendigen Einheit betrachten muß, um die ungeheure Wirksamkeit nicht zu verkennen, die solche auf Millionen ausüben, welche auch diese als eine erquickende Atmosphäre des Glaubens, der Liebe, der Gefühle ansehen, in der sie leben und sterben. Wozu will man nun mit dem zweischneidigen, feurigen Schwerte der Vernunft und Weisheit sich an unsere Glaubenstüre anzustemmen suchen, um mit dem spitzigen Pfeile des Spottes und dem scharfen Messer der Kritik unsere Zeremonien anzugreifen, an denen sich nicht nur gutmütige schwache, sondern auch erhabene große Seelen erquicken und erbauen? Wenn der christliche theologische Rationalismus die Reformen, die er so nötig an seinem kirchlichen Körper auszuüben hätte, nicht zu unternehmen sich getraut, wenn er solche Experimente so behutsam scheut, warum will er sie denn gerade an unserem Leibe machen, wie er dieses so ungestüm in seinem Verlangen kund gibt? So lange es ein christliches Dogmen- und Zeremonienwesen geben wird, so lange kann auch das jüdische nicht schwinden. — Doch wir kommen zu weit in das Gebiet der Polemik hinein und sollten nur in das des Glaubensfeldes ein wenig eindringen.

Man wollte, wie man es bei allen realen Dingen gewohnt war, auch unser Ideales, unsern Glauben, knechten, man wollte z. B. die Messiasidee (als das Prinzip eines theokratischen Staatenverhältnisses, wie man sie zu nennen pflegte) aus unsern Religionsbekenntnissen gestrichen haben, und da wir keineswegs damit zufrieden waren und sind, uns die bürgerliche Gleichstellung entziehen.

Ist es schon Barbarei genug, einen harmlosen Gedanken, der doch wahrhaftig, so lange er dieses ist, dem Staate nie gefährlich werden kann, zu unterdrücken, so es aber noch eine traurige Lächerlichkeit, uns das zum Vorwurfe machen zu wollen, was, während wir es hoffen, unsere christlichen Brüder nach ihrer festesten Überzeugung schon längst besitzen. Ob wir aber einen körperlichen Messias oder nur einen geistigen erwarten? — gewiß, wir gestehen es ja gerne zu, daß dieser in das Reich der historischen Wunder gehört, und dann lasse man doch die Gottheit handeln und opponiere nicht gegen ihre zukünftigen Zwecke.

Wenn man weiter unsern Glauben zu bekämpfen suchte, indem man uns die vermeintliche Intoleranz des Talmud vorwarf, so war dieses nichts als eine Oberflächlichkeit unserer Gegner. Der Talmud ist uns keineswegs ein Glaubenswerk, das uns in seinen ethischen und mystischen Ansichten bindend wäre, sondern nur als Tradition, in seinem zeremoniellen Kultus, da ist er unser Kodex, den wir als unantastbar verehren und dem wir pünktlichst folgen. Wie man uns nun den Fehdehandschuh hinwerfen konnte, weil jener einige inhumane Stellen gegen Nichtjuden aufzuweisen hat, die in einer Zeit verfaßt wurden, wo man die Juden unmenschlich behandelte; so bedarf er nicht einmal eines Apologeten, um wie viel weniger wir, die wir ja solche ungewohnte Intoleranz mit Recht nur den schrecklichen Zeitverhältnissen zuschreiben, — und unsere Philosophie schlägt um, wie unsere Pulse anders schlagen.

Hat ferner unsere Opposition, der es nie an Waffen gegen uns mangelte, kurzhin den Satz aufzustellen gewagt, daß wir treu an unsere Religion haltend, gar nicht in den Staatsdienst aufgenommen werden können, da unsere Feste uns an jeder Werktätigkeit hinderten: — so erwarte man keineswegs, daß ich von schimpflichen Zugeständnissen unserer Religion jetzt sprechen werde, — wir schachern und verkaufen nicht um Gold und Gut und nicht um Ehrenstellen und Fürstendienst unser Heiligstes auf Erden — handelten wir doch dann als wahre Sklaven, die selbst ihre individuelle Freiheit im Glauben und in den Zeremonien unterdrücken lassen —

behüte! ich nehme hierbei, bei dem scheinbar schwierigsten Widerlegungspunkte die Geschichte zur Hand, und zeige, wie im finstern Mittelalter, ja selbst früher, im talmudischen Zeitalter, an den bedeutendsten fürstlichen Höfen Juden in dem Staatsdienste waren, Juden, von deren wahrhaftester uneigenützigster Orthodoxie wir uns gar keinen Begriff machen können!! O arme Zeit der Aufklärung, die du nicht einmal so tolerant und nachsichtsvoll wie deine schwarze Ahnherrin handelst. — Wo das allgemeine Wohl des Staates gefährdet werden könnte, da sagt selbst das Gesetz, zur Beseitigung eines solchen Falles wäre kein Tag und keine Arbeit und kein Verbot zu scheuen, wo es sich aber um Privatinteressen handelt, nun da kann — und was vermag man nicht, so der gute Wille nicht fehlt — da kann gewiß auch durch andere Mittel dem Gesetze ganz unbeschadet abgeholfen werden.

Fassen wir bei unserer Lehre den Schluß, daß, je strenger und größer die religiöse Observanz sei, desto nützlicher es dem Staate selbst sein wird, weil desto mehr die Laster sinken, die seine Anordnungen umsonst zu verpönen suchten.—

Werfen wir nun aber auch einen Blick auf das Leben der Juden, so werden wir die Erfahrung machen, daß es im allgemeinen verhältnißmäßig auf einer größern Stufe der sittlichen Ausbildung, als das einer jeden andern Konfession stehe, da eben ihr strenges Zeremonienwesen und ihr Glaube es ist, die sie frugal und human heranbilden. Die Gebrechen aber, die man teilweise an ihnen erblickt, die hat der Staat durch sein Knechten und Unterdrücken, durch sein Hemmen jeder freieren Entwicklung selbst verschuldet*.

Und nun, hochherzige Volksvertreter! des teutschen Reiches schönste Hoffnung! werdet auch die eines mit Unrecht verfolgten Häufleins. Verschmäht es nicht, Euch eines Stammes anzunehmen, auf dem nicht der Fluch des Himmels, aber der Fluch des schrecklichsten Fanatismus so lange schon mit einer kaum zu ertragenden Last haftet. Möge doch endlich das freie teutsche Reich, dessen Repräsentanten Ihr seid, der Pflicht ersten und der Freiheit obersten Grundsatz, Gerechtigkeit, üben. Und wahrlich, die hohe Stunde des Rechtes, sie hat geschlagen; Ihr habt sie mutig erkämpft und errungen, lasset ihren günstigen Zeiger nicht zurück mehr sinken.

So empfanget denn, hohe Männer! diese schwachen Worte, die jetzt mein bewegtes Gemüt Euch und dem gewichtigen Momente gegenüber nur stammelnd und ungeordnet hervorbringen konnte, empfanget diese Worte als die leisesten, kaum vernehmbaren Töne einer mächtigen, durch die in sich tragende Wahrheit zauberhaft gewordenen Feuersprache, die aus Hunderttausender frisch atmenden Herzen wie Trompetenschall und Kanonendonner beim Gottesgerichte welterschütternd ertönt.

OFFENES WORT AN DEN CHRISTLICHEN KLERUS

Verzeiht es einem angehenden jüdischen Theologen, dem es vielleicht sonst weder nach seinen Jahren, noch nach seinen Kenntnissen anstehen möchte, daß er an Euch, würdige Priester, sein Wort richtet, und Eure Aufmerksamkeit für einen Gegenstand in Anspruch nimmt, zu dessen Veröffentlichung nur der mächtige,

---

*Verfasser dieses Sendschreibens konnte diese nur flüchtig erwähnten Punkte der Kürze der Zeit wegen nicht weiter ausführen. Es ist dieses Thema aber auch ein so oft schon verhandeltes, daß es ihm teilweise auch unnötig schien, das, was schon andere in ganzen Werken besprochen, hier zu wiederholen. Der edle Verteidiger seines Volkes, Hr. Dr. Riesser, Mitglied des Parlamentes, hat selbst in mehreren trefflichen Schriften diesen Gegenstand ausführlich erörtert.

unwiderstehliche Drang seines Herzens und der Wahrheit rückhaltlose Sprache ihn zwingen kann. Es ist die Zeit, die hochwichtige, in der wir leben, die ja der offnen Sprache gerne ihre Feder leiht, und den Unterschied des Alters und des Wissens im Gebiete des Gelehrtentums, da beseitigt, wo es gilt für das allgemeine Wohl ein Schärflein beizutragen; es ist die Zeit, die es auch dem Jünglinge erlaubt, daß er erfahrenen und ehrwürdigen Männern gegenüber kühn und unumwunden seine Meinung äußert, und die ihm erlaubt, auch die unzeitigen, erst in der Blüte begriffenen Gedanken in den Schoß der gereiftesten und der großartigsten niederzulegen. — Erwacht ist der Geist des Menschenrechtes. Die Ketten der Unterdrückten zu lösen, die Augen der Blinden und die Ohren der Tauben zu öffnen, das ist die Aufgabe, die er für sein Tagewerk sich setzt. Unaufhaltsam geht er seine Bahn, und groß sind die Aufgaben, die er bereits vollendet. Schon viele Blinde haben gesehen, schon viele Taube gehört, auch die Ketten vieler Unterdrückten wurden gelöst, doch noch viele schmachten in der Knechtschaft. Das Volk Israel muß sich leider auch noch unter sie rechnen. Noch immer ertönte nicht die Posaune seiner Freiheit, noch immer ist die Scheidewand nicht gestürzt, die zwischen ihm und dem Christentume gewaltsam aufgestellt wurde, noch immer lechzt es vergebens nach seiner Emanzipation. Zu Euch, Priester des christlichen Glaubens, zu Euch Repräsentanten einer Religion, die Ihr die der Milde und der Liebe nennet, zu Euch blickt dieses Volk jetzt in der Stunde der ernstesten Bedeutung, um aus Euren Händen seine Freiheit zu empfangen, um aus Eurem Munde die Kunde seiner Erlösung zu vernehmen. Ihr schüttelt verwundert Eure Häupter, nicht begreifend, wie ich eine solche Sprache gegen Euch führen kann, die doch nur an die Lenker und Führer der Regierungen zu richten ist. Nein! nicht zu jenen, sondern zu Euch und nur zu Euch kann ich so reden. Ihr nur seid es, die das beinahe zweitausendjährige Unrecht wieder gut machen, die Ihr jetzt der jüdischen Nation nebst Gott als Retter dienen könnet, Ihr nur seid es, die Ihr den erwachten Geist des Menschenrechtes nicht hemmen und seinen gesegneten Pfad mit unvergänglichen Blumen bestreuen sollt. —

Wohl mancher Staat hätte längstens schon die Gleichstellung der Juden ausgesprochen, wenn er nicht die unaufgeklärte, rohe, fanatische Masse fürchtete, die er dadurch aufs Äußerste bringen könnte; denn in ihr wurzelt leider noch immer der uralte furchtbare Judenhaß, der sich bei so vielen Gelegenheiten geltend macht, und die bedauerliche Fakten übergeht. Doch wie? wenn diese Unaufgeklärten aufgeklärt würden? wie? wenn man dieselben belehrt, daß das Judentum edel und würdig in seinen Religionsprinzipien, edel und würdig in seinen Vorschriften ist; wie? wenn man sie unterrichtet, wie das echte Christentum jede Inhumanität verpönt, und wie sein Stifter gleich Moses die Nächstenliebe gegen jedermann aufs strengste anempfiehlt? Wahrlich! der Fanatismus müßte schwinden und die Toleranz den Sieg davon tragen. —

Priester, ihr, die Lehrer des Volkes, Ihr, die Ihr doch die Grundsätze unserer Religion als die Pfeiler der Eurigen genau kennen müsset, Ihr vermögt dies alles zu bewirken, Ihr vermögt von der Kanzel aus den Samen des Guten und des Wahren zu streuen, von den Kanzeln aus, von wo doch Eure Macht und die Macht des lebendigen Wortes so imposant und so unendlich ist.

Kinder meines Gottes! wollt Ihr noch länger es mit ansehen, wie man Euren Brüdern — zur Schmach und zum Hohne der ganzen Menschheit — ihre Rechte vorenthält, wie Eure Brüder, als ob sie diese nicht wären, immer hintenangesetzt, immer verachtet, immer gedrückt bleiben? Haftet nicht genug des betrübendsten Makels an der finstern Vergangenheit, soll auch die lichtere Gegenwart uns solche graue Schandbilder aufweisen? Soll noch länger die Wahrheit zur Lüge gestempelt, das Licht zur Finsterniß verwandelt werden?

Welche schwierige Stellung die Kirche in unserer Neuzeit einnimmt, das ist auch Euch nicht unbekannt, — nur durch die Wahrheit kann sie sich retten, durch Schleichwege wäre sie auf immer verloren. In Eurem eigenen Interesse bitte und beschwöre ich Euch, sucht, daß dieselbe erhalten bleibe. Zeigt es jetzt der Welt, wie ungerecht man von der Kirche urtheilt, wenn man glaubt, daß sie den Fortschritt hemme, daß sie den freien Geist ersticke, daß sie der Wahrheit ihre Wege sperre. O Priester, bezeugt dieses durch Eure Lehren und die gute Sache wird triumphieren, und auch Ihr werdet Euch in der Farbe zeigen, in der Ihr Eurem hohen Stande gemäß erscheinen sollet. Unsre ganze Generation wird Eurem Verdienste Anerkennung zollen, das Volk Israel wird seinen Dank in Eure Urne legen, und die ganze Nachwelt Euer Angedenken segnen*.

Offne Antwort auf das offne Wort.

Du hast, Bruder vom Hause Israel! ein herzliches Wort gesprochen, das Dir eine bange Ahnung eingab, die sich verwirklichen möchte, wenn die erleuchteten Regierungen im Vereine mit den Vertretern der Völker die Emanzipation der Juden mit in die Grundgesetze ihrer Staaten einstellen. Du hast klar erkannt, wo das Haupthindernis liegt, das dem Zerbrechen der Knechtschaftsfesseln, die Euer Volk noch drücken, entgegensteht. Die Gebildeten aller Stände sind längst einig, daß des religiösen Bekenntnisses wegen kein Mensch, kein Volksstamm der bürgerlichen Rechte beraubt werden darf. Allein der seit bald zwei Jahrtausende gehegte und gepflegte Fanatismus des christlichen Volkes gegen die unschuldigen Nachkommen derjenigen, welche an dem Stifter unserer Religion den Justizmord begangen, ist die gerechte Quelle der Besorgnis aller Gutdenkenden und Wohlmeinenden für den Fall, daß die Israeliten in allem den Christen staatsbürgerlich gleichgestellt werden. Darum ergeht mit Recht an alle christlichen Religionslehrer die ernste Mahnung, und sie sollte von allen Bischöfen und Konsistorien amtlich erlassen werden, daß sie das Volk zweckmäßig vorbereiten auf die zur unabweislichen Forderung der Zeit gewordene und in kurzer Zeit überall in Europa durchzuführende staatsrechtliche Gleichstellung der Israeliten. Darum ruft auch ein katholischer Priester seinen Amtsbrüdern zu: Arbeitet an dem großen Werke der Veredlung des Euch anvertrauten Volkes mit Wort und Tat, stellt es auf den höhern Standpunkt der Erkenntnis und der allgemeinen Bruderliebe gleich dem Heiland, der den Samaritern eben so liebevoll begegnete wie den Juden, und erstere mehr als einmal den letzteren als Muster hinstellte. Zeigt dem Volke, daß die Nachkommen eben so wenig an der Tat ihrer Urahnen schuldig sind und dafür verantwortlich gemacht werden können, als überhaupt das Kind für die Fehler seiner Eltern. Derselbe Fanatismus, der jetzt, wie von jeher, so viele Christen und Christenpriester blendet, war auch zur Zeit Jesu die Haupttriebfeder der Hand-

---

*Dieser Artikel wurde während meiner Ferienzeit von Hürben (bei Augsburg) aus der deutschen konstitutionellen Zeitung überschickt, und in Nr. 134 abgedruckt. In dieser Zeitschrift Nr. 138 nun stand von München aus eine Erwiederung, die wir ihrer Vortrefflichkeit halber auch hier beizufügen uns erlauben.

lungsweise der Feinde Jesu. Sie wußten nicht was sie taten, so wie auch jetzt noch alle diejenigen, die den Samen des Hasses und der Zwietracht in die große Gottes-familie auf Erden säen, nicht wissen, was sie tun. Ziehet ab die Decke von Euren Augen, und erkennet in allen Menschen liebe Kinder eines und desselben liebenden Vaters, gleichviel auf welche Weise sie ihn ehren und zu ihm rufen. Erfüllet zuerst seinen Willen, sein heiliges, sein Hauptgesetz der Liebe, dann könnt Ihr auch ohne Mißgunst, Neid und Vorurteil die bisher zurückgesetzten, verachteten, gekränkten Brüder in Eure Familie aufnehmen. Streifet ab den Wahn, als ob die religiöse Erkenntnis und die Weltanschauung vergangener Jahrhunderte auch dann Norm für Gegenwart und Zukunft sein können, wenn sie den heiligsten Rechten der Menschheit, den untrüglichsten Gesetzen Gottes, wie sie in Schrift, Vernunft und Natur klar und stark ausgesprochen sind, schnurgerade widerstreben. Das histori-sche Recht beugt sich allenthalben dem Rufe der voranschreitenden Zeit: können wohl auf religiösem, oder vielmehr kirchlichem Gebiete noch länger die Schranken aufrecht gehalten werden, die nicht der Vater aller Menschen, nicht der Sohn Gottes gesetzt hat, sondern kurzsichtige, wahnbehaftete Menschen, die sich für die einzigen, für die unfehlbaren Ausleger der göttlichen Wahrheit und des Willens der Gottheit hielten? Hört drum auch auf, Ihr Priester der christlichen Religion! gegen Eure eigenen Amtsgenossen zu eifern, wenn der eine oder andere auch in richtigem Erfassen der Zeit und ihrer großen Aufgaben voraneilt: hetzt nicht Gemeinden gegen ihre Seelsorger auf, wenn diese unermüdet bestrebt sind, die Ihrigen auf eine höhere Stufe religiöser und selbst auch politischer Erkenntnisse zu heben. Laßt nie gehässige Worte gegen Christen eines anderen Bekenntnisses fallen, und arbeitet nach Kräften daran, daß Deutschland, wenn auch noch lange nicht in den Kon-fessionen, doch in Liebe einig werde. Von dieser Liebe schließet aber die Israeliten nicht aus, die flehend ihre Hände zu uns herüber reichen; führet sie ein ins Vater-haus, sie werden die Fehler ablegen, die eine natürliche Folge ihrer bisherigen Ausschließung, Zurücksetzung und Mißhandlung waren. Auf Euch, Ihr Prediger des Evangeliums! fällt die Schmach, wenn bei der bevorstehenden Emanzipation der Juden das christliche Volk dies nicht ertragen will, wenn Brutalität und teuf-lische Bosheit der Verblendeten, an der wehrlosen Minderzahl sich vergreifen und durch Exzesse sich schänden sollte, wie wir sie selbst in unserem Bayern erst kürzlich erlebten. Legt Hand ans Werk, ihr Verkünder des Friedens! und der Friede Jesu Christi den die Welt nicht geben kann, wird mit Euch sein. Und hiermit reiche ich dem jüdischen Theologen in Hürben die Bruderhand.

II

Petition Nr. 1170

Die Mündigerklärung der Israeliten im teutschen Völkerbunde und die Einsetzung derselben in alle bürgerlichen und staatlichen Rechte.

Eine Denkschrift an die Mitglieder der hohen Reichs-Versammlung in Frankfurt am Main, von J. G. Lehmann, evangelischer Pfarrer zu Nußdorf bei Landau in der Pfalz.

Groß ist die Zeit, in welcher wir leben, größer als jemals eine im deutschen Vaterlande gewesen! Früher stand wohl, im Laufe der Zeiten um Jahrhunderte, mancher große und tatkräftige Mann in Teutschland auf, um den Kampf zu bestehen für Freiheit und Menschenrechte, wie mehrere unter den teutschen Kaisern, aber ihre Macht zerstäubte entweder an dem furchtbaren Bollwerk der Priesterherrschaft (Hierarchie), oder an der Roheit des Zeitalters, und ihre Bemühungen trugen wenige, oder gar keine Früchte für das teutsche Vaterland. Wohl erhob sich auch im Beginne des XVI. Jahrhunderts ein Glaubensheld für die geistige Freiheit des Teutschen Volkes, allein sein großes Werk, so schön und herrlich begonnen, blieb unvollendet und statt gänzliche Befreiung des Geistes vom Glaubensjoche zu bringen, verlor sich dasselbe später größtenteils in gelehrten Zänkereien, oder ging unter im starren Festhalten am kalten, geisttötenden Buchstaben und in Schulweisheit. — Die französische Staatsumwälzung am Ende des vorigen Jahrhunderts erschütterte das teutsche Reich in seinen Grundfesten; das morsche, mürbe und veraltete Gebäude stürzte unaufhaltbar zusammen; alle Bande des Rechts und der Völker wurden dadurch gelöset; allein, statt daß sich mit dem neuen Jahrhunderte aus den Trümmern des alten Reiches ein neuer, mächtiger Staat entwickelt, statt daß eine starke kräftige Hand die Zügel ergriffen und den Geist der Zeit erkennend, durch Weisheit und Klugheit Teutschland zu neuer Größe und Hoheit geleitet hätte, wurde dasselbe leider! wieder zerstückelt und schmachtete dann lange Jahre unter dem schmählichen Drucke fremder, napoleonischer Zwangherrschaft!

Ein neuer Hoffnungsstern schien über den teutschen Landen aufzugehen, als in dem sogenannten Befreiungskriege die ganze Masse des teutschen Volkes, dem Rufe sowie den Verheißungen seiner tiefgedemütigten Fürsten treu und gerne folgend, aufstand um das verhaßte Franzosenjoch abzuschütteln. Das beinahe Unmögliche geschah, der Kampf für Gott, Fürst und Vaterland ward geschlagen, die furchtbare Macht des teutschen Erbfeindes wurde gebrochen, die entehrenden Fesseln abgestreift, der herrlichste Sieg, nach Strömen vergossenen edeln teutschen Blutes errungen, und glorreich entfaltete sich in Leipzigs Ebenen das Banner der goldenen Freiheit über die siegreichen teutschen Stämme, eine glückliche Zukunft verheißend. — Schöner Traum, eitle Täuschung! — Die im Streite erprobte Treue der Teutschen wurde nicht belohnt, der mit dem Herzblute der Völker erfochtene Sieg trug herbe Früchte; die von den Fürsten zur Zeit der Not gegebenen heiligen Zusagen gingen, schnöde verleugnet, nicht in Erfüllung; der errungene Lorbeer verwelkte; die im Völkerkampfe empfangenen Wunden heilten; aber durch die staatskünstlerischen (diplomatischen) Bestrebungen, Ränke und Deuteleien der durch treulose Berater verleiteten Größen, wurden der teutschen Freiheit tiefe tödliche Wunden geschlagen, sie konnte ihre Schwingen nicht entfalten, und unter zahllosen Quälereien, Plackereien und Erniedrigungen sank Teutschland abermals in Zerstücklung und in Schmach dahin! —

Da brach endlich mit den ewig denkwürdigen Februar- und Märztagen des Jahres 1848 ein neues Licht der Freiheit, der Geist der Einheit und Selbständigkeit über Teutschlands Gauen herein; das mühsam aufgeführte staatskünstlerische Gebäude sank in einigen Wochen zusammen vor dem Willen des mündig gewordenen Volkes; Ringen nach Einheit des Vaterlandes, nach Selbständigkeit und Wiederherstellung der dem Volke bisher, trotz aller Bitten und Bemühungen, schnöde vorenthaltenen Rechte, war das allgemeine Losungswort; Teutschland erwachte endlich aus seinem todähnlichen Schlummer und glühender Freiheitseifer beseelte und erfüllte jede Brust mit neuer großer Hoffnung. — Die Fürsten, den Mahnungen der ernsten Zeit Gehör gebend und den Geist des Jahrhunderts richtig erfassend, selbst befreit vom dem Drucke des österreichischen Hauptstaatskünstlers, der ihren völkerverderblichen Bund ins Leben gerufen und eingedenk der Zusagen ihrer Väter zur Zeit der Gefahr, bewilligten das Verlangen der Völker und gaben das feierliche Versprechen: die Verfassungen der teutschen Stämme zur Wahrheit zu erheben, sowie auch die Einheit und das Wohl des Gesamtvolkes zum Ziele ihres Strebens zu machen. Die Männer des Volkes traten rasch zusammen; ein teutscher Reichstag, zur Abstellung aller bisherigen Gebrechen, sowie zur Errichtung eines wohlbegründeten gesetzlichen Staatenbundes zum Heil und Wohl der einzelnen Stämme und des Ganzen, ward allgemein gefühltes Bedürfnis, sowie auch der innige Wunsch aller, und demzufolge wählte sofort das Volk die Männer seines Vertrauens, welche nun in Frankfurt a/M. zusammengetreten sind, um die Reichsverfassung zu entwerfen und über das künftige Geschick des gemeinsamen Teutschlands zu raten und zu taten. —

Schwer und wichtig, dies erkennt wohl jeder an, sind die Pflichten dieser freigewählten Vertreter aus allen teutschen Gauen; auf sie und auf ihr edles Streben sehen alle mit hingebendem Vertrauen, ja gleichsam mit hoffnungsvoller Sehnsucht, sowohl die Völker, als auch die Fürsten; allen sollen sie genügen, die gegenseitigen Rechte dieser wie jener wahren; alles sollen sie ordnen, befestigen und mit schaffendem tätigen Geiste den Grundstein legen zu einem mächtigen Gebäude, zu einem starken, einigen teutschen Reiche oder Staatenbunde. — Sie sollen alles ausgleichen, alle versöhnen, alles Unrecht wieder gut machen und auf den Hauptgrundpfeilern, auf Wahrheit und Recht, Teutschlands künftige Größe und Wohlfahrt erbauen. Groß und erhaben ist der Beruf dieser Vertrauensmänner, segenbringend ihre wichtige Aufgabe; möchten sie von Weisheit, Umsicht und echter Vaterlandsliebe geleitet, dieselbe ganz und vollständig lösen zum wahren Wohle aller Angehörigen des teutschen Völkerbundes.

Unter anderem haben die Männer des Reichstages auch ihr Hauptaugenmerk zu richten auf die Wiederherstellung der Freiheit jeglichen Glaubens und dessen ungestörte Ausübung, sowie auch auf Gleichheit aller Religionsbekenntnisse in bürgerlichen und staatlichen Rechten. — Denn, man schlage nur die Geschichtsbücher unseres Volkes aus den letztvergangenen Jahrhunderten nach, finden wir nicht auf jedem Blatte derselben das traurige Ergebnis, daß eben die Bevorzugung des einen, oder die Verfolgung des anderen Religionsteiles, oder auch die Erhebung eines Glaubens zur ausschließlichen Staatsreligion usw. freilich immer durch äußeren Einfluß von Süden her angeregt und unterhalten, jederzeit die hauptsächlichste Ursache zu Teutschlands Getrenntheit und Schmach gewesen sein und dessen Einheit und Gedeihen gehindert habe?! — Dies kann und darf fürder nicht mehr der Fall sein; keine Glaubensansicht soll künftig mehr den teutschen Bruder vom Bruder trennen und so wie — Gott gebe bald! — künftig nur ein Recht und ein Gesetz im teutschen Reiche walten und gelten wird, so kann und wird allgemeine Gewissensfreiheit mit der Zeit gewiß auch das ihrige dazu beitragen, daß

zur Befestigung des Völkerbundes später ebenfalls nur ein Glaube, ein Band der
Liebe und Eintracht, alle umschlinge und beglücke! —

An dem ältesten, merkwürdigsten und zugleich unglücklichsten Volke der Erde,
an den Israeliten ist in dieser Hinsicht auch großes Unrecht wieder gut zu machen,
was jetzt bei der geistigen Wiedergeburt und staatlichen Umgestaltung Teutschlands, durch Einsetzung derselben in alle ihnen gebührenden Menschenrechte
geschehen kann und muß. Wie gesagt, großes Unrecht ist hier zu vergüten; alle
kleinlichen und engherzigen Einwürfe, welche man bisher gegen die Mündigerklärung (Emanzipation) der Juden vorbrachte, müssen nun in den Hintergrund
treten, wenn Teutschlands Wohl, wenn Großes und Erhabenes beraten, begründet
und geschaffen werden soll; auch nicht der leiseste Mißton darf den Einklang
(Harmonie) stören, der jetzt alle teutschen Herzen durchbebt; keines Teutschen
Rechte dürfen gekränkt werden, oder unberücksichtigt bleiben, wenn wahrer
bleibender Segen für alle aus dieser Neugestaltung der Dinge erblühen soll. —

Damit also aufs künftige auch nicht mehr der geringste Vorwurf unser gutes
teutsches Vaterland treffen möge, so faßten wir den Entschluß, den in Frankfurt
zum Wohle aller Brüder versammelten Männern in den nachfolgenden wenigen
Bogen aus unseren Geschichtsbüchern die schreienden Ungerechtigkeiten vor
Augen zu führen, welche die Teutschen im Laufe der Jahrhunderte, an dem be-
dauernswerten jüdischen Volke begangen haben und dadurch zugleich das
Rechts- und Billigkeitsgefühl derselben in Anspruch zu nehmen, sowie auch den ein-
helligen Eifer bei ihnen zu erwecken, durch vollständige Mündigerklärung der
Israeliten und durch die Gleichstellung derselben mit allen übrigen Religionsgenossen in bürgerlicher und staatlicher Beziehung, den Schutzgeist (Genius) der
Menschheit wegen der den Bekennern des mosaischen Glaubens bisher unverdient
widerfahrenen Unbilden zu versöhnen, so daß demnach auf solche Weise die
Enkel das wiedergutmachen was die Väter gesündiget haben. Diese Mündigerklärung soll aber weder erbettelt, noch ertrotzt werden, sondern wie sich dies aus
der nachfolgenden geschichtlichen Darstellung und aus den teils eingestreuten,
teils angehängten Bemerkungen ergeben wird, sie muß zugestanden und ausgesprochen werden, als ein angeborenes Recht der Menschheit und zugleich als ein
Ausfluß der christlichen Religion, der Religion der Liebe. — Darum lautet auch
unser Wahlspruch: Wahrheit und Recht! —"

The author gives a detailed account of many atrocities committed against Jews, corroborated
— as is the rest of his text — by source references which have here been omitted. The extensive manuscript concludes with the following passages:

"Aber nicht nur die Liebe, sondern auch die Dankbarkeit machte es uns zur heiligen Pflicht, die Bekenner des mosaischen Glaubens für mündig zu erklären und sie
dadurch zu Teilnehmern an allen geistigen und bürgerlichen Rechten zu machen.
Denn, rühmen wir Christen uns reinerer Religionserkenntnisse, höherer Bildung,
überhaupt herrlicher Vorzüge, die wir in allen Zweigen des Wissens von den Juden
voraus haben, so ist dies alles im wahren Grunde nur eine Folge, ein Ausfluß der
Lehren des Evangeliums, was jeder unbefangene Wahrheitsfreund eingestehen und
zugeben muß. Gründet sich nun aber das Christentum nicht auf das Judentum, ist
es nicht aus demselben entsprungen und hervorgegangen? Müssen wir also nicht

dem merkwürdigen, ehrwürdigen und unglücklichen Volke Israels dafür danken, daß es auch unter allem Drucke und aller Verfolgung, welche schon in den vorchristlichen Zeiten über dasselbe ergingen, uns seine heiligen Bücher und die in denselben enthaltenen göttlichen Offenbarungen als die vorbereitende Grundlage des Christentums, in ihrer ursprünglichen Reinheit und Echtheit bewahret hat und dadurch der Beförderer des jetzigen, den Christen aller Länder und Weltteile eigentümlichen hohen Standes der wissenschaftlichen Bildung der Kenntnisse und Einsichten geworden ist? — Dürfen oder können wir es den Israeliten verargen, wenn sie noch jetzt bei der bisherigen geringen und mangelhaften Verwirklichung des göttlichen im Menschen durch die Lehren des Christentums, ja durch den Druck unter welchem sie von Seiten der undankbaren Christen schmachteten dazu bewogen und zurückgescheucht, sich immer mehr von denselben zurückzogen, um ihre höheren Offenbarungen und ihre Volkstümlichkeit rein zu erhalten? Dürfen wir es ihnen verübeln, wenn sie, unter den ungünstigen Umständen in welchen sie leben, überall gleichsam einen Staat im Staate bilden und sich gegen andere ganz abschließen, indem ihnen in dem christlichen Glauben bisher kein genügender Ersatz für das, was sie aufgeben sollten, geboten wurde? Hätten sie vor der Gründung des Christentums nicht nach eben diesen Grundsätzen gehandelt, hätten sie ihre heiligen Schriften dem Einflusse des jedesmaligen Zeitgeistes und ihrer äusseren traurigen Verhältnisse preisgegeben, würde denn da der Mosaismus sich nicht in dem Heidentum verloren haben und untergegangen sein und, falls dieses gewesen, könnten wir uns jetzt als Christen unseres glücklichen geistigen Zustandes rühmen? — Haben wir also nicht die dankbarsten Verpflichtungen gegen die Israeliten in dieser Beziehung und haben wir dieselben dadurch verwirklicht, daß wir sie durch unser Mißachten und unsere Verfolgung auf die niedrigste Stufe menschlicher Bildung und tätigen Wirkens herabbrachten und so tief sinken ließen? — Haben wir z.B. nur soviel für sie getan, als wir in neueren Zeiten zur Abschaffung der Sklaverei und zur Verbesserung des Zustandes der Heiden geleistet, denen wir doch nichts zu verdanken haben und deren wir uns nur aus reinem Mitgefühl und echter Menschenliebe annahmen, während wir die Juden, unsere geistigen Wohltäter, gefühllos von uns stießen, sie verfolgten und unterdrückten, wie uns die vorstehende geschichtliche Auseinandersetzung leider nur zu deutlich zeigt? — Sind wir also nicht aus Dankbarkeit schuldig und verbunden, ihre geistige und bürgerliche Freiheit möglichst und tunlichst zu befördern und auf solche Weise eine alte drückende Schuld gegen sie abzutragen? — Dies kann, soll und muß jetzt bei der Wiederbringung aller Dinge, bei der rechtlichen Ausgleichung aller Lebens- und Staatsverhältnisse, bei der Neugestaltung des deutschen Völkerbundes, durch die von dem allgemeinen Reichstage auszusprechende und festzusetzende Mündigerklärung der Israeliten, so wie auch durch die Einsetzung und Gleichstellung derselben mit allen übrigen Bewohnern Teutschlands in religiösen und staatlichen Rechten geschehen.

Haben wir denn nicht in der neuesten Zeit gesehen, welcher Geist sich auch in Israel regt? — Stehen nicht gegenwärtig viele jüdische Familien auf einer hohen geistigen Stufe, oder sind doch wenigstens in der Entwicklung zum Besseren begriffen? — Bemerken wir nicht überall unter der Mehrheit derselben eine ungemeine Tätigkeit, Wissenschaftlichkeit, steigende Bildung, zweckmäßigere Einrichtung ihrer Gottesverehrungen, Errichtung von Schulen usw. überhaupt ein Ringen nach geistiger Mündigkeit, ein Sprengen aller lästigen menschlichen Fesseln in Sachen des Glaubens und des Gewissens, durch Beseitigung unpassender, dem jetzigen Bildungsstande zuwiderlaufenden, aus ihrer früheren morgenländischen Heimat stammenden Gesetze und Gebräuche? — Ist es also nicht hohe Pflicht für die Christen, die Israeliten in diesem löblichen Streben zu unterstützen und ihnen in der, ihnen nach Vernunft, Wahrheit und Recht gebührenden Mündigerklärung und Gleichstellung mit den übrigen Religionsteilen die Mittel, darzureichen um sich geistig und bürgerlich von Tag zu Tag schneller und unbeengter entfalten und so durch und aus sich selbst mündig schaffen zu können? Also auch die Dankbarkeit gebietet uns, so tätig und wohlmeinend an den Besten der Brüder zu arbeiten.

Endlich verlangt dies aber auch noch das allgemeine Wohl und die Einheit des neu zu erstellenden teutschen Staatenbundes. Auf Wahrheit und Recht gegründet und auch in diesem Sinne gehandhabte und befolgte Gesetze und Verordnungen im geistigen und bürgerlichen Leben, müssen fortan die deutschen Stämme als Brüder untereinander verbinden, beglücken und sie zu einem einigen großen und mächtigen Volke heranbilden stark und kräftig im Innern, unüberwindlich, geehrt und Achtung gebietend nach Außen. Diese Einheit Teutschlands, die jetzt geschaffen werden soll, ist aber ohne innere und äußere Freiheit und Gleichheit aller Bundesangehörigen in religiösen und staatlichen Rechten nicht möglich. Das frühere geteilte, zerrissene und engherzige Wesen das immer Teutschlands Größe und Einheit hinderte, muß nun unbeschadet der einzelnen Regierungen und Staaten in einem Bunde aufgehen, in welchem der höchste Grundsatz der ist: einer für alle und alle für einen! —

War nicht bisher, wie uns leider die Geschichte der Teutschen lehrt, die innere Zerstückelung, sowie auch die Eingriffe von Außen, besonders in religiöser Hinsicht, die fortwährende betrübende Ursache des Verfalls und der Schmach unseres Vaterlandes? — Dies kann und darf künftig nicht mehr so sein, wenn Teutschland sich aus sich selbst entwickeln, erstarken und so zu seiner wahren Größe, Höhe und Einheit gelangen soll. Keine fremde oder welsche Hand darf sich fürder mehr verderbenbringend einmischen in die Entwicklung und in die Angelegenheiten unseres Vaterlandes, sei es in bürgerlicher oder kirchlicher Beziehung, denn das meiste Übel kam bisher von Außen über uns, jedoch auch vieles selbst verschuldet durch innere Zerrissenheit und Engherzigkeit.

Teutschland will und muß nun aber endlich im wahren Sinne des Wortes in und durch sich selbst ein Bruder- und Bundesstaat werden; denn wir wurden bisher oft, schwer und hart geprüft und die wichtigen Lehren, welche uns diese Prüfung verschafften, haben wir mit Zersplitterung unserer Kräfte, ja oft mit unserem warmen Herzblute bezahlt. Darum ist es jetzt hohe Zeit diese teuer erkauften Lehren ins Leben treten zu lassen und die Einheit des Vaterlandes zu erstreben. Darum darf kein Vorrecht, keine Bevorzugung aufs künftige mehr den Bruder vom Bruder, den Bürger vom Bürger, den Teutschen vom Teutschen scheiden, sondern alle bisherigen Sonderinteressen der einzelnen müssen sich nun auflösen in die Einheit des Ganzen; Liebe und Pflicht, Wahrheit und Recht müssen hinfort einer mit den andern und sie alle zusammen zum Gedeihen des großen Ganzen vereinen und verknüpfen. Werden diese Grundsätze in unserem lieben Vaterlande einheimisch und das heilige Eigentum eines jeden Teutschen, für welches er freudig Gut und Blut aufopfert, so wird dann keine Getrenntheit, weder im bürgerlichen noch im religiösen Leben, mehr unter uns sein oder aufkommen können.

Darum, wie schon oft und so auch zum Schlusse sei nochmals erwähnt, ist es eine Hauptverpflichtung und die vorzüglichste Aufgabe der Mitglieder des teutschen Reichstages, als eine notwendige Folge der allgemeinen Menschenrechte und als eine unabweisbare Forderung der Vernunft und des Christentums, die Freiheit des Glaubens und dessen ungestörte Ausübung, sowie die Gleichstellung aller Religionsgenossen in bürgerlichen und staatlichen Rechten als Grundgesetz aus-zusprechen und auf solche Weise Teutschlands wahres Heil auf ewige Zeiten zu begründen. Ja, wir wollen ein Volk sein und künftighin gelte unter den teutschen Brüdern nur noch der Vorzug, welcher sich dieser oder jener durch ihre höhere geistige Ausbildung erworben haben, um dann aber auch nur um so tätiger und kräftiger an dem Wohle des Ganzen arbeiten zu können. — Aus solchen Grund-sätzen kann sich nur Großes und Herrliches entfalten, daraus wird allgemeine Verbrüderung erstehen und aus geistiger und bürgerlicher Freiheit und Gleichheit muß die Einheit Teutschlands erblühen. — Dies der herzlichste Wunsch, dies die sehnlichste Hoffnung des gesamten teutschen Volkes, deren Verwirklichung es von seinen edlen, hochherzigen Abgeordneten zuversichtlich und vertrauensvoll erwartet! — Möchten letztere diese hohe Aufgabe würdig und völkerbeglückend lösen! Deswegen rufen wir nicht nur ihnen, sondern auch allen teutschen Brüdern in Ost und West, in Süd und Nord mit den Worten unseres größten vaterländischen Dichters zu:
Darum haltet fest zusammen — fest und ewig —
Kein Ort der Freiheit sei dem andern fremd —
Hochwachten stellet aus auf euren Bergen,
Daß sich der Bund zum Bunde rasch versammle —
Seid einig einig einig! —

Nußdorf im Juni 1848

J. G. Lehmann

III

Petition Nr. 2734

Hohe konstituierende Nationalversammlung!

Bitte der unterzeichneten israelitischen Lehrer Badens gegen Unterrichtsfreiheit und für Erklärung der Volksschulen zu Staatsanstalten und Einführung von Kommunalschulen; im Interesse des intellektuellen und materiellen Volkswohls, und namentlich aus Rücksicht der in paritätischen Gemeinden vorhandenen Minderheit von Religionsgenossenschaften.

Wenn ein großer Teil unseres deutschen Volkes seine Stimme erhebt für Trennung der Kirche vom Staate, diesem mißtrauend: er möchte, weil er alle Konfessionen gleich berechtigt, die ihrige beeinträchtigen, so wollen wir dagegen nichts einwenden. Die hohe konstituierende Nationalversammlung wird darüber entscheiden, ob sie den Wünschen solcher Gehör zu geben gut findet im Interesse aller Konfessionen. Wenn eben diese Klasse daraus auch die Notwendigkeit der Unterrichtsfreiheit folgert und beansprucht, so finden wir uns dazu berufen, hiergegen zu protestieren.

Fragen wir: Wer will Unterrichtsfreiheit? Antwort: Alle jene, denen es nicht um die religiöse Freiheit aller, sondern nur um die ihrige zu tun ist; diejenigen die wahrlich nicht schuld sind, daß der Grundsatz der Religionsfreiheit ausgesprochen worden, denen die Konfession, das Äußere, die Form, die Schale, das Alles ist; aber die Religion, das Innere, der Kern, das Wesen nur Nebensache. Es sind namentlich die Geistlichen, die das Volk hierzu veranlassen (fanatisieren), die es im Heiligtume, durch die Presse glauben machen, es sei durch die Religionsfreiheit ihre natürliche väterliche Religion in Gefahr, wenn nicht wieder wie ehedem die Schulen streng nach Konfessionen geschieden seien.

Fragen wir: Was will man mit Unterrichtsfreiheit und die Antwort ist: Man will die Schule ganz unter seiner Leitung, und die Lehrer vollständig am Gängelbande führen. Wer anders als wie die Geistlichen würden dann die Vorsteher der Schule werden? Was anders als Religionsunterricht würde da gelehrt werden bestehend in geisttötendem Mechanismus. Vor noch nicht langer Zeit hatten wir Israeliten Badens auch Unterrichtsfreiheit. Wir selbst können uns noch an jenen Zustand erinnern, haben auch lebendige Erinnerungszeichen an der Bildung eines großen Teiles der jetzigen Generation. Da schickte die Kinder in die Schule, wer nur wollte, und so lange man wollte, und wann man wollte, und zu wem man wollte. Es waren in einer jüdischen Gemeinde oft 4-6 Lehrer, in der kleinsten nicht selten 2; bei dieser Zahl hatten die Armen zuweilen nicht einen für ihre Kinder, weil die Reichen solche nur für die ihrigen hielten und bezahlten. Wir können solche Beispiele aus jeder Gemeinde anführen, wo allenthalben wegen Mangel an Mitteln ohne allen Unterricht aufgewachsene Männer und Frauen die Mehrzahl bilden. Und was lernten die Kinder der Reichen? Notdürftig Schreiben, Lesen, Rechnen, viel unverstandenes totes Zeug auswendig, welches das Gedächnis übermäßig anstrengte, die Denkkraft abstumpfte und den Verstand verdummte. So würde es werden bei dem großen denkenden deutschen Volke trotz seiner Philosophen. Auch wir hatten damals Gelehrte, aber die Masse war verdummt. Anstatt das Volk intellektuell zu bilden, würde es geistig verdummen, anstatt ihm materiell, namentlich dem armen Teil, zu erleichtern, würde es noch mehr belastet werden. Wir leben unter dem Volke und kennen den Geist desselben und vorzüglich den jener die solche Unterrichtsfreiheit wollen, es sind die Freiheitsliebenden wahrlich nicht. Es würde durch die Unterrichtsfreiheit dahin kommen, daß die Geistlichen Schulen errichten, und sie mit den ihnen zu Gebote stehenden kirchlichen Mittel unterhalten, wodurch der Unterricht wohlfeil würde. Allein das Wohlfeile würde hier am Ende teuer kommen, wie es uns die Schweiz lehrt.

So schädlich Unterrichtsfreiheit wäre, so nützlich und notwendig ist es, daß der

Staat die Schule zur Staatsanstalt erhebe und Kommunalschulen einführe. Die Notwendigkeit der Staatsanstaltschaft der Schule ist in der von unseren Kollegen eingereichten Petition nachgewiesen. Wir wollen nur hiermit die Notwendigkeit von Kommunalschulen, ihre Vorteile und Unschädlichkeit dartun, abermals gestützt auf unsere Erfahrung als israelitische Lehrer und als solche selbe im Interesse der kleinen Religionsgenossenschaften beanspruchend.

Daß Kommunalschulen der christlichen Religion ungefährlich sind das haben nicht nur Staatsmänner, die gute Christen sind, ausgesprochen, sondern es beweist dies ein christlicher Staat Deutschlands, das Großherzogtum Hessen, wo seit längerer Zeit solche unbeschadet der Religion bestehen. Auch wir haben ihre religiöse Unschädlichkeit in Bezug auf unsere Konfession erfahren. Denn seitdem den Israeliten gesetzlich die Erlernung der weltlichen Schulkenntnisse geboten ist, besuchen in den meisten Orten die israelitischen Kinder christliche Schulen, und wir haben noch nicht gefunden, daß aus diesen jüdischen Kindern christliche geworden sind. Warum nun soll nicht auch ein israelitischer Lehrer den christlichen, ein katholischer den evangelischen und ein evangelischer den katholischen Kindern Unterricht in den weltlichen Lehrgegenständen erteilen dürfen? Sind nicht auch die höhern Bürger- Industrieschulen, Gymnasien gemischt? Und schicken nicht selbst die Geistlichen ihre Kinder dahin, ohne eine Gefahr für ihre Religion zu befürchten? Nicht eine Trennung, sondern eine Einigung würde erreicht werden, dadurch, wenn es nicht jeder geistlichen Partei gestattet ist, die Schule zu Parteizwecken zu mißbrauchen.

In materieller Bezahlung sind Kommunalschulen insbesondere eine dringende Forderung der Zeit. In gemischten Gemeinden müssen mehrere Schulen unterhalten und mehrere Lehrer besoldet werden, wo oft nach der Schülerzahl ein Lehrer und eine Schule hinreichte. Wir können Orte namhaft machen, wo vier Lehrer sind und die Hälfte der dort angestellten Lehrer genügen würde, um dasselbe zu leisten. In dem großen Aufwande für die Konfessionsschulen, als durch die Gehalte der Lehrer, die Anschaffung und Unterhaltung der Schulhäuser, Einrichtung und Heizung der Schulzimmer, und mehrfache starke Prüfungsdiäten würde durch Vereinigung der Schulen ein bedeutendes Ersparnis erzielt werden, wo hingegen der status quo sofort immer größere und unerschwinglichere Lasten auflegen wird.

Wir stellen deshalb die Bitte:

Eine hohe Nationalversammlung wolle über die Eingaben um Unterrichtsfreiheit zur Tagesordnung übergehen, hingegen aber aussprechen, daß die bisherigen Konfessionsschulen zu Kommunalschulen umgeschaffen und diese als Staatsanstalten vom Staate unterhalten werden.

> In gebührender Hochachtung verharren
> Rohrbach bei Sinsheim,
> der 30. August 1848.

> Es folgen die Unterschriften

IV

Petition

[Covering letter]

Hohem Reichsministerium der Justiz.

Bei dem Unterzeichneten, als den Abgeordneten für Schwäbisch Hall, erscheint Dr. L. H. Löwenstein, aus Steinbach, O. A. Hall in Württemberg, und beklagte sich, daß er trotz eines 21 jährigen Aufenthalts in hiesiger Stadt Frankfurt, trotz einer Kaution, trotz Vermögens, das er in einer hiesigen Handlung habe, trotz einer an das königlich Württembergische Ministerium des Innern, von der Polizei-direktion zu Frankfurt, ergangenen Schreibens, daß man seinem Aufenthalt in der Stadt nichts in den Weg lege, neuerdings aus Frankfurt ausgewiesen worden, und zwar ohne Untersuchung, ohne Angabe eines Grundes, mit Mißachtung seiner wiederholten Bitte um gerichtliche Untersuchung.

Der Unterzeichnete wies den Beteiligten auf den Weg der Beschwerde an die Reichsministerien der Justiz u. des Innern und unterstützt und empfiehlt dessen Bitte, dahin zu wirken, daß vorläufig ihm der hiesige Aufenthalt gestattet, und sofort eine gerichtliche Untersuchung zur Erhebung seiner Unschuld eingeleitet werden möge.

Frankfurt d. 13. Oktob. 1848.

Der Abgeordnete zur Nationalversammlung

Dr. W. Zimmermann.

Petition

[Text]

An ein Hohes Reichsministerium der Justiz.

Gehorsamste Remonstration und Bitte des Orientalisten L. H. Löwenstein aus Steinbach im Königreich Württemberg, derzeit in Rödelheim, die Überweisung seiner Angelegenheit, polizeiliche Ausweisung aus Frankfurt betreffend, an das Hohe Reichsministerium des Innern und dessen Entscheidung betreffend.

Durch ein verehrliches Schreiben Seiner Exzellenz des Herrn Ministers des Innern, Herrn Baron von Schmerling, vom 25. dieses Monats wurde ich zu meinem tiefen Leidwesen benachrichtigt, daß ein hohes Reichsministerium der Justiz meine gehorsamste Vorstellung und Bitte vom 13. d.M., in betreff meiner mit Umgehung jeder rechtlichen Verhandlung erfolgten polizeilichen Ausweisung aus Frankfurt, nicht als eine Rechtssache selbst zur Hand genommen, sondern Seiner Exzellenz dem Herrn Reichsminister des Innern zur Erledigung übertragen, sonach als eine administrative Polizeisache zu behandeln sich veranlaßt gefunden. Schon hierdurch allein aber war der ganze Zweck meiner gehorsamsten Eingabe verfehlt und meine Bitte, die keineswegs etwa auf den Erlaß einer mir zuerkannten Strafe im Verwaltungswege, vielmehr lediglich auf eine gerichtliche Untersuchung und Konstatierung der Wahrheit abgezielt, brevi manu abgewiesen, und es konnte mich daher das aus erwähntem verehrlichen Schreiben weiter ersichtliche Ergebniß, der Herr Reichsminister des Innern habe sich nicht überzeugen können, daß ich von meinem Lebenswandel und meiner Tätigkeit nur die reine Wahrheit angegeben und die gegen mich verfügte Maßregel wirklich eine rein willkürliche gewesen, und ebenso wenig, daß die Frankfurter Behörde bei dieser Gelegenheit die zur Zeit in Frankfurt noch bestehenden Gesetze verletzt habe, und könne Se. Exzellenz daher meinem Gesuche nicht willfahren, um so weniger befremden, als allerdings jede, sowohl negative als positive Überzeugung zu den Unmöglichkeiten gehört, solange bloß ungeprüfte einseitige Angaben vorliegen und der Angeschuldigte auch nicht einmal vor Gericht geladen, vielweniger eigentlich zur Verantwortung gezogen und zur Rechtfertigung zugelassen worden ist.

Ich habe in meiner gehorsamsten Eingabe für angemessen erachtet, jeden Moment der Verteidigung, sowie überhaupt jede Einlassung in das Materielle des Prozesses, als bloß vor die Gerichtsbehörde gehörend, möglichst zu vermeiden und meine Bitte um Untersuchung lediglich in der Voraussetzung gestellt, daß nach der Gründung der hohen Zentralregierung Deutschlands
a) kein deutscher Bürger mehr in einem deutschen Lande als ein Ausländer betrachtet und
b) niemand, sei es auch selbst ein Ausländer, fortan in Deutschland ohne vorgängige richterliche Untersuchung, namentlich ohne Verhör und Urteil, mit irgend einer Verfügung beschwert werden könne.

In der Voraussetzung unstreitiger Gültigkeit dieser beiden Grundsätze, welche in dem gegen mich stattgehabten polizeilichen Verfahren offenbar verletzt worden, habe ich mir nun erlaubt, die Sache einem hohen Ministerium der Justiz vorzutragen und um die Veranlassung des bisher umgangenen gerichtlichen Verfahrens — falls dessen Unzulässigkeit nicht sofort anerkannt werden würde — zu bitten. Ich kann daher auch noch jetzt in meiner Bitte um Zuweisung an die Gerichtsbehörde nichts anderes als eine Rechtsache — den Fall einer Justizverweigerung — erblicken, wo ich bloß Recht, strenges, aber gesetz- und ordnungsmäßiges Recht für mich in Anspruch nehme. Aus diesen Gründen wage ich es wiederholt, ein hohes Reichsministerium ehrerbietigst zu bitten,
1) meine rubrizierte Angelegenheit, als zur Kompetenz hohen Reichsministeriums, der Justiz gehörig, der geeigneten Prüfung unterwerfen und demnächst
2) meiner gehorsamsten Bitte vom 13. d.M. gewährende Folge geben zu wollen.

Ich verharre in tiefster Ehrerbietung
eines hohen Reichsministeriums gehorsamster
Diener

L. H. Löwenstein

[Reply from the Minister]

An Dr. L. H. Löwenstein in Rödelheim.

Auf Ihre Eingabe vom 30/31. Oktober wird Ihnen Nachstehendes eröffnet: Sie erheben darüber Beschwerde, daß Ihre frühere Eingabe vom 13. Oktober in welcher Sie Zurücknahme der vom Senate der freien Stadt Frankfurt gegen Sie verfügten polizeilichen Ausweisung verlangten von hier, dem Reichsministerium des Innern als zu dessen Geschäftskreis gehörig, überwiesen worden ist.

Sie erachten Ihre Bitte um Zuweisung an eine Gerichtsbehörde als eine Rechtssache, und zwar gestützt auf die zwei Gründe, daß nach der Gründung der provisorischen Zentralgewalt
a) kein deutscher Bürger mehr in einem deutschen Lande als Ausländer betrachtet, und
b) niemand, sei es auch ein Ausländer, in Deutschland fortan ohne vorgängige richterliche Untersuchung, namentlich ohne Verhör und Urteil, mit irgend einer Verfügung beschwert werden könne. Demgemäß verlangen Sie, daß Ihre Angelegenheit, als zur Kompetenz des Reichsjustizministeriums gehörig, geprüft, und Ihrer früheren Bitte, welche auf sofortige Aufhebung Ihrer Ausweisung und Gestattung des Aufenthaltes in hiesiger Stadt, durch unmittelbare Verfügung des Reichsjustizministeriums; ferner auf Veranlassung einer gerichtlichen Untersuchung oder ausdrückliche Erklärung des Nichtstattfindens einer solchen von Seiten des Senates der Stadt Frankfurt gerichtet war, stattgegeben werde.

Das Reichsjustizministerium weiß auch nach nochmaliger Prüfung von seiner erstgefaßten Ansicht nicht abzugehen.

Vorerst ist zu bemerken, daß alle Voraussetzungen, auf welche Ihre Forderung gestützt ist, rechtlich und tatsächlich irrig sind.

Was nämlich den Satz betrifft, daß seit der Gründung der provis.[orischen] Zentralgewalt kein Deutscher mehr in einem deutschen Lande als Ausländer betrachtet werden dürfe; so hat die Schaffung einer Zentralgewalt mit den Ansprüchen des Einzelnen auf Bürgerrecht oder Aufenthalt in einem deutschen Einzelstaate lediglich nichts gemein, und ändert jene Einrichtung an der hierüber bestehenden Gesetzgebung nichts ab.

Eine solche Änderung wäre nur dann eingetreten, wenn die von der Reichsversammlung bei der ersten Lesung der Grundrechte gefaßten Beschlüsse über Freizügigkeit und Aufenthaltsrechte bereits Gesetzkraft erlangt hätten. Da dem nun aber bekanntlich bis itzt nicht so ist, vielmehr die definitive Beschlußnahme und Publikation der Grundrechte erst noch bevorsteht, so gelten auch bis zu diesem Zeitpunkte in Frankfurt die bisher bestehenden Gesetze. —

Zweitens wird auch nach dem Eintritte der Gesetzeskraft der neuen Grundrechte, der weitere von Ihnen aufgestellte Satz, daß niemand mehr mit irgendeiner Verfügung beschwert werden dürfe, ohne vorgängige richterliche Untersuchung, in solcher Allgemeinheit niemals richtig sein. Auch dann werden unzweifelhaft die Verwaltungs-, die Gemeinde-Behörden u.s.w. in ihrem Geschäfts- und Rechtskreise selbständige Verfügungen treffen können, durch welche Rechte und Interessen der Einzelnen berührt werden, ohne daß erst eine richterliche Untersuchung vorausgehen müßte, und ob dann, auch bei Aufhebung aller Verwaltungsrechtspflege, (falls solche zum Gesetze erhoben wird), zu einer nachfolgenden gerichtlichen Klage das Recht zusteht, wird teils das Gesetz, teils die materielle Beschaffenheit des einzelnen Falles bestimmen.

Endlich ist Ihre Annahme von der Zuständigkeit des Reichsjustizministeriums, als sei dasselbe zum unmittelbaren Einschreiten und zur Aufhebung der Verfügungen kompetenter Behörden eines deutschen Einzelstaates befugt, durchaus unbegründet. Das Reichsjustizministerium hat keinerlei Art von unmittelbarer Jurisdiktion.

Bei der Frage also, ob die Erledigung Ihrer Angelegenheit nach den itzt bestehenden Gesetzen zum Geschäftskreise des Reichsjustizministeriums gehörte, kann es sich lediglich darum handeln, ob Ihr Fall unter dem Art. 2. des Gesetzes vom 28. Juni fällt, das heißt, ob die allgemeine Sicherheit und Wohlfahrt Deutschlands dabei beteiligt ist, oder ob Verweigerung oder Verzögerung der Justiz gegen Sie begangen wurde? Da nun von Bejahung der ersteren Frage keine Rede ist, so wäre ein diesseitiges unmittelbares Einschreiten nur unter der Voraussetzung gesetzlich gestattet, wenn Sie entweder die Frankfurter Gerichte durch alle Instanzen hindurch vergeblich um Gehör angegangen hätten, oder wenn Ihnen durch irgend eine Maßregel der Regierung der Stadt der Zugang zu den Gerichten ganz verschlossen worden wäre, wobei noch bemerkt werden muß, daß in dem ersteren Falle das Justizministerium nur dann die Eröffnung des Rechtsweges verlangen würde und könnte, wenn es selbst der Ansicht wäre, daß Ihre Angelegenheit sich materiell zur gerichtlichen Verhandlung eigne, indem es natürlich nicht gegen seine eigene Überzeugung ein nicht passendes oder rechtsbegründetes Verfahren veranlassen dürfte.

Soviel nun aber aus Ihren Eingaben und den denselben beigefügten Aktenstücken erhellt, haben Sie bis itzt den Rechtsweg gar nicht betreten; es kann somit auch von einer gegen Sie begangenen Rechtsverweigerung keine Rede sein.

Ebensowenig ist ersichtlich, oder auch nur glaublich, daß der Senat der Stadt Frankfurt den Gerichten die Annahme einer Klage von Ihrer Seite untersagt hätte, damit ist aber auch die Unzuständigkeit des Reichsjustizministeriums schon aus formellen Gründen ganz unzweifelhaft ausgesprochen, und jede Untersuchung darüber, ob Ihre Beschwerde sich materiell zu einem gerichtlichen Verfahren eigne, erscheint als zeitig überflüssig.

Bei dieser Entscheidung bleibt das Reichsjustizministerium sowenig hinter seiner Pflicht zurück, daß vielmehr von demselben mehr, als ihm zunächst oblag, geschehen ist, als es aus eigenem Antriebe Ihre Angelegenheit, dem Reichsministerium des Innern zur Erledigung mitteilte.

Frankfurt, den 1. Nov. 1848.

Der Reichsminister der Justiz.

Petition

[Renewed application]

Rödelheim 5. November 1848.

An ein hohes Reichsministerium der Justiz

Gehorsamste Rückerklärung und Bitte des Orientalisten L. H. Löwenstein aus Steinbach in Württemberg, derzeit in Rödelheim, auf Verehrliches Reskript vom 1/4 dieses Monats, seine Ausweisung aus Frankfurt und Rechtsverweigerung betreffend.

Eines hohen Reichsministeriums der Justiz

Verehrliches Reskript vom 1/4 dieses Monats gereicht mir zu wahrer Beruhigung, indem ich darin meinen Anspruch auf Reichsschutz dem Grundsatze nach vollständig anerkannt und auf ein Reichsgesetz und dessen authentische Auslegung begründet finde, es sonach nur nach der einfachen Einsichtsnahme hohen Reichsministeriums in ein völlig notorisches und gar nicht zweifelhaftes faktisches Sachverhältnis bedarf, um der baldigen Gewährung meiner gehorsamsten Bitten und Beendigung meiner unverdienten Leiden in Anwendung der Aussprüche eben jenes hohen Reskripts mit ruhiger Zuversicht entgegensehen zu dürfen.

Wenn ich mich nämlich auch in einem Irrtum befunden, als ich von der bloßen Tatsache des Daseins einer Zentralgewalt für ganz Deutschland und von dem Prinzip deutscher Einheit, auf welches dieselbe gegründet ist, schon allein die Folge ableiten zu dürfen glaubte, daß fortan kein Deutscher mehr in Deutschland als Ausländer betrachtet werden könne, vielmehr jetzt dahin belehrt und überführt bin, daß die Zeit, wo die glorreichen Ergebnisse der Märzrevolution auch den einzelnen Bürger des freien Vaterlands zu gute kommen, erst noch für eine, übrigens hoffentlich ganz nahe Zukunft in Aussicht steht, so genügt doch für meinen gegenwärtigen Zweck vollkommen die unumwundene Erklärung hohen Reichsministeriums, wonach für die vorliegende Sache der Art. II. des Reichsgesetzes vom 28. Juni d.J. maßgebend und dieser so zu verstehen ist, daß dieselbe alsdann dem Geschäftskreise eines hohen Reichsministeriums der Justiz angehöre, wenn "Verweigerung oder Verzögerung der Justiz gegen mich begangen worden" d.h. der beigefügten authentischen Erläuterung zufolge, wenn ich entweder die

Frankfurter Gerichte durch alle Instanzen hindurch vergeblich um „Gehör angegangen hätte, oder wenn mir durch irgend eine Maßregel der Regierung der Stadt der Zugang zu den Gerichten ganz verschlossen worden wäre" wobei dann wieder die materielle Frage über die Zulässigkeit des gerichtlichen Verfahrens von dem Ermessen eines hohen Reichsministeriums der Justiz abhinge.

Mehr aber bedarf es keineswegs, um meine gehorsamsten Bitten vollkommen zu begründen und über jede Anfechtung hinauszusetzen.

Es ist nämlich gemeinkundig und unzweifelhaft, daß, nach der gegenwärtig in Frankfurt noch bestehenden Einrichtung, der Senat allerdings nicht allein die oberste administrative, sondern auch die höchste Justizbehörde dieses Staates ist, in welchem überhaupt eine Trennung zwischen Verwaltung und Rechtspflege dermalen nicht besteht, wohl aber die Befugnisse der Gerichtsstellen dahin beschränkt sind, daß diese, der längst bestehenden und allein üblichen Praxis nach, über Verfügungen der Verwaltungsbehörden niemals verhandeln, vielweniger erkennen, sondern bekanntlich allezeit angebrachte Klagen gegen administrative Maßregeln, als außer dem Bereich ihrer Zuständigkeit liegend, von vornherein abgewiesen haben; so daß es eines desfallsigen eigenen Verbots an die Gerichte seitens der Regierung in meiner Sache keineswegs bedurfte, da in dieser die Anrufung der Gerichtsbehörden, mit alleiniger Ausnahme der obersten, des Senats, nicht zulässig erschien. Letzterer aber hat meine wiederholte Bitte um Anstellung einer Untersuchung völlig unberücksichtigt, ja in seinem Bescheide vom 17. Juni selbst unerledigt gelassen, während er doch gleichwohl die Bestätigung der polizeilichen Verfügung aussprach.

Es liegt mithin allerdings hier der Fall vor, wo die oberste Justizbehörde eines Landes, welche in der Sache ganz allein im Rekurswege angegangen werden konnte und durfte, das formelle Rechtsverfahren nicht bloß verzögert, sondern sogar auch verweigert hat, während sie gleichzeitig eine ohne alles Rechtsverfahren ergangene Polizeimaßregel kraft der in ihr vereinigten administrativen und richterlichen Autorität guthieß.

Klarer und offenkundiger als hier möchte der, nach der eigenen Auslegung eines hohen Reichsministeriums in dem Art. II. des Gesetzes vom 28. Juni vorgesehenen Fall eines formellen Anlasses zur offiziellen Einschreitung der höchsten Reichsjustizbehörde schwerlich noch je vorgelegen haben und was die materielle Frage anbelangt, so steht es wohl außer Zweifel, daß, wenn ein hohes Reichsministerium — wie allerdings von meinem Standpunkte mit der größten Wahrscheinlichkeit erwartet wird und wie es auch die Meinung der Frankfurter Behörden selbst zu sein scheint — zur Einleitung einer Untersuchung in den Akten keine Veranlassung erblicken dürfte, diese hohe Stelle doch auch anderseits um so weniger eben darin einen Grund zur Fortsetzung meiner Strafe und Verfolgung erkennen wird. Sind die gegen mich angebrachten Beschuldigungen (wie z.B. daß die Arbeiter in Frankfurt mich nicht den „Doktor Löwenstein" sondern nur schlechtweg den „Arbeiter Löwenstein" tituliert hätten u.dgl. Unerheblichkeiten) wirklich so unwichtig, daß sie der Aufmerksamkeit der Gerichte nicht würdig erscheinen, dann werden sie doch wohl auch nicht verdienen, daß man deshalb einen seit einem halben Menschenalter unbescholten in der Stadt lebenden deutschen Bürger unaufhörlich gleich einem Missetäter behandle, ihn noch am Vorabend der

Verkündigung der Grundrechte des deutschen Volkes der Ungunst einer klein-
städtischen Laune zum Opfer bringe und mit den Seinigen dem Verderben preis-
gebe, wo es vielleicht eher am Platze wäre, daß die Frankfurter Regierung die
Worte des großen Rechtslehrers beherzigte: "Wer strenger ist als die Gesetze, der
ist ein Tyrann!"

Gestützt auf Art. II. des Reichsgesetzes vom 28. Juni 1848 und fußend auf die
Worte eines hohen Reichsministeriums vom 1/4 d.M. sehe ich daher hochgeneigter
Gewährung mit der sichersten Zuversicht entgegen, wenn ich hiermit meine
frühren Bitten, also begründet, zu wiederholen mir gehorsamst erlaube, indem ich
in tiefster Ehrerbietung verharre,

Eines hohen Reichsministeriums der Justiz gehorsamster Diener

L. H. Löwenstein.

[Reply from the Minister]

D. R. M. d. I.

An Herrn Dr. L. H. Löwenstein zu Rödelheim.

Da Ihre sehr geschätzte Rückerklärung vom 5/6. d.M. betreffend Ausweisung und
angebliche Rechtsverweigerung keine neuen tatsächlichen Umstände enthält, welche
nicht schon bei Prüfung Ihrer früheren Eingabe vom 30/31. v.M. in Erwägung
gezogen worden sind, so kann das Reichsministerium des Innern keine Veranlassung finden von seinem Erlaß vom 1. d.M. abzugehen, und werden Sie daher
lediglich auf diese Verfügung zurückverwiesen.

Frankfurt 6. November 1848.

V

Petition

Gehorsamstes Gesuch, der Frau Rebekka Bamberger in Berlin Königstraße 57
wohnhaft, betreffend die Realisation von westfälischen Reichsobligationen Lit. A.
Klassen und Serien der westfälischen Zwangs-Anleihen, aus den Jahren 1808, 1810
und 12 welche auf Veranlassung des königlich preußischen Gouvernements im
Jahre 1814 von dem Hofsteuerrat von Madai verifiziert und von denen die drei

am 31. Dezember 1813, 30. Juni 1814 und 31. Dezember 1814, fällig gewesenen Zinskupons mit dem königlich preußischen roten Stempel F.W. bezeichnet und in sämtlichen Kassen des vormaligen Königreichs Westfalen bei Entrichtung der Personalsteuern für voll an Zahlungsstatt angenommen worden sind.

Einem Hohen Reichsministerio der Justiz erlaube ich mir, nachstehendes Gesuch, ganz ehrerbietigst zum Vortrag bringen zu dürfen.

In dem Nachlasse, meines im August v. J. im 86. Lebensjahre verstorbenen sel. Vaters habe ich 20,000 Frcs. westfälische Reichsobligationen Lit. A. Serien und Klassen der nebenstehenden Kategorie vorgefunden.

Ich wendete mich an ein Königlich Hohes Finanzministerium, um zu erfahren, wann ich auf die Realisation dieser Obligationen rechnen dürfte, indem ich des Geldes, zur Ausstattung meiner Tochter, dringend benötigt sei.

Gedachte Hohe Behörde hat mir mittelst Verfügung anfangs Januar d.J. zum Bescheide erteilt, daß die Verhandlungen, wegen Anerkennung der westfälischen Staatsschuld, mit dem Hohen Reichsministerio zu Frankfurt a/Main noch nicht beendigt seien.
Ich erlaube mir deshalb die ganz untertänigste Bitte, mich gefälligst in Kenntnis setzen zu wollen, ob die Verhandlungen mit den betreffenden Regierungen in dieser Angelegenheit bereits so weit gediehen sind, daß ich auf eine baldige Realisation meiner Obligationen, welche ich zum angegebenen Zweck dringend benötigt bin, sicher rechnen kann.

Einer baldigen, geneigten Resolution hoffnungsvoll entgegensehend verharret in tiefster Hochachtung.

Berlin d. 9. Februar 1849.

Rebekka Bamberger
Königstraße 57

An Ein Hohes Reichsministerium zu Frankfurt a/M.
zu Händen Sr. Exzellenz des Herrn Justizministers Mohl.

[Reply from the Minister]

An Frau Rebekka Bamberger, zu Berlin. Königstraße 57.

Auf Ihre Anfrage vom 9/13. d.M. betr. den Stand der westfälischen Schulden-Angelegenheit, kann Ihnen nur erwidert werden, wie solches bereits von dem königl. preuß. Finanzministerium geschehen ist, daß die desfalsige mit den Regierungen von Preußen, Hannover, Kurhessen und Braunschweig eingeleitenden Verhandlungen noch nicht zum Abschluß gediehen sind.

Das Resultat derselben wird seiner Zeit öffentlich bekannt gemacht werden.

Frankfurt 13. Febr. 1849.

Mohl.

Petition

Berlin den 29. März 1849

An das Hochlöbliche Reichsministerium der Justiz zu Frankfurt a./M.

In der bekannten westfälischen Zentralschuldangelegenheit, bin ich auf meine Anfrage vom 9. v.M. unter Lit. E Nr. 194 vom 13. ejusd. dahin beschieden worden, daß die desfalligen mit den Regierungen von Preußen, Hannover, Kurhessen und Braunschweig eingeleiteten Verhandlungen noch nicht zum Abschluß gediehen sind. Ich hätte mich mit dieser Bescheidung beruhigt, wenn mich nicht die drükkenden Geldverhältnisse und die Ausstattung meiner Tochter in die Notwendigkeit versetzt hätten, auf meine nicht unbedeutenden Forderungen wenigstens einen Vorschuß zu verlangen.

Zur Erreichung dieses Zweckes trug ich beim hiesigen Finanzministerium unterm 21. v.M. darauf an, auf die in meinem Besitz befindlichen westfälischen Zwangsanleiheobligationen, welche von preußischen Untertanen, des vormaligen Königreichs Westfalen belegt, auch sämtlich nach der in dem Gouvernementsblatte erlassenen Bekanntmachung des Herrn Staatsministers von Klewitz in den Jahren 1813-1814 von der Verifikationskommission, durch den königlich-preußischen Hofsteuerrat von Madai verifiziert, sowie deren am 31. Dezember 1813, 30. Juni und 31. Dezember 1814 verfallene Kupons mit dem königlich-preußischen roten Stempel (F.W.) gestempelt und bei Entrichtung der Personalsteuer bei den sämtlichen Preußischen Kassen des vormaligen Königreichs Westfalen statt baren Geldes an Zahlungsstatt angenommen wurden, folglich unter allen Umständen die preußische Regierung verpflichten und zur Last fallen, ohne daß dabei es noch einer Auseinandersetzung mit den übrigen dabei beteiligten fremden Regierungen bedarf, mir einen angemessenen Vorschuß zu gewähren. Zu meinem größten Erstaunen erhielt aber gestern, das beiliegende Originalschreiben, de dato Berlin den 26. März, worin der zeitige Herr Finanzminister, nicht allein mein Gesuch förmlich abschlägt, sondern vielmehr sich auf die bekannte Kabinettsorder vom 3. März 1843 bezieht, wodurch damals der Ungerechtigkeit die Krone aufgesetzt wurde; denn nach dieser Kabinettsorder wurde bekanntlich den Gläubigern nicht allein ihre Forderungen nicht anerkannt, sondern ihnen noch dazu der Weg Rechtens verschlossen.

Der preußische Finanzminister scheint nach dieser von ihm ausgesprochenen Ansicht durchaus nicht wissen zu wollen, was in der 98. Sitzung der deutschen Nationalversammlung vom 17. Oktober v.J. zu Frankfurt a/M. beschlossen wurde, zu welcher Zeit auch die sämtlichen preußischen Abgeordneten die volle Zustimmung zu dieser Beschlußnahme gegeben, und hat dieses Ministerium wahrscheinlich meine Vorstellung vom 21. vorigen Monats, 5 Wochen in seinem Kabinette ruhen lassen, um erst die Gestaltung der Dinge in Frankfurt a/M. abzuwarten.

Nach meinem Dafürhalten hat aber die hohe Zentralgewalt an ihrer Kraft bis heute nichts verloren, denn sie besteht, und wer wagt's Hand an sie zu legen. Denn wenn sie die Macht besitzt, die Fürsten Deutschlands zu veranlassen, Truppen zum Kriege nach Dänemark zu schicken, so muß es ihr doch gewiß an moralischer Kraft auch nicht fehlen, die bei dem Königreich Westfalen beteiligten Regierungen zu veranlassen, ihre billigen Beschlüsse in Beziehung der westfälischen Zentralschuld in Ausführung zu bringen.

Demzufolge trage ich bei einem Hohen Justizministerio darauf an: die eingeleiteten Verhandlungen in dieser Angelegenheit zu beschleunigen, und das Resultat baldmöglichst zur Publikation zu bringen.

Einer recht baldigen geneigten Antwort hoffnungsvoll entgegensehend, verharret mit der vorzüglichsten Hochachtung

Rebekka Bamberger
Königstraße Nr. 57

VI

Petition

Wird zur Anzeige gebracht der Juden betreffend.

An die Sitzung zu Frankfurt.

Da demnach kein Reich mehr bestehen kann, wenn nicht die Juden aus dem Deutschland getrieben werden, denn diese sind nur zum Untergang des Volkes, sie verderben allen Handel sie stellen falsche Hypotheken-Scheine gegen einander aus um nur den Christen um das seinige zu bringen. Machen Bankrott, kurz sind nur zum Untergang der Christen, wenn diese nicht in ein anderes Land verwiesen werden, so sind wir genötigt, sie mit Gewalt hinaus zu treiben, wir hoffen aber, der Volksverein in Frankfurt werde diesen Übel abhelfen, denn sonst wird das deutsche Reich nicht einig werden oder bleiben, denn der Jud ist keinem Christen gut.

o.U. o.D.

VII

Petition Nr. 3651

Hohe Reichsversammlung!

Dem Vernehmen nach beabsichtigt eine hohe Nationalversammlung die Juden zu emanzipieren, und will die Gerichts- und Administrativ-Stellen den Nichtchristen in die Hände geben; wogegen wir, die wir die Stimmen des Volkes kennen, uns zu verwahren suchen.

Die Stimmen, welche die Emanzipation der "Juden" und die Gleichstellung der sogenannten "Deutschkatoliken" in die h. Nationalversammlung gebracht, sind nicht Volkesstimme!!!

Das deutsche Volk verlangt außer den eingeführten und von der Verfassung garantierten Konfessionen keine Gleichstellung, und am allerwenigsten will es die Emanzipation der Juden.

Baden, unser Großherzogtum, ist ein christlicher Staat wie es ganz Deutschland ist, — und dieser Charakter kann nicht aufgegeben werden. — Die Juden sind noch nicht um ein Haarbreit von ihrem Partikularismus abgegangen, ihre Unvermischbarkeit mit andern Völkern, woran sie so fest halten, und ihre religiösen Bekenntnisse zeichnen sie immer noch als Fremdlinge, nicht aber als "Deutsche", bei uns aus, und weder im Umgange noch im Handel findet man bei den Juden die geringste Sympathien, daß sie die staats- oder gemeindebürgerlichen Rechte, verdienen. Von dem uns bekannten Treiben der Juden in der Gegend des Odenwaldes und von ihrem Wuchern wollen wir aus zarter Schonung gegen dieselben schweigen, und bitten nur: uns von dem Druck der Juden zu befreien, statt dieselben den übrigen christlichen Konfessionen gleichzustellen; wodurch uns die hohe Reichsversammlung zum Danke verpflichten würde.

Walldürn den 28.ten September 1848.

> Der Gemeinderat im Namen
> der Stadtgemeinde.
> Es folgen die Unterschriften.

Aby Warburg (1866-1929) as Interpreter of Civilisation

BY HANS LIEBESCHÜTZ

Peter Gay in his recent book on the culture of the Weimar period has emphasised the importance of the Warburg Institute's position at the time of its initial activities in Hamburg. He describes the investigations into the connection of art and civilisation, which were stimulated by this library, as a glorious feature of the period. Professor Gombrich, the fourth successor of Aby Warburg as the guiding spirit of the Institute which is now incorporated in the University of London, has given us an intellectual biography of the founder.[1] His work is mainly based on an extensive amount of material taken from Warburg's unpublished notebooks, which are crammed with observations, reflections and sketches for academic courses. The book traces the intentions behind Warburg's scholarship and their development. The documentation is given both in German and in an English translation; owing to Warburg's individual language some passages of the English version make easier reading, even for people who share Warburg's mother tongue and dialect. The task of interpretation is performed with detachment, but also with respectful consideration for the personality of the man whose mind has remained a living force in the Institute he established. For a member of the older generation, who lived during the twenties in the same Hamburg suburb and was attracted by this treasure-house of books and its atmosphere of vigorous discussion, Gombrich's book recalls many memories. A compilation of such reminiscences may form a small contribution to the intellectual history of German Jewry in the final creative period.

I

In Warburg's life his family background played a great part. The banking firm had been established in Hamburg at the very end of the eighteenth century.[2] It obtained international importance in the last decade before the dawn of the twentieth. On the whole the importance of Hamburg Jewry did not reach quite the same level as that held by the merchants and bankers of the same group in Frankfurt and Berlin. However, the Warburgs enjoyed a position in Hanseatic society markedly different from that of other members of the community. They were almost accepted as belonging to the ruling stratum of lawyers and merchants and had adapted the

[1]Peter Gay, *Weimar Culture, the outsider as insider*, New York 1968, pp. 30-34. E. H. Gombrich, *Aby Warburg, an intellectual biography*, London 1970.
[2]Eduard Rosenbaum, 'M. M. Warburg & Co. Merchant Bankers of Hamburg', in *LBI Year Book VII* (1962), pp. 122 ff.

external circumstances of their life accordingly.[3] This social background formed one element in the preconditions of Aby Warburg's achievement. Essentially in consequence of his own mentality and character he remained a private scholar, who pursued his life's plan with exceptional single-mindedness; so he finally became the head of an Institute the authority of which was recognised beyond the limits of history of art. At every stage of his career he was able to obtain the support of his family. Moreover, his growing up in the midst of a commercial oligarchy ruling a small republic gave him a feeling of belonging, which very much encouraged his attempts to understand the bankers in fifteenth-century Florence. Their influence on the artists in their employment became an important object of his research. This sympathy, based on an impression of relationship between nineteenth-century Hamburg and the society of the early Italian Renaissance was qualified by a critical attitude concerning the manners and tastes of a rich bourgeoisie which were characteristic of both periods. Such ambivalence was unavoidable in the son of a banking family who dedicated his life to the study of art.

These features, however, represent only one aspect of the environment's impact on his personality. To his family's tendency towards assimilation there existed a very definite limit. A firm resolution loyally to preserve the religious tradition had been carried from one generation to the next. The majority of those Hamburg Jews who had been successful in business or a profession belonged either to the *Tempel*, the reform synagogue, or had given up any relation with a house of worship. The Warburgs, however, remained strong supporters of the community's orthodox section; Rabbi Nehemia Nobel officiated at the burial of Aby's father Moritz Warburg in 1910. It was an established custom that one member of the family served on the board which administered the general affairs of the Jewish community in Hamburg. Aby's father had done so, and his youngest brother Fritz Warburg filled this office till 1939. They all felt this attitude as a mark of distinction forming a dignified basis for their contact with Gentile society.[4]

Aby Warburg's mind was shaped more by revolt against this tradition than by its impact. His opposition to the commands of the ritual law started when he was still a schoolboy. His growing interest in works of art and their historical roots gave him the feeling that the pattern of life and belief in his parents' house was too narrow and therefore incompatible with the aims he set himself. Personal experience brought for some time an element of open conflict. In 1888, while working for his doctoral thesis in Florence, he met a young artist from Hamburg, Mary Hertz, whose mind was open to all that interested him most. They married nearly

[3]Shortly before the revolution of 1918 Max Warburg, who for many years had been an active and recognised member of the National Liberal Party *(Fraktion der Rechten)* in the city council, was proposed by the selection committee for the post of a senator; the second candidate on the short list, a coal merchant less well known in Hamburg, was chosen with the help of votes of Warburg's own parliamentary group. — Aby Warburg's social contacts around 1900 are illustrated by C. Mönckeberg, *Bürgermeister Mönckebergs Briefe und Aufzeichnungen*, 1918, pp. 208-215.

[4]Dr. Fritz Warburg, as chairman of the community's adult education committee, was with his vivacity and sense of humour always a reliable and valuable support for those who tried to preserve intellectual life under the Nazi rule.

ten years later. His fiancée was the daughter of a Hamburg senator. Her mother came from the Goszler family, who had joined the merchants' aristocracy at the end of the eighteenth century. But there was also a common element in the couple's social background. Mary's grandfather had been Jacob Hertz (1800-1866) who had been born a Jew and son of a stockbroker and became a successful entrepreneur and shipowner.[5] But the parents on both sides did not emphasise this link between the family histories; the antagonism between Jewish and Christian upbringing was paramount for them. The couple, however, had no doubts that they stood on common ground in all matters essential to them. The modernism which at the turn of the century experienced art as a creative force in the shaping of human life offered such a meeting-place undisturbed by the traditions of the past.

II

This tendency could lead Warburg to preferences which look paradoxical in a man whose name will always be linked to the study of antiquity's lasting impact on civilisation. He, as the eldest son of a banker, had been educated in the city's *Realgymnasium*, a grammar-school without Greek, with emphasis on modern languages, and Latin in a subsidiary rôle. When he had finished this course and decided to study history of art he was forced by faculty requirements to spend an additional period in a humanistic school to qualify in Greek. This experience did not prevent him about twenty years later from giving considered advice which led to a similar discrepancy of school and academic studies for a future historian. Max Schramm, a well-known lawyer, who some years later joined the Hamburg Senate, asked Warburg, as a friend and highly educated man, to what school he ought to send his promising son Percy. Without hesitation Warburg recommended the same *Realgymnasium* which he had himself attended. Percy Schramm, early in his academic career developed his research on the portraits of rulers as an important source for the understanding of politics and civilisation in close contact with Warburg's books and ideas. But when the study of Emperor Otto III led the budding *Privatdozent* into the sphere of Byzantium he also came across the fact that his own schooling was an obstacle in pursuing his professional task.

This slightly paradoxical preference for realistic modernity was not quite isolated in Warburg's mentality. The fact that he entered the world of secular values from an orthodox home brought more deeply rooted and more conspicuous consequences in this direction. He had broken his tie with Jewish tradition, but he did not intend to enter into intimate contacts with Christianity. When after four years of struggle against mental depression he returned to Hamburg in 1924 he inspected the rows of new books which in the meantime had gathered on his shelves. The extension of the section on the Middle Ages impressed him as rather exaggerated. The utterance: "My poor Renaissance!" expressed his feeling and at the same time marked the

[5]Hans W. Hertz, in *Neue Deutsche Biographie*, VIII, 1969, pp. 709 f.; Otto Mathies, *Hamburger Reederei 1814-1914*, 1924, pp. 53-56; portrait on p. 110.

difference of two succeeding generations of Jewish scholars. Fritz Saxl, his most important disciple, who was his librarian and became his successor, had been brought up during his student days in the tradition of the Viennese school of art history, going back to Alois Riegl and reaching to his own teacher Dvořák. Saxl had learnt to see his subject closely linked to the development of Christian religion from Late Antiquity to the Middle Ages. Consequently, the millennium between the final period of Roman civilisation and the Renaissance meant for Saxl more than a line of communication through which ideas and images travel in darkness from one creative period to their rebirth in a remote age. To him the study of ecclesiastical thought and institutions was indispensable for the analysis of European civilisation. As a scholar he was ready to see the windows of the church not only from the outside.

At the same time his Jewishness became for Saxl a positive factor. Earlier in his youth the clerical atmosphere of imperial Vienna had paralysed the influence of Hebrew learning, which his father, a lawyer of extensive erudition and a keen student of comparative linguistics, had encouraged during his boyhood.[6] Saxl's own experience in the Austrian world had made him see both Synagogue and Church as outdated antagonists of free thought. From this position he never explicitly retreated; but his attitude towards his own Jewish origin changed considerably. While his endeavour to understand works of art more deeply made him investigate their spiritual background, he discovered how helpful his Jewish inheritance was in this task. These were the years before 1914 when Herzl's message took root in the hearts of the rising generation. Saxl learnt to see his own universalist understanding of human achievements as a legacy of his ancestors. As a Jew, and therefore existentially an outsider, he was provided with the opportunity to practise independence of mind, including the study of religion, without any denominational ties. Moreover, he now liked to trace the origin of ecclesiastical piety in the Hebrew Bible and the religious life of his own people.

This combination remained alien to Warburg's mind. During the early twenties when Saxl gave some lectures to a Hamburg B'nai B'rith Lodge on synagogues and churches in the Hellenistic world, he knew well that the absent head of the library would not be pleased about this link between research inspired by his own work and specifically Jewish activities. For Warburg the barrier between both spheres remained permanent. A new-comer to his library might have been surprised by the good collection of books on Jewish history. But at that time these did not form a part of the section on Human Thought, as they now do on the shelves of the Institute in London. Their original function was a more private one. Warburg was aware of the antisemitic threat in the German environment. The feeling for his own status as a citizen in Hanseatic society did not encourage him to talk much about this issue, but at least once he felt the challenge of this problem so strongly that he jotted down some reflections as a preliminary draft for a public declaration of his personal commitment.

[6]Gertrud Bing, 'Fritz Saxl (1890-1948)', in *Fritz Saxl Memorial Essays*, edited by D. J. Gordon, London 1957, p. 1 f.

In the year 1900 the charge of ritual murder, which once had initiated destructive persecutions of Jewish communities during the late Middle Ages, had been revived in the provincial town of Konitz, south-west of Danzig. At this moment Warburg, at the age of thirty-five, felt a call to interpret the attitude of Jews who had grown to manhood during the twenty years since "Prussian Protestants" had opened the fight against Jewry with the exhortation "be slightly more modest".[7] Warburg confessed himself qualified and therefore obliged to attempt such a task: In comparison with other assimilated Jews he possessed a more intimate knowledge about their "fellows by descent"; he had himself been educated as an orthodox Jew and had remained a believer until he was a boy of fifteen. He added that the process of his liberation from the ancient traditions went through conflict with his environment and internal struggle until he dedicated his life as a private scholar to the service of learning. Warburg did not wish to claim any general interest for his personal experience, but he saw such development as a presupposition of his project to define the "typical character" of an enlightened and assimilated Jew. This article for which the intended title 'Psychologischer Querschnitt der deutschen Juden' is added in parentheses, was never written. Some fragmentary sentences reveal the conflict in the writer's mind. He cannot get over his antagonism to the ostentatiousness shown by wealthy Jews, an attitude which gave the antisemitic reaction an appearance of idealism. But further experience had shown Warburg that the very conspicuous complacency on the Jewish side was less dangerous than the "teutonic wrath" hidden behind a pretension of restraint. In this situation Warburg found it difficult to preserve in his mind the genuine composure corresponding to human dignity without which the gesture of self-control remains a mere mask. These sentences are written down with many corrections on some sheets of paper preserved in the Warburg archives of the London Institute.[8]

This knowledge about his own past and the attitude of his ancestors remained a silent but powerful force in his intellectual development. The Middle Ages, in which the artist's activities were dominated by Christian themes and ecclesiastical authorities, never had more than a marginal interest for him. It was a borderland without rights of its own, a source of attitudes which his analysis discovered as retarding elements in the art and society of fifteenth-century Florence. He described with respect the dignified devotion limiting the influence of such motifs by which Antiquity in literature and art had given a dense expression both of movement and excitement. Moreover, he dealt with medieval illustrated manuscripts which carried this legacy of the Ancients essentially unchanged to a new life in the Renaissance. But his real interest was concentrated on the change of mentality brought about in fifteenth-century Florence by these forces of Antiquity. That for Warburg the Middle Ages counted only as an interim and not as a genuine creative period is a more striking feature in his work than in that of other contemporary scholars working on similar problems: Warburg was increasingly inclined to see his special

---

[7]Treitschke.
[8]Miss A. M. Meyer encouraged me to look into the rich archives during a day's stay in the London Warburg Institute. I am grateful for her help.

subject in the context of universal history, as a part of the continuous stream of civilisation in which ideas and motifs run from land to land and from period to period. This comprehensive framework gave the white spot in his historical world picture its particular emphasis. Warburg intended to place himself and his work as a scholar on neutral ground, neither Jewish nor Christian. When he decided to dedicate his life to the study of artistic creativeness, he felt this step as a liberation from the shackles of tribal tradition into the freedom of enlightenment. To go further and investigate Christian thought as a positive force in the great process of history without the possession of a counter-balancing sympathy with the spiritual inheritance of Judaism would appear to him as an act of treason.[9] The experience of his own nonconformity as a first break in a way of life preserved by generations of ancestors gave him a self-consciousness from which the younger generation could free themselves by an untraditional but positive attitude towards their Jewishness. Warburg did not forget his roots, but he did not allow himself to be proud of them.

III

Perhaps it is possible to trace the effect of Warburg's position in the selection of ideas incorporated into his work from concepts presented by contemporary currents of thought. There were preferences fostered by Jewish tradition which did not lose their power completely by the process of secularisation. Moreover, the impact of German politics on everyday life created common problems for all members of an outsider group, despite their great differentiation. They might find contrasting answers; but the identity of the starting-point remained recognisable. Warburg's work was certainly not less unique than his personality; but his use of some concepts and judgments fit in with the pattern shaped, perhaps subconsciously, by the dialectics of assimilation. Warburg's interpretation of Luther can be seen as an example. In 1918 he completed for the Heidelberg Academy a study dealing with the contrast between the leader of the German Reformation and his most intimate collaborator Melanchthon concerning the validity of astrological prognosis. Luther's thoroughly critical attitude allows the representation of him as a champion of the emerging enlightenment; his friend Melanchthon, despite his broad erudition, remained caught in the dark superstition. The remnants of such an attitude in Luther's anxieties about natural monstrosities as signs of common disasters are carefully stated. But the emphasis is clearly on the power of rationality in his mind. Warburg's interpretation was written down at a time when Protestant research, well represented in his library, concentrated more and more on those aspects of Luther's theology which found expression in his fight against the doctrine of free will proclaimed by Erasmus. Warburg's choice of what for him was significant in

---

[9] C. G. Heise, *Persönliche Erinnerungen an Aby Warburg*, New York 1947, p. 47. The author witnessed an eruptive revelation of this feeling at the beginning of Warburg's mental depression.

Luther was not isolated. At the same time Ernst Cassirer, not yet in contact with the Hamburg art historian, gave a similar interpretation of Luther. In this he followed an idea which had always been important for his teacher's, Hermann Cohen's, understanding of the German mind. The leader of the Marburg Kant school had taken over this interpretation early in life from Heinrich Heine. The political and social situation of Jews in Germany fostered the tendency to establish a classical testimony for rationality and liberty in the nation's tradition.[10] In this way thinkers of very different outlook and loyalties were brought together by the sometimes esoteric character of outsiders.

A characteristic feature of Warburg's lectures points to a peculiar synthesis between highly individual experiences and the Jewish aspect of his biography. Some of his listeners — he liked to call regular visitors of his library the Institute's patients — felt a certain discrepancy between the speaker's passionate dedication to his themes and the scientific, often biological concepts and metaphors which characterised his interpretation. During the Weimar period academic writing and teaching on subjects of intellectual history was more or less influenced by Wilhelm Dilthey's philosophy of mind. Warburg bought all the books and periodicals following this trend, but himself made no concessions to it. The strong feeling pervading his description of human mentality might make his listeners expect that the speaker shared the prevailing antagonism against positivism. But Warburg kept firmly to the philosophy by which he had built up his understanding of the world since his student days in the eighties: fear, caused by sense impressions, remained a permanent element of human existence. Excitement and defensive movement accompanied by gestures were the natural reactions which artistic creation transformed in manifold symbols. These developments could lead the way to freedom when they helped to make possible *einen Raum der Besonnenheit*. Such pause for quiet consideration would break the chain of stimulus and automatic reaction. In this way the animal kingdom would show clearly the roots of civilisation.[11] What in man appears as a gesture, with other living beings is an act of self-preservation.

As an undergraduate in Bonn Warburg had attentively followed Hermann Usener's lectures on the origin of Greek mythology in primitive man's reaction to his environment. Such theories remained for him the classical model for the analysis of cultural phenomena. The universal application of his teacher's stimulating suggestion was made feasible for him, because his own mental state prevented him from recognising the Middle Ages as a period with a distinct character of its own, neither primitive nor modern. Otherwise the medieval background, from which the Florentine artists and connoisseurs started on a new course, would have put limitations to the use of ethnological concepts in a psychological interpretation of the Renaissance.

This emphasis on the close link between the biological preconditions of human

[10]'Heidnisch-antike Weissagung in Wort und Bild zu Luthers Zeiten', in Aby Warburg, *Gesammelte Schriften*, II, 1932, pp. 512, 531. Ernst Cassirer, *Freiheit und Form*, 1917, pp. 25-28. Hermann Cohen, *Jüdische Schriften*, vol. II, Berlin 1924, p. 361.
[11]Gombrich, *op. cit.*, pp. 235 ff., 252.

creativeness had deep roots in Warburg's personal experience. Never did he forget that the continuation of his own work was threatened by psychosomatic processes over which he had only limited control. His intense interest in the fear of demonic forces, which he traced as a characteristic feature in the mythological and astrological traditions, grew out of his knowledge of his own person. For him science, as a means of rational orientation in the world, and artistic creation were closely related; both were weapons in mankind's lasting struggle for liberation. This identification of his scholarship's object with his personal experience was certainly at the root of the intense influence which Warburg could exercise over pupils of very different age groups.

The same motive brought about a remarkable change in his views on civilisation in his later years. He generalised from his own consciousness that the fight between darkness and light, superstitious fear and rational understanding, was a permanent clement of man's inheritance. While his early research on the Florentine fifteenth century had been based on the concept of development by which one state of mind is replaced by another, he preferred during the last decade of his life to see the rhythm of civilisation represented by the model of polarity and oscillation. This scheme obviously corresponded to his personal experience. On the other hand, this attempt by a scholar completely devoted to historical research to eliminate the time factor as a creative force recalls Franz Rosenzweig's analysis of the Jewish mind which is outside the world and therefore essentially beyond its historical periods.[12] We must add that there is nothing more certain than that Warburg had no sympathetic interest in this aspect and not even a conscious knowledge of such a possible link between his position and his ideas.

IV

In the eighties, during Warburg's formative years, we can still preceive a trend which had come to Western Europe almost thirty years earlier, but had remained an effective ferment in Germany's intellectual situation. Its doctrines were especially attractive for Jewish students looking for a philosophy appropriate to their own position. John Stuart Mill and later Herbert Spencer, as representatives of English empirism, created an interest in the parallelism between biological and social evolution. London with its libraries and rich collections of ethnological material formed the remote centre of such studies. The whole current was antagonistic to the idealistic tradition of the German academic establishment, but the arising controversies were considered as a stimulating influence by a succession of younger scholars during the sixties and seventies, especially in Berlin. Here Moritz Lazarus and Heymann Steinthal, both followers of Herbart's philosophy, had since 1859

---

[12]*Gesammelte Schriften*, II, p. 492. Gombrich, *op. cit.*, p. 286 (Seminar 1927/28); Franz Rosenzweig, 'Geist und Epochen der jüdischen Geschichte', in *Kleinere Schriften*. 1919, pp. 12-25.

edited a periodical *Zeitschrift für Völkerpsychologie* which dealt with the development of language, mythology and poetry as various aspects of one comprehensive subject.[13] It was probably not mere chance that the two editors, pioneers of this movement, were Jews. Ethnological studies seemed to give opportunities for a serious study of religion, which was not determined by the principles and subject-matter of Christian theology. Mill had proclaimed a religion of humanity which would finally take the place of ecclesiastical belief.[14]

Warburg was very reticent about any link that might have existed between him and this Berlin school; even Adolph Bastian, the travelling ethnologist and founder of a great museum, does not seem to have been quoted in his notes.[15] But Warburg bought his books, and three volumes of Lazarus's periodical (1887-1889) bear witness to this link in his library. Perhaps more important is the relationship of thought between the theory used by Warburg as the philosophical basis of his interpretations and the doctrines about the anthropological roots of art characteristic of this periodical's contributors. The young Hermann Cohen was in family background, character and intellectual gifts as different from Warburg as one can imagine. But his writings during the late sixties dealt with the same problems from which Warburg started his research. Before Cohen discovered Kant as his life's taskmaster he believed in the psychology of associations as an instrument by which ethnological material could be shaped to form an introduction to the essence of civilisation. Cohen asserts that a general law controls the mechanism by which all forms of thought come into being. He traces the origin of poetry to the moment when man discovers that the mythological identification, for instance between a lightning-flash and the speed of a flying bird, is shaken by more precise observation. The simile, the origin of poetry, is called in to save the traditional recognition of one phenomenon by the other.[16]

The man who for Warburg built the bridge between such theories and historical research was, as we have now learnt, Karl Lamprecht (1856-1915). During the eighties he was lecturer at Bonn University. His link with the school of collective psychology was Wilhelm Wundt (1832-1920). In the field of historical studies Lamprecht became more and more the representative of naturalistic nonconformity, although he obtained in 1891 the important chair at Leipzig University and in his political views did not differ from the majority of his colleagues. But his lively fight for the recognition of laws determining the mental development of nations and also his quarrel with the idealistic inheritance in German historiography since Ranke gave

[13]The forthcoming volume I of the Lazarus-Steinthal correspondence, edited by Ingrid Belke, in Schriftenreihe wissenschaftlicher Abhandlungen des Leo Baeck Instituts, promises valuable information on this school of thought.

[14]Wilhelm Dilthey reports in his memorial article 'Wilhelm Scherer', 1884, on the impact of Western Europe, in *Gesammelte Schriften*, XI, Stuttgart and Göttingen 1960, pp. 236-253, especially p. 243.

[15]Gombrich, *op. cit.*, p. 89; Dilthey on Bastian: *Gesammelte Schriften*, XI, pp. 204-212.

[16]'Die dichterische Phantasie und der Mechanismus des Bewußtseins', 1869, reprinted in Hermann Cohen, *Schriften zur Philosophie und Zeitgeschichte*, I-II, Berlin 1928, pp. 141-228, especially pp. 141, 161 ff., 183.

him this position of an outsider.[17] During the session 1886/87 Warburg followed his lectures and preserved his carefully-written notes. In Lamprecht's interpretation of German history he found a new and promising approach to his own subject. Lamprecht brought together the study of society in the early Middle Ages with that of book illustrations belonging to the same period. This combination foreshadows clearly an essential idea of the research library, which Warburg built up twenty years later. Both men intended to trace in the particular object of their studies the universal law by which the human mind develops in the course of evolution. In Leipzig Lamprecht followed up his early specialised studies with a huge compilation, a German history in fourteen volumes which covered all periods from the primitive beginnings to the sophisticated age of the twentieth century. For him generalisation became more important than direct contact with the sources.

This way of working was utterly alien to Warburg. No comprehensive idea could overshadow his interest in every detail of all objects included in his research. He did not admit that any work of art, any sign of symbolic relevance could be understood without careful study of its particular appearance and environment. He continued to buy Lamprecht's books and pamphlets for his library and, as Professor Gombrich suggests, the foundation of the Leipzig *Institut für Kultur- und Universalgeschichte* in 1909 might have stimulated his plan for the development of the Warburg library in Hamburg.[18] The wide range of Lamprecht's concept for a comparative study of human civilisations must have appealed to the art historian who in his later years traced the migration of symbolic forms from Asia to Europe. But the difference in methodical approach remained considerable. Warburg did not quote Lamprecht in his published work and his name does not usually seem to be mentioned in the notes in which he attempted to formulate for his personal use the conclusions he drew from his research.

Secular patron saint of the Warburg library during its founder's life was Jacob Burckhardt. A metal paper-weight showing his bust in relief was visible on the left side of Warburg's writing-table in his private house, where portraits of other scholars were not so conspicuous. In the important publications on the relations between artist and employer in Florentine society and in the description of festival

---

[17]The lasting importance of Lamprecht's views on history for Warburg's idea of *Kulturwissenschaft* is a very stimulating result of Gombrich's interpretation. The argument had to be based on parallelism and differentiation in the structure of thought. After the period of Warburg's studies under Lamprecht in Bonn his teacher's name seems almost to fade away from his notes. Gombrich's book deals with Lamprecht's influence in the years of Warburg's maturity on 19 pages; only once (p. 144) is Lamprecht's name mentioned as a quoted authority in Warburg's notes. A summary of the methodical conflict: Th. Schieder, 'Die deutsche Geschichtswissenschaft im Spiegel der Historischen Zeitschrift', in *Historische Zeitschrift*, vol. 189, 1959, pp. 47-51. From 1905 Lamprecht attempted to make German foreign policy more effective and more moderate by improving mutual understanding of cultural trends. See Herbert Schönebaum, 'Karl Lamprechts Bemühen um innere und äußere Kulturpolitik', in *Die Welt als Geschichte*, XV, 1955, pp. 137-152. In this respect he was certainly in agreement with Warburg who always retained a critical respect for the imperial regime in Germany. See Gertrud Bing, *Aby Warburg*, Hamburger Vortrag, 1958, Hamburg 1958, pp. 30 f. For Lamprecht's activity in Bonn see P. E. Hübinger, *Das historische Seminar der Rheinischen Friedrich-Wilhelms-Universität zu Bonn* (Bonner Historische Forschungen, vol. 20), Bonn 1963, pp. 131-134, 140 f.
[18]P. 204.

performances as links between art and life Burckhardt is introduced as founding father of such studies. In 1892 Warburg had sent his dissertation on Botticelli to the old Basel professor, whose student he had never been. Burckhardt recognised the study as a sign of considerable progress in his own field and pointed to the Florentine painter's interest in mystical theology as a rewarding problem for future work. This answer reflects perhaps an aspect of Burckhardt's interpretation of the Renaissance which at that time was overlooked even by close followers.[19] In any case his advice did not give a new direction to Warburg. A certain criticism of the master arose from another angle.

Warburg thought of himself as a burgher of the Hamburg republic, but at the same time sensed a need always to dissociate himself from everything bordering on bourgeois taste. The tourist who with the help of his Baedecker performed his quota of admiration among Italian works of art as a valuable part of his holiday pursuits was the favourite target of his mockery or his wrath. From this point of view the sub-title of Burckhardt's *Cicerone, Guide to the enjoyment of art*, could suggest to him at certain moments an attitude different from his own.[20] Because he felt artistic creativeness as an act of liberation from deep anxieties he was inclined to depreciate any approach to the world of beauty as enjoyment and ornament of life. But his knowledge of Burckhardt was much too broadly based and deeply rooted to allow more than momentary significance to the remark by which he classified as hedonistic the scholar who had interpreted the Greek power of imagination and artistic creativeness as a reaction to suffering caused by antagonism in private and political life. In 1927 he drew his final image of Burckhardt for the concluding meeting of his seminar: here the older master appeared as a man who knew about the danger by which his insight into the depth of human nature threatened his very existence. He emphasised how Burckhardt preserved life and sanity by keeping a distance between himself and the powers of the past; Nietzsche, his former colleague, trespassed upon the zone of danger — and perished. When reading these lines we can scarcely avoid the impression that Warburg saw himself as the third figure in this Platonic myth about scholarship as sacrifice, just in the middle between Burckhardt and Nietzsche.[21] It was his knowledge about the danger of human creativeness which gave Warburg's personality the imprint differentiating him both from the type of the *viri doctissimi* who necessarily determine the atmosphere of the academic world, and from the class of successful and optimistic men of affairs who were the leaders of Germany's assimilated Jewry.

The uniqueness of his position was expressed by his way of communication, both in the spoken or written word addressed to the public and in his notes, by which he privately cleared his thoughts. For the purpose of summarizing his results he built

---

[19]Werner Kaegi, *Jacob Burckhardt. Eine Biographie*, vol. III, 1956, pp. 650 f., 693-701 f., 731 f., 739, 743 has shown that Burckhardt's image of the Renaissance is based on his profound understanding of the Middle Ages.

[20]Gombrich, *op. cit.*, p. 145.

[21]*Ibid.*, pp. 254-258. There seems still to be room for comparative investigation of Burckhardt and Warburg in their understanding of artistic imagination as product and symbol of the historical process.

up long and involved sentences with contrasting oppositions and qualifying subordinate clauses which well expressed the intensity of observation and feeling behind these reflections. In this framework he liked to place metaphors expressed in technological terms. The transmission of electrical signals, including the working of the nervous system, became a favoured image for the impact which the symbolic pictures created by antiquity had on the European mind through the interval of many centuries. The listener was left in doubt how far identification of spiritual forces with physical processes was meant; the approximation of both spheres was certainly intended.

The feeling of tenseness brought about by his construction of sentences pointed to a mystery rather than to rational enlightenment. In this way Warburg's style served him in the same function as the idealistic concepts of mind did for his twentieth-century contemporaries when they tried to define the spiritual power of creativeness in the language of their philosophy. The technological terms, inserted by Warburg at the key points of his argument, bore witness to the speaker's allegiance to a naturalistic interpretation of the world.

This aspect of his style as scholar and lecturer corresponded to his appearance in everyday life. Warburg liked soberness and directness of speech, which probably for him meant the homeliness of his Hamburg environment. This inclination made it possible for him to change quite suddenly from pathos to bathos. While interpreting Rembrandt's monumental picture of Claudius Civilis with intense sympathy, he stigmatises the artist's antagonists, who caused the painting's rejection by the description of *Lieferanten triumphaler Gegenwartsbejahung*.[22] It was the same way of speaking which he used in conversation, even when talking about serious experiences: on the last day of his life he entertained the Heidelberg medievalist Karl Hampe, who visited his library to select illustrations for his contribution to the *Propyläen-Weltgeschichte*. During that afternoon his family doctor, Heinrich Embden, telephoned to ask Warburg about his health. His answer was clearly heard from the next room: "All is well above the collar". On the evening of that day he died of a heart attack.

[22]Gombrich, *op. cit.*,p. 236.

Correspondence

Some Notes on Resistance

Helmut Eschwege's essay in Year Book XV[1] has met with a considerable response. We feel that at least some of the additional information on Jewish resistance in Germany which we have received should be printed in this Year Book, points raised or criticism voiced discussed, if only briefly, and bibliographical information made more complete.[2] It should be emphasised once more that it was only possible for selections from a much larger German manuscript, as yet unpublished, to be given in the Year Book and thus some, but by no means all, of the details given below will most likely be covered in the book edition which is in preparation; others, perhaps not known to the author, may be of supplementary value. Some previously published work on the topic had either been overlooked or came out at the same time as Eschwege's contribution.

Publication of Year Book XV coincided with Bulletin 45 of the Leo Baeck Institute, a booklet devoted entirely to the underground activities of Zionist youth in Germany.[3] This is a German version of the original Hebrew edition of the recollections of Yizchak Schwersenz[4] which was cursorily commented on in Year Book XV.[5] Strictly speaking, this record of the war-time clandestine activities of a Zionist youth group in Germany more properly belongs in the category of "defiance" rather than that of "resistance". But it has been related to it and evaluated within its historical context in a remarkable introduction by the Israeli historian Shaul Esh.[6] This essay, Esh's last work, was completed shortly before the author's tragic death in 1968.

In discussing non-Zionist youth Esh takes some small right-wing Jewish groups, who in the first years of the Nazi regime showed a certain predilection for the National Revolution (though eventually disabused of their illusions) and who set their hopes for a while on the likelihood of more conservative, respectable nationalists curbing the Nazi extremists, and contrasts them with those left-wing Jewish idealists who, as fierce opponents of fascist dictatorship and usually as adherents of German Socialist groups, had early resolved on clandestine anti-fascist acitivity.[7] The Communist underground decided at a certain stage to let its Jewish members

[1]'Resistance of German Jews against the Nazi Regime', in *LBI Year Book XV* (1970), pp. 143-180.
[2]The writer of these notes is particularly indebted to Lucien Steinberg, Paris and to Helmut Eschwege for helping to clarify a number of points.
[3]*Bulletin des Leo Baeck Instituts*, Tel Aviv, editor Hans Tramer, No. 45 (1969), 'Jüdische Jugend im Untergrund. Eine zionistische Gruppe in Deutschland während des Zweiten Weltkrieges', von Jizchak Schwersenz und Edith Wolff, Mit einer historischen Einführung von Shaul Esh. This German version was prepared by Heinz Gerling.
[4]*Machteret Chaluzim be-Germania ha-Nazit*, Ein Charod 1969.
[5]*LBI Year Book XV* (1970), pp. XVII-XVIII.
[6]*Loc. cit.*, pp. 5-25.
[7]*Ibid.*, pp. 9-11.

239

participate in the legal work of the various Jewish youth movements[8] and Herbert Baum apparently organised such "infiltration" and acted as contact for the Communist Party. It is not clear whether his younger comrades knew of this task of Baum's. The main organisations chosen, as all accounts agree, were the non-Zionist *Bund deutsch-jüdischer Jugend* (later called *Ring*) and the Zionist *Haschomer Hazair*. The choice of the latter, Esh comments,[9] was especially apt as its orthodox Marxism, albeit outwardly concealed, was generally known to Jewish youth in Germany (though the Gestapo, who on one occasion at least referred to the *Haschomer Hazair* as a Zionist boy scout movement, may have been unaware of these tendencies for a time). Specific Communist indoctrination would have been rejected sharply by the Jewish youth organisations and it is unlikely to have been conducted by the "emissaries",[10] but anti-fascism, and Marxism-Leninism in the case of the *Haschomer Hazair*, were preoccupations which united them anyway. And the fact is that such semi-legal activities were by no means restricted to the two named Jewish youth movements.[11] These few details are given here as they relate directly to the question of resistance and the reader is otherwise referred to Esh's excellent introduction.

Esh based his observations on the Baum group partly on a Hebrew study by Eliyahu Maoz[12] of which an English version (not formally published and therefore hitherto overlooked by us) also exists[13]. Maoz's study is particularly valuable as he was able to use the oral testimony of Charlotte Holzer, one of the two surviving members of the group, which she gave to Yad Vashem in Jerusalem in November 1963. According to her testimony the German Communist Party found it expedient as early as 1936/37 to withdraw Jews from the general underground movement and to organise them in separate cells (though the party neither prevented young Jews from emigrating nor necessarily forced them to belong to separate Jewish Communist groups). Apparently the Baum group was organised in accordance with this principle. This version is the only one to discuss in detail the possibility that the Baum group may have been betrayed (drawing an analogy between the firing

[8]*Ibid.*, p. 13. See also below and Eschwege, *loc. cit.*, p. 169. The various accounts differ somewhat as to motivation and organisational tasks.

[9]*Loc. cit.*, pp. 13-14.

[10]*Ibid.*, p. 13. Esh takes issue here with Margot Pikarski on whose *Die Rolle der Parteiorganisation der KPD in der Herbert-Baum-Gruppe, Berlin 1939-1942*, apart from Bernhard Mark, 'Die Gruppe von Herbert Baum. Eine jüdische Widerstandsgruppe in den Jahren 1937-1942', in *Blätter für Geschichte*, Warsaw 1961, vol. XIV (Yiddish) the more recent accounts lean. Esh had used Pikarski's manuscript which, under a somewhat different title, 'Über die führende Rolle der Parteiorganisation der KPD in der antifaschistischen Widerstandsgruppe Herbert Baum, Berlin 1939-1942' was published in *Beiträge zur Geschichte der deutschen Arbeiterbewegung*, Berlin 1966, No. 5.

[11]A conscious anti-fascism was widespread amongst Jewish youth. At the outbreak of the Spanish Civil War there was a considerable feeling of solidarity with the Spanish Republic in many Jewish youth movements and rumours were current in Berlin in the summer of 1936 that some young Jews alongside German workers had been involved in sabotaging war materials destined for Franco. This can, of course, not be substantiated now.

[12]In *Yalkut Moreshet*, 3, 1965, pp. 79-88.

[13]*A Jewish Underground in Germany*. The article was released by the Organisation Department of the World Zionist Organisation in March 1965 and contained in a 'Lecturers Kit' for the Anniversary of the Ghetto Revolts.

WERNER SCHARFF

JULIUS PHILIPPSON

German Jews who died defying the Nazis

HILDE MEISEL

By courtesy of the Centre de Documentation Juive Contemporaine, Paris

Herbert Baum and his resistance group honoured at Berlin-Weissensee

ber Gene. ....taatsanwalt
bei ..em Kammergericht   Berlin W 35, ..en 22 März 1945
                                          Elssholzstr. 32
13 OJs. 81.45

                              An
                              ..en Herrn Vorsitzer
                              ..es 3.Strafsenats ..es Kammergericht

                                        in B e r l i n

                    Anklage

gegen ..ie Ehefrau Pelagia K o z l o w s k i geb. Fengler aus
Berlin N 65, Utrechter Str. 33, geboren am 18.Dezember 1906
in Kriewen Bez. Kosten, Reichsdeutsche, verheiratet, katholisch,

      in ..ieser Sache im Gerichtsgefängnis Bayreuth in Unter-
      suchungshaft.

   Ich klage sie an:

           Sie hat sich in Berlin in ..en Jahren 1943 un.. 1944 ..er
           Vorbereitung zum Hochverrat un.. ..er Feindbegünstigung
           ..adurch schul..ig gemacht, ..aß sie ..ie für eine illegale
           antinationalsozialistische Organisation tätige Ju..in
           Bromberg bei sich beherbergte, beköstigte un.. ihr nach
           ..er Entweichen aus ..em Gefängnis zur weiteren Flucht
           behilflich war.
           - Verbrechen nach §§ 80 Abs.2, 83 Abs.2 un.. 3, Nr.1 un..
           3,91b, 73 StGB.-

                    Ermittlungsergebnis:

      In Luckenwal..e wur..e im Jahre 1943 von einem gewissen
Winkler, gegen ..en vom Oberreichsanwalt beim Volksgerichtshof
Anklage erhoben worden ist, in Gemeinschaft mit illegal leben..en
Ju..en eine Organisation ins Leben gerufen, ..ie sich mit ..er
Unterstützung un.. Betreuung von Ju..en befaßte, ..en Umsturz ..er
nationalsozialistischen Staatsregierung plante un.. sich auf ..ie
Übernahme ..er Macht vorbereitete. Von ..er Organisation wur..en
gefälschte Ausweise hergestellt, Drohbriefe un.. Femeurteile ver-
sandt un.. Hetzflugblätter in einer Auflage von etwa 3500 Stück
verbreitet.
      Die Angeschuldigte, ..ie le..iglich ..er ..AF. angehörte, ist
seit 1934 verheiratet. Ihr Ehemann steht zur Zeit an ..er Front.
Die Angeschuldigte ist als Verkäuferin in einem Damenbekleidungs-
geschäft tätig un.. bezieht, außerdem Familienunterstützung.Poli-
tisch ist sie bisher nachteilig nicht in Erscheinung getreten.
      In ..en Jahren 1934 bis 1938 war ..er Ehemann ..er Angeschul-
..igten als Fahrstuhlführer in einem jü..ischen Wäschenversan..ge-
schäft tätig. Hier hatte er einen jü..ischen Arbeitskollegen
namens Günther Samuel, ..en ..ie Angeschul..igte ..urch ihren Ehemann
kennen lernte. Durch Samuel machte sie dann ..ie Bekanntschaft ..es
bereits oben erwähnten Hans Winkler.Etwa im Dezember 1943 erschien dieser bei der Angeschul..igten un.. verlangte ihren Mann
zu sprechen. Er bat sie, ob er nicht bei ihr ..ie Jü..in Bromberg,
..ie aus Theresienstadt geflüchtet war, unterbringen könne. Die
Angeschuldigte kam ..iesem Ansinnen nach un.. nahm ..ie Bromberg
bei sich auf. Diese wohnte dann bei der Angeschuldigten mit
Unterbrechungen bis zu ihrer Festnahme im April 1944 un.. wur..e
von ..er Angeschul..igten auch mit Lebensmitteln un.. Geldbeträgen

                                          unterstützt.

Document from the court proceedings against members of the
Arbeitsgemeinschaft für Frieden und Freiheit

*From the Archives of the Institut Marxismus-
Leninismus beim ZK der SED, Berlin, DDR*

unterstützt. Meistens hielt sich die Bromberg in der Laube der
Angeschuldigten auf. Hier machte sie die von Winkler gelieferten
Hetzschriften versandfertig. Etwa Anfang April 1944 gab Winkler
durch eine Mittelsperson einen Karton mit etwa 500 Briefumschlägen
in dem Laden der Arbeitgeberin der Angeschuldigten ab, den diese
bei der Bromberg ablieferte.

Die Angeschuldigte will zunächst nichts von der illegalen
Tätigkeit der Bromberg gewußt haben. Erst im April 1944 will sie
von der Bromberg erfahren haben, daß diese für eine staatsfeindliche Organisation tätig und mit einem Flugblatt "geschnappt"
worden sei. Kurze Zeit danach will sie auch von Winkler darüber
unterrichtet worden sein. Nach Lage der Sache ist jedoch anzunehmen,
daß die Angeschuldigte von vornherein über das Treiben des Winkler
von der Bromberg unterrichtet war.

Am 14.November 1944 gelang es der Bromberg zusammen mit zwei
desertierten Soldaten, die sich mit ihr in einem Ausweichgefängnis
der Polizei befanden, auszubrechen. Ihr erster Weg war zu der
Angeschuldigten, die alle drei Personen mit Bekleidung, Lebens-
mittelmarken und Geld versah. Bei dieser Gelegenheit erzählte die
Bromberg der Angeschuldigten, daß sich Winkler wie ein Schwein
benommen und viele Leute preisgegeben habe.

Auf Grund des geschilderten Sachverhalts hat die Angeschuldigte während des Krieges bewußt staatsfeindliche Bestrebungen
gefördert, die auf den Sturz der nationalsozialistischen Staatsregierung gerichtet waren. Sie hat sich dadurch der Vorbereitung
zum Hochverrat und zugleich der landesverräterischen Feindbe-
günstigung schuldig gemacht.

Beweismittel:

1.) Einlassung der Angeschuldigten.
2.) Zeugen:

    a) Justizangestellter Hans Winkler, zur Zeit im Gefängnis
       Plötzensee in Untersuchungshaft,

    b) Hildegard Sara Bromberg, deren Anschrift noch angegeben
       wird.

Ich beantrage,

       Hauptverhandlung anzuordnen und Haftfortdauer
       zu beschließen.

               Im Auftrag
               gez.Keßler
               Oberstaatsanwalt.

of the anti-Soviet exhibition and the *Reichstag* fire). Again, according to Charlotte Holzer's testimony, the group was trapped and liquidated by the Gestapo which had planted forged propaganda material calling for incendiarism. She actually named Joachim Franke[14], the leader of the German group at the Kaiser Wilhelm Institute, as the "informer", a veteran Communist who "betrayed" the group to save his wife who was tortured in his presence.[15] Official Communist versions are silent on this aspect of the affair. This study is also a most percipient evaluation of the Jewish side of this and other Jewish underground groups.[16] It tells of young Jews who did not disown their Jewishness but despite everything continued to believe in a future Socialist Germany and were determined to stay on. Charlotte Holzer denied any "specifically Jewish ideology" of her group, but she did say that "the Jews had their duties". Maoz, who died recently,[17] has made here a significant contribution to German-Jewish historiography of this period.

In his book *La Révolte des Justes*,[18] which appeared at the same time as Year Book XV, Lucien Steinberg devotes sixty pages to the resistance of German Jews.[19] This is much more detailed than his previous German paper[20] and it also discusses Jewish participation in resistance in general with particular reference to the Baum group which here receives considerable space. Already in the German version Steinberg had referred briefly to the survivors' view that they had been "betrayed" from within their own ranks but he says that there is no evidence of this in the official records.[21] The book edition recounts in detail how Richard and Charlotte Holzer escaped and survived. We have drawn on Steinberg's book here for some other additional information.

Inge Berner, now living in New York, who as Inge Gerson had herself joined yet another small Jewish resistance group in Berlin, and some of whose closest friends were members of the Baum group, has put at the disposal of the Leo Baeck Institute the following moving account:

> The article by Helmut Eschwege in your Year Book XV touched me more deeply than anything I have read in the past years. So many names were familiar: Walter Sack was my *Zugführer* at the *Bund deutsch-jüdischer Jugend*, Ismar Zöllner was also in the *3. Zug*, Siegi Rotholz was for a time what the

---

[14]He is called Franka throughout this version which is obviously due to a mistake in translation.

[15]Franke's name (he was also executed) does not, unlike Steinbrink's, of the Kaiser Wilhelm Institute's group, appear on the memorial erected in Weissensee (see below, p. 243).

[16]All accounts agree that the Nazi invasion of Russia gave the actual impetus to the political work of the Baum group. As Maoz rightly observes, most Communist "sources of information fail to mention the period of the Ribbentrop-Molotov Pact, which must have been an awkward time for the members of the group".

[17]Maoz was a member of *Werkleute* and Kibbutz Hasorea. He contributed an essay on 'The Werkleute' to *LBI Year Book IV* (1959).

[18]*Les Juifs contre Hitler 1933-1945*, Fayard, Paris 1970.

[19]*Ibid.*, 'Les résistants juifs dans le IIIe Reich', p. 41ff. This section includes a detailed account of a mutiny by some Jewish inmates of Sachsenhausen. – Jewish resistance in concentration camps within Germany will also be extensively treated in Eschwege's forthcoming book.

[20]'Der Anteil der Juden am Widerstand in Deutschland', in *Studien und Berichte aus dem Forschungsinstitut der Friedrich-Ebert-Stiftung*, Bad Godesberg 1965, pp. 113-143.

[21]*Ibid.*, p. 134.

youngsters here call a "boy-friend"; and last but certainly not least, there were Hilde Loewy and Marianne Joachim, née Prager.

The last two were my class-mates at Große Hamburger Straße from *Sexta* to *Untersekunda*. Hilde and I became good friends when we once spent a summer vacation at Bad Salzelmen in the *Kinderheim*. She lived in Luitpold-straße, and she was the most intelligent girl in our class, if not even in our school. She had lost an arm in a tram-car accident but she never let that handicap her in any way. She was one of our best gymnasts and I can still see her unbuckle that heavy artificial hand, put a white stocking over the poor little stump and run and jump often better than all of us. We spent unforgettable days at her grandfather's place in Konradshöhe where we camped out and cooked terrible meals, but that didn't matter.

But of all the names mentioned in the article, none was as close to me as Marianne Joachim. We were best friends throughout our school life, I spent many hours at her parents' home at Belforter Straße, and also at their summer cottage in Krumme Lanke. Together we joined the *Bund deutsch-jüdischer Jugend* and here we listened and later participated in the serious discussions which later led to the forming of underground cells after all the Jewish youth orga-nisations were dissolved.

When Marianne and Hilde and Siegi Rotholz joined the Baum group our paths began to drift apart, mostly for ideological reasons. I joined a small group at the factory where I did forced labour, and we concentrated on the distribution of anti-fascist literature. Our leader, by the way, was a girl, Eva Mamlok of Berlin, Neuenburger Straße, who had been arrested twice before, once in 1934 for writing anti-Hitler slogans on the roof of a depart-ment store at Hallesches Tor (I don't remember whether it was Wertheim or Tietz), and once for putting flowers on the grave of Rosa Luxemburg.

Our group was denounced in September 1941 and I was arrested together with Eva Mamlok and another girl, Inge Levinson. During the three months I spent at the Alexanderplatz police jail I received no visitors, but was allowed to receive mail. Of course, my immediate family wrote regularly, but of all my friends only one young man and Marianne Joachim wrote to me. (Marianne had married shortly before I was arrested and I attended her wedding in a room above the partially-destroyed temple in Oranien-burger Straße.) To write to someone in prison on a charge of "Zersetzung der Wehrkraft des deutschen Volkes" was a very courageous act, but Marianne knew no fear and she wrote openly quoting her beloved Schiller, especially the Marquis Posa.

We were lucky. Though we were sentenced to death (without any trial of course), my dear Mother accomplished the impossible and found an official who could be bribed and who saw to it that our sentence was commuted to life imprisonment in a concentration camp. We were sent to Riga, and there I heard in 1943 from some people who had just been sent there from Berlin what had happened to Marianne, Hilde, Siegi and all the others. (Eva Mamlok must have perished either still at Riga or later at Stutthof concentration camp.)

Some thirteen or fourteen years ago I wrote a small article for the *Aufbau* in honour of Marianne Joachim, because I had felt that her name and that of all the members of the Baum group were forgotten, and I thought that they were heroes just as much as those of the Warsaw Ghetto. This article resulted in my getting in touch with Marianne's sister Ilse who now lives in Baltimore and who had been sent to England as a child.

I am most grateful that the Leo Baeck Institute has published this article, and I am glad that these brave young people are not forgotten.

The surviving members of the Baum group, Richard and Charlotte Holzer, succeeded shortly after the war in finding the remains of their executed friends
(probably with the aid of German police officials involved in the trial) and having
them re-buried at the Jewish cemetery in Berlin-Weissensee. There was opposition
to this from the Communist authorities, who favoured a re-interment of these
Jewish anti-fascist resistance fighters alongside their German comrades in the
revolutionary cemetery at Berlin-Friedrichsfelde.[22] This was regarded as far more
honourable than a separate Jewish burial and the authorities were rather surprised
at the request of the Holzers, but eventually agreed. There were, however, also
strong objections by the Jewish religious authorities as some members of the
Baum group had been Gentiles, and for a time they opposed the idea of Jews and
Gentiles being buried together in a Jewish cemetery. All obstacles were overcome,
though there are somewhat differing accounts as to the real difficulties the re-
interment encountered and how they were finally circumvented.* It would appear
that the memorial to the Baum group was erected hastily. Today the former
Lothringerstraße which leads to the Weissensee cemetery bears the name of
Herbert Baum.

Esh also made a brief reference to Jewish participants in the clandestine anti-Nazi
activities of the *Internationaler Sozialistischer Kampf-Bund (ISK)*,[23] a socialist organisation founded in 1925/26, the spiritual father of which was the Jewish philosopher
Leonard Nelson.[24] After its dissolution in 1933 the *ISK* re-restablished its organisation illegally in Germany under the leadership of the Jewish *Studien-Assessor* Julius
Philippson and engaged in extensive propaganda against the Nazi regime.
Philippson was arrested in the summer of 1937, which was the beginning of the
dissolution of the *ISK*. He resisted torture for months but eventually, faced with the
threatened seizure of his parents, made revelations which resulted in a series of
arrests.[25] All *ISK* resistance groups in Germany were liquidated in the winter of
1937/38. The trial of Philippson and his comrades took place before the *Volksgerichtshof* in December 1938,[26] immediately after the *Kristallnacht* and much was made of
Philippson's Jewish origin as an additional justification for the severe sentences
imposed. The *ISK* was described as an outpost of World Jewry in its fight against

---

[22]Steinberg, *La Révolte des Justes*, p. 77.
*While this Year Book was in print another account came from the German Democratic
Republic, differing substantially from the one given above which was based on Steinberg's
book, and other information previously received from the GDR. According to this the only
one buried under the memorial stone was Herbert Baum. After he was tortured to death
in prison his body was handed over to the cemetery authorities at Weissensee. The bodies
of the executed members of the Baum group were collected by the SS after medical experiments by the Anatomy Department of Berlin University.
[23]*Loc. cit.*, p. 12.
[24]On this organisation see: Werner Link, *Die Geschichte des Internationalen Jugendbundes (IJB)
und des Internationalen Sozialistischen Kampf-Bundes (ISK). Ein Beitrag zur Geschichte der Arbeiterbewegung in der Weimarer Republik und im Dritten Reich*, Marburger Abhandlungen zur politischen
Wissenschaft, I, Meisenheim am Glan 1964.
[25]*Ibid.*, p. 223.
[26]*Ibid.*, p. 228ff.

National Socialism. Philippson, who during the trial took all the guilt upon himself, was sentenced to life imprisonment. He perished in Auschwitz in 1943. Another Jewish member of the *ISK*, Hilde Meisel (the poet Hilde Monte) died during the last days of the Third Reich. She had often acted as a courier during the war, taking anti-Nazi leaflets across the German frontier and in the spring of 1945 had left Switzerland for Austria in order to co-ordinate resistance activities. On her return she was shot by an SS patrol while illegally crossing the border.[27]

Of another largely Jewish and almost unknown resistance group Lucien Steinberg has now given a fuller account.[28] He has provided the following English summary for the Year Book:

> Even less well known than the Herbert Baum group is that of Werner Scharff, known as *Arbeitsgemeinschaft für Frieden und Freiheit* (sometimes *Gemeinschaft für Frieden und Aufbau*). Günther Weisenborn published a leaflet of this group, whereas Hermann Maas and Gustav Radbruch quote a letter about Scharff, addressed to Ricarda Huch, in their *Den Unvergessenen. Opfer des Wahns 1933 bis 1945*, Heidelberg 1952, pp. 11-18.
>
> Scharff himself, like Baum, was born in 1912 and in the same region, namely Poznan (which was German at that time). Fair-haired and blue-eyed, he was far from being the "Jewish type".
>
> An electrician by trade, he was employed at the synagogue in Levetzow-straße which was the assembly point for the deportation of Berlin Jews. Here his resistance activity started. He helped the deportees in every possible way, even restoring personal property to them which had been confiscated. He even managed to hide cards, sometimes whole boxes of them, by putting those marked "for deportation" amongst those marked "deported". Later he endeavoured to gather round him several Germans in order to assist those Jews who had gone underground to go into hiding or even to change their identity.
>
> When the last employees of the *Reichsvereinigung* were deported (10th June 1943), Scharff himself went underground. His services as an electrician at the synagogue were no longer needed, and he risked immediate deportation.
>
> On the 14th July 1943 he was recognised by a Gestapo man. Although he was armed at the time he did not shoot, because the Gestapo man was accompanied by two Jews who had to act as auxiliaries, and Scharff did not wish to hurt them, so he made no resistance to his arrest. After spending three weeks in the "Jewish" *Bunker* of the Gestapo, he was deported to Theresienstadt, together with one of his resistance comrades, Friedel Fancia Grün.
>
> The two young people did not resign themselves to their fate and managed to escape from Theresienstadt five weeks later, on the 7th September. Back in Berlin, they succeeded in procuring false identity papers, Werner Scharff assuming the identity of Hans Wieczorek, travelling salesman, and was thus able to travel across Germany.
>
> His main base was at Luckenwalde, where Scharff recruited Hans Winkler, a clerk of the court. They set up the *Arbeitsgemeinschaft für Frieden und Freiheit*, headed by Winkler who adopted the title of *Reichsführer*. Among the members of this group one should mention the carpenter Walter Klatt, the agronomist

[27]Esh, *loc. cit.*, p. 12 and Link, *op cit.*, p. 318.
[28]Steinberg, *La Révolte des Justes*, pp. 78-84.

Alfred Stein, and the butcher Henry Landes, all from the vicinity of Luckenwalde and all of them "aryans". They set up a rescue fund which they called *Hoher Einsatz*, with which they helped Jews in hiding (including Fancia Grün, Hilde Bromberg and Gertrud Scharff, the wife of Werner). All these details are known from the trial briefs of the men of the group.

The money was collected simply by selling the donors membership cards of the *Arbeitsgemeinschaft*, purporting to be of help after the end of the Nazi regime. Significantly enough, quite a few members of the *Arbeitsgemeinschaft* had been or still were members of the Nazi Party. This was not so, however, in the case of a number of German women who actively helped Scharff, and who were somewhat older than the Jewish members: Pelagia Kozlowski, then aged thirty-eight, Johanna Schallschmidt, forty-two, Ida Röscher, forty-eight, Frieda Wiegel, fifty-three. A French-Jewish prisoner of war, Eric Sojka, interpreter at Stalag III A, was also in contact with the group.

There exists at least one leaflet of the group; it has been published by Günther Weisenborn in his *Der lautlose Aufstand. Bericht über die Widerstandsbewegung des deutschen Volkes 1933-1945*, Hamburg 1954, pp. 316-17. It is known that the group had contacts in Hamburg, Munich, Eisenach, and Berlin.

Of course, the Gestapo got wind of the existence of these people and succeeded in planting an informer. So Scharff's grandiose plan, the storming of the "Jewish" prison of Berlin, in the Schulstraße, to liberate the detainees, could not be carried out. Worse: Gertrud Scharff and Fancia Grün were arrested on the 12th October 1944. Werner was taken two days later, Winkler at about the same period, and the whole Luckenwalde network some time in December 1944. Scharff was quickly recognised as an escapee from Theresienstadt; he had left many traces behind in the form of pamphlets. He had to be made to talk, and the torture-chamber at the Oranienburger Straße had the reputation of being the most advanced of its kind. But Werner Scharff did not talk. He was subjected to a variety of tortures which only ceased when others talked. He was sent to Sachsenhausen where he was shot on the 16th March 1945. Fancia Grün and her husband, Gerhard Grün, suffered the same fate.

The German women, imprisoned at Fehrbellin concentration camp and in the Bayreuth gaol, survived until the liberation, as did Gertrud Scharff. Hildegard Bromberg, who also survived, committed suicide a few weeks after the liberation, in Berlin. I have been unable to find out anything about the fate of the Winkler-Klatt group.

As to the political affiliation of the *Arbeitsgemeinschaft*, one cannot arrive at any definite conclusion. In a statement before a West Berlin Reparations Court, Frieda Wiegel, who applied for a pension as a former resistance worker, said that the group had been Communist. Taking into account the place where the statement was made, it may be considered to have been made in good faith. On the other hand, however, the historiography of the German Democratic Republic does not mention the existence of the group at all, and this despite the fact that the source-material on which this modest paper is based is to be found in the *Zentrales Parteiarchiv* of the *Institut Marxismus-Leninismus beim ZK der SED*, Berlin to whom I am indebted for their assistance.*

*Steinberg studied this matter a few years ago. We understand from Helmut Eschwege that the *Arbeitsgemeinschaft* is now regarded as a Social Democratic resistance group by the *Institut für Marxismus-Leninismus*.

A serious criticism of Helmut Eschwege's essay is that many of those listed[29] as persecuted or murdered for resistance activities in the beginning of the Nazi era were merely the victims of Nazi revenge against their more prominent Jewish opponents who suffered solely for past political activities. This criticism is not entirely unjustified and we ourselves made an editorial qualification here.[30] Yet while some of those mentioned could probably not by any stretch of the imagination be classified as resistance fighters, there were many others who had begun to resort, even in the phase of neo-fascist twilight which preceded Hitler's ascent to power, to militant and semi-legal means and who did offer immediate resistance and organised clandestine activities from the very outset. Still, one must accept that the line between persecution and resistance in the earlier years is often blurred.

The point has been raised whether we can really speak of a "Jewish" resistance in Germany when so many of those engaged in underground activities in the Third Reich did so first and foremost on account of their Socialist or Communist convictions and in many instances regarded the semi-legal Jewish youth organisations as merely a cover for their political work. To some extent this is really a matter of terminology and we advisedly speak of the resistance of German Jews and not of the German-Jewish resistance. This is a complex question and no one could attempt a clear-cut division. That Jewish motives played an increasing rôle amongst most of those who saw themselves above all as adherents of the German working-class parties is self-evident — how could it have been otherwise? And the process of Jewish exclusion from German life was to necessitate, if for tactical reasons alone, as we have seen, the organisation of separate Jewish cells within the resistance network, with all the inevitable ideological problems attendant on such a division. With certain qualifications, keeping in mind that while resistance of German Jews runs the whole scale from *Jewish* youth groups to those members of the German resistance of Jewish origin who were without any Jewish involvement or consciousness, we are justified in assessing all the resistance of Jewish youth in Germany during this closing chapter of German-Jewish history also as a distinct Jewish phenomenon and their fate as a Jewish tragedy.

Accounts of the clandestine activities of German-Jewish youth in the Third Reich barely hint at, but do not otherwise discuss, the repercussions such illegal work, particularly sabotage, was likely to have for the Jewish community as a whole. Thus they relate for instance the frightful revenge the Nazi authorities exacted for the firing of the anti-Soviet exhibition by the Baum group but are cursory on the implications this or similar actions were likely to have had for all of Berlin's remaining Jews. Some members of the Baum group themselves, at any rate, regarded arson in the Lustgarten as too risky for the participants and likely to result in

---

[29]That the lists are not altogether satisfactory is freely admitted by the author. It was impossible to check all the facts as many eye-witnesses had perished likewise and documentary evidence had often been destroyed. He may also have included some Gentiles while the names of some Jewish victims eluded him. Hermann Liebmann (*LBI Year Book XV* (1970), p. 153), for instance, was not Jewish.

[30]*LBI Year Book XV* (1970), p. 153.

repressive measures against the Jewish population.[31] The activities of the Baum group belong, of course, already to the phase of the gradual liquidation of the Berlin community, but that militant anti-Nazi action by desperate or dedicated Jewish youth would have unforeseeable consequences for the exposed and isolated Jewish community was always feared by the remaining representative organs of Jewry in Nazi Germany and by many individual Jews. Who would say today that such concern was unwarranted? As to the Baum group, there are survivors from Berlin who state that its members were not only marked by a reckless and self-sacrificing disregard for their own lives but who also accuse them of indifference to the fate of all those Berlin Jews who might suffer in consequence of their activities. Such voices should be respected too, though there is sufficient evidence that the group had much support from Jews in Berlin. But the weighty argument that some actions were bound to cause more harm to innocent people than any tangible result achieved could possibly justify ("partisan warfare always endangers the civilian population") should perhaps not always be all that lightly dismissed — although we now know that the Jews were doomed anyway — by those who in retrospect demand that there should have been militant resistance at all costs.

It is perhaps symptomatic that a Seminar on Jewish Resistance recently organised in England by the World Union of Jewish Students[32] revolved largely round the accusation of the younger generation that insufficient resistance was offered by the Jews not only both before and after the outbreak of the Second World War but also prior to the establishment and consolidation of Nazi power.[33] To listen to this line of argument was to realise that it was obviously dictated by an unshakable conviction that the German-Jewish community could and should have attempted physical resistance from the very beginning (and this despite the total and ignominious collapse of all democratic bodies and institutions in Germany and the virtual disappearance of all actual or potential allies of the Jewish minority). These may be extreme views, easily contradicted as showing no genuine understanding of the real conditions which made mass revolt inconceivable at any time; and they are of course views which actually stem from the different historical context and consciousness of today. Yet what does emerge ever clearer from all the soul-searching, the discussions, and the diligent piecing together of the past is that there was, even in the very heart of the Nazi empire, a militant anti-fascist resistance of German-Jewish youth of dimensions not generally appreciated. It does not do to completely ignore some of the problems inherent in such resistance; but many of these courageous young men and women died unknown and forgotten and it is surely the duty of Jewish historiography to record them and their deeds and to rescue them from oblivion.

ARNOLD PAUCKER

---

[31]Steinberg, *La Révolte des Justes*, pp. 66-67.
[32]July 12th to 16th 1971 at the University of Reading.
[33]This writer has now covered this earlier phase in an English paper *The Jewish Defence against Antisemitism and Nazism in the Weimar Republic*, given at the Reading Seminar on Jewish Resistance, to be published shortly by the World Union of Jewish Students.

This letter was written by the twenty-one-year old Marianne Joachim,
a member of the Baum group, to her parents just before her
execution in Berlin-Plötzensee on the 4th March 1943

Berlin-Plötzensee, den 4. März 1943
Königsdamm 7
Haus

Name des Briefschreibers:
Joachim, Marianne Sara
Gelesen: RI

Mein geliebtes, einziges, kleines Muttchen, mein geliebter, guter Vati, wenn Ihr
diesen Brief erhaltet, bin ich schon nicht mehr am Leben. Ihr könnt mir glauben,
daß ich bis zur letzten Sekunde tapfer war. Wie gern hätte ich die Gewißheit, daß
Ihr jetzt auch stark dem Unabänderlichen begegnet. Mein letzter Wunsch ist,
daß Ihr Euch mit ganzer Kraft gesund erhaltet, um einst an unsrer Ille noch alle
die Freuden erleben zu können, die Ihr von mir leider umsonst erhofft habt. Mein
süßes Schwesterchen! Ich habe einen Brieftext für sie aufgesetzt, den ich Euch
bitte, ihr durchs Rote Kreuz zu schicken. Geliebtes Schwesterkläuschen, werde
kein Alltagsmensch, den nur sein Essen und Vergnügen interessiert. Gedenke der
Lieder, die wir gemein gesungen. Alles, alles Gute! Letzten Kuß Marianne.
Die Unterschrift könnt Ihr aus einem alten Brief ausschneiden und aufkleben.
 Schreibt aber vorher mit Eurem Absender, worum sich's handelt, damit der
Schreck nicht allzu groß ist. Ich will Euch als letzten Gruß noch ein paar Verse
senden, die mir vor kurzem eingefallen sind: Ich seh Euch Tag und Nacht die
Hände falten und beten zu der Macht, auf die Ihr baut. Ich hör' Euch innig-
flehend Zwiesprach' halten mit Eurem lieben Gott, dem Ihr vertraut. Ich weiß
um Euer Fühlen, Euer Denken, ich kenne Eurer Stunden bittre Qual. Wie gerne
wollt' Ihr mir das Leben schenken, zum zweiten, ach, zum millionsten Mal!
Unsagbar viel habt Ihr für mich getan von meinem ersten bis zum heut'gen Tage.
Jetzt sieht man's Euren lieben Zügen an: Ihr kanntet nichts als Arbeit, Müh' und
Plage. Seid stark und fest nun, da wir scheiden müssen, nehmt stark das Unab-
änderliche hin! laßt in Gedanken Euch herzinnigst küssen und glaubet mir, wie
dankbar ich Euch bin!
 Damit ist eigentlich alles gesagt. Noch einmal: Denkt an Ille und haltet Euch
ihretwegen tapfer! Mir fällt es nur Euretwegen schwer, aus dieser Welt zu gehen,
sonst habe ich ja nichts zu verlieren! Lebt wohl, meine geliebten Eltern! Grüßt
alle Lieben recht herzlich. Zum letzten Mal küsse ich Euch in Gedanken. Bis zuletzt
denke ich in Liebe und Dankbarkeit an Euch.

Eure Marianne.

Letters to the Editor

ERNST TOLLER

In Year Book XV Margarete Turnowsky-Pinner makes reference to the death of Bernhard Schottländer, in a footnote on p. 217 which I must correct. He was not killed (in Berlin) during the Spartacus rising (and not by the mob), but was abducted in Breslau by students of the extreme Right in March 1920, at the end of the Kapp-Putsch, and (probably after being knocked out by being beaten about the head) thrown into the Oder. His body was recovered from the water about a week later, and buried in the cemetery Lohestrasse in Breslau.

His literary remains which were handed over to me in 1922 were described and evaluated twenty-five years later, in 1947, by Professor Sadan in a long Hebrew essay in a volume of *Hapoel Hazair*. I have been told a great deal about the period at the end of the First World War, described by Margarete Turnowsky-Pinner, by my late wife Meta née Rossmann, who died in 1954. She, too, was a member of the Toller circle. I recall her mentioning Professor Lissauer's wife whose apartment in the Schloß-Wolfsbrunnen-Weg in Heidelberg even in 1919/20 was a meeting point of socialist-pacifist youth.

FRANZ MEYER

ANTONIE AND PAUL STRASSMANN

In Year Book XIII (1968), p. 224, Ernst Feder is quoted as saying that "der Kronprinz [sich] mehr für Frauen interessiert, so die Fliegerin Toni Strassmann, Tochter des Professors Strassmann."

Footnote 245 identifies, "The Jewish woman aviator Antonie Strassmann, daughter of Professor Paul Strassmann (b. 1866), the famous gynaecologist, who committed suicide after the *Machtübernahme*."

These statements are wholly or partly inaccurate. My father's sister, Antonie, was escorted by the *Kronprinz* during the 1920s but not as late as September 1932 when Feder wrote. As a matter of fact, Antonie arrived in the United States on the Hamburg-Amerika liner Albert Ballin on 29th March 1930 and then again in New York as an alien quota immigrant in January 1932. She lived in the United States until her death on 8th January 1952.

My grandfather was a member of the church council of an evangelical Lutheran church and, like his daughters, did not stress any Jewish heritage, identity, or affiliation.

He did not commit suicide. In January 1933, he dismissed his *Oberarzt*, Dr. Willy Jung, who had joined the Nazi party. An attempt was made to expropriate the Strassmann *Frauenklinik*. Hermann Göring, who, as a flyer, was acquainted with Antonie, is said to have frustrated this attempt. My grandfather continued to own and operate the *Frauenklinik* until the autumn of 1936 when he sold it, and it became part of the Charité hospital complex across the Luisenstrasse. It was shortly after his 70th birthday.

My grandfather died on vacation in Switzerland on the 15th August 1938.

WOLFGANG PAUL STRASSMANN

Corrections

KÄTHE LEICHTER

The Austrian Socialist Käthe Leichter née Pick who died in Ravensbrück concentration camp during the war was wrongly named Lester in Year Book XV on page 216 and in the General Index, page 322.

HANS BEYTH

Hans Beyth, the organiser of Youth Aliyah, was wrongly spelled Hans Bein in Year Book XV on page 76. In the General Index on page 317 the entry should not read Bein, Hans 76, 86 but there should be two entries:

Bein, Alexander,   86
Beyth, Hans,   76

HILDEGARD LOEWY and HELLA HIRSCH

A regrettable error has occurred in the captions to the pictures of Jewish resistance fighters executed by the Nazis, shown between pages 174-175 in Year Book XV which is apparently repeated in other publications. As Inge Berner, New York, informs us Hella Hirsch, on the left, was incorrectly identified as Hilde Loewy and Hilde Loewy, in the middle, as Hella Hirsch.

LILY ZADEK

Regarding the remark about the family roots of Lily Zadek in Year Book XV, page XIII, we are informed by Mrs. Gusta Rechav-Strumpf of Ramat Aviv (Israel), a life-long friend of Lily's, that her father was not a lawyer, as erroneously stated, but a physician in Berlin who had his practice for about fifty years in one of the working-class districts. For some time he was a Socialist member of the Berlin City Council.

MAX BROD

Another misprint occurred in Year Book XV, on page 97, line 8 in Curt Wormann's essay on German Jews in Israel. Max Brod left Prague on 15th March 1939, the day the German army marched in, not in May, as erroneously stated.

Abstracts of articles in this Year Book are included in *Historical Abstracts* and *America: History and Life.*

Post-War Publications on German Jewry

A Selected Bibliography of Books and Articles 1970

Compiled on behalf of the
LEO BAECK INSTITUTE
and
THE WIENER LIBRARY
by Bertha Cohn

Leo Baeck Institute
The Wiener Library
4, Devonshire Street
London W. 1.

CONTENTS

BIBLIOGRAPHY 1970

I. HISTORY

A. General

8405. BEN-SASSON, HAYIM HILLEL: *The Reformation in Contemporary Jewish Eyes.* Publ. by The Israel Academy of Sciences and Humanities. Proceedings. Vol. IV, No. 12. Jerusalem: Ahva Press, 1970. 88 pp.

8406. BUNDESZENTRALE FÜR POLITISCHE BILDUNG, ed.: *Das jüdische Volk in der Weltgeschichte.* Teil I: Von den Ursprüngen bis zur Emanzipation (Reiner Bernstein). Teil 2: Vom Zionismus bis zum Staat Israel der Gegenwart (Wanda Kampmann). Wiesbaden: Universum Verlagsanstalt, 1970. 24, 32 pp. [2 vols.] (Informationen zur politischen Bildung, Nr. 140/141.)

8407. COHEN, D. J.: *'Cossman zum Rade' — Emissary of the Jews of Germany in the 1560's.* [In]: 'Zion', Quarterly for Research in Jewish History. Vol. XXXV. Jerusalem, 1970. Pp. 117-126 + a summary in English. [Text in Hebrew with the documents in the original German.]

8408. *Conferences and Symposia on the Second World War 1968-1970.* [In]: Yad Vashem Studies. Vol. VIII. Jerusalem, 1970. Pp. 215-220. [Incl. The Conference on 'Research into the History of Central European Jewry from the Emancipation to its Destruction', organised by the Leo Baeck Institute in Jerusalem from 21-24 June 1970.] [See also No. 8505.]

8409. *Deutsches Judentum in Krieg und Revolution 1916-1923.* Ein Sammelband hrsg. von Werner E. Mosse unter Mitwirkung von Arnold Paucker. Tübingen: J. C. B. Mohr (Paul Siebeck), 1971. xi, 704 pp. bibl. (pp. 635-676). (Schriftenreihe wissenschaftlicher Abhandlungen des Leo Baeck Instituts, 25). [Conts.: Die Krise der europäischen Bourgeoisie und das deutsche Judentum (Werner E. Mosse). Die politischen Veränderungen der Kriegszeit und ihre Auswirkungen auf die Judenfrage (Saul Friedländer). Die Rolle der liberalen Presse (Werner Becker). Juden im politischen Leben der Revolutionszeit (Werner T. Angress). Der Beitrag der Juden zu Geist und Kultur (Hans Tramer). Zur Frage der wirtschaftlichen Motive im deutschen Antisemitismus (Wilhelm Treue). Die Ausbreitung des Antisemitismus (Werner Jochmann). Der Bewusstseinswandel der deutschen Juden (Eva G. Reichmann). Schlusswort (Robert Weltsch).]

8410. KATZ, JACOB: *Jews and Freemasons in Europe 1723-1939.* Transl. from the Hebrew by Leonard [Aryeh] Oschry. Cambridge, Mass.: Harvard University Press, 1970. viii, 293 pp., notes pp. 231-281. [Chap. IV: The Frankfurt Judenloge. VII: The Struggle for Masonic Emancipation in Prussia.]

8411. KISCH, GUIDO: *The Jews in Medieval Germany.* A Study of their Legal and Social Status. Second, rev. and enl. edition. New York: Ktav Publishing House, 1970. 655 pp., bibl. [First publ. in the U.S.A. in 1949.]

8412. LAMBERT, M.: *The Attempt to form a Jewish Bloc.* Jewish Notables and Politics in Wilhelmian Germany. [In]: 'Central European History'. Vol. 3, Nos. 1-2, March-June. Atlanta, Ga., 1970. Pp. 73-93.

8413. LEBOVICS, HERMAN: *Social Conservatism and the Middle Classes in Germany, 1914-1933.* Princeton: Princeton University Press, 1969. xi, 248 pp. [An analysis of the theories of Werner Sombart, Edgar Salin, Othmar Spann, Ernst Niekisch, Oswald Spengler and Ferdinand Fried against the background of the economic, political and social conditions of the period.]

8414. LOWENTHAL, MARVIN: *The Jews of Germany.* A Story of Sixteen Centuries. New York: Russell & Russell, 1970. 444 pp., bibl. [A reprint. The work was first publ. by Longmans, Green, New York, 1936.]

8415. MOSSE, WERNER E.: *The Conflict of Liberalism and Nationalism and its Effect on German Jewry.* [In]: LBI Year Book XV. London, 1970. Pp. 125-139.

253

8416. *Regesten zur Geschichte der Juden im Fränkischen und Deutschen Reiche bis zum Jahre 1273.* Hrsg. im Auftrage der Historischen Commission für Geschichte der Juden in Deutschland. Bearb. unter Mitwirkung von Albert Dresdner und Ludwig Lewinski von Julius Aronius. (Reprograf. Nachdruck der Ausgabe Berlin, Simion 1902.) Hildesheim: G. Olms Verlag, 1970. 370 pp.

8417. SCHUBERT, KURT [and others]: *Geschichte der deutschen Juden.* 13 Sendungen ab 28. Sept. 1969 im Studienprogramm des Bayerischen Rundfunk. München, 1969/1970.

8418. STERN-TAEUBLER, SELMA: *The First Generation of Emancipated Jews.* [In]: LBI Year Book XV. London, 1970. Pp. 3-40, ports. [of David Friedlaender, Naphtali Hartwig Wessely.]

8419. TOURY, JACOB: *Dokumente zur Juden-Emanzipation im Grossherzogtum Berg (1808).* [In]: 'LBI Bulletin'. 12. Jg., Nr. 46-47. Tel Aviv, 1969. Pp. 137-154. [Part of a documentation to be publ. in 1972/73.]

8420. *Zeitschrift für die Geschichte der Juden.* Hrsg. von Hugo Gold. Jg. VII. Nr. 1, 2/3, 4. Tel. Aviv: Olamenu, 1970. [Nr. 1 incl.: Neue Forschungen von Brilling (S. Neufeld). Joseph Roths lebenslange Auseinandersetzung mit dem Zionismus (David Bronsen). Nr. 2/3: Eine bedenkliche Ziffer. [Notes concerning the Jews of Elbing (S. Neufeld).] Nr. 4: Stefan Zweig, die Welt von Gestern (Walter A. Berendsohn).] [Some selected contributions are listed according to subject.]

LINGUISTICS

8421. CHAJES, SAUL: *Pseudonymen-Lexikon der hebräischen und jiddischen Literatur.* Thesaurus pseudonymorum quae in literatura Hebraica et Judaeo-Germanica inveniuntur. (Reprogr. Nachdr. der Ausgabe Wien 1933). Hildesheim: G. Olms Verlag, 1967. 421 pp.

8422. MARK, Y.: *The Yiddish Language, Its Cultural Impact.* [In]: American Jewish Historical Quarterly. Vol. 59, No. 2, Dec. Philadephia, 1969. Pp. 201-209.

8423. STEIN, SIEGFRIED: *Liebliche Tefilloh.* A Judaeo-German Prayer-Book printed in 1709. [In]: LBI Year Book XV. London, 1970. Pp. 41-72, facsims.

8424. WEISSBERG, J.: *Johann Christof Wagenseils 'Bericht Wie das Jüdisch-Teutsche zu lesen?'.* [In]: 'Zeitschrift für Deutsche Sprache'. 25. Jg., Nr. 3, Berlin, 1969. Pp. 154-168.

B. **Communal and Regional History**

1. **Germany**

8425. BAMBERG. PASCHKE, HANS: *Der Judenhof und die alte Judengasse zu Bamberg.* Bamberg: Kultur- und Sportamt, 1969. 44 pp., front. illus., illus., map.

8426. BERLIN. BRILLING, BERNHARD: *Das jüdische Goldschmiedegewerbe in Berlin 1700 bis 1900.* Ein Beitrag zur Kultur- und Gewerbegeschichte. [In]: Der Bär von Berlin. Jahrbuch des Vereins für die Geschichte Berlins. 19. Jg. Berlin, 1970. Pp. 106-138.

8427. BRUYN, GÜNTER DE: '*Berlin, Grosse Hamburger*'. [Chap. in]: Städte und Stationen in der DDR. Frankfurt a.M.: S. Fischer Verlag, 1970. [First publ. Rostock: Hinstorff Verlag, 1969.] [20 DDR authors describe places that seem important to them. The author remembers the Jewish Boy School, the Jewish old age home, which became the assembly point for deportation.]

8428. GILON, MEIR: *Eine Rechnungsprüfung in der Berliner Jüdischen Gemeinde im 18. Jahrhundert und ihre Folgen.* [In]: 'LBI Bulletin'. 12. Jg., Nr. 46-47. Tel Aviv, 1969. Pp. 101-136. [The essay is an introduction to a forthcoming study on 'Verfassung, Verwaltung und Finanzen der Berliner Gemeinde im 18. Jahrhundert'.]

8429. HAMBURGER, W.: *Aus alten Blättern der Jüdischen Reformgemeinde zu Berlin.* [In]: 'Tradition und Erneuerung'. Nr. 30, Nov. Bern, 1970. Pp. 542-551.

8430. LIANG, HSI-HUEY: *The Berlin Police Force in the Weimar Republic.* Berkeley, Los Angeles: University of California Press, 1970. xvi, 252 pp., ports., illus., maps, bibl. (pp. 231-243). [Incl. numerous references to Jews, in particular to Dr. Bernhard Weiss (1880-1951), Deputy Police President 1927-1932.]

8431. ROSE, PAUL: *Berlins grosse Theaterzeit.* Schauspieler-Porträts der zwanziger und dreissiger Jahre. Berlin: Rembrandt-Verlag, 1969. 176 pp., ports., illus.

8432. STRAUSS, HERBERT A. und KURT R. GROSSMANN, eds.: *Gegenwart im Rückblick. Festgabe für die Jüdische Gemeinde zu Berlin 25 Jahre nach dem Neubeginn.* Heidelberg: Lothar Stiehm Verlag, 1970. 374 pp., cover illus., + 82 ports., illus., facsims., gen. table [of Gebr. Veit (1780-1931), comp. by Hanns G. Reissner.] [Conts: Die preussische Bürokratie und die anti-jüdischen Unruhen im Jahre 1834 (Herbert A. Strauss). Jüdische Parlamentarier in Berlin 1848-1933 (Ernest Hamburger). Deutsche Juden auf der Linken. Ihre politische Aktivität in der Weimarer Republik (Kurt R. Grossmann). Fürsorge für das Volk. Anfänge einer neuen jüdischen Sozialpolitik in Deutschland 1919-1933 (Shalom Adler-Rudel). Die jüdische Bevölkerung in Preussen. Verteilung und wirtschaftliche Struktur im Jahre 1931 (Max P. Birnbaum). Austrittsbewegung und Berliner Adass Jisroel-Gemeinde 1869-1939 (Michael L. Munk). The Reactions of Reform Jews to the Nazi Rule (Wolfgang Hamburger). Zur Entstehung der 'Reichsvereinigung der Juden in Deutschland' (Hans-Erich Fabian). Die Ermordung von 35 000 Berliner Juden. Der Judenmordprozess in Berlin schreibt Geschichte (Robert M. W. Kempner). II. Teil: Franz Rosenzweig's Anecdotes about Hermann Cohen (Steven S. Schwarzschild). Out of the Root of Rabbis [On Leo Baeck.] (Manfred E. Swarsensky). In memoriam Rabbi Julius Galliner (Harris Hirschberg). A Rabbi under the Hitler Regime (Joachim Prinz). Ministry under Stress. A Rabbi's Recollections of Nazi Berlin 1935-1940 (Max Nussbaum). Erinnerungen an Berlin (Georg Salzberger). Berlins einstige Synagogen. Eine Erinnerung (Curt Wilk). Das Haus Minden (Felix Hirsch). Mein Vater Sigmund Feist. Erinnerungen an das Reichenheimsche Waisenhaus (Elisabeth Feist-Hirsch). Gebrüder Veit, Berlin (1780-1931) (Hanns G. Reissner). In memoriam Wilfrid Israel (Werner M. Behr). Meine aktive Verbundenheit mit dem jüdischen Sektor Berlins (Herman O. Pineas). Reflections on Berlin Jews: A Personal Memoir on Minority Status and its Lessons (Gerd W. Ehrlich). Erinnerungen an das Hansaviertel (Werner Rosenstock). Wiedergeburt in Berlin (Hans Steinitz). The Plural Worlds of German Jewry. A Postscript (Herbert A. Strauss). People, Places, and Documents. A Pictorial Record.]

8433. BRESLAU. BRILLING, BERNHARD: *Regesten zur Geschichte der Juden in Breslau vom 16.-18. Jahrhundert (1555-1749).* [In]: Hamburger Mittel- und Ostdeutsche Forschungen. Bd. VII. Hamburg: Ludwig Appel. 1970. Pp. 129-152.

8434. CHEMNITZ. DIAMANT, ADOLF: *Chronik der Juden in Chemnitz* (Heute Karl-Marx-Stadt). Aufstieg und Untergang einer jüdischen Gemeinde in Sachsen. Frankfurt a.M.: Verlag Wolfgang Weidlich (in Kommission), [1970]. II, 183 pp., ports., illus., tabs., diagr., facsims., bibl. (pp. 167-173).

8435. COLOGNE. JOSEPH, ARTUR: *Meines Vaters Haus.* Mit einem Vorwort von Heinrich Böll. 4. Aufl. Köln: Kiepenheuer & Witsch, 1970. 144 pp. [Reminiscences of a Cologne businessman first publ. 1959. See No. 1615 /YB.V.]

8436. LANGENBUCHER, KARL-OTTO: *Studien zur Sprache des Kölner Judenschreinsbuches 465 (Scabinorum) aus dem 14. Jahrhundert.* Bonn: Röhrscheid Verlag, 1970. 166 pp., 12 maps. (Rheinisches Archiv, 72). Diss. Bonn.

8437. DANZIG. *Die Geschichte der Juden in Danzig.* Zu einem Manuskript von Samuel Echt. [In]: 'Deutsche Studien', Vierteljahreshefte für vergleichende Gegenwartskunde. VIII. Jg., Juni. Bremen: Carl Schünemann Verlag, 1970. Pp. 145-153. [Cf. No. 4539/YB.X.]

8438. DUISBURG. FRANK, EMIL: *Jüdische Volksschule in Duisburg, 1927-1942.* [No date.] 10 pp. [Typescript].

8439. EAST and WEST PRUSSIA *(Provinces).* BRILLING, BERNHARD: *Zur Geschichte der Juden in Ost- und Westpreussen.* Besprechungen der Bücher von H. J. Krüger über Königsberg [see No. 5638/YB.XII] und M. Aschkewitz über Westpreussen [see No. 6260/YB.XIII.]. [In]: 'Zeitschrift für Ostforschung.' XIX. Jg. Marburg, 1970. Pp. 102-105.

8440. FRANKFURT/MAIN. ARNSBERG, PAUL: *Bilder aus dem jüdischen Leben im alten Frankfurt.* Frankfurt am Main: Verlag Waldemar Krämer, 1970. 272 pp., ports. illus.

8441. REINHARZ, J.: *The Lehrhaus in Frankfurt a.M.* A Renaissance in Jewish Adult Education. [In]: The Yavneh Review. Vol. 7. New York, 1969. Pp. 7-29.

8442. HALLE. KISCH, GUIDO: *Rechts- und Sozialgeschichte der Juden in Halle 1686-1730.* Berlin: Verlag Walter de Gruyter, 1970. ix, 244 pp., facsim., bibl. (pp. 213-220). (Veröffentlichungen der Historischen Kommission zu Berlin beim Friedrich-Meinecke-Institut der Freien Universität Berlin. Bd. 32.)

8443. HAMBURG. Brilling, Bernhard: *Aus der rabbinischen Tätigkeit des Rabbiners Jonathan Eibenschütz.* [In]: 'Udim', Zeitschrift der Rabbinerkonferenz in der Bundesrepublik Deutschland. Jg. I, H.1. Frankfurt a.M., 1970. Pp. 27-32.

8444. HESSE. Goldmann, S.: *Streiflichter zur Geschichte der Juden in Hessen. I. Friedberg.* [In]: 'Zeitschrift für die Geschichte der Juden'. Nr. 2/3, 1970. Pp. 89-93. [See No. 8420.]

8445. HORNBURG b. HALBERSTADT. Schulze, Hans: *Juden in Hornburg.* [In]: 'Wolfenbütteler Zeitung'. 18., 25. April, 1. Mai. Wolfenbüttel, 1970.

8446. ICHENHAUSEN (BAVARIA). Ganzenmüller, Eugen: *Ichenhausen: Vom Dorf zum Markt zur Stadt.* Im Auftrag der Stadt hrsg. Ichenhausen, 1970. ports., illus. [Incl. the history of the once flourishing Jewish community.]

8447. LANDAU/PALATINATE. Hess, Hans: *Die Landauer Judengemeinde. Ein Abriss ihrer Geschichte.* Hrsg. von der Stadtverwaltung — Stadtarchiv. Landau/Pfalz, 1969. 87 pp., ports., illus. facsim.

8448. LAUPHEIM. Schenk, G.: *Die Juden in Laupheim.* [In]: 'Rosch Haschana 5731/1970'. Hrsg.: Die Israelitische Religionsgemeinschaft Württembergs. Sept. Stuttgart, 1970. Pp. 24-32, illus.

8449. Lowenthal, E. G.: *In the Shadow of Doom.* Post-War Publications on Jewish Communal History in Germany (II). [In]: LBI Year Book XV. London, 1970. Pp. 223-242. [For part I see No. 5600/YB. XII.]

8450. LÜBECK. Brilling, Bernhard: *Zur Geschichte der Juden in Lübeck und Moisling.* Bemerkungen zum Buche von D.A. Winter: Geschichte der jüdischen Gemeinde in Moisling/Lübeck. [In]: 'Zeitschrift des Vereins für Lübeckische Geschichte und Altertumskunde'. Bd. 49, 1969. Pp. 139-145. [See No. 6929/YB.XIV.]

8451. MUNICH. Schwarz, S.: *Streiflichter auf die Frühzeit der Judenemanzipation in München.* [In]: Israel-Forum. 12. Jg., Nr. 5. Okt. Rothenburg ob der Tauber, 1970. Pp. 31-38.

8452. OSNABRÜCK. Asaria, Zwi: *Zur Geschichte der Juden in Osnabrück und Umgebung.* Festschrift zur Weihe der Synagoge und des Jüdischen Kulturzentrums in Osnabrück, 15. Siwan 5729— 1. Juni 1969. Hrsg. von der Stadt Osnabrück, 1969. 60 pp., ports., illus., facsims., biogr. notes, bibl. [6 essays.]

8453. POMERANIA. Keněž, Csaba: *Geschichte des Judentums in Pommern.* [In]: 'Pommern'. Nr. 8. [Würzburg: Holzner Verlag?], 1970. Pp. 8-17.

8454. PRUSSIA. Feuchtwanger, E. J.: *Prussia: Myth and Reality.* London: Oswald Wolff, 1970. 262 pp. [Incl.: The position of the Jews in Prussia.]

8455. Stern, Selma: *Der preussische Staat und die Juden.* Dritter Teil: Die Zeit Friedrichs des Grossen. Erste Abtlg.: Darstellung. Zweite Abtlg.: Akten (in 2 Halbbdn.) Tübingen: J. C. B. Mohr (Paul Siebeck), 1971. xv, 426 pp.,; v, 814 pp.; v, pp. 815-1615. (Schriftenreihe wissenschaftlicher Abhandlungen des Leo Baeck Instituts, 24/1 und 24/2, 1-2.) [For parts I and II see No. 3030/YB.VIII.]

8456. REGENSBURG. Hable, Guido: *Juden.* [Chap. in]: Geschichte Regensburgs. Eine Übersicht nach Sachgebieten. Unter Mitarbeit von W. Sterl. Regensburg: Mittelbayerische Druckerei- und Verlags-Gesellschaft, 1970. 269 pp. (Studien und Quellen zur Geschichte Regensburgs, Bd. 1).

8457. SIEGERLAND. Thiemann, Walter, ed.: *Von den Juden im Siegerland.* 2., wenig veränderte Aufl. Siegen: Verlag der Gesellschaft für christlich-jüdische Zusammenarbeit, 1970. 57 pp., ports., illus., tabs., plan, facsims., bibl. [1st ed. 1968. See No. 6939/YB.XIV.]

8458. SILESIA. Brilling, Bernhard: *Mittelalterliche jüdische Grabsteine aus Schlesien (Breslau-Brieg).* [And]: *Friedrich der Grosse und der Waad Arba Arazoth.* Ein Kapitel aus der Geschichte der Juden in Breslau im 18. Jahrhundert. [In]: Theokratia. Pp. 88-96, illus.; pp. 97-143, bibl. (pp. 142-143). [See No. 8500.]

8459. Hupka, Herbert, ed.: *Grosse Deutsche aus Schlesien.* München: Gräfe und Unzer Verlag, 1970. 344 pp., ports., illus. [Incl. Ferdinand Lassalle, Paul Ehrlich, Fritz Haber, Edith Stein, Ludwig Meidner.]

8460. SWABIA/WÜRTTEMBERG. Veitshans, Helmut: *Die Judensiedlungen der schwäbischen Reichsstädte und der württembergischen Landstädte im Mittelalter.* [And]: *Kartographische Darstellung der Judensiedlungen* ... Stuttgart: Kohlhammer Verlag, 1970. Textteil: xii, 64 pp.; Kartenteil: v, 26 pp., maps pp. 7-26. (Arbeiten zum historischen Atlas von Südwestdeutschland, H.5, 6.)

8461. WORMS. Böcher, Otto: *Der alte Judenfriedhof in Worms.* Ein Führer durch seine Geschichte und Grabmäler. 4., neu durchges. Aufl. Worms: Stadtarchiv, 1968. 28 pp., front. illus., illus., map. [1st ed. 1958, see No. 1377/YB.IV. 3., veränderte Aufl. 1962, see No. 6261/YB.XIII.]

8462. WÜRZBURG. Schuster, David: 850 *Jahre Juden in Würzburg.* Einweihung der Synagoge Würzburg, 24. März 1970-16. Adar 5731. Würzburg, 1970. 24 pp., illus. [Also lists the names of all former Jewish communities within the district of Lower Franconia (Unterfranken).]

8463. WÜRTTEMBERG. Israelitische Religionsgemeinschaft Württemberg, ed.: *Pessach-Festschrift 5729/1969, 5730/1970.* Stuttgart, 1969/1970. 2 vols. [Incl.]: Erinnerungen von Julius Wissmann. Beiträge zur Geschichte der jüdischen Gemeinden von Schwäbisch-Gmünd, Künzelsau. [Cf. also No. 6944 and 6945/YB.XIV.] Erinnerungen an Rabbi Josef Carlebach (S. Neufeld).

8464. Israelitische Religionsgemeinschaft Württemberg, ed.: *Rosch Haschana 5730/1969, 5731/1970.* Stuttgart, 1969/70. 2 vols.

8465. Zülz *(Upper Silesia)*. Brilling, Bernhard: *Dr. Simon Fränkel aus Zülz O/S. — der erste jüdische Arzt in Jerusalem im 19. Jahrhundert.* [In]: 'Mitteilungen des Verbandes ehemaliger Breslauer und Schlesier in Israel'. Nr. 28, Sept. Tel Aviv, 1970.

8466. ZÜNDORF/PORZ. Rieger, Reinhard: *Die Zündorfer Judengemeinde.* [In]: Unser Porz. Beiträge zur Geschichte von Amt und Stadt Porz. Hrsg. vom Heimatverein Porz in Verbindung mit dem Stadtarchiv Porz. H.12. Porz, 1970. Pp. 1-50, ports. illus., facsims., tabs.

2. Austria

8467. Barkai, A[vraham]: *The Austrian Social Democrats and the Jews.* Part I-II. [In]: 'The Wiener Library Bulletin'. Vol.XXIV, No. 1-2, New Series No. 18-19. London, 1970. Pp. 32-40, bibl.; pp. 16-21, bibl.

8468. Fraenkel, Josef, ed.: *The Jews of Austria.* Essays on their Life, History and Destruction. 2nd, rev. ed. London: Vallentine, Mitchell, 1970. xv, 585 pp., cover ports., bibl. (pp. 547-566. [30 essays in English and 6 in German. For 1st ed. see No. 6262/YB.XIII.]

8468a. Grossberg, Mimi: *Österreichs literarische Emigration in den Vereinigten Staaten 1938.* Wien, Frankfurt a.M.: Europa Verlag, 1970. 67 pp. (Monographien zur Zeitgeschichte.)

8469. Veiter, Theodor: *Das Recht der Volksgruppen und Sprachminderheiten in Österreich.* Mit einer ethnosoziologischen Grundlegung und einem Anhang (Materialien). Wien-Stuttgart: Wilhelm Braumüller, 1970. xxv, 890 pp., bibl. (pp. 813-859). [II. Teil: Die Volksgruppen und Sprachminderheiten in der Republik Österreich. Die Juden (pp. 199-215).]

8470. Zuckerkandl, Bertha: *Österreich intim.* Erinnerungen 1892-1942. Hrsg. von Reinhard Federmann. Frankfurt a.M./Berlin: Verlag Ullstein, Propyläen, 1970. 228 pp., cover ports., ports., illus., facsims. [A picture of old Vienna at the turn of the century. — Bertha Zuckerkandl née Szeps (1862-1945) was the daughter of the editor of 'Neues Wiener Tagblatt'.]

8471. BURGENLAND. Gold, Hugo, ed.: *Gedenkbuch der untergegangenen Judengemeinden des Burgenlandes.* Tel Aviv: Olamenu, 1970. 148 pp., ports., illus., maps, facsims., bibl. (pp. 147-148).

8472. GRAZ. Salzer-Eibenstein, Gerd W.: *Die räumliche Lage der Grazer Judensiedlung im Mittelalter.* [In]: Historisches Jahrbuch der Stadt Graz. Bd. 3. 1970. Pp. 35-42.

3. Czechoslovakia

8473. BOHEMIA. Demetz, Hanna: *Ein Haus in Böhmen.* Roman. Berlin: Ullstein Verlag, 1970. 208 pp. [The autobiographical story of a 'Mischling'.]

8474. *'Judaica Bohemiae'.* Vol. V, No. 2. Praha: Státni Židovské Muzeum, 1969. [Incl. Die Rabbiner der Altneuschul (O. Muneles, pp. 92-107). Die hebräische Literatur auf dem Boden der ČSSR, pp. 108-139. Der Begriff 'erlerntes Handwerk' in den Prager Judenprivilegien von 1627 und 1648 (B. Brilling, pp. 140-143). Aus der Handschriftensammlung des Staatl. Jüd. Museums in Prag (illuminierte Handschriften des 18. Jahrhunderts (V. Sadek, pp. 144-151).]

8475. FLEISCHMANN, GISI. Neumann, Yirmeyahu Oscar: *Gisi Fleischmann.* The Story of a Heroic Woman. Transl. from the German and supplemented by Karen Gershon. Publ. by the World Wizo Dept. of Organisation and Education. Tel Aviv, 1970. 35 pp., cover port. [?-1944 Auschwitz.]

8476. GOLDSTÜCKER, EDUARD. GOLDSTÜCKER, EDUARD: *Dankrede bei der Übernahme des Preises für Germanistik im Ausland 1969.* [In]: Jahrbuch 1969. Hrsg.: Deutsche Akademie für Sprache und Dichtung Darmstadt. Heidelberg: Verlag Lambert Schneider, 1970. Pp. 63-67.

8477. *Kunstschätze.* Staatl. Jüd. Museum Prag. Ausstellung, veranstaltet von der Österreichischen Kulturvereinigung, 24. März bis 28. Juni 1970. Wien, Hofburg Museum für Völkerkunde. Katalogtext: Josef Hrasky. Wien: Österr. Kulturvereinigung, 1970. 88 pp., 32 pp. illus.

8478. PRAGUE. BENDA, VILÉM: *Die Prager jüdischen Sehenswürdigkeiten.* Übertragung aus dem Tschechischen: Bedřich Král. Prag: Olympia Verlag, 1968. 81 pp., illus. (Miniinformator-Reihe.)

8479. SCHMOLKA, MARIE. ENGEL, NELLY: *In Memoriam Marie Schmolka.* Publ. by the World Wizo Department of Organisation and Education. Tel Aviv, 1970. 36 pp., front. illus., port. (Wizo's Little Reference Library, No. 4.) [First issued in 1944 by Wizo and the Marie Schmolka Group of Women Zionists from Czechoslovakia, London. Contributors incl.: Jan Masaryk, Rebecca D. Sieff, Frederick Thieberger, Felix Weltsch, Max Brod, Irma Polák. Marie Schmolka 1884-1940.]

8480. SLÁNSKÝ, RUDOLF. LONDON, ARTUR: *Ich gestehe.* Der Prozess um Rudolf Slánský. Hamburg: Hoffmann und Campe Verlag, 1970. 463 pp. [Cf. No. 7671/YB.XV.]

8481. STEINER, HANNAH. *Hannah Steiner.* Publ. by the World Wizo Dep. of Organisation and Education. [Tel Aviv, n.d.]. 3 pp. [typed.] [The last chairman of the CSR Wizo Federation, 1894-1944 Auschwitz).]

8482. URZIDIL, JOHANNES. URZIDIL, JOHANNES: *Die erbeuteten Frauen.* 7 dramatische Geschichten. München: Deutscher Taschenbuch-Verlag, 1970. 170 pp. (Lizenz des Artemis-Verl., Zürich). [Johannes Urzidil (1895-1970). Obituaries by Hilde Spiel [in]: Börsenblatt für den deutschen Buchhandel, 13. Nov., Frankfurt a.M. 1970. and 'F.A.Z.', 4. Nov. 1970. Peter Stadelmayer [in]: 'Aufbau', Febr. 5, New York, 1970. Robert Weltsch [in]: LBI Year Book XV and LBI News, Fall, New York 1970, port. [Also in]: 'NZZ', 6. Nov., Zürich, 1970, and in many other papers.]

4. Hungary

8483. BRAHAM, RANDOLPH L., ed.: *Hungarian Jewish Studies II.* New York: World Federation of Hungarian Jews, 1969. xiv, 300 pp. [Studies in the history and sociology of Jews in Hungary.]

8484. KATZBURG, NATHANIEL: *Antishemiut b'Hungaria, 1867-1914.* Tel Aviv: Bar Ilan University and Dvir Publishing House, 1969. 294 pp. [In Hebrew.] [Cf. B. Vago: *The Roots of Hungarian Antisemitism.* A New Standard Work by Katzburg. [In]: The Wiener Library Bulletin. Vol. XXIV, No. 2, New Series No. 19. London, 1970. Pp. 27-30.]

8485. SCHEIBER, SANDOR (AEXANDER): *Evkönyv.* Budapest: Magyar Izraelitak Orszagos Kapviselete, 1970. 267 pp. [An annual publ. by the Central Council of Hungarian Jewry containing articles on Hungarian-Jewish history.]

8486. SCHEIBER, ALEXANDER: *Monumenta Hungariae Judaica (1414-1748).* Ed. and publ. with the collaboration of J. Hazi, J. Pataki and J. Zsoldos. Nr. 12. Budapest: Landesvereinigung ungarischer Juden, 1969. 547 pp., 4 pp. facsims.

5. Switzerland

8487. LOWENTHAL, E. G.: *Im Spiegel des Leo-Baeck-Institut-Katalogs.* Neuere Geschichte der Juden in der Schweiz. [In]: 'Das Neue Israel'. 23. Jg., H.5, Nov. Zürich, 1970. Pp. 367-369.

8488. BASLE. KISCH, GUIDO: *Historiographie der Juden in Basel.* [In]: Forschung am Judentum. Pp. 77-90. [See No. 8657.]

8489. BIEL. SILBERSTEIN, A[RON]: *Juden in Biel.* [And]: *Ein Pionier der zionistischen Bewegung von Biel.* Dr. Camille Levy (1869-1953). [In]: 'Israelitisches Wochenblatt'. 70. Jg., 1. Mai. Zürich, 1970. Pp. 17-19, illus.; pp. 21-23, facsim. of a letter by Chaim Weizmann. [Rabbi Silberstein died in 1970 aged 65.]

C. German Jews in Various Countries

8490. ANNENBERG, WALTER. FONZI, GAETO: *Annenberg*. A Biography of Power. New York: Weybright & Talley, 1970. 256 pp. [The life of the publisher and philanthropist, at present US Ambassador in London, and of his father, the late Moses Annenberg, born 1865 in East Prussia.]

8491. BELLER, JACOB: *Jews in Latin America*. New York: Jonathan David Publishers, 1969. xii, 303 pp.

8492. CUNNINGHAM, WILLIAM: *Alien Immigrants to England*. London: Frank Cass, 1969. 286 pp. [The book, a reprint, deals partly with Jewish immigration to England.]

8493. FRANKFURTER, FELIX. BRAITERMAN, MARVIN: *Felix Frankfuter and the Paradox of Restraint*. [In]: 'Midstream'. Vol. XVI, No. 9, Nov. New York, 1970. Pp. 12-22.

8494. GLANZ, RUDOLF: *The German Jewish Mass Emigration 1820-1880*. [In]: American Jewish Archives. Vol. XXII, No. 1, Apr. Cincinnati: Hebrew Union College — Jewish Institute of Religion, 1970. Pp. 49-66, illus. [Cf. No. 7685/YB.XV.]

—— GROSSBERG, MIMI: *Österreichs literarische Emigration in den Vereinigten Staaten 1938*. [See No. 8468a.]

8495. HAGEN, VICTOR H. VON: *Der Ruf der Neuen Welt — Deutsche bauen Amerika*. Aus dem Amerikanischen von Peter de Mendelssohn und D. Dörr. München: Droemer Knaur Verlag, 1970. 368 pp., ports., illus. [Incl. the mass immigration of Jewish intellectuals after 1933.]

8496. STRAUSS, HERBERT A.: *Die kulturelle Anpassung der deutschen Juden in den Vereinigten Staaten von Amerika*. Eine Übersicht. [And]: REICHMANN, EVA G.: *Deutsche Juden in England*. [In]: 'Emuna-Horizonte'. Nr. 1, Jan. 1970. Pp. 19-36, bibl.; pp. 37-42.

8497. TAFT, R. and J. GOLDLUST: *The Current Status of Former Jewish Refugees in Melbourne*. [In]: 'The Australian and New Zealand Journal of Sociology'. Vol. 6, No. 1, Apr. Canberra, 1970. Pp. 28-48.

II. RESEARCH AND BIBLIOGRAPHY

A. Libraries and Institutes

8498. EDELMANN, RAFAEL: *Report on the Activities of the Association of Libraries of Judaica and Hebraica in Europe during the period February 1969 to June 1970*. Copenhagen, 1970. 6 pp. [Mimeog.] [The Association, formed in 1955, is preparing a Union Catalogue of Judaica and Hebraica in European libraries. A progress report by the retiring chairman.]

8499. FEINBERG, NATHAN: *The Jewish League of Nations Societies*. A chapter in the history of the struggle of the Jews for their rights. Jerusalem: The Magnes Press, The Hebrew University, 1967. 205 pp. [In Hebrew, documents quoted in their original language.]

8500. INSTITUTUM JUDAICUM DELITZSCHIANUM. *Theokratia*. Jahrbuch des Institutum Judaicum Delitzschianum. Hrsg. von Karl Heinrich Rengstorf [and others]. Jg. 1, 1967-1969. Leiden: E. J. Brill, 1970. 223 pp., illus. [Some selected contributions are listed according to subject. See Nos. 8458, 8672, 8686, 8820.]

8501. LEO BAECK INSTITUTE. *Bulletin des Leo Baeck Instituts*. Hrsg. Hans Tramer. 12. Jg., Nr. 45, 46-47. Tel Aviv: Verlag Bitaon, 1969. Pp. 1-100, 101-218, illus., facsims. [Individual contributions are listed according to subject.]

8502. *Year Book XV*. Precursors of Integration. Defiance in Destruction. An annual Collection of Essays on the history and activity of Jews in Germany during the past century. Ed.: Robert Weltsch. London: East and West Library, 1970. xviii, 326 pp., front. port. [of Selma Stern-Taeubler], ports., illus., facsims., bibl. [Individual contributions are listed according to subject.]

8503. LBI-NEW YORK. *LBI News*. Ed.: Margaret T. Muehsam. Vol. XI. Nos. 1-2. Spring. Fall. New York: Leo Baeck Institute, 1970. 10 pp., ports., illus., facsims.; 10 pp., ports. [of Erich v. Kahler and Johannes Urzidil], illus.

—— *LBI New York Bibliothek und Archiv: Katalog Band I*. [See No. 8517.]

8504. HAMBURGER, ERNEST: *Das Leo-Baeck-Institut*. [In]: 'Geschichte in Wissenschaft und Unterricht'. Zeitschrift des Verbandes der Geschichtslehrer Deutschlands. Jg. 21, H. 3, März. Stuttgart: Ernst Klett Verlag, 1970. Pp. 131-143.

8505. MOSES, SIEGFRIED: *Tätigkeit und Ziele des Leo Baeck Instituts*. Übersetzung der hebräischen Ansprache des Präsidenten des Instituts zur Eröffnung der wissenschaftlichen Tagung am 21. Juni 1970 in Jerusalem. [In]: 'MB', 26. Juni, Tel Aviv, 1970. [Also]: TRAMER, HANS: *15 Jahre Leo Baeck Institut*. Zur Tagung in Jerusalem. [And]: *Die Tagung des Leo Baeck Instituts* — Ein historisches Ereignis. [In]: 'MB', 19. Juni, 3. Juli. Tel Aviv, 1970. Port. [of S. Moses]. [See also No. 8408.]

8506. SCHABER, WILL: *Leo Baeck-Institut erhält Zunz-Briefe*. [In]: 'Aufbau', June 26. New York, 1970, port. [of Leopold Zunz]. [Also]: *Leopold Zunz Letters Recovered*. [In]: LBI News, Spring. New York, 1970, facsim.

8507. YAD VASHEM STUDIES on the European Jewish Catastrophe and Resistance. Ed. by Livia Rothkirchen. Vol. VIII. Jerusalem: Yad Vashem, 1970. 232 pp., facsims., map. [Some selected contributions are listed according to subject. See Nos. 8408, 8550, 8551, 8560, 8561, 8569, 8586.]

B. Bibliographies and Catalogues

8508. BERENDSOHN, WALTER A., ed.: *Personen- und Sachverzeichnis zu 'Deutsche Literatur der Flüchtlinge aus dem Dritten Reich'*. Zusammengestellt von Anatol Akerman, hrsg. von der Koordinationsstelle zur Erforschung der deutschsprachigen Exilliteratur. Stockholm, April 1970. 41 pp. [Typescript.]

—— BRAHAM, RANDOLPH L.: *The Eichmann Case*. A Source Book. [See No. 8535.]

8509. COLEMAN, EDWARD D.: *The Jew in English Drama together with the Jew in Western Drama*: an Essay and a check list (1968) by Edgar Rosenberg. New York: Public Library and Ktav, 1970. 50, 265 pp. [An annotated bibliography of plays from earliest times to 1938 with a survey of 500 Jewish plays by Western authors of the past four centuries.]

8510. DAN, ROBERT: *Jahrbuch für Jüdische Geschichte und Literatur*. Repertorium. [In]: 'Zeitschrift für die Geschichte der Juden'. Nr. 2/3. Tel Aviv, 1970. Pp. 133-153. [The 1st vol. was publ. 1898 by Verein für Jüdische Geschichte und Literatur in Deutschland.]

8511. DEUTSCHER KOORDINIERUNGSRAT DER GESELLSCHAFTEN FÜR CHRISTLICH-JÜDISCHE ZUSAMMENARBEIT, ed.: *Übersicht zur Lehre der Wissenschaft vom Judentum an den deutschen Universitäten und Kirchlichen Hochschulen*. Ausgabe 1, Wintersemester 1969/70; Ausgabe 2, Sommersemester 1970; Ausgabe 3, Wintersemester 1970/71. Frankfurt a.M., 1970. 7, 17, 17 pp. [3 vols.]

8512. EICHSTÄDT, VOLKMAR, comp.: *Bibliographie zur Geschichte der Judenfrage*. Bd. 1: 1750-1848. Nachdruck der Ausgabe Hamburg 1939. (Schriften des Reichsinstituts für Geschichte des Neuen Deutschlands). Westmead Farnborough Hants. (England): Gregg International Publishers Limited, 1970. 278 pp.

8513. EPPLER, ELIZABETH E.: *The Jewish View of the Jew*. A Bibliography and Catalogue of an exhibition. London: World Jewish Congress, British Section, 1970. 16 pp.

—— *Israel im deutschsprachigen Schrifttum*. Ein Verzeichnis zur Buchausstellung. [See No. 9151.]

8514. *Jewish Population Studies 1961-1968*. Ed. by Usiel Oskar Schmelz and Paul Glikson. With an Introduction by Prof. Bachi. Jerusalem: The Hebrew University, Institute of Contemporary History. London ed.: Institute of Jewish Affairs, 1970. 174 pp., bibl. (pp. 125-173).

8515. JOEL, ISSACHAR, comp.: *Index of Articles on Jewish Studies*. No. 2: 5727-1967 (with additions to 5726-1966). Issued by The Editorial Board of 'Kirjath Sepher', Bibliographical Quarterly of the Jewish National and University Library. Jerusalem: The Magnes Press, The Hebrew University, 1970. xviii, 186 pp. + 15 pp. annexed. [In Hebrew and English. For Vol. I see No. 7705/YB. XV.]

8516. KISCH, GUIDO: *Die deutsch-jüdische Bibliographie seit dem 19. Jahrhundert* [In]: 'Zeitschrift für Religions- und Geistesgeschichte'. Bd. XXII, H. 2. Köln: E. J. Brill, 1970. Pp. 143-152.

8517. *LBI New York Bibliothek und Archiv: Katalog Band I*: Deutschsprachige jüdische Gemeinden, Zeitungen, Zeitschriften, Jahrbücher, Almanache und Kalender. Unveröffentlichte Memoiren und Erinnerungsschriften. Hrsg. von Max Kreutzberger unter Mitarbeit von Irmgard Foerg. Tübingen: J. C. B. Mohr (Paul Siebeck), 1970. xli, 623 pp., front. illus., illus., facsims. (Schriftenreihe wissenschaftlicher Abhandlungen des Leo Baeck Instituts 22.)

8518. *(The) New Standard Jewish Encyclopedia.* Chief eds.: Cecil Roth and Geoffrey Wigoder. New, rev. ed. Jerusalem: Massada Publ. Co., 1970. 2028 cols., ports. illus., facsims.

8519. *Österreichisches biographisches Lexikon, 1815-1950.* Hrsg. von der Österr. Akademie der Wissenschaft. Unter der Leitung von Leo Santifaller, bearb. von Eva Obermayer-Marnach. Wien/Graz: Böhlau Verlag, 1970. Pp. 97-192. (Bd. 5, Lfg. 22.) [For Vol. IV see No. 5847/YB. XII.]

8520. *Post-War Publications on German Jewry.* A Selected Bibliography of Books and Articles 1969. Comp. on behalf of the Leo Baeck Institute and The Wiener Library by Bertha Cohn. [In]: LBI Year Book XV. London, 1970. Pp. 251-312.

8521. SCHLAWE, FRITZ: *Briefsammlungen des 19. Jahrhunderts.* Bibliographie der Briefausgaben und Gesamtregister der Briefschreiber und Briefempfänger 1815-1915. Stuttgart: J. B. Metzler, 1969. xvi, 1173 pp. (2 Halbbände). (Repertorien zur Deutschen Literaturgeschichte, hrsg. von Paul Raabe.)

8522. SENDREY, ALFRED: *Bibliography of Jewish Music.* New York: Kraus Reprint, 1969. xli, 404 pp. [A reprint of the 1951 Bibliography of Jewish Music from 1545 to the present.]

8523. SHUNAMI, SHLOMO, comp.: *Bibliography of Jewish Bibliographies.* Photographic reprint of 'Second Edition Enlarged' 1965 with corrections. Jerusalem: The Magnes Press, The Hebrew University, 1969. xxiv. 997, xxiii pp. [Cf. No. 5060/YB. XI.]

8524. STERN, DESIDER, comp.: *Werke von Autoren jüdischer Herkunft in deutscher Sprache.* Eine Bio-Bibliographie. 3., rev. und erw. Aufl. Wien: Selbstverlag, (Wollzeile 20), 1970. 455 pp [For 1st ed. see No. 6298/YB. XIII, 2nd ed. No. 6978/YB. XIV.]

8525. STERNFELD, WILHELM, EVA TIEDEMANN, comps.: *Deutsche Exil-Literatur 1933-1945.* Eine Bio-Bibliographie. Zweite, verbesserte und stark erweiterte Auflage. Mit einem Vorwort von Hanns W. Eppelsheimer. Heidelberg: Verlag Lambert Schneider, 1970. 606 pp. (Veröffentlichungen der Deutschen Akademie für Sprache und Dichtung Darmstadt. Bd. 29 A.) [First ed. 1962. See No. 3073/YB. VIII.]

8526. *Veröffentlichungen deutscher sozialistischer Schriftsteller in der revolutionären und demokratischen Presse 1918-1945.* Bibliographie. 2., durchgesehene Aufl. Bearb.: Edith Zenker. Berlin [East]: Aufbau Verlag, 1969, xvi, 657 pp. (Hrsg. von der Deutschen Akademie der Künste zu Berlin [East]). [1st ed. 1966.]

8527. *Verzeichnis der Judaica-Sammlung des Historischen Seminars/Abt. Neuere Geschichte der Ludwig-Maximilans-Universität.* München, 1970. 72 pp. [Typescript.]

8528. WEISSER, ALBERT: *Bibliography of Publications and other Resources on Jewish Music.* Rev. and enl. edition. Based in part on the 'Bibliography of Jewish Music' by Joseph Yasser . . . 1955. New York: National Jewish Music Council, 1969. 117 pp.

8529. ZAFREN, HERBERT C., comp.: *Jewish Reference Books: A Select List.* [In]: Jewish Book Annual. Vol. 28. New York: Jewish Book Council of America/National Jewish Welfare Board, 5731/1970-71. Pp. 56-71.

III. THE NAZI PERIOD

A. General

8530. AUSLÄNDER, CILLY, comp.: *Bibliographie des ouvrages traitant des dommages physiques dont souffrent les persécutés du Nazisme, les anciens résistants, les anciens combattants et les prisonniers de guerre, ainsi que des travaux traitant de l'activité criminelle des médecins SS.* Edition Complétée, élaborée et rédigée par Cilli Ausländer, éditée à l'occasion du Ve Congrès Medical International de la F.I.R. Septembre. Wien: Internationale Föderation der Widerstandskämpfer (F.I.R.), 1968. 168 pp. [Mimeog. bound vol.]

8531. BAEYER, WALTER VON: *Über die Auswirkungen rassischer Verfolgung und Konzentrationslagerhaft vom Standpunkt des Psychiaters.* [In]: 'Emuna-Horizonte'. Nr. 1, Jan. 1970. Pp. 65-68. [See No. 9158.]

8532. BAUMINGER, ARJE, ed.: *Roll of Honour.* Introduction by Abba Eban. Jerusalem: Yad Vashem, 1970. [Non-Jews who risked their lives in order to save Jews persecuted by the Nazis.]

8533. BERGEN-BELSEN. LANDESVERBAND DER JÜDISCHEN GEMEINDEN VON NIEDERSACHSEN, ed.: *Bergen-Belsen.* Von der Knechtschaft in die Befreiung. Denkschrift zur 25. Wiederkehr der Befreiung. Hannover: Verlag für Literatur und Zeitgeschehen, 1970. 95 pp., illus., facsims.

8534. BOYENS, ARMIN: *Kirchenkampf und Ökumene 1933-1939*. Darstellung und Dokumentation. München: Christian Kaiser Verlag, 1969. 486 pp., facsims. [Incl.: Die Judenfrage.]

8535. BRAHAM, RANDOLPH L.: *The Eichmann Case: A Source Book*. New York: World Federation of Hungarian Jews, 1969. xi, 186 pp. [A bibliography.]

8536. BROSZAT, MARTIN, ed.: *Studien zur Geschichte der Konzentrationslager*. Stuttgart: Deutsche Verlags-Anstalt, 1970. 202 pp., bibl. (Schriftenreihe der Vierteljahrshefte für Zeitgeschichte, Nr. 21.)

8537. BUCHAU AM FEDERSEE. MOHN, JOSEPH: *Der Leidensweg unter dem Hakenkreuz*. Aus der Geschichte von Stadt und Stift Buchau am Federsee. Eine im Auftrag der Stadt verfasste Gedenkschrift. Bad Buchau, 1970. 197 pp., ports. [of Albert Einstein], illus., map, family tree, bibl.

8538. CONWAY, JOHN S.: *Die nationalsozialistische Kirchenpolitik 1933-1945*. Ihre Ziele, Widersprüche und Fehlschläge. Aus dem Engl. von Carsten Nicolaisen. München: Christian Kaiser Verlag, 1969. 383 pp., facsims.

8539. DENMARK. YAHIL, LENI: *The Rescue of Danish Jewry*. Test of a Democracy. Transl. from the Hebrew by Morris Gradel. Philadelphia: The Jewish Publication Society of America, 5730/1969. xx, 536 pp., facsim., bibl. (pp. 521-530). [Hebrew ed. 1966. See No. 6322/YB. XIII.]

8540. DEUTSCHER KOORDINIERUNGSRAT DER GESELLSCHAFTEN FÜR CHRISTLICH-JÜDISCHE ZUSAMMENARBEIT, ed.: . . . *Die dem Gewissen gehorchten*. Frankfurt a.M., 1969. 68 pp., illus., map, bibl.

8541. DOBSCHINER, JOHANNA-RUTH: *Selected to Live*. Memories. London: Pickering & Inglis, 1970. 255 pp., front. port., illus., facsims. (First ed. 1968.) [The story of a Dutch Jewish girl who survived Nazi camps due to the help of Dutch Catholics, and later converted to Christianity.]

8542. ELIAV, ARIE L.: *The Voyage of the 'ULUA'*. Transl. from the Hebrew by Israel I. Taslitt. New York: Funk and Wagnalls, 1969. 191 pp., map. (A Sabra Book.) ["ULUA" was the Latin-American name of the Haganah immigrant ship "Haim Arlosoroff".]

8543. FEINGOLD, HENRY L.: *The Politics of Rescue*. The Roosevelt Administration and the Holocaust, 1938-1945. New Brunswick, N. J.: Rutgers University Press, 1970. xiii, 394 pp., bibl. (pp. 351-366). [Cf. No. 7723/YB.XV.]

8544. FRANK, ANNE. FRANK, ANNE: *Das Tagebuch*. 12. Juni 1942 - 1. Aug. 1944. Aus dem Holländischen übertragen von Anneliese Schütz. Mit einem Vorwort von Albrecht Goes. Frankfurt a.M.: Fischer-Bücherei, 1970. 200 pp., ports. illus. (Fischer-Bücherei, 77.)

8545. *Weerklank van Anne Frank*. Response to Anne Frank. Geredigeerd door Anna G. Steenmeijer in samenwerking met Otto Frank, Henri van Praag, voorzitter van de Anne Frank Stichting. Amsterdam: Uitgeverij Contact N.V., 1970. 120 pp., ports., illus., facsims., bibl. [A.F.'s diary was publ. in 1947, transl. into 40 languages, 9 million copies have been sold. This book ['Widerhall von Anne Frank'] shows the response the Diary has had. Incl. are some hitherto unpubl. short stories written by Anne, photographs, and letters received by her father, Otto Frank, from world leaders.]

8546. HALPERIN, IRVING: *Messengers from the Dead*. Literature of the Holocaust. Philadelphia: The Westminster Press, [1969]. 144 pp., bibl. (pp. 141-144).

8547. HOCHHEIMER, ALBERT: *Die Passagiere der Penelope*. Roman. Zürich/ Stuttgart: Werner Classen Verlag, 1970. 213 pp. [The adventurous flight, in 1941, of Jews from Europe who eventually reached Palestine.]

8548. HUDSON, DARILL: *Ökumene und Politik*. Aus dem Amerikanischen von Ulrich Braker. Stuttgart: W. Kohlhammer Verlag, 1970. 224 pp. [The Christian attitude towards Nazi persecution of the Jews.]

8549. HUNGARY. SANDBERG, MOSHE: *My longest year*. In the Hungarian Labour Service and in the Nazi Camps. Ed., with an historical survey by Livia Rothkirchen: Development of Anti-Semitism and Persecution of the Jews in Hungary, 1920-1945. Transl. from the Hebrew by S.C. Hyman. Jerusalem: Yad Vashem, 1968. xxxiv, 114 pp., illus., maps, bibl. [Since 1971 the author has been President of the State Bank of Israel.]

8550. SZENES, KATHERINE: *On the Threshold of Liberation.* Reminiscences. [In]: Yad Vashem Studies. Vol. VIII. Jerusalem, 1970. Pp. 107-126. [See No. 8507].

8551. VAGO, BÉLA: *Budapest Jewry in the Summer of 1944.* Otto Komoly's Diaries. [In]: Yad Vashem Studies. Vol. VIII. Jerusalem, 1970. Pp. 81-105, facsims. [See No. 8507.]

8552. KAHN, HENRY F.: *Concentration Camp and Ghetto Mail System under the Nazi Regime.* Photos by Arnold Engel. [In]: 'Postal History Journal'. Official Organ of the Postal History Society of the Americas. Vol. X, No. 1 (15). New York, 1966. Pp. 3-30, illus., facsims., maps, bibl.

8553. KANTOROWICZ, ALFRED: *The Story of the Library of the Burned Books.* [In]: 'The Wiener Library Bulletin'. Vol. XXIV, No. 4. New Series No. 21. London, 1970/71. Pp. 36-41. [La Bibliothèque Allemande des Livres Brulés — or The German Freedom Library, was founded in Paris on 10th May 1934, the first anniversary of the Nazi book burning.]

8554. KREHBIEL-DARMSTÄDTER, MARIA: *Briefe aus Gurs und Limonest 1940-1943.* Ausgewählt, erläutert und hrsg. von Walter Schmitthenner. Heidelberg: Verlag Lambert Schneider, 1970. 383 pp., front. port., list of names pp. 366-383. [The author, born 1892, converted to Christianity 1921, became a social worker, was deported from Mannheim 1940, sent to Auschwitz 1943.]

8555. *Living with the Knowledge of the Holocaust 1945-1970.* [In]: 'Midstream'. Vol. XVI, No. 6, June/July. New York, 1970. Pp. 3-26. [Cont.: Living with the Holocaust (Alfred Kazin). A Generation Later (Arthur Hertzberg). Fiction of the Holocaust (Ernst Pawel).]

8556. MANNING, OLIVIA: *The Tragedy of the Struma — the Ship that never had a Chance.* [In]: 'The Observer Magazine'. 1st March, London, 1970. Pp. 8-19, ports. illus.

8557. NORDEN, GÜNTHER VAN: *Nationalsozialistische Judenverfolgung.* Didaktische und methodische Überlegungen zu einem Unterrichtsproblem. [In]: 'Geschichte in Wissenschaft und Unterricht'. Zeitschrift des Verbandes der Geschichtslehrer Deutschlands. Hrsg.: K. D. Erdmann und F. Messerschmid. Jg. 21, H. 11, Nov. Stuttgart: Ernst Klett Verlag, 1970. Pp. 660-671. [An extract from 'Das Dritte Reich im Unterricht', Frankfurt a.M.: Hirschgraben Verlag.]

8558. ROBINSON, JACOB: *Psychoanalysis in a Vacuum.* Bruno Bettelheim and the Holocaust. New York: Yad Vashem-YIVO Documentary Projects, 1970. 36 pp. [With special reference to Bettelheim's work: 'The Informed Heart'. The Human Condition in Modern Mass Society. London: Thames and Hudson, 1961. German ed.: Aufstand gegen die Masse. Die Chance des Individuums in der modernen Gesellschaft. München: Szczesny, 1964.]

8559. ROBINSON, JACOB and YEHUDA BAUER, eds.: *Guide to Unpublished Materials of the Holocaust Period.* Vol. I. Jerusalem: Hebrew University — Institute of Contemporary Jewry, 1970. 245 pp.

8560. ROTHKIRCHEN, LIVIA: *The 'Final Solution' in its Last Stages.* [In]: Yad Vashem Studies. Vol. VIII. Jerusalem 1970. Pp. 7-29. [See No. 8507.]

8561. ROTHKIRCHEN, LIVIA, ed.: *Rescue Efforts with the Assistance of International Organizations.* Documents from the Archives of Dr. A. Silberschein. [In]: Yad Vashem Studies. Vol. VIII. Jerusalem, 1970. Pp. 69-80, facsims. [See No. 8507.]

8562. ROUMANIA. FISHER, JULIUS S.: *Transnistria: The Forgotten Cemetery.* New York: Thomas Yoseloff, 1969. 161 pp., bibl. (pp. 154-156).

8563. SCHOEPS, HANS-JOACHIM: *Preussen und Deutschland.* Wandlungen seit 1763. 2., veränderte Aufl. Berlin: Haude & Spener, 1970. 306 pp. [Pp. 217-223: Die Judenverfolgung.]

8564. SLOVAKIA. JELINEK, YESHAYAHU: *The 'Final Solution' — The Slovak Version.* [In]: 'East European Quarterly'. Vol. IV, No. 4. Boulder, Colorado: University of Colorado, 1970. Pp. 431-441.

8565. STEINERT, MARLIS G.: *Hitlers Krieg und die Deutschen.* Düsseldorf: Econ Verlag, 1970. 646 pp., bibl.

8566. SWITZERLAND. BONJOUR, EDGAR CONRAD: *Schweizerische Flüchtlingspolitik 1943-1945.* Basel: Verlag Helbing & Lichtenhahn, 1970, illus.

8567. HÄSLER, ALFRED A.: *The Lifeboat is Full.* Switzerland and the Refugees, 1933-1945. Transl. from the German by Charles L. Markmann. New York: Funk & Wagnalls, 1969. 366 pp., ports., illus., facsims. [For German original see No. 6339/YB. XIII.]

8568. SZAJKOWSKI, ZOSA: *A Note on the American-Jewish Struggle against Nazism and Communism in the 1930's.* (Pp. 272-289.) *American Editorial Response to the Rise of Adolf Hitler.* A Preliminary Consideration (M.K. Norden, pp. 290-301). *The Berlin Riots of 1935 and their Repercussions in America* (M. Gottlieb, pp. 302-328). [In]: American Jewish Historical Quarterly. Vol. 59, No. 3, March. Philadelphia, 1970. Pp. 272-328.

8569. WALK, JOSEPH: *The Diary of Günther Marcuse — the Last Days of the Gross-Breesen Training Centre.* [In]: Yad Vashem Studies. Vol. VIII. Jerusalem, 1970. Pp. 159-181, facsims., map. (See No. 8507. Cf. also No. 5068/YB. XI.]

8570. WIESENTHAL, SIMON: *Die Sonnenblume.* Von Schuld und Vergebung. Übertragung der fremdsprachigen Texte ins Deutsche von Eva Gärtner. Hamburg: Hoffmann und Campe Verlag, 1970. 247 pp. [The author, in doubt whether his attitude was the right one, asked 43 well known personalities whether he should have acceded to a dying young Nazi criminal's request for forgiveness. — For English ed. see No. 7749/YB. XV.]

B. Jewish Resistance

8571. DWORZECKI, MARK: *Historia de la Resistencia Antinazi Judía (1933-1945).* Problemática y Metodología. Traducido del francés por Roberto A. Gombert. Buenos Aires: Ejecutivo Sudamericano del Congreso Judío Mundial, 1970. 48 pp., illus., facsims. (Biblioteca Popular Judía, 38). [For French original see No. 5712/YB. XII.]

8572. ESCHWEGE, HELMUT: *Resistance of German Jews against the Nazi Regime.* [In]: LBI Year Book XV. London, 1970. Pp. 143-180, ports., illus., facsims.

8573. FROMMHOLD, ERHARD: *Kunst im Widerstand.* (Malerei, Graphik, Plastik 1922-1945). Frankfurt a.M.: Röderberg Verlag, 1970. 663 illus.

8574. INSTITUT FÜR MARXISMUS-LENINISMUS BEIM ZENTRALKOMITEE DER SED., ed.: *Deutsche Widerstandskämpfer 1933-1945.* Biographien und Briefe. Bd. 1-2. Berlin [East]: Dietz Verlag, 1970. 659, 582 pp., ports., facsims. [2 vols.] [Incl. many Jewish resistance fighters.]

8575. JAHNKE, KARL-HEINZ: *Entscheidungen.* Jugend im Widerstand 1933-1945. Frankfurt a.M.: Röderberg Verlag, 1970. 252 pp., ports. illus., facsims., bibl. (pp. 249-252).

8576. *Jewish Resistance During the Holocaust.* With an Introduction by Arieh Tartakower. Proceedings of the Conference on Manifestations of Jewish Resistance, Jerusalem, 7-11 April 1968. Jerusalem: Yad Vashem, 1970. 463 pp., illus. [In Hebrew.]

8577. LATOUR, ANNY: *La Résistance juive en France. (1940-1944).* Paris: Edition Stock, 1970. 301 pp., ports., illus., facsims., maps, bibl. (pp. 271-282), chronology pp. 283-286. (Témoins de notre temps.)

8578. *Literatur und Widerstand.* Anthologie Europäischer Poesie und Prosa. Hrsg. von der Internationalen Föderation der Widerstandskämpfer (FIR). Frankfurt a.M.: Röderberg-Verlag, 1969. 799 pp., front. facsims., biographies of authors pp. 741-783, bibl. (pp. 784-792).

8579. MAOZ, ELI[Y]AHU [i.e. Ernst Mosbacher]: *A Jewish Underground in Germany.* Transl. from the Hebrew. Jerusalem: Org. Dept., World Zionist Organisation, March 1965. 11 pp., notes. [Typescript.] [The article was contained in a 'Lecturers Kit' for the Anniversary of the Ghetto Revolts.]

8580. PIKARSKI, MARGOT: *Über die führende Rolle der Parteiorganisation der KPD in der antifaschistischen Widerstandsgruppe Herbert Baum Berlin 1939 bis 1942.* [In]: Beiträge zur Geschichte der deutschen Arbeiterbewegung. Jg. 8. Berlin [East]: Dietz Verlag, 1966. Pp. 867-881.

8581. SCHWERSENZ, JIZCHAK und EDITH WOLFF: *Jüdische Jugend im Untergrund.* Eine zionistische Gruppe in Deutschland während des zweiten Weltkrieges. Mit einer historischen Einführung von Shaul Esh. (Deutsche, von Heinz Gerling hergestellte Fassung mit Anmerkungen von Shaul Esh.) [In]: Bulletin des Leo Baeck Instituts. 12. Jg., Nr. 45. Tel Aviv: Verlag Bitaon, 1969. 100 pp., illus., facsims. [For the unabridged Hebrew original see No. 7759/YB. XV.]

8582. STEINBERG, LUCIEN: *Der Anteil der Juden am Widerstand in Deutschland.* [In]: Stand und Problematik der Erforschung des Widerstandes gegen den Nationalsozialismus. Hrsg.: Forschungsinstitut der Friedrich-Ebert-Stiftung. Bad Godesberg, 1965. Pp. 113-143, bibl. [Mimeog.] (Studien und Berichte aus dem Forschungsinstitut der Friedrich-Ebert-Stiftung.)

8583. STEINBERG, LUCIEN: *La Révolte des Justes*. Les Juifs contre Hitler 1933-1945. Paris: Fayard, 1970. 605 pp., bibl. (pp. 593-602). (Grands Documents Contemporains. Collection Dirigée par Constantin Melnik). [Incl. Part II: Au Coeur de l'Empire Nazi. Les Résistants Juifs dans le IIIᵉ Reich. Le Combat de Herbert Baum. L'Union pour la Paix et la Liberté. L'Emeute des Détenus Juifs de Sachsenhausen, pp. 39-95.]

IV. POST WAR

A. General

8584. ARETZ, EMIL: *Hexen-Einmal-Eins einer Lüge*. 2. Aufl. Pähl: Franz von Bebenburg Verlag, 1970. 384 pp., bibl. (pp. 365-369). [Author contests the 'political lie' of 6 million Jewish victims.]

8585. AUSTRIA. WILDER-OKLADEK, F.: *The Return Movement of Jews to Austria after the Second World War*. With special consideration of the return from Israel. The Hague: Martinus Nijhoff, 1969. x, 130 pp., tabs., bibl. (pp. 103-106). (Publications of the Research Group for European Migration Problems, XVI.)

8586. BAVARIA. BAUER, YEHUDA: *The Initial Organization of the Holocaust Survivors in Bavaria*. [In]: Yad Vashem Studies. Vol. VIII. Jerusalem, 1970. Pp. 127-157. [See No. 8507, cf. also No. 8693.]

8587. BUND JÜDISCHER VERVOLGTER DES NAZIREGIMES, ed.: *Angriff auf das Dokumentationszentrum des B.J.V.N. und Simon Wiesenthal und die Reaktion aus aller Welt*. Wien, 1970. 64 pp.

8588. BURG, J. G. [i.e. Josef Ginsburg]: *NS-Verbrechen Prozesse des schlechten Gewissens*. Von Deutschen gegen Deutsche unter Zions Regie geführt. München: G. Fischer — Buchversand Otto Nagl, 1968. 192 pp. (Eine Reihe der 'Auslese'- Bibliothek.) [The Jewish author, a contributor to 'Deutsche National- und Soldatenzeitung', wants the prosecution of Nazi criminals discontinued and attacks the State of Israel.]

8589. BURG, J. G.: *Sündenböcke*. Grossangriffe des Zionismus auf Papst Pius XII. und auf die deutschen Regierungen. 2. Aufl. München: G. Fischer Verlag, 1968. 334 pp., illus.

8590. CZECHOSLOVAKIA. *Informationsbulletin*. Hrsg.: Rat der jüdischen Gemeinden in der Tschechoslowakischen Sozialistischen Republik und vom Zentralverband der jüdischen Gemeinden in der Slowakischen Sozialistischen Republik. Redakteur: Rudolf Iltis. Nr. 1-4. Prag: Kirchenzentral-Verlag, 1970. [Nr. 3 incl.: Gottesdienst am 24. Mai 1970 anlässlich des Siebenhundertjahr-Jubiläums der Altneusynagoge zu Prag. (Pp. 1-17.) — Rabbi Prof. Feder, who lost his 9 sons in Theresienstadt, died in March 1971 in Prague aged 95.]

8591. KOLÁR, FRANTIŠEK J.: *Sionismus A Antisemitismus*. [Zionism and Antisemitism]. Praha: Svoboda, 1970. 88 pp. (Dialogy, 12.) [In Czech.]

8592. OSCHLIES, WOLF: *'Antizionismus' in der Tschechoslowakei*. Teil I-III. [In]: 'Berichte' des Bundesinstituts für Ostwissenschaftliche und Internationale Studien. Nr. 31, 41, 50, Juni-Aug., Köln, 1970, 18, 40, 30 pp. [3 vols., mimeog.]

8593. OSCHLIES, WOLF: *Phases and Faces of Czech Antisemitism*. [In]: 'The Wiener Library Bulletin'. Vol. XXIV, No. 4, New Series No. 21. London, 1970/71. Pp. 22-28.

8594. *ŽIDOVSKÁ ROČENKA 5731/1970-1971* [Jewish Year Book]. Prag: Rat der Jüdischen Kultusgemeinden, 1970. 141 pp.

8595. DEUTSCH, HANS. EMMENEGGER, KURT: *Der Fall Deutsch*. Tatsachen zu einem Justizskandal. New Haven (Conn.)/Zürich: '1789 Editions', 1970. 335 pp., ports.

8596. ECKERT, WILLEHAD PAUL: *Juden in Deutschland — deutsche Juden in der Welt. Jüdisch-deutsche Transmigration* (Harry Maor). *Jüdische Jugend in Deutschland* (Walter W. Jacob Oppenheimer). *Judentum ohne Heimat*. Aus der Sicht eines jüdischen Jugendlichen in Deutschland (Georg Heuberger). [In.]: 'Emuna-Horizonte'. Nr. 1, Jan. 1970. Pp. 1-18. [See No. 9158.]

8597. ENGELMANN, BERNT: *Deutschland ohne Juden*. Eine Bilanz. München: Verlag Franz Schneekluth, 1970. 524 pp., ports., illus., facsims., list of Jewish physicians pp. 471-496, bibl. (pp. 501-507).

8598. Fejtö, François: *Judentum und Kommunismus*. Antisemitismus in Osteuropa. Deutsche Übersetzung [from the French] von Gertraud Kanda und Elisabeth Eberan. Wien: Europa Verlag, 1967. 263 pp. (Europäische Perspektiven.]

8599. Fürstenau, Justus: *Entnazifizierung*. Ein Kapitel deutscher Nachkriegspolitik. Neuwied: Luchterhand Verlag, 1969. xii, 274 pp. (Politica, Bd. 40). (Diss. Frankfurt a.M.)

8600. GERMAN DEMOCRATIC REPUBLIC. '*Nachrichtenblatt*' der Jüdischen Gemeinde von Gross-Berlin und des Verbandes der Jüdischen Gemeinden in der Deutschen Demokratischen Republik, März u. Juni. Berlin-Dresden, 1970. 26 pp., illus., 15 pp., illus. [Incl. Die Isr. Religionsgemeinde zu Dresden (Max Lesser). History up to 1939 when the community ceased to exist.] [Heinz Schenk, chairman of the Berlin Jewish community, died in June 1971. Obituary in: 'AJR Information', London, July 1971 by Werner Rosenstock.]

8601. Häsler, Alfred A., ed.: *Leben mit dem Hass*. 21 Gespräche. Reinbek b. Hamburg: Rowohlt Verlag, 1969. 187 pp. [Incl. Ernst Bloch, David Ben-Gurion, Herbert Marcuse.]

8602. Hellendall, F.: *Nazi Crime before German Courts*. The Immediate Post-War Era. [In]: 'The Wiener Library Bulletin'. Vol. XXIV, No. 3. New Series No. 20. London 1970. Pp. 14-20.

8603. Karger-Karin, Mendel, ed.: *Israel und Wir*. Keren Hayessod-Jahrbuch der jüdischen Gemeinschaft in Deutschland 1967-1970/5727-5730. Frankfurt A.M.: Keren Hayessod Verlag, 1970. 540 pp., ports., illus., tabs. [Incl. Obituaries of Rabbi I.E. Lichtigfeld (1894-1967) by Israel Goldstein, Manfred Rosenthal (1904-1966) by Hans Tramer.]

8604. Littmann, Wolf: *Juden in Deutschland*. Pp. 54-80 in: Minderheiten in der Bundesrepublik. Hrsg. von Bernhard Doerdelmann. München: Delp Verlag, 1969. 254 pp.

8605. *Reports on Jewish Communities in Central Europe: West Germany* (Hans Lamm, pp. 443-459). *Czechoslovakia*, pp. 473-477. *Hungary* (Leon Shapiro, pp. 478-481). *Romania* (Jerry Goodman, pp. 482-490) [In]: American Jewish Year Book 1970. Vol. 71. New York: The American Jewish Committee, Philadelphia: The Jewish Publication Society of America, 1970. xi, 686 pp., tabs.

8606. Sittig, Gerhard: *Das Bild der Juden bei Schulabgängern des 9. Schuljahres*. H. 3 der Schriftenreihe 'protokoll' des Seminars für Politische Bildung und Didaktik der Geschichte der Pädagogischen Hochschule Rheinland, Abt. Bonn, 1970. 64 pp.

B. Restitution

8607. Balabkins, Nicholas: *West German-Israel Negotiations of 1952*. A Case Study in 'Wiedergutmachung' Diplomacy. [In]: Wissenschaft, Wirtschaft und Technik. Studien. Wilhelm Treue zum 60. Geburtstag. Hrsg. von Karl-Heinz Manegold. München: Verlag F. Bruckmann, 1969. Pp. 98-116.

8608. Bentwich, Norman: *The United Restitution Organisation, 1948-1968*. London: Vallentine, Mitchell, 1969. 47 pp.

8609. [Bentwich, Norman] *In Memory of Norman Bentwich, Feb. 28, 1883-April 8, 1971*. [Obituaries in]: 'The Times', April 10, London 1971; 'Jewish Chronicle, Apr. 23, port.; 'AJR Information', No. 5, May, London [by] Werner Rosenstock, Eva G. Reichmann; 'Allgemeine', 23. April, Düsseldorf, [by] E. G. Lowenthal; 'MB', 23. April, Tel Aviv, [by] Hans Tramer.

8610. *Bundesentschädigungsgesetz (BEG-Schlussgesetz) und Rechtsverordnungen*. Kommentar von Walter Brunn, Richard Hebenstreit unter Mitwirkung von Heinz Klee. Schlussnachtrag 1966-1969. Berlin: Erich Schmidt Verlag, 1970. 262 pp.

8611. *Entscheidungen des Obersten Rückerstattungsgerichts für Berlin*. Bd. 21 — Bd. 27, Entscheidungen Nr. 717-996, 1965-1969. Berlin: Oberstes Rückerstattungsgericht, 1965-1969. Berlin: Oberstes Rückerstattungsgericht, 1965/69. [7 vols.]

8612. Hoog, Günter, comp.: *Völkerrecht, Staatsangehörigkeit, Entschädigung*. 21 in der Periode 1966-1969 erstattete Gutachten. Hrsg.: Forschungsstelle für Völkerrecht und ausländisches Recht der Universität Hamburg. Frankfurt a.M.: Metzner Verlag (in Kommission), 1970.

8613. Kossoy, Edward: *Deutsche Wiedergutmachung aus israelischer Sicht*. Geschichte, Auswirkung, Gesetzgebung und Rechtsprechung. Inaug. Diss. . . . Rechtswissenschaftliche Fakultät der Universität zu Köln, 1970. xvi, 369 pp., bibl. (pp. xi-xvi).

8614. Oberstes Rückerstattungsgericht, Dritter Senat: *Entscheidungen Nr. 762-784*. Veröffentlicht im Auftrage: Edward A. Marsden. Bd. XIII. Herford/Westf., 1967-1969.

V. JUDAISM

A. Jewish Learning and Scholars

8615. BEN CHORIN, SCHALOM: *Das Judentum der Gegenwart.* Freising: Kyrios-Verlag Meitingen, 1970. 38 pp. (Meitinger Kleinschriften.)

8616. BERGMAN, S. HUGO: *The Quality of Faith.* Essays on Judaism and Morality. Introduction by Mordechai Bar-On. Transl. from the Hebrew by Yehuda Hanegbi. Jerusalem: Youth and Hechalutz Department of the World Zionist Organisation, 1970. 89 pp. [Hebrew title: Hashamayim VeHaaretz, Tel Aviv: Schdemot 1969.]

8617. BERGMAN, SHMUEL HUGO: *Toldot haphilosophia h-chadaschah, mi Nicolaus Cusanus ad t'kufath ha-Haskalah.* Bd. 1. Jerusalem: Mossad Bialik, 1970. 512 pp. [Cf. Robert Weltsch: Keine Scheidewand mehr zwischen 'Jude' und Mensch. Zu Hugo Bergmans 'Geschichte der Philosophie'. [In]: 'Allgemeine', 16. Apr., Düsseldorf, 1971.]

8618. BUBER, MARTIN. BUBER, MARTIN: *Des Baal-Schem-Tov Unterweisung im Umgang mit Gott.* Köln: Verlag Jakob Hegner, 1970. 117 pp. (Hegner-Bücherei, Texte der nicht-christlichen Religionen.)

8619. BUBER, MARTIN (gemeinsam mit Franz Rosenzweig): *Biblische Gestalten aus der Schrift.* Köln: Verlag Jakob Hegner, 1970. 372 pp. [A selection from 'Die Schrift'.]

8620. BUBER, MARTIN: *The Legend of the Baal Shem.* Transl. by Maurice Friedman. New York: Schocken, 1969. 223 pp. [First publ. in German 1908.]

8621. BUBER, MARTIN: *Ten Rungs.* Hasidic Sayings. Transl. by Olga Marx. 4th printing. New York: Schocken Books, 1968. 126 pp. (Schocken paperbacks, 18.)

8622. FRIEDMAN, MAURICE: *Martin Buber and the Theatre.* New York: Funk & Wagnalls, 1969. 192 pp. [Translation of four essays on the theatre by Buber, and his play 'Elijah', with three essays by Friedman on Buber's relation to the theatre.]

8623. GRUNWALD, DETLEV: *Das dialogische Prinzip Martin Bubers.* Seine Dimensionen, sein Anspruch auf Integrität und seine Konzeption des Seins als Begegnung. Phil. Diss. Wien, 1970. v, 495 pp., bibl. (pp. 481-495). [Typed Ms.]

8624. LEWIS, H. D.: *The Elusive Self and the I Thou Relation (Buber).* [In]: Royal Institute of Philosophy Lectures. Vol. 2, 1967/68. London, 1969. Pp. 168-184.

8625. ROLLINS, E. WILLIAM and HARRY ZOHN, eds.: *Martin Buber and Albrecht Goes: Men of Dialogue.* Preface by Maurice Friedman. New York: Funk & Wagnalls, 1969. xxxi, 228 pp. [See also No. 7062/YB. XIV.]

8626. SIMON, CHARLIE MAY (HOGUE): *Martin Buber.* Wisdom in our time. The story of an outstanding Jewish thinker and humanist. New York: E. P. Dutton, 1969. 191 pp., ports., illus., bibl. (pp. 181-183).

8627. TALMON, SHMARIAHU: *Martin Bubers Wege in der Bibel.* [And]: RENDTORFF, ROLF: *Martin Bubers Bibelübersetzung.* [In]: 'Emuna-Horizonte'. Jg. V, Nr. 2, März. Frankfurt a.M., 1970. Pp. 93-95, 96-103. [See No. 9158.]

8628. VOHEL, M.: *The Concept of Responsibility in the Thought of Martin Buber.* [In]: Harvard Theological Review. Vol. 63, No. 2, April. Cambridge, Mass., 1970. Pp. 159-182.

8629. WACHINGER, LORENZ: *Der Glaubensbegriff Martin Bubers.* München: Max Hueber Verlag, 1970. 298 pp. (Beiträge zur ökumenischen Theologie, Bd. IV.)

8630. WOOD, ROBERT E.: *Martin Buber's Ontology: An Analysis of 'I and Thou'.* Evanston: Northwestern University, 1970. 139 pp.

8631. COHEN, ARTHUR A[LLEN], ed.: *Arguments and Doctrines.* A reader of Jewish thinking in the aftermath of the Holocaust. Selected with introductory essays. Philadelphia: Jewish Publication Society of America, 1970. xviii, 541 pp. [Incl.: The Jew as pariah; a hidden tradition (H. Arendt). Simone Weil, prophet out of Israel (L. Fiedler). Franz Kafka and the tree of knowledge (N. N. Glatzer). From Marxism to Judaism (W. Herberg). Uniqueness and universality of Jewish history (J. L. Talmon). God and man in modern thought (S. H. Bergman). Are we Israelis still Jews? (E. Simon). How live by Jewish law today (H. J. Schoeps)].

8632. COHEN, HERMANN. HOLZHEY, HELMUT: *Zwei Briefe Hermann Cohens an Heinrich von Treitschke.* [In]: 'LBI Bulletin'. 12. Jg., Nr. 46-47. Tel Aviv, 1969. Pp. 183-204. [Helmut Holzhey is director of the Hermann Cohen Archives at Zurich University.]

8633. *Darmstädter Pessach Haggadah.* Faksimile Druck. Berlin: Propyläen Verlag, 1970. Illus. [Written by Israel ben Meir of Heidelberg at about 1430. The first facsimile copy was presented by Axel Springer to the Berlin Jewish Community at its jubilee celebration in December 1970. Cf. Eine bibliophile Grosstat. [In]: 'Aufbau', March 5, 1971.]

8634. EBAN, ABBA: *Dies ist mein Volk — Die Geschichte der Juden.* Aus dem Engl. übersetzt von Gerda Kurz und Siglinde Summerer. München: Droemersche Verlagsanstalt, 1970. 448 pp., ports., illus., maps. [For Engl. eds. see Nos. 7072/YB. XIV, 7804/YB. XV.]

8635. EHRLICH, ERNST LUDWIG: *Geschichte Israels.* Von den Anfängen bis zur Zerstörung des Tempels (70 n. Chr.). 2. Aufl. Berlin: de Gruyter, 1970. 158 pp., map. (Sammlung Göschen, Bd. 231/231 a.)

8636. ELBOGEN, ISMAR: *Der jüdische Gottesdienst in seiner geschichtlichen Entwicklung.* Nachdruck der 3., verb. Aufl. Frankfurt 1931. Hildesheim: Georg Olms, 1970. xv, 635 pp. (Grundriss der Gesamtwissenschaft des Judentums.)

8637. FINKELSTEIN, LOUIS, ed.: *The Jews: Their History.* 4th ed. New York: Schocken Books, 1970. xiv, 556 pp. [3 vols.] (Schocken paperbacks, SB 271.)

8638. GOLDSCHMIDT, ERNST DANIEL., ed.: *Kritische Ausgabe des Machsor Aschkenaz für die Hohen Feiertage.* (Machsor Lejamim Hanoraim). Mit historischer Einleitung, Vorwort und Anmerkungen. Jerusalem: Leo Baeck Institute/Verlag Koren, 1970. 2 vols. [Dr. Goldschmidt received the Raav Kook Prize for this work.]

8639. HIRSCH, SAMSON RAPHAEL. ASARIA, Z.: *Samson Raphael Hirsch's Wirken im Lande Niedersachsen.* [In]: 'Udim'. Jg. 1, Nr. 1. 1970. Pp. 1-22. [See No. 8671.]

8640. JOSPE, ALFRED, ed.: *Tradition and Contemporary Experience: Essays on Jewish Thought and Life.* New York: Schocken, 1970. 372 pp.

8641. LIEBESCHÜTZ, HANS: *Von Georg Simmel zu Franz Rosenzweig.* Studien zum jüdischen Denken im deutschen Kulturbereich. Mit einem Nachwort von Robert Weltsch. Tübingen: J. C. B. Mohr (Paul Siebeck), 1970. 258 pp., bibl. (pp. 239-244). (Schriftenreihe wissenschaftlicher Abhandlungen des Leo Baeck Instituts 23.)

8642. MARTIN, BERNARD: *Great 20th Century Jewish Philosophers: Shestov, Rosenzweig, Buber.* With Selections from their Writings. New York: Macmillan, 1970. 336 pp. [Lev S[c]hestov orig. Lev Isakovich Schwarzman, 1866-1938, was a Russian philosopher who emigrated to France in 1917.]

8643. MENDELSSOHN, MOSES. KRAUT, S.: *The Relation of Reason and Revelation in the Thought of Locke, Bayle, and Mendelssohn.* [In]: 'The Yavneh Review'. Vol. 7. New York, 1969. Pp. 100-129.

8644. NÁDOR, GEORG: *Moses Mendelssohn.* Hannover: Niedersächsische Landeszentrale für politische Bildung, 1969. 64 pp. (Deutsch-Jüdisches Gespräch.)

8645. *Mendelssohn-Miszellen.* Hanns Günther Reissner und Gerhard Ballin in: 'LBI Bulletin'. 12. Jg., Nr. 46-47. Pp. 212-214. [See No. 8501.]

8646. OPPENHEIM, DAVID ABRAHAM. NOSEK, B. and V. SADEK: *Georgio Diodato und David Oppenheim.* [In]: 'Judaica Bohemiae'. Jg. VI, No. 1. Prag, 1970. Pp. 5-27. [Rabbi, 1664 Worms — 1736 Prague.]

8647. PELLI, MOSHE: *Intimations of Religious Reform in the German Hebrew Haskalah Literature.* [In]: 'Jewish Social Studies'. Vol. XXXII, No. 1. New York: Conference on Jewish Social Studies, 1970. Pp. 3-13.

8648. PETUCHOWSKI, JAKOB J.: *Prayerbook Reform in Europe.* The Liturgy of European Liberal and Reform Judaism. Foreword by Solomon B. Freehof. New York: The World Union for Progressive Judaism, 1968. xxii. 407 pp.

8649. RABINOWICZ, HARRY M.: *The World of Hasidism.* London: Vallentine, Mitchell, Hartford: Hartmore House, 1970. 271 pp., ports., illus., facsims., bibl. (pp. 259-264.)

8650. RAPOPORT [SHIR], SHLOMO YEHUDAH. BARZILAY, ISAAC: *Shlomoh Yehuda Rapoport (Shir) 1790-1867 and his Contemporaries.* Some Aspects of Jewish Scholarship of the Nineteenth Century. [Ramat Gan]: Massada Press, 1969. 214 pp., front. port., bibl. (pp. 197-206).

8651. RASCHI [SALOMO BEN ISAAK]. MENDELSON, JOSÉ: *Raschi.* Buenos Aires: Congreso Judío Mundial, 1970. 38 pp., illus. (Grandes Figuras Del Judaísmo, LV). [Raschi (1040-1105) lived from 1055 to 1065 in Worms.]

8652. ROSENHEIM, JACOB. ROSENHEIM, JACOB: *Erinnerungen 1870-1920.* Hrsg. von Heinrich Eisemann und Herbert N. Kruskal. Frankfurt a.M.: Verlag Waldemar Kramer, 1970. 164 pp., front. port., illus. [1870 Frankfurt — 1965 Jerusalem. Founder and president of the Aguda World Organisation.]

8653. ROSENZWEIG, FRANZ. *Kohav Hageulah.* (Stern der Erlösung). Ins Hebräische übersetzt und mit Anmerkungen versehen von Jehoshua Amir. Eingeleitet und erklärt von Moshe Schwarz. Jerusalem: Leo Baeck Institute gemeinsam mit Mossad Bialik, 1970. 437 pp., front. port., facsim. [First publ. in German 1921.]

8654. HORWITZ, RIVKA: *Franz Rosenzweig's Unpublished Writings.* [In]: 'The Journal of Jewish Studies'. Vol. XX, Nos. 1-4, 1969. Publ. by The Institute of Jewish Studies, The Society for Jewish Study. London: Jewish Chronicle Publications, 1970. Pp. 57-80.

8655. MAYBAUM, IGNAZ: *Das Gesetz.* Franz Rosenzweigs Ringen mit den jüdischen Traditionen. [Also]: *Franz Rosenzweig — Martin Buber: Ein Briefwechsel über Tradition im Judentum.* Zusammengestellt von Edith Scheinmann-Rosenzweig. [In]: 'Emuna-Horizonte'. Jg. V, Nr. 2. Frankfurt a.M., 1970. Pp. 82-89, bibl., pp. 90-92. [See No. 9158.]

8656. TEWES, JOSEPH: *Zum Existenzbegriff Franz Rosenzweigs.* Meisenheim am Glan: Anton Hain Verlag, 1970. viii, 157 pp. (Monographien zur philosophischen Forschung. Bd. 62). (Diss. München.)

8657. ROTHSCHILD, LOTHAR. *Forschung am Judentum.* Festschrift zum sechzigsten Geburtstag von Rabbiner Dr. Dr. h.c. Lothar Rothschild. Dargereicht von der Vereinigung für religiös-liberales Judentum in der Schweiz. Bern: Verlag Herbert Lang, 1970. [Incl. contributions by Victor Loeb, Max Horkheimer, Ernst Ludwig Ehrlich. Also: Der Name Maram (Marum). Zur Geschichte der Familien Guggenheim, Weil und anderer Nachkommen des Meir von Rothenburg. (Bernhard Brilling, pp. 99-125).]

8658. SCHOLEM, GERSHOM G. SCHOLEM, GERSHOM: *Die Erforschung der Kabbala von Reuchlin bis zur Gegenwart.* Vortrag anlässlich der Entgegennahme des Reuchlin-Preises der Stadt Pforzheim . . . , 1969. Pforzheim: Im Selbstverlag der Stadt, 1969. 24 pp., port. [Also in: 'NZZ', 8. Nov., Zürich, 1970. Pp. 49-50.]

8659. SCHOLEM, GERSHOM: *Judaica II.* Frankfurt a.M.: Suhrkamp Verlag, 1970. 226 pp. (Bibliothek Suhrkamp, Bd. 263). [A collection of lectures and essays previously publ.; Judaica I was publ. in 1963. in No. 3895/YB. IX.]

8660. SCHOLEM, GERSHOM: *Die Krise der Tradition im jüdischen Messianismus.* [In]: Eranos-Jahrbuch 1968. Jg. 37. Zürich: Rhein Verlag, 1970. Pp. 9-44.

8661. SCHOLEM, GERHARD G.: *On the Kabbalah and its Symbolism.* New York: Schocken, 1970. viii, 215 pp.

8662. SCHOLEM, G. G.: *Reflections on the Possibility of Jewish Mysticism in our Time.* [In]: 'Ariel'. No. 26, Spring. Jerusalem, 1970. Pp. 43-52. [Also in]: The Israel Year Book, Tel Aviv, 1971. Pp. 133-139.

8663. SCHOLEM, GERSHOM: *The Neutralisation of the Messianic Element in Early Hasidism.* [In]: 'The Journal of Jewish Studies'. Vol. XX, Nos. 1-4, 1969. London: The Institute of Jewish Studies, The Society for Jewish Study, 1970. Pp. 25-55. [This contribution is devoted to the memory of Joseph George Weiss, Hebrew scholar, (1918 Budapest-1969 London). The Journal also cont. an obituary of J. G. Weiss].

8664. SCHOLEM, GERSHOM: *Über einige Grundbegriffe des Judentums.* Frankfurt a.M.: Suhrkamp Verlag, 1970. 169 pp. (edition suhrkamp, Bd. 414). [Cont. 4 lectures delivered at Eranos meetings in Ascona 1957-1965.]

8665. WIJNHOVEN, JOCHANAN H. A.: *Gershom G. Scholem: The Study of Jewish Mysticism.* [In]: 'Judaism'. Vol. 19, No. 4, Fall. New York: The American Jewish Congress, 1970. Pp. 468-481.

8666. SELIGMANN, CAESAR. MEYER, MICHEL A.: *Caesar Seligmann and the Development of Liberal Judaism in Germany at the Beginning of the Twentieth Century.* [In]: Hebrew Union College Annual. Vols. XL-XLI, 1969/1970. Ed.: Matitjahu Tsevat. Cincinnati/Ohio, 1970. [The vol. also contains: Salomon Maimon's Doctrine of Fiction and Imagination (Samuel Atlas). Joshua Heschel Schorr [scholar, 1814-1895 Brody] (Ezra Spicehandler.)]

8667. SIMON. ERNST: *Das Volk der Überlieferung in Zeit und Ewigkeit.* [In]: Vom Sinn der Tradition. [See No. 8763.]

8668. TALMON, J. L.: *Israel among the Nations.* London: Weidenfeld and Nicolson, 1970. 199 pp.

8669. '*Tradition und Erneuerung*'. Zeitschrift der Vereinigung für religiös-liberales Judentum in der Schweiz. H. 30, Nov. Bern, 1970. [Incl.: Aus alten Blättern der Jüdischen Reformgemeinde zu Berlin (Wolfgang Hamburger). Dank und Gesang: Louis Lewandowski, ein Reformer der synagogalen Musik (Hermann Herz). Streit um die deutsche Beschriftung jüdischer Grabsteine [mainly in Silesian communities] (Bernhard Brilling).]

8670. TREPP, LEO: *Das Judentum. Geschichte und lebendige Gegenwart.* Aus dem Amerik. übersetzt von Karl-Heinz Laier. Reinbek b. Hamburg: Rowohlt Verlag, 1970. 254 pp., bibl. (pp. 243-246). (rowohlts deutsche enzyklopädie. 325/326.) [Orig. title: Judaism, Development and Life. — Author was, until his emigration to the USA, the last Rabbi of the Oldenburg district.]

8671. *'Udim'.* Zeitschrift der Rabbinerkonferenz in der Bundesrepublik Deutschland. 1. Jg., H. 1. Frankfurt a.M., 1970. [Incl.: Das Thoratreue Judentum in Bayern vor seiner Zerstörung (F. Bloch). Die Gründung der Rabbinerkonferenz in Deutschland (S. Neufeld). See also Nos. 8443, 8639, 8909.

8672. WILHELM, KURT. TRAMER, HANS: *Kurt Wilhelm (1900-1965).* [In]: Theokratia. Bd. I. Pp. 106-182. [See No. 8500.]

8673. ZUNZ, LEOPOLD. RAPHAEL, J.: *Die Zeitschrift des Dr. Leopold Zunz.* [In]: 'Zeitschrift für die Geschichte der Juden'. 7. Jg., Nr. 1. 1970. Pp. 31-36, bibl. (pp. 35-36). [See No. 8420.]

B. The Jewish Problem

8674. KAHLE, WOLFGANG: *Von Juden in Frankreich.* Assimilierung — geglückt oder misslungen? [In]: 'Monat'. H. 263, 22. Jahr, Aug., Berlin, 1970. Pp. 63-72. [Incl. the Ashkenazim from Alsace whose number was increased by German Jews from the Rhineland.]

8675. KOCHAN, LIONEL: *Jewish Self-Hatred.* Publ. by The World Jewish Congress, British Section. London, 1970. 20 pp. (Noah Barou Memorial Lecture 1970). [Incl. Theodor Lessing, Karl Kraus, Maximilian Harden, Otto Weininger, Paul Rée (philosopher, 1849-1901).]

8676. PIERSON, RUTH: *German-Jewish Identity in the Weimar Republic.* A Dissertation presented . . . Yale University, 1970. 347 pp. + 13 pp. Appendix A: Jewish Periodicals published in Germany during the Weimar Republic + bibl. (pp. i-xxix). [Mimeog.]

C. Jewish Life and Organisations

8677. COMMISSION INTERNATIONALE POUR UNE HISTOIRE DU DÉVELOPPEMENT SCIENTIFIQUE ET CULTUREL DE L'HUMANITÉ, ed.: *Social Life and Social Values of the Jewish People.* [In]: 'Journal of World History'. Vol. XI, Nos. 1-2. Neuchâtel: Éditions de la Baconnière, 1968. 344 pp.

8678. ELIAV, MORDECHAI: *Philippsons Allgemeine Zeitung des Judentums und Erez Israel.* [In]: 'LBI Bulletin'. 12. Jg., Nr. 46-47. Tel Aviv, 1969. Pp. 155-182. [The paper, founded by Rabbi Ludwig Philippson (1811-1889) in 1837, was publ. until 1922.]

8679. JACOBSON-SCHULE, SEESEN. BALLIN, GERHARD: *Ein Brief Benedikt Schotts an Israel Jacobson.* [In]: 'LBI Bulletin'. 12. Jg., Nr. 46-47. Tel Aviv, 1969. Pp. 205-211, facsim. (Publ. by courtesy of the Staatsarchiv Wolfenbüttel.) [Israel Jacobson (1768-1828) was the founder and patron of the school, Benedikt Schott (orig. Schottländer), 1763-1846, its director from 1806-1838.]

8680. BALLIN, GERHARD: *Gästebuch der Jacobson-Schule für die Jahre 1804-1831.* [In]: Braunschweigisches Jahrbuch, Bd. 51, 1970.

8681. BALLIN, GERHARD: *Geschichte des Gebäudes der nach ihrem Gründer Israel Jacobson (1768-1828) benannten Jacobson-Schule in Seesen.* [In]: 'Beobachter'. Seesen, 1970.

8682. MARGALITH, ELKANA: *Die sozialen und intellektuellen Ursprünge der jüdischen Jugendbewegung 'Haschomer Hazair', 1913-1920.* Pp. 261-289 [in]: Archiv für Sozialgeschichte. Hrsg. von der Friedrich-Ebert-Stiftung. Bd. X. Hannover: Verlag für Literatur und Zeitgeschehen, 1970. 524 pp.

8683. PAPPENHEIM, BERTHA. JENSEN, ELLEN M.: *Anna O. — A Study of her Later Life.* [In]: 'The Psychoanalytic Quarterly'. Vol. XXXIX, No. 2. New York, 1970. Pp. 269-293, bibl. (pp. 292-293). [Rev. and enlarged English version first publ. in 1961. See No. 2652/YB. VII. — Under the pseudonym Anna O. Bertha Pappenheim was one of Sigmund Freud's first patients.]

8684. SCHATZKER, CHAIM: *The Jewish Youth Movement in Germany between the Years 1900-1933.* Thesis, submitted . . . Senate of the Hebrew University, February. Jerusalem, 1969. xvi pp. [In English], 323 pp. [in Hebrew.] [Mimeog.] [Text in Hebrew, Summary in English.]

8685. SCHLOSS, FRIEDRICH: *Die Dotalprivilegien der Jüdinnen.* Ein Beitrag zur Dogmengeschichte des gemeinen Civilrechts. (Nachdruck d. Ausg. Giessen, Ferber, 1856). Amsterdam: Rodopi, 1970. xiv, 96 pp., bibl. (pp. 1-9).

8686. [(The) Wiener Library, London]. ARONSFELD, C. C.: *Alfred Wiener (1885-1964).* [In]: Theokratia. Pp. 144-159. [See No. 8500]. [Alfred Wiener was the founder and director of the Wiener Library, London.]

8687. WIZO, *The Women's International Zionist Organisation. The Saga of a Movement: WIZO 1920-1970.* Publ. by the Department of Organisation and Education of WIZO. Ed. by Fay Grove-Pollak. Tel Aviv, 1970. xiii, 264 pp., ports. illus.

8688. *Zur Geschichte der jüdischen Krankenhäuser.* Symposium der Deutschen Gesellschaft für Krankenhausgeschichte in Heidelberg. [A report in]: 'Allgemeine'. Nr. XXV/12, 20. März. Düsseldorf, 1970.

D. Jewish Art and Music

8689. BAUMGARTEN, JOSEPH M.: *Art in the Synagogue.* Some Talmudic Views. [In]: 'Judaism'. Vol. 19. No. 2, Spring. New York: American Jewish Congress, 1970. Pp. 196-206.

8690. SAALSCHÜTZ, JOSEPH LEVIN: *Geschichte und Würdigung der Musik bei den Hebräern,* im Verhältnis zur sonstigen Ausbildung dieser Kunst in alter und neuer Zeit. Nebst einem Anhang über die hebräische Orgel. Unveränderter Neudruck der Ausgabe 1829. Niederwalluf b. Wiesbaden: M. Sändig, 1970. x, 141 pp., front. illus., music score.

—— SENDREY, ALFRED: *Bibliography of Jewish Music.* [See No. 8522.]

8691. SULZER, SALOMON. WOHLBERG, MAX: *Salomon Sulzer and the Seitenstettengasse Temple.* [In]: 'Journal of Synagogue Music'. Vol. 2, No. 4, April. New York, 1970. Pp. 19-24. [The same issue of the journal cont. 'Chasidism in Jazz' (J. Katz), pp. 28-33.]

—— WEISSER, ALBERT: *Bibliography of Publications and other Resources on Jewish Music.* [See No. 8528.]

8692. WERNER, ERIC: *From Generation to Generation.* Studies on Jewish Musical Tradition. New York: American Conference of Cantors, 1969. 168 pp., illus., music score [Incl. Solomon Sulzer, Abraham Zvi Idelsohn].

VI. ZIONISM AND ISRAEL

8693. BAUER, YEHUDA: *Flight and Rescue: Brichah.* New York: Random House, 1970. x, 369 pp., bibl. (pp. 360-362.) (Contemporary Jewish Civilization Series. In cooperation with Institute of Contemporary Jewry, The Hebrew University of Jerusalem, ed.: Moshe Davis.) [The documented history of the organised escape of the Jewish survivors of Eastern Europe, 1944-1948.] [See also No. 8586.]

8694. BAUER, YEHUDA: *From Diplomacy to Resistance.* A History of Jewish Palestine 1939-1945. Transl. from the Hebrew by Alton M. Winters. Philadelphia: The Jewish Publication Society of America, 1970. 432 pp., bibl. (pp. 421-424).

8695. BIRAM, ARTHUR. HALPERIN, SARA: *Dr. Arthur Biram und seine Realschule.* Jerusalem: Verlag Rubin Mass. 1970. [In Hebrew.] [Cf. Ernst Simon: Arthur Biram und Richard Lichtheim — ein Vergleich. [In]: 'MB', Nr. 15/16, 9. Apr. Tel Aviv, 1971. Arthur Biram (1878-1967). See also No. 8716.]

8696. BRAUN, SIEGFRIED. JACOBI, HANS: *Nostradamus.* In Memoriam Dr. Siegfried Braun. [And]: *Dr. Siegfried Braun (1885-1969),* (Hans Chanoch Meyer). [In]: 'Zeitschrift für die Geschichte der Juden', Nr. 1, 1970. Pp. 27-30, 45-47. [See No. 8420.]

8697. CARPI, DANIEL, ed.: *Zionism.* Studies in the History of the Zionist Movement and of the Jews in Palestine. Vol. I. Tel Aviv: Tel Aviv University, Hakibbutz Hameuchad Publ. House, 1970. 503 pp., bibls. [In Hebrew, with some essays in English and German.] [Incl.: Der 'Judentag'-Plan and the Zionists in Germany (Jacob Toury), pp. 9-56, bibl. (pp. 34-45). The German Consulate in Jerusalem and the Jews in Jerusalem in the 19th Century (Mordechai Eliav, pp. 57-83, bibl. (pp. 74-83). [For German version see No. 7866/YB. XV.] The editions of 'The Jewish State' by Theodor Herzl (A. Bein, H. Avrahami, pp. 464-474. [A bibliography.]

8698. COHEN, AHARON: *Israel and the Arab World*. Preface by Martin Buber. Transl. [from the Hebrew] by Aubrey Hodes, Naomi Handelman, and Miriam Shimeoni. London: W. H. Allen, 1970. xvi, 576 pp., maps. [Publ. 1964 in Israel by Sifriat Poalim. The last chapter has been completely revised for the English ed.]

8699. COHEN-REISS, EPHRAIM: *Memories of a Son of Jerusalem*. Second Ed. Jerusalem: Sifriyat Hayishouv, 1967. 447 pp. [In Hebrew, with a short introductory note in English. First publ. 1932 in 2 vols. Author (1862 Jerusalem — 1942 Nice), studied in Germany and became the sole representative of the 'Hilfsverein der deutschen Juden' and its educational work in Palestine.]

8700. DINER, DANY: *Der Zionismus und die jüdische Frage heute*. (pp. 153-159). *Die Neue Linke und jüdische Identität*. Assimilation durch den Zionismus. (Zwi Lamm, pp. 160-170). *Zionismus und Antizionismus — Thesen und Fragen* (Friedrich-Wilhelm Marquardt, pp. 171-176). [In]: 'Emuna-Horizonte'. Nr. 3, Juni, 1970. Pp. 153-176. [See No. 9158.]

8701. ELIAV, MORDECHAI: *Love of Zion and Men of Hod*. German Jewry and the settlement of Eretz-Israel in the 19th Century. Publ. by The Institute for Zionist Research at Tel Aviv University. [Tel Aviv]: Hakibbutz Hameuchad, 1970. 442 pp., facsims., tabs., bibl. (pp. 413-428). [In Hebrew.]

8702. FOERDER, YESCHAYAHU (HERBERT). D'AVIGDOR-GOLDSMID, SIR HENRY: *Dr. Y. Foerder (1901-1970)*. Leading Israeli Businessman. [Obituary in]: 'The Times', June 27, London, 1970. [Other obituaries in]: 'MB', June 19 and July 10 (Kurt Tuchler). 'Jewish Chronicle', June 11, London. 'Jewish Observer', June 19, port., London. 'Aufbau', June 26, New York (Joachim Prinz). 'Isr. Wochenblatt', June 19, Zürich. 'Das Neue Israel', July, port., Zürich. 'AJR Information', August, London. LBI Year Book XV, London (Robert Weltsch).

8703. CAPELL, HANS: *Yeschayahu Herbert Foerder*. Ein Jahr nach seinem Tode. [In]: 'MB', 11. Juni. Tel Aviv, 1971.

8704. SCHOCKEN, GERSCHOM: *Die Juden Deutschlands in Israel*. Zum Gedenken an Dr. Herbert Foerder. Aus dem 'Haaretz', [June 19], übersetzt. [In]: Jüdischer Presse Dienst'. Nr 7-8. Hrsg.: Zentralrat der Juden in Deutschland. Düsseldorf, 1970. Pp. 9-12. [Also in]: 'Müncher Jüdische Nachrichten', Nr. 25, 3. Juli, 1970. [Transl. from the Hebrew by Baruch Graubard.] [In reply, a letter was publ. by G. R. Tamarin in 'Haaretz', 24th June 1970, pointing out some of the reasons for the situation described by Mr. Schocken. Cf. Robert Weltsch [In]: LBI Year Book XV, London 1970, pp. XV-XVI.]

8705. FRAENKEL, JOSEF: *Von Theodor Herzl bis Golda Meir*. Die Geschichte des Zionistischen Zentralarchivs in Jerusalem. [In]: 'Aufbau', May 22, New York, 1970. [After their beginnings in Vienna and Cologne, the archives in Berlin, under the expert guidance of Georg Herlitz, were greatly expanded and, in 1934, transferred to Jerusalem.]

8706. FREEDEN, HERBERT: *Deutsche Juden in Israel*. Pp. 43-46. *Aus Deutschland nach Erez Israel emigrierte jüdische Künstler*, (Sima Miron, pp. 47-60 + 8 pp. illus.). *Was bedeutet mir als Juden aus Deutschland in Israel das Land meiner Herkunft?* (Walter Preuss, pp. 62-63.) *Wie stehen Kinder deutsch-jüdischer Immigranten in Israel zum Herkunftsland ihrer Eltern?* (Edna Brocke, pp. 63-65.) [In]: 'Emuna-Horizonte', Nr. 1, Jan., 1970. Pp. 43-65, illus. [See No. 9158.]

8707. GEISS, IMANUEL: *Israel — Frühjahr 1969*. Ein politischer Reisebericht. [In]: 'Junge Kirche'. Eine Zeitschrift europäischer Christen. Okt. Dortmund, 1969. 31 pp. [Author was twice visiting lecturer at Tel Aviv University. — Cf. Nos. 8723 and 8708.]

8708. GEISS, IMANUEL: *Judentum, Zionismus und Israel*. Erwiderung auf Fritz Sonnenberg. [In]: 'Werkhefte', Zeitschrift für Probleme der Gesellschaft und des Katholizismus. 24. Jg., Nr. 5-6, Mai-Juni. München, 1970. Pp. 129-137, 166-172. [See Nos. 8707 and 8723.]

8709. *Gespräche mit israelischen Soldaten*. Hrsg. von der Kibbuzbewegung. Aus dem Hebräischen von Susanne Euler. Frankfurt a.M.: Joseph Melzer Verlag, 1970. 404 pp.

8710. GOLDMANN, NAHUM: *The Future of Israel*. [In]: 'Foreign Affairs'. Publ. by Council on Foreign Relations. Vol. 48, No. 3. New York, 1970. Pp. 443-459.

8711. GOLDMANN, NAHUM: *Memories*. The Autobiography of Nahum Goldmann. The Story of a Lifelong Battle by World Jewry's Ambassador-at-large. Transl. by Helen Sebba. London: Weidenfeld and Nicolson, 1970. 358 pp., ports., illus., facsim. [For American ed. see No. 7870/YB. XV.] [German edition]: *Staatsmann ohne Staat*. Autobiography. Köln: Kiepenheuer & Witsch, 1970. 474 pp., front. port., ports., illus., facsim.

8712. GOLDMANN, NAHUM: *'Die Zeit arbeitet gegen Israel'*. Spiegel-Gespräch mit Nahum Goldmann. [In]: 'Der Spiegel'. Jg. 24, Nr. 18, 27. April. Hamburg, 1970. Pp. 131-136.

8713. HERZL, THEODOR. HERZL, THEODOR: *The Jewish State* (Der Judenstaat). A new translation by Harry Zohn. New York: Herzl Press, 1970. 110 pp.

8714. COHN, HENRY J.: *Theodor Herzl's Conversion to Zionism*. [In]: 'Jewish Social Studies'. Vol. XXXII, No. 2. Apr. New York: Conference on Jewish Social Studies, 1970. Pp. 101-110.

8715. LEVINE, NORMAN: *Karl Marx and the Arab-Israeli Conflict*. [In]: 'Judaism', Vol. 19, No. 2, Spring. New York, 1970. Pp. 145-157.

8716. LICHTHEIM, RICHARD: *Rückkehr*. Lebenserinnerungen aus der Frühzeit des deutschen Zionismus. Mit einer Einleitung von Pinchas Rosen. Stuttgart: Deutsche Verlags-Anstalt, 1970. 387 pp., front. port., facsim. (Veröffentlichung des Leo Baeck Insituts Jerusalem.) [Richard Lichtheim (1885-1963).] [See No. 8695.]

8717. MEIER-CRONEMEYER, ROLF RENDTORFF, ULRICH KUSCHE: *Israel*. Geschichte des Zionismus. Religion und Gesellschaft. Der Nahost-Konflikt. Hannover: Verlag für Literatur und Zeitgeschehen, 1970. 182 pp., tabs., maps, chronology, bibl. (pp. 171-174).

8718. NORDAU, MAX [orig. Südfeld]: SCHALLMAN, LAZARO: *Max Nordau*. Editado por el Ejecutivo Sudamericano del Congreso Judío Mundial. Buenos Aires, 1970. 48 pp., port. (Biblioteca Popular Judía, Grandes Figuras del Judaísmo, No. 51.)

8719. PARZEN, HERBERT: *The Magnes-Weizmann-Einstein Controversy*. [In]: 'Jewish Social Studies'. Vol. XXXII, No. 3, July. New York: Conference on Jewish Social Studies, 1970. Pp. 187-213. [The controversy concerned the Hebrew University Jerusalem.]

8720. RAPAPORT, DAVID: *Die Kibbutz-Erziehung und ihre Bedeutung für die Entwicklungspsychologie*. [In]: Kinder im Kollektiv. Anleitung für eine revolutionäre Erziehung. 2. Aufl. mit Kritik und Selbstkritik. Nr. 5, Sept. Hrsg.: Zentralrat der Sozialistischen Kinderläden, Berlin (1 Berlin 12, Wielandstr. 13), 1969. Pp. 8-20. [The same issue contains: Anna Freud: Kinder im KZ, pp. 32-76.]

8721. ROTHSCHILD, ELI: *Die Juden und das Heilige Land*. Zur Geschichte des Heimkehrwillens eines Volkes. 2., verb. Aufl. Hannover: Niedersächsische Landeszentrale für Politische Bildung, 1968. 94 pp. (Schriftenreihe der . . ., Probleme des Judentums, 2.) [First ed. see No. 9574/YB. X.]

8722. SIMON, ERNST: *Der Wandel des jüdischen Menschenbildes im heutigen Israel*. [In]: Jüdisches Volk — gelobtes Land. [See No. 9161.]

8723. SONNENBERG, FRITZ: *Israel — oder: Der Anti-Philosemitismus und die liberale Linke*. [In]: 'werkhefte'. 24. Jg. März. München, 1970. Pp. 75-84. [A critical examination of the article by Imanuel Geiss. See Nos. 8707 and 8708.]

8724. SPITZER, MORITZ. ROSENKRANZ, HERBERT: *Dr. [Moritz] Spitzer im Israel-Museum*. [In]: 'Das Neue Israel'. 23. Jg., H. 5, Nov. Zürich, 1970. Pp. 346-349, illus. [Dr. Spitzer, prior to his emigration to Israel, was reader at the Schocken publishing house, Berlin. He recently celebrated his 70th birthday.]

8725. WORMANN, CURT D.: *German Jews in Israel: Their Cultural Situation since 1933*. [In]: LBI Year Book XV. London, 1970. Pp. 73-103, ports. [of Jakob Sandbank, Georg Landauer], illus.

8726. YOUTH ALIYAH. PINCUS, CHASYA: *Come from the Four Winds*. The Story of Youth Aliyah. New York: Herzl Press, 1970. 332 pp. [Inspired by Recha Freier, the story began at a meeting in Berlin in January 1933.]

8727. ZADEK, LILY: *D'varim mi-shelah ve-alehah*. (Memoirs and Memories.) Tel Aviv, 1969. [A niece of Eduard Bernstein, Lily Zadek became a very active member of the 'Volksheim' in Berlin. She went to Palestine in 1921, and died in 1969. Cf. Uri Benjamin: Eine deutsche Jüdin aus der 3. Alijah. [In]: 'MB', 18. Juli, Tel Aviv, 1969 [and] Robert Weltsch [In]: LBI Year Book XV, pp. XIII-XIV.

VII. PARTICIPATION IN
CULTURAL AND PUBLIC LIFE

A. General

8728. ARENDT, HANNAH: *Men in Dark Times.* London: Jonathan Cape, 1970. x, 272 pp. [Incl. Rosa Luxemburg, Hermann Broch, Walter Benjamin. Essays and articles written over a period of 12 years. First publ. in USA 1968.]

8729. ARIS, STEPHEN: *The Jews in Business.* London: Jonathan Cape, 1970. 255 pp., ports., illus., bibl. (pp. 243-246). [Incl. Sir Siegmund Warburg, Sir Jules Thorn.]

8730. ASSION, P.: *Jakob von Landshut: Zur Geschichte der jüdischen Ärzte in Deutschland.* [In]: Sudhoffs Archiv. Jg. 53, Nr. 3, Nov. Wiesbaden, 1969. Pp. 270-291.

8731. *Austromarxismus.* Texte zu 'Ideologie und Klassenkampf' von Otto Bauer, Max Adler, Karl Renner, Sigmund Kunfi, Béla Fogarasi und Julius Lengyel. Hrsg. und eingel. von Hans-Jörg Sandkühler und Rafael de la Vega. Frankfurt a.M./Wien: Europäische Verlagsanstalt/Europa Verlag, 1970. 408 pp., bibl. (pp. 403-408). (Politische Texte.)

8732. BACHMANN, DIETER: *Essay und Essayismus.* Stuttgart: W. Kohlhammer Verlag, 1970. [Incl. Walter Benjamin, Hermann Broch.]

8733. BEYER, WILHELM RAIMUND: *Vier Kritiken: Heidegger — Sartre — Adorno — Lukács.* Köln: Pahl-Rugenstein Verlag, 1970. 232 pp. (Kleine Bibliothek, Politik, Wissenschaft, Zukunft, Bd. 5.)

8734. BÜCHLER, FRANZ: *Wasserscheide zweier Zeitalter.* Essais. Heidelberg: Lothar Stiehm Verlag, 1970. 127 pp. (Poesie und Wissenschaft, Bd. XII). [Incl.: Eräugtes Dunkel (Paul Celan). Siderische Sicht (Alfred Mombert). Schizoider Zeitgeist (von Kassner über Kafka zu Beckett).]

8735. DEUTSCHE BANK. SEIDENZAHL, FRITZ: *Hundert Jahre Deutsche Bank, 1870-1970.* Im Auftrag des Vorstandes der Deutschen Bank hrsg. Frankfurt a.M.: Dt. Bank, 1970. xi, 459 pp., ports., illus., facsim., map.

8736. ENZENSBERGER, HANS MAGNUS, ed.: *Freisprüche.* Revolutionäre vor Gericht. Frankfurt a.M.: Suhrkamp Verlag, 1970. 458 pp., bibls. at end of chapters. [Incl.: Karl Marx, Alexander Parvus-Helphand, Rosa Luxemburg, Eugen Leviné.]

8737. *(Die) erschreckende Zivilisation.* Salzburger Humanismusgespräche. Hrsg. von Oskar Schatz, Erich Fromm und Herbert Marcuse. Wien: Europa Verlag, 1970. 240 pp.

8738. EXILE LITERATURE. BENJAMIN, URI: *Der Antiquar und die Exilliteratur.* Oder: Der noch unentdeckte Anteil des Buchhandels am Aufbau der seltenen Sammlungen. [In]: 'Börsenblatt für den Deutschen Buchhandel', Nr. 49, 19. Juni. Frankfurt a.M., 1970. Pp. A 82—A 84.

8739. BERENDSOHN, WALTER A.: *'Innere Emigration'.* Bromma, Schweden, o.J., 4 pp. [Typescript.]

—— BERENDSOHN, WALTER A., ed.: *Personen- und Sachverzeichnis zu 'Deutsche Literatur der Flüchtlinge aus dem Dritten Reich'.* [See No. 8508.]

8740. CAZDEN, ROBERT: *German Exile Literature in America 1933-1950.* Chicago: American Library Association, 1970. 250 pp. [Cf. No. 7682/YB. XV.]

8741. DEUTSCHE BÜCHEREI LEIPZIG, ed.: *Die Sammlung der Exil-Literatur 1933-1945.* Überarb. Neudruck. Leipzig: Deutsche Bücherei, 1969. 5 pp. (Neue Mitteilungen aus der Deutschen Bücherei, Nr. 44.)

8742. KANTOROWICZ, ALFRED: *Der deutsche Geist in der Diaspora.* Reprinted from 'Moderna Sprak' 1968. Stockholm [o.J.]. Pp. 259-284. (Vortrag, geh. am 20.4.1968 auf Einladung der schwedisch-deutschen Gesellschaft in Stockholm anlässlich der Eröffnung der Buchausstellung 'Exilliteratur 1933-1945' in der Königl. Bibliothek.)

8743. MIERENDORFF, MARTA: *Unersetzliches geht täglich verloren.* Kritisches zur Exilforschung. [In]: 'Frankfurter Rundschau', 8. Aug. Frankfurt a.M., 1970. [A reply from] Berthold Werner: Exil-Literatur. [In]: 'FR.', 15. Aug. 1970.

8744. MÜSSENER, HELMUT, comp.: *Bericht I.* Stockholmer Koordinationsstelle zur Erforschung der deutschsprachigen Exil-Literatur. Hrsg. vom Deutschen Institut der Universität Stockholm, 1970. v, 157 pp.

8745. Müssener, Helmut: *Die deutschsprachige Emigration nach 1933—Aufgaben und Probleme ihrer Erforschung.* Saltsjö-Duvnäs: Moderna Sprak, [1970]. 15 pp. (Language Monographs 10.] (Vortrag, geh. auf dem Stockholmer Symposium über 'Die deutsche Literatur der Flüchtlinge aus dem Dritten Reich', im September 1969.)

8746. Stahlberger, Peter: *Der Zürcher Verleger Emil Oprecht und die deutsche politische Emigration 1933-1945.* Mit einem Vorwort von J. R. von Salis. Zürich: Europa Verlag, 1970. 407 pp., bibl. (pp. 377-399). (Diss. Univ. Zürich.)

—— Sternfeld, Wilhelm, Eva Tiedemann, comps.: *Deutsche Exil-Literatur 1933-1945.* [See No. 8525.]

8747. Gay, Peter: *Die Republik der Aussenseiter.* Geist und Kultur in der Weimarer Zeit: 1918-1933. Aus dem Engl. von Helmut Lindemann. Mit einem Vorwort zur deutschen Ausgabe von Karl Dietrich Bracher. Frankfurt a.M.: S. Fischer Verlag, 1970. 256 pp., ports., illus., bibl. (pp. 219-249). [Incl. Alfred Adler, Albert Einstein, Hannah Arendt, Kurt Weill.]

8748. Grossner, Claus, ed.: *Politik deutscher Philosophen — Ende der Wissenschaft?* Hamburg: Christian Wegner Verlag, 1970, bibl. [An abbreviated version was serialised under the title 'Philosophie in Deutschland' [In]: 'Zeit', Nr. 11-22, 12. März — 29. Mai. Hamburg, 1970. — A description and analysis of the most important teachings of the modern German philosophers, incl. Theodor W. Adorno, Max Horkheimer, Herbert Marcuse, Ernst Bloch, Karl R. Popper.]

8749. Heilbroner, Robert L.: *The Worldly Philosophers.* The Great Economic Thinkers. London: Allen Lane The Penguin Press, 1969. 320 pp. [Incl. Karl Marx.]

8750. Heise, Carl Georg and Johannes Langner, eds.: *Karl Scheffler.* Eine Auswahl seiner Essays aus Kunst und Leben 1905-1950. Hamburg: Ernst Hauswedell Verlag, 1970. 187 pp. [Incl. the article Scheffler wrote in 1933 challenging the Nazis, on Max Liebermann's portrait of Sauerbruch, as a result of which he was silenced.]

8751. Heiseler, Johannes Heinrich von [and others], ed.: *Die Frankfurter Schule im Lichte des Marxismus.* Zur Kritik der Philosophie und Soziologie von Horkheimer, Adorno, Marcuse, Habermas. Materialien einer wissenschaftlichen Tagung aus Anlass des 100. Geburtstages von W.I. Lenin, veranstaltet vom Institut f. Marxistische Studien und Forschungen (IMSF) am 21.u. 22. Febr. 1970 in Frankfurt a.M. Frankfurt a.M.: Verlag Marxistische Blätter, 1970. 184 pp. (Marxistische Taschenbücher.)

8752. Hermand, Jost: *Unbequeme Literatur.* Eine Beispielreihe. Heidelberg: Lothar Stiehm Verlag, 1970. 225 pp. (Literatur und Geschichte, Bd. 3.) [Incl. Ernst Toller, Karl Emil Franzos.]

8753. Hochhuth, Rolf and Herbert Reinoss, eds.: *Ruhm und Ehre.* Die Nobelpreisträger für Literatur. Mit einem Vorwort von Martin Walser. Illustrationen von Manfred Bluth u.a. Gütersloh: Bertelsmann Verlag, 1970. 991 pp., ports. [Incl. S. Agnon, Nelly Sachs. Paul Heyse (1830-1914) a half-Jew, was the first German writer to receive the Nobel Prize (1910).]

8754. Holländer, Alfred: *Von der Bibel bis Buber.* Wien: Wartburg Buchhandlung, 1970. 24 pp.

8755. '(DER) JÜNGSTE TAG'. Neu hrsg. und mit einem dokumentarischen Anhang versehen von Heinz Schöffler. Frankfurt a.M.: Verlag Heinrich Scheffler, 1970. 1805, 1867 pp. [2 vols.] [Many German Jews contributed to the 86 vols. which Kurt Wolff publ. between 1913 and 1921.]

8756. Kessler, Harry Graf: *The Diaries of a Cosmopolitan: Count Harry Kessler, 1918-1937.* Transl. and ed. by Charles Kessler. London: Weidenfeld and Nicolson, 1970. 544 pp. ports., illus., [For German orig. see No. 2688/YB. VII. A large number of well known German-Jewish personalities are mentioned in the diaries.]

8757. Koch, Thilo: *Die goldenen zwanziger Jahre.* Das Porträt eines Jahrzehnts. Graphische Gestaltung: Jürgen Seuss. Frankfurt a.M.: Akademische Verlagsgesellschaft, 1970. 172 pp., 150 ports. and illus.

8758. Kolinsky, Eva: *Engagierter Expressionismus.* Politik und Literatur zwischen Weltkrieg und Weimarer Republik. Eine Analyse expressionistischer Zeitschriften. Stuttgart: J. B. Metzler, 1970. viii, 232 pp., bibl. (pp. 217-227). (Diss. F.U. Berlin.)

8759. Masur, Gerhard: *Propheten von Gestern.* Zur europäischen Kultur 1890 — 1914. Aus dem Amerikanischen von Alfred Dunkel. Frankfurt a.M.: S. Fischer Verlag, 1965. 489 pp., bibl. (pp. 443-479). [Prophets of Yesterday was first publ. in 1961.]

8760. MATULL, WILHELM, ed.: *Grosse Deutsche aus Ostpreussen.* München: Gräfe und Unzer Verlag, 1970. 259 pp., ports., bibl. [The 28 biographies incl.: Eduard von Simson (1810-1899) by Immanuel Birnbaum. Leopold Jessner (1878-1945) by Horst Schroeder.]

8761. OTTENDORF-SIMROCK, WALTHER: *Von Otto Hahn bis Max Liebermann.* Begegnungen. Wuppertal: Henn Verlag, 1970. 109 pp., ports.

8762. POLL, BERNHARD, ed.: *Rheinische Lebensbilder.* Hrsg. im Auftrag der Gesellschaft für Rheinische Geschichtskunde, Bd. 4. Düsseldorf: Rheinland-Verlag, 1970. 304 pp., ports., illus. [Incl. biographies of Peter Hasenclever, 1716-1793 (Hermann Kellenbenz). Heinrich Heine, 1797-1856 (Eberhard Galley). Walter Hasenclever, 1890-1940 (Victor Conzemius). Ludwig Strauß, 1892-1953 (Werner Kraft).]

8763. REINISCH, LEONHARD, ed.: *Vom Sinn der Tradition.* Zehn Beiträge. München: C. H. Beck, 1970. ix, 181 pp. [Incl.: Gibt es Zukunft in der Vergangenheit? (Ernst Bloch). Das Volk der Überlieferung in Zeit und Ewigkeit (Ernst Simon).]

8764. RIEFF, PHILIP, ed.: *On Intellectuals.* Theoretical Studies, Case Studies. Garden City, N.Y.: Doubleday, 1969. x, 347 pp. [Incl. The Life and Opinions of Moses Hess (Isaiah Berlin). The Case of Dr. Julius Robert Oppenheimer (Philip Rieff).]

8765. ROHNER, LUDWIG: *Deutsche Essays.* Prosa aus zwei Jahrhunderten. Neuwied: Luchterhand Verlag, 1970. 470, 674, 626 pp. [3 vols.] [Incl. Gustav Landauer, Alfred Kerr, Alfred Polgar's 'Max Pallenberg', Georg Lukács, Th. W. Adorno and others.]

8766. ROLOFF, ERNST-AUGUST: *Exkommunisten.* Abtrünnige des Weltkommunismus, ihr Leben und ihr Bruch mit der Partei in Selbstdarstellungen. Mainz: v. Hase & Koehler Verlag, 1969. 432 pp., tab., bibl. (pp. 415-429). [Incl. Louis Fischer, Alfred Kantorowicz, Arthur Koestler, Manès Sperber, Carola Stern, Ralph Giordano.]

8767. ROSENBERG, BERNHARD-MARIA: *Die ostpreussischen Abgeordneten in Frankfurt 1848/49.* Köln u. Berlin: G. Grotesche Verlagsbuchhandlung, 1970. (Veröffentlichungen aus den Archiven Preussischer Kulturbesitz, Bd. 6.) [Incl. Eduard v. Simson (1810-1889), Johann Jacoby (1805-1877).]

8768. ROTHE, WOLFGANG, ed.: *Expressionismus als Literatur.* Gesammelte Studien. Bern: Francke Verlag, 1969. 797 pp. [50 contributions.]

8769. RUPRECHT, ERICH/DIETER BÄNSCH, eds.: *Literarische Manifeste der Jahrhundertwende 1890-1918.* Stuttgart: J. B. Metzler, 1970. 579 pp. [Incl. Samuel Lublinski (1863-1910), Ludwig Jacobowski (1860-1900).]

8770. SANDKÜHLER, HANS JÖRG and RAFAEL DE LA VEGA, eds.: *Marxismus und Ethik.* Texte zum Neukantianischen Sozialismus. Frankfurt a.M.: Suhrkamp Verlag, 1970. 320 pp. [Incl. texts by Max Adler, Hermann Cohen, Georg Lukács.]

8771. SCHOLZ, HARRY/PAUL SCHROEDER, eds.: *Ärzte in Ost- und Westpreussen.* Leben und Leistung seit dem 18. Jahrhundert. Würzburg: Holzner Verlag, 1970. 340 pp., ports. (Ostdeutsche Beiträge aus dem Göttinger Arbeitskreis, Bd. XLVIII.)

8772. SOKEL, WALTER HERBERT: *Der literarische Expressionismus.* Der Expressionismus in der deutschen Literatur des 20. Jahrhunderts. Vom Verf. durchgesehene und autorisierte Übersetzung von Jutta und Theodor Knust. 2. Aufl. München: Langen/Müller, 1970. 310 pp., bibl. (pp. 285-302). [Title of the American original: The Writer in Extremis.]

8773. STEINER, GEORGE: *Language and Silence.* Essays 1958-1966. Harmondsworth, Middlesex, England: Penguin Books, 1969. 368 pp. [First publ. by Faber & Faber, London, 1967.] [German edition]: *Sprache und Schweigen.* Essays über Sprache, Literatur und das Unmenschliche. Aus dem Engl. von Axel Kaun. Frankfurt a.M.: Suhrkamp Verlag, 1969. 275 pp. [A critical examination of events in Germany during the last 30 years. The essays incl.: The Pythagorean Genre. A conjecture in honour of Ernst Bloch. (1965). A Kind of Survivor. For Elie Wiesel (1965). K (Kafka) (1963). Schoenberg's Moses and Aron (1965). Georg Lukács and His Devil's Pact (1960).]

8774. ('DER) STURM'. *'Der Sturm'.* Wochenschrift (später Halbmonats-, dann Monatsschrift). Hrsg. von Herwarth Walden, Berlin 1910-1932. Nendeln (Lichtenstein): Kraus Reprint, 1970. 20 vols., ports., illus. [Herwarth Walden, orig. Georg Lewin, expressionist writer, born 1878 in Berlin, fled to Russia in 1933. 1941 banished to Siberia, never to be heard of again. 'Der Sturm' was a centre of expressionism. Else Lasker-Schüler (Walden's first wife), Döblin, Ludwig Rubiner, Alfred Lichtenstein, van Hoddis, Mynona, Alfred Kerr, and many other German Jews contributed to this important magazine.]

8775. Töpner, Kurt: *Gelehrte Politiker und politisierende Gelehrte.* Die Revolution von 1918 im Urteil deutscher Hochschullehrer. Göttingen: Musterschmidt-Verlag, 1970. 290 pp., bibl. (pp. 270-284). (Veröffentlichungen der Gesellschaft für Geistesgeschichte, Bd. 5.) [Incl.: Professoren in Eisners Diensten. Hugo Preuss und die Weimarer Reichsverfassung. Also: Moritz J. Bonn, Jonas Cohn, Paul Nikolas Cossman, Ernst Feder, Otto v. Gierke, Ludwig Haas, Hugo Haase, Gustav Landauer, Paul Landsberg, Erich Mühsam, Franz Oppenheimer, Walther Rathenau, Hugo Sinzheimer.]

8776. Torberg, Friedrich (i.e. Friedrich Kantor Berg): *Der Beifall war endenwollend.* Theaterkritiken und Glossen. Hrsg. von Eberhard Gaupp. München: Dt. Taschenbuch-Verlag, 1970. 245 pp.

8777. Wiese, Benno von, ed.: *Deutsche Dichter des 19. Jahrhunderts.* Ihr Leben und Werk. Berlin: Erich Schmidt Verlag, 1969. 600 pp., bibls. [See also No. 5857/YB. XII.]

8778. Wiese, Benno von, ed.: *Deutsche Dramaturgie vom Naturalismus bis zur Gegenwart.* Tübingen: Max Niemeyer Verlag, 1970. 190 pp., bibl. (Deutsche Texte.) [Incl. Hofmannsthal, Julius Bab, Karl Kraus, Rudolf Borchardt, Kurt Pinthus, Hasenclever, Sternheim, Schnitzler, Benjamin.]

8779. Wiesner, Herbert, ed.: *Handbuch der deutschen Gegenwartsliteratur in drei Bänden.* Zweite, verb. und erw. Aufl. München: Nymphenburger Verlagshandlung, 1970. [3 vols.] [Vol. I: Die deutsche Gegenwartsdichtung (Hermann Kunisch). Vol. II: Der Expressionismus: Anreger, Herausgeber, Verleger (Günther Erken). Deutsche Literatur im Exil 1933-1947 (Hildegard Brenner). Die innerdeutsche Literatur im Widerstand, 1933-1945 (Herbert Wiesner). Vol. III: Bibliographie der Personalbibliographien (Herbert Wiesner, Irena Zivsa, Christoph Stoll).- For 1st ed. in one vol., ed. by H. Kunisch and Hans Hennecke, 1965, see No. 5227/YB. XI.]

B. Individual

8780. ADLER, ALFRED. Adler, Alfred: *Menschenkenntnis.* 71.-82. Tsd. Frankfurt a.M.: Fischer Bücherei, 1970. 254 pp., bibl. A.A. pp. 252-253. (Fischer-Bücherei, Bd. 6080.)

8781. Sperber, Manès: *Alfred Adler oder Das Elend der Psychologie.* Wien: Fritz Molden Verlag, 1970. 304 pp., ports., illus. (Reihe: Glanz und Elend der Meister). [Cf. Seelenkunde im Kreuzfeuer der Kritik (Jean Améry). [In]: 'Merkur', 24. Jg., H. 10, 1970. Pp. 978-984.]

8782. ADORNO, THEODOR W. Adorno, Theodor W.: *Ästhetische Theorie.* Gesammelte Schriften, Bd. 7. Hrsg. von Gretel Adorno und Rolf Tiedemann. Frankfurt a.M.: Suhrkamp Verlag, 1970. 544 pp.

8783. Adorno, Theodor W.: *Aufsätze zur Gesellschaftstheorie und Methodologie.* Frankfurt a.M.: Suhrkamp Verlag, 1970. 244 pp. [Cf. Post Mortem. Ein Umstrittener wurde zum Klassiker (Wolf Lepenies). [In]: 'FAZ', 29. Aug. 1970.]

8784. Adorno, Theodor W.: *Dissonanzen.* Musik in der verwalteten Welt. 4. Ausg. Göttingen: Vandenhoeck u. Ruprecht, 1969. 159 pp. (Kleine Vandenhoeck-Reihe 28/29/29a.)

8785. Adorno, Theodor W.: *Erziehung zur Mündigkeit.* Vorträge und Gespräche mit Hellmut Becker, 1959-1969. Hrsg. von Gerd Kadelbach. Frankfurt a.M.: S. Suhrkamp Verlag, 1970. 156 pp.

8786. Adorno, Theodor W.: *Die Freudsche Theorie und die Struktur der faschistischen Propaganda.* [In]: 'Psyche'. Juli. Stuttgart: Ernst Klett Verlag. 1970.

8787. Adorno, Theodor W. and others: *Der Positivismusstreit in der deutschen Soziologie.* 2. Aufl. Neuwied: Luchterhand Verlag, 1970. 347 pp. (Soziologische Texte, Bd. 58.)

8788. Massing, Otwin: *Adorno und die Folgen.* Über das hermetische Prinzip der 'Kritischen Theorie' Neuwied: Luchterhand Verlag, 1970. 67 pp.

8789. Anders, Günther [i.e. Günther Stern]: *Der Blick vom Mond.* Reflexionen über Weltraumflüge. München: C. H. Beck, 1970. 190 pp.

8790. Andrian, Leopold: *Der Garten der Erkenntnis.* Mit Dokumenten und zeitgenössischen Stimmen. Hrsg. von Walter H. Perl. Frankfurt a.M.: S. Fischer Verlag, 1970. 116 pp. [The work by the grandson of G. Meyerbeer was first publ. 1895, and later transl. into French and Dutch. Incl. are comments by S. Fischer, Felix Salten, H. v. Hofmannsthal, Karl Kraus.]

8791. Arendt, Hannah: *Macht und Gewalt.* Von der Verf. durchges. Übersetzung aus dem Englischen (On Violence) von Gisela Uellenberg. München: Piper Verlag, 1970. 107 pp. (Serie Piper, Bd. 1.)

8792. (H.) AUFHÄUSER, *Bankhaus, München. 100 Jahre Bankhaus H. Aufhäuser 1870/1970.* Festschrift. (München), 1970, n.p., ports., illus., facsim. [Heinrich Aufhäuser (1842-1917), his sons Martin (1842-1917 USA), Siegfried (18 ?-1949 USA).]

8793. BARNOWSKY, VICTOR. RICHTER, RENATE: *Das deutsche Künstler-Theater (in Berlin) unter Victor Barnowsky (1915-1924).* Eine Untersuchung unter besonderer Berücksichtigung der zeitgenössischen Kritik. Berlin: Colloquium Verlag, 1970. 144 pp. (Theater und Drama, Bd. 33.)

8794. BAUER, OTTO. LEICHTER, OTTO: *Otto Bauer.* Tragödie oder Triumph. Wien: Europa Verlag, 1970. 395 pp., front. port., bibl. O.B. pp. 381-392. [Austromarxist (1882-1938).]

8795. BEN-HAIM, PAUL. PAUL BEN-HAIM. A short biography and appreciation published on the occasion of the composer's 70th birthday, on July 5, 1967. Tel Aviv: Israeli Music Publications, [1967]. 27 pp., port., music. [Paul Ben-Haim, i.e. Paul Frankenburger, was born in Munich.]

8796. BENJAMIN, WALTER. BENJAMIN, WALTER: *Die Aufgabe des Übersetzers.* (Vorwort zu): Charles Baudelaire: Ausgewählte Gedichte. Deutsch von Walter Benjamin. Frankfurt a.M.: Suhrkamp Verlag, 1970. (Bibliothek Suhrkamp, Bd. 257.)

8797. BENJAMIN, WALTER: *Berliner Chronik.* Hrsg. und mit einem Nachwort versehen von Gershom Scholem. Frankfurt a.M.: Suhrkamp Verlag, 1970. 133 pp. (Bibliothek Suhrkamp, Bd. 251.)

8798. ADORNO, THEODOR W.: *Über Walter Benjamin.* Hrsg. und mit Anmerkungen versehen von Rolf Tiedemann. Frankfurt a.M.: Suhrkamp Verlag, 1970. 187 pp. (Bibliothek Suhrkamp, Bd. 260).

8799. BERGMANN, HUGO: *Das philosophische Werk Bernhard Bolzanos.* Mit Benutzung ungedruckter Quellen kritisch untersucht. Nebst einem Anhang: Bolzanos Beiträge zur philosophischen Grundlegung der Mathematik. Reprograf. Nachdruck der Ausgabe Halle/Saale, Niemeyer 1909. Hildesheim: G. Olms, 1970. xiv, 230 pp., bibls. B.B. pp. 212-219.

8800. BERNAYS, JACOB. BERNAYS, JACOB: *Grundzüge der verlorenen Abhandlung des Aristoteles über Wirkung der Tragödie.* Eingel. von Karlfried Gründer. Reprograf. Nachdruck der Ausgabe Breslau, Trewendt 1858. Hildesheim: G. Olms Verlag, 1970. xi, 70 pp. [Philologist (1824-1881).]

8801. BERNFELD, SIEGFRIED [and others]: *Psychoanalyse und Marxismus.* Dokumentation einer Kontroverse. Einleitung von Hans Jörg Sandkühler. Frankfurt a.M.: Suhrkamp Verlag, 1970. 314 pp., bibl. (Reihe Theorie.)

8802. BERNSTEIN, EDUARD: *Die Voraussetzungen des Sozialismus und die Aufgaben der Sozialdemokratie.* Hrsg. von Günther Hillmann. 2. Aufl. Reinbek b. Hamburg: Rowohlt Verlag, 1970. 250 pp., bibl. E.B., bibl. (pp. 242-247). (Texte des Sozialismus und Anarchismus 1800-1950, Bd. 14.)

8803. BLOCH, ERNST. BLOCH, ERNST: *Freiheit und Ordnung.* Abriss der Sozialutopien. Mit Quellentexten. 2. Aufl. Reinbek b. Hamburg: Rowohlt Verlag, 1970. 251 pp. (Rowohlts deutsche Enzyklopädie 318/319: Sachgebiet Philosophie.) [First publ. New York: Aurora, 1946.]

8804. BLOCH, ERNST: *Politische Messungen, Pestzeit, Vormärz.* Frankfurt a.M.: Suhrkamp Verlag, 1970. 490 pp. (Bd. 11 der Gesamtausgabe). [Political essays written 1902-1970.]

8805. BLOCH, ERNST: *Spuren.* Neue, erw. Ausg. Frankfurt a.M.: Suhrkamp Verlag, 1970. 220 pp. (Bibliothek Suhrkamp, Bd. 54.)

8806. BLOCH, ERNST: *Tübinger Einleitung in die Philosophie.* Neue, erw. Ausg. Frankfurt a.M.: Suhrkamp Verlag, 1970. 384 pp. (Gesammelte Werke, Bd. 13.) [First publ. 1963/1964. See No. 5263/YB. XI.]

8807. BLOCH, ERNST: *Über Methode und System bei Hegel.* Frankfurt a.M.: Suhrkamp Verlag, 1970. (edition suhrkamp, Bd. 413.)

8808. *Ernst Bloch zum 85.* Hrsg. von HAP Grieshaber. Gedichte von Margarete Hannsmann. Zeichnungen von Grieshaber. Hamburg: Claassen Verlag, 1970.

8809. KARLOW, GERT, ed.: *Es spricht Ernst Bloch.* Ernst Bloch zum 85. Geburtstag. Kassette mit 2 Schallplatten und Textheft. Frankfurt a.M.: Suhrkamp Verlag, 1970. [Cont. 4 speeches by Bloch.]

8810. KRÄNZLE, KARL: *Utopie und Ideologie*. Gesellschaftskritik und politisches Engagement im Werk Ernst Blochs. Bern: Lang Verlag, 1970. 211 pp. (Europäische Hochschulschriften, Reihe Philosophie, Bd. 1.) (Diss. Univ. Basel.)

8811. PASTERK, URSULA: *Das Phänomen der Utopie im Denken Ernst Blochs*. Zur kritischen Fundierung der menschlichen Hoffnung in einer 'Ontologie des Noch-Nicht-Seins'. Wien: Phil. Diss., 1969. vii, 354 pp., bibl. (pp. 349-354.) [Typescript.]

8812. PIERRE, RONALD: *Ernst Bloch als jüdisch-marxistischer Philosoph und Schriftsteller*. Luxemburg: Selbstverlag (Rue des Celtes 8), 1966. xiii, 114 pp., bibl. E.B., bibl. (pp. i-xii.)

8813. RATSCHOW, CARL HEINZ: *Atheismus im Christentum?* Eine Auseinandersetzung mit Ernst Bloch. Gütersloh: Mohn Verlag, 1970. 119 pp. [Cf. Ernst Bloch: Atheismus im Christentum. No. 7975/YB. XV.]

8814. UEDING, GERT: *Schein und Vor-Schein in der Kunst*. Zur Ästhetik Ernst Blochs. [In]: 'Neue Deutsche Hefte'. Nr. 121, H.1. Gütersloh: S. Mohn Verlag, 1969. Pp. 109-129.

8815. BOHR, NIELS. MOORE, RUTH: *Niels Bohr*. Ein Mann und sein Werk verändern die Welt. Aus dem Amerik. von F. A. Thorn. München: Paul List Verlag, 1970. 423 pp. [Physicist (1885-1962).]

8816. BONDI, GEORG. PAWLOWSKY, PETER: *Helmut Küpper, vormals Georg Bondi, 1895-1970*. Düsseldorf und München: Helmut Küpper vormals Georg Bondi, 1970. 75 pp., ports., illus., facsims., bibl. (pp. 53-54). [Georg Bondi was the publisher of the Stefan George circle.]

8817. BORCHARDT, RUDOLF. HILLARD, GUSTAV: *Rudolf Borchardt als metapolitischer Dichter*. [In]: Festschrift für Prof. Hans Barion zum 70. Geburtstag. Wuppertal: Brockhaus Verlag, 1970.

8818. HILLARD, GUSTAV: *Zwei Borchardt-Anthologien*. [In]: 'Merkur', 24. Jg., H. 5 (265). Stuttgart: Ernst Klett Verlag, 1970. Pp. 491-494. [Gedichte. Auswahl und Einleitung von Theodor W. Adorno [and] Auswahl aus dem Werk. See Nos. 7212, 7214/YB. XIV.]

8819. KRAFT, WERNER: *Rudolf Borchardts 'Jamben'* [In].: 'Hochland'. 31. Jg., Sept./Okt. München: Kösel Verlag, 1969. Pp. 414-433. [See No. 5882/YB. XII.]

8820. BRILLING, BERNHARD. *Bibliographie Bernhard Brilling 1928-1968*. (283 Nummern mit Orts-, Namen- und Sachindex). [In]: Theokratia. Bd. 1. Pp. 195-223. [See No. 8500.]

8821. BROCH, HERMANN. BROCH, HERMANN: *Gedanken zur Politik*. Ausgewählt von Dieter Hildebrandt. Frankfurt a.M.: Suhrkamp Verlag, 1970. 186 pp. (Bibliothek Suhrkamp, Bd. 245.)

8822. BROCH, HERMANN: *Huguenau oder die Sachlichkeit*. Roman. Frankfurt a.M.: Suhrkamp Verlag, 1970. 324 pp. (Bibliothek Suhrkamp, Bd. 187.) [Part III of 'Die Schlafwandler'. For Parts I-II see No. 4015/YB. IX.]

8823. BROCH, HERMANN: *Die Schuldlosen*. Roman. Mit einer Einführung von Hermann J. Weigand und einem Nachwort von Viktor Suchy. Wien, Frankfurt a.M.: Büchergilde Gutenberg, 1970. 299 pp. (Lizenz des Suhrkamp Verl.)

8824. DURZAK, MANFRED: *Hermann Brochs 'Der Tod des Vergil'* — Echo und Wirkung. Ein Forschungsbericht. [In]: Literaturwissenschaftliches Jahrbuch. Im Auftrag der Goerres-Gesellschaft hrsg. von Hermann Kunisch. N.F. Bd. 10, 1969. Berlin: Duncker & Humblot, 1970. vi, 438 pp., front. port., illus.

8825. HEYDEMANN, KLAUS: *Die Stilebenen in Hermann Brochs Roman 'Der Tod des Vergil'*. Diss. Wien, 1970. 197 pp., bibl. (pp. 191-196).

8826. JONAS, KLAUS W.: *Von Mexico bis Teesdorf: Begegnungen im Zeichen von Hermann Broch*. [In]: 'Börsenblatt für den Deutschen Buchhandel'. Nr. 103. 30. Dez. Frankfurt a.M., 1970. Pp. 339-346, illus., facsim. [The author's search for material for his Broch bibliography.]

8827. MENGES, KARL: *Kritische Studien zur Wertphilosophie Hermann Brochs*. Tübingen: Max Niemeyer Verlag, 1970. vii, 181 pp. (Studien zur deutschen Literatur, Bd. 22.)

8828. STEINECKE, HARTMUT: *Hermann Broch als politischer Dichter*. [In]: Deutsche Beiträge zur geistigen Überlieferung. Ein Jahrbuch. Hrsg. von George J. Metcalf und H. Stefan Schultz. Bd. VI. Heidelberg: Lothar Stiehm Verlag, 1970. 199 pp.

8829. STEINECKE, HARTMUT: *Hermann Broch und der polyhistorische Roman*. Studien zur Theorie und Technik eines Romantyps der Moderne. Bonn: H. Bouvier Verlag, 1970. 221 pp.

8830. BROD, MAX. BROD, MAX: *Paganism — Christianity — Judaism: A Confession of Faith*. Transl. from the German by William Wolf. Tuscaloosa: University of Alabama Press, 1970. 276 pp. ['Heidentum, Christentum, Judentum. Ein Bekenntnisbuch' was publ. 1921.]

8831. BROD, MAX: *Soll die Geschichte des Judentums neu geschrieben werden?* [In]: 'Isr. Wochenblatt'. 25. Sept. Zürich, 1970.

8832. HEBEL, FRIEDA: *Max Brod.* Zum ersten Todestag. [In]: 'Zeitschrift für die Geschichte der Juden'. 7. Jg., Nr. 1, 1970. Pp. 5-13. [See No. 8420.]

8833. *Max Brod.* Eingeleitet von Willy Haas und Jörg Mager. Hamburg: Hans Christians Verlag, 1970, port., facsim. bibl. M. B. (Hamburger Bibliographien. Bd. 12.)

8834. PAZI, MARGARITA: *Max Brod — Werk und Persönlichkeit.* Bonn: H. Bouvier, 1970. vi, 177 pp., bibl. M. B. pp. 170-173, bibl. (pp. 174-177). (Abhandlungen zur Kunst-, Musik- und Literaturwissenschaft, Bd. 95.)

8835. WELTSCH, ROBERT: *Max Brod and his Age.* New York: Leo Baeck Institute, 1970. 30 pp. (The Leo Baeck Memorial Lecture, 13.)

8836. CANETTI, ELIAS. CANETTI, ELIAS: *Alle Vergeudete Verehrung.* Aufzeichnungen 1949-1960. München: Carl Hanser Verlag, 1970. 160 pp. (Reihe Hanser, Bd. 50.)

8837. HELWIG, WERNER: *Die Gesichter des Elias Canetti.* [In]: 'Merkur'. 24. Jg., H. 8 (268), Aug. Stuttgart: Ernst Klett Verlag, 1970. Pp. 786-787.

8838. CASSIRER, ERNST. CASSIRER, ERNST: *Individuum und Kosmos in der Philosophie der Renaissance.* 3., unveränd. Aufl. Reprograf. Nachdruck der 1. Aufl. Leipzig und Berlin 1927. Darmstadt: Wissenschaftliche Buchgesellschaft, 1969. 458 pp., illus.

8839. HERTZBERG, ARTHUR: *A Reminiscence of Ernst Cassirer.* [In]: LBI Year Book XV. London, 1970. Pp. 245-246.

8840. CELAN, PAUL [Orig. Paul Anczel, also Antschel]: CELAN, PAUL: *Ausgewählte Gedichte.* Auswahl von Klaus Reichert. Frankfurt a.M.: Suhrkamp Verlag, 1970. 194 pp.

8841. CELAN, PAUL: *Lichtzwang.* Frankfurt a.M.: Suhrkamp Verlag, 1970. 108 pp. [Celan's last vol. of poetry.]

8842. CELAN, PAUL: *'Auf, werde licht'.* Zu einem Gedicht von Paul Celan. [In]: 'NZZ', 29. März. Zürich, 1970.

8843. FRIEDLANDER, ALBERT HOSCHANDER: *Paul Celan.* [In]: European Judaism. Vol. 5, No. 2. London, 1970. Pp. 19-22.

8844. GADAMER, HANS-GEORG: *Wer bin ich und wer bist Du?* Zu einem Gedicht von Paul Celan. [In]: 'NZZ', Nr. 223. 17. Mai. Zürich, 1970. Pp. 49/50, port.

8845. MAYER, PETER: *Paul Celan als jüdischer Dichter.* Diss. Universität Heidelberg, 1969. [And]: Pp. 190-195 in: 'Emuna-Horizonte'. 5. Jg., Nr. 3, 1970. [See No. 9158.]

8846. MEINECKE, DIETLIND, ed.: *Über Paul Celan.* Frankfurt a.M.: Suhrkamp Verlag, 1970. 322 pp., bibl. P.C. pp. 291-319. (edition suhrkamp, Bd. 495.)

8847. MEINECKE, DIETLIND: *Wort und Name bei Paul Celan.* Zur Widerruflichkeit des Gedichts. Bad Homburg v.d.H.: Gehlen Verlag, 1970. (Literatur und Reflexion, Bd. 2.)

8848. *Paul Celan, 23.11.1920 Czernowitz - 1.5.1970 Paris* (suicide) [Obituaries]: Gedenken an Paul Celan (Franz Büchler), 'Neue Rundschau', 81. Jg., H. 3, Frankfurt a.M.: S. Fischer, 1970. Pp. 628-634. Und er ging den Weg des Unmöglichen (Siegfried Einstein, 'Isr. Wochenblatt', 20. Nov., Zürich, 1970. Sind noch Lieder zu singen? Zur Lyrik Paul Celans, 'FAZ', 20. Juni, Frankfurt a.M. 1970, port. Paul Celan. A broadcast (Michael Hamburger), August 18th, British Broadcasting Corp. (B.B.C.), London, 1970. Das Grab eines Dichters (Hans Jürgen Heise), 'Welt der Literatur', 6. Aug., Hamburg, 1970, illus. Zum Tode Paul Celans (Dieter Hoffmann), 'Tribüne', H. 34, Frankfurt a.M., 1970. Erinnerung an Paul Celan (Hans Mayer), 'Merkur', 24 Jg., H. 12 (272), Dez., Stuttgart, Ernst Klett Verlag, 1970. Pp. 1150-1163. [This vol. also cont. 'Letzte Gedichte' by Paul Celan, pp. 1148-1149.] Kaddisch für Paul Celan, 'AJR Information', June, London, 1970. Gedenkblatt für Paul Celan 'NZZ', Nr. 317, 12. Juli, Zürich 1970. Du sei wie du, (Werner Weber), 'Zeit', 15. Mai, Hamburg, 1970, port.

8849. CHAGALL, MARC. CRESPELLE, JEAN PAUL: *Marc Chagall — Liebe, Traum und Leben.* Eine Biographie. Aus dem Französischen von Peter Kamnitzer. Hamburg: Marion von Schröder Verlag, 1970. 323 pp., bibl. [French title: Chagall — l'amour, le rêve et la vie.]

8850. ROTERMUND, HANS-MARTIN: *Marc Chagall und die Bibel.* Lahr/Schwarzwald: Verlag Ernst Kaufmann, 1970. 176 pp., illus.

8851. COHN, JONAS. COHN, JONAS: *Vom Sinn der Erziehung.* Ausgewählte Texte, hrsg. von Dieter Jürgen Löwisch. Paderborn: Schöningh Verlag, 1970. 258 pp., front. port., bibl. J. C., bibl. (pp. 235-238). (Quellen zur Geschichte der Pädagogik). [Incl. Jonas Cohn's System der Pädagogik (Dieter-Jürgen Löwisch).] [Jonas Cohn (1869-1947), philosopher.]

8852. DÖBLIN, ALFRED. DÖBLIN, ALFRED: *Die drei Sprünge des Wang-lun*. Chinesischer Roman. Mit einem Nachwort von Walter Muschg. Ungek. Ausgabe. München: Dt. Taschenbuch-Verlag, 1970. 501 pp. (Lizenz d. Walter Verl., Olten.)

8853. DÖBLIN, ALFRED: *Gesammelte Erzählungen*. Hrsg. und mit einem Nachwort versehen von Walter Muschg. Reinbek b. Hamburg: Rowohlt Verlag, 1970. 432 pp.

8854. GRASS, GÜNTER: *Über meinen Lehrer Döblin und andere Vorträge*. Berlin: Literarisches Colloquium, 1969. 77 pp.

8855. KORT, WOLFGANG: *Alfred Döblin*. Das Bild des Menschen in seinen Romanen. Bonn: Verlag H. Bouvier, 1970. 149 pp., bibl. A.D., bibl. (pp. 139-143). (Studien zur Germanistik, Anglistik und Komparatistik, Bd. 8.)

8856. KREUTZER, LEO: *Alfred Döblin*. Sein Werk bis 1933. Stuttgart: Kohlhammer Verlag, 1970. 196 pp., port. (Sprache und Literatur, Bd. 66.)

8857. RIBBAT, ERNST: *Die Wahrheit des Lebens im frühen Werk Alfred Döblins*. Münster (Westf.): Aschendorff Verlag, 1970. 237 pp. (Münstersche Beiträge zur deutschen Literaturwissenschaft, Bd. 4). (Diss. Münster/Westf.)

8858. WEYEMBERGH-BOUSSART, MONIQUE: *Alfred Döblin*. Seine Religiosität in Persönlichkeit und Werk. Bonn: H. Bouvier Verlag, 1970. 426 pp., bibl. A.D. pp. 381-398. (Abhandlungen zur Kunst-, Musik- und Literaturwissenschaft, Bd. 76.)

8859. EHRENSTEIN, ALBERT. DREWS, JÖRG: *Die Lyrik Albert Ehrensteins*. Wandlungen in Thematik und Sprachstil von 1910 bis 1931. Ein Beitrag zur Expressionismus-Forschung. München, Diss. 1969. iii, 228 pp. [Poet, writer (1886-1950).]

8860. EINSTEIN, ALBERT. *Einstein anekdotisch*. Ein Genie, zum Lachen. Hrsg. von Steffi und Armin Hermann. München: Kindler Verlag, 1970. 127 pp., front. port., illus.

8861. WAGNER, JOSEF: *Was Einstein wirklich sagte*. Wien: Verlag Fritz Molden, 1970. 208 pp., illus., biogr. notes. (Reihe: 'Was sie wirklich sagten'.)

8862. EINSTEIN, CARL. PENKERT, SIBYLLE: *Carl Einstein — Existenz und Ästhetik*. Einf. mit einem Anhang unveröffentlichter Nachlasstexte von Sibylle Penkert. Wiesbaden: Franz Steiner Verlag, 1970. 100 pp., ports., facsims. (Verschollene und Vergessene.) [See also No. 8009/YB. XV.] [Art historian (1885-1940), committed suicide.]

8863. EISLER, HANNS. BUNGE, HANS-JOACHIM: *Fragen sie mehr über Brecht*. Hanns Eisler im Gespräch. Mit einem Nachwort von Stephan Hermlin. München: Rogner und Bernhard, 380 pp., front. illus., ports., illus., bibl. H. E. pp. 352-355. [The composer (1898-1962) talks about his co-operation with Brecht, the twenties in Berlin, Schönberg, Adorno, Herbert Marcuse and others.]

8864. ELOESSER, ARTHUR. SCHAAF, DORIS: *Der Theaterkritiker Arthur Eloesser*. Berlin: Colloquium Verlag, 1970. 172 pp. (Theater und Drama, 21). [1870-1938.] [See also appreciations on the occasion of the centenary of his birth in: 'AJR Information' (Fritz Friedlaender), Apr. London 1970. 'Allgemeine' (E.G. Lowenthal), 20. März, Düsseldorf 1970.]

8865. FISCHER, S. – S. FISCHER VERLAG. FREUND, J[OACHIM] HELLMUT, ed.: *Almanach S. Fischer Verlag*. Bilder aus dem S. Fischer Verlag 1886-1914 und 1915-1934. Frankfurt a.M.: S. Fischer Verlag, 1969/1970. 164, 181 pp., ports., illus. facsims. [2 vols., complementary to No. 8866.]

8866. MENDELSSOHN, PETER DE: *S. Fischer und sein Verlag*. Frankfurt a. M.: S. Fischer Verlag, 1970. 1487 pp., front. port., bibl. (pp. 1349-1373.)

8867. FRANZOS, KARL EMIL. FRANZOS, KARL EMIL: *Ein Kampf ums Recht*. Illustrationen von Erhard Schreier, Berlin [East]: Verlag Neues Leben, 1970. 414 pp., illus. [1848-1904.]

8868. FREUD, SIGMUND. FREUD, SIGMUND: *Abriss der Psychoanalyse. Das Unbehagen in der Kultur*. Mit einer Rede von Thomas Mann als Nachwort. (379.-408. Tsd.) Frankfurt a.M./Hamburg: Fischer-Bücherei, 1970. 150 pp. (Fischer-Bücherei, 6043.)

8869. FREUD, SIGMUND: *Gesammelte Werke*. Chronologisch geordnet. Unter Mitwirkung von ... hrsg. von Anna Freud. Frankfurt a.M.: S. Fischer Verlag, 1966/1970. [17 vols.]

8870. ALTHUSSER, LOUIS: *Freud und Lacan*. Aus dem Franz. übersetzt von Hanns-Henning Ritter und Herbert Nagel. Berlin: Merve Verlag, 1970. 41 pp. (Internationale marxistische Diskussion, 10.) [Jacques de Lacan, psychologist, 1901-   .]

8871. BIRK, KASIMIR: *Sigmund Freud und die Religion*. Münsterschwarzach: Vier-Türme-Verlag, 1970. xv, 125 pp., bibl. (pp. ix-xv.) (Münsterschwarzacher Studien, Bd. 10.)

8872. DREWS, JÖRG, ed.: *Freud anekdotisch*. München: Kindler Verlag, 1970. 110 pp., front. port.

8873. HUCH, KURT JÜRGEN: *Freuds Exil.* [In]: 'Merkur'. 24. Jg., H. 1 (261), Jan. Stuttgart: Ernst Klett Verlag, 1970. Pp. 65-78.

8874. LEE, ROY STUART: *Freud and Christianity.* Harmondsworth, Middlesex: Penguin Books, 1967. 185 pp., bibl. (pp. 177-178.)

8875. LOEWENBERG, P.: *A Hidden Zionist Theme in Freud's 'My son, the Myops . . .' dream.* [In]: 'Journal of the History of Ideas'. Vol. 31, No. 1, Jan. -March. Philadelphia, 1970. Pp. 129-132.

8876. MANNONI, OSCAR: *Freud.* Paris: Editions du Seuil, 1970. 188 pp., ports., illus., facsims., bibl. (pp. 184-188). (Ecrivains de toujours, 82.)

8877. MITSCHERLICH, ALEXANDER: *Versuch, die Welt besser zu bestehen.* Fünf Plädoyers in Sachen Psychoanalyse. Frankfurt a.M.: Suhrkamp Verlag, 1970. 173 pp. (Bibliothek Suhrkamp, Bd. 246.)

8878. POLITZER, HEINZ: *Sigmund Freud als Deuter seiner Träume.* [In]: 'Merkur'. 24. Jg., H. 1 (261), Jan. Stuttgart: Ernst Klett Verlag, 1970. Pp. 34-48.

8879. ROAZEN, PAUL: *Brother Animal: The Story of Freud and Tausk.* London: Allen Lane, The Penguin Press, 1970. 245 pp., ports., illus. [Cf. No. 8034/YB. XV.]

8880. SCHIFF, B.: *The Wisdom and Humour of Sigmund Freud.* New York: Fleet, 1969.

8881. SONNEMANN, ULRICH: *Hegel und Freud.* [In]: 'Psyche'. Zeitschrift für Psychoanalyse und ihre Anwendungen. Hrsg. Alexander Mitscherlich. Nr. 24, März. Stuttgart: Ernst Klett Verlag, 1970. Pp. 208-218.

8882. STONE, IRVING: *Der Seele dunkle Pfade.* Ein Roman um Sigmund Freud. Aus dem Amerik. von Norbert Wölfl. München: Drömersche Verlagsanstalt, 1970. 895 pp. [Orig. title: The Passions of the Mind: A Novel of Sigmund Freud. London: Cassell, 1970. 895 pp.]

8882a. WYSS, DIETER: *Marx und Freud.* Ihr Verhältnis zur modernen Anthropologie. Göttingen: Vandenhoek u. Ruprecht, 1969. 114 pp. (Kleine Vandenhoek-Reihe. 309/311.)

8883. FRISCH, SIEGFRIED. RUTKOWSKI, ERNST R. VON: *Einer der Tapfersten Offiziere im Regimente: Oberleutnant in Reserve Dr. Siegfried Frisch im Weltkrieg 1914-1918.* [In]: 'Zeitschrift für die Geschichte der Juden'. Nr. 2/3, 1970. Pp. 97-129, bibl. (pp. 125-129). [See No. 8420.] [Born 1886 in Galicia — ?].

8884. FROMM, ERICH: *Analytische Sozialpsychologie und Gesellschaftstheorie.* Frankfurt a.M.: Suhrkamp Verlag, 1970. 233 pp. (edition suhrkamp, 425.) [Cont. 9 essays written 1932-1970.]

8885. FROMM, ERICH: *Die Herausforderung Gottes und des Menschen.* Aus dem Amerik. übertragen von Harry Maor. Konstanz: Diana Verlag, 1970. 235 pp. [Orig. title 'You shall be as Gods'. See No. 5908/YB. XII.]

8886. GOLDSTEIN, MORITZ. [Pseud. Inquit.] SCHABER, WILL: *Nestor des deutschen Journalismus.* Zum 90. Geburtstag von Moritz Goldstein. [In]: 'Aufbau', No. XXXVI/13, March 27. New York, 1970, port. ['Inquit' of the 'Vossische Zeitung' publ. 1912 in 'Kunstwart' the provocative essay 'Deutsch-Jüdischer Parnass', recognising the danger of German antisemitism. Cf. Robert Weltsch [in]: LBI Year Book XV, London 1970, p.X.]

8887. GOLL, YVAN. GOLL, YVAN: *Oeuvres complètes.* Tome I. Paris: Emilie-Paul, 1969. [Orig. Lang (1891-1950).]

8888. PERKINS, VIVIEN: *Yvan Goll.* An iconographical study of his poetry. Bonn: H. Bouvier, 1970. vi, 198 pp., bibl. Y.G. pp. 183-185. (Studien zur Germanistik, Anglistik und Komparatistik, Bd. 5.)

8889. GOMBRICH, E. H.: *In Search of Cultural History.* Oxford: Clarendon Press, 1969. 55 pp.

8890. GOTHEIN, GEORG. KINDER, ELISABETH: *Nachlass Georg Gothein.* Bearb. Als Manuskript gedruckt. Koblenz: Bundesarchiv 1970. iv, 29 pp. (Findbücher zu Beständen des Bundesarchivs, Bd. 7.) [Georg Gothein (1857-1940), father Jewish. 1918/19 co-founder of the German Democratic Party, Reichsschatzminister.]

8891. GROS-GALLINER, GABRIELLA: *Glas.* A Guide for Collectors. London: Frederick Muller, 1970. 174 pp., illus. [Born in Berlin, daughter of the painter and art historian Arthur Galliner.]

8892. GUTFREUND, OTO. *Oto Gutfreund.* Ausstellung 7.12.1969-25.1.1970, Städt. Kunstgalerie, Bochum. Ausstellungskatalog. Bochum: Städt. Kunstgalerie, 1969/70. 12 pp. with illus., 29 pp. illus., bibl. O.G. [Cf. No. 8044/YB. XV.]

8893. HABER, FRITZ. HABER, CHARLOTTE: *Mein Leben mit Fritz Haber.* Spiegelungen der Vergangenheit. Düsseldorf: Econ Verlag, 1970. 293 pp., front. port.

8894. HAHN, KURT. *Kurt Hahn.* Ed. by H. Rohrs and H. Tunstall-Behrens. London: Routledge, 1970. 268 pp. [Kurt Hahn recently celebrated his 85th birthday.]

8895. HARDEN, MAXIMILIAN. HILLARD, GUSTAV [i.e. Gustav Steinbömer]: *Maximilian Harden zum 100. Geburtstag*. [In]: Recht auf Vergangenheit. Essay, Glossen, Veduten. 2. Veränd. Aufl. Hamburg: Hoffmann und Campe, 1970. 239 pp. [First ed. 1966.]

8896. MOMMSEN, WOLFGANG, ed.: *Nachlass Maximilian Harden*. Bearb. unter Mitwirkung von Gertrud Winter. Als Ms. gedruckt. Koblenz: Bundesarchiv, 1970. 111 pp. (Findbücher zu Beständen des Bundesarchivs, Bd. 4.)

8897. WELLER, B[jörn] UWE: *Imperialismus und Resignation*. Maximilian Hardens politische Publizistik. [In]: 'Publizistik'. 15. Jg., H. 4. Konstanz: Druckerei und Verlagsanstalt Konstanz, 1970. Pp. 319-334.

8898. WELLER, B[jörn] UWE: *Maximilian Harden und die 'Zukunft'*. Bremen: Carl Schünemann Verlag, 1970. 485 pp., ports., facsim., bibl. M.H. pp. 453-458, bibl. (pp. 458-470.) (Studien zur Publizistik. Bremer Reihe — Deutsche Presseforschung, Bd. 13.) (Diss. Univ. Münster/Westf.)

8899. HEINE, HEINRICH. HEINE, HEINRICH: *Säkularausgabe*. Werke, Briefwechsel, Lebenszeugnisse. Hrsg. von den Nationalen Forschungs- und Gedenkstätten der klassischen deutschen Literatur in Weimar und dem Centre National de la Recherche Scientifique in Paris. 50 Bde.: I. Heines Werke in deutscher Sprache. II. Heines Werke in französischer Sprache. III. Heines Briefwechsel. IV. Heines Lebenszeugnisse und Gesamtregister. Berlin [East]: Akademie-Verlag, 1970. Bd. 5: *Reisebilder I* (1824-1828) (Karl Wolfgang Becker), 214 pp. Bd. 7: *Über Frankreich 1831-1837*. Berichte über Kunst und Politik (Ed. Fritz Mende), 315 pp. Bd. 20: *Briefe 1815-1831*. Bd. 21: *Briefe 1831-1841*. (Ed. Fritz H. Eisner), 448, 450 pp.

8900. ALTENHOFER, NORBERT, ed.: *Heinrich Heine*. Mit Anmerkungen, Zeittafel und Registern. München: Heimeran-Verlag, 1970. 600 pp. (Reihe 'Dichter über ihre Dichtungen', Bd. 8/I, II, III.)

8901. BERENDSOHN, WALTER ARTUR: *Die künstlerische Entwicklung Heines im Buch der Lieder*. Struktur- und Stilstudien. Stockholm: Almqvist u. Wiksell, 1970. 209 pp. (Acta universitatis Stockholmiensis. Stockholmer germanist. Forschungen, 7.)

8902. BETZ, ALBRECHT: *Ästhetik und Politik*. Heinrich Heines Prosa. München: Hanser Verlag, 1970. 192 pp. (Literatur als Kunst.)

8903. BORRIES, MEGHTHILD: *Ein Angriff auf Heinrich Heine*. Kritische Betrachtungen zu Karl Kraus. Stuttgart: W. Kohlhammer Verlag, 1970. 108 pp. (Studien zur Poetik und Geschichte der Literatur, Bd. 13.)

8904. FLAKE, OTTO: *Heine*. [In]: Die Verurteilung des Sokrates. Biographische Essays aus sechs Jahrzehnten. Hrsg. von Fredy Gröbli-Schaub und Rolf Hochhuth. Nachwort von Kurt Scheid. Heidelberg: Verlag Lambert Schneider, 1970. 351 pp., front. port. (Veröffentlichungen der Deutschen Akademie für Sprache und Dichtung Darmstadt, 44.) [The Heine essay was written in 1947.]

8905. *Heine-Jahrbuch 1971*. Hrsg.: Heine Archiv, Düsseldorf, Landes- und Stadtbibliothek u. Heinrich-Heine-Gesellschaft. Schriftltg.: Eberhard Galley. Hamburg: Hoffmann und Campe, 1970. 153 pp., ports., illus., bibl. H.H. pp. 148-153. [Incl. Glossen zum Notizblatt Heines für den Rabbi von Bacharach (Ludwig Rosenthal). Heine und Büchner (Heinz Fischer).]

8906. HULTBERG, HELGE: *Heine*. Levned, Meninger, Boger. (Lebenslauf, Meinungen, Bücher.) Kopenhagen, 1969. [In Danish]. [Cf. Walter A. Berendsohn: Die neueste Heine Forschung. [In]: 'MB', 9. April. Tel Aviv, 1971.]

8907. KAUFMANN, HANS: *Heinrich Heine*. Geistige Entwicklung und künstlerisches Werk. 2. Aufl. Berlin [East]: Aufbau Verlag, 1970. 290 pp., ports., illus. [1st ed. 1967.]

8908. KREUTZER, LEO: *Heine und der Kommunismus*. (Erw. Fassung eines Vortrags). Göttingen: Verlag Vandenhoeck & Ruprecht, 1970. 38 pp. (Kleine Vandenhoeck-Reihe, 322.)

8909. LEHRMANN, C. CH.: *Heine — ein deutscher, französischer oder jüdischer Dichter?* [In]: 'Udim'. 1. Jg., Nr. 1. Frankfurt a.M., 1970. Pp. 47-66. [See No. 8671.]

8910. MARCUSE, LUDWIG: *Heinrich Heine in Selbstzeugnissen und Bilddokumenten*. Dokumentarischer und bibliographischer Anhang: Paul Raabe. 7. Aufl. Reinbek b. Hamburg: Verlag Rowohlt, 1969. 181 pp. (rowohlts monographien.)

8911. MENDE, FRITZ: *Heinrich Heine*. Chronik seines Lebens und Werkes. Hrsg. von den Nationalen Forschungs- und Gedenkstätten der klassischen deutschen Literatur in Weimar. Berlin [East]: Akademie-Verlag, 1970. xiv, 418 pp., gen. table [of the Heine and van Geldern families].

8912. '*Mitteilungen der Heinrich-Heine-Gesellschaft Düsseldorf'*. H. 1-2. Düsseldorf, 1970. 12 pp., 12 pp., ports., facsims.

8913. PRAWER, SIEGBERT: *Heine's Shakespeare*. A Study in Contexts. An Inaugural Lecture delivered before the University of Oxford on 5 May 1970. Oxford: Clarendon Press, 1970. 40 pp.

8914. ROS, GUIDO: *Heinrich Heine und die 'Pariser Zeitung' von 1838*. Ein Beitrag zur Geschichte der deutschen Emigrantenpresse in Paris 1830-1848. [In]: 'Publizistik'. 15. Jg., H.3. Konstanz: Druckerei und Verlagsanstalt, 1970. Pp. 216-228.

8915. TAUBES, J. S.: *Eine Botschaft vom Geiste Heinrich Heines*. Nebst d. Essay 'Heinrich Heines Heimkehr zu Gott'. Toluca Lake/Calif.: Pacifia House, 1968. 133 pp.

8916. VICTOR, WALTHER: *Marx und Heine*. Tatsachen und Spekulation in der Darstellung ihrer Beziehungen. 4. Aufl. Berlin [East]: Henschel Verlag, 1970. 150 pp.

8917. VORDTRIEDE, WERNER: *Heine Kommentar*. Unter Mitarbeit von Uwe Schweikert. Bd. 1: *Zu den Dichtungen*. [Contained also in: Heinrich Heine: Sämtliche Werke, München: Winkler, 1969. See No. 8052/YB. XV.] Bd. 2: *Kommentare zu den Schriften zur Literatur und Politik*. München: Winkler Verlag, 1970. 148 pp., 190 pp.

8918. HEINE, THOMAS THEODOR. LANG, LOTHAR: *Thomas Theodor Heine*. München: Rogner & Bernhard, 1970. 160 pp., ports., facsims. (Klassiker der Karikatur, Bd. 1.)

8919. HERMANN, GEORG [i.e. Georg Borchardt]. HERMANN, GEORG: *Grenadier Wordelmann*. Roman. Hrsg. von Bernhard Kaufhold. Berlin [East]: Verlag Das Neue Berlin, 1970. 383 pp. (Ausgew. Werke in Einzelausgaben.)

8920. HERMANN, GEORG: *Rosenemil*. Ein Roman aus dem alten Berlin. Hrsg. von Bernhard Kaufhold. Berlin [East]: Verlag Das Neue Berlin, 1969. 457 pp. (Lizenz d. Südd. Verl., München.) [See No. 3328/YB. VIII.] [Georg Hermann (1871-1943 Auschwitz).]

8921. HILLER, KURT. FRITZSCHE, KLAUS: *Rationalismus als Ideologie am Beispiel Kurt Hillers*. [In]: 'Frankfurter Hefte'. 25. Jg., H.1, Jan. Neuwied: Hermann Luchterhand Verlag, 1970.

8922. SCHUMANN, THOMAS B.: *Schöpfer des Aktivismus*. Kurt Hiller zum 85. Geburtstag. [In]: 'Allgemeine'. Nr. XXV/33, 14. Aug. Düsseldorf, 1970.

8923. HODDIS, JAKOB VAN [i.e. Hans Davidsohn.] REITER, UDO: *Jakob von Hoddis*. Leben und lyrisches Werk. Göppingen: Kümmerle Verlag, 1970. 214 pp., front .port., facsims. (Göppinger Arbeiten zur Germanistik, Nr. 16.) (Diss. Univ. München.) [Expressionist (1887-1942).]

8924. HÖNIGSWALD, RICHARD. HÖNIGSWALD, RICHARD: *Die Grundlagen der Allgemeinen Methodenlehre*. Teil II. Hrsg. von Hariolf Oberer. Bonn: Verlag H. Bouvier, 1970. xii, 316 pp. (Veröffentlichung durch das Hönigswald-Archiv am Philosophischen Seminar A der Univ. Bonn. Schriften aus dem Nachlass Bd. 8.) [For part I see No. 8077/YB. XV.]

8925. HÖNIGSWALD, RICHARD: *Philosophie und Sprache*. Problemkritik und System. Reprograf. Nachdr. der Ausg. Basel 1937. Darmstadt: Wissenschaftl. Buchgesellschaft, 1970. x, 461 pp.

8926. HOFFNUNG, GERARD. HOFFNUNG, GERARD: *Hoffnungs grosses Orchester*. Cartoons. München: Verlag Langen-Müller, 1969. 254 pp., illus. [Also]: Teilsammlung. Frankfurt a.M. u. Hamburg: Fischer-Bücherei, 1970. 123 pp., illus. (Fischer-Bücherei, 1144.)

8927. HOFFNUNG, GERARD: *Vögel, Bienen, Klapperstörche*. Hoffnungs Sprösslinge. Cartoons. Aus dem Englischen. München: Dt. Taschenbuch-Verlag, 1969. 53 pp. illus. with text, [Engl. title: Birds, Bees and Storks]. [Musician and Cartoonist (1925-1959).]

8928. HOFMANNSTHAL, HUGO VON. HOFMANNSTHAL, HUGO VON: *Gedichte und lyrische Dramen*. *Dramen*. Gesammelte Werke in Einzelausgaben, hrsg. von Herbert Steiner. Frankfurt a.M.: S. Fischer Verlag, 1970. 544, 512 pp.

8929. HAUPT, JÜRGEN: *Konstellationen Hugo von Hofmannsthals*. Harry Graf Kessler, Ernst Stadler, Bertolt Brecht. Mit einem Essay: *Hofmannsthal und die Nachwelt von Hans Mayer*. Salzburg: Residenz Verlag, 1970. 145 pp., bibl.

8930. HUGO VON HOFMANNSTHAL. Zeugnisse und Dokumente. [In]: 'Hofmannsthal Blätter'. Veröffentlichungen der Hugo von Hofmannsthal-Gesellschaft. Hrsg. Martin Stern. H.5, Herbst. Frankfurt a.M., 1970. Pp. 321-405, facsim., bibl.: Die Hofmannsthal Forschung 1970(2) mit Nachtrag 1964-1969 [comp. by] Norbert Altenhofer (pp. 402-405). [Contributions incl.: Ein Brief Hofmannsthals an Samuel Fischer. Mitgeteilt von Mario Uzielli. Eine frühe Rezension von Karl Kraus: H. 's 'Gestern' (Eugene Weber). H.'s Antwort auf Richard Dehmels weltpolitischen 'Warnruf' 1918 (Martin Stern). Joseph Roth, Hofmannsthal und das Kunstgewerbe (Hartmut Scheible).] [See also No. 9112.]

8931. KILIAN, ERNST RUDOLF: *Die verfremdete Wirklichkeit in den Erzählungen Hugo von Hofmannsthals und Franz Kafkas.* Diss. Wien, 1970. 346 pp., bibl. (pp. 337-345.)

8932. KOBEL, ERWIN: *Hugo von Hofmannsthal.* Berlin: Verlag Walter de Gruyter, 1970. x, 377 pp. (Habil.-Schrift Zürich.)

8933. TAROT, ROLF: *Hugo von Hofmannsthal.* Daseinsformen und dichterische Struktur. Tübingen: Max Niemeyer Verlag, 1970. x, 425 pp., bibl. H. v. H. pp. 407-408. (Habil.-Schrift Zürich.)

8934. HOLLÄNDER, Felix. NOVAK, RUDOLF: *Das epische Werk von Felix Holländer.* Phil. Diss. Wien, 1970. vi, 313 pp., bibl. (pp. 309-313.) [Typed Ms.] [Novelist, critic (1867-1931).]

8935. HORKHEIMER, MAX. HORKHEIMER, MAX: *Anfänge der bürgerlichen Geschichtsphilosophie.* Hegel und das Problem der Metaphysik. Montaigne und die Funktion der Skepsis. Einleitung von Alfred Schmidt. Frankfurt a.M.: Fischer Bücherei, 1970. 144 pp.

8936. HORKHEIMER, MAX: '*Die Sehnsucht nach dem ganz Anderen*' — Ein Interview mit Kommentar von Helmut Gumnior. Hamburg: Furche Verlag, 1970. 90 pp. (Stundenbücher, Bd. 97.) [See also No. 8942.]

8937. HORKHEIMER, MAX: *Traditionelle und kritische Theorie.* Vier Aufsätze. Frankfurt a.M.: Fischer Bücherei, 1970. 230 pp. (Fischer Bücherei, Bd. 6015 BdW.)

8938. HORKHEIMER, MAX: *Vernunft und Selbsterhaltung.* Erstausgabe. Frankfurt a.M.: S. Fischer Verlag, 1970. 57 pp. [The essay, written in 1941/42, following Walter Benjamin's death, is contained in 'Festschrift für Walter Benjamin', ed. by Max Horkheimer and Theodor W. Adorno in 1942.]

8939. HORKHEIMER, MAX: *Verwaltete Welt.* Gespräch zwischen Max Horkheimer und Otmar Hersche. Zürich: Verlag Die Arche, 1970. 42 pp. (Arche Nova.)

8940. HOLZ, HANS HEINZ: *Impuls und Verfall der kritischen Theorie.* Zum 75. Geburtstag ihres Begründers Max Horkheimer am 14. Febr. [In]: 'Frankfurter Rundschau', 14. Febr. 1970, port. [Also]: Dialektik kennt keinen Stillstand (Karl Korn) [In]: 'FAZ', 13. Febr. 1970, port. [And]: Kritik, nicht Götzendienst (Günter Zehm) [In]: 'Die Welt', 13. Febr. Hamburg, 1970, port. [Max Horkheimer is the first recipient of the "Stuttgart Medal". He also received the Lessing Prize for 1970.]

8941. STÖHR, MARTIN: *Max Horkheimer und die Theologie.* Kirchenfunksendung, Hessischer Rundfunk, 21. April 1970. 5 pp. [Typescript.]

8942. '*Was wir "Sinn" nennen, wird verschwinden*'. Spiegel-Gespräch der Spiegel-Redakteure Georg Wolff und Helmut Gumnior mit dem Philosophen Max Horkheimer. [In]: 'Der Spiegel'. 24. Jg., Nr. 1/2, 5. Jan. Hamburg, 1970. Pp. 76-84, ports., illus. [See also No. 8936.]

8943. WESTARP, MICHAEL-VIKTOR GRAF: '*Kritische Theorie*' *in der Sackgasse.* Weg und Werk von Max Horkheimer. [In]: 'Merkur'. 24. Jg., H. 5 (265), Mai. Stuttgart: Ernst Klett Verlag, 1970. Pp. 477-484.

8944. HUSSERL, EDMUND. FEIN, HUBERT: *Genesis und Geltung in Husserls Phänomenologie.* Frankfurt a.M.: Europäische Verlagsanstalt, 1970. 126 pp.

8945. JACOBI, CARL GUSTAV [orig. Jacques Simon]. KOENIGSBERGER, LEO: *Carl Gustav Jacobi.* Festschrift zur Feier der hundertsten Wiederkehr seines Geburtstages. Neudruck der Ausgabe Leipzig 1904. (Nachdruck mit Genehmigung des Verlages B. G. Teubner, Stuttgart). Hildesheim: Verlag H. A. Gerstenberg, 1970. xviii, 554 pp., port., facsim. [Mathematician knight of the order Pour le Mérite (1804-1851).]

8946. JACOBS, MONTY (Montague). PREUSS, JOACHIM WERNER: *Der Theaterkritiker Monty Jacobs (1875-1945.)* Berlin: Colloquium Verlag, 1970. 212 pp. (Theater und Drama, 28.)

8947. JACOBY, JOHANN. SILBERNER, EDMUND: *Johann Jacoby 1843-1846.* Beitrag zur Geschichte des Vormärz. [In]: International Review of Social History. Vol. 14, No. 3. Assen, 1969. Pp. 353-411.

8948. SILBERNER, EDMUND: *Johann Jacoby in der Revolution von 1848/49.* [Pp. 153-259 in]: Archiv für Sozialgeschichte. Hrsg. von der Friedrich-Ebert-Stiftung. X. Bd. Hannover: Verlag für Literatur und Zeitgeschehen, 1970. 524 pp.

8949. SILBERNER, EDMUND: *Zur Jugendbiographie von Johann Jacoby.* [In]: Archiv für Sozialgeschichte. Hrsg. von der Friedrich-Ebert-Stiftung. IX. Bd. Hannover: Verlag für Literatur und Zeitgeschehen, 1969. Pp. 5-112. [J. Jacoby, physician and politician (1805-1877.]

8950. JEITTELES, ALOIS. WOLF, SALOMON: *Alois Jeitteles*. Beitrag zum Beethovenjahr. [In]: 'Allgemeine', Düsseldorf, 'MB', Tel Aviv, 23 .Okt. 1970. [Alois Jeitteles (1794-1858) as a student of philosophy and medicine wrote the texts of Beethoven's 'Liederkreis: An die ferne Geliebte'.]

8951. JELLINEK, GEORG: *Ausgewählte Schriften und Reden*. Neudruck der Ausgabe Berlin 1911, vermehrt um ein Lebensbild. In 2 Bden. Bd. 1: *Georg Jellinek. Ein Lebensbild von Camilla Jellinek*. Aalen: Scientia Verlag, 1970. 140, xxxii, 454 pp., ports.; x, 584 pp. [2 vols.]

8952. JONAS, HANS: *Wandel und Bestand*. Frankfurt a.M.: Vittorio Klostermann, 1970. 30 pp. [Cf. Hugo Bergman: Zu einem Vortrage und einem Buche von Hans Jonas [In]: 'MB', 8. Jan. Tel Aviv, 1971.]

8953. KAFKA, FRANZ. BINDER, HARTMUT: *'Kafkas Briefscherze' und 'Sein Verhältnis zu Josef David'*. [In]: Jahrbuch der Deutschen Schillergesellschaft. 13. Jg. Marbach a.L. 1969. Pp. 536-559.

8954. FREY, EBERHARD: *Franz Kafkas Erzählstil*. Eine Demonstration neuer stilanalytischer Methoden in Kafkas Erzählung 'Ein Hungerkünstler'. Bern: Lang Verlag, 1970. xiii, 372 pp. (Europäische Hochschulschriften. Reihe 1: Deutsche Literatur und Germanistik. Bd. 31.) (Diss., Cornell Univ. Ithaca/N.Y.)

8955. HENEL, HEINRICH: *Kafka's Der Bau, or How to Ecsape from a Maze*. [In]: The Discontinuous Tradition. Studies in German Literature in honour of Ernest Ludwig Stahl. Ed. by P. F. Ganz. Oxford: Clarendon Press, 1970.

8956. KOBS, JÖRGEN: *'Kafka' — Untersuchungen zu Bewusstsein und Sprache seiner Gestalten*. Hrsg. von Ursula Brech. Bad Homburg: Athenäum Verlag, 1970. 560 pp., bibl. (pp. 544-550.)

8957. KRAFT, WERNER: *Die 'Fackel' als eine Quelle für Kafka*. [In]: 'Neue Zürcher Zeitung', Nr. 39, 25. Jan. Zürich, 1970, facsim.

8958. LINSIDER, J. A. :*Kafka and Judaism*. [In]: The' Yavneh Review'. Vol. 7. New York, 1969. Pp. 130-138.

8959. *New Views on Franz Kafka*. Articles and Essays. [In]: 'Mosaic'. Vol. 3, No. 4, Summer. Winnipeg, 1970. 190 pp.

8960. KAHLER, ERICH VON: *Untergang und Übergang*. Essays. München: Deutscher Taschenbuch-Verlag, 1970. 248 pp. (dtv-Taschenbücher, 638.) [Essays written 1952-1967.] [Erich v. Kahler (1885-1970). Obituaries: Gerson D. Cohen [In]: LBI News Letter, Fall, New York, 1970, port. Walter Müller-Seidel [In]: Deutsche Rundschau, H. 4, 1970. Pp. 822-829. Robert Weltsch [In]: LBI Year Book XV, London 1970. P. xviii, port. Victor Lange: Gedenkwort für Erich v. Kahler [In]: Jahrbuch 1970. Deutsche Akademie für Sprache und Dichtung Darmstadt. Heidelberg: Verlag Lambert Schneider, 1971. Pp. 95-97.]

8961. KAHNWEILER, DANIEL-HENRY. KAHNWEILER, DANIEL-HENRY: Ästhetische Betrachtungen. Köln: Verlag Du Mont Schauberg, 1970. (Dokumente.)

8962. FEHSENBECKER, EVA: *Hommage à Kahnweiler*. Zu der Verleihung des Ehrenringes der Stadt Mannheim an Daniel-Henry Kahnweiler. [And]: Zur Ausstellung des Mannheimer Kunstvereins. [In]: 'Mannheimer Hefte'. Nr. 1, Mannheim, 1970. Pp. 28-33, port., illus. [The noted art-dealer and historian was born in Mannheim in 1884.]

8963. KANTOROWICZ, HERMANN: *Rechtshistorische Schriften*. Hrsg. von Helmut Coing und Gerhard Immel. Karlsruhe: Verlag C. F. Müller, 1970. xiv, 468 pp., bibl. H.K. pp. 465-468. [Prof. of law (1877-1940).]

8964. KERR, ALFRED [*i.e. Alfred Kempner.*] CORINO, K.: *Robert Musil und Alfred Kerr. Der Dichter und sein Kritiker*. [In]: Robert Musil. Studien zu seinem Werk. Im Auftrag der Vereinigung Robert-Musil-Archiv Klagenfurt hrsg. von Karl Dinklage u. a. Reinbek b. Hamburg: Rowohlt Verlag, 1970. 410 pp., port.

8965. DROSS, FRIEDRICH: *Ernst Barlach und Alfred Kerr*. [In]: 'NZZ', FA. Nr. 3, 4. Jan. Zürich, 1970. Pp. 39/40. [Ernst Barlach (1870-1938) and his art were much attacked by the Nazis who also maintained that he was a Jew or "Judenknecht". His harshest critic and adversary, however, was Alfred Kerr who showed no understanding for his work.]

8966. PEM: *Erinnerungen an Alfred Kerr*. [On the occasion of an Alfred Kerr exhibition organised by the German Institute in London and opened by Michael Kerr. [In]: 'Allgemeine', 19. Juni. Düsseldorf, 1970 and 'Aufbau', June 26, New York.]

8967. KESTEN, HERMANN: *Ein Optimist.* Beobachtungen unterwegs... München: Kurt Desch, 1970. 189 pp., bibl. H.K.

8968. KISCH, EGON ERWIN: *Zyankali gegen den Generalstab.* 10 Reportagen. Berlin [East] und Weimar: Aufbau Verlag, 1970. 125 pp.

8969. KLAAR, ALFRED. ANTOINE, RAINER: *Alfred Klaar — Theaterkritiker der Vossischen Zeitung.* Berlin: Colloquium Verlag, 1970. 104 pp. (Theater und Drama, 25.) [1848-1927.]

8970. KORTNER, FRITZ. KAUL, WALTER/ROBERT G. SCHEUER, eds.: *Fritz Kortner.* Berlin: Deutsche Kinemathek, 1970. 36 pp., ports., illus. (Schriftenreihe der DKB, Nr. 21.)

8971. LAMM, HANS: *Juden auf der Bühne.* [In]: 'Emuna-Horizonte'. Nr. 5, Okt. 1970. [Mainly on Kortner. See No. 9158.]

8972. LANDSITTER, CLAUS, ed.: *Kortner anekdotisch.* München: Dt. Taschenbuch-Verlag, 1970. 122 pp. [For original ed. see No. 6631/YB.XIII.]

8973. MEUSCHEL, STEFAN, IVAN NAGEL, HENNING RISCHBIETER and others: *Fritz Kortner oder das unerbittliche Theater.* Eine Monographie über Kortners Beitrag zur Theatergeschichte. Velber: Verlag Friedrich, 1970. 220 pp., ports., illus. [12 May 1892 Vienna — 22 July 1970 Munich. Many Jewish and non-Jewish papers carried obituaries.]

8974. KRACAUER, SIEGFRIED. KRACAUER, SIEGFRIED: *History.* The Last Things Before the Last. New York: Oxford University Press, 1969. 284 pp. [The last work of the sociologist (1889-1966), published posthumously.]

8975. SUHRBIER, HARTWIG: *Ein falsches Bild zu korrigieren.* Plädoyer für eine Siegfried-Kracauer-Gesamtedition. [In]: 'Frankfurter Rundschau'. 25. April. Frankfurt a.M., 1970, port.

8976. KRAUS, KARL. KRAUS, KARL, ed.: *Die Fackel.* Hrsg. des photomechanischen Nachdrucks: Heinrich Fischer. Bd. 13, Jg. 9, 1907/08, Nr. 223/249, 620 pp.; Bd. 14, Jg. 10, 1908/09, Nr. 250/278, 734 pp.; Bd. 15, Jg. 11, 1909/10, Nr. 279/300, 604 pp.; Bd. 16, Jg. 12, 1910/11, Nr. 301/320, 576 pp. München: Kösel Verlag, 1970. (Literarische Zeitschriften in Neudrucken.) [For vols. 1-8 see No. 7335/YB. XIV, 9-12 No. 8115/YB. XV. Cf. also No. 8957.]

8977. KRAUS, KARL: *Die Letzten Tage der Menschheit.* Tragödie in 5 Akten. Mit Vorspiel und Epilog. (2. Aufl.) München: Kösel Verlag, 1970. 769 pp., front. port., illus. (Werke. Bd. 5.) [First book edition 1922.]

8978. KRAUS, KARL: *Sittlichkeit und Kriminalität.* Hrsg. von Heinrich Fischer. München: Kösel Verlag, 1970. 348 pp. (Die Bücher der Neunzehn, Bd. 191, Sonderausgabe. Werke. Bd. 8.) [First publ. 1910.]

—— BORRIES, MECHTHILD: *Ein Angriff auf Heinrich Heine.* Kritische Betrachtungen zu Karl Kraus. [See No. 8903.]

8979. HARTL, EDWIN: *Karl Kraus im Spiegel der Literaturgeschichte oder Literaturgeschichte im Spiegel von Karl Kraus.* [In]: 'Österreich in Geschichte und Literatur'. 13. Jg., Graz: Stiasny Verlag, 1969. Pp. 183-196.

8980. KERRY, OTTO, comp.: *Karl-Kraus-Bibliographie.* Mit einem Register der Aphorismen, Gedichte, Glossen und Satiren. München: Kösel Verlag, 1970. 480 pp. [With a short introductory biography. — Cf. Karl Kraus und seine geistige Ausstrahlung. Ein literarisches Denkmal in Form einer Bibliographie. [In]: 'NZZ', 20. Nov. Zürich, 1970.]

8981. PERL, WALTER H.: *Die demolierte Literatur.* Eine frühe Streitschrift von Karl Kraus gegen 'Jung-Wien' (1897). [In]: 'Du'. August. Zürich, 1970, illus.

8982. *Polemik um Karl Kraus.* Polemik un einen grossen Polemiker (Jeannie Ebner). Verblendete Hellseher und Schwarzseher. Überlegungen zu den Gegnern von Karl Kraus (Edwin Hartl). Protest (Friedrich Jenaczek). Egon Erwin Kisch über Karl Kraus (Josef Polácek). Dokumentation einer Polemik. [In]: 'Literatur und Kritik'. Österreichische Monatsschrift. Jänner. Salzburg: Otto Müller Verlag, 1970. Pp. 1-36.

8983. TORBERG, FRIEDRICH: *Als die ersten 'Fackel'-Hefte erschienen.* Vortrag, geh. in der Österreichischen Gesellschaft für Literatur am 20. Mai 1969 und im Werkraumtheater der Münchner Kammerspiele am 3. Dez. 1969. [And]: G. J. Carr: *Zu den Briefen Else Lasker-Schülers an Karl Kraus.* [And]: Sigurd Paul Scheichl: *Publikationen des Auslandes über Karl Kraus.* [In]: 'Literatur und Kritik'. H. 49. Okt. Salzburg: Verlag Otto Müller, 1970. Pp. 531-545, 549-556, 557-560.

8984. URBACH, REINHARD: *Karl Kraus und Arthur Schnitzler*. Eine Dokumentation. [In]: 'Literatur und Kritik'. H. 49, Okt. Salzburg: Otto Müller Verlag, 1970. Pp. 513-530. (Karl Kraus: Briefe an Arthur Schnitzler. Arthur Schnitzler: Notizen über Karl Kraus.)

8985. LANDAUER, GUSTAV. BORRIES, ACHIM VON: *Gustav Landauer: 7. April 1870-2. Mai 1919*. [In]: 'Werkhefte', 24. Jg., H. 5, Mai. München, 1970. Pp. 141-145. [Articles on the centenary of his birth in many newspapers.]

8986. LANDSHUT, SIEGFRIED. LANDSHUT, SIEGFRIED: *Kritik der Soziologie und andere Schriften zur Politik*. Neuwied: Hermann Luchterhand Verlag, 1969. 372 pp. (Schriften zur Politik. Reihe Politica, Bd. 27.)

8987. HENNIS, WILHELM: *Siegfried Landshut (1897-1968)*. [In]: 'Zeitschrift für Politik'. Nr. 1. Köln: Carl Heymanns Verlag, 1970. [Since his return from Israel in 1951 the sociologist has held the first chair of Political Science in Hamburg.]

8988. LASKER-SCHÜLER, ELSE. GOTTGETREU, ERICH: '*War da . . . Jussuf*'. Neue Else Lasker-Schüler-Funde. Zum 25. Todestag der Dichterin am 22. Januar. [In]: 'MB', 23. Jan., Tel Aviv, 1970. [And in]: 'Das Neue Israel', 22. Jg., H. 8 u. 9, Febr./März. Zürich 1970. Pp. 637-639, 711-713. [Also]: Mirror of a Tormented Soul [In]: 'Jerusalem Post Magazine', 23 Jan., 1970.

8989. KRAFT, WERNER: *Else Lasker-Schüler*. Eine Gedenkrede anlässlich ihres 100jährigen Geburtstages in der Deutschen Bibliothek Tel Aviv, am 11. Februar 1969. Tel Aviv, 1969. 18 pp.

8990. LASSALLE, FERDINAND. LASSALLE, FERDINAND: *Reden und Schriften*. Aus der Arbeiteragitation 1862-1864. Mit einer Lassalle-Chronik. Hrsg. von Friedrich Jenaczek. München: Dt. Taschenbuch-Verlag, 1970. 528 pp.

8991. NA'AMAN, SHLOMO: *Lassalle*. Hannover: Verlag für Literatur und Zeitgeschehen, 1970. xv, 890 pp., chron., bibl. (Veröffentlichungen des Instituts für Sozialgeschichte, Braunschweig.)

8992. LESSING, THEODOR. LESSING, THEODOR: *Geschichte als Sinngebung des Sinnlosen, oder Die Geburt der Geschichte aus dem Mythos*. Nachwort von Christian Gneuss. Hamburg: Rütten & Loening Verlag, 1962. 348 pp. [First publ. in 1916, completely rev. in 1927. The epilogue (pp. 319-337) was written in 1962.]

8993. SCHRÖDER, HANS EGGERT: *Theodor Lessings autobiographische Schriften*. Ein Kommentar. Bonn: H. Bouvier Verlag, 1970. 166 pp., bibl. Th.L. pp. 9-11. [Cf. No. 8287/YB.XV: Theodor Lessing: Einmal und nie wieder. Lebenserinnerungen. The philosopher and physician was murdered by the Nazis in 1933.]

8994. LEVI, HERMANN. STERN, JOSEF: *Hermann Levi und seine jüdische Welt*. [In]: 'Zeitschrift für die Geschichte der Juden'. 7. Jg., Nr. 1, 1970. Pp. 17-25, bibl. [See No. 8420.] Hermann Levi (1839-1900), was the first conductor of Wagner's Parsifal in Bayreuth, 1882.]

8995. LEVI, PAUL. WIEGENSTEIN, ROLAND: *Zwischen Spartakus und Sozialdemokratie*. [In]: 'Merkur'. 24. Jg., H. 2, Febr. Stuttgart: Ernst Klett Verlag, 1970. Pp. 185-188. [With ref. to: Paul Levi, ein demokratischer Sozialist in der Weimarer Republik. See Nos. 8130/8131/YB.XV.]

8996. LEWIN, KURT. LEWIN, KURT: *Die Entwicklung der experimentellen Willenspsychologie und die Psychotherapie*. Unveränd. reprograf. Nachdr. der Ausgabe Leipzig 1929. Darmstadt: Wissenschaftl. Buchgesellschaft, 1970. 28 pp., illus. (Libelle, Bd. 307.)

8997. MARROW, ALFRED J.: *The Practical Theorist: The Life and Work of Kurt Lewin*. New York: Basic Books, 1969. 290 pp. [Psychologist (1890-1947).]

8998. LUKÁCS, GEORG. LUKÁCS, GEORG: *Essays über Realismus*. Probleme des Realismus. Neuwied: Luchterhand Verlag, 1970. 678 pp. (Werke, Bd. 4). [Cf. Jürgen Rühle: Lukács, der grosse Mann von gestern: wie Marx. [In]: 'Welt der Literatur', 29. Apr., Hamburg, 1971, pp. 11-12, port.]

8999. LUKÁCS, GEORG: *Die Grablegung des alten Deutschland*. Essays zur deutschen Literatur des 19. Jahrhunderts. 2. Aufl. Reinbek b. Hamburg: Rowohlt Verlag, 1970. 172 pp. (rowohlts deutsche enzyklopädie, Bd. 276.)

9000. LUKÁCS, GEORG: *Marxismus und Stalinismus*. Politische Aufsätze. Hamburg: rowohlt Verlag, 1970. 251 pp. (rowohlts deutsche enzyklopädie, 327/328. Ausgewählte Schriften, Bd. 4.)

9001. LUKÁCS, GEORG: *Skizze einer Geschichte der neueren deutschen Literatur:* 1. Fortschritt und Reaktion in der deutschen Literatur. 2. Deutsche Literatur im Zeitalter des Imperialismus. Neuwied a.Rh.: Luchterhand Verlag, 1970. 247 pp.

9002. BAHR, EHRHARD: *Georg Lukács.* Berlin: Colloquium Verlag, 1970. 93 pp., front. port., chronology, bibl. (pp. 89-91). (Köpfe des XX. Jahrhunderts, Bd. 61.)

9003. DEMETZ, PAUL: *Der linke Humanismus und sein Schatten.* Zur Verleihung des Goethe-Preises an Georg Lukács. [In]: 'Merkur'. 24. Jg., H. 11 (271), Nov. Stuttgart: Ernst Klett Verlag, 1970. Pp. 1091-1093.

9004. PARKINSON, G. H. R., ed.: *Georg Lukács.* The Man, his Work and his Ideas. London: Weidenfeld and Nicolson, 1970. 254 pp., bibl. G.L. pp. 237-243, bibl. (pp. 244-247). (Reading University Studies on Contemporary Europe, 4.)

9005. SOZIOLOGISCHES LEKTORAT, ed.: *ad lectores.* Goethepreis. Georg Lukács zum 13. April 1970. Neuwied: Luchterhand Verlag, 1970. 198 pp., ports., illus.

9006. STAHL, KARL HEINZ: *Georg Lukács und die Zerstörung der Vernunft.* Eine Würdigung des Goethe-Preisträgers 1970. [In]: 'Tribüne', 9. Jg., H. 35, 1970. Pp. 3808-3816. [See No. 9145.] [On the occasion of his 85th birthday, on 13th April 1970, newspapers in many countries carried appreciations of his work. Georg Lukács died on 4th June 1971.]

9007. LUXEMBURG, ROSA. ABOSCH, HEINZ: *Das Ärgernis Rosa Luxemburg.* [In]: 'Neue Rundschau'. 81. Jg., H. 1. Berlin-Frankfurt a.M.: S. Fischer Verlag, 1970. Pp. 149-157.

9008. FRÖLICH, PAUL: *Rosa Luxemburg — Gedanke und Tat.* Mit einem Nachwort von Iring Fetscher. Durchsicht und Bearbeitung von Rose Frölich. Frankfurt a.M.: Europäische Verlagsanstalt, 1970. 377 pp., ports.

9009. NETTL, [JOHN] PETER: *Rosa Luxemburg.* Vom Autor gekürzte und bearbeitete Volksausgabe. Aus dem Engl. von Karl Römer. Die Zitate aus den polnischen Briefen R.L.'s ins Deutsche übertragen von Wanda Bronska-Pampuch. Köln: Kiepenheuer & Witsch, 1969. 576 pp., bibl. R.L. pp. 573-576. [First German ed. see No. 6659/YB. XIII, English ed. No. 5988/YB. XII.]

9010. [SCHULZE-]WILDE, HARRY: *Rosa Luxemburg — Ich war — ich bin — ich werde sein.* Eine Biographie mit Auszügen aus Rosa Luxemburgs Reden und Schriften. Wien: Fritz Molden Verlag, 1970. 264 pp., bibl. (pp. 253-258).

9011. MARCUSE, HERBERT. MARCUSE, HERBERT: *Ideen zu einer kritischen Theorie der Gesellschaft.* 2. Aufl. Frankfurt a.M.: Suhrkamp Verlag, 1969. 191 pp. (edition suhrkamp, Bd. 300.)

9012. GOLDSCHMIDT, GEORGES-ARTHUR: *Thomas Mann et Marcuse.* La Culture en Question. [In]: 'Allemagne D'Aujourd'hui'. Revue française d'information sur l'Allemagne. Nouvelle Série, No. 22. Mars-Avril. Paris 1970. Pp. 45-56, bibl.

9013. KATEB, GEORGE: *The Political Thought of Herbert Marcuse.* [In]: 'Commentary'. Vol. 49, No. 1, January. New York: American Jewish Committee, 1970. Pp. 48-63.

9014. MARKO, KURT: *Herbert Marcuse in der Sicht Moskaus.* Analyse. Hrsg.: Bundesinstitut für Ostwissenschaftliche und Internationale Studien. Köln, 1968. 4 pp. (Berichte des Bundesinstitut ..., Nr. 39.)

9015. MARX, KARL. ALTHUSSER, LOUIS: *For Marx.* London: Allen Lane The Penguin Press, 1970. 272 pp. [To rescue Marxism from ideological deviation, and Marx's own work from ideological distortion.]

9016. BERLIN, ISAIAH: *Benjamin Disraeli, Karl Marx and the Search for Identity.* [In]: 'Midstream'. Vol. 16, No. 7, Aug.-Sept. New York, 1970. Pp. 29-49.

9017. BOSSE, HANS: *Marx — Weber — Troeltsch.* Religionssoziologie und marxistische Ideologiekritik. Mainz: Matthias Grünewald Verlag, 1970. 240 pp.

9018. EUCHNER, WALTER and ALFRED SCHMIDT, eds.: *Kritik der politischen Ökonomie heute. 100 Jahre 'Kapital'.* Referate und Diskussionen vom Frankfurter Colloquium im September 1967, veranstaltet vom Institut für Politikwissenschaft der Johann Wolfgang Goethe-Universität und der Europäischen Verlagsanstalt. Frankfurt a.M.: Europäische Verlagsanstalt, 1968. 358 pp. (Politische Ökonomie, Geschichte und Kritik.)

9019. HARTMANN, KLAUS: *Die Marxsche Theorie.* Eine philosophische Untersuchung zu den Hauptschriften. Berlin: Walter de Gruyter, 1970. xii, 593 pp.

9020. HASTINGS, MICHAEL: *Tussy is Me.* London: Weidenfeld and Nicolson, 1970. 432 pp. [Eleanor (Tussy) Aveling, the youngest and favourite daughter of Karl Marx, was born in London in 1855, committed suicide in 1898.]

9021. KADENBACH, JOHANNES: *Das Religionsverständnis von Karl Marx.* Paderborn: Verlag Schöningh, 1970. lxxx, 420 pp., bibl. K.M. pp. xviii-xxx. (Abhandlungen zur Philosophie, Psychologie, Soziologie der Religion und Ökumenik. H. 24/26.)

9022. *Karl Marx und seine Familie.* 24 Fotos. Zusammengestellt vom Institut für Marxismus-Leninismus b.ZK der SED. Reichenbach im Vogtland: Verlag Bild und Heimat, 1968. 24 pp.

9023. LÖWENSTEIN, JULIUS ISAAC: *Vision und Wirklichkeit.* Marx contra Marxismus. Basel: Kyklos-Verlag, Tübingen: J. C. B. Mohr (Paul Siebeck Verlag), 1970. xiv, 170 pp. (Veröffentlichungen der List Gesellschaft, Bd. 65.)

9024. *Marx und die Revolution.* Vorträge von Ernst Bloch, Herbert Marcuse, Jürgen Habermas. Frankfurt a.m.: Suhrkamp Verlag, 1970. 141 pp. (edition suhrkamp, 430.)

9025. PRINZ, ARTHUR: *New Perspectives on Marx as a Jew.* [In]: LBI Year Book XV. London, 1970. Pp. 107-124, facsim.

9026. STEUSSLOFF, HANS: *Marxismus und sozialistischer Humanismus.* Ein Beitrag zu ethischen Grundfragen der ethischen Konzeption von Karl Marx. Beilage zu: 'Universität', Jg. 17, H. 1. Leipzig: Karl Marx Universität, 1968. 51 pp. (Gesellschafts- und sprachwissenschaftl. Reihe.)

9027. MARXISM. MACINTYER, ALASDAIR: *Marxism and Christianity.* Rev. edition. London: Gerald Duckworth, 1969. ix, 143 pp. [Also publ. in 1968 by Schocken Books, New York.]

9028. OSBORN, REUBEN [i.e. Reuben Osbert]: *Marxismus und Psychoanalyse.* Mit einer Einleitung von John Strachey .Aus dem Engl. übers. von André Wohlleben. Frankfurt a.M.: März-Verlag, 1970. 210 pp.

9029. MEITNER, LISA [LISE]. CRAWFORD, DEBORAH: *Lisa Meitner, Atomic Pioneer.* York: Crown, 1970. 192 pp. [1878-1968.]

9030. MENDELSSOHN, FELIX. REICH, WILLI, ed.: *Felix Mendelssohn im Spiegel eigener Aussagen und zeitgenössischer Dokumente.* Zürich: Manesse Verlag, 1970. 448 pp., port. (Manesse Bibliothek der Weltliteratur.)

9031. MEYERBEER, GIACOMO. MEYERBEER, GIACOMO: *Sizilianische Volkslieder.* Hrsg. von Fritz Bose. Berlin: De Gruyter Verlag, 1970. 77 pp. music with text.

9032. MÜHSAM, PAUL. MÜHSAM, PAUL: *... seit der Schöpfung wurde gehämmert an diesem Haus.* Paul Mühsam — Eine Werkauswahl. Mit einem Geleitwort von Zenta Maurina. Unter Mitarbeit von Else Levi-Mühsam hrsg. Konstanz: Seekreis Verlag, 1970. 204 pp., port.

9033. MÜHSAM, PAUL: *Tao, der Sinn des Lebens.* Eingeleitet von K. O. Schmidt. (Neuaufl.) München: Drei-Eichen-Verlag, 1970. 96 pp. (Wissen für jedermann.) [Paul Mühsam (1876 Brandenburg-1960 Israel).]

9034. MUNI, PAUL [i.e. Muni Weisenfreund]. FARBERMAN, BORIS: *Paul Muni.* Buenos Aires: Ejecutivo Sudamericano del Congreso Judío Mundial, 1970. 46 pp., front. port., ports. (Grandes Figuras Del Judaísmo, LVII). [Film actor.]

9035. NELSON, LEONARD. NELSON, LEONARD: *Die Schule der kritischen Philosophie und ihre Methode.* Mit einem Geleitwort von Paul Bernays, einem Vorwort von Grete Henry-Hermann und einem Beitrag von Julius Kraft: *Leonard Nelson und die Philosophie des 20. Jahrhunderts.* Bd. 1. Hamburg: Verlag F. Meiner, 1970. xxiv, 329 pp. Gesammelte Schriften in 9 Bden. Hrsg. von Paul Bernays u.a. [Also]: *System der philosophischen Ethik und Pädagogik.* Aus dem Nachlass hrsg. von Grete (Henry-)Hermann und Minna Specht. 3., unveränd. Aufl. Bd. 5. xix, 535 pp. *System der philosophischen Rechtslehre und Politik.* Bd. 6. 566 pp. [For vol. 3 see No. 4769/YB.X, vol. 7 No. 3402/YB. VIII.]

9036. NEUTRA, RICHARD. *Richard Neutra — Naturnahes Bauen.* Ein Bildband. Stuttgart: Verlag Alexander Koch, 1970.

9036a. ROTH, ALFRED: *Richard Neutra 1892-1970.* Anmerkungen zu seinem architektonischen Werk. [In]: 'NZZ', 10. Mai. Zürich, 1970. Pp. 49-50, illus.

9037. NOETHER, EMMY. DICK, AUGUSTE: *Emmy Noether, 1882-1935.* Basel: Birkhäuser Verlag, 1970. 72 pp., port., bibl. E.N. pp. 40-43. [Mathematician (1882-1935).]

9038. OPPENHEIM, FRIEDRICH CARL, *Freiherr von.* TREUE, WILHELM: *Der Privatbankier an der Wende vom 19. zum 20. Jahrhundert.* Dem Privatbankier Friedrich Carl Freiherr von Oppenheim zum 70. Geburtstag. [In]: 'Tradition', Zeitschrift für Firmen-Geschichte und Unternehmer-Biographie. 15. Jg., H. 5. Sept./Okt. München: Verlag F. Bruckmann, 1970. Pp. 225-238.

9039. OPPENHEIM, MAX, Freiherr von. TREUE, WILHELM: *Max Freiherr von Oppenheim —*
Der Archäologe und die Politik. [In]: 'Historische Zeitschrift'. Bd. 209, H. 1. München,
1970. Pp. 37-74. [Archaeologist, diplomat (1860-1946). Founder of Deutsches Orient-
Institut.]

9040. OPPENHEIMER, JULIUS ROBERT. MICHELMORE, PETER: *The Swift Years: Robert*
Oppenheimer's Story. Garden City, N.Y.: Doubleday, 1969. 320 pp.

9041. PAIS, ABRAHAM, ed.: *Oppenheimer.* New York: Scribner, 1969. 128 pp. [A collective
appreciation, especially of his contribution to physics, by five of his students and asso-
ciates.] [1904-1967.]

9042. ORLIK, EMIL. SCHREMMER, ERNST: *Pioneers in Art: Orlik, Hoffmann, Loos, Metzner.*
[In]: 'Central Europe Journal'. Vol. 18, No. 9, Sept. München: Sudetendeutsches
Archiv, 1970. Pp. 329-341, illus.

9043. POLGAR, ALFRED. POLGAR, ALFRED: *Bei Lichte betrachtet.* Texte aus vier Jahrzehnten.
Zusammengestellt von Bernt Richter. Reinbek b. Hamburg: Rowohlt Verlag, 1970.
205 pp. (rororo Taschenbuch, Bd. 1326/27). [Essayist, 1875-1955.]

9044. RATHENAU, WALTHER. BERGLAR, PETER: *Walter Rathenau.* Seine Zeit. Sein Werk.
Seine Persönlichkeit. Bremen: Carl Schünemann Verlag, 1970. 416 pp., front. port.,
notes, pp. 321-378, bibl. W.R., pp. 379-390, bibl. (pp. 390-408).

9045. BURCHARDT, LOTHAR: *Walther Rathenau und die Anfänge der deutschen Rohstoffbewirtschaf-*
tung im Ersten Weltkrieg. [In]: 'Tradition'. Zeitschrift für Firmen-Geschichte und Unternehmer-Biographie. 15. Jg., 4. H., Juli/Aug. München: Verlag F. Bruckmann, 1970.
Pp. 169-196, ports., facsim.

9046. FELIX, D.: *Walther Rathenau.* [In]: 'History Today'. Vol. 20, No. 9, Sept. London, 1970.
Pp. 638-647.

9047. MEYER, HENRY CORD: *Naumann and Rathenau: Their Paths to the Weimar Republic.* [Pp.
301-314 in]: The Responsibility of Power. Historical Essays in Honor of Hajo Holborn.
Ed. by Leonard Krieger and Fritz Stern. London: Macmillan, 1968. xiv, 464 pp.

9048. SWARSENSKY, HARDI: *Walther Rathenau.* Leben, Werk und Wollen. [In]: 'Zeitschrift für
die Geschichte der Juden'. 5. Jg., Nr. 1. Tel Aviv, 1968. Pp. 1-20.

9049. RÉE, PAUL. PFEIFFER, ERNST, ed.: *Friedrich Nietzsche, Paul Rée und Lou von Salomé —*
Die Dokumente ihrer Begegnung. Frankfurt a.M.: Insel Verlag, 1970. 600 pp. [Philosopher,
1849-1901.]

9050. REINHARDT, MAX. REINHARDT, MAX: *Regiebuch zu 'Macbeth'.* Köln: Schäuble
Verlag, 1970. xxiv, 169 pp., illus.

9051. HILLARD, GUSTAV [i.e. Gustav Steinbömer]: *Das Erbe Max Reinhardts.* [Pp. 84-97 in]:
Recht auf Vergangenheit. Essays, Glossen, Veduten. 2., durchges. Aufl. Hamburg:
Hoffmann und Campe Verlag, 1970. 239 pp. [First ed. 1966.]

9052. LEISLER, EDDA and GISELA PROSSNITZ, eds.: *Max Reinhardt und die Welt der Commedia*
dell'arte. Text- und Bilddokumentation. Salzburg: Otto Müller Verlag, 1970. (Erste
Veröffentlichung der Max-Reinhardt-Forschungsstätte in Salzburg.)

9053. ROTH, JOSEPH. ROTH, JOSEPH: *Der Neue Tag. Unbekannte politische Arbeiten, 1919 bis*
1927, Wien, Berlin, Moskau. Hrsg. und mit einem Vorwort von Ingeborg Sültemeyer.
Köln: Kiepenheuer & Witsch, 1970. 280 pp., front. port.

9054. BRONSEN, DAVID: *Joseph Roths Beziehung zur Habsburger Monarchie.* Ein Kapitel öster-
reichisch-jüdischer Geschichte. [In]: 'Tribüne' 9. Jg., H. 33., 1970. Pp. 3556-3564.
[See No. 9145.]

9055. BRONSEN, DAVID: *Die journalistischen Anfänge Joseph Roths, Wien 1918-1920.* [In]: 'Literatur
und Kritik'. Österreichische Monatsschrift. Nr. 41, Jänner. Salzburg: Otto Müller
Verlag, 1970. Pp. 37-54.

9056. BRONSEN, DAVID: *Der unwillkommene Gast: Joseph Roths Übersiedlung nach Wien.* [And]:
Joseph Roth im Widerspruch zum Zionismus, (Hansotto Ausserhofer). [In]: 'Emuna-Horizonte'. Nr. 5, Okt. 1970. Pp. 320-330. [See No. 9158.]

9057. SCHEIBLE, HARTMUT: *Joseph Roth.* Mit einem Essay über Gustave Flaubert. Stuttgart:
W. Kohlhammer Verlag, 1970. 199 pp., bibl. (pp. 195-199). (Studien zur Poetik und
Geschichte der Literatur. Bd. 16.) (Diss., Univ. Frankfurt a.M.)

9058. SACHS, NELLY. SACHS, NELLY: *The Seeker and other poems.* New York: Farrar, Straus &
Cudahy, 1970. 399 pp. [A bilingual edition of the German original and English translation.]

9059. SACHS, NELLY: *Verzauberung.* Späte szenische Dichtungen. Frankfurt a.M.: Suhrkamp
Verlag, 1970. 156 pp. (Bibliothek Suhrkamp, Bd. 276.)

9060. BEZZEL-DISCHNER: *Poetik des modernen Gedichts*. Zur Lyrik von Nelly Sachs. Bad Homburg v. d. Höhe: Gehlen Verlag, 1970. 148 pp. (Frankfurter Beiträge zur Germanistik, Bd. 10.) (Diss., Univ. Frankfurt/M.)

9061. BLUMENTHAL-WEISS, ILSE: *Die wahre Lebensretterin von Nelly Sachs*. [In]: 'Aufbau', 20. Nov. New York, 1970. [Gudrun Dähnert née Harlan, now living in Dresden.]

9062. KERSTEN, PAUL: *Die Metaphorik in der Lyrik von Nelly Sachs*. Mit einer Wort-Konkordanz und einer Nelly Sachs-Bibliographie. Hamburg: Lüdke Verlag, 1970. xi, 424, 143 pp. (Geistes- und sozialwissenschaftliche Dissertationen, 7. Diss., Univ. Hamburg.)

9063. SAGER, P.: *Die Lyrikerin Nelly Sachs*. [In]: 'Neue Deutsche Hefte'. Jg. 17, Nr. 4 (128). Gütersloh: S. Mohn Verlag, 1970. Pp. 26-45.

9064. UNSELD, SIEGFRIED: *'Mit meinem Untergang nähre ich dich'*. Zum Tode von Nelly Sachs, Friedenspreisträgerin 1965. [In]: 'Börsenblatt für den Deutschen Buchhandel'. 26. Jg., Nr. 45, 5. Juni. Frankfurt a.M., 1970. Pp. 1286-1290, port., facsim. [Nelly Sachs, born 10 Dec. 1891 in Berlin, died 12 May 1970 in Stockholm. Appreciations appeared in many countries.]

9065. SCHELER, MAX. BURGER, HUBERT: *Wert und Person bei Max Scheler*. Diss., Wien, 1969. v, 179 pp., bibl. (pp. 175-178).

9066. SCHNITZLER, ARTHUR. SCHNITZLER, ARTHUR: *Zug der Schatten*. Drama in 9 Bildern (unvollendet). Aus dem Nachlass hrsg. und eingel. von Françoise Derré. Frankfurt a.M.: S. Fischer Verlag, 1970. 119 pp.

——— URBACH, REINHARD: *Karl Kraus und Arthur Schnitzler*. Eine Dokumentation. [See No. 8984].

9067. SCHOENBERG, ARNOLD. BORETZ, BENJAMIN and EDWARD T. CONE, eds.: *Perspectives on Schoenberg and Stravinsky*. An Anthology. London: Oxford University Press, 1969. 294 pp., music scores. (Perspectives of New Music.)

9068. SCHOEPS, HANS-JOACHIM. SCHOEPS, HANS-JOACHIM: *'Bereit für Deutschland!'* Der Patriotismus deutscher Juden und der Nationalsozialismus. Frühe Schriften 1930 bis 1939. Eine historische Dokumentation. Berlin: Haude & Spenersche Verlagsbuchhandlung, 1970. 316 pp. [Cf. Robert Neumann: Bei 'Arischen': 'Anständiger' Jude, H. Schoeps. [In]: 'Tribüne'. H. 36, 1970. Pp. 3952-3955.] [See No. 9145.]

9069. SCHOEPS, HANS-JOACHIM: *Rufmord 1970*. Beiheft zu 'Bereit für Deutschland!' Der Patriotismus deutscher Juden und der Nationalsozialismus. Erlangen und Berlin: Im Selbstverlag des Verfassers, 1970.

9070. SEGHERS, ANNA. SEGHERS, ANNA: *Aufstellen eines Maschinengewehrs im Wohnzimmer der Frau Kamptschik*. Erzählungen. Mit einem Nachwort von Christa Wolf. Neuwied: Luchterhand Verlag, 1970. 164 pp. (Sammlung Luchterhand, 14.)

9071. *Anna Seghers*. Anlässlich des 70. Geburtstages von Anna Seghers am 19. 11. 1970 zusammengestellt von Ewald Birr unter Mitarbeit von Gertrud Saito. Hrsg. Hilde Weise. [In]: Bibliographische Kalenderblätter. Sonderblatt 28. Berlin [East]: Berliner Stadtbibliothek, 1970. 42 pp., front. port.

9072. NEUGEBAUER, HEINZ: *Anna Seghers*. Ihr Leben und Werk. Hrsg. vom Kollektiv für Literaturgeschichte. Leitung: Kurt Böttcher. Red.: Paul Günter Krohn. Berlin [East]: Verlag Volk und Wissen ,1970. 208 pp., bibl. A.S. pp. 200-201. (Schriftsteller der Gegenwart. 4: Deutsche Reihe.)

9073. SONNEMANN, LEOPOLD. GERTEIS, KLAUS: *Leopold Sonnemann*. Ein Beitrag zur Geschichte des demokratischen Nationalstaatsgedankens in Deutschland. Frankfurt a.M.: Waldemar Kramer Verlag, 1970. 116 pp., ports., illus., facsims. (Studien zur Frankfurter Geschichte. H. 3. Diss., Univ. Frankfurt.)

9074. SONNENFELS, JOSEPH VON. OSTERLOH, KARL-HEINZ: *Joseph von Sonnenfels und die österreichische Reformbewegung im Zeitalter des aufgeklärten Absolutismus*. Eine Studie zum Zusammenhang von Kameralwiss. und Verwaltungspraxis. Lübeck und Hamburg: Matthiesen Verlag, 1970. 271 pp. (Historische Studien, H. 409. Diss., Univ. Marburg.)

9075. SONNWALD, LEO. HERZ, PETER: *Leo Sonnwald*. Blut und Erdöl. Ein Schicksalsbericht. Wien: Europäischer Verlag, 1969. 31 pp., port. [Promoter of the petrol industry in Galicia.]

9076. STERNHEIM, CARL. STERNHEIM, CARL: *Lyrik, Dramenfragmente, Prosa*. Unveröffentlichtes Frühwerk II. Hrsg. von Wilhelm Emrich unter Mitarb. von Manfred Linke. Neuwied: Luchterhand Verlag, 1970. 650 pp. (Gesamtwerke Bd. 9.)

9077. SEBALD, W. G.: *Carl Sternheim — Kritiker und Opfer der Wilhelminischen Ära*. Stuttgart: W. Kohlhammer Verlag, 1970. 160 pp. (Sprache und Literatur, Bd. 58.)

9078. STRAUSS, LUDWIG. STRAUSS, LUDWIG: *Dichtungen und Schriften*, Hrsg. von Werner Kraft. München: Kösel Verlag, 1970. 836 pp. [See also No. 8762.]

9079. STRICH, FRITZ. STRICH, FRITZ: *Die Mythologie in der deutschen Literatur*. Von Klopstock bis Wagner. Unveränd. Nachdruck der 1. Aufl. Halle a. d. Saale, Niemeyer 1910. Bern u. München: Verlag Francke, 1970. xi, 483 pp., vii, 490 pp. [2 vols.]

9080. TARRASCH, SIEGBERT. TARRASCH, SIEGBERT: *Das Schachspiel*. Systemat. Lehrbuch für Anfänger und Geübte. Neu bearb. im allgemeinen Teil von Karl Junker. Eröffnungen von Rudolf Teschner. Stuttgart: Dt. Bücherbund, 1970. 407 pp. [The physician and world chess champion (1862-1934) had a great influence on the development of the game.]

9081. TOLLER, ERNST. TURNOWSKY-PINNER, MARGARETE: *A Student's Friendship with Ernst Toller*. [In]: LBI Year Book XV. London, 1970. Pp. 211-222.

9082. TUCHOLSKY, KURT. TUCHOLSKY, KURT: *Ausgewählte Werke*. Hrsg. von Ronald Links unter Mitarbeit von Christa Links. Mit einem Nachwort der Hrsg. Berlin [East]: Verlag Volk und Welt, 1969/70. [3 vols.]

9083. TUCHOLSKY, KURT: *Etwas ist immer*. Freiburg i.Br.: Hyperion Verlag, 1969. 166 pp. (Hyperion-Bücherei.)

9084. TUCHOLSKY, KURT: *Gedichte*. Berlin [East]: Verlag Neues Leben, 1970. 31 pp. (Reihe Poesiealbum, H. 34.)

9085. TUCHOLSKY, KURT: *Politische Justiz*. Zusammengestellt von Martin Swarzenski. Mit einem Vorwort von Franz Josef Degenhardt. Reinbek b. Hamburg: Rowohlt Verlag, 1970. 132 pp. (rororo Taschenbuch 1336.)

9086. BORRIES, ACHIM VON: *Kurt Tucholsky 1933-1935, oder: Das absolute Exil*. [In]: 'Werkhefte'. 24. Jg., H. 6, Juni. München: Arbeitsgemeinschaft Werkhefte, 1970. Pp. 153-159.

9087. VIERTEL, BERTHOLD. VIERTEL, BERTHOLD: *Schriften zum Theater*. Hrsg. von Gert Heidenreich unter Mitarbeit von Manfred Nöbel. Mit einem Geleitwort von Herbert Ihering: Berthold Viertel — Der Schriftsteller als Regisseur. München: Kösel Verlag, 1970. 574 pp., bibl. B.V. pp. 535-552. [1885-1953.]

9088. VIERTEL, SALKA. VIERTEL, SALKA: *Das unbelehrbare Herz*. Ein Leben in der Welt des Theaters, der Literatur und des Films. Mit einem Vorwort von Carl Zuckmayer. Von der Autorin bearb. Übers. aus dem Amerikanischen von Helmut Degner. Hamburg und Düsseldorf: Claassen Verlag, 1970. 495 pp.

9089. WARBURG, ABY. GOMBRICH, E. H.: *Aby Warburg*. An Intellectual Biography. With a Memoir on the History of the Library by F. Saxl. London: The Warburg Institute University of London, 1970. 376 pp., front. port. + 65 pp. illus., bibl. A. W. pp. 339-347, bibl. (pp. 348-352). [Art Historian (1866-1929), founder and director of the Kulturwissenschaftliche Bibliothek Warburg in Hamburg which was transferred to London in 1933 and as The Warburg Institute forms part of the University of London. Cf. Robert Weltsch: Ein Pionier der Kulturforschung. [In]: 'Allgemeine', 26. März, Düsseldorf, 1971.]

9090. WASSERMANN, JAKOB. KAYSER, RUDOLF: *Jakob Wassermann*. [In]: 'Zeitschrift für die Geschichte der Juden'. 7. Jg., Nr. 1, 1970. Pp. 37-44. [See No. 8420.]

9091. WEICHMANN, HERBERT: *Gesellschaftlicher Fortschritt im humanen Geist*. Regierungserklärung vor der hamburgischen Bürgerschaft am 27. Mai 1970. Hamburg: Senat der Freien und Hansestadt Hamburg, Staatl. Pressestelle, 1970. 34 pp. (Hamburgische Dokumente. 1/70.)

9092. WEILL, KURT. WILLNAUER, FRANZ: *Vom Schiffbauerdamm zum Broadway — Weg und Werk Kurt Weills*. [In]: 'Opernwelt'. April. Velber: Friedrich Verlag, 1970. Pp. 44-48, port., illus. [Slightly rev. text of a tel. broadcast of Zweites Deutsches Fernsehen on Feb. 27, 1970. Composer (1900-1950).]

9093. WEISS, ERNST. WOLLHEIM, MONA: *Begegnung mit Ernst Weiss. Paris 1936-1940*. Icking und München: Kreisselmeier Verlag, 1970. 84 pp. [Physician and author (1884-1940), committed suicide.]

9094. WEISS, PETER. BEST, OTTO F.: *Selbstbefreiung und Selbstvergewaltigung*. Der Weg des Peter Weiss. [In]: 'Merkur'. 24. Jg., H. 10 (270), Okt. Stuttgart: Ernst Klett Verlag, 1970. Pp. 933-948.

9095. CANARIS, VOLKER, ed.: *Über Peter Weiss*. Frankfurt a.M.: Suhrkamp Verlag, 1970. 184 pp., bibl. P.W. and bibl. pp. 151-183.

9096. WOLFSKEHL, KARL. *Karl Wolfskehl, 1869-1969.* Leben und Werk in Dokumenten. Eine Ausstellung der Hessischen Landes- und Hochschulbibliothek vom 20. Okt. bis 14. Dez. 1969. Ausstellungskatalog: Manfred Schlösser. Darmstadt: Agora-Verlag [1969.] 396 pp., ports., illus., facsims., gen. table. (Schriftenreihe Agora, Bd. 22.)

9097. HERING, GERHARD F.: *Wolfskehl, der Literaturhistoriker.* Text der am 17. Okt. 1969 im Justus-Liebig Haus-zu Darmstadt frei gehaltenen Gedenkrede zu Karl Wolfskehls 100. Geburtstag (pp. 145-158). *Ansprache zur Eröffnung der Wolfskehl-Ausstellung* (Erich Zimmermann, pp. 159-163). *Symbol und Verkündigung im Lebenswerk von Karl Wolfskehl* (Jan Aler, pp. 164-182). [In]: Jahrbuch 1969. Hrsg.: Deutsche Akademie für Sprache und Dichtung Darmstadt. Heidelberg: Verlag Lambert Schneider, 1970. 213 pp. (pp. 145-182.)

9098. ZUCKER, PAUL. ZUCKER, PAUL: *Fascination of Decay.* Ridgewood, N.J.: The Gregg Press, 1968. 271 pp., illus. [The aesthetics of ruins and their impression on modern man.] [Paul Zucker (1890 Berlin — 1971 New York), architect, art historian. He was the husband of the singer Rose Walter.]

9099. ZUCKMAYER, CARL. ZUCKMAYER, CARL: *Über die musische Bestimmung des Menschen.* Rede zur Eröffnung der Salzburger Festspiele 1970. Hrsg. von Max Kaindl-Hönig. Engl. Übersetzung von Richard Rickett, franz. von Martha Eissler. Salzburg: Festungsverlag, 1970. 91 pp. (Salzburger Festreden, 7. Text deutsch, engl. und franz.)

9100. BAUER, ARNOLD: *Carl Zuckmayer.* Berlin: Colloquium Verlag, 1970. 93 pp., front. port., facsim., chron., bibl. (Köpfe des XX. Jahrhunderts, Bd. 62.)

9101. LANGE, RUDOLF: *Carl Zuckmayer.* Velber b. Hannover: Verlag Friedrich, 1969. 123 pp., ports., illus. (pp. 97-112). (Friedrichs Dramatiker des Welttheaters. Bd. 33.)

VIII. AUTOBIOGRAPHY

MEMOIRS, LETTERS, GENEALOGY

9102. (THE) AUERBACH FAMILY. AUERBACH, SIEGFRIED M[ORITZ]: *The Auerbach Family.* The Descendants of Abraham Auerbach. Supplement IV. London: M. Sulzbacher (distributor), 1970. 14 pp. [This supplement covers the years 1966-1969; altogether the genealogy covers 8 generations. Cf. Nos. 1136/YB. III, 2351/YB. VI, 3482/YB. VIII, 5451/YB. XI. — Siegfried M. Auerbach (1886 Frankfurt a.M.-1971 London).]

9103. BERNSTEIN, EDUARD. HIRSCH, HELMUT, ed.: *Eduard Bernstein und Friedrich Engels: Briefwechsel.* Assen: Van Gorcum Verlag, 1970. xxxvi, 452 pp., ports., illus. (Quellen und Untersuchungen zur Geschichte der deutschen und österreichischen Arbeiterbewegung. N.F.1.)

9104. *Das bin ich.* Ernst Deutsch, Tilla Durieux, Willy Haas, Daniel-Henry Kahnweiler, Joseph Keilberth, Oskar Kokoschka, Heinz Tietjen, Carl Zuckmayer erzählen ihr Leben. Hrsg. und mit einem Vorwort von Hannes Reinhardt. München: Verlag Piper, 1970. 267 pp., ports.

9105. DÖBLIN, ALFRED: *Briefe.* In Verbindung mit den Söhnen des Dichters hrsg. von Walter Muschg. Weitergeführt und mit einem Nachwort versehen von Heinz Graber. Olten/Freiburg i. Br.: Walter Verlag, 1970. 685 pp., ports., illus., facsims. (Ausgewählte Werke, Bd. 13.)

9106. EMBDEN, CHARLOTTE NÉE HEINE. RAPHAEL, J.: *Über die Nachkommen der Charlotte Embden aus Hamburg.* [In]: 'Zeitschrift für die Geschichte der Juden'. Nr. 2/3, 1970. Pp. 65-72. [See No. 8420.] [H. Heine's only sister.]

9107. EPHRAIM, VEITEL HEINE. HOPPE, HANS: *Der friderizianische Münzpächter Ephraim und seine Nachkommen.* [In]: 'Der Herold', Zeitschrift für Heraldik, Genealogie und verwandte Wissenschaften. Nr. 4, Okt./Dez. Berlin, 1969.

9108. FEDER, ERNST. FEDER, ERNST: *Heute sprach ich mit ...* Tagebücher eines Berliner Publizisten 1926-1932. Hrsg. und eingeleitet von Cécile Lowenthal-Hensel und Arnold Paucker. Mit einem biographischen Register von Ernst G. Lowenthal. Stuttgart: Deutsche Verlags-Anstalt, 1971. 432 pp., front. port., ports., bibl. E.F., biogr. register pp. 329-432.

9109. FEILCHENFELDT, K.: *Die Beziehungen der Familie Carel und Rose Asser-Levin zu ihren Berliner Verwandten.* [In]: 'Studia Rosenthaliana'. Vol. 4, No. 2, July. Assen (Holland), 1970. Pp. 181-212.

9110. FRANKEL, MAX: *You can't go home to Weissenfels.* Godesberg: Inter Nationes, n.d. [1970?]· 8 pp. [The author, diplomatic correspondent of the New York Times, was born in Weissenfels/Thuringia.]

9111. FREUD, SIGMUND—ZWEIG, ARNOLD. FREUD, ERNST L., ed.: *The Letters of Sigmund Freud and Arnold Zweig.* Transl. by Prof. and Mrs. W. D. Robson-Scott. London: The Hogarth Press and the Institute of Psycho-Analysis, 1970. ix, 190 pp., ports. (The International Psycho-Analytical Library, No. 84.) [For German orig. see No. 7503/ YB. XIV.]

9112. FRISCH, EFRAIM. *Hofmannsthal und Efraim Frisch.* Zwölf Briefe 1910-1927. Mitgeteilt und eingeleitet von Max Kreutzberger. [In]: 'Hofmannsthal Blätter'. H. 5, Herbst. Frankfurt a.M., 1970. Pp. 356-370, notes. (Veröffentlichungen der Hugo von Hofmannsthal-Gesellschaft. Hrsg. Martin Stern. [The correspondence is in the archives of the Leo Baeck Institute in New York]. [Essayist (1873-1942).] [Cf. also No. 8930.]

9113. HEINE, HEINRICH: *Briefe.* 1815-1831, 1831-1841. Bd. 20-21. Hrsg. von Fritz H. Eisner. Berlin [East]: Akademie Verlag, 1970. 445, 436 pp. [2 vols.] (Säkularausgabe Werke, Briefwechsel, Lebenszeugnisse. Hrsg. von den Nationalen Forschungs- und Gedenkstätten der klassischen deutschen Literatur in Weimar und dem Centre national de la recherche scientifique in Paris.)

9114. HERRMANN, LENE. HERRMANN, ROBERT, ed.: *'Lene' Wozu die Flügel* . . . Eine Autobiographie in Gedichten. Rothenburg o.d. Tauber: J. P. Peter, Gebr. Holstein, 1970. 77 pp., front. port., facsim. [Priv. publ. in London, 1966. Cf. No. 6091/YB. XII. Born in Brno, Lene Herrmann died during a visit to Slovakia in 1965.]

9115. HOFMANNSTHAL, HUGO VON. BRADISCH, JOSEPH A. and NORBERT ALTENHOFER, eds.: *Hugo von Hofmannsthal/Anton Wildgans: Briefwechsel.* Erw. und verb. Neuaufl. Heidelberg: Lothar Stiehm Verlag, 1970.

9116. HUGO VON HOFMANNSTHAL/WILLY HAAS: *Ein Briefwechsel.* Mit einer Einführung von Rudolf Hirsch. Berlin: Propyläen Verlag, 1969. 111 pp.

9117. KOESTLER, ARTHUR: *Frühe Empörung.* Aus dem Engl. übertragen von Eduard Thorsch und Franziska Becker. Wien/München/Zürich: Fritz Molden Verlag, 1970. 552 pp., front. port., ports., illus. (Gesammelte autobiographische Schriften, Bd. 1.)

9118. KOLMAR, GERTRUD [orig. Chodziesner]: *Briefe an die Schwester Hilde (1938-1943).* Hrsg. von Johanna Zeitler. München: Kösel Verlag, 1970. 247 pp., front. port., facsims. [Poet, interpreter at the German Foreign Office (1894-1943), died in a concentration camp.]

9119. LANDAUER, ELIAS and KAROLINE. FRENKEL, ELIAS KARL, comp.: *Family Tree Elias and Karoline Landauer (Hürben-Krumbach-Munich).* Jerusalem: [no impr.]. 59 pp., gen. table. [Mimeog.]

9120. LASKER-SCHÜLER, ELSE. BAUSCHINGER, SIGRID: *Else Lasker-Schüler in ihren Briefen.* [In]: 'Neue Rundschau'. 81. Jg., H. 2. Berlin-Frankfurt: S. Fischer Verlag, 1970. Pp. 366-374.

9121. KUPPER, MARGARETE: *Der Nachlass Else Lasker-Schülers in Jerusalem.* Verzeichnis der Briefe an Else Lasker-Schüler. [In]: Literaturwissenschaftliches Jahrbuch. Im Auftrag der Görres-Gesellschaft hrsg. von Hermann Kunisch. N.F. Bd. 10. Berlin 1969. Pp. 175-230.

9122. LEPMAN, JELLA: *A Bridge of Children's Books.* Memoirs. Frankfurt a.M.: S. Fischer, English Language Edition. Leicester: Brockhampton Press, 1968. 'Die Kinderbuchbrücke' — A volume of reminiscences. Cf. Egon Larsen [In]: 'AJR Information', Dec. London, 1970. [Jella Lepman (1891 Stuttgart-1970 Zürich), journalist and founder of 'International Youth Library'.]

9123. LIND, JAKOV: *Counting my Steps.* Autobiography. London: Jonathan Cape, 1970. 223 pp., cover illus., port. [Born Jakob Landwirt in Vienna, the novelist and short story writer, now living in London, recounts his life as a child refugee from the Nazis.]

9124. LIND, JAKOV: *Selbstporträt.* Autorisierte Übersetzung aus dem Englischen von Günther Danehl. Frankfurt a.M.: S. Fischer, 1970. 216 pp., cover port.

9125. LOEWENBERG, JAKOB. LOEWENBERG, ERNST L.: *Jakob Loewenberg*. Excerpts from his Diaries and Letters. [In]: LBI Year Book XV. London, 1970. Pp. 183-209, poit., illus. [Author, educationalist (1856-1929).]

9126. MEIDNER, LUDWIG. FRITSCHE, HERBERT, ed.: *Briefe von Ludwig Meidner.* [In]: 'Neue Deutsche Hefte'. Nr. 121, H. 1. Gütersloh: S. Mohn Verlag, 1969. Pp. 3-21.

9127. MEYERBEER, GIACOMO: *Briefwechsel und Tagebücher.* Hrsg. von Heinz Becker im Auftrag der Akademie der Künste und unter Mitwirkung des Staatlichen Instituts für Musik-forschung, Berlin. Bd. 2: 1825-1836. Berlin: Verlag Walter de Gruyter, 1970. 725 pp., ports., illus., facsims., music. [For vol. I: 'Bis 1824' see No. 2371/YB. VI. — Cf. Robert Weltsch: Meyerbeer steigt aus der Versenkung. [In]: 'Allgemeine', 1. Jan. Berlin, 1971 [and in]: 'MB', Nr. 19/20, 7. Mai, Tel Aviv 1971.]

9128. PAULI, HERTHA: *Der Riss der Zeit geht durch mein Herz.* Ein Erlebnisbericht. Wien: Paul Zsolnay Verlag, 1970. 270 pp.

9129. PICARD, MAX: *Briefe an den Freund Karl Pfleger.* Mit Beiträgen von Karl Pfleger und Michael Picard zur geistigen und religiösen Problematik von Max Picard. Erlenbach-Zürich: Eugen Rentsch Verlag, 1970. 159 pp. [Physician and author (1888-1965), converted to Catholicism in 1939, but later returned to the Jewish faith.]

9130. ROTH, JOSEPH. *Joseph Roth Briefe 1911-1939.* Hrsg. und eingel. von Hermann Kesten. Köln: Kiepenheuer & Witsch, 1970. 642 pp., bibl. J.R. pp. 617-618. [Incl. letters from Stefan Zweig to Roth.]

9131. SANDER, CLARA: *Alte Geschichten.* Erinnerungen. London, 1970. 97 pp. [Photocopy of typescript.]

9132. (THE) SCHEYER FAMILY OF KOSCHMIN/POSEN. HERTZ, IRENE: *Die Scheyer von Koschmin.* [In]: 'Isr. Wochenblatt', 2. Okt. Zürich, 1970.

9133. SCHNITZLER, ARTHUR. SCHNITZLER, ARTHUR: *My Youth in Vienna.* Foreword by Frederic Morton. Transl. from the German by Catherine Hutter. New York: Holt, Rinehart and Winston, London: Weidenfeld and Nicolson, 1970. xiv, 304 pp., ports., illus. [For the German orig. see No. 7515/YB. XIV. Cf. also: Robert Weltsch: Eros and Sorrow [In]: 'Jewish Chronicle', July 2, London, 1971.]

9134. NICKL, THERESE and HEINRICH SCHNITZLER, eds.: *Arthur Schnitzler/Olga Waissnix: Liebe, die starb vor der Zeit.* Ein Briefwechsel. Mit einem Vorwort von Hans Weigel. Wien, München: Fritz Molden Verlag, 1970. 424 pp., ports., illus., facsims.

9135. WAGNER, RENATE: *Arthur Schnitzlers Beziehung zu Otto Brahm und zu Max Reinhardt.* Zu zwei Briefwechseln des Dichters. [In]: 'NZZ', 13. Sept. Zürich, 1970. [Also]: *Arthur Schnitzler an Max Reinhardt.* (A letter dated Vienna, Dec. 24, 1909). [And]: *Arthur Schnitzlers Grabrede für Otto Brahm.* (Dated Nov. 30, 1912.) [In]: 'NZZ', 13. Sept., Zürich, 1970. Pp. 51-52, facsim. [Both texts, publ. for the first time, with an acknowledgement to Heinrich Schnitzler, the author's son.]

9136. SIMONSON, WERNER: *The last Judgement.* An autobiography. Gerrards Cross (Bucks.): C. Smythe, 1969. 181 pp., ports., illus., facsims.

9137. STERN, HEINEMANN: *Warum hassen sie uns eigentlich?* Jüdisches Leben zwischen den Kriegen. Erinnerungen, hrsg. und kommentiert von Hans Ch. Meyer. Düsseldorf: Droste Verlag, 1970. 372 pp., ports., illus., facsim., notes pp. 320-350, bibl. (pp. 367-368). [Educationist (1878-1957).]

9138. TUCHOLSKY, KURT: *Briefe an eine Katholikin 1929-1931.* Reinbek b. Hamburg: Ernst Rowohlt Verlag, 1970. 89 pp., front. port., facsim. [Recipient of the 27 letters, only recently discovered and publ. for the first time, was Marierose Fuchs.]

9139. *(Das) Volk braucht Licht — Frauen zur Zeit des Aufbruchs 1790-1848 in ihren Briefen.* Nach-wort, Zeittafel und Texterläuterungen von Manfred Schlösser. Mit zeitgenössischen Scherenschnitten. Darmstadt/Zürich: Agora-Schriftenreihe, 1970. 794 pp. [Incl. Dorothea Schlegel, Rahel Varnhagen.]

9140. (THE) WARBURG FAMILY. *'Granny Gerta Warburg und die Ihren'.* Hamburger Schick-sale, berichtet von Gertrud Wenzel-Burchard. Hamburg: Hans Christians Verlag, 1970. 237 pp., front. port., ports., illus. [The history of the W.'s of Altona.]

9141. ZWEIG, STEFAN: *Die Welt von gestern.* Erinnerungen eines Europäers (Ungek. Ausg). Frankfurt a.M./Hamburg: Fischer-Bücherei, 1970. 317 pp. (Fischer-Bücherei Nr. 1152). [First publ. 1941.]

IX. GERMAN - JEWISH RELATIONS

A. General

9142. *Diskussion über die deutsch-jüdische Situation*. [Contributions by]: Wolfgang Abendroth, Ernst Ludwig Ehrlich, Jean Améry, Erich Fried, Barbara Just-Dahlmann, Alfred Kantorowicz, Hermann Kesten, Hermann Langbein, Rudolf Walter Leonhardt, Eva G. Reichmann, Hilde Rubinstein, J. R. von Salis, Alphons Silbermann, Dietrich Strothmann, Robert Neumann. [In]: 'Tribüne', 9. Jg., H. 34, 1970. Pp. 3643-3661. [The discussion arose from Robert Neumann's review of the play 'Die Kannibalen' by George Tabori in 'Tribüne', H. 33, 1970.]

9143. MOSSE, GEORGE L.: *Germans and Jews. The Right, The Left, and the Search for a 'Third Force' in Pre-Nazi Germany.* New York: Howard Fertig, 1970. 260 pp., bibl. notes (pp. 229-253).

9144. REICHMANN, EVA G.: *Verfemt, verfolgt, geduldet?* Soziologische Aspekte des Problems der Minderheiten. Hrsg.: Gesellschaft für Christlich-Jüdische Zusammenarbeit, Düsseldorf, 1970. 12 pp. (Vortrag, geh. anlässlich einer Arbeitstagung in der 'Woche der Brüderlichkeit' . . . vor Düsseldorfer Oberschülern.]

9145. *'Tribüne'*, Zeitschrift zum Verständnis des Judentums. Hrsg. von Elisabeth Reisch. 9. Jg., H. 33-36. Frankfurt a.M.: Tribüne Verlag, 1970. [H. 33 incl.: Die konstruierte Krise. Stellungnahme zu Deutsch-Israelischen Beziehungen (Otto Brenner, Franz Böhm). H. 34: Oberammergau bleibt Oberammergau. Antworten auf Fragen von Julius Kardinal Döpfner und Bischof Heinrich Tenhumberg. Nelly Sachs zu ehren (Walter Jens, obituary). Zur Ausstellung der Woche jüdischer Autoren in der Akademie der Künste, Berlin. H. 35: Good Bye, Fritz Kortner (Robert Neumann). Emigration (Ernst Bloch). See also No. 9142.]

B. German-Israeli Relations

9146. BENTWICH, NORMAN: *A German Christian Brotherhood in Israel.* [In]: 'AJR Information'. Vol. XXV No. 7, July. London, 1970.

9147. BÜHRING, LARS [and others]: *Untersuchung der israelischen Wirtschaft im Hinblick auf eine Ausweitung des Exports in die Bundesrepublik Deutschland.* Ergebnisbericht des Forschungsinstituts der Friedrich-Ebert-Stiftung über Studienreisen nach Israel im Sommer 1968. Bad Godesberg: Dt. Gesellschaft zur Förderung der Wirtschaftsbeziehungen mit Israel, 1968. 68 pp.

9148. DEUTSCHKRON, INGE: *Israel und die Deutschen.* Zwischen Ressentiment und Ratio. Mit einem Geleitwort von Asher Ben Nathan. Köln: Verlag Wissenschaft und Politik, 1970. 368 pp. [Engl. edition]: *Bonn and Jerusalem. The Strange Coalition.* Philadelphia/London: Chilton, 1970. 357 pp.

9149. *'deutschland-berichte'* Hrsg. Rolf Vogel. 6. Jg., Nr. 1-12, Bonn, 1970.

9150. HÄSLER, ALFRED A.: *Wie es dazu kam . . .* Gespräch mit Prof. Wolfgang Gentner, Direktor des Max-Planck-Instituts für Kernphysik in Heidelberg und Vorsitzender des Komitees für Zusammenarbeit zwischen deutschen und Wissenschaftlern des Weizmann-Instituts. [In]: 'modell'. Hrsg.: Europäisches Komitee des Weizmann Institute of Science Rehovot. Zürich, 1970. Pp. 2-5, ports.

9151. *Israel im deutschsprachigen Schrifttum.* Ein Verzeichnis zur Buchausstellung. Israel-Woche in Stuttgart 1969. Stuttgart: Kulturamt, Stadtbücherei 1969. 63 pp., illus.

9152. LEWAN, KENNETH M.: *Der Nahostkrieg in der westdeutschen Presse.* Köln: Pahl-Rugenstein Verlag, 1970. 180 pp. (Kleine Bibliothek, Politik-Wissenschaft-Zukunft, 9.)

9153. SEELBACH, JÖRG: *Die Aufnahme der diplomatischen Beziehungen zu Israel als Problem der deutschen Politik seit 1955.* Meisenheim am Glan: Verlag Anton Hain, 1970. xviii, 299 pp., chron. table, bibl. (pp. 277-294). (Marburger Abhandlungen zur Politischen Wissenschaft. Hrsg. von Wolfgang Abendroth, Bd. 19.)

C. Church and Synagogue

9154. Ben Chorin, Schalom: *Jesus im Judentum.* Wuppertal: Theologischer Verlag Brockhaus, 1970. 79 pp. (Schriftenreihe für christlich-jüdische Begegnung, Bd. 4.)

9155. Ben Chorin, Schalom: *Paulus.* Der Völkerapostel in jüdischer Sicht. München: Paul List Verlag, 1970. 239 pp., annotated bibl. (pp. 223-230). [Vol. II of the trilogy. For vol. I 'Bruder Jesus' see No. 6836/YB. XIII.]

9156. Ben Chorin, Schalom: *Wachsame Brüderlichkeit.* Trier: Paulinus Verlag, 1970. 84 pp.

9157. Davies, Alan T.: *Anti-Semitism and the Christian Mind.* The Crisis of Conscience after Auschwitz. New York: Herder, 1969. 192 pp. [A Catholic view of contemporary Christian-Jewish relations.]

9158. *'Emuna-Horizonte'.* Zur Diskussion über Israel und das Judentum. Hrsg.: Willehad Paul Eckert, Jutta Bohnke-Kollwitz, Ulrich Kusche, N. Peter Levinson, Rolf Rendtorff [for] Deutscher Koordinierungsrat der Gesellschaften für Christl.-Jüd. Zusammenarbeit, Deutsch-Israelische Gesellschaft, Bundesverband Deutsch-Israelischer Studiengruppen in Verbindung mit dem Bundesverband Jüdischer Studenten in Deutschland, Germania-Judaica-Kölner Bibliothek zur Geschichte des deutschen Judentums. V.Jg., Nr. 1-6, Jan.-Dez. Frankfurt a.M., 1970. Pp. 1-435, illus., facsims. [6 vols.] [Nr. 2 incl.: Tradition als jüdisches Selbstverständnis (Pinchas Erich Rosenblüth). Erinnerung an Lion Feuchtwanger (Alfred Kantorowicz). Nr. 3: Israelische Künstler — ehemalige Bauhausschüler (Claire Lachmann). Nr. 4: Eva G. Reichmann und Robert Raphael Geis zu Ehren (Hans-Joachim Kraus) [the two recipients of the Buber-Rosenzweig Medaille 1970]. Lambert Schneider zum Gedenken (Willehad Paul Eckert). Some selected contributions are listed according to subject.]

9159. *'Freiburger Rundbrief'.* Beiträge zur Förderung der Freundschaft zwischen dem Alten und dem Neuen Gottesvolk im Geiste beider Testamente. Hrsg. von Willehad Paul Eckert, Rupert Giessler, Georg Hüssler, Ludwig Kaufmann, Gertrud Luckner u.a. Jg. XXII, Nr. 81/84. Freiburg i.Br.: Freiburger Rundbrief, 1970. 164 pp., illus. — See also No. 9167.]

9160. Holsten, W.: *Judentum, Heidentum, Christentum.* [In]: 'Theologische Rundschau'. Jg. 35, Nr. 1-2. Tübingen, 1970. Pp. 65-86, 94-163.

9161. *Jüdisches Volk — gelobtes Land.* Die biblischen Landverheissungen als Problem des jüdischen Selbstverständnisses und der christlichen Theologie. Hrsg. von Willehad Paul Eckert, Nathan Peter Levinson und Martin Stöhr. München: Christian Kaiser Verlag, 1970. 334 pp.; (Abhandlungen zum christlich-jüdischen Dialog. Hrsg. von Helmut Gollwitzer.) [Incl. Der unwiderrufliche Rückzug auf Zion (Jochanan Bloch). Eine Theologie der 'Galut' bei Franz Rosenzweig (Reinhold Mayer). Israel und die Diaspora bei Leo Baeck (Albert H. Friedlander). Der Wandel des jüdischen Menschenbildes im heutigen Israel (Ernst Simon). Christentum und Zionismus (Friedrich-Wilhelm Marquardt).]

9162. *Kirche und Synagoge.* Handbuch zur Geschichte von Christen und Juden. Darstellung mit Quellen. Hrsg. von Karl Heinrich Rengstorf und Siegfried v. Kortzfleisch. Bd. II. Stuttgart: Ernst Klett Verlag, 1970. 745 pp. [Vol. I documented the history of relations between church and synagogue up to the 16th century. This vol. continues it to 1933. Chaps. incl.: Der Heilige Stuhl und die Juden. Die deutschen Katholiken und die Juden in der Zeit von 1850 bis zur Machtübernahme Hitlers (Rudolf Lill). Jüdische Renaissance im 19. und 20. Jahrhundert (Hans Tramer). — For vol. I see No. 6841/YB. XIII.]

9163. Lapide, Pinchas E.: *Jesus in Israel.* Gladbeck: Schriftenmissions-Verlag, 1970. 108 pp. (Wahrheit und Wagnis.) [Incl.: Jesus in der israelischen Literatur.]

9164. Miskotte, Kornelis Heiko: *Das Judentum als Frage an die Kirche.* Aus dem Holländ. übersetzt von Brigitte Toet-Kahlert. Wuppertal: Theologischer Verlag Brockhaus, 1970. 86 pp. (Schriftenreihe für christlich-jüdische Begegnung, Bd. 5.)

9165. Oesterreicher, John M., ed.: *The Bridge.* Brothers in Hope. A Yearbook of Judaeo-Christian Studies. Vol. V. New York: Herder & Herder, 1970. 350 pp.

9166. Schoeps, Hans J.: *Jewish Christianity.* Factional Disputes in the early Church. Philadelphia: Fortress, 1969. 163 pp.

9167. TAL, URIEL: *Martin Buber und das christlich-jüdische Zwiegespräch.* Vortrag, geh. auf dem Symposium 'In memoriam Martin Buber' an der Hebräischen Universität, anlässlich der Grundsteinlegung des 'Mordechai Martin Buber Zentrum' . . . am 30. Okt. 1967. [In]: 'Freiburger Rundbrief', pp. 3-7. [See No. 9159.]

9168. *The Vatican Declaration on the Jews . . . October 28th 1965 — October 28th 1970 — 5 Years Later.* Report of the Commission to implement the Vatican Declaration on the Jews. Christopher Hollis, Chairman of the Commission. London (17, Chepstow Villas, W.11), 12 pp.

9169. VOGEL, M.: *Some Reflections on the Jewish-Christian Dialogue in the Light of the Six-Day War.* [In]: The Annals of the American Academy of Political and Social Science. Vol. 387, Jan. Philadelphia, 1970. Pp. 96-108.

D. Antisemitism

9170. BEGOV, LUCIE: *Das verkannte Volk.* Die Judenfrage — ein christliches Problem. Mit einer Einleitung von Ernst Platz. Wien: Verlag Typographische Anstalt, 1969. 55 pp. [Author, a survivor of Auschwitz, is editor of 'Aktion gegen den Antisemitismus in Österreich'.]

9171. CHIARLONI, A. PEGORARO: *Antisemitismo in Germania 1848-1970.* [In]: 'Studi Storici'. Vol. 11, No. 1, Jan.-March. Roma 1970. Pp. 97-112.

9172. GLAUS, BEAT: *Die nationale Front.* Eine Schweizer Faschistische Bewegung 1930-1940. Zürich/Köln: Benziger Verlag, 1969. 503 pp., ports., illus., facsims., bibl. (pp. 479-486). (Diss. Basel.)

9173. HEER, FRIEDRICH: *God's First Love.* Transl. from the German. London: Weidenfeld and Nicolson, 1970. 560 pp. [For German orig. see No. 6854/YB. XIII.]

9174. JAFFÉ, ANIELA: *Aus Leben und Werkstatt von C. G. Jung.* Parapsychologie, Alchemie, Nationalsozialismus. Erinnerungen aus den letzten Jahren. Zürich/Stuttgart: Rascher Verlag, 1968. 156 pp., facsim., notes (pp. 149-156). [Jung's attitude to Nazism and Jews, pp. 87-104.]

9175. KATZ, J.: *A State within a State* — The History of an Anti-Semitic Slogan. Publ. by The Israel Academy of Sciences and Humanities. Proceedings Vol. IV, No. 3. Jerusalem: Ahva Press, 1969. 30 pp. [Author is rector of the Jerusalem University.]

9176. KUPISCH, KARL: *Adolf Stoecker.* Hofprediger und Volkstribun. Ein historisches Porträt. Berlin: Haude & Spener, 1970. 94 pp., ports., illus. (Berlinische Reminiszenzen, 29.)

9177. LOHALM, UWE: *Völkischer Radikalismus.* Die Geschichte des Deutschvölkischen Schutz- und Trutz-Bundes, 1919-1923. Hamburg: Leibniz Verlag, 1970. 492 pp., bibl. (pp. 446-481).

9178. OBERAMMERGAU. AMERICAN JEWISH COMMITTEE, ed.: *Oberammergau, 1960 and 1970.* A Study in Religious Anti-Semitism. New York, July 1970. 24 pp.

9179. CORATIEL, ELISABETH H. C.: *Oberammergau and its Passion Play.* London: Burns & Oates, 1970. 128 pp.

9180. FINK, ROMAN/HORST SCHWARZER: *Die ewige Passion.* Phänomen Oberammergau. Düsseldorf: Econ Verlag, 1970. 240 pp. + 48 pp. illus. [Cf. Oberammergau — eine Schande. [In]: 'Der Zeuge', Organ der Internationalen Judenchristlichen Allianz. Jg. XXI, Nr. 43, Mai. London, 1970.]

9181. SANDERS, WILM: *Antisemitismus bei den Christen?* Gedanken zur christlichen Judenfeindschaft am Beispiel der Oberammergauer Passionsspiele. Leutesdorf: Johannes Verlag, 1970. 45 pp. [Author is a Catholic priest.]

9182. SCHWAIGHOFER, HANS: *Für ein neues Oberammergauer Passionsspiel.* Mit einer Einführung von Alois Fink. München: Verlag Karl Thiemig, 1970. 22 pp., illus.

9183. *(Der) Streit um Oberammergau.* [In]: 'Emuna-Horizonte'. Jg. 5, Nr. 4, August, 1970. Pp. 217-256, illus. [Contributors: Willehad Paul Eckert, Hans Conrad Zander, Georg R. Schroubek, Hans-H. Mallau, Wilm Sanders. — See No. 9158.]

9184. VOGEL, CARL LUDWIG: *Oberammergau's 36th Season.* [In]: 'Central Europe Journal'. Publ. by Sudetendeutsches Archiv, München. Vol. XVIII, No. 3, March. Bonn, 1970. Pp. 96-106, ports., illus. [The history of the passion-play which started during the Thirty Years' War in 1634.]

9185. REICHMANN, EVA G.: *Hostages of Civilisation*. The Social Sources of National Socialist Anti-Semitism. Westport, Connecticut: Greenwood Press, 1970. 281 pp., bibl. (pp. 268-277). [First English edition, London: Gollancz, 1950. First German ed., Flucht in den Hass, Frankfurt a.M.: Europäische Verlagsanstalt, 1956. See No. 7560/YB. XIV.]

9186. ROSENBERG, HANS: *Moderner Antisemitismus und vorfaschistische Strömungen*. [Pp. 88-117 in]: Grosse Depression und Bismarckzeit. Wirtschaftsablauf, Gesellschaft und Politik in Mitteleuropa. Berlin: Walter de Gruyter, 1967. xii, 301 pp., bibl. (pp. 274-287). (Veröffentlichungen der Historischen Kommission zu Berlin beim Friedrich-Meinecke-Institut der Freien Universität Berlin. Bd. 24.)

9187. STRAUSS, HERBERT A.: *Jewish Defense against Antisemitism and National Socialism in the Last Years of the Weimar Republic*. New York: American Jewish Committee, 1969. 37 pp. [Mimeog.] [An English summary of the book by Arnold Paucker: Der Jüdische Abwehrkampf gegen Antisemitismus und Nationalsozialismus in den letzten Jahren der Weimarer Republik. Hamburg: Leibniz-Verlag, 1968. See No. 8349/YB. XV.]

9188. *(The) U.N. Convention on the Elimination of All Forms of Racial Discrimination*. A Commentary by Natan Lerner. Publ. for the Institute of Jewish Affairs in association with the World Jewish Congress, London. Leyden: A. W. Sijthoff, 1970. 132 pp.

9189. WEINZIERL, ERIKA: *Stereotypen christlicher Judenfeindschaft*. [In]: 'Wort und Wahrheit'. Jg. 25, Nr. 4, Juli-Aug. Freiburg i.Br.: 1970. Pp. 343-355.

E. Noted Germans and Jews

9190. BUSCH, FRITZ. BUSCH, GRETE: *Fritz Busch, Dirigent*. Frankfurt a.M.: S. Fischer Verlag, 1970. 369 pp., with discography F.B., comp. by Jacques Delalande, pp. 335-354. [His widow describes mainly the years following his emigration in 1933, his work at Glyndebourne, in Copenhagen, Buenos Aires and New York.]

9191. FONTANE, THEODOR. JOLLES, CHARLOTTE: *Theodor Fontanes Korrespondenzen aus London*. [In]: 'NZZ', 8. März. Zürich, 1970. Pp. 49/50. [Herrn Marcus' Bilderladen.]

9192. SIMON, ERNST: *Theodor Fontanes jüdischer Komplex*. [In]: 'NZZ'. 16. Aug. Zürich, 1970. P. 39-40.

9193. HEGEL, GEORG WILH. FRIEDRICH. FACKENHEIM, EMIL.: *The Religious Dimension in Hegel's Thought*. Bloomington, Indiana: Indiana University Press, 1967. 274 pp. [Cf. Nathan Rotenstreich [In]: 'Judaism'. Vol. 18, No. 4, Fall, New York: American Jewish Congress, 1969. Pp. 508-509.]

9194. HEUSS, THEODOR. HEUSS, THEODOR: *Tagebuchbriefe 1955-1963*. Eine Auswahl aus Briefen an Toni Stolper. Hrsg. und eingeleitet von Eberhard Pikart. Tübingen/Stuttgart: Rainer Wunderlich Verlag Hermann Leins, 1970. 644 pp., cover facsim. (Veröffentlichung des Theodor Heuss Archivs). [His letters to the Jewish widow of Gustav Stolper cont. many references to Jews, Jewish friends, his visit to the Wiener Library, London, and to Israel.]

9195. KOLB, ANNETTE. BENYOETZ, ELAZAR: *Annette Kolb und Israel*. Heidelberg: Lothar Stiehm Verlag, 1970. 174 pp., ports. (Literatur und Geschichte. Bd. 2.)

9196. LUTHER, MARTIN. MILLS, EDGAR: *Martin Luther and the Jews*. A refutation of his book 'The Jews and their Lies'. Wien: Europäischer Verlag, 1969. 37 pp.

9197. MANN, THOMAS. MANN, THOMAS: *The Letters of Thomas Mann*. Selected, translated and annotated by Richard and Clara Winston. London: Secker and Warburg, 1970. 2 vols.

9198. JONAS, KLAUS W., comp.: *Die Thomas-Mann-Literatur*. Bd. 1: Bibliographie der Kritik 1901-1955. Berlin: Erich Schmidt Verlag, 1970.

9199. KARST, ROMAN: *Thomas Mann oder Der Deutsche Zwiespalt*. Aus dem polnischen Originalmanuskript übertragen von Edda Werfel. Wien/München: Verlag Fritz Molden, 1970. 360 pp., ports., illus., facsim. (Glanz und Elend der Meister.)

9200. MANN, GOLO: *Mein Vater Thomas Mann*. (Vortrag). Lübeck: Weiland Verlag, 1970. 33 pp.

9201. SCHNEIDER, LAMBERT. Georgi, Arthur: *Dank an Lambert Schneider*. [In]: 'Börsenblatt für den Deutschen Buchhandel'. 26. Jg., 19. Juni. Frankfurt a.M., 1970. Pp. 1350-1352, port. [of L. Schneider and Martin Buber]. [On his meetings with Martin Buber and Salman Schocken which led to the establishment of his publishing firm.]

9202. Mayer, Hans-Otto: *Lambert Schneider 70 Jahre*. [In]: 'Börsenblatt für den Deutschen Buchhandel'. 26. Jg., 14. Apr. Frankfurt a.M., 1970. Pp. 862-865, port. [Lambert Schneider (1900-1970). Cf. No. 9158.]

9203. WAGNER, RICHARD. Goldman, Albert and Evert Sprinchorn, eds.: *Wagner on Music and Drama*. With an Introduction and a Selection from Wagner's Prose Works. Transl. by H. Ashton Ellis. London: Victor Gollancz, 1970. 448 pp., bibl. (pp. 445-447.)

9204. Gutman, Robert W.: *Richard Wagner*. Der Mensch, sein Werk, seine Zeit. Aus dem Amerik. von Horst Leuchtmann. München: Piper Verlag, 1970. 573 pp., ports., illus. [For English ed. see No. 7577/YB. XIV.] [Wagner's antisemitism is treated extensively.]

9205. Magee, Bryan: *Aspects of Wagner*. London: Alan Ross, 1968. [Incl. a chapter on Wagner as one of the initiators of cultural antisemitism. Cf.: Wagner in our Time. A new assessment (H. W. Freyhan) [In]: 'AJR Information', Feb. London, 1971.]

9206. WIECHERT, ERNST. Kirshner, S.: '*Even if they were Guilty*'. An unpublished letter by Ernst Wiechert about the Jews. [In]: 'German Life and Letters'. Vol. 23, No. 2, Jan. Oxford, 1970. Pp. 138-143. [Writer (1887-1950) was, in 1938, imprisoned for a few months in a concentration camp.]

X. FICTION, POETRY AND HUMOUR

9207. Aloni, Jenny: *Zypressen zerbrechen nicht*. Roman. 2. Aufl. Witten/Berlin: Eckart-Verlag, 1970. 251 pp.

9208. Ben-Gavriel, M. Y.: *Frieden und Krieg des Bürgers Mahaschavi*. Alte und neue Abenteuer. Roman. Frankfurt a.M.: Fischer-Bücherei, 1970. 277 pp. (Fischer-Bücherei. Bd. 1113.)

9209. Dahn, Ben Amotz: *Masken in Frankfurt*. Roman. Autoris. Übersetzung aus dem Hebräischen von Ulrike Zimmermann. Darmstadt/Frankfurt a.M.: Joseph Melzer Verlag, 1970. 477 pp. [Autobiographical novel of an Israeli who comes to Germany for his restitution claim.]

9210. Domin, Hilde: *Ich will dich*. Gedichte. München: Piper Verlag, 1970. 48 pp.

9211. Domin, Hilde: *Nachkrieg und Unfrieden*. Gedichte als Index 1945-1970. Neuwied: Luchterhand Verlag, 1970. 195 pp.

9212. Fischer, Wolfgang Georg: *Wohnungen*. 1. Band einer Trilogie. München: Carl Hanser Verlag, 1969. 206 pp., front. illus. [A documentary novel. The author, born in Vienna in 1933, is a director of the London Marlborough Fine Arts Gallery, founded by his father. He was awarded the Charles Veillon Prize 1970.]

9213. Fried, Erich: *Unter Nebenfeinden*. 50 Gedichte. Berlin: Verlag Klaus Wagenbach, 1970. 66 pp. (Reihe Quarthefte, Bd. 44.) [Political poetry.]

9214. Jacobson, Dan: *The Rape of Tamar*. London: Weidenfeld and Nicolson, 1970. 192 pp. [Cf. A Biblical Narrative in Modern Garb (J. Maitlis). [In]: 'AJR Information', June. London, 1971.

9215. Jones, Eva: *Just a Woman*. Ed. by Léonie Scott-Matthews. London: Magpie Press, 1969. 39 pp., cover drawing. [Eva Jones née Solon, born in Berlin in 1913, emigrated to Paris, escaped during the war with her journalist husband [orig. Jonas] to Spain, and now lives in London.]

9216. Kishon, Ephraim: *Nicht so laut vor Jericho*. Neue Satiren. Übersetzt von Friedrich Torberg. München: Langen Müller Verlag, 1970. 248 pp.

9217. Laor, Eran [orig. Erich Landstein]: *Der Himmel stürzt ein, die Welt geht unter*. Gedichte. Wien: Verlag Typographische Anstalt, 1970. 70 pp.

9218. '*Rachels Lyrik*'. Ausgewählte Lieder. Aus dem Hebräischen übertragen von Rita Goldberg. Mit Zeichnungen von David Davidov. Tel Aviv: Davar Verlag, 1970.

9219. RASP-NURI, GRACE: *Siegfried — oder die Zerstörung des Menschen*. Freiburg i.Br.: Alsatia Verlag, 1969. 260 pp. [The story of a patriotic Berlin Jewish family].

9220. SAALFELD, MARTHA: *Isi oder die Gerechtigkeit*. Roman. München: Kurt Desch Verlag, 1970. 190 pp.

9221. UHLMAN, FRED: *Reunion*. A Novel. London: Adam Books, 1970. [The story of a Jewish doctor's son in Württemberg, in 1932, whose aristocratic friend turned Nazi, but was later executed for his part in the July anti-Hitler plot.]

9222. WIESEL, ELIE: *Der Bettler von Jerusalem*. Roman. Aus dem Französischen von Christian Sturm. München: Bechtle Verlag, 1970. 208 pp. [Le Mendiant de Jérusalem]. [Engl. ed.: A Beggar in Jerusalem. New York: Random House, 1970.]

9223. ZEITLIN, AARON: *Poems of the Holocaust and Poems of Faith*. New York — Tel Aviv: Bergen-Belsen Memorial Press of the World Federation of Bergen-Belsen Associations, 1967, 471 pp. [In Yiddish.]

Index to Bibliography

Index to Bibliography

List of Contributors

JENKS, William A., Ph.D., b. 1918 in Jacksonville, Fla. William R. Kenan Jr. Professor of History, Washington and Lee University, Lexington, Va. Author of *The Austrian Electoral Reform of 1907* (1950); *Vienna and the Young Hitler* (1960); *Austria under the Iron Ring, 1879-1893* (1965).

LIEBESCHÜTZ, Hans, Ph.D., Fellow of the Royal Historical Society, b. 1893 in Hamburg. Lives in Liverpool. Late Reader in Medieval History, Liverpool University, Prof. Ext. Hamburg University. Field of studies: Intellectual History of the Middle Ages; Historiography. Author of a.o. *Das Judentum im deutschen Geschichtsbild von Hegel bis Max Weber* (1967); *Mediaeval Humanism of John of Salisbury* (1968); *Von Georg Simmel zu Franz Rosenzweig. Studien zum Jüdischen Denken im deutschen Kulturbereich* (1970) and contributor to many learned periodicals. Member of the London Board of the LBI. (Contributor to Year Books I, II, IV, V, VII, VIII, IX, XI and XIII).

MEYER, Michael A., Ph.D., b. 1937 in Berlin. Associate Professor of Jewish History, Hebrew Union College — Jewish Institute of Religion, Cincinnati, Ohio. Author of *The Origins of the Modern Jew: Jewish Identity and European Culture, 1749-1824* (1967) and of contributions to various periodicals. (Contributor to Year Book XI).

MOLDENHAUER, R. Dr. phil., b. 1911 in Berlin. Director, Bundesarchiv Frankfurt/Main. Author of a number of contributions to various historical journals on Petitions to the German National Assembly 1848/49.

MOSSE, George L., Ph.D., b. 1918 in Berlin. Bascom Professor of History, University of Wisconsin; co-editor, *Journal of Contemporary History*. Author of a.o. *The Struggle for Sovereignty in England* (1950); *The Reformation* (1953); The *Culture o j Western Europe. The Nineteenth and Twentieth Centuries* (1961); *The Crisis of German Ideology. Intellectual Origins of the Third Reich* (1964); 'Die deutsche Rechte und die Juden' in *Entscheidungsjahr 1932* (1965); *Nazi Culture. Intellectual, Cultural and Social Life in the Third Reich* (1966); *Germans and Jews. The Right, the Left, and the Search for a "Third Force" in Pre-Nazi Germany* (1971); co-editor of *Europe in Review* (1964). (Contributor to Year Book II).

NIEWYK, Donald L., Ph.D., b. 1940 in Grand Rapids, Mich. Assistant Professor of History, Ithaca College, Ithaca, N.Y. Author of *Socialist, Anti-Semite, and Jew: German Social Democracy Confronts the Problem of Anti-Semitism, 1918-1933* (1971).

PAUCKER, Arnold, M. A., b. 1921 in Berlin. Director of the Leo Baeck Institute, London. Author of *Der jüdische Abwehrkampf gegen Antisemitismus und Nationalsozialismus in den letzten Jahren der Weimarer Republik* (2nd. ed. 1969); collaborated in the editing of *Entscheidungsjahr 1932* (2nd ed. 1966) and *Deutsches Judentum in Krieg und Revolution 1916-1923* (1971); co-editor of Ernst Feder: *Heute sprach ich mit . . .* (1971); essays on historical and philological subjects. (Contributor to Year Books V, VIII, XI and XIII).

SAUER, Wolfgang, Ph. D., b. 1920 in Berlin. Professor of History, University of California, Berkeley, Cal. Co-author of *Die nationalsozialistische Machtergreifung* (1960); contributed to Karl Dietrich Bracher, *Die Auflösung der Weimarer Republik* (1955); author of a.o. 'Das Problem des deutschen Nationalstaates', in *Moderne deutsche Sozialgeschichte* (1966).

SCHWARCZ, Moshe, Ph.D., b. 1925 in Hungary. Chairman, Department of Philosophy, Bar-Ilan University, Ramat Gan. Author of *The realistic Conception of Myth in Schelling's late Philosophy* (diss., 1958); *Language, Myth, Art* (1967); *Introduction and Commentary to the Hebrew Translation of Rosenzweig's "Star of Redemption"* (1970); and of articles on modern general and Jewish philosophy and aesthetics.

SIMON, WALTER B., Ph. D., b. 1918 in Vienna. Visiting Professor of Sociology at the University of Guelph, Ontario, Canada. Author of numerous articles on sociology, social psychology etc. in German and North American journals.

STEINBERG, Lucien, Dipl. Sciences Pol., b. 1926 in Bucharest. Now lives in Paris. Historian. Author of *Les Autorités Allemandes en France Occupeé* (1966); *La Révolte des Justes. Les Juifs contre Hitler* (1970); numerous essays and studies published in Germany and Israel, contributor to the *Encyclopaedia Judaica*.

STRAUSS, Herbert A., Dr.phil., b. 1918 in Würzburg. Professor of History, The City College, New York. Executive Vice President, American Federation of Jews from Central Europe, New York. Author of *Staat, Bürger, Mensch* (1948); *Botschaften der Präsidenten der Vereinigten Staaten von Amerika, 1793-1948* (1956); editor of *Conference on Acculturation* (1965); *Conference on Anti-Semitism* (1969); *Conference on American-Jewish Dilemmas* (1971); co-editor of *Gegenwart im Rückblick. Festgabe für die Jüdische Gemeinde Berlin 25 Jahre nach dem Neubeginn* (1970); and author of numerous articles. Fellow of the LBI, New York. (Contributor to Year Books VI and XI).

TOURY, Jacob, Ph.D., b. 1915 in Beuthen. Associate Professor of Modern Jewish History in the West, Tel Aviv University. Author of a.o. *Die politischen Orientierungen der Juden in Deutschland — Von Jena bis Weimar* (1966); *Turmoil and Confusion in the Revolution of 1948* (Hebrew, 1968); of textbooks and of numerous contributions to learned periodicals in Hebrew and German. (Contributor to Year Books XI and XIII).

WHITESIDE, Andrew G., Ph.D., b. 1921 in New York. Professor of History, Queens College of the City University of New York. Author of *Austrian National Socialism before 1918* (1962); 'The Austrian Right, 1867-1938' in *The European Right: A Historical Profile* (1965); and of numerous articles and reviews in Austrian, German, and American publications.

Index

General Index to Year Book XVI
of the Leo Baeck Institute

NEW PUBLICATIONS OF THE
LEO BAECK INSTITUTE

The First Catalogue-Volume of the
Collections of the Leo Baeck Institute

Leo Baeck Institute New York
Bibliothek und Archiv

Katalog Band I

herausgegeben von

MAX KREUTZBERGER

unter Mitarbeit von

IRMGARD FOERG

(Schriftenreihe wissenschaftlicher Abhandlungen des Leo Baeck Instituts 22)

1970. XLI, 623 Seiten, mit 23 Kunstdrucktafeln

J. C. B. MOHR (PAUL SIEBECK), TÜBINGEN

NEW PUBLICATIONS OF THE
LEO BAECK INSTITUTE

A Second Symposium on the Jewish Question in Twentieth-Century Germany

Deutsches Judentum in Krieg und Revolution 1916-1923

Ein Sammelband herausgegeben von WERNER E. MOSSE unter Mitwirkung von ARNOLD PAUCKER
(Schriftenreihe wissenschaftlicher Abhandlungen des Leo Baeck Instituts 25)
1971. XI, 704 Seiten

INHALT

J. C. B. MOHR (PAUL SIEBECK), TÜBINGEN

NEW PUBLICATIONS OF THE LEO BAECK INSTITUTE

ROBERT WELTSCH

An der Wende des modernen Judentums

Betrachtungen aus fünf Jahrzehnten

J. C. B. MOHR (PAUL SIEBECK), TÜBINGEN

*

Diaries from the Weimar Republic

ERNST FEDER

Heute sprach ich mit...
Tagebücher eines Berliner Publizisten
1926 - 1932

herausgegeben von

Cécile Lowenthal-Hensel und Arnold Paucker
mit einem Biographischen Register
von Ernst G. Lowenthal

Deutsche Verlags-Anstalt, Stuttgart

NEW PUBLICATIONS OF THE
LEO BAECK INSTITUTE

Schriftenreihe wissenschaftlicher Abhandlungen des Leo Baeck Instituts

The Monumental Work on Prussian Jewry

24

SELMA STERN

Der Preussische Staat und die Juden
Dritter Teil: Die Zeit Friedrichs des Grossen

1. Abt.: Darstellung
2. Abt.: Akten

1971. XV, 426 Seiten (Text)
1615 Seiten (Documents in two volumes)

*

21

MORITZ LAZARUS

und

HEYMANN STEINTHAL

Die Begründer der Völkerpsychologie in ihren Briefen

Mit einer Einleitung herausgegeben
von INGRID BELKE

1971. IX, 421 Seiten

J. C. B. MOHR (PAUL SIEBECK), TÜBINGEN